PUBLIC FREEDOM

PUBLIC FREEDOM | Dana Villa

PRINCETON UNIVERSITY PRESS   Princeton and Oxford

Copyright © 2008 by Princeton University Press

Published by Princeton University Press, 41 William Street, Princeton, New Jersey 08540

In the United Kingdom: Princeton University Press, 6 Oxford Street, Woodstock, Oxfordshire OX20 1TW

All Rights Reserved
Library of Congress Cataloging-in-Publication Data
Villa, Dana Richard.
Public freedom / Dana Villa.
   p. cm.
Includes bibliographical references and index.
ISBN 978-0-691-13593-9 (hardback : alk. paper)—ISBN 978-0-691-13594-6 (pbk. : alk. paper)
1. Liberty.   I. Title.
JC585.V45 2008
320.01'1—dc22
2008003033

British Library Cataloging-in-Publication Data is available

This book has been composed in Minion and Myriad

Printed on acid-free paper. ∞

press.princeton.edu

Printed in the United States of America

10 9 8 7 6 5 4 3 2 1

To my father, Alfred L. Villa,

and to the memory of my mother, Virginia Barrett Villa

CONTENTS

ACKNOWLEDGMENTS

The chapters in this book were written over several years and at a number of institutions, including the University of California, Santa Barbara; Harvard University; the American Academy in Berlin; the University of Southern California; and the University of Notre Dame. I would like to acknowledge colleagues at all these institutions. In one way or another, they provided time and resources for the writing here. Special thanks go to my theory colleague at UCSB, Peter Digeser.

Two thousand and six was Hannah Arendt's centenary year, and I was fortunate to be invited to conferences in New Haven, New York, Princeton, Paris, Bari, Oslo, Berlin, Helsinki, and Tel Aviv. Attendees at these events heard early versions of chapters 6 and 10 of the present volume, and I am grateful for the many, often spirited, comments I received. In particular, I would like to thank Seyla Benhabib, Jim Schmidt, Patchen Markell, Jay Bernstein, Richard J. Bernstein, Rocio Zambrana, Nancy Fraser, Anson Rabinbach, Antonia Grunenberg, Wolfgang Heuer, Martine Leibovici, Etienne Tassin, Geraldine Muhlmann, Anne Kupiec, Krista Johansson, Julia Honkasalo, Francesco Fistetti, Francesca R. Recchia Luciani, Steven Aschheim, Edith Zertal, Jerry Kohn, and Elisabeth Young-Bruehl. I would also like to thank Michael Steinberg, whose gracious invitation to deliver the Hannah Arendt Seminar inaugural lecture at Brown University's Cogut Humanities Center gave the initial impetus to formulations in both chapters.

Chapter 3 (on Hegel and Tocqueville) was presented at a variety of venues, including the University of Southern California, the University of California at San Diego, the University of California at Los Angeles, the

University of Notre Dame, Boston University, and the University of Chicago. I would like to thank the audiences at all these events for their questions and discussion. Chapter 4 (on Tocqueville and Arendt) was originally the Haniel Lecture at the American Academy in Berlin (fall, 2003). It was subsequently given at political theory colloquia at Princeton and at Johns Hopkins University. A shorter version of chapter 5 (on Mill) was presented at the J. S. Mill Bicentennial Conference at University College, London, in April 2006. Again, I am indebted to audience members at these various events for many pointed and illuminating questions.

Chapter 2, "Tocqueville and Civil Society," originally appeared in *The Cambridge Companion to Tocqueville*, edited by Cheryl Welch (copyright © Cambridge University Press, 2006). Reprinted with permission. Chapter 10 appeared in the *Graduate Faculty Philosophy Journal* 28, no. 1 (2007), pp. 29–46. An abbreviated version of chapter 3 appeared in *The Review of Politics* 67, no. 4 (2005), pp. 659–686. Finally, a slightly different version of chapter 7, "Genealogies of Total Domination," appeared in *New German Critique* 34, no. 100 (2007), pp. 1–45. Copyright © 2007. Used by permission of the publisher, Duke University Press.

I would like to thank Peter Eli Gordon, who graciously vacated his office at Harvard's Center for European Studies for two consecutive summers, enabling me to work at his desk, ransack his library, and listen to his music. The writing of chapters 6 and 7 was much facilitated thereby, and by the always accommodating staff at the Center, Anna Popiel in particular. Much of what appears in chapters 2, 3, 6, 7, and 8 was initially inspired—if that's the right word—by a lecture course on continental political thought I had the pleasure of giving twice (first in the spring semester of 2002, then again in the fall of the same year) as visiting associate professor of government at Harvard. I want to thank the undergraduate (and graduate) students in both classes for providing my most satisfying teaching experience to date. And I want to thank Michael Sandel for extending the original invitation to teach at Harvard.

When I wasn't at Harvard, Svetlana Boym put up with prolonged absences and what can only be described as a less than fully developed telephonic persona. Needless to say, I owe her more than any passing "acknowledgment" could possibly convey.

Similarly, I owe a debt of gratitude to my teachers, including George Kateb, Norman Birnbaum, and Tracy Strong at Amherst and Sheldon Wolin and the late Richard Rorty at Princeton. Academics have a bad habit of reducing one another to emanations of thesis or dissertation advisors. As a rule, this works only for the blandest (or most ideologically motivated) of epigones. Suffice it to say most real learning is done on one's own, and in one's own way. However, it's good to occasionally be pointed in the right direction, and Professors Kateb, Birnbaum, Strong, Rorty, and Wolin provided me this invaluable service again and again.

Finally, the book is dedicated to my father, Alfred L. Villa, who—in addition to providing my first (and probably longest lasting) political education—has been unstinting in his support over all too many years. If I have a genuinely skeptical bone in my body, it is due to my father's insight and influence. I am much indebted.

The book is also dedicated to my late mother, Virginia Villa, who died after a long illness in 2004. My mother, a feminist and scholar of Henry James, Virginia Woolf, and Walt Whitman, spent over thirty years teaching many underprivileged and grateful students at Greater Hartford Community College. As all who knew her can attest, she was one of a kind: keenly intelligent, cuttingly witty, hugely sympathetic, and (last but not least) very beautiful. She will be missed.

PUBLIC FREEDOM

1 | INTRODUCTION: PUBLIC FREEDOM TODAY

The Liberty of a Subject, lyeth therefore only in those things, which in regulating their actions, the Soveraign hath praetermitted: such as is the Liberty to buy, and sell, and otherwise contract with one another; to choose their own aboad, their own diet, their own trade of life, and institute their children as they themselves think fit; & the like.... There is written on the Turrets of the city of *Luca* in great characters at this day, the word *LIBERTAS;* yet no man can thence inferre, that a particular man has more Liberties, or Immunitie from the service of the Commonwealth there than in *Constantinople*. Whether a Commonwealth be Monarchicall, or Popular, the Freedome is still the same.
—Thomas Hobbes, *Leviathan,* chap. 21

To the state as an essentially political entity belongs the *jus belli,* i.e., the real possibility of deciding in a concrete situation upon the enemy and the ability to fight him with the power emanating from the entity.... The state as the decisive political entity possesses an enormous power: the possibility of waging war and thereby publicly disposing of the lives
of men.
—Carl Schmitt, *The Concept of the Political*

Sovereign is he who decides on the exception.
—Carl Schmitt, *Political Theology*

I have heard the voices, I read the front page. But I'm the decider.
—President George W. Bush, April 18, 2006

Americans, we are repeatedly told, cherish freedom more than almost any other value or good. Yet the freedom we cherish is peculiarly one-sided. It is, first and foremost, a freedom of choice: the individual's freedom to decide on a career path, choose a religion, a life partner, a place of residence, a lifestyle, how to raise and educate their children. While it is tempting to view this identification of freedom with individual choice as a more or less direct outgrowth of consumer culture, it is important to remember that its fundamental presupposition is *not* the market. Rather, it is the absence of an authoritarian or tutorial state that tells us how to live and what to believe. As liberal political theorists have long insisted, freedom as choice depends upon freedom from interference—by the state or by any other powerful social body.

This "negative" form of freedom—the freedom *from* something—is often contrasted with more positive (and potentially authoritarian) forms.[1] Americans, in large part, instinctively reject the latter. Whatever freedom is, Americans believe, it *cannot* be the "freedom" that supposedly results when we are coerced to conform to *someone else's* idea of civic, moral, or religious virtue. Realizing one's best self—pursuing one's own good in one's own way, as J. S. Mill famously put it—may be a laudable *private* goal. However, the Rousseauian notion that we can somehow be "forced to be free" by public authority—that is, forced to rise above our individual desires and interests, so that we might better recognize and support the "common good"—elicits an instinctive abhorrence.

Rousseau, of course, is one of the two great political theorists of the civic republican tradition (the other is Machiavelli). This tradition has been competing with liberalism for over 200 years, although as a tradition it is much older. Whereas the liberal tradition has emphasized constitutional limits on governmental power and the priority of individual rights, the civic republican tradition has focused far more on active citizenship and the preconditions of *public* liberty. As readers of Machiavelli's *Discourses* and Rousseau's *Social Contract* are well aware, the theoretical results of this focus are not always pretty. Whether it's Machiavelli's insistence on military discipline and civil religion as the two most important "schools" of citizenship, or Rousseau's anti-cosmopolitan image of upright peasants deciding their common affairs under an oak tree, the civic republican tradition has often displayed a deep-seated resistance to pluralism and any-thing resembling open-ended argument. It has valued unanimity over difference, and a quasi–a priori idea of the public good over the more ad hoc kind that emerges through robust debate and argument.[2]

Appeals to civic virtue, patriotism, and the Roman Republic have never gone completely out of style in Western political thought, and they have been more influential on American political development than many of us would care to admit.[3] The contemporary American cult of the mili-tary as the one remaining locus of authentic civic virtue is but a single example. However that may be, most Americans would heartily endorse the criticism Benjamin Constant made of Rousseau and the civic republi-can tradition generally in his 1819 lecture "The Liberty of the Ancients Compared with that of the Moderns."[4] Drawing a contrast between the "freedom as collective sovereignty" idea found in ancient republics with the type of freedom offered by modern representative governments, Con-stant poses his audience a rhetorical question: "Ask yourselves, Gentle-men, what an Englishman, a Frenchman, and a citizen of the United States of America understand today by the word 'liberty.'" His answer continues to resonate:

> For each of them it is the right to be subjected only to the laws, and to be neither arrested, detained, put to death or maltreated in any way by the arbitrary will of one or more individuals. It is the right of everyone to express their opinion, choose a profession and practice it, to dispose of property, and even to abuse it; to come and go without permission, and without having to account for their motives and undertakings. It is everyone's right to asso-ciate with other individuals, either to discuss their interests, or to profess the religion which they and their associates prefer, or even simply to occupy their days or hours in a way which is most com-patible with their inclinations and whims. Finally, it is everyone's right to exercise some influence on the administration of the gov-ernment, either by electing all or particular officials, or through representations, petitions, demands to which the authorities are more or less compelled to pay heed.[5]

The liberty of the ancients, on the other hand, "consists in exercising collectively, but directly, several parts of the complete sovereignty; in de-liberating, in the public square, over war and peace; in forming alliances with foreign governments; in voting laws and pronouncing judgments; in examining the accounts, the acts, the stewardship of the magistrates; in calling them to appear in front of the assembled people, in accusing, condemning or absolving them."[6] Such "collective" freedom—which Rousseau-inspired Jacobins futilely tried to resurrect during the French Revolution—was, as Constant points out, entirely compatible with "the complete subjection of the individual to the authority of the community," a subjection no *modern* individual would find bearable. The "liberty of the moderns," then, is irreducibly and for the most part *individual* freedom. If the achievement and preservation of this liberty came at the price of older, possibly more "edifying" notions of *public* freedom, so be it. As Constant implies, it is a price we moderns simply have to pay.

Constant's manner of posing the alternatives apparently pays tribute to what has become our contemporary "common sense." We know better than to yearn after direct democracy and collective sovereignty; we realize that such a system is impractical in large nation-states; and we flatter ourselves that we have exchanged the "bellicose spirit" of the ancient republics for the far more benign "spirit of commerce." In short, we know (albeit intuitively and often inarticulately) that "we can no longer enjoy the liberty of the ancients," and that (as a result) "our freedom must consist of peaceful enjoyment and private independence."[7] *Public* freedom, Constant seems to be telling us, is a thing of the past. Any attempt to revive it would result in a miserable abortion. Most Americans—even those utterly unfamiliar with the history, ideological origins, and political excesses of the French Revolution—would probably agree. An individual and essentially privatized liberty is "the true modern liberty."

Yet this self-flattering conclusion is grossly premature. Even Constant, his praise of the spirit of commerce and the romantic idea of self-development notwithstanding, did not carry through on the exhaustive either/or his lecture *seems* to construct. Unlike ourselves, the choice for Constant is not between *political or public* freedom (on the one hand) and *individual* freedom (on the other). The latter may, in fact, be the "true modern liberty," but the former "is its guarantee." While commerce may have made people more alike and wars less likely, the fact remains that even representative governments have a tendency to enlarge their powers, with or without the excuse of war.[8] As a result, Constant warned, "the danger of modern liberty is that, absorbed in the enjoyment of our private independence, and in the pursuit of our particular interests, we should surrender our right to share in political power too easily."[9] For this very reason, "political liberty"—public freedom—"is indispensable."[10]

This warning—echoed by Alexis de Tocqueville and J. S. Mill in the nineteenth century, and by Hannah Arendt in the twentieth—has largely fallen on deaf ears in America, and never with more disastrous results than in the present. What Constant, Tocqueville, and Mill saw as essential components of modern liberty—namely, the protection of individual rights and the recognition of individual interests—has become, in twenty-first century America, a defining creed and epistemological limit. The dyad of rights and interests effectively circumscribes our moral, political, and social world, as well as our conception of what freedom is or can be. The fact that group rights loom larger these days (thanks to the so-called "politics of recognition") does little to alter the basic equation. "Rights" supposedly hold overweening governmental (or corporate) power in check, while "interests" propel our associations or affinity groups to enter the public realm episodically, if at all.

Our attitude toward what Constant called political liberty is, as a result, almost entirely instrumental. Occasionally such liberty is invoked in the struggle to gain or redeem certain basic rights, such as citizenship, the right to vote, the right to strike, the right to a decent education, and so on. More often than not, however, it is exploited to further the agenda of a particular interest group and its members. "The public" is less an arena for the exercise of a distinctive (nonprivate) form of freedom than it is an all-purpose container or scrim for the endless lobbying, bogus "citizen initiatives," and staged political events that presently define our political lives.

The most striking feature of the contemporary public realm is how uniformly the attitudes of manipulation and opportunism characterize all who enter it. From the moralizing evangelical to the politically correct academic; from industry lobbying groups to those protesting "illegal aliens"; from unions to corporate boards—virtually everyone treats "the public" as a stage that can be briefly seized in order to get their particular "message" (and interest) across. This effort—what passes today for the exercise of "political liberty"—is the result of a strictly strategic calculation, one predicated on the media-dominated nature of our public sphere and the resulting tyranny of public relations and advertising.[11] In the past, Constant observed, war was the primary means of "getting what one wants." In modern times, commerce took its place, but the goal was the same.[12] To this basic "world-historical" schema we might well add: and where commerce fails, "politics" as public relations provides the most obvious avenue for "getting what one wants."

This is not to say that interests have no place in the public realm, or in motivating our exercise of political freedom. Ever since Hegel and Tocqueville attempted to renovate the civic republican tradition, the legitimacy of interests (properly mediated) has been seen by political theorists as an absolutely essential component of modern politics.[13] Rather, my point is that the pursuit of interest (understood in its most vulgar and unmediated form) has become so ingrained in our political culture and character that it has made other, more authentically political attitudes and practices all but impossible. By universally taking up an exploitative, instrumental, and fundamentally strategic approach to politics and political action, we have rendered the public sphere an unfit place for human habitation.

The result is that many of us who still feel the tug of civic obligation (to use an old-fashioned term) participate at arm's length. We write checks to well-meaning NGOs and political action groups, the better to combat the disproportionate influence of multinational corporations and other "sinister interests" on the political and legislative process. There is an obvious irony here, one that is compounded when we take to the streets in protest over some new outrage. Our government views such public demonstrations—and there were many, both here and abroad, in the run-up to the Iraq War—as little more than "letting off steam." Where political action actually transcends the opening of a checkbook—where it is relatively popular, spontaneous, and civic-minded in character—it is treated by our leaders as little more than white noise, irrelevant to the political "process." The resulting impression is that of enormous, interlocking corporate and governmental structures far removed from the "noise" emanating from an emaciated and impoverished public sphere.

This configuration doesn't exactly mirror the nightmare of "administrative despotism" that Tocqueville outlined in the second volume of *Democracy in America*, but there are eerie resemblances nonetheless. Tocqueville worried about how the advent of democratic equality would destroy "intermediary powers," leaving equal but impotent individuals to confront an enormous, albeit attentive, bureaucratic state. Without organization, Tocqueville thought, such a "confused mass" would be unable to "raise new secondary powers." As a result, it would soon find itself relegated to the status of a well-tended herd.[14]

Such an over-centralized sovereign power—one that usurps the educational, economic, and welfare functions of civil society—has not exactly been our fate. Libertarians to the contrary, market forces play far too large a role in our daily lives for our government to convincingly fill the role of the omni-competent Leviathan Tocqueville sketches. The contemporary reader is, however, struck by Tocqueville's descriptions of popular impotence and docility. It is these passages—rather than his description of a single, towering, and omnipotent central power—that resonate in the present. For what Tocqueville saw with unparalleled clarity was the way in which a people unused to the exercise of public freedom would soon forget both its practice and its value. Given broad social equality by recent revolutions, divorced from the corporate or caste affiliations of the feudal past, relieved of the exercise of traditional local freedoms—in such a condition, the dissociated "democratic individual" would invariably turn in upon himself, his family, his friends, and his material interests. He would value public order more than public freedom, and would view the latter's demands as a set of irritating obstacles to the untrammeled pursuit of his self-interest.[15]

There is, then, a "bourgeois" and not merely a socialist "road to servitude," a fact that Tocqueville, if not his twentieth-century disciples, knew all too well. The distinguishing characteristic of the former is that it prefers tranquility, order, and the accumulation of wealth to a "dangerous freedom." It is one of the ironies of Tocqueville's legacy that the peculiar danger he saw American democracy as successfully eluding—thanks to a pervasive public spirit, an intense attention to political matters and local administration, and a habit of association for all sorts of purposes—has returned to haunt us with a vengeance. What was once a pathology peculiar to the haute bourgeois class in Europe has become a universal affliction. The "taste for physical gratification" that Tocqueville saw reflected in but contained by American middle-class mores has become an obsessive pursuit for nearly everyone. In our hyped-up consumer culture, the public realm and the responsibilities of citizenship are, for the most part, well and truly neglected. Our sense of political powerlessness grows as our creature comforts accumulate.

Of course, such impotence isn't entirely self-incurred. For many, the neglect of public freedom is not simply a function of the desire for additional comforts. A large percentage of Americans have abandoned the public sphere less out of craven materialism than out of a relentless, daily anxiety about their (and their families') future. The lesson that everyone is replaceable and, in a sense, disposable is a lesson taught again and again by the business pages of our newspapers, as well as by countless individual stories of down-sized or out-sourced workers.[16] It is increasingly taken for granted—by politicians, policymakers, editorial page writers, and the people themselves—that our "national mission" is less to realize democracy than to "be competitive" in the international marketplace—even if this means layoffs in the tens of millions.[17]

An ingrained sense of one's own relative superfluousness in the maw of global capitalism in not exactly a recipe for "empowerment." In recent years, the work of "atomization"—that is, the spread of the dissociative tendencies that Tocqueville ascribed to a "democratic social condition"— has been radicalized and accelerated by the advent of a robustly global competition. Far more than government, the marketplace throws us back upon ourselves, enforcing the practice of a distinctly non-Emersonian form of self-reliance. When it comes to the production and reproduction of citizen docility—the phenomenon Tocqueville feared most—nothing works better than the iron discipline and myriad shocks of the labor market. It is to *this* discipline—and the perpetual anxiety that underlies it— that captains of industry and all too many governmental leaders would like to see us subjected, sans intermediaries. A "disciplined" and fearful workforce—one that lacks both the organization and elementary solidarity necessary to assert itself—is no recipe for a self-governing citizen body.

This last observation may seem more Marx than Tocqueville. However, it is extremely important to remember two things if we are to register Tocqueville's lessons about the threats to public and political freedom in the modern, democratic world. The first is that he thought the "art of association"—and especially association for *political* purposes—was essential if the disempowering tendencies of privatism (or what he called "individualism") were to be combated.[18] The second is that, while writing of a still largely pre-capitalist and pre-industrial America, he surveyed the future with intense anxiety. Even in 1840, Tocqueville sensed the emergence of a new, un-democratic world built on the foundation of industrial capitalism. In a chapter entitled "How an Aristocracy May be Created by Manufactures," he writes:

> In proportion as the principle of the division of labor is more extensively applied, the workman becomes more weak, more narrow-minded, and more dependent. The art advances, the artisan recedes. On the other hand, in proportion as it becomes more manifest that the productions of manufactures are by so much the cheaper and better as the manufacture is larger and the amount of capital employed more considerable, wealthy and educated men come forward to embark on manufactures. . . . This

man resembles more and more the administrator of a vast empire; that man a brute.

The master and the workman have then here no similarity, and their differences increase every day. They are connected only ·like the two rings at the extremities of a long chain. Each of them fills the station which is made for him, and which he does not leave; the one is continually, closely, and necessarily dependent upon the other and seems as much born to obey as the other is to command. What is this but aristocracy?[19]

Such *structural* dependence and inequality were, of course, defining characteristics of classical capitalism, and created the kind of abyss between classes that Tocqueville, with the French experience very much in mind, could not help but see as the prelude to perpetual, low-grade civil war. While America today is far from the class warfare that characterized much of Europe in the middle and late nineteenth century, we have clearly advanced well down the road toward the creation of a new form of caste society. This is a society is which decent health care, education, job security, and political influence are the prerogatives of those in middle-management or above, and in which everyone—with the possible exception of the super-rich—lives in a perpetual "fear of falling." As a result, many of us have indeed become part of what Tocqueville described as a "flock of timid and industrious animals"—except that we can hardly count on the government to be our "shepherd."[20]

In addition to privatism, materialism, rising economic anxiety, and increasing structural inequality, we have to contend—after September 11, two wars, and an open-ended "war on terror"—with an atmosphere of generalized fear. This fear sometimes recedes, but it is perpetually on call, the better to guard the expanding prerogatives of the national security state and the interests of corporate power.

I want to be clear here, since some academic critics of the "war on terror" have treated it as if there were no concrete threat whatsoever. Of course there are people and organizations who wish us great harm. The challenge they present, however, is to police work, intelligence-gathering, and international cooperation (not to mention the "winning of hearts and minds" despite enormous cultural differences). To treat the "war on terror" as a literal and open-ended war is to create a perpetual state of emergency in which the executive branch can demand, and to a surprising extent receive, the deference of the other two branches of government—branches that the founders intended to check and balance. It is to create a situation in which constitutional democracy threatens to transform into a state of the old-style European variety. In such a polity the government lays claim to a virtual monopoly on all meaningful power, action, and judgment. The great accomplishment of the founders—their creation of an ingenious system of decentralized power, their theoretical and practical overcoming of the idea of the centralized, sovereign state—is tossed onto the ash heap of history.

Fear, then, is every bit as disempowering as privatism and pervasive economic anxiety. And—as Tocqueville, Constant, and their theoretical mentor, Montesquieu, knew all too well—fear is the perpetual accomplice of despotism, of whatever variety. It is in the interest of the despot to create and perpetuate a climate of fear, the better to further separate his subjects, make joint action less likely, and solidify his monopoly on public force and public judgment.[21]

In our own time, fear has been used to make dissent look unpatriotic; to suspend or make conditional many of the constitutional protections we take for granted; to provide an excuse for ever-heightened levels of government secrecy and non-transparency; and to hijack American foreign policy. The "trust us" attitude of the George W. Bush administration flies in the face not only of democratic self-understanding ("distrust" being a constitutive element not only of our system of checks and balances, but any and all forms of liberal constitutionalism). It also collides with the most basic principles of the Enlightenment war against absolutist authority. In "An Answer to the Question: What is Enlightenment?" (1784), Immanuel Kant argued that *maturity* and an escape from the infantilizing paternalism of the old regime were predicated upon the "courage to use one's own understanding."[22] Since September 11, 2001, it has been clear that our leaders prefer we not follow Kant's advice.

This leads to an obvious conclusion, one I think that neither Constant nor Tocqueville would disavow. The "daddy state"—the state that fights, that decides who is friend and who is enemy—is an even greater threat to democratic maturity and self-government than the so-called "mommy state" (the European welfare state of the latter half of the twentieth century). "Democratic despotism" may take the "soft" form Tocqueville outlined at the end of *Democracy in America* (a centralized state power that is "absolute, minute, regular, provident and mild"). But it may also take the "hard" form of a neo-Hobbesian entity, one that cuts civil society out of the circuit of political debate and decision, all the while maintaining an increased surveillance of the "nonpolitical" sphere.[23]

What to do in this situation? The political theorists who grappled with the problem of public freedom after Rousseau hardly provide a list of handy answers for our situation. They do, however, provide a set of alternative understandings and conceptual mappings of the terrain that is the public-political realm. This is a terrain that the traditional American understanding of politics as the clash of interests tends to obscure.[24] Many of the theorists addressed in this volume were motivated by the desire to find avenues through which a sense of agency and public power could be either generated or restored amongst a "crowd" of increasingly dispersed and privatized individuals.

In this regard, much of what Hegel, Tocqueville, Mill, and Arendt have to say about public-political freedom can be viewed as drawing out the implications of the fraught passage from being subjects to becoming citizens. With the possible exception of Arendt, none of them depend on the time-honored republican trope of looking to the ancient Greeks or Romans for images of freedom in the present.[25] Rather, they all see *modern* political freedom as a distinctive synthesis of liberal and republican elements—the kind of synthesis Constant gestured to strongly (if inadequately) at the end of his famous lecture. Modern political freedom is thus not a question of literal self-government or "direct democracy." But neither is it a question of government by others, of rulers and ruled. If it were, it could be hardly be called *political* freedom. Rather, it would be that pure "freedom from interference" which Hobbes—the first modern theorist of despotism—thought perfectly compatible with absolutist government. For absolutist government (of a rule-based, non-arbitrary sort) provides that perfect "freedom *from* politics" that leaves us free to pursue the essentially nonpolitical goal of "commodious living." The price of this "freedom from" politics and political responsibility is, of course, a willingness to trade the status of citizens for that of subjects.

The huge accomplishments of political modernity notwithstanding, I think we are well on the way to becoming subjects once again. This danger was felt intensely by Tocqueville, but also by Hegel, Mill, and Arendt. Reworking civic republican themes within a modern (liberal or individualist) context, they were all concerned to identify the new forms of despotism and self-incurred immaturity that threaten the newly won "freedom of the moderns." In this respect, at least, their work is continuous with the more "totalizing" critiques of theorists like Adorno, Marcuse, and Foucault. What separates the thinkers in the first group from those in the second is the sense that a good portion of the dangers *are* self-incurred, and remediable by concrete practices, revived distinctions, and specific institutional reforms. None of this first group of theorists denies or papers over the structural constraints of modern politics. But— just as important—none of them buy into the idea that the public as such is a privileged site of disciplinary power, the repression of difference, or "total domination." In other words, none of them comes close to suggesting (as Adorno, Marcuse, and Foucault unfortunately do) that the distinction between "citizen" and "subject" no longer signifies.

In this regard, we could do worse than understand the sequence of Hegel, Tocqueville, Mill, and Arendt as attempting to create and expand a place for difference within the (previously homogenizing and repressive) civic public. True, their "solutions" to this dilemma—whether we consider Hegel's rationally differentiated state, Tocqueville's idea of civil society, Mill's notion of a liberal public, or Arendt's emphasis on human plurality— often fail to strike a convincing balance between the "universal" and the "particular," the common good and the (enlightened) individual or group interest. But striking or at least articulating that balance is indeed their joint project. It is, in fact, the defining problem of all post-Rousseauian theories of public freedom. How to do justice to the legitimate claims of individual rights and private liberty (on the one hand) and public freedom and political action (on the other)? How to conceive a realm of social or political experience in which particular interests are gradually educated or "mediated," reaching a higher level of generality (albeit one far removed from the fantasy of an inclusive harmony or unity)?

Needless to say, it is a lot easier to solve these problems if we focus on one side of the rights/public liberty equation. This is what Rousseau and Machiavelli did, in their distinct but related ways. It is what many liberal thinkers have also done, but starting from the standpoint of individual rights rather than that of public freedom. From Madison's famous argument in *Federalist* 10 to the hegemony of interest group politics in America today, the tendency has been to downplay if not eliminate the need to "educate" one's interests to what I have called higher levels of generality.[26] The clash of interests, we like to believe, will take care of itself, even if the spectacle of that clash is by no means edifying and largely serves as a breeding ground for cynicism.

Cynicism toward the very idea of a fruitful mediation between particular and general interests is, of course, what drives Karl Marx's famous critique of the state/civil society distinction in his early essay "On the Jewish Question" (1843). Marx argued that a secular, liberal, or constitutional republic consigned human beings to living a divided, double life: half as community-minded *citoyen*, half as self-interested *bourgeois*:

> Where the political state has attained to its full development, man leads, not only in thought, in consciousness, but in *reality*, in *life*, a double existence—celestial and terrestrial. He lives in the *political community*, where he regards himself as a *communal being*, and in *civil society* where he acts simply as a *private individual*, treats other men as means, degrades himself to the role of a mere means, and becomes the plaything of alien powers. The political state, in relation to civil society, is just as spiritual as is heaven in relation to earth.[27]

Marx—with his ideas of an all-sided, integrated and (above all) social existence as a normative ideal—thought such a "divided" existence was a necessarily alienated one. Whereas Tocqueville expressed delight and wonderment at the fact that "an American attends to his private concerns as if he were alone in the world, and the next minute he gives himself up to the common welfare as if he had forgotten them," Marx saw such a "double existence" as an unstable and untenable compound—one that, in the end, was a fraud.[28] It was based on the illusion that human beings could be two very different things at once (or, at least, in very rapid succession): public-minded citizens and relentlessly egoistic maximizers of their own utility.

While the institutions of a secular republic are built upon the idea of such a "split" between public and private existence (codified in the "rights of the citizen" and the "rights of man," respectively), Marx argued that the tension between the two would always resolve itself in favor of the self-interested forces of civil society (the sphere of the market and particular interests). In this regard, Marx thought post-revolutionary French realities proved a less misleading guide than the American experience, at least as it had been interpreted by Tocqueville. Scratch a *citoyen*, Marx claimed, and you will always find a *bourgeois*. The latter is the real or "concrete" individual, whereas the former is a kind of religious projection or cover-up, the "political lion-skin" under whose cover we pursue our selfish interests. Such is the inevitable outcome of a social body divided up into an "unreal" universality (the state) and an all-too-real particularism (civil society).

Marx's tracing of our "double existence" back to what he calls the "universal secular contradiction between the political state and civil society" provides the backdrop to his breathtaking and (to liberals, at least) scandalous deconstruction of the "rights of man." These rights provide the moral basis for the constitutional regimes brought forth by the French and American Revolutions. It is in the name of the "rights of man" that governmental power is limited, and it is to preserve them that the "rights of the citizen" are promulgated and protected. But what, Marx asks rhetorically, do the "rights of man" really amount to? Who is the "man" (as opposed to the "citizen") that possesses these rights, and how does the "schism" between state and civil society effect their shape and content?

Marx turns to the texts of the French *Declaration of the Rights of Man and of the Citizen* of 1791, the French Constitutions of 1793 and 1795, and the state constitutions of Pennsylvania and New Hampshire to provide an answer.[29] The human rights of equality, liberty, security, and property are revealed, one by one, to be rights of the selfish individual—the individual as civil society knows and makes him. Thus liberty—"the power which man has to do everything which does not harm the rights of others"—is, according to Marx, the power of the "isolated monad" to do whatever he wants within his own little world, so long as it does not harm the (equally selfish) rights of others in their own little worlds. The idea that freedom might have something to do with, or even be constituted by, relations with others is never seriously entertained.

Likewise, the right to property is, according to Marx, essentially the right to self-interest. It is the defining right of man considered as a creature of the egoistic realm of civil society. The rights to equality and security are, respectively, the right to be considered equal before the law as any other member of civil society; and the right to have one's individual person, rights, and property secured by what is, at bottom, a "night watchman state."[30]

Marx's deconstruction of the "rights of man" (and—by extension—the "liberty of the moderns" articulated by Constant) will be seen as persuasive by those who are convinced (as he was) that our "social" nature—the fact that we are constituted as individuals by networks of language, practices, and relations that are irreducibly social—implies a normative and binding idea of what a genuinely free individual looks like. Such a genuinely free individual will view social relations not as a limit to his or her freedom, but as the very medium and substance of their freedom. This is the gist of Marx's much misunderstood notion of man's species-being (*Gattungswesen*).[31]

Leaving aside the controversy of whether the human subject or self is, or should be, viewed more like a "network of relations" than an "isolated monad," we are able to see Marx's deeper critical point. Title notwithstanding, the real subject of "On the Jewish Question" is the disaggregation of various spheres of life that occurs with the collapse of feudalism and the *ancien régime*. With the transition to modernity—consummated politically by the "bourgeois" revolutions in America and France—the public-political sphere finally separates out from the theological. This separation is paralleled by the dismantling of the so-called "embedded" economy and the emergence of an autonomous market and social sphere (the "private" realm that constitutional regimes are designed to protect). This new constellation generates the distinction between state and civil society, a distinction that lies at the heart of Hegel's political philosophy but that is also presumed (albeit in a somewhat confused way) by such proto-liberal thinkers such as John Locke and Thomas Paine. From this point on, the common or "universal" will be the province of the state or government, while "particular" interests will find their home in civil society.

However, the emerging independence of society in the late seventeenth and early eighteenth centuries actually expressed a newfound strength. The state, once the director and arbiter of virtually everything of import, increasingly found itself recast as the servant and protector of powerful "social" interests. Thus, what Arendt described as the "rise of the social" in the early modern age actually created a new (and largely instrumental) configuration between state and society. In this new dispensation, the political realm was increasingly subservient to the social. One result was that the "public good" increasingly came to be viewed—by economists, utilitarian philosophers, and a rising middle class—as little more than the aggregate of numerous individual preferences.

Unsurprisingly, this reversal of relative priority—the newfound hegemony of the social over the political—had broad implications for the relative "dignity" of the political world. As Marx observes, with this reversal "the citizen is declared to be the servant of egoistic 'man.' . . . The sphere in which man functions as a species-being is degraded to a level below the sphere in which he functions as a partial being."[32] This can be seen in the way the "rights of the citizen" are retrofitted (so to speak) to serve what Marx viewed as the essentially egoistic core of the "rights of man"—namely, man as a creature of market society.

It is this reconfiguration of "social" (market or economic) and "political" powers that explains why Marx was so dismissive of the idea that the institutions of a liberal republic could successfully "mediate" (that is, educate and expand) the partial or particular interests of "civil society."[33]

The dissolution of feudal society may have liberated civil society from direct and personalized *political* domination, but it did nothing to transform ("revolutionize") the constitutive elements of that society. In Marx's pithy summation, "Feudal society was dissolved into its basic element, *man*; but into *egoistic* man who was its real foundation."[34]

Given the depressing realities of the present, I must say that I share more than a little of Marx's skepticism concerning the liberal-republican project of mediation, even as I reject the utopianism of his notion of our "species-being" (and the idea of a "relational" freedom that goes along with it).

Confronted by the contemporary realities of lobbying, the intrusion of business into the process of legislation and regulation (to the point where many industries, such as energy and pharmaceuticals, more or less write the laws intended to regulate them), and ever-proliferating interest groups, only the most shameless of corporate shills could possibly maintain that our public-political realm works to further the generalization (or "education") of interests. To the contrary, it is increasingly assumed—by politicians and business leaders, but also by average citizens, educators, and even legal theorists—that the *raison d'être* of American constitutional government is to facilitate economic activity. We have become, in Sheldon Wolin's apt phrase, an "economic polity," one in which the curtailment or education of interests is seen as unworkable, unnecessary, and un-American.[35]

In the face of this unquestioned bit of "common sense," the reintroduction to the broad problematic shared by Hegel, Tocqueville, Mill, and Arendt is a salutary exercise. However fraught their individual attempts to renovate certain aspects of the civic republican tradition may be, these theorists remind us that the public-political world has a significance and purpose beyond the protection of property and the securing of public order, two goods that can be provided by even the most authoritarian of regimes (for example, China).

The starting point of this diverse set of theorists—the thing that makes them all "modern" in Constant's sense of the word—is that they recognize the pursuit of interest as a large and legitimate sphere of activity, all the while insisting that the public-political cannot be reduced to—or made an epiphenomenon of—such activity. Or, to put it in a more positive formulation: Hegel, Tocqueville, Mill, and Arendt all insist on the relative autonomy or dignity of the public realm.[36] They remind us that unless citizens are able to see the difference between the pursuit of interest (on the one hand) and their joint responsibility for a common world (on the other), an exploitatively instrumental configuration of the sort Marx postulated would invariably result. Hence their shared emphasis on what (for want of a better word) I will call the "educational" experience of public participation and sustained attention to public affairs.

But isn't this a return to the most dubious dimension of the civic republican tradition—namely, the heavy emphasis on the "formative" project, the project of "correct" socialization urged by Machiavelli and Rousseau? And doesn't this, in turn, summon up the specter of a tutorial or paternalistic state?

It is indeed jarring when we read a liberal theorist like Constant stating that "institutions must achieve the moral education of the citizens."[37] By this, however, he did not mean the institutional stamping of civic "form" onto the more or less promising "raw material" of the people. The latter was, indeed, the project of republican theorists like Machiavelli and Rousseau. Above everything else, they wanted to create a morality of the common good among citizens. Such a morality demanded a root-and-branch socialization, one that Machiavelli and Rousseau saw as proceeding through such "neo-Roman" institutions as military service, civil religion, and a rigorous censorship.[38] Corruption—the gradual dissolution of this civic form through the rise of particular or selfish interests—would be kept at bay only so long as laws, institutions, and mores worked together to effectively contain those who might exploit public institutions for private advantage (usually, the wealthy or noble class, the "overmighty"). However, once the lure of inequality, luxury, and private interest took hold, a "corrupt" people would be able to retain its liberty only with the greatest difficulty.[39] For unreconstructed civic republicans like Machiavelli and Rousseau, commerce and representative government are, respectively, a great accelerator and a clear symptom of civic corruption. They attest to the substantial loss of public freedom.[40]

As a champion of both representative government and the spirit of commerce, such a robustly republican "formative" project was the furthest thing from Constant's mind. What, then, did he mean when he said that "institutions must achieve the moral education of the citizens"?

The answer—one echoed, in various ways, in Hegel, Tocqueville, Mill, and Arendt—was that citizens must be given something to do for the public if they were to become capable of exercising the "active and constant surveillance" of governmental authorities that a representative system demands.[41] As already noted, Constant thought that the danger of modern liberty was that, "absorbed in the enjoyment of our private independence, and in the pursuit of our particular interests, we should surrender our right to a share in political power too easily."[42] This danger was hardly speculative. The French bourgeoisie embraced Napoleonic despotism not one but twice—first in 1804, then again in 1851—preferring public order to public liberty. The former condition was, after all, much more conducive to the steady accumulation of profit. As Tocqueville ruefully observed in volume 2 of *Democracy in America*:

> When the taste for physical gratification among them [a demo-cratic people] has grown more rapidly than their education and their experience of free institutions, the time will come when men are carried away and lose all self-restraint at the sight of the new possessions they are about to obtain. In their intense and exclusive anxiety to make a fortune they lose sight of the close connection between the private fortune of each and the prosper-ity of all. It is not necessary to do violence to such a people in order to strip them of the rights they enjoy; they themselves will-ingly loosen their hold. The discharge of political duties appears to them to be a troublesome impediment which diverts them from their occupations and business.[43]

Hence the imperative of *some* political involvement on the part of or-dinary citizens, an involvement that transcends the (occasionally mean-ingless) ritual of electoral participation. As early as 1820, Hegel wrote: "As for popular suffrage, it may further be remarked that especially in large states it leads inevitably to electoral indifference, since the casting of a sin-gle vote is of no significance where there is a multitude of electors."[44] Civic virtue in the strong republican sense might well be a dangerous anachro-nism in the modern world. Nevertheless, political theorists still had to find a way to enable the *citoyen* to coexist with the *bourgeois*, and not merely as the latter's "political lion-skin." They had to find a way, in other words, to replace old-style civic republicanism with a distinctively modern form of public spirit—what Arendt would call "care for the public world."

The primary *modern* avenue for the cultivation of public-political traits was—as Hegel, Tocqueville, and Mill all emphasized—participation in associational life, understood in both its political and social dimen-sions.[45] But the cultivation of public spirit also depended on a real consti-tutional or institutional presence, a "public space" that was both durable and accessible to ordinary people. Tocqueville did not call political associations and participation in local administration the "large free schools" of democratic citizenship for nothing. Mill gave a classic formulation of the moral-political benefits of such expanded participation in his *Considerations on Representative Government* (1861):

> It is not sufficiently considered how little there is in most men's ordinary life to give any largeness either to their conceptions or to their sentiments. Their work is routine; not a labor of love, but of self-interest in the most elementary form, the satisfaction of daily wants; neither the thing done, nor the process of doing it, introduces the mind to thoughts or feelings extending beyond individuals; if instructive books are within reach, there is no stimulus to read them; and in most cases the individual has no access to any person of cultivation much superior to his own. *Giving him something to do for the public, supplies, in a measure, all these deficiencies.* If circumstances allow the amount of public duty assigned to him to be considerable, it makes him an educated man. . . . He is called upon, while so engaged, to weigh interests not his own; to be guided, in the case of conflicting claims, by another rule than his private partialities; to apply, at every turn, principles and maxims which have for their reason of existence the common good. . . . He is made to feel himself one of the public, and whatever is for their benefit to be for his benefit. Where this *school of public spirit* does not exist, scarcely any sense is entertained that private persons, in no eminent social situation, owe any duties to society, except to obey the laws and submit to the government.[46]

The predominant image here is less that of a "school of public spirit" constructed by a great lawgiver (such as Moses, Lycurgus, or Romulus—the preferred examples of Machiavelli and Rousseau) than a constitutional arrangement that provides ample and open-ended opportunity for ordinary citizens to learn basic civic arts (and modes of judgment) by doing. As the passage above attests, Mill tended to view such self-instruction as dependent upon limited and indirect guidance from the more enlightened or instructed classes.[47] Nevertheless, he is building on a key insight, one we find articulated in both Hegel and Tocqueville.

The gist of this insight might be put as follows. The only way we can cultivate "care for the public realm" in a world where people's primary energies are (necessarily) devoted to the pursuit of private interest is to make sure that associational life and political participation provide ample opportunities for the gradual education and generalization of interests. What Tocqueville famously described as the "close tie that unites general to private interest" can be drawn out by experience in the political or associational realm. Such experience invariably presses us to revise our understanding of the nexus between ourselves, our interests, and our identities and the rights, interests, and identities of others. The "public"—conceived broadly as an institutional *and* associational space, one that cuts across the state/civil society distinction[48]—is the place where such mediation occurs, if it occurs at all.

Many of the chapters in this volume are devoted to teasing out the nature and prospects of such mediation, as Hegel, Tocqueville, Mill, and Arendt conceived it. My primary concern is to show how representative institutions, a pluralistic associational life, and what I call a "decentered" or highly differentiated state structure opened up a new and varied range of public spaces—at least in theory. The post-Rousseauian problematic of public freedom in European political thought of the first half of the nineteenth century is thus not characterized by any nostalgia for a world we have lost (the "beautiful freedom" of the Athenian polis or Roman Republic), nor is it animated by a sense of inevitable closure. While well aware of the potential pathologies arising from a democratic social condition (including privatism, the rule of public opinion, and the strong tendency toward bureaucratic despotism), Hegel, Tocqueville, Mill, and Arendt are all marked by what we might call a sober or disillusioning form of hopefulness. Like Constant, they are ruthless in their hunting down of anachronisms in political theory and practice. Unlike him, they offer very specific recommendations for actualizing the potential of the new spaces of public freedom opened up in the post-revolutionary world.

Of course, many of their hopes have failed to bear fruit, the recent celebratory literature on the topic of "civil society" notwithstanding. Why is this the case?

One answer is that the complex structures of representation, mediation, deliberation, and decision they envisioned presumed not just substantial public spirit and attentiveness on the part of ordinary citizens but also a balance between the political and the economic spheres. The world Hegel, Tocqueville, and Mill inhabited was a world in which the systemic colonization of the public-political world by economic forces and categories had only just begun. This is the context for Hegel's elaborate attempt in *The Philosophy of Right* to demonstrate how the modern, "rational" state could give civil (market) society its due without being overwhelmed by its particularistic, egoistic spirit. It is also the context for Tocqueville's intense focus on the political arrangements and cultural preconditions (the "free *moeurs*") that made American democracy possible—a focus that permitted only the most hurried glance at the rising "aristocracy of manufactures." It is, finally, the context for Mill's endorsement (in his *Principles of Political Economy*) of free markets as a crucial facilitator of the value of autonomy, an endorsement combined—only somewhat paradoxically—with an oft-expressed frustration that the only outlet for individual energy and creativity in mid-nineteenth century Britain was business.

All of these analyses depart from what seems the ungrounded assumption that political and cultural factors either outweigh or are equal to the troubling expansion of strictly economic forces. Whatever inequities the latter introduced (and Hegel, Tocqueville, and Mill were far from blind to these), they could still be coped with by flexible yet vigilant political arrangements. For these theorists, the real threats to public freedom remained: (a) the state as a potentially mechanical and enervating (centralized) structure; and (b) the rise of an intolerant and potentially monolithic public opinion. If Hegel, Tocqueville, and Mill look a bit quaint to us today, it is because they lived not just in a pre-Marxian but also in a pre-Weberian world. They lived, in other words, in a world in which neither capitalism nor bureaucracy had become pervasive and seemingly all-determining structural realities. Such structures of congealed political and economic power were still largely threats on the horizon, rather than overwhelming actualities in the present.

It is not surprising, then, that the *social* theories of Marx and Weber often seem to speak much more directly to our situation. Marx's recurring image of economic instrumentalities that become ends-in-themselves, dominating those who created them, or Weber's metaphor of an "iron cage" of administrative rationality capture the ubiquitous sense of disempowerment that accompanies life in the late modern world. Wherever one turns, one confronts enormous structures of governmental, bureaucratic, and corporate power, structures that do indeed have a "life of their own" and that often (if not necessarily always) treat us as means rather than ends. In such a structurally recalcitrant world, it is hardly surprising that many conservatives prefer to address the problems of American democracy strictly in terms of the vocabulary provided by Tocqueville. Our problems, they insist, are a function of the decline of our manners and mores, our lack of attention to virtue and to a still needed education in character.

Would that things were so simple. No amount of "moral" education will prevent America from devolving into a superpower caste society, one whose relationship to democracy is formal or notional at best. Even in the terms provided by Tocqueville and Mill (for obvious reasons, Hegel is rarely cited by American conservatives), the critics on the right get it wrong. The "education" envisioned by the great political thinkers of the first half of the nineteenth century was an education in the rudiments of self-government and public life. It was an education not of "character," but of political judgment and agency for classes who had been excluded from any political participation for centuries on end. Yet even if we get Hegel, Tocqueville, and Mill "right"—that is, even if we see the "educational" dimension of their political theories as political rather than merely or mostly moral—we may still feel they haven't begun to address the most difficult aspects of the late modern condition. Popular ignorance, apathy, and distraction present huge impediments to recovering what is left of our diminishing democracy. It is sobering to realize that these are hardly the only, or indeed the largest, obstacles to that project.

Confronted by grim contemporary reality, politically engaged students (not to mention their professors) often swing to the opposite side of the theoretical spectrum. They opt for a theory of "total" or systemic domination such as we find in "classic" Frankfurt School theorists (Horkheimer, Adorno, and Marcuse) and in mid-career Foucault (the Foucault of *Discipline and Punish*).

The relentlessly downbeat analyses of neo-Marxism in the middle of the last century are eminently understandable once they are placed in their historical context, a context that included the defeat of the left, the rise of fascism, and the horrific destruction of European Jewry. What is more surprising is how these analyses were appropriated and simplified by movement we know as postmodernism. From the standpoint of political theory, postmodernism was notable for installing a new manic-depressive dialectic, a dialectic we only now seem to be emerging from. Swinging relentlessly between the poles of claustrophobic forms of total domination (on the one hand) and new forms of vitalism and subjectivism (on the other), postmodernism promised that all could be changed if only we adjusted our attitude. The unsurprising result was a complete lack of concern for, or engagement with, the problem of how to institutionalize freedom in the late modern world.

I say "unsurprising" because so much of what is written today flows directly from Weber's iron cage metaphor, through Adorno and Horkheimer's idea of total domination (*totale Herrschaft*), to (finally) Foucault's notion of a disciplinary society ("the carceral"). With each step in this progression, the terms of domination are ratcheted up. In the end, the only move left is to rise, Peter Pan–like, above the entire terrain of political parties, institutions, debates, etc. of one's local or national political scene. One imagines oneself part of a larger, utterly deterritorialized mass of the oppressed, a mass engaged in globally networked, decentralized struggle against new forms of imperial hegemony (the rule of multinational corporations backed up by American military might).

This vision—Hardt and Negri's "multitude"—is an appealing one for many on the "theory left."[49] It chimes with the ingrained Marxist presumption that representative democracy and liberalism more generally were a sham from the very beginning, updating it by declaring "sovereignty" to be an outmoded and anachronistic concept. Global hegemony requires global resistance—*la lotta continua*, albeit this time outside of any specific set of institutions and without any politically organized people. In this way, one moves from feeling absolutely impotent (as an atomized member of a more or less marginalized American left) to feeling enormous empowerment (as part of a trans-subjective, global, and vitalist mass). Suffice it to say that this fantasy of global solidarity and resistance, based on a dubious neo-Spinozist metaphysics, is precisely that. More troubling, perhaps, is that it feeds on the human, all too human, desire to feel at one with larger-than-human forces. As Arendt pointed out long ago in *The Origins of Totalitarianism*, such a desire is a highly dubious motivation for political action.

Arendt was responding to the rise of rise of tribalist conceptions of political identity following World War I. During this period, she thought, political romanticism truly came into its own, as the idea of political membership was shorn of its public, constitutional, and "worldly" dimensions. For the Pan-Germanist and Pan-Slavist movements of this period, what remained was (respectively) the appeal to one's racial identity or to one's "Slavic soul." What at first seemed like a forward-looking deterritorialization of political identity—born of the yearning to go beyond the institutional confines of the nation-state—was actually a regress to a vulgarized version of the cult of romantic inwardness. Who one is, politically speaking, was held to have nothing to do with the finite, artificial, and institutionally defined space one inhabited, and everything to do with the pre-institutional, pre-political identity of one's race or "soul." Of course, today's political romantics are proud of having overcome all such "particularist" identities.

However, they are at one with those of yesteryear in seeing political identity in supra-institutional (and supra-constitutional) terms.

As I already suggested, this move is to be expected in a post-Weberian world where institutions are experienced largely as cages or as more or less subtle vehicles for domination. The move from political action as the joint action of citizens in the public realm (Arendt) to political action as a radically decentered and mobile resistance (to corporations, the state, and the everyday discipline of schools, hospitals, and prisons: Foucault, Hardt and Negri) is a move designed to make us question the sheer tenability of the public/private distinction, a distinction that underlies both the liberal and civic republican traditions and the idea of constitutional democracy itself.

One can, of course, recognize the less-than-benign impact of multinational corporations, and the less-than-liberal operation of everyday disciplines, without abandoning the normative ideals of limited government and critical, vigilant citizenship of the sort called for by Locke, Constant, and Arendt. It is true that the public/private distinction can, in a reified or "naturalized" form, blind us to exercises of power that are not "state-centered." But it is a long way from the acknowledgment that the liberal and republican conceptions of power are often inadequate to the analysis of new economic and disciplinary configurations, to the conclusion that the point of these political vocabularies was—from the very beginning, as it were—to conceal the operations of power and facilitate the production of "docile subjects." Nothing could be further from the truth, even if we acknowledge the contributions made by late-eighteenth- and early-nineteenth-century reformers (such as Bentham) to the project of disciplinary surveillance.[50]

Political or social institutions are often sites of "normalizing surveillance," just as the public itself (at least in its robust republican formulation) was clearly intended to create a certain shame-inducing transparency.[51] In this sense, Foucault was right: being "forced to be seen" is just as troubling a project as being "forced to be free." But there is an enormous difference between the civic republican's inveterate suspicion of the private (a suspicion noted and rebuked by Constant in the strongest possible terms) and the idea that republican government itself exists primarily as a vehicle of and for surveillance. Similarly, we can acknowledge that liberal constitutionalism is often ineffectual in dealing with the "politics of everyday life." However, that does not render it essentially a Trojan horse for the operation of disciplinary practices. To think that it is requires falling back on the notion of conspiratorial class rule (something Foucault himself was not always above).[52] It also demands the conflation of the origins of specific disciplinary "technologies" with their contemporary functions. Foucault, good Nietzschean that he was, was always careful to distinguish the two. His epigones have largely thrown such methodological precautions to the wind.

Even if public-political institutions are not just vehicles of domination (as both Weber and Adorno, in addition to Marcuse and Foucault, suggest), we are still left with a troubling question. What can "the public" and political institutions be in a world so dramatically constrained by the imperatives of the global marketplace and the ubiquity of bureaucratic hierarchy and bureaucratic process?

The essays in this volume do not pretend to offer any easy answers to this question—in many respects, *the* question of political theory in the "late modern" age. Rather, they are intended to show two things: first, how a "liberal republican" range of theoretical possibilities was opened in the wake of the French Revolution; and second, how fears about bureaucratic despotism and "social tyranny" transformed into something altogether different with the advent of the twentieth century—namely, the idea of a "soft totalitarianism" that supposedly afflicts the liberal democratic regimes of the present.

Anyone who has studied either the thought of Hannah Arendt or genuinely totalitarian regimes will find the latter locution—probably first deployed by Herbert Marcuse in *One Dimensional Man*—irresponsible and misleading. It is irresponsible because it is, quite simply, an example of unconstrained hyperbole. As such, it has no place in political or social theory. It is misleading because it blinds us to the real nature of the dangers we face in the present. These, I would suggest, are far closer to the "neo-absolutism" recently analyzed by Elaine Scarry than to the "total system" suggested by Marcuse.

The political world we inhabit is increasingly Schmittian in nature. It is a world in which "national emergency" and the so-called "war on terror" have seemingly revealed the profoundly conditional—not to say ultimately fictitious—nature of constitutional restraints. Schmitt—and before him, Hobbes—apparently has been proven right: the rule of law stops at (and depends on) the moment of sovereign definition and decision. The only way of combating this bogus inevitability is to reclaim our capacity for action as *citizens*, rather than as members of single-issue focused interest groups. We must insist *as citizens* that the increasingly regular suspension of constitutional limits and restraints (for example, warrantless wiretapping) is both unconstitutional and un-American. We must reject the mindless (Schmittian) patriotism of the call to "strike back" for the *constitutional* patriotism that lies at the heart of the "American experiment."[53]

This is not easy to do in a political context where virtual one-party rule has effectively neutered constitutional checks and balances.[54] Yet it is a duty incumbent on anyone who views politics as something more than a "decision procedure," or a way of deciding "who gets what, when, where and how." As I note in chapter 5, Mill once observed that a "political machinery does not run by act of itself. As it is first made, so it has to be worked, by men, and even by ordinary men. It needs, not their simple acquiescence, but their active participation."[55] We Americans have been used to thinking of our Constitution as a "machine that runs by itself" for far too long. As the last six years have shown, the institutional machine—the multi-tiered system of power put in place by the Constitution—can break down, and its checks and balances all but neutralized. It can be retooled for what are, essentially, illiberal or authoritarian purposes.

Beyond the realization of our political liberty, the purpose of public freedom is to make concrete—to actualize—the "active and constant surveillance over their [the people's] representatives." This is something Constant, echoing Locke, thought essential to any constitutional regime. In this regard, public freedom is not the alternative to, or antithesis of, representative government.[56] It is, rather, an absolutely essential element of any representative system.[57] Where trust has been betrayed by officeholders and bureaucrats, public freedom is one crucial avenue for restoring the balance. We cheat ourselves, our country, and our children if, like Hobbes, we think such freedom doesn't exist, or that—between elections, at least—we are subjects rather than citizens, utterly bereft of the power to act and, indeed, to decide.

2 | TOCQUEVILLE AND CIVIL SOCIETY

The Rebirth of Civil Society

Tocqueville's reflections on civil society have proven to be one of his most enduring theoretical legacies. They have also proven to be one of the most contested and promiscuously appropriated. This is especially so in America, where in recent years there has been an explosion of academic and journalistic writing on the topic of civil society. Authors from across the ideological spectrum have turned to Tocqueville for guidance in figuring out how the resources of civil society—the diverse array of political, charitable, educational, religious, neighborhood, and professional associations—might best be deployed in the fight against a wide range of social ills. These include perceived declines in civic engagement and individual responsibility, the loss of trust and a sense of community, and the spread of urban decay, apathy, and selfishness.

Perusing this literature, the casual reader might well conclude that "civil society" has become little more than a feel-good slogan in a time of generalized distrust of (or impatience with) governmental institutions. The core of Tocqueville's idea—civil society as the sphere of intermediary organizations standing between the individual and the state—has been worked and reworked to the point where it is no longer clear where the primary importance of this realm lies. Is it in the moralizing potential of churches, synagogues, and schools? In the ability of the "private sector" to counterbalance or outperform government bureaucracy?[1] In the pluralism inherent in associational life, the fact that this sphere offers no particular setting for a singular vision of the good life, but rather (in the words of Michael Walzer) a "setting of settings"?[2] Or might it be in the way civil society functions as a seedbed for civic virtue, fostering a sense of citizenship and public life through what Tocqueville called "the habit of association"?

These reworkings result in a confusing picture, one not made any clearer by the fact that when Tocqueville used the phrase "civil society" (*société civile*) he did so to distinguish a sociocultural realm of ideas, feelings, and habits (*moeurs*) from the institutions and practices of government (*le monde politique*). This distinction frames the respective discussions of *Democracy in America*'s two volumes, the first (1835) focusing on the "political public world," the second (1840) on the attitudes and sustaining *moeurs* of American democracy. Invoked in the introduction to volume 1 and the author's preface to volume 2, Tocqueville's "official" separation of *political* from *civil* society promotes a focus on manners and nonpolitical associations—a focus well-suited to the moralizing intentions of many contemporary neo-Tocquevillians.

However, it would be a great mistake to see the reemergence of "civil society"—and the corresponding rise in Tocqueville's theoretical profile— as solely, or even chiefly, the function of specifically American worries and debates. Beyond the chorus praising "membership" and the role of "mediating institutions" in American life, a deeper conceptual sea change has occurred, one born of very real social and political upheavals that have shaken much of the globe over the last thirty years. These upheavals include the crisis of the welfare state in Western Europe (beginning in the 1970s and continuing to this day); the collapse of state socialism in Eastern Europe and the former Soviet Union; the protracted struggle against right-wing authoritarian regimes in Central and South America; and the gradual abandonment of state-directed programs of modernization in the developing world.[3]

Outside the limited confines of the American debate, "civil society" came to represent a newly born, newly active political and associational life—one without the official sponsorship of the state. It appeared as a marker of broad but fitful democratization, often the result of intense political struggle. It referred to a diverse array of trade, women's, political, and student groups, all of whom were determined to defend not just private but also *local* and *public* liberty. It came, in a word, to stand for a decentralized and pluralistic public realm, one capable of advancing society's claims not only against the bureaucratic/authoritarian state, but also against large economic interests (such as multinational corporations). It was outside America that "civil society" recovered, as both concept and reality, the public-political dimension that made it such an important idea for Tocqueville—indeed, his master idea.

This fact raises a number of questions. First, how is it that "civil society" has such radically different connotations in different parts of the world? Second, why has the "civil society movement" in the United States focused so intently on community, character, and volunteerism rather than dissent, joint action, and the activity of self-government? Third, which broad conception of civil society—the largely nonpolitical one familiar from the American debate, or the self-consciously political one familiar from other parts of the world—is more in line with Tocqueville's theoretical intentions?

The first two questions have elicited a great deal of comment but fall outside the purview of this chapter.[4] I will focus, instead, on the third. Answering it will demand an exploration of why intermediate organizations—associational life in the broadest sense—loom so large in Tocqueville's view of democracy, its potential pathologies, and its possibilities for freedom. I will begin with a brief consideration of the history of "civil society" in Western political thought, the better to highlight the nature and extent of Tocqueville's theoretical innovation (an innovation often obscured by his "official" distinction between *le monde politique* and *société civile*). I will then turn to consider Tocqueville's discussion of local and political associations in volume 1 of *Democracy in America*. This will provide a broader, more political context for consideration of volume 2's well-known discussion of "civil associations" (a discussion which provides the point of departure for the American debate on the value of voluntary association).[5] I will conclude by briefly considering the relative valence of public freedom and religious belief in Tocqueville's account of civil society.

I believe that any adequate discussion of "Tocqueville and civil society" must proceed in terms of his overarching theoretical questions. First, are democratic societies fated to be centralized (bureaucratic) nonparticipatory societies? The example of post-revolutionary France seemed to point in this direction. Second, how, if at all, can democracy and meaningful decentralization be combined in the modern world?[6] It was the drive to answer these questions that led Tocqueville to focus on the role of intermediate organizations in the first place, and to construe this category in very broad terms indeed. Thus, in Tocqueville's understanding, the "intermediate" sphere of American democracy included (as content or precondition) the following: town meetings, a free press, the separation of church and state, a federal structure of government, political associations, and nonpolitical ("civil") associations.[7]

If we want to understand civil society in terms of Tocqueville's political theory, we must see that the central distinction for him is not between *société politique* and *société civile*, nor between political associations and nonpolitical ones. Rather, the crucial distinction is between local and centralized organizations of power, action, and administration. This broadly Montesquieuian approach to civil society shifts its center of gravity away from the idea of a (seemingly self-contained) realm of manners and mores, and toward the questions of politics, participation, and public life generally. Indeed, as I shall argue, Tocqueville's conception of civil society is one in which the "priority of the political" is very much in evidence—a fact that distinguishes him from both his immediate predecessors (Guizot, Constant, and the *Doctrinaires*) and many of his contemporary appropriators.

The Theoretical Background

As Hegel—the touchstone for virtually all theoretical discussions of civil society—observed in *The Philosophy of Right*, civil society is "the achievement of the modern world."[8] The idea that *state* and *society* are separate and distinct entities is a relatively recent one in Western political thought, going back only a few centuries. The fact that it comes so naturally to us obscures the long and often painful process by which the spheres of religious belief, market relations, and public opinion gradually emancipated themselves from the state. One need only look back to the ancient Greek notion of a *koinonia politike*, or the feudal Christian idea of a *communitas civilis sive politica*, to see that—for much of our tradition—state and society formed a kind of identity. Functional or "organic" differentiation was recognized early on (most memorably in Plato's *Republic*), as was the idea of political society as a plurality of associations (the famous family/village/polis schema of Aristotle's *Politics*). But it was never doubted that what *we* think of as a relatively independent social sphere inhered, in some way, in a larger, more comprehensive political association (a point of view Hegel tried to revive for the modern age, his stress on social differentiation notwithstanding).

For the longer part of its history, then, the term "civil society" referred to *political* society in this broad, inclusive sense. As late as the 1680s, we find John Locke contrasting "civil society" not with the state, but with the *state of nature*.[9] Civil society was, for Locke, *politically organized* society, a body characterized by a "common established law," a judicature to decide controversies, and a magistrate to "punish Offenders." Where these three elements were lacking, Locke claimed, one remained "in the perfect state of nature."[10] At the same time, however, we find in Locke the beginnings of a systematic distinction between *society* and *government*, the latter being understood as the "trustee" of a collective political power created by a society-forming pact of association (itself designed to remedy the "inconveniences" of the state of nature).[11] It was on the basis of this emergent distinction that Locke famously grounded the right to revolution.[12]

With the Enlightenment, a noticeable shift in the meaning of civil society occurs. This shift has two moments. The first is due to the leading figures of the Scottish Enlightenment (Adam Smith, David Hume, Sir James Steuart, and Adam Ferguson), who delineate a new, essentially economic conception of civil society. Pressing for the separation of economic relations from the state, these thinkers conceived of civil society as a more or less self-regulating sphere of interests and markets.[13] The goal was not merely to liberate commercial society from the fetters of the "embedded" economy, but to suggest that the pursuit of self-interest could actually hold society together more efficiently, producing greater freedom and public goods than any political apparatus could. This suggestion received a sharp rebuke from Rousseau, who saw self-interest and "partial associations" as invariably corrupting. Against emergent market society, he reaffirmed the traditional civic republican idea of a "common good" that occupied a moral plane distinct from (and opposed to) that of individual interest.[14]

The second moment of the Enlightenment shift comes with the emergence of what Habermas has called the "bourgeois public sphere" in the course of the eighteenth century.[15] Arising in the coffeehouses, salons, and table societies of the period, a "culture debating public" gradually turned its critical attention to public-political affairs, an arena previously monopolized by the monarchical state. Guided by controversialists like Diderot and Voltaire and given theoretical articulation by Kant, the "republic of letters" gave birth to a new idea of civil society: the idea of a social space where private persons came together to make public use of their reason.[16] In this sphere, public opinion appeared as a critical, rationalizing force, one that challenged the authoritarian and secretive imperatives of *raison d'état.*

It was Hegel who first brought these two moments at least partly together, giving civil society its first fully modern articulation in political theory. *The Philosophy of Right* famously identifies civil society as a dimension of ethical life, a sphere of difference that "intervenes" between the natural community of the family and the universal (but highly differentiated) moral life of the state.[17]

At first glance, Hegel's concept of civil society seems merely to reiterate that of the Scottish Enlightenment—albeit this time with an emphasis on the socially disintegrative effects of an unconstrained market economy.[18] It is indeed true that Hegel saw civil society as (chiefly) the sphere of "particularity"—that is, as a sphere of more or less universal egoism in which individuals go about pursuing their self-interest.[19] However, Hegel also saw civil society as having an integrative and educative dimension, one that militates against its atomizing, individualistic core.[20] Thus, Hegel's full conception of civil society includes those organs of public authority that regulate and support economic activities. It also includes the main social "estates" or classes (*Stände*), plus professional associations, religious bodies, learned societies, and town councils (a collection Hegel dubs "the corporation"). The institutions of civil authority protect the welfare and rights of members of civil society, while those of the "corporation" provide a sense of membership, solidarity, and recognition to individuals in an otherwise competitive and egoistic sphere.[21]

Of course, Hegel thought that civil society—the sphere of modern individualism and particularity par excellence—could realize its potential *only* when integrated into the higher (more universal and concrete) ethical life of the state. He worried that the self-seeking "spirit of civil society" would—if given too free a rein—infect the political state, subordinating it to the "free play of interests and the subjective opinions of individual citizens."[22] His solution (such as it was) was to provide a limited role for public opinion, participation, and deliberation, while reserving an expansive one for executive organs, cabinet ministers, and the civil service (the "universal" class).

Yet, despite these flaws, Hegel's concept of civil society successfully articulated a sphere of intermediate interests and associations, filling in the terrain between the particularity of self-interest (on the one hand) and the abstract universality of the state (on the other).[23] Not only that: Hegel also showed how the institutions of civil society (corporations, estates, and municipalities) educated citizens to progressively more general levels of interest. Hegel's idea of civil society thus went a long way toward bridging the apparent abyss between *bourgeois* and *citoyen*, an abyss opened up by Rousseau's vehement critique of the Scots' vision of a commercial society held together by self-interest and an increasingly specialized division of labor.[24]

Tocqueville was barely aware of Hegel, and hardly shared his enthusiasm for the modern, "rational" state (the state created by Louis XIV and "perfected" by the Revolution and Napoleon). However, on the issue of civil society, there is an important but largely overlooked parallel between their works.[25] Both Hegel and Tocqueville focused on the associational middle ground ignored by political economists and civic republicans alike. More to the point, both thinkers were deeply worried about the unchecked spread of modern (what Tocqueville labeled "democratic") individualism. In response, they drew attention to the public dimensions and significance of some of civil society's central institutions. This simultaneous emphasis on civil society's distinctness from *government* and its overlap with *public-political* life is perhaps their greatest shared legacy (less surprising when we recall their mutual debt to Montesquieu).

Two factors enabled Tocqueville to highlight this continuity between civil society and public life in a more profound manner than Hegel. First, there was Tocqueville's deep distaste for the idea of the bureaucratic state as *the* repository of the public good. Second, there was his eye-opening journey to America. When Hegel contemplated America from his Berlin lecture podium in 1830, he saw a country that appeared to be *all* civil society: the young nation lacked, in his view, a developed state and (thus) a meaningful public life.[26] When Tocqueville visited America in 1831–32, he too was struck by the "absence of government" and the spectacle of a society that "goes along by itself."[27] But he also saw that public life had hardly vanished. On the contrary, it had dispersed to a host of local sites and organizations scattered throughout the country.

In America, the Enlightenment's dream of overcoming the state's monopoly on public affairs had been realized, but in a way that neither the *philosophes* nor Hegel could quite have imagined. The centralized state was gone, and public-political life inhabited (to a large extent) the terrain of what we now call social life.[28] This was the great discovery of *Democracy in America*, and the reason why Tocqueville's conception of civil society has proven, ultimately, to be richer and more politically suggestive than Hegel's (his only serious competitor in this regard).

When contemporary social scientists and political commentators turn to Tocqueville on civil society, they invariably cite his declaration that "nothing . . . is more deserving of our attention than the intellectual and moral associations of America."[29] It is certainly true that Tocqueville was struck by how the Americans made use of the "means" of voluntary association to achieve an almost comical variety of ends.[30] Yet the reflexive reference to one short chapter in volume 2 of Tocqueville's masterpiece has had the effect of seriously impairing our grasp of his political conception of civil society and associational life. This can be seen from the fact that Tocqueville's treatment of "civil associations" in volume 2 is situated in terms of a much broader discussion about how democratic equality fosters individualism, privatism, and the decline of public virtues. Associations—both political and civil—are vital means for combating this tendency, for preserving a robust form of citizenship and public life. Indeed, a case can be made that many of the essentials of Tocqueville's *political* theory of civil society are contained (paradoxically enough) in volume 1.

In volume 1—and again at the beginning of volume 2—Tocqueville distinguishes between civil society and the "political world" (*le monde politique*). While fundamental to his theoretical enterprise and the structure of his work, this distinction is also misleading. Like Hegel's apparently clear-cut distinction between civil society and the state, Tocqueville's distinction invites us to place all public-political institutions and activities in one sphere, and all cultural, charitable, business, and social organizations in another. To do so, however, would make a travesty of Tocqueville's central argument about the role of associations *qua* intermediary organizations in American political life. Further, we would be unable to fully grasp his distinctions between *permanent, political,* and *civil* associations, or see how these categories map out a social and political space *between* equal individuals and their government. If we want to grasp Tocqueville's idea of civil society, we must conceive it not as a seemingly self-contained realm of mores, habits, and feelings, but rather as a sphere of politically invaluable mediating organizations, a sphere sustained by the "free *moeurs*" these organizations help to create and maintain.

Tocqueville's use of the term "permanent associations" varies according to context. Used with respect to Europe, it refers to the various corporate identities (aristocratic, bourgeois, peasant) that made up the "estates" of the *ancien régime*. One became a member of such an estate by being born into it, and there was very little chance of changing one's place in a social hierarchy composed of such "permanent" associations.[31] In contexts of democratic equality (such as post-revolutionary France or America) there were no "permanent" associations in this sense. However, in volume 1 of *Democracy in America* (*DAI*) Tocqueville does not drop the term. Rather, he now uses it to refer to local, legally established political entities, such as townships, cities, counties, and other sites of local political administration and participation.[32] These are not "involuntary" in the way that social classes are in an aristocratic society, but neither are they as episodic or as shifting in membership as many voluntary associations.

By "political associations" Tocqueville meant those voluntary groups formed by like-minded individuals intent on advancing a particular political doctrine or opinion, or achieving a specific political goal. Such associations may be small and limited to a single end, or they may be larger and more durable groupings with local chapters and regular meetings. The largest of such groups are political parties who aspire to "rule the state" through the mechanisms of representation and election.[33] Finally, by "civil associations" Tocqueville meant not only "commercial and manufacturing companies," but "associations of a thousand other kinds, religious, moral, serious, futile, general or restricted, enormous or diminutive."[34] Somewhat surprisingly, Tocqueville's notion of civil association also includes the press and newspapers, the latter making possible discussion of political issues by large numbers of people dispersed over great distances.

Merely listing these three types (or levels) of association indicates the expansive character of Tocqueville's idea of civil society. It also serves to underline the priority of the political in his conception. By construing civil society in loosely Montesquieuian terms—as including virtually every kind of intermediary organization imaginable—Tocqueville signals that he is interested, first and foremost, in the political uses and effects of associational life. Associations serve not only to decentralize administrative and political power; they also enable ordinary citizens to attain a degree of positive political freedom it would otherwise be hard to imagine. Associations empower by fostering the habit of joint action amongst the equal, isolated, and privatized individuals of modern democratic societies. They are the primary means by which modern fragmentation and powerlessness are overcome, and "democratic despotism" kept at bay.[35]

I want to take a closer look at each of the three "levels" of associational life that Tocqueville distinguishes, the better to understand his political conception of civil society—a conception that escapes any simple state/society dichotomy.

First there is the level of *permanent association*—the townships, municipalities, and counties that Tocqueville identifies with local administration. From a contemporary standpoint, this represents the most counterintuitive of Tocqueville's uses of the word "association." Yet is also the most fundamental. The reason for this is obvious enough. Seen through Tocqueville's Montesquieuian lens, the new democratic world appears bereft of the kind of intermediary powers characteristic of an aristocratic society (noble families, but also guilds, *parlements*, manorial courts, and so on). In America, where such aristocratic institutions simply did not exist, the "permanent associations" of township, city, and county stepped into the breach, occupying a critical part of the terrain between individual and government. Tocqueville clearly saw these "permanent" American associations as highly effective functional substitutes for the old-style *pouvoirs intermédiares* that had hedged in royal power.[36] Indeed, these associations were so successful at dispersing authority that Tocqueville even writes of an "excessive decentralization," one that makes America appear (to European eyes, at least) to be characterized by an utter "absence of government."[37]

What appeared to be an "absence of government" was, in fact, the absence of centralized administration—something made possible by the local authority exercised by the townships. Tocqueville's fascination with this particular form of "permanent association" is well documented.[38] Dating back to the mid-seventeenth century and imported from the "mother country," the institution of the township had, in Tocqueville's view, an enormous impact on America's political development. The tradition of local administration and political participation it created helped America avoid—at least until the 1830s—the more characteristic pathologies of a "democratic social condition" (hypercentralized government; majority tyranny; a mass of equal yet powerless individuals). Calling township independence the "life and mainspring of American liberty at the present day," Tocqueville gives a remarkable description of the townships' historical role in fostering a democratic civil society:

> The independence of the township was the nucleus round which the local interests, passions, rights, and duties collected and clung. It gave scope to the activity of a real political life, thoroughly democratic and republican. The colonies still recognized

the supremacy of the mother country; monarchy was still the law of the state; but the republic was already established in every township.

The towns named their own magistrates of every kind, assessed themselves, and levied their own taxes. In the New England town the law of representation was not adopted; but the affairs of the community were discussed, as at Athens, in the marketplace, by a general assembly of citizens.[39]

This surprising portrait of a Puritan *polis* is revised and expanded in volume 1's chapter on townships and municipalities. If anything, the basic characteristics of the colonial township have, in Tocqueville's view, grown more pronounced over time. Indeed, he saw the early nineteenth-century township as the concrete instantiation of the American principle of popular sovereignty. It provided a local, participatory form of democracy, one with roots in the colonial town meeting. As a result, it was able to dispense with ruling municipal councils and what Tocqueville calls "the system of representation."[40]

The other outstanding characteristic of the New England township was its *independence* as a political entity. Historically antecedent to both state and federal governments, each township formed, as it were, an "independent nation" jealous of its interests, prerogatives, and capacity for self-government.[41] This independence was most clearly manifest in the township's administrative autonomy and authority—an authority that extended to all aspects of community life (from taxation and education to the maintenance of roads and welfare of the poor) as well as to the enforcement and execution (if not the actual legislation) of the law.[42] Finally, and perhaps most important, the township functioned as a "school" for citizenship and public-spiritedness, affording ordinary people not merely the chance to govern themselves, but an insight into the deep continuity between individual and community interests:

> The native of New England is attached to his township because it is independent and free: his cooperation in its affairs ensures his attachment to its interests; the well-being it affords him secures his affections; and its welfare is the aim of his ambition and of his future exertions. He takes a part in every occurrence in the place; he practices the art of government in the small sphere within his reach; he accustoms himself to those forms without which liberty can advance only by revolutions.[43]

Viewed as a whole, the "permanent associations" of township, municipality, and county create a nexus of local democracy second only to the federal constitution as a bulwark against "administrative despotism" and the threat of majority tyranny.[44] In addition, these associations cultivate a "taste for freedom and the art of being free" at the grassroots level. They create, in other words, an experience and expectation of citizenship *directly opposed* to that fostered by a centralized, administrative state.[45]

Tocqueville's treatment of democratic "permanent" associations does much to scramble his official distinction between civil society and *le monde politique*. The same can be said of his treatment of political and civil associations, although first impressions suggest otherwise.

In *DAI*, Tocqueville—haunted by the specter of political instability in post-revolutionary France—offers only a qualified defense of freedom of political association. Presenting American political organizations as a special case of a much broader associative tendency, he is keen to demonstrate how different they are from their European counterparts.[46] In America, "partisans of an opinion" associate mainly to promote a particular political, economic, or social doctrine, and see *persuasion*—not the seizure of power—as their primary task. Through regular discussions and meetings, they articulate their shared opinion more precisely. Through the creation of local chapters or centers, they diffuse it. Should the association become quite large, its members "unite in electoral bodies and choose delegates to represent them in a central assembly."[47] While political associations in Europe can pretend to represent a disenfranchised majority, and remain almost exclusively oriented toward the struggle for power, in America their primary function was to challenge the moral authority of an actually governing majority. Freedom of political association—a somewhat ambiguous blessing in Europe—is, in America, a "necessary guarantee against the tyranny of the majority."[48]

At first glance, this limited (and largely negative) defense of political association seems to confirm the view that, for Tocqueville, the heart and soul of associational life is to be found in the "civil" (social or nonpolitical) arena. Repelled by the dominance of the centralized state and fearful of the violent turbulence born of class-based political struggle, Tocqueville, it seems, can hardly conceal his delight at the energy, peacefulness, and pluralism manifest in American civil society. Applying the "art of association" across the social sphere, the Americans succeed in bringing together—through "artificial" but largely nonpolitical means—what democratic equality effectively tears asunder:

Americans of all ages, all conditions, and all dispositions constantly form associations. They have not only commercial and manufacturing companies, in which all take part, but associations of a thousand other kinds, religious, moral, serious, futile, general or restricted, enormous or diminutive. The Americans make associations to give entertainments, to found seminaries, to build inns, to construct churches, to diffuse books, to send missionaries to the antipodes; in this manner they found hospitals, prisons, and schools. If it is proposed to inculcate some truth or foster some feeling by the encouragement of a great example, they form a society.[49]

Tocqueville's astonished description of the number and variety of voluntary associations in America seems to announce the definitive triumph of society—not only over a self-centered individualism, but over the state and *le monde politique* as well. The "do it yourself" spirit of voluntary ("civil") associations demotes government, politics, and political association itself to an apparently secondary, if not completely peripheral, status. This, at any rate, is how many conservative and communitarian writers have preferred to read Tocqueville, detaching the all important "habit of association" from its roots in politics and public life.

An alternative interpretation of the nature and importance of "civil associations" is suggested the moment we place the passage cited above in its textual context. Tocqueville's description of the spirit of civil association occurs just after his famous analysis of the "atomizing" or socially dissolvent effects of democratic equality. "Aristocracy," he writes, "had made a chain of all the members of the community from the peasant to the king; democracy breaks that chain and severs every link of it."[50] A society in which all are equal may be a society without "natural" hierarchy, but it is also a society without corporate identity and the kind of recognition that goes along with it.

Such a society promotes *individualisme,* which, as Tocqueville notes, is something quite different from mere selfishness. It is a "mature and calm feeling," more an "erroneous judgment" than a "depraved passion." It disposes citizens to withdraw from society into the small circle of family and friends, and to imagine that "their whole destiny is in their own hands."[51] The resulting privatization, isolation, and relative powerlessness of democratic individuals saps not only public virtues; it creates an unprecedented opportunity for new forms of despotism. One can speak, in this regard, of a "fatal alliance" between democratic individualism and government centralization (and control) of public life.[52]

Now, Tocqueville clearly thought that *civil* associations have an important role to play in combating the disempowering effects of democratic equality.[53] However, when it comes to avoiding the "administrative despotism" that is the focus of his fears for the future, nonpolitical associations turn out to be of limited value. Indeed, as Tocqueville observes, they may even be encouraged by governments eager to see popular energies channeled away from the political realm.[54] By themselves, "civil" associations fail to teach what Tocqueville considers the basic moral-political lesson: that there is a "close tie that unites private to general interest."[55] Only public freedom and political associations (of both the "permanent" and more episodic, voluntary kinds) effectively impart this insight, helping thereby to dissolve the abstract opposition between self-interest and the common good. As Tocqueville remarks, "As soon as a man begins to treat of public affairs in public, he begins to perceive that he is not so independent of his fellow men as he first imagined, and that in order to obtain their support he must often lend them his cooperation."[56]

Tocqueville is adamant about the fundamental role public freedom and political participation play in combating individualism and avoiding despotism:

> The Americans have combated by free institutions the tendency of equality to keep men asunder, and they have subdued it. The legislators of America did not suppose that a general representation of the whole nation would suffice to ward off a disorder at once so natural to the frame of democratic society and so fatal; they also thought it would be well to infuse political life into each portion of the territory in order to multiply to an infinite extent opportunities of acting in concert for all the members of the community and to make them constantly feel their mutual dependence.[57]

Political associations, more than civil ones, reinforce this basic accomplishment of the founders and of "permanent" associations. Like local freedom and the "administration of minor affairs," they draw individuals out of their narrow circle of friends and family, teaching them the "art of association" for *public* ends. Along with local freedom, Tocqueville asserts, freedom of political association is the thing most feared by centralizing government. Its very principle challenges the sovereign state's claim to a monopoly of judgment in public matters.[58] In *DAII*, Tocqueville insists that while freedom of *political* association may periodically disturb public tranquility, this is a relatively small price to pay for the preservation of public liberty—especially when the alternative is the transformation of citizens into a "flock of timid and industrious animals, of which the government is the shepherd."[59]

The idea of a "robust" civil society, separate and distinct from the realm of political affairs, is, then, hardly an end-in-itself for Tocqueville. This point is driven home by his consideration of the relation between political and civil associations (*DAII*, book 2, chap. 7). While *Democracy in America* gives ample evidence of Tocqueville's acceptance of Guizot's distinction between social condition and political institutions, it by no means supports the currently popular view that "civil" associations are the seedbed of, or a substitute for, political association and engaged citizenship.[60] In fact, when it comes to learning the fundamentals of the "art of association" (an art essential to the practice of nondocile citizenship), Tocqueville again leaves little doubt as to the priority of political associations. It is they, rather than civil associations, which are the "large free schools" where "all the members of the community go to learn the general theory of association."[61] As Tocqueville explains:

> In their political associations the Americans of all conditions, minds, and ages daily acquire a general taste for association and grow accustomed to the use of it. There they meet together in large numbers, they converse, they listen to one another, and they are mutually stimulated to all sorts of undertakings. They afterwards transfer to civil life the notions they have thus acquired and make them subservient to a thousand purposes.[62]

Tocqueville's insistence on the causal priority of political associations raises the question of why so many "neo-Tocquevillians" assert the exact contrary. *Civil* associations—churches, clubs, charities, professional and social organizations of all kinds—these, they maintain, are our real schools of joint action and civic virtue. One explanation for this otherwise curious inversion is the relative scarcity of spaces of "local freedom" in contemporary society. Where local democracy and self-government are an increasingly dim memory, the hope of many is that civic engagement can be encouraged through more diffuse and generic forms of membership. An alternative explanation is found in the longstanding tendency of liberals and conservatives alike to view commercial associations and the market as the real counterbalance to the state, and religious association as the most important counterweight to individualism (in the distinctly pejorative sense Tocqueville gives this term).

Tocqueville's emphasis on public liberty and the importance of political participation stands as an effective riposte to recent advocates of membership, trust, and "social capital." As for the idea that political associations are, ultimately, less crucial in the fight against centralization and individualism than either commercial or religious association, I should note the following.

First, while it is true that Tocqueville thought government intrusion into the economy would constrict liberty and be damaging to the "morals and intellect" of citizens, it is also true that he harbored little love for the commercial or "bourgeois" spirit.[63] Democratic equality creates a society of more or less universal competition and moral isolation, with an unhealthy focus on physical gratification. Left to itself, the self-interest praised by the Scottish economists yields a corrosive materialism, one destructive not only of public virtues, but of public freedom and liberal rights:

> When the taste for physical gratification among them [a democratic people] has grown more rapidly than their education and their experience of free institutions, the time will come when men are carried away and lose all self-restraint at the sight of new possessions they are about to obtain. In their intense and exclusive anxiety to make a fortune they lose sight of the close connection that exists between the private fortune of each and the prosperity of all. It is not necessary to do violence to such a people in order to strip them of the rights they enjoy; they themselves willingly loosen their hold. The discharge of political duties appears to them to be a troublesome impediment which diverts them from their occupation and business.[64]

A people driven by competition, self-interest, and the quest for material well-being will fear popular unrest, not authoritarian government. Their desire for public order will be so intense that they will be ready, in Tocqueville's words, to "fling away their freedom at the first disturbance."[65] Thus, Tocqueville thought, Napoleonic despotism was made possible (at least in part) by the cravenness of the French bourgeoisie (a verdict he repeats with even greater disgust at the coming of the Second Empire).[66]

What prevented a similar fate from befalling American democracy was not any supposed link between the "spirit of free enterprise" and that of political freedom. On the contrary, Tocqueville saw everything hinging on the containment of the "spirit of civil society" (in Hegel's sense) by a republican-democratic form of civic spirit.[67] The co-presence of these elements on the American scene, and in the American character, led Tocqueville to observe (again, with a certain amount of astonishment), that "an American attends to his private concerns as if he were alone in the world, and the next minute he gives himself up to the common welfare. At one time he seems animated by the most selfish cupidity; at another by the most lively patriotism."[68] Such an energetic double life was possible only so long as traditions of local freedom and political association mediated the drive for material well-being and social advancement.[69] So long as they did, a certain balance or continuity (if not identity) of private and public interest appeared to be commonsensical to the Americans.[70]

But if the unalloyed "spirit of civil society" provides no substitute for the moral achievement wrought by political association (the expansion of narrow self-interest into something far broader in scope), might not the "spirit of religion" overcome the moral isolation created by a democratic social condition? Might not religion help fill the gap left by the demise of "local freedom," demonstrating, in its own way, the "close tie" between individual and community interest? Conservative followers of Tocqueville have been quick to seize upon this idea, drawing support from the strong link he establishes (in *DAI*) between "the spirit of religion" and the "spirit of liberty."

There is little doubt that Tocqueville saw religion as an essential social institution.[71] And there is little doubt that he, like Machiavelli and Rousseau (albeit without their anti-Christian instrumentalism), thought belief was "necessary for the maintenance of republican institutions."[72] But while Tocqueville saw Christianity as underwriting norms of liberal justice and civic equality, he did not think that religious associations, by themselves, could provide anything like a viable substitute for the kind of public culture that democratic freedom presupposed.[73] The positive contribution he saw religion making in the New World was due, in no small part, to the fact that the Americans had fashioned a "democratic and republican" form of Christianity; one clearly distinct and separate from the state; one at odds with the docility and apolitical worldlessness of both early and orthodox Christianity.[74]

In sum, Tocqueville did not think that civil associations, narrowly construed, could do the moral work of political association and participation.[75] This is not to say that he thought civil association had no contribution to make to the public political world. In addition to spreading the habit of association and a spirit of self-reliance (no small achievement), the proliferation of voluntary associations in America challenged the otherwise unfettered dominance of majority feeling and opinion. Tocqueville saw this challenge in terms analogous to those outlined by Madison in *Federalist* 10. By vastly multiplying the number of interests and opinions, civil associations undercut the possibility of any "rule of faction," including that of the majority.[76]

But the proliferation of civil associations also had a more positive contribution to make to *le monde politique*. As Tocqueville explains in *DAII* (book 2, chap. 6), "There is a necessary connection between public [civil] associations and newspapers; newspapers make associations, and associations make newspapers."[77] Newspapers serve not only to bring the dispersed but like-minded together, thereby bolstering the judgment of a minority against the "public opinion" of the majority. They "maintain civilization" by informing private individuals every day about public affairs, establishing a diverse, many-voiced public argument and conversation across vast distances. In other words, through the exploitation of freedom of association and of the press, the Americans had created a *decentered public sphere*: one not dominated by a particular party or city; one free of central government control and—potentially, at least—the dictates of majority opinion. Thus is the *agora* reborn in a society that is no longer face to face and no longer ruled by a single conception of the good life.

Tocqueville's analysis of the close tie between civil associations, newspapers, and the daily experience of citizenship effectively repudiated Rousseau's civic republican dread of "partial" associations, while avoiding the familiar utilitarian conclusion that political life is little more than the clash between conflicting interests and preferences (which need to be effectively "aggregated" at the governmental level). The terrain between individual interests and the "common good" is filled in by ever larger configurations of associational interest. This would approximate our contemporary picture of interest group politics were it not for Tocqueville's repeated stress (parallel to Hegel's) on the political and educational dimensions of associational life, its close tie (through the press and the principle of acting together) to the public realm. The result, in both cases, is a conception of civil society that is intrinsically pluralist—not merely in terms of interests, but also in terms of *values*.[78] The difference between the two theorists is that while Hegel looks to the corporate bodies of the past (the *Stände*) to embody these values within the "Gothic architecture" of the modern state, Tocqueville looks to voluntary associations and local freedom in the context of a decentered public sphere.[79]

And it is here that we encounter Tocqueville's greatest theoretical innovation—an innovation we remain blind to as long as we conceive "civil society" in predominantly economic or moralistic terms. What is this innovation? As I indicated above, it has little to do with Tocqueville's distinction between *société civile* and *le monde politique*. Nor does it have much to do with his focus, in *DAII*, on the realm of habits, opinions, and *moeurs*. Rather, Tocqueville's unique contribution to the "discourse of civil society" is to be found in his remarkable re-visioning of public-political life as dispersed over a nonstate terrain. It is in the realm of "permanent," political, and civil associations that citizenship is learned, self-government effected, and debate and argument suffused throughout society. Civil society, comprised of these three levels of association, effectively ends the reign of the sovereign state over public life.

This is not to say that Tocqueville conflates the social and the political (as did the revolutionaries of 1848), or that he wanted republican civic values to penetrate every nook of democratic society (the disastrous ambition of Rousseau and the Jacobins). It is to say that *public freedom, public virtues,* and the "spirit of liberty" remained his guiding passions in a post-revolutionary world—a world in which peasants, workers, and the bourgeoisie were all too ready to make their accommodation with a centralized, tutelary state. He could not help but view American civil society as a seedbed for civic virtue and the "habit of association" (the forces opposed to individualism), as well as providing the actual space for (decentralized) political participation. Thus, while retaining and expanding the liberal "art of separation," Tocqueville was able to fashion a concept of civil society that was political at its very core.[80] *Democracy in America* signals the moment, fleeting though it might have been, when public life—like economic and religious life before it—slips the confines of the sovereign state and takes on a new, distinctively modern, form.[81]

Conclusion

To read Tocqueville on American democracy and civil society is to be reminded of just how far we have come—or, perhaps, of just how far we have fallen. For if Tocqueville demonstrated, through his updating of Montesquieu's *pouvoirs intermédiaires*, the extent to which the public realm could inhabit the space of civil society, our fate has been to see these two spheres separate out once again. What we are left with is the familiar array of economic "special interests" (on the one hand), and the arena of media spectacle (on the other). "Public virtues" now denote little more than the politician's adeptness at the performance of authenticity, or the average citizen's essentially unpolitical willingness to volunteer (for charity, community work, or military duty). "Public life" has been reduced to the moralizing cliché of public service or the unholy cult of celebrity. Nothing could be further from Tocqueville's distinctive brand of liberal republicanism, with its emphasis on limited government, free *moeurs*, and extensive participation in (and attention to) public affairs.

In part, this sad development has to do with the kind of broad cultural shifts described by Hannah Arendt in *The Human Condition* and by Richard Sennett in *The Fall of Public Man*.[82] In part, it has to with what Habermas calls the "structural transformation" of the public sphere—a transformation wrought by the fusion of corporate capitalism, the bureaucratic state, and a newly "mediatized" public realm. This fusion creates the conditions for a pervasive manipulation and management of public opinion, which loses its critical function and becomes just one more input in "the administered society."[83] But the twilight of public life in America also has roots in a deeply ingrained cultural tendency, one not given much attention by recent theorists of the public realm or by Frankfurt School-inspired critical theory. This is the tendency to view *religion*, not politics or public life, as the only *real* antidote to the pathologies wrought by individualism, materialism, and the unfettered pursuit of self-interest.

Here we need to be clear about Tocqueville's own position. While he drew attention to the "wonderful alliance" between the spirit of religion and the spirit of liberty in the New World, reminding his readers that "it must never be forgotten that religion gave birth to the Anglo-Americans," he did so in order to draw a political lesson.[84] He stressed how Protestant/ Puritan/congregationalist beliefs served to cultivate self-reliance, the habit of free association, and the practice of debating and settling collective affairs. He celebrated colonial Protestantism not for its religious content, or even because it would serve as a "countervailing force" against growing materialism and anomie.[85] Rather, he celebrated it as the soil of habits and attitudes characteristic of a *free people*—a people used to managing its own affairs; a people who did not reflexively look to the state for help in resolving, or instruction in administering, public matters.[86]

In contemporary America, this "democratic and republican" form of religion has become yet another dim memory. Tocqueville's attention to the unsuspected civic resources of specific strains of seventeenth- and eighteenth-century Anglo-American Christianity has given way to a ubiquitous concern with the individual's "personal relationship with God"—a concern that pervades not only much of contemporary American Protestantism, but Catholicism and non-Orthodox Judaism as well. This exclusive focus on subjective belief and a personal relationship with the divine would not have surprised Hegel, who dissected the "law of the heart" and the ethical egomania of romantic Protestantism in his *Phenomenology*.[87] But it would have surprised Tocqueville, who saw the American religion as a great resource in the fight against privatizing individualism, and as "otherworldly" only in the benign sense of reminding a perpetually restless people of matters greater than worldly success.[88]

The point here is that Tocqueville considered religion less for its own sake than for its contribution to the creation of free *moeurs*, nondocile citizens, and the preservation of a public culture. Yet it is precisely this conception of religion as supportive of a publicly oriented culture—as secondary to the value of public freedom—that has become most problematic, and indeed most alien, for us.[89] We look to religion to fulfill the spiritual and therapeutic needs of the individual. When religion does enter the public realm, it is usually to cement a misplaced sense of national rectitude (as manifest in the phrase "for God and Country"). Tocqueville, in contrast, sought out those cultural aspects of religion that supported self-reliance, public freedom, and civil equality.

The contemporary American discourse of civil society betrays a similar foreshortening and depoliticization. We are inclined to view this realm in accordance with a strict separation between society and government, *société civile* and *le monde politique*. This allows us to assert the basic Lockean-liberal lesson—that government should serve society, not vice versa—and to count the many blessings of limited government. But it also blinds us to the essential role civil society plays in creating a new kind of space for the public realm; in fostering the "habit of association" and joint action so crucial to public-political life itself. This is, to a large degree, a willful blindness—one born of our desire to be free of the burdens, responsibilities, and argument that characterize public life; one born of our desire to safeguard our *freedom from politics* as best we know how.

Like his liberal predecessor and near contemporary Benjamin Constant, Tocqueville had no desire to resurrect the myth of ancient collective sovereignty in the modern world.[90] Where popular sovereignty did appear (in the fictional rule of *le peuple* during the French Revolution, or in the "tyranny of majority opinion" threatening America), it was often destructive of freedom. Often, but not always. The lesson of American democracy was that civil society could provide new spaces for, and new forms of, political participation, popular sovereignty and public freedom; that it could preserve the *moeurs* necessary to self-government in an age of individual powerlessness; and that it could challenge—and, indeed, undercut—the monolith of majority opinion in a democracy. It is an irony of history that the political conception of civil society Tocqueville introduced to Europe must now be reintroduced to America—from, of all places, a democratic and secular Europe.

3 | HEGEL, TOCQUEVILLE, AND "INDIVIDUALISM"

In his early essay "On the Scientific Ways of Treating Natural Law" (1802–03), Hegel performed a critical move that was later to form the core of *Phenomenology of Spirit* (1807).[1] This was the move from a philosophical-epistemological critique of "atomism" (understood as both method and general explanatory device, such as we find in Hobbes) to a broader, cultural-psychological critique of modern individualism (in both its moral and "bourgeois" or possessive forms).

What in 1802 and 1807 was a novelty has, of course, become a widespread intellectual tendency. Again and again, we find critics of liberal individualism—whether communitarian, post-Marxist, or post-modernist—following Hegel's lead, more or less repeating his objections. Solid arguments about the salience of shared language, practices, and culture are deployed to refute the methodological individualism found, say, in Rawls or Nozick. This refutation then quickly (and often unself-consciously) devolves into a repudiation of "individualism" in all its tangled moral, political, and historical complexity.[2] The logic is simple, albeit fallacious: if methodological individualism ("atomism") is untenable, then moral individualism must be as well. Thus is the baby disposed with the bath water.

There is a certain irony to this, not least because Hegel viewed "freedom of subjectivity"—individual freedom—as "the principle of the modern world." He judged any political constitution that did not institutionally recognize this fact as "unacceptable."[3] But—at the same time—Hegel devoted an enormous amount of philosophical energy to correcting what he saw as a misleading and false picture of social reality (one born of Hobbes and the social contract tradition, and given wider currency by the utilitarian social philosophies of the Enlightenment). He made this effort less because he was obsessed with method than with the character of our self-understanding.[4] To misconstrue the relative priority of language, laws, institutions, and practices vis-à-vis the individual was not merely to stand the social world on its head, mistaking the effect for the cause. It was to deprive oneself and one's society of the possibility of ever achieving genuine freedom. Considered as a stubbornly persistent worldview, individualism seemed to condemn Western culture to the pursuit of a phantom freedom—the freedom of individual self-assertion or self-sufficiency.[5]

Hegel, then, saw the methodological presuppositions of modern Natural Law and utilitarianism as *symptoms* of a deeper, historically and culturally rooted, misunderstanding of our place in the world. This misunderstanding, he argued, fundamentally distorted the nature of our moral and political experience. Thus, while Hegel can with some justice be blamed for setting the pattern by which epistemological-methodological argument substitutes for (or bears the brunt of) cultural critique, we need to keep one thing very firmly in mind. Unlike many of his inheritors, Hegel insisted on making a distinction between *subjectivity* (which he saw as the great achievement of the modern age) and *subjectivism* (which he saw as an increasingly dangerous moral *and* methodological fetish).[6] Hegel's clear grasp of this distinction enabled him to appreciate the moral-political achievement of modernity—individual liberty—while simultaneously mounting one of the most powerful critiques ever made of individualism *qua* worldview. On this score, he bears a striking resemblance to Tocqueville—their massive dissimilarities (regarding the nature of the state, civil society, and democracy—to say nothing of sheer style of thought) notwithstanding.

In this chapter, I look at Hegel's indictment of individualism, contrasting it with Tocqueville's more limited, but in many ways parallel, critique. My hope is that bringing these two disparate thinkers together not only illuminates the origins of what has become a reflexive intellectual tendency, but will also clarify what is at stake—morally and politically speaking—in any responsible critique of individualism.

At the outset, we have to note two fundamental points that separate Hegel and Tocqueville from their inheritors. The first is that while both saw individualism (or "atomism") as premised on a faulty idea of freedom as independence, Hegel and Tocqueville nevertheless upheld individual rights as the basis of a distinctively "modern" form of liberty.[7] No reader of their work can doubt the fact that each saw the right of "subjective" freedom as central to (if not definitive of) the "rational" state and any morally defensible democracy. Second—and this is the complicating factor—both Hegel and Tocqueville valued public life, public norms, and public freedom as much or more than they valued individual rights. In different but parallel ways, they tried to combine a substantial "liberal" moment with an updated, modern form of civic humanism.[8]

Just how successful they were in effecting this synthesis is, of course, the subject of much interpretive debate. One thing, however, is clear. From the standpoint of both Hegel and Tocqueville, the "liberty of the moderns" could not be reduced (à la Constant at his most polemical) to individual rights and negative freedom.[9] But neither could modern liberty be formulated in terms of a "common good" that stood in stark opposition to individual (or group) interests. This heritage of civic republicanism from Machiavelli to Rousseau was one that Hegel and Tocqueville—in their unique but parallel ways—definitively transformed. As a result, civic virtue and public liberty would never look quite the same.

This dual emphasis on individual rights and public liberty—on "negative" and "positive" freedom—distinguishes Hegel and Tocqueville not only from their precursors, but the majority of their inheritors as well. It makes the critiques offered by the latter seem both shrill and one-dimensional in comparison. This is not to say that Hegel and Tocqueville's criticisms of individualism are unproblematic. The slide from the critique of methodological individualism ("atomism") to that of moral or democratic individualism *tout court* is more or less built into their respective theories, as is the dangerous idea that thought and action must never become too independent.

Tocqueville and Individualism

In his preface to *The Old Regime and the Revolution*, Tocqueville writes:

> People today, no longer attached to one another by ties of caste, class, guild, or family, are all too inclined to be preoccupied with their own private interests, too given to looking out for themselves alone and withdrawing into a narrow individualism where all public virtues are smothered. Despotism, rather than struggling

against this tendency, makes it irresistible, because it takes away from citizens all common feeling, all common needs, all need for communication, all occasion for common action. It walls them up inside their private lives. They already tend to keep themselves apart from one another: despotism isolates them; it chills their relations; it freezes them.[10]

This passage reveals, in a highly compact way, the inner connections Tocqueville saw between democratic equality, atomization, and the rise of the administrative despotism of the modern (centralized) state. Once the corporate ties of a feudal society are dissolved by a democratic social revolution (such as occurred in France), nothing prevents the retreat of equal yet powerless individuals to the private realm. Here they will single-mindedly pursue their self-interest, with little or no regard for the public realm or the common good (the brief intermezzo of revolutionary republicanism notwithstanding). The state encourages this change in *moeurs* (from *citoyen* to *bourgeois*) since it guarantees the new Leviathan a monopoly on public administration, public action, and—perhaps most important—public judgment. With the social space cleared of all the old *pouvoirs intermédiaires* and structures of corporate affiliation, nothing prevents a new despotism from "eventually seeping into every private home."[11]

These themes all trace back to *Democracy in America*.[12] But while the closing chapters of that work are full of fear for a future in which "each nation is reduced to nothing better than a flock of timid and industrious animals, of which the government is the shepherd," it was written in order to point a path around—or out of—the abyss. That path was the one laid out by decentralized American democracy, where "the habit of association" worked in tandem with local administration to produce a thriving public culture on the basis of a democratic *condition sociale*. Indeed, from Tocqueville's standpoint, American federalism—when combined with localism and a robust civil society—pointed to a democratic future in which the very idea of the sovereign or centralized state would be overcome once and for all.

This is not to say that the Americans did not have to contend with their own brand of *individualisme*, or that their own public-oriented culture somehow came naturally. On the contrary, in volume 2 of *Democracy in America* Tocqueville consistently emphasized how American democracy produced effects parallel to the dissociating bourgeois attitudes he so loathed on the continent, sometimes exaggerating or excelling them. Thus, democratic equality helped foster a cult of private judgment in the New World, making the Americans unself-conscious Cartesians in their everyday lives.[13] As in Europe, equality in America dissolved the ties between generations and social groups, making a man "forget his ancestors" while simultaneously "separat[ing] his contemporaries from him."[14] It encouraged a love of physical gratification, as well as the pervasive and curiously American habit of understanding all actions in terms of "self-interest, rightly understood."[15] Finally, it produced the illusion of a total personal independence, an illusion that made Americans think they "owe[d] nothing to any man" and that they held "their whole destiny in their own hands."[16]

Individualism, in short, was clearly an American *problem*, not an American virtue.[17] It was, in Tocqueville's view, an unavoidable syndrome in any modern republic, given the power of democratic equality to dissolve existing ties of corporate solidarity and recognition (or prevent them from taking root in the first place). By its very nature, democratic equality produced atomized and isolated individuals. It was inevitable that such radically dissociated individuals would turn in upon themselves and be prone to live entirely privatized lives. This is the background of Tocqueville's famous definition of the "novel expression" *individualisme*, a term he carefully distinguishes from selfishness (*égoïsme*):

> Individualism is a mature and calm feeling [*un sentiment réfléchi et paisable*], which disposes each member of the community to sever himself from the mass of his fellows and to draw apart with his family and his friends, so that after he has formed a little circle of his own, he willingly leaves society at large to itself. Selfishness originates in blind instinct [*un instinct aveugle*]; individualism proceeds from *erroneous judgment* more than from depraved feelings; it originates as much in deficiencies of the mind as in perversity of the heart [*il prend sa source dans les défauts de l'esprit autant que dans les vices du coeur*].[18]

But while the French bourgeoisie succumbed entirely to this tendency, withdrawing into private affairs while viewing self-interest as the driving force of society, the Americans (in Tocqueville's judgment) "combated by free institutions the tendency of equality to keep men asunder, and they have subdued it."[19] Torn asunder by the dissociative tendencies of democratic equality, the Americans deployed the "art of association" (learned from their unique political experience) in order to create a web of artificial social ties. The result was a society that—though bereft of the kind of "permanent associations" (classes, estates, guilds, and so on) that held the *ancien régime* together—succeeded in cultivating a deep sense of community and an appreciation of "the close tie that unites private to general interest."[20] The "erroneous judgment" (*jugement erroné*) fostered by individualism was not thereby completely eliminated. Rather, it was balanced and held in check by the experience of local freedom and the habit of association—a habit manifest in a wide variety of projects, both political and "civil."[21]

The creation of a civic and self-reliant culture on the unpromising ground of democratic equality was, for Tocqueville, a tremendous achievement—especially when compared with the French experience. However, this achievement did not prevent the Americans from *misinterpreting* their experience—that is, from habitually articulating it in terms more liberal and utilitarian than democratic or republican. This fact emerges with special clarity in Tocqueville's chapter "How the Americans Combat Individualism by the Principle of Self-Interest Rightly Understood."

At first glance, the very title of this chapter contains a paradox, if not an outright contradiction. How can one hope to combat individualism through the appeal to self-interest, however we understand the latter idea? Tocqueville's answer is that the Americans not only modify the definition of self-interest in a community-friendly way (linking private and public interest through an expanded idea of utility); they also deceive themselves into thinking their public-political spirit (which Tocqueville elsewhere describes as substantial)[22] is nothing other than the application of "the doctrine of interest rightly understood."[23] They take the eighteenth-century doctrine of enlightened self-interest and apply it universally, even when it is clear that other motivations—such as the spirit of local independence or a love of public liberty—underlie their actions. As Tocqueville observes:

> The Americans . . . are fond of explaining almost all the actions of their lives by the principle of self-interest rightly understood; they show with complacency how an enlightened regard for themselves constantly prompts them to assist one another and inclines them willingly to sacrifice a portion of their time and property to the welfare of the state. *In this respect I think they frequently fail to do themselves justice;* for in the United States as well as else-

where people are sometimes seen to give way to those disinterested and spontaneous impulses that are natural to man; but the Americans seldom admit that they yield to emotions of this kind; they are more anxious to do honor to their philosophy than to themselves.[24]

It is true that Tocqueville praises the doctrine of "self-interest, rightly understood" as making a nonheroic, less demanding form of civic virtue available to all.[25] But it is also true that he sees it as an *idée fixe* of the Americans. It is a kind of optical trick that a restlessly commercial people performs upon themselves, the better to reconcile their substantial moments of "disinterested" patriotism and public spirit with their more practical workday lives and worldview. The Americans may combat *individualisme* by time- and energy-consuming participation in "free institutions," but they placate their self-interested side by repeating the cliché that "it is in the interest of every man to be virtuous."[26] Having learned through political participation and local administration about the "close tie that unites private to general interest," they (as it were) reteach themselves the same lesson so that it conforms to the doctrine of self-interest.[27]

The result is not a seamless integration of the public and private dimensions of life (such as Hegel claimed for the *polis* and unreflective Greek *Sittlichkeit*), but a strange, and slightly schizophrenic, double-life; one in which the *mentalités* of bourgeois and *citoyen* alternate in apparent confusion. One minute, "an American attends to his private concerns as if he were alone in the world"; the next, "he gives himself up to the common welfare as if he had forgotten them."[28] The "contradiction" of a people that has learned the habit of duty and joint action through local administration and public affairs, but which restlessly pursues material gratification and individual advancement, is resolved by the belief—the ideology, if you will—that "their chief business is to secure for themselves a government which will allow them to acquire the things they covet."[29]

That Tocqueville did not think that either the public spirit or the "free *moeurs*" of the Americans could be reduced to modalities of self-interest is made clear by volume 1's analysis of township democracy and volume 2's analysis of the "art of association." It is also strongly conveyed by his insistence that "if an American were condemned to confine his activity to his own affairs, he would be robbed of one half of his existence; he would feel an immense void in the life which he is accustomed to lead, and his wretchedness would be unbearable."[30] The Americans, then, are less "bourgeois" than their universal acceptance of the "doctrine of self-interest, rightly understood" would lead one to believe. Their idea of the "public good" hardly excludes individual or group interests; but neither (in the end) is it reducible to either. "Self-interest, rightly understood" turns out to be a form of interest that has been mediated and transformed by the learning experience provided in the "schools" of political association and local self-government.[31]

A similar gap between ideology and experience opens up when we attempt to square the "philosophical method" of the Americans with the reality of public opinion and religious belief. As Tocqueville notes at the beginning of volume 2, the Americans may not read Descartes, but in no country are his precepts better or more universally applied.[32] This is because America—as an egalitarian society bereft of any clear social hierarchy—deprives its members of authoritative elites. There is, as a result, no authority to turn to, no basis for the cultivation of habits of deference. As with so much else, the Americans are thrown back upon themselves. Hence their intuitive, unself-conscious "Cartesianism," their habit (as Tocqueville describes it) of "fixing the standard of their judgment in themselves alone."[33] The cult of private judgment—of moral and intellectual *independence* from authority—thus receives its first full cultural instantiation in the everyday "philosophical" method of the Americans.

Having articulated the American self-understanding on this score, Tocqueville immediately turns to examine the social forces that restrain if not refute it. The first of these, familiar from the first volume of *Democracy in America*, is that of public or majority opinion. Where democratic equality prevails, individuals have little reason to resign their judgment up to any class, group, or elite. However, their "readiness to believe the multitude" increases in direct proportion to their growing freedom from traditional authorities. Equal and isolated individuals—painfully aware of their own fallibility—place their faith in the "judgment of the public," trusting it to serve as guide and bannister for their own feeble (but still supposedly independent) judgment.[34] Doubt, skepticism, and a genuine desire to understand wane as public opinion becomes (in Tocqueville's famous phrase) the "mistress of the world."

The democratic individual thus comes to view "what everybody thinks" as a convenient source of ready-made opinions. This reflex relieves him of "the necessity of forming opinions" of his own.[35] While perhaps the most palpable manifestation of a general eclipse of independent thought, this is by no means the only one. Even more striking, from Tocqueville's perspective, is the spread of what he calls a "courtier-spirit" amongst democratic writers and politicians. Those who might have served as paradigms of independent thought and judgment bow down before the "irresistible authority" of public opinion. Thus, the ideology of private judgment notwithstanding, Tocqueville could honestly claim that he knew of "no country in which there is so little independence of mind and real freedom of discussion as America."[36]

This last remark was made in 1835, as part of Tocqueville's worries about an emerging "tyranny of the majority." In 1840, however, he seems to stress the positive side of this turn away from the fetish of independent judgment (at least on the level of practice).[37] It is not that Tocqueville came to see the dominance of "majority thought and feeling" (Mill) as a *good* thing. Rather, the focus of his attention has shifted. Thus, the beginning of volume 2 is devoted to showing how private judgment is rarely, if ever, *really* private in America. The "superstructure" of everyday Cartesianism— the ideology of private judgment—turns out to rest upon a firm foundation of religious dogma and shared belief.

If this is true, it would seem to give democratic conformism an additional (and largely unfortunate) boost. However, his fears of the looming tyranny of public opinion notwithstanding, Tocqueville saw dogmatic belief as the inescapable basis of all social stability. One need only look to Europe, where the "private judgment" lauded by Luther, Descartes, and Voltaire snowballed from a bounded (religious and philosophical) skepticism into the revolutionary destruction of an entire social structure.[38] Without the limiting force of authoritative shared belief (something that had "gone dead" in Europe), Descartes's principle of independent thought had the capacity to become quickly and endlessly dissolvent. In Tocqueville's view, this is exactly what happened during the Enlightenment and the Revolution. Throughout this period of French history, nearly every social practice and institution was brought before the bar of an essentially private and abstract reason. Unsurprisingly, they were all found lacking, worthy only of destruction.[39]

The contrast with American "Cartesianism" is striking. In America, Tocqueville observed, conformist public opinion effectively socialized (and to that extent tamed) a potentially anarchic principle of judgment.[40] Not only that. The alliance between the "spirit of liberty" and the "spirit of religion" in colonial America had held firm, thus ensuring that "general ideas respecting God and human nature" were placed beyond the reach of doubt and private judgment.[41] The nigh-universal American acceptance of the basic tenets of Christianity imposed a "salutary restraint on the intellect," saving them from the spiritual enervation of doubt (which Tocqueville saw—however odd it may sound to us—as a precondition of despotism).[42] Christianity also reminded a restless and striving people of their duties toward each other, promoting an everyday moral egalitarianism that (in turn) helped underwrite norms of liberal justice.[43] Religion thus served to combat the illusion of complete independence in much the same manner as "free institutions." It drew the individual out of himself and his daily (self- and family-centered) concern.[44]

Stepping back, we see that Tocqueville has painted a curious picture. On the one hand, there is the intuitive "Cartesianism" of the Americans, their inveterate tendency to ignore tradition and "make frequent use their private judgment." On the other, there is a substantial body of dogmatic belief, a body largely untouched by the claims of skepticism and individual reason. Part of this dogma is social and conventional—it is based on the (seemingly) unchallengeable authority of public opinion in a world of democratic equality. But an even more substantial part of it is religious and spiritual in nature—it is based on the peculiarly American linkage of the "spirit of liberty" with the "spirit of religion," a connection that Tocqueville traces back to the Puritans.[45] The result is that the dangers of American "Cartesianism" (a kind of moral atomism, to use Hegel's term) are defused thanks to what Tocqueville considers a large (and overwhelmingly benign) body of common belief. This body is not only substantial; it also transcends the *doxa* of the day thanks to its firm grounding in religion, custom, and mores.[46] If, in their political lives, the Americans successfully combat individualism through participation in their "free institutions," so—in their moral and intellectual lives—they successfully (albeit unconsciously) combat the pathologies of an untethered, and potentially anarchic, private judgment.

There is, then, a large and clear gap between the Americans' self-understanding (individualism, private judgment, "Cartesianism") and their sociopolitical experience (which occurs in a world of local freedom and association, a world made possible by shared attitudes, habits, and beliefs). When it comes to the crucial realms of membership and judgment, the Americans are not nearly as independent or individualist as they take themselves to be. But here we need to be clear that, *contra* Marx, this self-misunderstanding (or "erroneous judgment") is not mere ideological obfuscation. Its roots are to be found in the very real (and very novel) experience of atomization produced by democratic equality. As

Tocqueville observes, if "aristocracy had made a chain of all the members of the community, from the peasant to the king," democracy in effect "breaks that chain and severs every link of it."[47] This is the "natural" result of a "democratic social condition," and it was as real in America (despite the absence of aristocratic structures to break up) as it was in Europe. The form of consciousness—the state of mind or worldview—denoted by "individualism" accurately represents this condition of modern, "democratic" dissociation. But, as Tocqueville points out, this form of consciousness also blinds us to the myriad ways we continue to depend on one another. It obscures the "close tie" between our private interest and the public good.

It is this myopia born of *individualisme* that Tocqueville sets out to correct in volume 2's famous discussion of political and civil associations in America and of the "art of association" more generally.[48] But Tocqueville also corrects it by reminding us just how much we share—or once shared— in terms of habits, beliefs, and attitudes. These constituted the "free *moeurs*" he saw as supporting American democracy—*moeurs* the like of which he hoped free institutions would eventually create in France. Combined with the "free institutions" of early America, such *moeurs* constituted a kind of *Sittlichkeit* or collective "ethical life" with which the average American citizen could readily identify himself—at least when he wasn't restlessly pursuing dreams of material gratification and self-advancement in a society characterized by universal competition.[49]

Hegel and the Social Integration of the Modern Individual

The concept of *Sittlichkeit* refers us, of course, to Hegel. No doubt he would have found the suggestion that Tocqueville discovered a democratic form of "ethical life" in America absurd. Assessing America in his 1830 lectures on the philosophy of world history, Hegel saw a republic which was, so to speak, all civil society and no state.[50] Since the state was, in Hegel's understanding, the only adequate vehicle of modern "ethical life," a society without a developed state would (at best) be a voluntary arrangement for the protection of life and property.[51] What such a society lacked, in Hegel's view, was the organic yet differentiated totality of law, social relations, and political institutions that, together, composed "the actuality of concrete freedom."[52] Such a complex structure—the "rational" state of Hegel's political philosophy—expressed a set of common principles, ends, or ideals of the good life, while simultaneously creating and preserving individual rights by means of rationally codified public law. It gave civil society (the arena of needs and individual interests) its due without being overwhelmed by it. Hence Hegel's famous statement in *The Philosophy of Right* that "the principle of modern states has enormous strength and depth because it allows the principle of subjectivity to attain fulfillment in the *self-sufficient extreme* of personal particularity, while at the same time *bringing it back to substantial unity* and so preserving this unity in the principle of subjectivity itself."[53]

However we feel about Hegel's claim to have demonstrated the possibility of combining a substantive community life, individual freedom, and a relatively autonomous social sphere ("civil society") all within the confines of the modern state, one thing seems clear: he and Tocqueville are working at cross purposes. Tocqueville, after all, saw the modern democratic state—the state born of the French Revolution—as the centralizing force par excellence; an administrative edifice that reduces, potentially, its "citizens" to the status of a relatively well-tended herd.[54] Hence his delight at discovering in America a society that seemed to run by itself, and his subsequent reputation as not only a classical liberal, but as *the* theorist of civil society.[55] In contrast, Hegel remains—for his admirers as well as his critics—a philosopher of the state. He is the philosopher who saw in the Napoleonic reforms of the early nineteenth century not the advent of a new form of despotism (Tocqueville's nightmare), but rather the dawning of "concrete freedom" after the long night of feudal (hyper-decentralized) irrationality.

This is true as far as it goes, and one should not underestimate the distance—both in terms of native political culture and political ideals—between the two theorists.[56] However, viewing Hegel and Tocqueville as polar opposites—as the patron saints of the state and civil society, respectively—is highly misleading. This is especially so when it comes to grasping the theoretical intention behind their respective critiques of individualism. The widely accepted caricatures of Tocqueville as the champion of local freedom and participatory politics (on the one hand), and Hegel as the apologist for the bureaucratic or "rational" state (on the other), are—it turns out—more than a little wide of the mark. Consider the following passage from Hegel's early (1798–1802) essay on *Die Verfassung Deutschlands* ("The German Constitution"):

> How dull and spiritless a life is engendered in a modern state where everything is regulated from the top downwards, where

nothing with any general implication is left to the management and execution of interested parties of the people—in a state like what the French Republic has made itself—is to be experienced only in the future, if indeed this pitch of pedantry in domination can persist. But what life and what sterility reigns in another equally regulated state, in the Prussian, strikes anyone who sets foot in the first town there or sees its complete lack of scientific or artistic genius, or assesses its strength otherwise than by the ephemeral energy by which a single genius has been able to generate in it for a time by pressure.[57]

The dominating image here, as in Tocqueville, is of a dissociated aggregate of equal subjects confronting the "mechanistic" structure of the modern administrative state. Whether this state is Jacobin or Frederician in origin makes little difference to Hegel. The end result is the same: atomized individuals—a "formless mass"—dominated by an enormous bureaucratic apparatus, one that regulates everything "from the top downwards."[58] It is this image of the state as a lifeless machine producing "docile subjects" (to use Foucault's phrase) that haunts Hegel as well as Tocqueville.[59] That this fear was not confined to his "radical" youth is confirmed by the following passage, written twenty years later, from *The Philosophy of Right*:

> But this [the "expedient" of appointing a prime minister or cabinet council] may have the result that *everything is again controlled from above* by ministerial power, and that functions are, to use the common expression, centralized. This is associated with a high degree of facility, speed, and effectiveness in measures adopted for the universal interest of the state. A regime of this kind was introduced by the French Revolution and further developed by Napoleon, and it still exists in France today. On the other hand, France *lacks corporations and communal associations*—that is, *circles in which particular and universal interests come together*. Admittedly, these circles gained too great a degree of self-sufficiency in the Middle Ages, when they became states within the state. . . . But although this ought not to happen, it can still be argued that the proper strength of states resides in their [internal] communities.[60]

These passages contain *in nuce* Tocqueville's critique of—and solution to—the enervating qualities of the centralized state. Yet even when appraised of these sentiments on Hegel's part, most Anglo-American readers will continue to view the "living" state of *The Philosophy of Right* with skepticism. The Hegelian state, it has often been argued, swallows up both individuality and popular political participation, all in the misguided attempt to revive Aristotelian organicism in modern form (one respectful of private property and freedom of conscience).[61]

This too is a caricature. Not only does Hegel go out of his way to give free play to the "principle of subjective freedom" in his political philosophy (distinguishing himself from the ancients in precisely this regard);[62] he also promotes what is—for his place and time—a surprisingly large role for popular representation and participation.[63] True, political representation (as presented in sections 301–320 of *The Philosophy of Right*) is totally mediated through membership in the "estates" (*Stände*). But even Hegel's reservations about direct popular suffrage have an oddly Tocquevillian ring, and not merely because he is afraid of a "rabble" [*Pöbel*] asserting itself in a "barbarous manner."[64] In *The Philosophy of Right* he states:

> The idea that those communities which are already present in the circles [of association] referred to above can be split up again into a collection of individuals as soon as they enter the sphere of politics—i.e., the sphere of the *highest concrete universality*— involves separating civil and political life from each other and leaves political life hanging, so to speak, in the air; for its basis is then merely the *abstract individuality of arbitrary will and opinion*.[65]

As with Tocqueville, the primary concern here is to integrate "circles of association" into the public-political realm, even when these circles have their basis in profession or social class. What needs to be avoided at all costs is the effacement of the sphere of associations, since it is this sphere that mediates between individuals and the (political) state:

> Viewed as a *mediating* organ, the Estates stand between the government at large on the one hand and the people in their division into particular spheres and individuals on the other. . . . At the same time, this position means that they share the mediating function of the organized power of the executive, ensuring on the one hand that the power of the sovereign does not appear as an isolated *extreme*—and hence simply as an arbitrary power of domination—and on the other, that the particular interests of communities, corporations, and individuals do not become

isolated either. Or more important still, they ensure that individuals do not present themselves as a *crowd* or *aggregate*, unorganized in their opinions and volition, and do not become a massive power in opposition to the organic state.[66]

Mediation and *integration* through associational life are thus the keys to avoiding radical atomization and "democratic despotism." It is precisely because Hegel thinks that modern individuals focus too much on their rights and withdraw into the realm of "subjectivity" that he emphasizes (again like Tocqueville) the crucial role of estates, corporations, and so on.[67] The main difference between them, in this regard, is that while Tocqueville emphasized the importance of associations, he also insisted upon the crucial educative role played by direct participation in local affairs.[68] This comes out in his admiring pages about the New England township (which he unblushingly compares to Athenian democracy) in volume 1, as well as his praise of local "free institutions" in volume 2. In a passage already alluded to above, Tocqueville writes:

> It is difficult to draw a man out of his own circle to interest him in the destiny of the state, because he does not clearly understand what influence the destiny of the state can have upon his own lot. But if it is proposed to make a road cross the end of his estate, he will see at a glance that there is a connection between this small public affair and his greatest private affairs; and he will discover, without its being shown to him, the *close tie that unites private to general interest* [*le lien étroit qui unit ici l'intérêt particulier à l'intérêt général*]. Thus, far more may be done by entrusting to the citizens the administration of minor affairs than by surrendering to them the control of important ones, towards interesting them in the public welfare and convincing them that they constantly stand in need of one another in order to provide for it.[69]

Local administration and direct (township) democracy mediate between individual and general interests, educating the former to a higher level of what Hegel would call "universality." The gap between *bourgeois* and *citoyen* that so bedeviled continental political thought after Rousseau is here bridged, and not by any merely conceptual innovation. Like Rousseau, Tocqueville saw a real "moralizing" potential in political participation; unlike him—and, indeed, unlike the bulk of the civic republican tradition—he did not see actualization of this potential as hinging on the stern repression of self-interest.[70] One discovers the "close tie" that unites private to general interest through direct participation; one learns the basic moral lesson by doing, by direct involvement in matters of local administration.

Like Tocqueville, Hegel believed that "particular interests should not be set aside, let alone suppressed; on the contrary, they should be harmonized with the universal, so that both they themselves and the universal are preserved."[71] The individual citizen learns about this potential harmony or integration over a lifetime, and on a number of levels. The family, civil society, and the state all have their educative functions, which boil down to educating "self-will" in the (progressively more universal) needs of the community (whether this be the intimate moral community of the family, the universal interdependence of civil society, or the "concrete universality" of the state).[72] The "close tie" uniting general to private interest is revealed gradually, and in a number of distinctly different contexts. At no point, however, is it assumed that the general or universal interest can be reduced to aggregated private preferences (as in utilitarianism), or endowed with the status of a qualitatively different (and somewhat mysterious) *a priori*, such as Rousseau suggested with his famous characterization of the General Will as "constant, unalterable, and pure."

Thanks partly to these different strata of social existence, and partly to the complex character of the modern state, Hegel (*contra* Tocqueville) does not think that the all-important insight into the "close tie" hinges upon direct and regular political involvement by the individual citizen.[73] Rather, such insight is achieved on one level (that of civil society) through membership in estates and corporations; on another (that of the state), through law, representation, open assembly debates, and a free press.[74] It becomes most explicit and self-conscious through the philosophical comprehension of the state as "a great architectonic edifice, a hieroglyph of reason which becomes manifest in actuality"[75]—a comprehension *The Philosophy of Right* tries to cultivate.[76] Such is the multilayered and decentered process of civic education that Hegel sees the modern state as effecting. No Machiavellian founder, no Rousseauian legislator is needed for communal consciousness of the general interest to become a reality. Rather, such consciousness is "the emergent outcome of [a] lengthy process of *Bildung*."[77]

While ingenious conceptually, Hegel's schema does limit the role and importance of political participation by average citizens, at least in comparison to Tocqueville. This more limited role is a function of Hegel's ambivalent attitude toward public opinion (which he characterized as something that "deserves to be respected and despised") and his suspicion of the undifferentiated idea of "the people" that underlies most doctrines of popular sovereignty.[78] One might see Hegel's insistence on the representative principle as replacing Tocqueville's "learning by doing" (as an active citizen) with a more passive "learning by being" (as a member of an estate or corporation). Such membership promotes a sense of the internal differentiation of the modern state. It is thus the basis for "learning by understanding"—grasping how the parts function together in an organic way—which, for Hegel, constitutes the essence of civic education.

Yet though there is ample basis for such a contrast, we should exercise caution when distinguishing between Tocqueville's "participatory" model of integration and Hegel's more social (and intellectual) one. There are several reasons why we need to qualify any such distinction. The first and most obvious concerns the utterly divergent political realities of Prussia (on the one hand) and France and America (on the other), the reforms of vom Stein and Hardenberg notwithstanding. The second concerns the limited penetration of the early-nineteenth-century German world by a democratic *condition sociale* and its dissolvent effects. Because this penetration was limited, "atomization" was not nearly as extensive. Many of the corporate bases of identity (the *Stände*, trade and professional associations, and so on) were left relatively intact, and these provided Hegel with "ready-made" components for his differentiated yet rationally structured state (they also accounted for its occasional, but misleading, resemblance to Plato's *Republic*).[79] The third has to do with the fact that Hegel *does* include political participation as one important "moment" amongst others in his civic learning process. He leaves no doubt that the "voice of the people" should be heard, even if it is clear that he does not think they should rule.[80] It is his quasi-Tocquevillian horror at the prospect of a "formless mass" ruling through public opinion that leads him to insist on the (undemocratic) corporate forms of voting and representation he does.

But perhaps the most important reason for qualifying the distinction between a "political" or participatory Tocqueville and a "philosophical"or intellectualist Hegel is that it blinds us to the deeper sources of their disagreement. In fact, the most basic dispute between Tocqueville and Hegel doesn't center on how best to "combat" individualism and atomization at all. As we have seen, they both focus on associations—voluntary and/or corporate in character—as the most important mediators between individuals and the state, and as the most important sites of nongovernmental (decentralized) power. At the most general level, then, Hegel and Tocqueville are intent on recovering spaces of public freedom, whether these take the form of township democracy, voluntary associations, or the array of institutions that make up "objective spirit." Their *real* dispute—the fundamental source of tension between their overlapping yet divergent political visions—concerns their radically different views on the origins, nature, and depth of individualism as a force in Western culture. It is this disagreement—rather than any simple verdict "for" or "against" popular sovereignty and democratic institutions—which molds their respective conceptions of the problem of atomization, and which subtly colors their respective solutions.

For Tocqueville, individualism (understood as privatism) is a relatively new phenomenon, one born of democracy and the destruction of an aristocratic social condition. *"Individualisme,"* he writes, is *"un expression récente qu'une idée novelle a fait naître."* For Hegel, individualism (understood as *subjectivism* or the tendency to promote inwardness [*Innerlichkeit*] to a privileged moral and epistemic position) first appears with Socrates. Its appearance is a function of the necessary decline of the "beautiful freedom" of the Greek city-state, and is clearly manifest in Socrates' novel claims concerning the priority of individual reason and conscience.[81]

As a broad cultural tendency away from public life, individualism tremendously expands its realm with the overturning of the Roman republic. Under the Empire, public culture could no longer be viewed as an extension of the self of the individual citizen nor as an expression of individual will.[82] "All political freedom vanished," and with it the average citizen's hope for immortality through participation and political action. According to Hegel, at this point "death must have become something terrifying, since nothing survived" the individual citizen beyond private property.[83] This sets the stage for Christianity's "flight from the world" in the late Roman Empire, a flight that focuses on personal salvation and that permanently displaces the idea of the political community as the "absolute end" of humanity.

The resulting alienation from public life—the "unhappy consciousness" born of Christianity—is the ground of modern individualism and its decidedly "instrumentalist" view of the state (one already on full display in Augustine's *City of God*). Like Machiavelli and Rousseau before him, Hegel sees his primary task as challenging this view and the seemingly boundless alienation on which it rests.[84] However, unlike them, Hegel's challenge does not hinge upon the idea of reviving the kind of public life found in either the *polis* or the Roman republic. His resoluteness in this regard—his refusal of the theoretical nostalgia of a Rousseau or a Schiller—accounts for the intensity of his focus on *recognition, representation,* and *comprehension,* as opposed to *participation, self-government,* and civic *virtu.*

For Hegel, then, "individualism" is hardly an "erroneous judgment" that can be overcome by increased community involvement and participation in "free institutions." It is, rather, one of the defining elements of our identity as Western and modern—perhaps the defining element. The question for Hegel is how we can come to see it as a central strand of our tradition, and not as an irreducible starting point (as it is for the social contract tradition) or an ultimate reality (as it is for the bourgeois-romantic view of the world). We cannot go home again—the modern individual cannot *fully* identify with the public norms and practices of his community in the naive and natural manner of the ancient Athenians.[85] But we can—with the philosopher's aid—see the way in which the modern state creates and protects a space for subjective ("negative") freedom, while simultaneously embodying the concrete freedom of the community in its laws, institutions, and public practices.

In this manner, "atomism" as a method or mode of understanding social and political reality is refuted, while *the individual*—understood as the conjunction of "free subjectivity" and the principle of particularity [*Partikularität*]—is given his rightful (limited and institutionally protected) place.[86] Hegel, in other words, tries to pry individualism—or, better, the *truth* of this hugely important dimension of our culture—free from the distorting grasp of otherworldly Christians, reductionist utilitarians, and hopelessly egocentric "beautiful souls." All have grossly exaggerated the nature, bounds, and explanatory power of the self, to the point where the reality of the public world—the objective world of shared law, practices, language and institutions, of determinate ethical obligations—dissolves in a haze of good motives, base interests, and entirely external instrumental structures.

We might, then, characterize the crucial difference between Tocqueville and Hegel in the following terms. Tocqueville wants us to overcome the enervating (modern and democratic) condition of individualism through expanded participation, association, and self-government. These avenues will remind us of our mutual dependence and the importance of public freedom. Hegel, on the other hand, wants us to contextualize individualism, to understand its origins and variations, and ultimately to tame it. He wants us to see it as the central, but also as the most potentially pathological, strand of our culture. Again and again in the history of the West, "free subjectivity" devolves into one form or another of subjectivism. Hegel demonstrates this thesis at length in the *Phenomenology* and in the lectures on the philosophy of world history. In *The Philosophy of Right* he shows us how the social and political complexity of the modern state is able to give individualism its due while curbing its more anarchic or subjectivist tendencies (whether these are generated by the market, Protestant "enthusiasm," or romantic self-indulgence).[87]

This major difference on the question of the historical roots of individualism gives rise to a more important difference on the question of freedom generally. While both Hegel and Tocqueville sought to reemphasize the public dimensions of liberty in a modern context, Hegel's historical/ cultural/psychological approach to the evolution of consciousness led him to stigmatize independence in all its forms.[88] This is a mistake Tocqueville was able to avoid, even though he agreed with Hegel that anyone who thought they stood alone, with their destiny fully in hand, was delusional. Independence conceived as a basic mode of social being was, for Tocqueville, clearly a mistake, a *jugement erroné*. Independence as an element of freedom, however, was not, as Tocqueville's emphasis on local independence and the last book of *Democracy in America, volume 2,* makes plain. Ironically, it was Tocqueville's appreciation of what he considered to be the "German contribution" to the Western idea of freedom that prevented him from making Hegel's error, from dismissing independence entirely.[89]

Hegel, Tocqueville, and Freedom as Independence

Why did Hegel—who clearly appreciated both the role of individual interests in modern society and the significance of the "principle of subjective freedom" in Western culture—remain deaf to the claims of independence as an element of modern freedom? Why did he insist that individual moral and political judgment stood in vital and perpetual need of the education, mediation, and sublimation provided by membership in professions, estates, and the state itself? Finally, why did he marginalize the importance of dissent, insisting time and again on something like a "my station and its duties" morality?[90] These and similar questions take us to the heart of a real tension with Tocqueville, their shared emphasis on the importance of public freedom and "ethical life" notwithstanding.

At first glance, this set of issues seems to return us to the question of the relative valence of "the political" in Hegel versus Tocqueville. One need not be a radical democrat to observe that Hegel focuses on recognition, integration, and reconciliation in his social philosophy, whereas Tocqueville focuses on the roots of civic engagement, as well as on the social forces that undermine public spirit and public liberty. There is more than a kernel of truth to this assessment. Hegel, after all, defines freedom as essentially a form of self-consciousness or (self) knowledge.[91] However, framing matters in such broad terms blinds us to the intensely political motivation underlying Hegel's mapping of the evolution of Western consciousness in the *Phenomenology* (and again in *Lectures on the Philosophy of World History*).

As already noted, Hegel saw individualism *qua* subjectivism as symptomatic of Western culture *as a whole*.[92] The illusion of autonomy—of self-sufficiency or self-contained independence—was one that plagued European man for virtually the whole of his post-*polis* history, from the fall of the Roman republic onward. In Hegel's time, this illusion took the form of the Romantic cult of alienation, fostering—in conjunction with Kant's philosophy and the legacy of radical Protestantism—an ethos of personal conviction built on disdain for the established structures and duties of the public moral-political world. Such an ethos—in which the "is" stands as a cold and dead refutation of the "ought"—could easily flip, in Hegel's view, into a fuzzy-headed, anti-institutional nationalism.[93] For many in Hegel's time (and since), the gap between the "I" and the "we" seemed to have broadened to the point where the only "solution" was a self-obliterating submergence in the *Volk*.

Even where the temptation to immediately identify the "I" with the "we" was successfully resisted, the spread of such culturally entrenched alienation from the public world (given further impetus by the growth of a universal market mentality) gave rise to a society in which the majority "too stubbornly insisted on their rights or withdrew into their subjectivity."[94] Increasingly—and to the detriment of their prospects of ever attaining happiness or genuine freedom—people became oblivious to any end larger than the family or the self, and to any ties beyond those of sentiment or self-interest. In Hegel's view, the twin dangers of privatism and a *völkisch* nationalism demanded a critique of individualism as a broad and deep cultural phenomenon; a *philosophical* critique that probed its roots far more deeply than any merely political or sociological analysis could.

The paradox, of course, is that the very profundity of Hegel's cultural, psychological, and philosophical dissection of individualism *qua* worldview is undercut by its sheer scope and historical comprehensiveness. If individualism is not the (limited) product of recent social and political transformations, but rather a basic mode or paradigm of consciousness (one that takes a variety of forms over nearly 2,000 years), then there seems little reason to hope that this peculiarly Western bad habit will ever be transcended. Rather, it appears far more likely that "free subjectivity" will repeatedly devolve into yet another form of subjectivism (something the *Phenomenology* apparently confirms). The only hope seems to reside in the possibility that we have truly come to the end of the "highway of despair," the long historical-cultural road that traces the development of self-consciousness (and, thus, the consciousness of freedom) in the West. It was this unlikely possibility that Hegel tried to demonstrate as accomplished fact through his complicated notion of philosophy as a kind of remembrance, and through his much-maligned theory of the modern state.

In Hegel's theory as (his)story, the idea of independence recurs *almost* eternally as the primary roadblock to recognition of self in the other; to achievement of transparency in our sociopolitical relations; and to *freedom*, to "being with oneself in another" (*Beisichselbtsein in einem Andern*).[95] It is an idea whose myriad historical incarnations prevent us from grasping that our *true* being lies in the ethical life of the state; that particularity and universality are (in that context, at least) only *seemingly* opposed. Hence the need to root out the idea of independence, to expose its obsessive and long-lived hold on the Western imagination after the fall of the Roman republic. Only when this idea has been rooted out will rational social and political institutions reveal themselves as reflections of our will, and as the concrete actuality of our freedom.

This goes a long way to explaining Hegel's unremitting hostility toward Socratic moral individualism, Roman Stoicism, the "unhappy consciousness" of Christianity, Cartesian rationalism, utilitarianism, Kantian notions of autonomy, and (last but not least) Jacobin radicalism.[96] From Hegel's perspective, these various forms of consciousness all make the mistake of putting individual conscience (or reason, or desire, or will) at the center of the moral world. As a result, they prevent us from seeing that reason, morality, and freedom are inherently and necessarily *social* in character, embodied in specific cultural practices, forms of interaction, and public institutions. Once Hegel's broad critical point is accepted—

and, as I indicated at the outset, it is hard *not* to accept it these days—it seems but a short and eminently reasonable step to conclude that the form and content of the moral life is *simply* a function of society and one's place in it. As Hegel somewhat notoriously put it in the introduction to his *Lectures on the Philosophy of World History*, "all the worth which the human being possesses, all spiritual reality, he possesses through the state. . . . Thus only is he fully conscious; thus only is he a partaker of morality—of a just and moral social and political life."[97]

In drawing this conclusion, Hegel did not intend to reduce the individual to the status of mere means of some supra-individual entity. Neither should he be read as holding that *all* societies and *all* practices are to be presumed moral until proven otherwise. His dictum that no individual can leap over their own time notwithstanding, the last thing we can accuse Hegel of is relativism.[98] What he *can* be accused of is the perpetuation of an ontological prejudice, one that presumes that Spirit (and with it, ethical life, *Sittlichkeit*) can find its adequate embodiment *only* in the public norms, practices, and institutions of a society with a developed state.[99] Such a prejudice—more or less demanded by the quasi-Aristotelian metaphysics of *Geist's* development[100]—predisposes us to view all deviations from said norms, practices, and institutions as either instances of supreme self-indulgence (the "beautiful soul" who cultivates *Innerlichkeit*), or as harbingers of the imminent dissolution of the life of the *Volk*.[101]

As a world-historical figure, Socrates clearly falls into both categories for Hegel. With his discovery of individual conscience, Socrates more or less invents "subjective inwardness," and (thus) initiates the movement away from an integrated public culture toward various (and increasingly irrationalist) forms of privatism. With Socrates, what Hegel refers to as the "descent into the self" begins. This descent entails the "evaporation" (*verflüchtigt*) of all "substantial" (that is to say, social) ethical content.[102] Hence the dual significance of Socrates for Hegel, a significance he sums up in *The Philosophy of Right*:

> Socrates made his appearance at the time when Athenian democracy had fallen into ruin. He evaporated the existing world and retreated into himself in search of the right and the good. Even in our times it happens that reverence for the existing order is in varying degrees absent, and people seek to equate accepted values with their own will, with what they [as individual selves] have recognized.[103]

Of course, this process—the emergence of "free subjectivity" out of more "natural," substantive forms of consciousness—has its positive side as well. After all, it is only through such diremption that the goal of history—*self*-conscious freedom—can be achieved. Thus, the whole subsequent development from Socrates to the present (and the seemingly endless cycles of alienation and moral *mèconnaisance* it involves) is, as Hegel repeatedly reminds us, necessary.

What should concern us here, however, is not the imputation of any logical or historical inevitability. Rather, the cause of concern is the larger and more troubling Hegelian vision of freedom as—first and foremost—a species of integration or (better) *re*-integration. Hegel's negative view of "subjective" dissent—his persistent contempt for those who uphold the claims of subjective conscience against the law, or who "wrongheadedly" point out the gap between the "is" and the "ought"[104]—is premised on the assumption that modern freedom is, and should be, a form of *being at home in the world*. This is the ultimate philosophical content of "being with oneself in another," as well as the idea that freedom is actual when individuals are "with themselves" in their social lives.[105]

One cannot emphasize strongly enough that the institutions and norms Hegel wanted individual citizens to identify with were relatively liberal and (for his place and time) progressive. Moreover, while he saw Socratic conscience as the avatar of an alienated individualism and (thus) of subjectivism, Hegel would hardly have viewed the unreflective obedience of an Adolf Eichmann (or a "my country right or wrong" American) as an appropriate paradigm of modern freedom. To be authentic, one's identification with a given set of sociopolitical institutions and practices has to be mediated through a reflective subjectivity. It cannot—repeat, cannot—take the form of sheer "positivity."[106] As Hegel put it in *The Philosophy of Right*, "In modern times . . . we expect to have our own view, our own volition, and our own conscience."[107] As moderns, personal judgment is both our right and our duty; hence, our identification with the world of "objective spirit"—the public world—must pass through this subjective dimension. We must will this world, its practices and institutions, as (rational) individuals.[108]

But here a problem arises. If genuine freedom hinges on my ability to identify with the institutions and practices of my community—if my freedom hinges on "feeling myself to be part of them, and feeling them to be part of me"[109]—then overcoming alienation becomes *the* central philosophical-political task. This may well seem an impossible project, particularly given the alienation many of us feel toward the institutions and norms of our own society. But, Hegel thinks, much of this alienation is not rooted in anything real. It is, rather, a function of the "principle of atomicity's" broad and baneful influence.[110] Get rid of an atomistic understanding of political society and its purposes, and the larger part of this alienation will disappear. Such, at any rate, is the premise behind Hegel's social philosophy. It is also the reason why he places so much weight on the achievement of rational insight into what is *already there*. Insight begins with the recognition that an atomistic understanding of society—the sort of understanding promoted by the social contract theorists of the seventeenth century—is a false and superficial one. It is consummated in the realization that the laws, institutions, and duties of our society are not obstacles to, but rather the (concrete) vehicles of, our freedom.[111]

However "mediated" Hegel's idea of social integration is, we may still find ourselves skeptical toward his ideal of identification with public norms and institutions. As the children of a liberal (or formerly liberal) political culture, we are inclined to see distrust rather than identification as the *sine qua non* of a healthy political constitution. Such, at any rate, is the lesson of Locke and Paine. One can get around this aversion to "strong" forms of identification by simply pointing out that "bringing about what already is"—realizing the *Sitte* in *Sittlichkeit*—hardly entails the deification of the status quo. A good Hegelian citizen is not one who mindlessly obeys the authorities, or who toils robotically in his profession. He is, rather, one who strives to articulate, and to actualize, the best possibilities of his society and political constitution.[112]

One could claim along these lines (as both George Grote and Michael Walzer have) that Socrates was precisely this sort of citizen, Hegel's misreading of his "world-historical" significance to the contrary. Instead of viewing Socrates as a "moral revolutionary," one who upholds the claims of the conscientious self *against* the polis, we should view him as an "immanent critic" of Athenian democracy. That is to say, we should view Socrates as someone who fully accepted democratic Athens's basic institutions, values, and practices, and who saw himself as helping his fellow citizens live up to their best democratic selves.[113]

While appealing, such a "Hegelianized" Socrates is unpersuasive. Here we have to acknowledge that Hegel did get something essentially right about Socrates, however much we may disagree with his final assessment. Socrates' insistence on "care for one's soul" did, in fact, introduce a principle destructive of the "beautiful freedom" of the Athenians.

Unlike the "immanent" critic or the reformer, Socrates engaged in his philosophical activity because he felt that something was fundamentally wrong with the values and practices of Athenian democracy. His turn to conscience—to the *internal* dialogue of the thinking self—is motivated largely by a desire to escape the necessary injustice of a *merely civic* morality. In this respect, he truly was a moral revolutionary, something the rhetoric of the *Apology*—and his unique position in Western thought—makes luminously clear.[114]

Hegel, while radical philosophically, was no moral or political revolutionary. He was a reformer at heart, and for what he considered good historical and scientific (*wissenschaftlich*) reasons.[115] Following the importation of modern constitutional principles by Napoleon, and the subsequent modernization of the Prussian state by vom Stein and Hardenberg, it seemed clear (to Hegel, at least) that the basic structure of the "rational" state was in place, even though adequate representative institutions and freedom of the press had yet to be realized. This certainty that history was nearing its end led Hegel to view all calls for radical change, democracy, and universal (manhood) suffrage with impatience and unease.[116] America may indeed be the "land of the future," but there was no doubt in Hegel's mind that the soon-to-be-perfected European constitutional monarchy—one characterized by strong representative institutions, the rule of law, and a fair amount of social and associational pluralism—was more than worthy of its citizen-subjects' identification and support. From his world-historical perspective, *independence* was an outmoded and destructive form of freedom, one that encouraged alienation by making rational insight into the achievement of the modern state more or less impossible.

Returning to Tocqueville, we can see the emergence of a quite distinctive—one might almost say, post-Hegelian—conception of what "healthy" sociopolitical integration looks like. To be sure, Tocqueville's conception presumes no small degree of identification on the part of the average citizen (in terms of public spirit, shared values, *moeurs*, and a willingness to sacrifice). It is this dimension that endears him to contemporary communitarians. However, unlike them—and, indeed, unlike Hegel—Tocqueville is careful to make room for the idea and practice of freedom as independence (although not in the classically negative sense of *personal* independence we find in Hobbes and Mill).[117] What he has in mind is summed up by his politically incorrect phrase "manly liberty." By this Tocqueville meant a kind of independent or risk-taking action; the kind taken out of commitment to a principle, an idea, or a sense of honor;

the kind that flows from the desire to retain at least the semblance of self-mastery.

What is Tocqueville's motivation in arguing for independence in *this* sense? The answer is that he did not believe that atomization and the specter of centralization could be contained by the art of association, "hands-on" civic education, and shared *moeurs* alone. What was also needed, and desperately so, was the kind of self-assertion made possible by freedom of association, a robust pluralism, and a fiercely independent localism.

Tocqueville readily admitted that unlimited freedom of association carries dangers, as does a combative pluralism, or an exaggerated sense of local independence.[118] While sensitive to such potentially "fatal results," he was willing to run the risk of a certain amount of civic turbulence for one simple reason. Only the unapologetic assertion of minority opinion and local interests (by means of a free press and free association) could, in his view, preserve freedom in the face of majority tyranny and looming administrative despotism.[119] Independent, "manly" action was needed to stave off a future in which "every man allows himself to be put in leading strings."[120]

Phrases like this—as well as the one about "timid and industrious animals" cited above—mark Tocqueville as a precursor not only to Mill, but to Nietzsche, Weber, and Foucault as well.[121] They reveal a not-so-tacit philosophy of history, one in which the seemingly inevitable destiny of equality leads not to the triumph of liberty, but to the creation of a "herd man" and a pervasive docility.[122] The prospect of such a post-political destiny—an administrative despotism that renders *political* governance obsolete—should call forth concerted resistance on the part of all those who value freedom as independence. The theoretical-historical project of Tocqueville's two major works can thus be seen as a romantic and democratic protest at the prospect of an overly integrated and administered world. Tocqueville fears atomization not because it produces dangerous levels of anomie and social pathology (the complaint of contemporary conservatives), but because it results in a generalized retreat from the public realm and the self-assertion necessary to self-government.[123]

This, it seems to me, marks the fundamental fault line between Hegel and Tocqueville. For while both theorists vehemently attack the "individualist" idea that people can be free by withdrawing from either society or the public world, Hegel can hardly be said to fear the prospect of too much integration. This can be explained by "geographical" and historical circumstances, notably the fact that Hegel did not have the kind of first-hand experience of a rational, yet overly centralized, state that Tocqueville and the French did.[124] But it can also be explained in terms of Hegel's reaction to the Terror and to his overreaction to Romanticism. These two factors impelled him to repudiate, or at least chasten, all forms of rebellious subjectivity.[125] Misdirected passion, combined with subjectivism, was in Hegel's view the great enemy of the public realm, the realm of "objective spirit."

For Tocqueville, the primary threat came from apathy and indifference of a bourgeois sort.[126] This very substantial diagnostic difference accounts for Tocqueville's greater proximity to contemporary sensibility, a sensibility that fears the deadening hand of liberal proceduralism and yearns for more "agonistic" forms of political action. Even in his most dispirited moments, Tocqueville retains a youthful enthusiasm for the possibilities of political—rebellious or "great"—action.[127] Such enthusiasm is utterly foreign to the mature Hegel.[128]

The *topos* of rebellious subjectivity vs. the centralized state takes us only so far, however, in explaining why independence could, in a political context, retain such a positive connotation for Tocqueville. To fully appreciate the difference between Tocqueville and Hegel on this score, we must return to volume 1 of *Democracy in America*. Here the fears for the future revolve around the victory of the "democratic revolution" and the principle of popular sovereignty—a victory Hegel saw as temporary and due for assimilation by the structures of the "rational" state.[129] For Tocqueville, in contrast, this victory was both complete and epoch-making, in America as well as France. The Hegelian halfway house between the old, aristocratic and hierarchical, world and the new democratic one was clearly no longer an option. The only *real* alternative, in Tocqueville's view, was between functional and dysfunctional popular sovereignty; between a democracy where popular sovereignty "worked" through a decentralized participation in local administration (America), and one where it was too weak, inexperienced, and lacking in self-confidence to take up the burdens of self-government (France).[130]

But even where the "democratic revolution" did not abort, dangers lurked. The "absolute sovereignty of the majority" was, after all, the "very essence of democratic government." And absolute sovereignty contained within it, always and everywhere, the "germ of tyranny."[131] In America, this germ developed into the "tyranny of the majority," a tyranny exercised through both legislative and "moral" channels. In Tocqueville's view, there were relatively few institutional restraints to the majority at the state level, especially given elected officials' lack of independence. Only a robust pluralism, combined with a widespread respect for law and a religiously inspired rejection of the "impious adage" that "everything is permissible in the interests of society," kept the potential "legal despotism of the legislature" more or less in check.[132]

The same could not be said about the realm of thought and opinion in America. There the tyranny of the majority came fully into its own, making the absolute monarchs of Europe look like duffers:

> In America, the majority raises formidable barriers around the liberty of opinion; within these barriers an author may write what he pleases, but woe to him if he goes beyond them. Not that he is in danger of an auto-da-fé, but he is exposed to obloquy and persecution. His political career is closed forever, since he has offended the only authority that is able to open it. Every sort of compensation, even that of celebrity, is refused to him. Before making public his opinions he thought he had sympathizers; now it seems to him that he has none any more since he revealed himself to everyone; then those who blame him criticize loudly and those who think as he does keep quiet and move away without courage. He yields at length, overcome by the daily effort which he has to make, and subsides into silence, as if he felt remorse for having spoken the truth.[133]

The spiritual tyranny exercised by an irritable and intolerant majority renders independence of thought and action all but impossible. Not only does it block the careers of would-be public men: it goes further, corrupting the best minds of the day through the creation of a "courtier mentality." According to Tocqueville, writers and political actors in the United States invariably devote the greatest part of their energy to praising the wisdom and virtue of the American people. In this aspect, they exceed the sycophants of Louis XIV in both their flattery and their slavishness. The result of this willful self-prostitution is a generalized "debasement of character," a debasement most acute among men of letters and politicians. The "manly candor and masculine independence of opinion" that characterized the generation of the founders is, in Tocqueville's time, nowhere to be seen.[134] Dissenting judgments may win the agreement of a few, but never in public.

It may appear that what Tocqueville had to say about majority tyranny in volume 1 of *Democracy in America* conflicts with his later analysis of the "herd-like" majority in volume 2. The majority in volume 1 appears restive, eager to assert its will through legislation and "spiritual tyranny" in the realm of opinion. However, in volume 2 the majority is docile and easily administered.[135]

There is a grain of truth to this, but it obscures the underlying continuity of Tocqueville's thought. In both volumes, independence is presented as a kind of official American ideology. And, in both volumes, actual American social and political practice is presented as quite the reverse. "Bad" independence—the kind born of *individualisme* and the dissociative effects of democratic equality—is daily overcome through participation in "free institutions." "Good independence"—the kind Tocqueville associates with local self-government and the "manly" generation of the founders—disappears as majority opinion comes to monopolize the empty space of authoritative judgment. Indeed, the rule of an increasingly monolithic public opinion threatens to overwhelm the salutary effects of both associative pluralism and governmental decentralization. In neither volume of *Democracy in America* does Tocqueville conceal his dismay at a democratic world that (so to speak) naturally extinguishes independence of thought and action.[136] Whether this independence is extinguished by the moral authority of the majority, or by the "benign and tutelary power" of the administrative state, makes little difference in the end.

But—as always with Tocqueville—there is another side to things. The dread of a world without "good" independence is more than balanced by his horror at an increasingly disenchanted world; a world infected by skepticism and characterized by the rapid evaporation of tradition, custom, and instinctive patriotism. In the first volume of *Democracy in America* Tocqueville writes:

> Epochs sometimes occur in the life of a nation when the old customs of a people are changed, public morality is destroyed, religious belief is shaken, and the spell of tradition broken. . . . The country then assumes a dim and dubious shape in the eyes of its citizens; they no longer behold it in the soil which they inhabit, for that soil is to them an inanimate clod; nor in the usages of their forefathers, which they have learned to regard as a debasing yoke; nor in religion, for of that they doubt; nor in the laws, which do not originate in their own authority; nor in the legislator, whom they fear and despise. The country is lost to their senses; they can discover it neither under its own nor under

borrowed features, and they retire into a narrow and unenlightened selfishness.[137]

The only hope in such circumstances lies not in the artificial and futile attempt to resurrect antique virtue, but in accelerating what Tocqueville calls the "union of private and public interests."[138] However, Tocqueville believes that any structure of mediation or participation designed to overcome or transcend the abstract Rousseauian opposition between individual and general interests will founder unless it too is grounded on a foundation of shared *moeurs*, religious belief, and public spirit.

Tocqueville's "reflective" patriotism (*patriotisme réfléchi*) is therefore not nearly as intellectual as its name makes it sound. While providing a place for "enlightened" self-interest, it too rests on *moeurs*, customs, and beliefs—on pre-reflective "habits of the heart" that provide a modern substitute for ancient *moeurs* that have gone dead.[139] Thus, while Tocqueville fears a future in which the monolith of public opinion effectively crushes independent thought and action, he simultaneously affirms the necessity of a deep and far-reaching moral consensus, one grounded, ultimately, in shared belief. "One cannot establish the reign of liberty without that of *moeurs*, and *moeurs* cannot be firmly founded without beliefs."[140]

That this is not simply a matter of social theory (the question of "social glue") is confirmed by Tocqueville's Burkean attack on the *philosophes* in *The Old Regime and the Revolution*, as well as by his indictment of skepticism and materialism ("*une maladie dangereuse de l'espirit humain*") in volume 2 of *Democracy in America*.[141] It is also confirmed by his disgracefully approving citation of an American judge's refusal to take evidence from a nonbeliever.[142] In these and similar passages, we run up against the narrow limits of Tocqueville's endorsement of independence of mind (to say nothing of independence of action or life-style). While fully alive to the ways in which public opinion can become despotic and exercise a "social tyranny," Tocqueville manages to remain oblivious to what Mill was to call the "despotism of custom."[143]

The reason for this, I would suggest, is that Tocqueville, like Hegel, viewed custom (*moeurs*, *Sitten*) as the irreducible substance of "ethical life." Where one regime of custom (the aristocratic) subsided, another—hopefully republican, Christian, and industrious, such as Tocqueville found in the Americans—would have to take its place. The only alternative was a full-blown atomism, one in which the prudentially based social contract of Hobbes, Locke, et al. became a social and political reality.[144] This possibility—in which the political community was reduced to a means for the preservation of life, liberty, and property—was as anathema to Tocqueville as it was to Hegel.

From the perspective of Hegel and Tocqueville, the survival of public liberty in the modern age demanded more—much more—than fair rules of the game and a known and indifferent "umpire" to oversee them. It required a firm bed of *moeurs* or *Sitten*. It also demanded a structure of participatory and/or representative institutions through which the pursuit of self-interest could be educated, mediated, and (so to speak) domesticated. The outline of such a firmly grounded structure was precisely what Hegel and Tocqueville sought to provide: the one through his elaboration of the "gothic architecture" of the modern state, the other through his analysis of American democracy and its substantive moral preconditions.

Conclusion

Hegel and Tocqueville were right to see bourgeois individualism and more extreme forms of romanticism as signaling a dangerous alienation from public life. Their joint project of reminding us of the importance of the public realm stands as a high point of nineteenth-century political thought—especially when compared to subsequent developments in liberal and socialist theory, in which economism moves to the fore. They were wrong, however, in seeing strong identification with society's basic institutions and norms as the only real counter to this alienation, as the *sine qua non* of a renewed public life. Love of public liberty expresses itself far more through dissent than through identification, even if (as Hannah Arendt observed) dissent implies consent.[145] This truth finds greater resonance in Tocqueville than in Hegel. While it is true that equality, atomization, and social homogenization are intimately tied and potentially pathological phenomena, it is also true that the kind of "meaningful differentiation" celebrated by Hegel and Tocqueville depends—in the last instance—upon shared ends, common mores, and a shared moral idiom.[146] It depends, in other words, on a "thick theory of the good," a theory made flesh in the mores and customs of a particular people and a particular (coherent and unfragmented) way of life.

This is not to deny that Hegel and Tocqueville perform much of the theoretical heavy lifting required to arrive at a pluralist conception of politics. It is, rather, to underline the limits of the nascent pluralism of their accounts. What we find in their theories is a pluralism of interests and associations, professions and social spheres. What we do not find is anything approaching a real moral pluralism—the kind of pluralism born of deep cultural and religious differences, and which manifests itself in allegiance to different ultimate values.[147] Such "radical" pluralism characterizes all modern, multicultural societies, and makes hopes for "an expressive state" or a "post-industrial *Sittlichkeit*" look dim indeed.[148]

From the historical perspective of Hegel and Tocqueville, however, grounding the renewal of public life on *moeurs* or *Sitten* that citizens consciously identified with looked eminently possible. After all, they lived in an age where one could speak, without fear of contradiction, of the "spirit of the people" (*Volksgeist*) or the "national character of the Americans."[149] That age—the age of an Anglo-Christian America, in which Catholicism formed the most novel and exotic cultural strand[150]—is long gone, and with it the hopes for civic engagement grounded on moral consensus or "free *moeurs*." Hegel has a bit of an advantage in this regard, given his more consistent institutional emphasis. But for institutions to be vehicles of identification and self-recognition (rather than simply the required machinery of a complex society), they too must be expressive of "the spirit of a people."

Today, the promotion of such "self-recognition" in our institutional life would demand hefty measures of self-deception and ideological fiction, and not simply because the bureaucracies and political parties of a mass society are in and of themselves alienating.[151] More clearly than ever before, America and the European nations are "imagined communities." The original collective subjects presumed by Hegel and Tocqueville's accounts (the *Volk*; "the Americans") have gone missing. In their place are much more diverse, polyglot, morally pluralist populations; populations that lack the kind of aesthetic wholeness presumed by Tocqueville's comparative method and Hegel's historical sensibility.[152]

In addition to being radically pluralist in nature, the late modern condition is also (as Max Weber reminded us) an essentially fragmented one. The centrifugal forces of atomization have been matched by the accelerated disaggregation of value-spheres (for example, religion, art, science, family, and citizenship) on the one hand, and by the increasing coordination of economic and political "subsystems" on the other. This, needless to say, has been a hard pill for both neo-Hegelians and neo-Tocquevillians to swallow.

The integrated structure of institutions, practices, and moral ends they wish for has little or no place in the late modern world.

This very absence, however, explains why Hegelian/Tocquevillian images of moral coherence and sociopolitical integration continue to exercise such a powerful appeal. Torn between the conflicting demands of numerous and autonomous spheres of life, the late modern individual well may experience nostalgia for the (relative) simplicity of the "double life" depicted by Tocqueville.[153] *If only* family, civil society, and political life interlocked and complemented each other in the way both Tocqueville and Hegel described; *if only* these spheres worked together to create an integrated structure of mediation, one in which universal and particular, community and individual interest, gradually came together. Such, however, is not our fate. Nor is it possible to imagine a version of the late modern world in which it could be.

This brings me to the most troubling aspect of Hegel and Tocqueville's attempt to foster a return to public life through strategies of integration and identification (strategies they pursue by deploying vocabularies of shared *moeurs* and associational membership). It has long been a cliché of postwar thought that totalitarianism's rise was made possible by the collapse of the class system in Europe, a collapse brought on by the trauma of World War I, economic crisis, and revolutionary turmoil.[154] More recently, communitarian political theory has pointed out how social homogenization, when combined with a liberal-proceduralist public philosophy, generates unprecedented levels of anomie and a receptiveness to fundamentalisms (whether nationalist or religious in character).[155] Each of these diagnoses of the pathologies of our time makes reintegration through corporate or community membership look like our most pressing—and obvious—need.

But *are* atomization and alienation at the root of our most fundamental sociopolitical problems? An affirmative answer would, in my view, have to ignore the myriad ways in which mass culture and our economic system supply alternative, often highly effective, forms of integration and belonging. "Estates" in the Hegelian sense may be obsolete, but "demographics" (as the advertising industry calls them) are not.[156] Similarly, local self-government and "township independence" may be a thing of the past, but membership in communities of leisure or faith is stronger than ever. There are, of course, broad tendencies toward disorganization and disaffiliation. For example, unions are in decline and the contemporary underclass has many of the same troubling characteristics Hegel detected in the "rabble" of his day. However, the fact remains that consumer society and celebrity culture effect broad and deep cathexis by untold millions from every social class. Combine this considerable investment of desire with the perpetual anxiety born of a "global economy" and you have a recipe for over-identification (what Marcuse called "the happy consciousness")[157] *and* docility.

In other words, we would do well to at least entertain the possibility that we currently suffer from too much, rather than too little, identification and integration.[158] Moderate alienation as a form of minimal critical distance has become an increasingly scarce commodity—and not because the majority of us are radically alienated. Quite the contrary. The possibility that mass culture would prove to be a such a potent source of the wrong kind of integration was thematized by Mill in *On Liberty's* famous discussions of the "social tyranny" and "despotism of custom" that afflict a modern, mass society. Mill was, of course, building on Tocqueville's insights about majority tyranny in the "moral" realm. But Tocqueville himself did not draw Mill's lesson: he did not jump to the defense of the person with heretical ideas or an eccentric lifestyle. While valuing a certain "manly" independence in political affairs, Tocqueville—like Hegel—wound up attacking those who had drifted a bit too far from the established *moeurs* of their culture.

Hegel and Tocqueville's attacks on individualism *qua* subjectivism need to be substantially qualified. Contrary to what they imply, there is no internal link between moral individualism and privatism or quietism (however strong this link might be in the case of "possessive" or bourgeois individualism). Hegel and Tocqueville's serial conflations of this score are highly misleading. The *real* danger confronting the present comes from rampant over-identification with the *moeurs* and opinions of one's class, nation, or religion. Wherever dissent and independent judgment are identified with idiosyncrasy and decline; wherever established customs, laws, and institutions are endowed with a substantiality only a metaphysician could doubt; *there* the moral achievement of the modern world—the *aspiration* to autonomy—has been undercut, if not exactly abandoned.[159]

Preserving this aspiration does not demand the resurrection of "atomism," or the defensive insistence that "the subject" really is "master in its own house" thanks to free will or pure practical reason. It does not, in other words, entail the effective repudiation of philosophical and social thought after Nietzsche. Rather, all it demands is that we recognize that the struggle to "realize what already is" must be balanced by an ever-present suspicion of the given, public interpretation of our "world" (manifest in its norms, institutions, practices, and *moeurs*). This is true even when that interpretation appears to us cloaked in its most somber and "edifying" garb.[160]

4 | TOCQUEVILLE AND ARENDT: PUBLIC FREEDOM,

PLURALITY, AND THE PRECONDITIONS OF LIBERTY

But how difficult it is to establish liberty solidly among people
who have lost the practice of it, and even the correct notion of
it! What greater impotence than that of institutions, when ideas
and mores do not nourish them.
—Tocqueville to Gustave de Beaumont, February 27, 1858

In *The Structural Transformation of the Public Sphere*, Jürgen Habermas
presents a narrative about the birth, growth, and (possibly fatal) decline
of the "bourgeois public sphere" over the course of two and a half centuries. Habermas's narrative provides a useful touchstone when considering Arendt and Tocqueville on the promise and perils of American
democracy. I say "useful" not because I think Habermas is right—far
from it. Rather, *Structural Transformation* highlights the divergence of
Habermas's rationalist conception of the public sphere from both Arendt
and Tocqueville's interpretations of American democracy, and—more
broadly—from the presuppositions of American democracy itself.

Does this mean Arendt and/or Tocqueville are right where Habermas is
wrong? Hardly. For anyone who thinks that moral and political pluralism
are a constitutive feature of liberal democracy, Arendt and Tocqueville's interpretations of the American republic are almost (but not quite) as problematic as Habermas's idea of the role of a properly functioning public

sphere. For Habermas, the "bourgeois public sphere" was the venue in which private persons came together and "rationalized" state policies and laws through the public use of their reason. The goal was to reach consensus about the "common good" in a discursive arena where participants recognized no authority other than that of the "force of the better argument."

To anyone schooled in liberal or Enlightenment political thought, Habermas's idea of a properly functioning public sphere is remarkable in its assumption that the "public use" of our reason tends toward consensus—an assumption even more remarkable when one considers his assertion that such rationally guided consensus is first discovered in debates about culture and judgments of taste.[1] Habermas gives us a public realm in which rational-critical debate not only clarifies and purifies plural opinions, but produces *opinion publique,* which has the force (if not the epistemological status) of truth.[2] What is surprising here is not only the bracketing of the "passions and the interests" that so preoccupied the founders, but the (Kantian) modeling of the public sphere on the example of the scholarly exchange of ideas.[3]

Habermas's construal of the functioning of "enlightened public opinion" is a long way from Arendt's emphasis on "public freedom, public spirit, and public happiness," as well as from Tocqueville's picture of a vibrant associational life. Indeed, for both Arendt and Tocqueville, "public opinion" looms more as a despotic than as a rationalizing force. Arendt rejects "public opinion" in no uncertain terms, just as Tocqueville warns of the potential for a democratic "tyranny of the majority."[4] They reject "public opinion" not simply for its irrationalism (as a vehicle of popular sentiment), but for its potential unanimity. Both Arendt and Tocqueville are responding, in somewhat different ways, to the provocation of Rousseau and the very idea of a General Will or Sovereign People. Arendt rejects the idea of a General Will in the name of human plurality and the plurality of (individual) opinions; Tocqueville in the name of civil society and a radically decentered political life. The idea that debate and deliberation—whether in Arendt's "public realm" or Tocqueville's sphere of associations—should aim, even ideally, at unanimity or a general consensus is foreign to them both.[5]

But if, compared to Habermas, both Arendt and Tocqueville look like friends of pluralism and plurality of opinion in politics, they are both sorely lacking from a liberal standpoint. One need not be an Isaiah Berlin to detect in both thinkers traces of the overvaluation of moral consensus that is so characteristic of the Western tradition of political thought. While

Tocqueville famously saw himself as providing a "new political science for a new world," and Arendt saw herself as breaking with the main lines of the Western tradition precisely on the issue of human plurality, in the end neither goes nearly far enough in exploring the relation between plurality and pluralism, diversity of opinion and diversity of ultimate values or worldviews.

In this chapter I examine Tocqueville and Arendt's main arguments concerning public freedom, participation, the looming threat of "public opinion," and independent judgment. I contend (uncontroversially) that Arendt's interpretation of American democracy and its discontents is deeply indebted to Tocqueville. I also contend (perhaps somewhat controversially) that this debt extends to the most dubious part of Tocqueville's analysis, namely, his insistence that religion (or something like it) is required to underwrite manners, mores, and responsible citizenship in a democracy. While Arendt would hardly endorse Tocquville's sentiment that "Christianity must be maintained at any cost in the bosom of modern democracies,"[6] her republicanism leads her to be strangely unconcerned with the role moral pluralism plays in modern public life. In this regard, she is disturbingly celebratory of the role that something close to myth or civil religion plays in the preservation of American democracy.

Tocqueville: The Priority of the Political

As any reader of *Democracy in America* and *On Revolution* knows, there is a good deal of thematic continuity, if not narrative structure, between the two works. Tocqueville's depiction of American democracy highlights the relative social equality of the Americans; the importance of the townships to self-government; the way freedom of association teaches the "art of association" and joint action; and the need for a radical decentralization of power if a free way of life is to be preserved. All of these themes are echoed—and amplified—in *On Revolution*. Even more striking, however, is the way Arendt appropriates Tocqueville's diagnosis of the nascent pathologies of American democracy, a diagnosis she sees as fully born out by the passage of time. Thus, Tocqueville's fears about individualism, withdrawal, materialism, and centralization are all reiterated in *On Revolution*. The difference, of course, is that whereas Tocqueville worried prospectively about the effects these tendencies would have on the democratic future, Arendt cast herself in the role of the owl of Minerva, dismally confirming the "loss of the revolutionary spirit" wrought by the causes Tocqueville had identified.

But—it will be objected—Arendt hardly shared Tocqueville's enthusiasm for civil society. Her civic republican interpretation of the American Revolution stands at some distance from Tocqueville's focus (in volume 2 of *Democracy in America*) on associational life and American manners and mores. Unlike Tocqueville, she buys into the Rousseauian/civic republican distinction between *hommes* and *citoyens*, a distinction Tocqueville partly blurs with his analysis of the relation between "public" and "civil" associations, and with the idea of "self-interest rightly understood."[7] Thus, the public realm as it emerges in Tocqueville is one of "private individuals appearing in public," attending to the kinds of matters that run afoul of Arendt's rigorous (and much criticized) distinction between the social and the political.[8]

This objection has obvious weight, but it exaggerates the distance separating the two theorists. In fact, the model of political action that emerges in *On Revolution* is far more associational in character than the Greek (or agonistic) model we find in *The Human Condition*.[9] The later paradigm is one of ordinary people coming together in joint action, rather than virtuosic actors competing on a public stage. As actual or potential "participators in government," these ordinary people are *citizens*, first and foremost. They are attuned to *public matters*, and not simply the activity and regulation of civil society (understood here in the Hegelian sense of the "system of needs"). But even this is less opposed to Tocqueville than first glance might suggest. For despite his anti-Rousseauian focus on the interface between *homme* and *citoyen*, Tocqueville leaves little doubt that it is as members of political associations—that is, as *citizens*—that we learn the art of association so essential to a vibrant civil society.[10] As with Arendt, there is a distinct "priority of the political" in Tocqueville—a fact many of his contemporary American admirers seem genuinely unable to appreciate.[11]

How does this priority of the political manifest itself in Tocqueville? First through his emphasis on the value of citizenship and participation in government. With the possible exceptions of Rousseau and Arendt, it is hard to think of a canonical thinker who places greater weight on the value of self-government and the participation of ordinary people in public life. It might be objected that Tocqueville's enthusiasm for the local autonomy and civic spirit he encountered in America was largely a function of his desire to *avoid* a certain outcome, namely, the rise of the bureaucratic, centralized state. So viewed, his emphasis on participation is largely liberal or strategic in character, at odds with Arendt's more overtly republican emphasis on the intrinsic value of participation.[12] But this objection fails to appreciate the extent to which Tocqueville saw participation in moral as well as instrumental (or defensive) terms. Participation and self-government were the means to fend off the bureaucratic night in which all cats are grey; but they also served to cultivate the habits and attitudes—the free *moeurs*—necessary to the formation of energetic and self-reliant citizens, rather than docile or privatized subjects. Arendt may avoid Tocqueville's moralizing rhetoric, but they share this essential point.[13]

Second, the priority of the political is manifest in Tocqueville's fear of atomization and withdrawal, and in his foreboding that democracies may well sacrifice political liberty to their passion for social equality.[14] This is not a worry about the possible breakdown of social capital and networks of trust. Rather, it is a worry about the ways in which a body of citizens can gradually dissolve through lack of public spirit and political participation, yielding a disaggregated mass where there was once a politically organized people. The resulting separation and isolation are, Tocqueville maintains, the crucial preconditions for the emergence of a new form of despotism—a sociological point that Arendt makes the center of her analysis of totalitarianism's rise in Europe.[15]

Third, the priority of the political informs Tocqueville's quest for a non-sovereign form of political power, a form he thought he discovered in American democracy.[16] Our liberal instincts tell us that decentralization of government is necessary to overturn the sovereign model of power that so threatened individual rights in Europe, even after the democratic revolutions. But decentralization is necessary not only to limit *state* power. It is necessary for the generation of dispersed public power, and for the creation and preservation of freedom and self-government. In other words, while a nonsovereign, decentralized form of government is necessary to preserve freedom *from* politics, it is even more necessary to preserve public freedom, the freedom *for* politics. This is a point that both Tocqueville and Arendt—in different but parallel ways—never tire of emphasizing.[17]

Fourth, the priority of the political is found where we least expect it, namely, in Tocqueville's description of associational life in America. We have been conditioned by Robert Putnam and a legion of civil society enthusiasts to read Tocqueville's chapters on association as a paean to membership and such "mediating structures" as families, neighborhoods, churches, and clubs.[18] Perusing this literature, one would never guess that the primary reason Tocqueville celebrated "civil associations" (or what we call "voluntary associations") was because he saw them as both consolidating and facilitating the effects of political association.[19] Indeed, when it came to learning the distinctively political art of joint action (what Arendt, following Tocqueville, calls "acting in concert"), it was political and not "civil" associations that Tocqueville called the "large free schools" of democracy. In political associations "all the members of the community go to learn the general theory of association."[20] The Tocquevillian idea of political action as *joint* action, emerging from the art of association, is one Arendt made her own and consistently emphasized in a variety of contexts.[21]

Finally, Tocqueville's description (in book 4 of volume 2) of an emergent form of democratic despotism, one founded on a compromise of sorts between popular sovereignty and administrative despotism, attests to the essential importance of citizenship and a vibrant public life.[22] The picture Tocqueville paints of a passive, submissive populace cared for by the "immense and tutelary power" of a centralized, bureaucratic state apparatus is not—or not merely—a proto-libertarian (or proto-Foucauldian) vision of the welfare state run amok. It is, far more importantly, a vision of the end of public life and the obliteration of political freedom and political government.[23] It is this nightmare—the fear of a depoliticized, bureaucratic world in which administration triumphs over political governance—which drives Tocqueville's hopeful analysis of decentralized American democracy. This form of democracy is the last, best hope for an increasingly centralized (post-aristocratic) world; a world stripped of the stability born of social hierarchy and *pouvoirs intermédiaires*; a world astonishingly vulnerable to bureaucratic centralization and the eclipse of public freedom.

Readers of the last chapters of Tocqueville's second volume have the experience of being wrenched, suddenly, back to France. But while the centralized French state (and a passive French citizenry) stood as a stark warning about one possible route to the closure of the political, Tocqueville was not so blind to think that all was well with American democracy.[24] Its robust associational life and habits of self-reliance notwithstanding, American democracy was threatened by the rule of public opinion, "individualism," and a creeping focus on physical gratification and materialism. I want briefly to consider how Tocqueville construed each of these dangers before turning to his preferred antidote: religion.

If, unlike their French counterparts, Americans did not have to worry about a statist interpretation of popular sovereignty, they still had to worry about their own native version of "the voice of the people is the voice of God." While Tocqueville was primarily concerned to point out the dangers of the legislative power of the majority, his analysis famously revealed a deeper and more insidious form of tyranny, one that captured souls and not just bodies. In a world bereft of aristocratic structures of authority, the majority naturally tended to make its own judgment the highest and most unquestionable standard, the sole authority.[25] Indeed, Tocqueville thought that "ages of equality" bolstered the individual's faith in the judgment of the multitude, making public opinion "the mistress of the world."[26] Thus, in the American democracy, "as long as the majority is still undecided, discussion is carried on; but as soon as its decision is irrevocably pronounced, everyone is silent, and the friends as well as the opponents of the measure unite in assenting to it propriety."[27] A "courtier-spirit" ruled, as writers and politicians outdid themselves to pay tribute to the virtues and judgment of their fellow citizens. To do otherwise—to challenge the "irresistible authority" of public opinion—was to invite "obloquy and persecution" as well as banishment from public life.[28] Hence, American freedom and equality notwithstanding, Tocqueville could claim that he knew of "no country in which there is so little independence of mind and real freedom of discussion as America."[29]

The key feature of Tocqueville's analysis is not (as Habermas contends) that "public opinion" emerges as an arbitrary and irrational power, impervious to the rationalizing force of critical debate.[30] Rather, it is his linkage of democracy, equality, and conformity—a linkage later liberal thinkers (from J. S. Mill to David Riesman) elaborated in terms of mass culture. The striking thing about this thesis is the way Tocqueville reconstructs the logic of sovereignty in terms of a democratic "common sense." The evacuation of the concept of sovereignty from the world of institutions (the achievement of the founders) hardly guarantees a robust pluralism in the realm of opinion or *doxa*. On the contrary: it ironically helps to create conditions necessary for the emergence of a virtual sovereign—public opinion—one that is, in many respects, more oppressive than any absolute monarch.[31]

This brings us to the second of Tocqueville's American/democratic pathologies: individualism. If liberals have fixated on the Tocquevillian themes of majority tyranny and the quashing of "heretical" dissent, then communitarians have responded by erecting an entire political philosophy on the basis of three short chapters of *Democracy in America*. As a result, the notion that something called "individualism" is at the root of most of America's ills has become fixed in the imaginations not only of communitarian intellectuals, but of the public at large.[32] Vague notions of the "malaise" of individualism, however, obscure as much as they reveal about Tocqueville's original meaning, which is framed by constant reference to the decline of public life and the public self.

Unlike his contemporary appropriators, Tocqueville defines individualism in pointed contrast to egoism and selfishness. Selfishness is "a vice as old as the world," whereas "individualism is of democratic origin."[33] It refers to the pronounced tendency for "each member of the community to sever himself from the mass of his fellows and to draw apart with his family and friends," thereby leaving "society at large" to itself.[34] A "mature and calm feeling," individualism flows not from any "exaggerated love of self," but from the tendency of democratic society to dissolve the ties between families, generations, and classes.[35] Finding himself detached from the past and more "organic" forms of membership, the democratic individual wrongly concludes that the self is the center of mental, moral, emotional, and material life.[36] Thus, individualism is not really (or not originally) a vice at all: it proceeds from an "erroneous judgment" rather than a "depraved feeling." The chief moral effect of individualism is that it "saps the virtues of public life."[37] Encouraging privatism and withdrawal, individualism drains civic life not by promoting selfishness (the perennial claim of conservatives and communitarians) but by fostering a specifically democratic form of moral obtuseness.[38]

Withdrawn into family and self, deaf to the moral claims of politics and public life, the democratic individual is prone to concentrate his energy on the pursuit of physical gratification and material well-being. This is the third pathological tendency Tocqueville detects in the American democracy, but one he regarded as more potential than real. Given the exorbitant quality of contemporary American materialism and consumerism, this is clearly one instance in which the prophetic Tocqueville was blind to his own insight. What accounts for this blindness, and how does it connect to Tocqueville's hopes for containing individualism and the rule of public opinion?

In the second volume of *Democracy in America*, Tocqueville writes:

When the taste for physical gratifications among [a democratic people] has grown more rapidly than their education and their experience of free institutions, the time will come when men are carried away and lose all self-restraint at the sight of the new possessions they are about to obtain. In their intense and exclusive anxiety to make a fortune they lose sight of the close connection that exists between the private fortune of each and the prosperity of all. It is not necessary to do violence to such a people in order to strip them of the rights they enjoy; they themselves willingly loosen their hold. The discharge of political duties appears to them to be a troublesome impediment which diverts them from their occupations and business.[39]

This is about as accurate a description of current American attitudes toward public life and its "burdens" as one could ask for. Yet Tocqueville—strangely, to us—thought the immoderate pursuit of physical gratification and private interest was largely a continental malady, and not one the Americans had to worry too much about. In the new world, one need not live in fear of the despotism of faction (an omnipresent danger when the majority are "engrossed by private affairs" and too busy to protect their own liberty). Rather, "an American attends to his private concerns as if he were alone in the world, and the next minute he gives himself up to the common welfare as if he had forgotten them."[40]

What made this energetic double life possible was, partly, the idea of "self-interest, rightly understood," which militated against any stark opposition of private vs. public interest and worked to prevent the corruption of the public sphere by "sinister interests." More fundamentally, however, it was *religious belief*—and the basic moral education it provided in the form of habits and *moeurs*—that Tocqueville saw as containing the nascent pathological tendencies of American democracy. Thus, while the "taste for physical well-being in America" was intense, it remained (in Tocqueville's view) firmly within the limits of a middle-class morality, itself the product of regular church attendance and an unquestioning (and universal) belief in the central dogmas of Christianity.[41]

Similarly, individualism was kept in bounds not merely through the horizon-expanding effects of "free institutions" and participation in public life, but also by shared belief in the fundamental tenets of Christian morality, which Tocqueville saw as providing a foundation for everyday egalitarianism and the norms of liberal justice.[42] Even the threat of majority tyranny and the rule of public opinion was kept within limits, thanks again to America's universal subscription to Christianity. As Tocqueville writes in volume 1:

Hitherto no one in the United States has dared to advance the maxim that everything is permissible for the interests of society, an impious adage which seems to have been invented in an age of freedom to shelter all future tyrants. Thus, while the law permits the Americans to do what they please, religion prevents them from conceiving, and forbids them to commit, what is rash or unjust.[43]

What keeps would-be "revolutionists" and tyrants in line also serves to limit public opinion's belief in its own ultimate authority.

It is, of course, hardly original to point to the central role Tocqueville assigned to Christianity in undergirding the American democracy. What is striking, however, is how Tocqueville frames religion—and the idea of a shared basis in belief—as essential to the health and viability of the American regime. Without Christianity, he argues, democratic freedom would provide the kind of atmosphere conducive to the full development of these pathologies, realizing their anti-democratic potential. With Christianity, not only are free *moeurs* securely established, but the pathologies themselves lose much of their power. So long as American democracy has a firm basis in Christian morality, the dangers Tocqueville enumerates are (on his analysis, at least) held in check. Christianity and moral consensus are the antidotes to the democratic distemper.

While his depiction of the benign effects of Christianity was clearly intended for a French audience, it is important to note that Tocqueville prescribed religion not simply as a remedy for the class conflict and moral dissensus found in so-called "transitional" societies. There can be little doubt that Tocqueville saw religion as "the most basic of all political institutions" and as playing a foundational role in democracy *tout court*.[44]

This fact, combined with his vehement attack on skepticism and "materialism" (read atheism), places Tocqueville's critique of Rousseau-ism in a peculiar light.[45] For if the structure of American democracy signaled the overcoming of the idea of a unitary sovereign will, Tocqueville's view of the role religion played cultivating "free *moeurs*" signaled a regression to one of the most anti-pluralistic (and anti-liberal) of Rousseau's ideas. This is the notion that the "real constitution of the state" is to be found not in laws, rights, and institutional protections, but in the "hearts of the citizens," in their "manners and morals."[46] So long as one holds to this idea, it is impossible to acknowledge (and properly value) the place of moral and political pluralism in a democracy. Indeed, from this perspective the very idea of an "overlapping consensus"—and of political liberalism in John Rawls's sense—must seem a chimera.

Tocqueville's analysis thus leaves us with a quandary. On the one hand, he has few equals in his appreciation of American democracy's successful move beyond the concept of sovereignty, toward a decentered political system based on local administration and complete liberty of association. This is, so to speak, the "pluralistic" and participatory Tocqueville. On the other, however, he felt that such freedom and liberation from centralized authority demanded the moral bedrock of a shared Christian faith. We have become so accustomed to communitarian readings of Tocqueville on civil society that we tend to forget the paradox at the center of his thought. How is it that the most insightful analyst of the dynamic of majority tyranny, the conformist character of public opinion, and the democratic suppression of dissent should urge, in so single-minded a fashion, the imperative of a deep, thoroughgoing moral and religious consensus as the basis of any healthy democracy?[47]

Arendt: Founding, Preserving, Worshiping

In turning to Arendt's interpretation of the early triumph (and subsequent vicissitudes) of American democracy in *On Revolution*, one is struck by both her reliance on—and distance from—Tocqueville's basic story. I have already mentioned their joint emphasis on relative equality of condition in America; on the importance of participation, free institutions, and local administration; and their shared fear that citizens may well forget the "art of being free" should they channel their energies too single-mindedly into the pursuit of *private* happiness. But if much of *On Revolution* reads like a gloss upon (or updating of) *Democracy in America*, there is one aspect in which this is clearly not the case. Nowhere in *On Revolution* do we find Arendt following Tocqueville's lead on the question of religion and politics (her appreciation of the Mayflower Compact and the Protestant roots of promising and agreement as political activities notwithstanding).[48] What accounts for this fact? Does it mean that Arendt's version of the "priority of the political" is, in the end, more accommodating of pluralism and plurality than Tocqueville's?

Of course, one could hardly expect a Jewish intellectual refugee from Hitler's Germany to take as sanguine a view of the political role of Christianity as Tocqueville. Her early work on Augustine notwithstanding, Arendt harbored a deep suspicion of the religious impulse in politics, especially Christian otherworldliness. Unlike Tocqueville (who viewed the remnants of this otherworldliness as an edifying restraint on this-worldly material-ism), Arendt sides with Machiavelli, Rousseau, and the rest of the republi-can tradition in pointing out the opposition between the quest for salvation and the desire to establish and preserve worldly freedom. Like them, she thinks that care for one's soul undermines care for the world, and that any moderately responsible citizen must make "the world"—the public-political world—the central object of their concern. *Amor mundi* and *amor Dei* are—as Augustine would have agreed—in the greatest tension with one another.[49]

For Arendt, the "priority of the political" meant precisely that: the need to construct and care for such a world, one in which citizens could come to experience worldly freedom through action, debate, and delibera-tion with their peers. The resulting space—the "public realm"—was insti-tutionally articulated, but its primary function was to provide a stage upon which speech, persuasion, and the exchange of opinion could take place. It is this "Greek" view of the essence of the political that Arendt op-poses to Plato's authoritarian politics of truth in *The Human Condition*. It lies at the root of her quarrel with any conception that subjects politics and the realm of opinion to the coercive force of an extra-political Absolute (whether this Absolute is discovered by reason or revelation).[50]

Did Arendt then view Tocqueville as a closet "authoritarian" thinker, in the mold of Plato or Marx? Not at all. In fact, like Tocqueville, she drew on Montesquieu's analysis of mores to excavate the moral under-pinnings of pre-revolutionary Europe.[51] But she parted company with him on the significance of Montesquieu's analysis. For Tocqueville, writ-ing in the 1830s, Montesquieu provided a model for thinking about the role of *moeurs* and *pouvoirs intermédiares* in creating and preserving nondespotic polities. For Arendt, writing in light of the calamitous politi-cal history of the twentieth century, Montesquieu provided no sociologi-cal model but rather a prescient analysis of the rot at work on the moral (and legal) foundations of Western polities. By the eighteenth century, the authority of these structures—their "legitimacy"—came to rest solely (and all too perilously) on the manners and mores of their subjects. They remained in place strictly out of habit, nothing more.[52] All that was re-quired was for new political forces to break the already weakened hold of tradition, and to take up a political power that, for all intents and pur-poses, had lost its foundation.[53]

Might Christianity step in and provide the moral ballast necessary for a political world made new, a political world bereft of the interlocking supports of tradition, religion, and authority? Arendt was highly dubious about this Tocquevillian proposition. For one thing, she didn't believe (as he fervently did) that the moral kernel of Christianity—human equality before God—provided anything like adequate support for equal civil and political rights. For another, she had a far more skeptical view of the relevance of manners and mores to the body politic.[54] She preferred to put her faith in durable man-made structures of law and institutions. But she was well aware that such constructions demanded something more energetic than habit—and more expressly political than Christian morality—if they were to constitute an edifice that could guarantee tangible, public freedom for generations to come.

On Revolution can be read, at least in part, as Arendt's attempt to specify what such a republican—and distinctively political—foundation looks like. One could even go so far as to call it her attempt to rethink authority in a "disenchanted" age. This is not to deny the force of Jeremy Waldron's argument that *On Revolution* testifies to Arendt's intense and oft-neglected interest in the institutional "housing" of freedom, or Albrecht Wellmer's contention that it represents her coming to terms with the two antagonistic revolutionary traditions (Marxist and liberal) that grew out of the Enlightenment.[55] But neither of these characterizations fully does justice to Arendt's central endeavor in her 1963 work, which is to give a reading of the meaning of the American Revolution through the dual lenses of civic republicanism and existential philosophy.

For Americans schooled in a Lockean-liberal interpretation of the Revolution, Arendt's focus on "public freedom, public happiness, and public spirit," combined with her tendency to denigrate civil liberties as pre-political, merely "negative" freedoms, came as something of a shock.[56] It still does. But what makes the book of enduring theoretical interest is not Arendt's Jeffersonian insistence that "political freedom, generally speaking, means the right 'to be a participator in government,' or it means nothing," or the overly stark choice between participatory and representative democracy this seemingly implies.[57] Rather, it is the way Arendt struggles to combine an understanding of revolution as radical beginning with an equally strong emphasis on the creation of enduring structures of freedom.

"Founding and preserving" is, of course, a topos familiar from the civic republican tradition. Arendt stands firmly within this tradition when she notes that the "republican form of government" recommended itself to the American founders precisely because of its "promise of greater durability."[58] She begins to depart from it, however, when she explains why the founders viewed democracy as an inherently unstable form a government, one unlikely to establish a *novus ordo saeclorum*. "Democracy," she writes, "was abhorred because *public opinion* was held to rule where the public spirit ought to prevail, and the sign of this perversion was the unanimity of the citizenry."[59] Glossing Madison's arguments in *Federalist* 10 and 50, she reaches the following conclusion:

> The truth of the matter is that no formation of opinion is ever possible where all opinions have become the same. Since no one is capable of forming his own opinion without the benefit of a multitude of opinions held by others, the rule of public opinion endangers even the opinion of those few who may have the strength not to share it. . . . Public opinion, by virtue of its unanimity, provokes a unanimous opposition and thus kills true opinions everywhere.[60]

This leads Arendt to take up the all-important distinction between opinions and interests. Interests, she notes, are politically relevant "only as group interests," whereas opinions "never belong to groups but exclusively to individuals, who 'exert their reason cooly and freely,' and no multitude, be it the multitude of a part or of the whole society, will ever be capable of forming an opinion."[61]

This is a key point for Arendt, and for two reasons. First, if opinions are the property of individuals and not groups, then public opinion is no opinion at all. It is, rather, "the death of opinions"—that is, the death of the most important political manifestation of human plurality.[62] Second, if opinions and interests are, in fact, opposed phenomena (something neither Madison nor Tocqueville would have maintained), they are so because interests are largely given, functions of a particular group's identity, position, and desires. Opinions, on the other hand, can never be given or assumed, since they are always formed through a process of debate, deliberation, testing, and purification.[63] The political world is the realm of *doxa*, not truth, and *doxa* is always an achievement, the result of communication and exchange between a wide variety of individual perspectives or standpoints on a common world.[64]

Arendt's recuperation of opinion as a rational faculty of individuals is central to her broader conception of politics as open-ended talk and deliberation. In the present context, it is important to see how this recuperation places her interpretation of the American revolution at some distance from both liberal and civic republican views. Liberal interpretations emphasize not just the protection of civil liberties and the creation of limited (constitutional) government, but the Madisonian idea that what prevents majority tyranny is less the jostling of opinions than that of interests. Yet Arendt repudiates this notion, seeing it as encouraging an instrumental attitude toward the public-political realm, an attitude ultimately destructive of the preconditions of responsible citizenship.[65] There is and must be a clear distinction between *homme* and *citoyen*, between private interests and care for the (common) world. (In this regard, it is fairly clear that Arendt would also object to Tocqueville's attempt to split the difference between the two with the notion of "self-interest, rightly understood.")

Such an insistence would seem to put us—and Arendt—firmly back in the civic republican camp. While she is acidly critical of Rousseau's General Will, she clearly agrees with him on this basic distinction between public and private selves.[66] And, of course, there is *On Revolution's* persistent emphasis on the fundamental importance of public spiritedness (the "revolutionary spirit") and the tragedy resulting from its loss. But for someone so interested in active citizenship, Arendt is curiously uninterested in the educative process by which civic virtues are inculcated and public-spirited citizens are molded. This process—which Michael Sandel has dubbed "the formative project"[67]—is at the heart of Aristotle, Machiavelli, Rousseau, and the civic republican tradition generally. Why, then, does Arendt scarcely touch upon it, and (indeed) avoid it?

Part of the answer is that she (like Mill) accepts the Tocquevillian argument that, when it comes to citizenship, one learns by doing. But the stronger reason is that she, like any good liberal, is repelled by a tutelary model of the polity, and by the idea of like-minded, "patriotic" citizens being stamped out from a common mold.[68] The "inculcation of civic virtues" may thus be central to the republican idea of public spiritedness, but it is utterly tangential—in fact, opposed—to Arendt's. If we remember what she says about politics as the realm of *doxa* (on the one hand) and public opinion as a form of tyranny (on the other), this is not especially surprising.[69] Insofar as the inculcation of civic virtue tends to promote sameness, unity, and a convergence of viewpoints (or deference to the views of elites), it undermines human plurality and the infinite richness that flows from distinct perspectives on the same world.[70] In other words, the "formative project"—the heart of civic republicanism—directly undermines the anti-Platonic, plurality- and opinion-centered politics of debate and deliberation that Arendt championed throughout her career.

When we juxtapose Arendt's distaste for factional interests and patriotic solidarity with her strong emphasis on the uniqueness of individual perspectives and the importance of independent judgment, we might well be tempted to view her as advocating a species of public-spirited individualism. Again, the paradox is only seeming, since individualism and citizenship are opposites only if we accept Tocqueville's definition of the first term. The contribution of *The Human Condition* and essays like "Philosophy and Politics" (1954) is to remind us that public-spirited individualism is no oxymoron, and that the great achievement of the Athenians was the creation of a culture in which such individualism—both civic and philosophical in temper—could flourish.[71] Like Mill, Arendt's heroes are Pericles and Socrates.[72]

Following Margaret Canovan's suggestion, we might frame the difference between civic republicanism and Arendt as the difference between a moralizing conception of public spirit (one that aims at moral consensus or concord [Aristotle's *homonoia*]) and one that views politics as a form of *culture*.[73] What matters to the former conception is the foundation of manners, habits, and virtues found in the souls of citizens. What matters to Arendt's *cultural* conception is the feeling citizens have for a common (shared) world of appearances, an artificial and institutionally articulated world that makes civilization, beauty, and a meaningful life possible. Debate and deliberation, judgment and action, depend above all on this shared world of appearances, and not on the inculcation of collective virtues or reference to any revealed or rational Truth. As Arendt puts it in her essay "The Crisis in Culture,"

> Culture and politics . . . belong together because it is not knowledge or truth which is at stake, but rather judgment and decision, the judicious exchange of opinion about the sphere of public life and the common world, and the decision what manner of action is to be taken in it, as well as to how it is to look henceforth, what kind of things are to appear in it.[74]

Public culture and the politics of opinion hang together: it is impossible to have one without the presence (and preservation) of the other.[75] Arendt's use of "public spirit" to describe the origins of the American republic is thus designed not to focus her readers on stern neo-Roman virtues possessed by manly founders and sadly lacking in contemporary life.

On the contrary: it is designed to remind us of the possibilities and enjoyments created by a culture different from our own, one animated by public (non-materialistic, non-economic) concerns and a joy in argument. Public spirit is to be valued not because it preserves the *patria*, but because it is essential to tangible public freedom, and this (in turn) makes public happiness possible. And it is public happiness that—as Arendt asserts in chapter 3 of *On Revolution*—recent generations of Americans have forgotten.

◆

Why have we forgotten it? The causes that transform a culture centered on local political participation, public spirit, and the creation of a public space of freedom (the *constitutio libertatis*) to one centered on free enterprise, consumption, and private happiness are many. As noted above, Arendt tends to be at her least original (and often least persuasive) in enumerating them.[76] The debt to Tocqueville is large: privatism, atomization, materialism, the elimination of local spaces of freedom (the townships)—all come into play, as does a fairly dubious generalization about the effects of European immigration to America during the nineteenth and early twentieth centuries.[77]

Arendt is more original, complex, and—ultimately—disturbing on how the American founding solved the "problems" of power, legitimacy, and authority in a secular, free society. In chapter 4 of *On Revolution*, she examines how the Constitution—as the creation of a new form of government and nonsovereign system of power—erected a new space for freedom, thus fulfilling the promise of revolution as a form of initiatory action, of radical beginning. She also describes how political change in the European context always ended in a gesture toward a "new absolute"—a sovereign popular will, the Nation, History—in order to create the semblance of legitimacy and rightful authority. In contrast, the American founders avoided recourse to such dubious absolutes by focusing on institutional design (seeing constitution-making itself as "the noblest of all revolutionary deeds") and by following the ratification process they did.[78] Rather than postulate a fictional "will of the nation" as a *pouvoir constituant* (one that remained "outside and above all governments and all laws"), they grounded the legitimacy of their creation on the very notions of "binding and promising, combining and convenanting" that had established the original colonies. These activities could now serve as the basis for the new system of power.[79] In other words, it was only in America that the chief lesson of the social contract tradition—that the legitimacy of political power flows from the uncoerced agreement of equals, and has no other source—was fully grasped and implemented.

But if the establishment of a new system of power—the Constitution—could be achieved through promising and consent, the establishment of the authority of the new form of government could not. For better or worse, the (Roman) distinction between power and authority is central to Arendt's political thought, and to her interpretation of the American Revolution in particular. Power can be generated by an institutional framework and by citizens "acting together, acting in concert."[80] It can be endowed with legitimacy through the human capacity to promise, to bind oneself for the future. But authority is a different matter. Separate from power, it eschews both coercion and persuasion.[81] It operates through belief, and retains its vitality only so long as the branch of government (or constitutional instrument) in question is *believed* to be authoritative by citizens (shades of Max Weber).

Authority as the basis of political life has, in Arendt's view, a largely unsavory past, consisting primarily in the legitimation of a ruling hierarchy by appeal to some transcendental source or standards.[82] Nevertheless, Arendt believes that some form of authority must underwrite public-political life, especially if the public world is to have the relative permanence and durability required for "tangible freedom." Yet the modern world has been generally hostile to the principle of authority and the kind of credulity it demands. The radical beginning effected by the modern revolutionary tradition only heightens the problem. As Arendt notes, "It is in the very nature of a beginning to carry with itself [*sic*] a measure of complete arbitrariness."[83] How could a new constitution, obviously created through the joint action, promises, and conventions of men, be vested with the kind of authority necessary to make it "a standard, a pillar, and a bond" rather than "a kite or balloon, flying in the air"?[84]

The answer to this riddle is found by making the act of foundation/beginning itself the source of authority. In Arendt's view, the pattern for such a nonmetaphysical (and specifically political) concept of authority was set by the Romans, who identified authority (*auctoritas*) not with any set of transcendent standards (given by the Ideas, Nature, or God), but with the act of foundation itself, which took on for them a correspondingly sacred aura. The "great deed" of the founders of the city created the opportunity for subsequent generations to "augment, to increase and enlarge, the foundations as they had been laid down by the ancestors."[85] Thus the Roman Senate wielded authority because, as the *patres* or elders of the Republic, they represented the founding ancestors. Foundation, augmentation, and conservation were, on the Roman understanding, intimately related. The most important quality of political authority was precisely this tie back to the beginning, a tie manifest in an "unbroken line of successors" and in "pious remembrance and conservation" of one's own beginnings.[86]

Arendt argues that it was precisely the Roman understanding that the American founders drew upon, and that accounts for the success of the American Revolution in creating a durable "house for freedom":

> The great measure of success the American founders could book for themselves, the simple fact that their revolution succeeded where all others were to fail, namely, in founding a new body politic stable enough to survive the onslaught of centuries to come, one is tempted to think, was decided the very moment when the Constitution began to be 'worshiped,' even though it had hardly begun to operate. And since it was in this respect that the American Revolution was most conspicuously different from all other revolutions which were to follow, one is tempted to conclude that it was the authority which the act of foundation carried within itself, rather than the belief in an Immortal Legislator, or the promises of reward and the threats of punishment in a 'future state,' or even the doubtful self-evidence of the truths enumerated in the preamble of the Declaration of Independence, that assured stability for the new republic. . . . It was ultimately the great Roman model that asserted itself almost automatically and almost blindly in the minds of those who, in all deliberate consciousness, had turned to Roman history and Roman political institutions in order to prepare themselves for their own task.[87]

Arendt's suggestion that the Roman idea of authority underlies the "success" of the American Constitution is ingenious for a number of reasons. It reconciles the fundamental revolutionary experience of radical beginning with the human need for continuity and permanence. It thus enables Arendt to offer an "existentialized" version of civic republicanism, something that might otherwise seem a contradiction in terms. Moreover, by understanding the American founding as an act that contains its principle (namely, public freedom, the self-government of civic equals) within itself, Arendt enables us to view legislative and judicial activity not in terms of transcendental standards (God-given "inalienable rights") or the elusive intent of the framers, but in terms of their contribution to the "preservation and augmentation" of this new space (or house) for freedom.

But while Arendt's turn to the Romans solves certain thorny theoretical problems for the modern revolutionary tradition (the problem of authority and the need for a "new absolute" most of all), it comes at a price—a price secular liberals like myself are loath to pay, and one that undermines the suggestion of a public-spirited individualism found elsewhere in her work.

As Arendt notes in several places, authority in the Roman sense—*auctoritas*—was inseparable from piety toward the ancestors and toward the founding of the city. As a result, "religious and political activity could be considered as almost identical," particularly since (for the Romans) "religion literally meant *re-ligare*: to be tied back, obligated to the enormous, almost superhuman and hence always legendary effort to lay the foundations, to build the cornerstone, to found for eternity."[88] In this way, Roman religion, tradition, and authority formed an incredibly solid (and self-renewing) foundation for the polity, a true "groundwork of the world."[89]

Now Arendt hardly thought that Americans could go back to the Romans and reconstruct such a "groundwork" for their world. She was not in the business of peddling civil religion *à la* Rousseau. Modernity and secularization have demolished the possibility of authority in its full-blooded Roman sense.[90] Nevertheless, she did think that the one thing which saved the American Constitution from the fate of all subsequent (European) constitutions was precisely this piety toward it, and toward the myth of the founders.

Thus, in the passage from *On Revolution* cited above, she emphasizes how "worship" of the Constitution is the distinguishing characteristic of the American post-revolutionary experience. Similarly, she singled out the "atmosphere of reverent awe" surrounding the Constitution as the element that "has shielded both event and document against the onslaught of time and changed circumstances" (as well as "a hundred years of minute scrutiny and violent critical debunking").[91] She concluded by writing that "one may be tempted even to predict that the authority of the republic will be safe and intact as long as the act itself, the beginning as such, is remembered whenever constitutional questions in the narrower sense come into play."[92]

These and similar passages make it clear that one very important purpose of *On Revolution* was to construct a salutary myth about the act of founding/constitution itself, and its importance to the survival of the republic. For while the American Revolution "did not break out but was made by men in common deliberation and on the strength of mutual pledges," the durability of the "new space of freedom" did not hinge upon the promise or consent of subsequent generations. Rather, it resulted from the living memory of the act of beginning itself, forever hallowed and "augmented." This act—the founding—carried "its own principle within itself," and "inspires the deeds that are to follow."[93] And while Arendt's approach to politics is, in many respects, directed against Plato and his influence, she nevertheless completely agrees with his remark that "the beginning is like a god which as long as it dwells among men saves all things" (*Laws*, 775). She glosses this as follows: "For the beginning, because it contains its own principle, is also a god who, as long as he dwells among men, as long as he inspires their deeds, saves everything."[94] America will remain a "house of freedom" so long as the memory of this pure beginning—preserved from debunkings and the dissolvent effect of what Nietzsche called "critical history"—occupies a central, if not the central, place in American consciousness.[95]

This, of course, is not the way things have worked out. According to *On Revolution's* own narrative, forgetfulness and the failure to preserve the revolutionary spirit have more or less killed off the beginning, reducing the *constitio libertatis* to the creation of limited government or—worse—to the founding of the "free enterprise system." But this, obviously, is why Arendt wrote *On Revolution* in the first place: to revive the memory of the beginning, a beginning construed as the foundation of freedom through a system of decentralized, participatory self-government. Representative government may have transformed the American political system into what Arendt calls a "de facto oligarchy," but hope is not lost so long as the myth of a beginning devoted to "public freedom, public spirit, and public happiness" can be revived.

Conclusion

The fact of Tocqueville's reliance upon religion, coupled with Arendt's turn to authority and what I have been calling the myth of the founding, might lead some to conclude that Habermas is, in the end, the preferable guide. Better "the public use of one's reason" than a democracy grounded on Christian faith or a neo-Roman cult of the founders. But it is important to see that Habermas's appeal to the "force of the better argument" is—and always has been—largely rhetorical, gaining its force from the original tension between public argument (on the one hand) and *raison d'état* (on the other). Given a more general and contemporary formulation, the ideal is largely vacuous outside of highly conventionalized (some might say stylized) discursive contexts, such as we find in academic disciplines.[96] But even here, in arenas largely unburdened of political coercion and naked political passion, there is precious little agreement as to where the force of the "better argument" resides. And there is the even more obvious point that, in contentious moral and political matters, reasonable people will disagree about the "force of the better argument." It should come as no surprise that the most recent wave in the literature on deliberative democracy has made the irreducibility of *disagreement*, and not the consensus-generating power of public argument, its theme.[97]

Tocqueville and Arendt are, in my opinion, more insightful than Habermas when it comes to elucidating the nature of democratic politics and its preconditions. Their shared emphasis on participation and plurality (whether of associations or individuals, projects or opinions) places them in the first rank of canonical thinkers who have tried to overcome the baneful consequences of the Western political theory's fascination with the idea of a sovereign will or power. But—as I have tried to show—both Tocqueville and Arendt felt the need to ground participation and the "priority of the political" in something apparently sturdier than constitutional law and institutional frameworks. Tocqueville turned to the moralizing potential of religion, while Arendt placed a significant portion of her hopes on the preservation of a quasi-religious deference to the founding itself. Each thought that republican institutions—and public life itself—must be anchored in something beyond "mere" respect for law and rights: Tocqueville because he thought such respect was (ultimately) the creature of a specific religious tradition; Arendt because she felt law and rights were inadequate when it came to creating and sustaining a "shared feeling for the world," a *sensus communis*.

It may well be that any attempt to assert the priority of the political must have recourse to such horizon-sustaining *moeurs* or myths. Where participation and self-government have priority, a large area of agreement is obviously presumed. The "active, self-governing citizen" can be a widespread species only where the clash of values and opinions has been effectively narrowed and focused by the strictures of public life, public institutions, and public virtues. True, one can speak—as Arendt does—of a self-chosen political elite, but this avenue will hardly yield the kind of public culture both she and Tocqueville so strongly desired. At some point—and usually through questionable means—the "formative project" reasserts itself. "Educating the demos" becomes the linchpin of all calls for renewed civic engagement and increased political participation.

The need for a common set of *moeurs*, or virtues, or sense of the world, clashes with the moral pluralism characteristic of contemporary liberal democracies. This clash has produced a flood of books and articles, not only by participatory or deliberative democrats, but by liberal theorists anxious to square the circle, to show that, beneath it all, there exists a set of (liberal) values or virtues on which all can agree. Yet even these efforts tend to fall back on the imperative of a renewed and enlarged program of civic education—albeit this time from a liberal point of view. However, if full-blown Millian liberalism is itself (as the later Rawls would say) a "controversial philosophy of life," then it must be pared down to its political and legal-institutional essentials. Only in this way does it have any hope of becoming the object of an "overlapping consensus" in an increasingly fragmented and pluralistic world.

Viewed from the sadder but wiser perspective of political liberalism, the projects of resurrecting shared *moeurs* or reconstituting authority look dubious indeed. We can agree with Tocqueville and Arendt that a privatized culture, sunk under the weight of a mind-numbing and enervating consumerism, is one possible road to despotism. But we can disagree when they argue that hopes for a more public-oriented, participatory society rest (ultimately) on either shared morals or the renewal of a shared sense of the (durable, tangible) public world. Like it or not, the world we inhabit as citizens is irreducibly pluralist, fragmented, and elusive. Civic reengagement begins not by denying or repudiating this situation (the reflexive Tocquevillian and Arendtian response), but by owning up to it.

5 | MATURITY, PATERNALISM, AND DEMOCRATIC EDUCATION IN J. S. MILL

With regard to the advance of democracy, there are two different positions which it is possible for a rational person to take up, according as he thinks the masses prepared, or unprepared, to exercise the control which they are acquiring over their destiny.... If he thinks them prepared, he will aid the democratic movement.... If, on the contrary, he thinks them unprepared for complete control over the government—seeing at the same time that, prepared or not, they cannot be prevented from acquiring it—he will exert his utmost efforts in contributing to prepare them; using all means, on the one hand, for making the masses themselves wiser and better; on the other for so rousing the slumbering energy of the opulent and lettered classes, so storing the youth of those classes with the profoundest and most valuable knowledge, so calling forth whatever of individual greatness exists or can be raised up in the country, as to create a power which might partially rival the mere power of the masses, and must exercise the most salutary influence over them, for their own good.
—J. S. Mill, "Civilization" (1836)

The object of this Essay is to assert one very simple principle.... That principle is, that the sole end for which mankind are

warranted, individually or collectively, in interfering with the liberty of action of any of their number, is self-protection. That the only purpose for which power can be rightfully exercised over any member of a civilized community, against his will, is to prevent harm to others. His own good, either physical or moral, is not a sufficient warrant.
—J. S. Mill, *On Liberty* (1859)

A government is to be judged by its action upon men, and by its action upon things; by what it makes of the citizens, and what it does with them; its tendency to improve or deteriorate the people themselves; and the goodness or badness of the work it performs for them, and by means of them.
—J. S. Mill, *Considerations on Representative Government* (1861)

"Maturity" and the Liberty/Paternalism Conundrum

Over the last 150 years, Mill's reputation has waxed and waned. In the United States it is safe to say that it has reached its lowest ebb. A number of factors are to blame. Outside of the academy, there is a widespread disenchantment with the ideals of autonomy and moral individualism. We live in an age in which most people prefer to think of themselves as "encumbered selves"—as kitted out (from birth, as it were) with an array of moral, political, and religious commitments that they cannot and will not stand back from. To question these commitments is to question their identity and their authenticity; it is to question who they are and to imply that they, and not just their beliefs, are in need a radical rethinking and reformulation.

Encouraged by forces too numerous to list to think of themselves essentially in terms of group identities (gay, straight, Christian, Jewish, white, black, Hispanic, Asian, etc.), Americans no longer look kindly, if they ever did, on anyone who suggests that the web of our moral customs and beliefs is in need of constant examination, reform, and rearticulation. The idea that "we" (whether Christian or secular, conservative or liberal) might be fundamentally wrong about anything, or that our truths are merely half-truths, is rejected out of hand as an attack on our "values." And "values," as nearly every American has come to believe, are essentially pre-rational and sacrosanct. This, needless to say, is not very fertile ground for the Millian idea of individuality to take root, no matter how superficially hospitable American ideas of individualism and self-reliance may look to Mill's basic message.

The situation is not all that different within the academy. There are, of course, utilitarian philosophers of various kinds and not a few Mill scholars. Generally speaking, however, the consensus is that Mill richly deserves his apparent resting place on the ash heap of history. Individualism, as many a college sophomore will tell you, is not only a transparent ideology that serves the super-rich; it is also a flawed social epistemology, one that hides the myriad ways power relations constitute agents and their identities. As Foucault famously put it, "The individual . . . is not the *vis à vis* of power; it is . . . one of its prime effects."[1] Forget Mill's sensitivity to matters of power, gender, and class, and his firm rejection of social contract methodology: the verdict is in.

Besides, the same sophomore will tell you, there is the irreducible fact of Mill's elitism and his rampant Eurocentrism. Even though *On Liberty* presents itself as the anti-paternalistic tract par excellence, Mill clearly does advocate paternalism for those nations and cultures he deems insufficiently civilized: these are not yet ready to be improved by "free and equal discussion" alone. The glaring irony of *On Liberty* is that Mill's plea for individual freedom from political and social tyranny is joined to a philosophy of cultural development that virtually mandates paternalistic intervention in the case of either "immature" or overly ripe civilizations. From this perspective, Millian liberalism only *seems* to be in favor of freedom and diversity. In fact, it heavy-handedly deploys arch-European ideas of progress and cultural maturity, ideas that justify picking up the "white man's burden" abroad while undermining more traditionalist communities at home. Mill's liberalism is, as the current lingo has it, a form of "comprehensive" liberalism—that is, an aggressive form of liberalism that won't be satisfied until everyone buys into *its* ideas of secular individuality and self-development.

What are we to make of the (remarkably widespread) charge that Millian liberalism foists autonomy and humanism on those who do not want it at home, while providing essential "fuel for empire" abroad?

At first glance, the prospects for defending Mill against this indictment look rather bleak. The whole project of retrenchment John Rawls undertook in his *Political Liberalism* (1993) was, after all, predicated on a *mea culpa* by one of liberalism's most celebrated twentieth-century representatives. The admission of guilt centered on the idea that the liberalism of *A Theory of Justice* (1971) was itself a form of comprehensive liberalism, and thus intrinsically hostile to cultural and moral pluralism.

Like Mill, the early Rawls apparently wanted to foist an ideal of individual autonomy upon all the members of his just society. But, as the later Rawls came to realize (with the help of communitarian critics like Michael Sandel and Charles Taylor), the liberal idea of "the good life" as a form of autonomy had no place when it came to tracing the outline of just institutions for a pluralist society. Thus, the claim that political liberalism successfully evades the charge of foisting a "thick conception of the good" upon citizens came to rest on Rawls's specific rejection of the idea that Millian individuality is, or can be, in any way normative for a liberal pluralist society.[2] To paraphrase Mill's famous line from *Utilitarianism*: it may be better to be a Socrates dissatisfied than a "fool" or a "pig" satisfied; however, political liberalism deems *that* judgment firmly outside the (now strictly circumscribed) "domain of the political."[3]

Things get even worse when we turn to the "fuel for empire" charge. Here, evidently, we confront the smoking gun of Mill's own words. I need only remind the reader of two passages from *On Liberty*—the first from the "Introductory" chapter, the second from the last few pages of chapter 3 ("Of Individuality").

The first passage is well known, and is often cited as proof of Mill's more-than-implicit imperialist leanings. Immediately following his statement of the "one very simple principle" that is "entitled to govern absolutely the dealings of society with the individual in the way of compulsion and control" (the so-called "principle of liberty"), Mill writes:

> It is, perhaps, hardly necessary to say that this doctrine is meant to apply only to human beings in the maturity of their faculties. We are not speaking of children, or of young persons below the age which the law may fix as that of manhood or womanhood. Those who are still in a state to require being *taken care of by others*, must be protected against their own actions as well as against external injury. *For the same reason*, we may leave out of consideration *those backward states of society* in which the race itself may be considered in it nonage. The early difficulties in the way of spontaneous progress are so great that there is seldom any choice of means for overcoming them; and a ruler full of the spirit of improvement is warranted in the use of *any expedients* that will attain an end, perhaps otherwise unattainable. *Despotism is a legitimate mode of government* in dealing with *barbarians*, provided the end be their improvement, and the means justified by

actually effecting that end. Liberty, as a principle, has *no applica-tion* to any state of things anterior to the time when mankind have become capable of being improved by free and equal discussion. Until then, there is nothing for them but implicit obedience to an Akbar or Charlemagne, if they are so fortunate to find one.[4]

The trope of equality and freedom limited by its subject's stage of development is one that has a lengthy pedigree in liberal thought, going back (at least) to Locke's famous declaration in the *Second Treatise* that only "state of maturity" makes us *truly* free and equal beings.[5] Locke, of course, made attainment of reason and understanding the *sine qua non* of individual equality and independence, a qualification that legitimately placed children, "Lunaticks and Ideots" under paternalistic rule.[6] Mill is making much the same move, albeit minus the Lockean foundation of natural rights and the "law of Nature."[7] Once reason, understanding, and "maturity" are seen as *cultural-civilizational attainments* rather than as (temporally realized) God-given faculties, the ground is laid for distinguishing not only between "mature" and "immature" types of persons (the child or "Ideot" vs. the rational adult), but also between social classes and (indeed) between different cultures.

For many critics, it is Mill's typically nineteenth-century/utilitarian rejection of "the idea of abstract right" that enables him to move so blithely from a stern rejection of the tutorial state (and "social tyranny") to the advocacy of enlightened despotism—at least when it comes to dealing with "barbarians" (that is, with the culturally immature). That the patron saint of individual liberty should so easily avail himself of such an "end justifies the means"-type argument suggests that—morally speaking— something truly fundamental changes when minimal adult rationality is no longer identified with the "age of majority," but rather with a stage of cultural development. Once this move is made, it seems but a short step to the conclusion that entire social classes are in need of remedial "care," as are entire civilizations—particularly those, like India, laboring under the weight of a "barbaric" caste system.[8]

Those who have imbibed, over a thousand years, the status of "slaves" cannot, Mill thinks, effect a system of self-government. Already knowing how to obey, they are not in need of a "despot," an "Akbar or a Charlemagne." But—as Mill writes in chapter 2 of *Representative Government*— "they have to be *taught* self-government, and this, in its initial stages, means the capacity to act on general instructions. What they require is not a government of force, but one of *guidance*."[9] Such a "government of leading strings" seems to Mill to be "the one required to carry such a people the most rapidly through the next necessary stage of social progress."[10] The Tocquevillian idea of "learning by doing" will not work until such a people has been brought up to speed, as it were, by a benign superintendence. Of course, Mill adds, "the leading strings are only admissible as a means of gradually training the people to walk alone."[11]

The image of "leading strings" calls to mind another theorist of enlightened maturity, Immanuel Kant. At first glance, Kant might well seem the more consistent opponent of paternalism. Our immaturity, he famously wrote, is "self-incurred"—that is, largely a function of our lack of moral courage and our general intellectual shiftlessness. "It is because of laziness and cowardice that it is so easy for others to usurp the role of guardians."[12] Yet even in Kant the call to "have the courage to use your own understanding" is limited, in large part, to his fellow (propertied and literate) Europeans, and is strictly circumscribed in its political effects. The "public use of a man's reason must be free at all times," but such "public use" is for general (scholarly) discussion only, and should have no bearing on the individual's performance of his socially assigned duties and doctrinal obligations.[13] Even an age and culture of enlightenment—an age and culture far removed from the kind of "immaturity" Mill has in mind—requires its authority figure, namely, the ruler of a "free state," who says, "Argue as much as you want and about whatever you want, but obey!"[14]

Mill's historical and cultural consciousness was, of course, much deeper than Kant's, thanks in large part to his reading of Coleridge and the Romantics. Hence his Hegelian-historicist insistence in "The Spirit of the Age" (1831) that to criticize the Middle Ages for a failure to erect constitutional, popular government amounts to a non sequitur: "To find fault with our ancestors for not having annual parliaments, universal suffrage, and vote by ballot, would be like quarreling with the Greeks and the Romans for not using stem navigation. . . . Human nature must proceed step by step, in politics as well as physics."[15] However, the point that no political culture can overleap its own age apparently inscribes a linear idea of cultural-historical development; one that proceeds by discrete and clearly ordered stages ("step by step"), and in a distinctly progressive direction. On such a view, the realm of political possibility depends absolutely on what stage in the (more or less universal) process of maturation a particular people has reached.[16] If it is "immature," how immature? Is its immaturity that of rude and uncultured independence (like the Bedouins or Malays, to cite Mill's examples), or is it more like that of a "civilized" slavery (like the Chinese and "Oriental" peoples generally)?

These considerations appear to plant Mill himself firmly in his own time, prey to such dubious nineteenth-century ideas as an "inevitable" progress or ontogeny recapitulating phylogeny. But do we best understand Mill's emphasis on cultural preconditions in terms of a linear historical progression from "immaturity" (and fitness for despotism or "guidance") to "maturity" (and fitness for popular or representative government)?

Any minimally responsible answer to this question would have to take into account Mill's repeated emphasis that "things left to themselves inevitably decay."[17] This classically republican formulation, taken from the *Considerations*, reminds us that—in Mill's view—there is no such thing as a necessary and linear progress in moral and political affairs. Civilizational and cultural development occur at different times and rates for different peoples, but in no case does Mill's idea of development imply an inevitable (or even likely) attainment of robust "adulthood." Always and everywhere, inertia and the tyranny of custom threaten to turn a given stage of development into one form or another of an iron cage.

This is so not only in the East—Mill's well-known and politically incorrect examples are of a caste-bound India and a senescent China—but in the West as well. What, after all, is *On Liberty* about if not the *new* form of the "despotism of custom" that has come to dominate the modern, "progressive" West? Social tyranny, conformity, and the rule of public opinion are, in Mill's view, the inescapable accompaniments of a mass democratic society. No matter what "stage" we have attained, we are always in danger of succumbing to a master; of creating new and more deadly forms of stasis, despotism, and cultural stagnation. "If there is anything certain in human affairs," Mill writes, "it is that valuable acquisitions are only to be retained by the continuation of the same energies which gained them."[18] Such continuation is never a sure thing in any cultural context. It is, as Mill insists in a number of places, the exception rather than the rule.

This is made clear by a famous statement in chapter 3 of *On Liberty*. There, in the context of a larger discussion about the "social utility" of the truly creative "persons of genius," Mill writes: "But these few are the salt of the earth. Without them, human life would become a stagnant pool."[19] Mill's impassioned plea for individuality, originality, and eccentricity flows from this bedrock conviction. The fact that Europe has thus far escaped the fate of "becoming another China" has nothing to do with a higher per capita production of genius. Rather than some "superior excellence" in them, Westerners should appreciate the central role played by Europe's "remarkable diversity of culture and character."[20]

It is this historical/geographic/cultural set of *contingencies* that produced a "plurality of paths" and (with it) a "progressive and many-sided development."[21] And—as Mill reminds us—the pluralizing effects of this set of contingencies is rapidly disappearing as Europe moves toward a politically egalitarian and economically integrated social form. The stage is set for the ascendency of "public opinion in the State" and the hegemony of received (mass) opinion. The latter is distinguished from the "despotism of Custom" in China less by any qualitative measure (such as Hegel's supposedly "Eurocentric" criterion of the consciousness of freedom) than by a purely *quantitative* measure (so to speak) of relative *comprehensiveness.*[22]

What appears at first glance to be a gratuitously Orientalizing vision of Europe's possible fate is, in fact, an emphatic insistence on the danger confronting all social forms and cultures: the danger of stagnation. If Mill can be accused of anything, it is that he comes close to ontologizing the omnipresent threat of social stagnation and eclipse of the individual in a manner weirdly parallel to Heidegger's *Being and Time*. China, from this point of view, is not the "other." Rather, it is us—our future—unless we take dramatic steps to ensure that "tearing one's self away" from what Heidegger called the tyranny of everydayness remains a concrete possibility in the (ever-homogenizing) West.[23] As Alan Kahan and numerous other scholars have pointed out, Mill is not overly sanguine about our prospects for escaping this new form of despotism.[24]

These remarks provide something of a corrective context for my second notorious passage, taken (once again) from *On Liberty*. The passage comes at the beginning of Mill's warning about Europe's possible fate, and seems—like the justification of despotism for "rude" or uncivilized peoples—to offer ample cover for an aggressively imperialist form of paternalism. Mill writes:

> We have a warning example in China—a nation of much talent, and, in some respects, even wisdom, owing to the rare good fortune of having been provided at an early period with a particularly good set of customs, the work, in some measure of men to whom even the most enlightened European must accord, under

certain limitations, the title of sages and philosophers. They are remarkable, too, in the excellence of their apparatus for impressing, as far as possible, the best wisdom they possess upon every mind in the community, and securing that those who have appropriated the most of it shall occupy the posts of honor and power. Surely the people who did this have discovered the secret of human progressiveness, and must have kept themselves steadily at the head of the movements of the world. On the contrary, they have become stationary—have remained so for thousands of years; and if they are ever to be farther improved, it must be by foreigners.[25]

The (typically Millian) juxtaposition of "progressiveness," "stationariness," and "improvement" (by foreigners, if need be) seems to provide carte blanche for European intrusiveness the world over. Is your culture too "rude" and "uncivilized" for self-government? Don't worry, the East India Company (or some similar entity) will come to your aid. Is it too old and inert? Don't worry, European intervention will provide the necessary "goose" to start it going again. If "progressiveness" is what matters, both the "primitive" and the overly cultivated must be lent a helping—and, if need be, administratively despotic—hand.

To be sure, Mill's rhetoric lends itself to imperialist ideologues who would like to present their rapacious exercises in domination in the guise of paternalistic intervention. But here as elsewhere we need to remind ourselves that what Mill says cuts mainly against the dominant tendencies within Western (modern) culture, and provides as much justification for intervention (or "shock therapy") in our culture as it does for others. In one of the most famous (and famously resonant) passages of *On Liberty*, Mill writes:

> There is only too great a tendency in the best beliefs and practices to degenerate into the mechanical; and unless there were a succession of persons whose ever-recurring originality prevents the grounds of those beliefs and practices from becoming merely traditional, such dead matter would not resist the smallest shock from anything really alive, and there would be no reason why civilization should not die out, as in the Byzantine Empire.[26]

Of course, in the West, Mill's case is not for the intrusion of a "progressive" principle from the outside, but for an "atmosphere of freedom" which would allow persons of genius to do their thing, to "discover new truths" and "commence new practices."[27] But the overarching sense is that *any* culture which has degenerated into the mechanical—even a British middle-class society—will (or deserves to be) "shaken up" from the outside. If there is an implicit brutality in Mill's view of culture, history, and progress, it is his willingness to entertain—indeed welcome—the verdict of history on those cultures that have ceased to be (or failed to ever become) "progressive."

Mill is at his closest to Hegel here.[28] Like Hegel, he seems to think that a nation's "maturity" is also the moment when the "rule of habit" will come to the fore.[29] Unlike Hegel, Mill holds out the possibility that a culture may reform and renew itself through the broad freedom to experiment in practices and lifestyles it allows its individual members. This seems to stack the cards firmly in favor of the (Anglo-American) West, until we remember that Mill sees such freedom as under attack by the dominant tendencies of the age. There is, in other words, nothing remotely "triumphalist" about his diagnosis of the "spirit of the age," nor about the state of Anglo-American culture. We are on the edge—not of a precipice, but of a long and slow decline that neither political power nor economic might can reverse.[30]

But say all this is true—that Mill's "philosophy of history" (if we can call it that) plays no favorites, even if the criteria of "individuality" and "progressiveness" are clearly derived from the humanist threads of the Western European tradition.[31] What about the criteria he sets out in chapter 1 of *Considerations on Representative Government* to determine whether a "people" is fit for the activity of self-government?

Here the idea of relative "maturity" returns with a vengeance, and (apparently) without the proto-existentialist dimension that made it a kind of critical floating signifier in *On Liberty*. In the *Considerations*, fitness or maturity is a clear-cut and apparently unproblematic standard, one that militates against underdeveloped non-European (and southern European) nations. If, Mill writes, a constitution "does not act by itself"—if it requires the "active participation" of citizens—then the "qualities and capacities" of a given people must be taken into account, and the institutional "machinery" adjusted accordingly.[32] There are, Mill thinks, three necessary conditions for any constitution with even a minimally "popular" character. First, "the people for whom the form of government is intended must be willing to accept it." Second, "they must be willing and able to do what is necessary to keep it standing." And third, "they must be willing and able to do what it requires of them to enable it to fulfill its purposes."³³ The "failure of any of these conditions," Mill tells us, "renders a form of government, whatever favorable promise it might otherwise hold out, unsuitable to a particular case."³⁴

With these criteria in place, Mill proceeds to supply the post-colonial critic with ample ammunition for the "fuel for empire" charge. He illustrates "repugnance of a people for [a] particular form of government" by pointing to the native Americans: "Nothing but foreign force would induce a tribe of North American Indians to submit to the restraints of a regular and civilized government."³⁵ His examples of "a people unwilling or unable to fulfill the conditions" of a government they otherwise accept or even desire are "Hindoos" and southern Europeans. These, he thinks, are peoples who habitually view the authorities and the rule of law as troublesome impositions on the traditional fabric of everyday life. In such "backward" cultures, the people "regard the law as made for other ends than their good, and its administrators as worse enemies than those who openly violate it."³⁶ The end result is that "the public authorities will have to be armed with much sterner powers of repression than elsewhere."

Finally, Mill's example of a people incapable of "doing what is required" to enable its government to achieve its purposes is a "popular" or representative system in which "the generality of electors are not sufficiently interested in their own government to give their vote, or, if they vote at all, do not bestow their suffrages on public grounds, but sell them for money, or vote at the beck of some one who has control over them, or whom for private reasons they desire to propitiate." Where the people are thus apathetic or corrupt, popular election, instead of being a "security against misgovernment," is but "an additional wheel in its machinery."³⁷ Mill gives no specific illustrations of this last case, but it is easy to guess that he has various southern European populations in mind, as well as the politically underdeveloped English working class (which he viewed as lacking the most rudimentary education in public spirit).³⁸

The general point behind these examples is that institutions and forms of government are not organic givens, but (within broad cultural parameters) matters of will and choice. A people that is not "barbaric" (as the native Americans, in Mill's estimation, were), or "rude" (like the southern Europeans), or utterly lacking in public spirit, is a more or less fit candidate for a popular form of government, one that promotes both energy and progress (the criteria of a "good form"). Recognizably drawing on the classical and civic republican traditions, Mill departs from them in advocating representative government as the most likely to "educate" the broad mass of people in the responsibilities of citizenship while making the best use of socially available talents and expertise:

> A representative constitution is a means of bringing the general standard of intelligence and honesty existing in the community, and the individual intellect and virtue of its wisest members, more directly to bear upon the government, and investing them with greater influence in it, than they would in general have under any other mode of organization.[39]

But, of course, such active improvement and "diffusion of intelligence" can come about only when the human "material" in question is neither so "barbaric," nor so "corrupt," that free institutions will only render it more intransigent. Everything depends on the form of government being correctly "adapted" to a people's "particular stage of advancement." Thus,

> a people in a state of savage independence, in which every one lives for himself, exempt, unless by fits, from any external control, is practically incapable of making any progress in civilization until it has *learnt to obey*. The indispensable virtue, therefore, in a government which establishes itself over a people of this sort is, that it make itself obeyed. To enable it to do this, the constitution of the government must be nearly, or quite, despotic. A constitution in any degree popular, dependent on the voluntary surrender by the different members of the community of their individual freedom of action, would fail to enforce the first lesson which the *pupils*, in this stage of their progress, require.[40]

Now, I would like to suggest that such passages—however off-putting and ripe for critical exploitation they might be—are not the real problem in Mill. We need to remind ourselves that the issue they address is that of broad historical-cultural readiness to accept the rule of law and (ultimately) limited, constitutional government. We may well take exception to Mill's specific examples of "immaturity." However, his general point— that not all peoples at all places and times are ready (or willing) to accept the rule of law and the self-restraint it requires—is indisputable. We should not let our horror at his easy, totalizing judgments about the "national character" of the "envious" Chinese, the "impulsive" French, or the "self-helping and self-struggling" Anglo-Americans to obscure this fact.[41]

The real problem in Mill—the root of the liberty/paternalism conundrum in his thought—has to do with the robustly educational agenda he sets for politics and government generally. This comes out early on in the *Considerations*. In chapter 2 of that work ("The Criterion of a Good Form of Government") Mill observes:

> Government consists of acts done by human beings; and if the agents, or those who choose the agents, or those to whom the agents are responsible, or the lookers-on whose opinion ought to influence and check all these, are mere masses of ignorance, stupidity, and baleful prejudice, every operation of government will go wrong; while, in proportion as the men rise above this standard, so will government improve in quality. . . . The first element of good government, therefore, being the virtue and intelligence of the human beings composing the community, the most important point of excellence which any form of government can possess is to promote the virtue and intelligence of the people themselves. The first question in respect to any political institutions is, how far they tend to foster in the members of the community the various desirable qualities, moral and intellectual; or rather (following Bentham's more complete classification), moral, intellectual and active.[42]

However much one might agree with Mill's statement that a constitution is not a "machine that runs by itself," one can still be taken aback by how deeply invested he apparently is in something that looks a lot like the anti-liberal "formative project" of the civic republican tradition, or the equally anti-liberal "education in virtue" drawn from the classical tradition.

There is no disputing the fact that Mill does view governments (and their constitutional-institutional forms) as, first and foremost, vehicles for the moral and mental improvement of citizens. In this sense, they are indeed educational in nature, and the public-political realm looks increasingly like a school. Hence the undeniably classical echoes in passages like the following from *Representative Government*: "A government is to be judged by its action upon men, and by its action upon things; by what it makes of the citizens, and what it does with them; its tendency to improve or deteriorate the people themselves; and the goodness or badness of the work it performs for them, and by means of them."[43]

This broadly tutorial conception does not render us "raw material" awaiting the shaping hand of the political artist of character (the Platonic philosopher-king, for example). But it does have the effect of turning each and every generation into a class of potential pupils, waiting to imbibe the set of (fairly direct and concrete) lessons in public spirit Mill sees representative government as teaching them. The "improvement of the people themselves"—the making of them active, informed, and mentally alert—is the grand and justifying purpose of this, the "ideally best" form of government.[44] It is to Mill's credit that he saw such "education" as, in the long run, making a people capable of self-government. However, it is to his discredit that he saw such improvement as perpetuating a teacher/student relationship at the heart of representative government itself (I return to this problem below).[45]

For the post-colonialist critic, this advocacy of a broadly "tutorial" form of government merely confirms what was suggested at the outset—namely, that the "real" Mill is an inveterate paternalist and elitist, one who never really outgrew the stance outlined in "Civilization." His commitment to "improvement" evidently leads him to view virtually *all* human beings—but especially those in "backward" cultures or classes—as children in need of educational or therapeutic intervention (what sort of intervention—despotism or benign superintendence—will depend on the given culture or class's "state of development"). And this, of course, sits uncomfortably with his official commitment to adult autonomy. From Rousseau down to the present, all such educations "to" autonomy—the government of visible or invisible "leading strings"—wind up being not very convincing pantomimes. The "child" in question comes to feel as if he is making his own decisions, forging his own destiny, when in fact it is actually Emile's tutor, the "instructed classes," or the colonial administrators who are really pulling the strings.[46]

Yet even if we reject a people's "improvement" as the chief or even a valid end of government, the problem of their relative maturity and energy remains. Here I think that Mill would have been on firmer ground if he, like Tocqueville, had presented the problem more straightforwardly as one of public spirit and the desire for liberty. A people can be highly civilized and amenable to order, and yet have little or no feeling for public liberty. They are too busy tending to their private business and private interests.

As Tocqueville noted, individualism, born of democratic "equality of condition," leads to privatism, and thence to the withering of all public virtues. It was this condition that he found pervasive on the continent, and which led him to view American democracy as far in advance of the bastardized French (bourgeois) version. Most important, Tocqueville's Americans demonstrated that "improvement" in a democratic context must always be self-improvement. The "close tie" linking public and private interest is something ordinary citizens reveal to themselves, through the habits of political participation and decentralized, local administration.[47] How such local institutions (and the "free *moeurs*" they presupposed) could be transposed to a post-revolutionary France was a mystery Tocqueville never quite solved.

Mill faced a similar problem with respect to the British people, the vast majority of whom had been excluded from "participation in government" for many generations. Extending the franchise (if not universal manhood suffrage) was an obvious and necessary reform, even if Mill did not share Bentham's and his father's naive faith in majoritarianism.[48] The more pressing question, however, was how the habits and attitudes necessary for active citizenship could be cultivated amongst those who had been excluded from the public world for so long.

Mill's answer to this question is starkly un-Tocquevillian. What is evidently needed is education from above, whether by the government, its agencies, or an "instructed" elite. This impression is strengthened by the fact that—whether he is analyzing the phenomenon of social tyranny in *On Liberty* or the case for representative government in the *Considerations*—Mill invariably addresses an audience of fellow elites, urging them to use their positions, persuasive powers, and expertise to help bring about the civic formation (and moral *Bildung*) of people in the middling and working classes. It is this "elitist" rhetorical stance of Mill as author that makes him so problematic, if not anathema, to many today.[49]

This, however, is more a question of the atmospherics of Mill's prose than it is evidence of an unreconstructed "aristocratic liberalism."[50] To repeat, the real problem in Mill—one that cuts across the categories of developed and undeveloped populations, "sophisticated" and "rude" peoples—is that he makes pedagogic purposes of a moral and civic sort trump the more traditionally liberal demands of justice, rights, and fair representation.[51] More than anything else, it is this fact that accounts for much of the "top down" feeling of his political theory.

To be sure, the creation and preservation of the legal-institutional structures of a liberal republic depend on a certain minimal degree of intelligence, civic virtue, and public spirit. However, it is exceedingly dubious to see the *primary* point of the representative system as being "educational" in nature; as residing in the mission to help citizens attain "a higher level of civilization."[52] This is, at best, a secondary and indirect feature of representative government, one that ranks a distant third behind the preservation of rights and the periodic chastisement of elected holders of political power. Indeed, as we inhabitants of a long-established (and relatively stable) representative democracy have come to realize, "improvement" is at best a sporadic and all-too-fleeting occurrence. Unlike Mill, we cannot assume that it provides the basis for, or a moral justification of, liberal representative government.

Why, then, did Mill insist on labeling the tendency toward improvement "*the* criterion of a good form of government"? If he wasn't an inveterate elitist, why did he place so much emphasis on the "educational" dimension of representative government? And why did he feel the need to frame the public-political realm—in the manner of Plato, Aristotle, and other elitist anti-democrats—as, *au fond*, a kind of "school"?

In what follows, I examine these questions in terms of Mill's broad conception of the public-political sphere; his thoughts about the kind of goods expanded political participation would bring about; and his numerous worries about the relative "competence" of the middle and working classes of his day.

Addressing the question of "improvement" from these angles helps us to see that Mill hoped for something substantially more than the pantomime of self-government we find in the *Emile* and in many contemporary liberal democracies. It allows us to see that Mill really did want ordinary people to understand political processes and to have some say in the decisions that shaped their lives. His commitment to autonomy and freedom from political or social interference (in *On Liberty*) is thus no mere fig leaf for a philosophy of semi-paternalistic government, such as some commentators are inclined to find in the *Considerations*. The non-negligible traces of paternalism we do find in the latter work attest more to Mill's residual pessimism about human nature and education itself than to any desire to create a permanent hegemony of the "instructed classes."

This pessimism is often lost sight of in a thinker for whom the concepts of human development and improvement loomed so large.[53] But even at a fairly high stage of cultural development, human beings can be, as Mill notes, "mere masses of ignorance, stupidity, and baleful prejudice." And, as he observes in the *Considerations*, "We ought not to forget that there is an incessant and ever-flowing current of human affairs toward the worse, consisting of all the follies, all the vices, all the negligences, indolences, and suppinenesses of mankind."[54] There is nothing remotely Pollyannaish about his hopes for the future.

Mill—like Hegel and Tocqueville—knew that any morally defensible form of representative government would have to rest on the mediation and gradual universalization of "private" or group interests. However, he was less optimistic than they were about the capacity of either institutional design, or "local" political participation, to effectively perform this mediation, and the "education in public spirit" that went along with it. In this regard, his repeated invocation of the classical trope of the public-political realm as a "school for virtue" testifies to his skepticism about the average man's capacity to (at least partially) break out of the orbit of individual or group interest. Hence the need for "benign superintendence" at what we might call the "introductory" level of popular government. Hence (more problematically) the need for the greatest possible diffusion of the intelligence, judgment, and political competence of the instructed or "wisest" class at a more "intermediate" level of democratic development. Hence, finally, the disturbing possibility that even a relatively "mature" people—a people that possesses the literacy, experience, and self-restraint necessary for self-government—may ultimately prove itself "unfit for liberty" through its "indolence, or carelessness, or cowardice, or want of public spirit."[55]

What *Kind* of Political Education?
The Problem of an "Educative" Democracy

What kind of political education, then, did Mill want? How could a politically inexperienced people—a people accustomed, perhaps, to looking after their own interests, but not much else—be "taught" to be more "public-spirited," more attuned to the "close tie" linking public and private interest?

Mill's father, James Mill, and Jeremy Bentham had a ready and seemingly persuasive answer to this question. They viewed democracy less as a political or moral good in itself than as a mechanism for securing the "greatest good for the greatest number." They also viewed human beings as utility maximizing machines who were largely products of psychological association and their environmental conditioning. Alter that conditioning, they thought, and a reformer could change the kind of pleasures a given group of human beings pursued. If one wanted to lift a largely illiterate and politically inexperienced working class up from bondage to base or merely selfish pleasures, all one had to do was provide the educational conditioning that would encourage members of this class to seek out higher and more long-term pleasures. Reinforcing a certain set of psychological associations would inculcate a sense of "enlightened self-interest" in this neglected and undereducated group. And this, in turn, would pave the way to a more effective (and longer term) aggregation of interests through the mechanism of democratic procedures.

The younger Mill, in his capacity as a propagandist for the philosophical radicalism of Bentham and his father, initially endorsed this view. But, as the *Autobiography* makes painfully clear, Mill's loss of faith in the utilitarian approach to political education played no small role in facilitating his "mental crisis."[56] The reduction of human beings to essentially hedonistic creatures, intent on maximizing pleasures and subject to the laws of associationist psychology, was tantamount to a denial of human freedom and the capacity for autonomy. It is no coincidence that Mill's way out of the mental hell created by his father and Bentham's psychological determinism proceeded by way of Coleridge, Carlyle, Goethe, Humboldt, and other European writers of a self-consciously "Romantic" bent.[57]

It was these thinkers who taught Mill the value of autonomy and—even more important—the value of self-development or *Bildung*. It was only after imbibing the ideal of self-development from Humboldt and other Germans that Mill became interested in mounting what Nicholas Capaldi has called a Romantic defense of liberal institutions (such as limited government, the rule of law, free markets, and a secular culture).[58]

That project came to fruition in *On Liberty's* vehement defense of negative liberty as the absolutely essential precondition for self-discovery and self-development. Humboldt's rejection of the Prussian tradition of paternalistic government (a tradition that justified itself explicitly in terms of the subject's welfare and happiness)[59] provided Mill with his limiting principle: "the only purpose for which power can be rightfully exercised over any member of a civilized community, against his will, is to prevent harm to others. *His own good, either physical or moral, is not a sufficient warrant.*"[60]

Mill's rejection of paternalism in his "one very simple principle" is categorical. Indeed, it reaches beyond the powers of the state to the social forms of tyranny and intolerance that are his chief target in *On Liberty*. However, this uncompromising stance against paternalism in any form (Platonic, feudal, absolutist, utilitarian)—raises an obvious and unavoidable question. Did Mill forget himself when, in the *Considerations*, he turned to the crucial question of education for citizenship?

The answer—perhaps unsurprisingly, given the epigraph to this chapter from "Civilization"—is both yes and no. It is "no" because Mill staunchly advocates the superiority of an active, self-reliant character in the *Considerations*.[61] This advocacy—framed, it is true, in the politically incorrect terms of "national character"—carries *On Liberty's* paean to "energy" and an "energetic character" into the political realm.[62] In both works, Mill leaves little doubt as to his conviction that paternalism (whether in a political or more diffusely social form) enervates and relaxes our mental and moral powers, making further self-development and "improvement" all but impossible.

Nowhere is this clearer than in the opening of chapter 3 of the *Considerations*, where Mill takes on the popular misconception that "if a good despot could be ensured, despotic monarchy would be the best form of government."[63] Even assuming the availability of an all-seeing and omnicompetent monarch, one capable of overseeing all aspects of legislation and administration, what would be the practical result?

> A good despotism means a government in which, so far as depends on the despot, there is no positive oppression by officers of state, but in which all the collective interests of the people are managed for them, all the thinking that has relation to collective interests done for them, and in which their minds are formed by, and consenting to, this abdication of their own energies. Leaving things to the Government, like leaving them to Providence, is synonymous with caring nothing about them, and accepting their results, when disagreeable, as visitations of Nature. With the exception, therefore, of a few studious men who take an intellectual interest in speculation for its own sake, the intelligence and sentiments of the whole people are given up to the material interests, and when these are provided for, to the amusement and ornamentation of private life. But to say this is to say, if the whole testimony of history is worth anything, that the era of national decline has arrived; that is, if the nation had ever attained anything to decline from.[64]

Any regime that relieves its people of the "burdens" of political judgment and political action inevitably produces privatism, and privatism—"if the whole testimony of history is worth anything"—is the road to barbarism (Mill is echoing both Tocqueville and Hegel here). Much if not all of the superiority of a popular or "free" form of government consists in the fact that it opens the arena of political judgment and action to the people themselves, thereby freeing them from what we might call the mental and moral idiocy of a strictly private life.[65] A "good despotism," Mill concludes, is "an altogether false ideal." Indeed,

> There is no difficulty in showing that the ideally best form of government is that in which the sovereignty, or the supreme controlling power in the last resort, is vested in the *entire aggregate of the community*; every citizen not only having a voice in the exercise of that ultimate sovereignty, but being, at least occasionally, called on to take an actual part in the government, by the personal discharge of some public function, local or general.[66]

The "pre-eminence" of a "completely popular form of government" consists in the capacity to improve the "existing faculties, mental, moral, and active, of its various members," and the ability to better utilize these energies and talents for "the good management of the affairs of society."[67] In making these rather large claims for the superiority of popular government, Mill goes well beyond the Constant-like stance of *On Liberty*.[68] His instinctive repugnance to the monopolization of political power and pervasive privatization places him much closer to the liberal republicanism of Tocqueville and the latter's faith in the "moralizing" potential of public-political action.

This last point—and the importance of political participation in general for Mill—is born out if we turn to Mill's 1840 review of volume 2 of Tocqueville's *Democracy in America* (published the same year). This essay is frequently cited as the high point of the young Mill's "conservative" reaction to the radicalism of his father and Bentham.[69] This is true if we attend chiefly to what Mill has to say about the tyranny of public opinion and the need for some form of elite "countervailing power." But the 1840 review is also notable for the way Mill underlines Tocqueville's assertion that it is the "dissemination of public business as widely as possible among the people" that gives them the habit of regularly attending to public affairs and to their civic responsibilities. It is the dispersal of political power and local administration in America that makes the people "fit" to wield their ultimate sovereign power.[70]

Such "learning by doing" in the political realm appears eminently useful to Mill, his doubts about majority opinion notwithstanding. It is useful both as a means of civic education and as a vehicle for the cultivation of a broader moral horizon. Without substantive participation in the public-political sphere, the natural tendency is the contraction of the sphere of interest to self, family, and friends. As Mill writes:

The main branch of education of human beings is their habitual employment. . . . The private money-getting occupation of almost everyone, is more or less a mechanical routine; it brings but few of his faculties into action, while its exclusive pursuit tends to fasten his attention and interest solely upon himself, and upon his family as an appendage of himself;—making him indifferent to the public, to the more generous objects and the nobler interests, and, in his inordinate regard for his personal comforts, selfish and cowardly. Balance these tendencies by contrary ones; give him something to do for the public, whether as a vestryman, a juryman, or an elector; and in that degree his ideas and feeling are taken out of this narrow circle. . . . He is made to feel that besides the interests which separate him from his fellow citizens, he has interests which connect him with them; that not only the common weal is his weal, but that it partly depends on his exertions. Whatever might be the case in some other constitutions of society, the spirit of a commercial people will be, we are persuaded, *essentially mean and slavish whenever public spirit is not cultivated by extensive participation of the people in the business of government in detail.*[71]

Mill is largely paraphrasing Tocqueville here. What is surprising—particularly for those who think of Mill as little more than a spokesperson for an elite-heavy or "aristocratic" form of representative government—is that he returns to the same point, in pretty much the same terms, twenty-one years later in the *Considerations*:

It is not sufficiently considered how little there is in most men's ordinary life to given any largeness to their conceptions or to their sentiments. Their work is routine; not a labour of love, but of self-interest in the most rudimentary form, the satisfaction of daily wants; neither the thing done, nor the process of doing it, introduces the mind to thoughts or feelings extending beyond individuals; if instructive books are within their reach, there is no stimulus to read them; and in most cases the individual has no access to any person of cultivation much superior to his own. Giving him something to do for the public, supplies, in a measure, all these deficiencies. If circumstances allow the amount of public duty assigned him to be considerable, it makes him an educated man.[72]

After citing the very considerable "public education" every Athenian citizen received from his democratic institutions, Mill turns explicitly to the moral effects of political participation; that is, to the broadening of moral horizons that accompanies the development of a civic (that is, politically attentive) consciousness:

> Still more salutary is the moral part of the instruction afforded by the participation of the private citizen, if even rarely, in public functions. He is called upon, while so engaged, to weigh interests not his own; to be guided, in case of conflicting claims, by another rule than his private partialities; to apply, at every turn, principles and maxims which have for their reason of existence the common good. . . . Where *this school of public spirit* does not exist, scarcely any sense is entertained that private persons, in no eminent situation, owe any duties to society, except to obey the laws and submit to the government. There is no unselfish identification with the public. . . . The man never thinks of any collective interest, of any objects to be pursued jointly with others, but only in competition with them, and in some measure at their expense. A neighbor, not being an ally or an associate, since he is never engaged in any common undertaking for joint benefit, is therefore only a rival. Thus even private morality suffers, while public is actually extinct.[73]

The lessons Mill's "school of public spirit" teaches are not reducible to the kind of selfless devotion to the common good praised by Pericles in his Funeral Oration, or by Machiavelli in his *Discourses*.[74] Mill's "public spirit" is indeed related to what we would call patriotism (he sometimes uses the words interchangeably). However, his insistence upon the importance of an agonistic or "conflictual" public realm (in *On Liberty*), combined with his substantive concern for minority rights and "voice" (in the *Considerations*), demonstrates that ideological homogeneity has absolutely no place in his conception of public-spiritedness. The point of participation is to energize and develop the mental and moral faculties that would otherwise wither or grow flabby through inaction. Such development—such education—cannot possibly occur in a public world that reduces political judgment to a reflexive and unanimous patriotism, the collective (literal or figurative) banging of spears on shields.

All of Mill's points—the "barbarizing" effects of privatism; the importance of participation for the expansion of one's moral horizon; the need for a plurality of interests and the preservation of "antagonism"—are extremely Tocquevillian in character. The break comes when he considers the question of whether a given people can develop the capacity for self-government out of itself, "spontaneously" (so to speak) without the intervention of Rousseauian legislators, "enlightened" despots, or a guiding elite.

Tocqueville's answer to this question was complex. On the one hand, he emphasized to his French audience that only a specific constellation of qualities and conditions enabled the habit of self-government to emerge spontaneously amongst the Anglo-Americans. The absence of poverty; the tradition of township and congregational self-government brought by the Puritans from England; the literacy, intelligence, and independence of the original immigrants to New England; the emergence of a robust associational life—these and other factors made it possible for self-government to establish deep local roots early on in colonial America.[75] On the other hand, Tocqueville thought that specific institutional reforms (such as a radical decentralization of the hyper-centralized French state) would help stimulate the emergence of the "free *moeurs*" amongst a politically infantilized French people (*moeurs* that the Anglo-Americans could mostly take for granted).

With Mill—and, indeed, with an industrializing England in the middle of the nineteenth century—things are quite different. The continuing monopolization of political power and judgment by an anti-intellectual, lazy, and largely out of touch aristocracy; the growth in social power of a commercial middle class that devoted itself to the pursuit of selfish interests; and an ever-expanding urban proletariat, largely illiterate and without political experience—these factors combined to make Mill skeptical of any "natural" or spontaneous emergence of political maturity in his native country. The "informal curricula" of basic skills necessary to democratic citizenship—a curricula supplied by Tocqueville's free *moeurs*—were lacking.[76] Radical reform—not revolution—was needed, but it would have to be led (or so Mill thought) by opinion leaders such as himself and others from the "instructed classes." Then and only then would the threat of rule by a conformist and untutored "public opinion" be avoided. Then and only then could the "improvement of mankind" proceed apace.

This makes it sound as if Mill, confronted by "facts on the ground" in England, fell back on the theory/practice schema favored by "philosophical radicals" such as Bentham and his father. That would be incorrect. As I already noted, after his mental crisis Mill rejected the deterministic assumptions built into his father's and Bentham's idea of "political education." As a result, for the mature Mill, such education could never be a form of conditioning determined from on high. But neither could it be a simple and straightforward "learning by doing" such as Tocqueville had described in his work on American democracy. The preconditions of such learning, Mill thought, were simply not available in England, where class division, hierarchy, "sinister interests," and political illiteracy were the order of the day.

Thus, one of the primary reasons Mill endorses representative government in the *Considerations* as the "ideally best form" is that—potentially at least—it enlists more of the intelligence of the nation, from across a wider social spectrum, than any other form.[77] But this remains only a possibility if the doctrines of popular sovereignty and "one man, one vote" are allowed to completely define the structure of representative government. "The natural tendency of representative government," Mill writes, "as of modern civilization, is toward collective mediocrity: and this tendency is increased by all the reductions and extensions of the franchise, their effect being to place the principal power in the hand of classes more and more below the highest level of instruction in the community."[78]

Tocqueville, then, was right to emphasize the importance of political participation for the "mental cultivation" of the "mass of mankind." However, his analysis revealed that while "political life in America is indeed a most valuable school" in this respect, it is also "a school from which the ablest teachers are excluded; the first minds in the country being as effectually shut out from the national representation, and from public functions generally, as if they were under a formal disqualification."[79] English representative government must find a way around the exclusion of "distinguished talent" that Tocqueville had identified as one of the hallmarks of American democracy.[80]

This explains Mill's otherwise inexplicable enthusiasm for London lawyer Thomas Hare's scheme of proportional representation and transferable votes, a scheme that would open Parliament and municipal government (Mill thought) to "hundreds of able men of independent thought, who would have no chance whatsoever of being chosen by any existing constituency."[81] Through the introduction of the "aristocratic principle" (a "natural" aristocracy of the best educated and most competent), the "difficulty of popular representation" identified by Tocqueville—the tyranny of majority opinion and the "mediocre minds" that represent it—could be at least partly overcome. Mill went so far as to write Hare in order to tell him that the 1859 book in which he proposed his scheme (*The Election of*

Representatives, Parliamentary and Municipal) had "raised up the cloud of gloom and uncertainty which hung over the futurity of representative government and therefore of civilization."[82]

Mill's enthusiasm for Hare's plan was motivated, first and foremost, by his desire to reduce the influence of incompetent representatives as well as dangers of class legislation.[83] But it was also motivated by the desire to give voice to what was, to his mind, the class most threatened by permanent under-representation in an increasingly democratic system. This was the "intellectual" class of writers, professors, reformers, and so on whose political base was largely outside the emerging party system. In a representative system built on parties and representation of localities, it was the voice of this minority that was least likely to be heard.

This has potentially dire implications for the "school of public spirit" that representative democracy brings into being. That school will do nothing but reproduce mediocrity unless it is given a higher, more ideal and more competent, tone by the "instructed class." As Mill writes: "It is what men think that determines how they act; and though the persuasions and convictions of average men are in a much greater degree determined by their personal position than by reason, no little power is exercised over them by the persuasions and convictions of those whose personal position is different, and by *the united authority of the instructed*."[84]

Now, even in these terms, Mill's proposed "liberal" modification of representative democracy might appear unjustifiably elitist, a regress to the Saint-Simonian and Coleridgian opinions of his earlier years.[85] But while Mill undoubtedly was an "aristocratic liberal" of sorts, we need to be extremely careful about how we parse this term. It is wrong to identify him (as Leo Strauss explicitly does in his essay on "Liberal Education and Responsibility") as an advocate of "rule by the gentlemen."[86] Similarly, it would be wrong to see him (as some contemporary "radical democrats" do) as wanting to throw the democratic principle—the principle of popular government and limited popular sovereignty—out with the bath water of "majority tyranny."[87] The emphasis on participation—learned from Tocqueville's study and placed front and center in the *Considerations*—is far too strong. It is clearly intended to be something more than a mask for a hoped for "rule by the elite."

The complexity of the *Considerations* is obviously a function of its attempted synthesis of popular and "aristocratic" principles. The resulting tense equilibrium between these principles goes to the heart of Mill's conception of an "educative" democracy. The idea of a "school for public spirit" is relatively unproblematic if, like Tocqueville, we rely on civil society, political associations, and the "informal curricula" of free *moeurs* to do the educating. It becomes appreciably more problematic if, like Mill, we demand there to be *teachers* in the school as well. That Mill wanted "teachers"—that he believed them to be absolutely imperative given "the present low state of the human mind"—is indisputable.[88] The real question is: what kind of teachers, armed with what kind of authority, did he desire?

One answer—the "maximalist" version, in line with his younger "conservative" self—would be that Mill wanted, if not rule by an elite, then something approximating a "government of leading strings." This would be an elite-heavy form of representative government, one designed to gradually bring about the capacities for self-government in a population too inexperienced, too self-interested, and too "immature" to care much about the "public thing." This answer finds support in the large role the *Considerations* gives to the expert knowledge of trained civil servants, as well as Mill's surprisingly tight restrictions on the "proper function" of an elected representative assembly.[89] It also finds considerable support in such "notorious" passages as the following, taken from the chapter on "Individuality" in *On Liberty*:

> No government by a democracy or a numerous aristocracy, either in its political acts or in the opinions, qualities, and tone of mind which it fosters, ever did or could rise above mediocrity, except insofar as the sovereign Many have let themselves be guided (which in the best of times they always have done) by the counsels and influence of a more highly gifted and instructed One or Few. The initiation of all wise or noble things, comes and must come from individuals; generally at first from some one individual. The honor and glory of the average man is that he is capable of following that initiative; that he can respond internally to wise and noble things, and be led to them with his eyes open.[90]

This and other passages suggest that, when it comes to of popular participation in government, Mill never really abandoned the position he took in an 1832 *Examiner* article, a position rife with "Platonic" (paternalist) associations:

> The true idea of popular representation is not that the people govern in their own persons, but that they choose their governors. In

a good government public questions are not referred to the suf-frages of the people themselves, but to those of the most judicious persons whom the people can find. . . . If the House of Commons were constituted in the most perfect manner, whom would it con-sist of? Surely of the wisest and best men in the nation, or those whom the people believe to be such. Now, if I vote for a person because I think him the wisest man I know, am I afterwards to set myself up as his instructor, as if I were wiser than him? . . . We shall never have wise legislators, until legislation is a profession . . . when the value of knowledge is adequately felt, a man will choose his legislator as he chooses his physician. No man pretends to in-struct his physician.[91]

A quite different answer—not quite minimalist, but certainly less robustly "aristocratic"—is found in what I call Mill's "trickle down" theory of political judgment. On this view, the later Mill considerably modified, if not outright repudiated, his earlier statement that "the best government, (need it be said?) must be the government of the wisest, and these must always be few."[92] The "diffusion of intelligence" he stresses in the *Consider-ations* aims not at establishing a relation of authority and obedience—of rulers and ruled, or physicians and patients—between the "few" and the "many." Rather, the goal of such diffusion is a higher level of debate, a more informed public opinion, and (ultimately) better public policy. This diffusion is facilitated by an awareness on the part of "less instructed" classes that the views of the better educated—those who have a knowledge of public affairs and a demonstrated commitment to the public good—are worthy of attention and a certain amount of deference.[93]

Such men—the "men of talent and instruction" whose views Mill wanted to save from oblivion in an increasingly "mass-centric" world—should at least have their voices heard on important questions of public policy, legislation, and reform. We can learn from them, Mill argues, precisely because their opinions depart from the mainstream of public opinion (which is well represented by the professional politicians and the political parties).[94] Needless to say, listening to and learning from the views of a "better instructed" minority is hardly the same thing as obeying a Guardian-like elite or deferring to a "rational" bureaucracy. Nor is it quite the same as the people's "cheerful acknowledgment" of the superior judgment of the instructed class that Mill describes in his 1835 review of volume 1 of *Democracy in America*.[95]

Which is closer to Mill's true position, the maximalist or the quasi-minimalist account? If we stay within the confines of the *Considerations*, one would have to say that Mill comes down squarely in the middle. On the one hand his plea for participation and inclusion is vehement and seriously meant. On the other, his distrust of untutored public opinion—a distrust warranted by the same Tocqueville who emphasized the importance of participation—manifests itself on just about every page.

Thus, in chapter 3 of the *Considerations* we can read Mill praising "the practice of the dicastery and the ecclesia" in raising "the intellectual standard of an average Athenian citizen far beyond anything of which there is yet an example in any other mass of men, ancient or modern," while in chapter 5 we can see him insisting on strict functional limits to the work of popular (representative) assemblies. The "proper function" of the latter is to "indicate wants, to be an organ for popular demands, and a place of adverse discussion for all opinions relating to public matters, both great and small; and, along with this, to check by criticism, and eventually by withdrawing their support, those high public officers who really conduct the public business, or who appoint those by whom it is conducted."[96] Only in this (highly restricted) fashion can the public sphere and representative organs go about their "control and criticism" function without unduly interfering in the specialized business of "skilled legislation and administration" performed by a "specially trained and experienced Few."[97] If in chapter 3 Mill sounds like the "participatory" Tocqueville, in chapter 5 he sounds like an "Anglo" Hegel—complete with the latter's faith in the so-called "universal class" (the specially trained civil service or bureaucracy).[98]

Leaving aside the issue of the "specialized" character of public administration and legislation, we see that Mill is actually trying to walk a very fine line between the cultivation of a participatory ethos (inspired by his reading of the classics and Tocqueville) and a more deferential one (in which the people recognize themselves as attentive pupils in matters relating to the art of government, public affairs, and the pathologies of democracy). It is safe to say that contemporary American readers—unless they happen to be arrogant technocrats or philosophical elitists of a Straussian or similar persuasion—will find the latter ethos both off-putting and incomprehensible. Why should we abdicate our privilege of judging and thinking for ourselves? Why should we defer to the authority of the "best and the brightest" (to use a non-Millian phrase)?

Of course, Mill doesn't want anyone to abdicate the privilege of judging and thinking for themselves. If nothing else, *On Liberty* is a vehement refutation of intellectual passivity and the "Calvinistic" ethos of obedience to regnant norms and ideas.[99] The despotism of custom and the tyranny of (mass) public opinion have combined to breed a herd-like docility in the face of "what everyone thinks" (a force made even more potent by the amplified voice of spokesmen for "what everyone thinks"—our politicians and radio talk show hosts).

Against this ethos—the ethos of contemporary mass culture democracy—Mill argues passionately for an agonistic public realm, one in which competing ideas clash; one in which truth emerges through conflict and the antagonism of views. He wanted to find avenues through which the deadening hand of custom, mass opinion, and what his friend George Grote called "King Nomos" might be escaped.[100] Above all, he wanted to increase the level of moral and intellectual energy amongst the ordinary people of his age. Unless this level is increased (and it can only be increased by education in the true sense of the word, that is, by the "guided" awakening of intellectual curiosity and energy *à la* Socrates), the best of our beliefs and practices will invariably "degenerate into the mechanical," losing whatever truth and moral value they might once have possessed.[101]

This is the context in which the passage cited above about "the Sovereign Many" allowing themselves to be "guided" by the "counsels and influence of a more highly gifted or instructed One or Few" should be read. Appearances to the contrary, this remark is not intended to empower philosopher-kings or call forth a cult of genius-worship on the part of the "mediocre mass." As Mill observes, new ideas and practices are commenced by individuals who possess originality and who think against the grain. It is the "honor and glory" of the average man that he can, and often does, "respond internally to wise and noble things," following the initiative of those more "gifted" with "his eyes open."[102] The latter have no power to compel (that would be inconsistent with the freedom for self-development that is *On Liberty*'s chief goal), but only "to point out the way."

The questioning and intellectual combat that form the substance of Mill's ideal public sphere are here not done away with. Rather, they are raised to the status of a moral principle, the better for heterodox ideas to emerge and "blaze out far and wide."[103] In an age in which "the opinions of masses of merely average men are everywhere become or becoming the dominant power," the "corrective and counterpoise" is found in the new practices, ideas, and perspectives offered by those of "more pronounced individuality." These do not legislate and they do not "rule" in any political sense of the word. What they offer—at least in a world where freedom of thought and discussion has not been completely quashed by the intolerance of a "self-adoring" majority—is a step beyond socially inscribed dogma. This, in turn, opens up the possibility of that rare but not completely unheard of species, an "intellectually active people"—one that has liberated itself from the "general atmosphere of mental slavery."[104]

As I have argued elsewhere, this Socratic ethos guides *On Liberty* and Mill's idea of education.[105] In his "Inaugural Address" to St. Andrews University (1867), Mill charged the faculty and students:

> To question all things; never to turn away from any difficulty; to accept no doctrine either from ourselves or from other people without a rigid scrutiny by negative criticism, letting no fallacy, or incoherence, or confusion of thought, slip by unperceived; above all, to insist upon having the meaning of a word clearly understood before using it, and the meaning of a proposition before assenting to it; these are the lessons we learn from the ancient dialecticians.[106]

To be sure, this charge is laid upon an "elite" audience of university graduates, not a group of undereducated and disenfranchised workers.[107] But it is telling insofar as it identifies the very *process* of classroom education with free dialectical debate. Only in this way are minds awakened rather than put to sleep. And, of course, the ethos of debate—and education through debate—carries over into the political sphere as well. Thus, in his 1859 essay "Recent Writers on Reform," Mill describes the House of Commons as "not only the most powerful branch of the Legislature; it is also the great council of the nation; the place where the opinions which divide the public on great subjects of national interest, meet in a common arena, do battle, and are victorious or vanquished."[108] The central importance of antagonism and debate to Mill's view of both politics and education makes his assimilation to any of the prevalent (Platonically inspired) ideas of the "tutorial" or educational state all but impossible.

The problem, of course, is that an ethos of debate and antagonism sits uncomfortably with an ethos of deference (however limited) toward one's intellectual betters. Even if the latter ethos is modified in the way I have suggested Mill wants to modify it, the fact remains that the authority of the "teachers" looms over their "students." The "students"—the citizens or potential citizens who lack the largeness of view possessed by people like Mill and other writers on reform—may or may not accept what their "teachers" have to say, but they do owe them a serious (and ongoing) hearing. Thus, the articulation of any debate, and the actual process of debate itself, seems to happen on a stage at a critical remove from the lives and contributions of ordinary citizens. It is not, I think, a coincidence that Mill presents his ancient Athenians—the most political of all peoples—engaged in the audience-like activities of listening to and delivering judgment upon competing orators.[109] *Qua* "student," the "average man" is primarily an audience member, albeit a particularly attentive one.[110]

Mill's "educative democracy," then, aims at the cultivation of the intellectual and moral energies necessary for self-government; it aims at increased publicity and participation, as well as increased inclusion of hitherto disenfranchised social groups. Its reticence toward the idea of a full, active form of popular sovereignty flows, in part, from good liberal (Constant and Tocqueville-inspired) worries about individual and minority rights in the face of an unrestrained majority principle. But it also flows from Mill's sense of the ingrained political immaturity of the people—an immaturity that no amount of association, party activism, or expansion of voting rights would eradicate by itself.

As a result, political education and the attainment of political maturity is rarely, if ever, a do-it-yourself project. In Mill's estimation, it must be guided—not only abroad, but in Europe and (more to the point) in England itself. To be sure, the indirect quality of guidance Mill proposes for his fellow countrymen stands at an enormous remove from the untrammeled bureaucratic rule he recommends for the Indian subcontinent. But it is guidance nonetheless, predicated on the firm belief that political education should not be left to chance or to the periodic fluctuations of public opinion. If it is, the "incessant and ever-flowing current of human affairs toward the worse" will become a raging torrent.

Conclusion: The Future of "Educative" Democracy

In any account of what is living and what is dead in Mill's thought, his hopes for a science of ethology—a science that would uncover "universal laws of the Formation of Character"—would rank high on the list of dead items.[111] So would his many confident assertions about the "national character" of, say, the Spanish and the French, as well as about the relative cultural health (and maturity) of the Indians or the Chinese. Another clear candidate for such a list would be Mill's persistent identification of "social utility" with "progress," and his presumption that both of these terms have a clear and more or less objective content.

Viewed from the perspective of today, these elements of Mill's philosophy seem thoroughly mired in the intellectual milieu of the nineteenth century, clear but unconvincing results of his attempted synthesis of utilitarian with Romantic principles. The question is whether his hopes for an "educative democracy"—and the conception of political "maturity" from which it takes its bearings—belongs on this list of "dead items" as well.

At first glance, there is much that seems to argue in the affirmative. It is difficult if not impossible for us to imagine a form of representative democracy that combines Mill's insistence on the need for an active, energetic character with the habits of intellectual deference he urged upon the "average man." The idea that contemporary Americans should pay more attention to their public intellectuals and university-trained specialists when making up their minds about the issues of the day seems, perhaps unfortunately, a nonstarter. Our culture is too big, too diverse, and too driven by popular media and market imperatives for Mill's "trickle down" theory of political judgment to have much relevance. There is no agreed upon "slate" of public intellectuals or voices for reform who wield the kind of authority, and receive the kind of deference, that Mill's "educative" democracy more or less depends on.

What we have, instead, is a series of increasingly fragmented "demographic publics," each with its representative spokespeople, media figures, and bloggers.[112] Our public sphere lacks not only the kind of national wholeness presumed by Mill; it also lacks the kind of intellectual seriousness and attention he thought "mature" citizenship demanded.[113] Thus, while we have made tremendous strides in public education, increasingly universal enfranchisement, and the sheer proliferation of outlets for political discourse, we have also regressed in a number of notable ways. The "marketplace of ideas" (never a phrase Mill used) is now simply a market, one that hawks ideological half-thinking, outright lies, and sound bites to the already persuaded or the too disinterested to care. Political debate, like everything else, is largely defined by what Martin Amis has rightly dubbed the "moronic inferno" of popular (consumer) culture. Rarely, if ever, has the terrain of social, cultural, and political life seemed less hospitable to the vision of democratic education Mill envisioned.

But it is precisely the seeming irrelevance of Mill's idea of representative government as a vehicle for the *improvement* of people's moral, intellectual, and "active" faculties that should give us pause. Since this improvement has obviously not happened in the American case (at least not in anything like the terms Mill had in mind), we are inclined to dismiss the entire notion out of hand. Recent history suggests that substantial numbers of the American *demos* are anxious and willing to believe virtually anything their leaders say. Such unfiltered credulity in the face of cynical manipulation of fear demonstrates two things: first, that the "school" of representative democracy is anything but that; second, that the cultivation of "deference" is the last thing we need.

Confronted with these criticisms, Mill would entirely agree. But he would stick to his guns. The fact that Americans often seem only marginally more "competent," "mature," or "public-spirited" than the citizens of much younger democracies suggests that our characteristic faith in the machinery of representative government is radically misplaced. This faith—the faith that political attentiveness is not all that important because our leaders are trustworthy and our "checks and balances" intact—has, once again, been shown to be without foundation. Nor can we fall back on the "free *moeurs*"—the habits, attitudes, and ideas—that Tocqueville saw animating an earlier, public-spirited America. These have decayed and mostly disappeared—in part, because the landscape of American political life has altered so dramatically over the past 175 years, but also because consumer culture and the crushing discipline of a globalized labor market has effectively destroyed the last tattered remnants of our civic culture.

In such straits, Mill would argue all the more strenuously for his brand of "educative" democracy. In the case of America, the education would have to be remedial. We suffer, apparently, from national attention deficit disorder. This disorder makes people think we can suspend many of the defining features of liberal constitutional democracy with little or no cost to ourselves or to the future. This fact, combined with pervasive ignorance of constitutional basics and a privatism that deepens daily, has helped turn the United States into a dangerously underachieving democracy. This is especially so if we take the standard of achievement to be fidelity to representative democracy's underlying principles, rather than the accumulation of wealth or power.[114]

Mill's prescription for our ills—a forthrightly "educative" democracy, with a substantial elite component—would hardly work in our context, for reasons I have already mentioned. But even if the prescription is problematic, the fundamental analysis remains stingingly correct. A constitution must be "worked by men, and even by ordinary men. It needs not their simple acquiescence, but their active participation."[115] Today, the most important form of participation would be a vigilant and informed attentiveness, one driven by the desire to hold our representatives to account. Only when this is the case can we be at all confident that our institutional machinery will secure us not just negative liberty—the freedom from undue government interference—but an even more important liberty: the liberty from subjection.[116] As Mill himself observes in the *Considerations*:

> Political checks will no more act of themselves, than a bridle will direct a horse without a rider. If the checking functionaries are as corrupt or as negligent as those whom they out to check, and if the public, *the mainspring of the checking machinery*, are too ignorant, too passive, or too careless and inattentive, to do their part, little benefit will be derived from the best administrative apparatus.[117]

A passive and inattentive public, combined with a supine Congress and a Supreme Court that rarely meets an expansion of executive power it doesn't like, has brought our representative democracy to the brink—not of fascism, but of a purely formal liberal democracy. This is a "liberal democracy" in which governmental hierarchy and secrecy combines with corporate prerogative to produce an order of power virtually unconstrained by any checking machinery whatever. Again and again, one has the sickening feeling of watching a train wreck occur in slow motion—but from the sidelines, as a politically impotent spectator for whom the word "public" has neither an active nor a critical connotation.

A good deal of the blame lies with our representatives, but—as I have argued—a decent share also lies with us, the constituents of "the public." The willingness to let executive power expand almost indefinitely; to allow torture, warrantless wiretapping, and the deprivation of basic civil rights; to forgo even the most minimal democratic processing of the critically important foreign policy decisions—these are less the result of well-considered judgments concerning the threats we face as a representative democracy than they are evidence of a growing tendency to accept our elected officials as de facto rulers, replete with the powers and prerogatives of rulers.

This tendency will only increase as the United States—through the more or less spontaneous collaboration of its leading economic, political, and educational institutions—devotes its energies to turning out ravenous consumers and anxious employees, but not *citizens*. As Mill again reminds us, the function of citizens is not to support the national economy through purchasing power or to reflexively sacrifice themselves during wartime. It is to devote at least part of their moral, intellectual, and "active" powers to the all-important work of checking the holders of power.

This brings us, finally, back to Mill's criteria for deciding whether a given people is suited for representative government—that is, whether it has achieved the minimum necessary level of cultural development and political "maturity." The three "fundamental conditions" that must be filled are: "(1) That the people should be willing to receive it. (2) That they should be willing and able to do what is necessary for its preservation. (3) That they should be willing and able to fulfill the duties and discharge the functions which it imposes on them."[118] A detached and abbreviated judgment with respect to the American people's claim to fulfill these criteria would run something like this: (1) Yes, we are more than willing to receive it (from our ancestors); (2) We are partly willing and partly able to do what is necessary for its preservation; and (3) We are all too often unwilling or unable to fulfill the duties and discharge the functions—especially the all-important checking function—that it imposes on us. The latter assumes an energetic focus of attention on public affairs. This is something increasingly few seem willing, or even able, to undertake.[119]

It is all too easy to use Mill's theory of political development to score easy post-colonial points in these troubled times. I would like to suggest that it may be more fruitful to turn his theoretical mirror, and his criteria of "maturity," back upon ourselves, and the state of our democracy. The results, as indicated, are not especially encouraging. This suggests another point on which the *Considerations* was fundamentally correct: things left to themselves invariably decay.

Americans have gotten far too used to treating representative government as a mechanism that frees them from the "burdens" of public life and attention to public affairs. The great virtue of John Stuart Mill—his overestimation of the role of an educated "clerisy" in politics and his Anglo-Saxon ethnic prejudices notwithstanding—is that he reminds us that "liberation" from public affairs was never the point of representative government, properly understood. Representative government is as much a freedom for politics as it is a freedom from politics. If the *Considerations* teaches us but one essential lesson, this is it.

6 | THE FRANKFURT SCHOOL AND THE PUBLIC SPHERE

Aufklärung ist der Ausgang der Menschen aus seiner selbstver-
schuldeten Unmündigkeit.
—Immanuel Kant

"Enlightenment," Kant famously wrote in 1784, "is man's emergence from
his self-incurred immaturity." And immaturity, he continued, is

> the inability to use one's own understanding without the guid-
> ance of another. This immaturity is *self-incurred* if its cause is not
> lack of understanding, but lack of resolution and courage to use it
> without the guidance of another. The motto of the enlightenment
> is therefore: *Sapere aude!* Have the courage to use your *own* un-
> derstanding.[1]

Kant's formulation—which presents laziness, cowardice, and a general
propensity for "dogma and formulas" as holding back the majority of
human beings from the attainment of a rational "maturity"—has been
tremendously influential, extending even to philosophical and theoretical tendencies that vigorously dispute the idea of a rational or "autonomous" subject. It has been centrally and explicitly influential on the
main figures of the Frankfurt School—Horkheimer, Adorno, Marcuse,
and Habermas. These theorists all cast their philosophical projects as

part of a generalized effort to remove persistent ideological obstacles, obstacles that block our emergence from "self-incurred immaturity."

While indebted to Kant, the *Ideologiekritik* of the Frankfurt School stands in an ambivalent—some might say strained—relationship to him. On the one hand, it takes the Kantian project of gradually rationalizing (and thus dissolving) structures of domination with the utmost seriousness. On the other, it rejects the Kantian assumption that our immaturity is, in essence, "*self*-incurred." No matter how far any of the major Frankfurt School figures stray from Marx, they are one in their acceptance of the basic Marxian teaching that ideological obfuscations—forms of "mystified" consciousness—have their roots in the material structures of capitalist reproduction. This assumption is made quite explicitly in Horkheimer's programmatic essay "Traditional and Critical Theory" (1937), and remains in place throughout the Frankfurt School's diverse and twisting itinerary (well laid out in Rolf Wiggerhaus's magisterial history).[2] The fact that many if not most of us reproduce the "spiritual conditions of our own domination" (to use the classic Marxian formulation)[3] is, as a result, not due to any lack of resolve or courage. It is, rather, the result of late capitalism's secretion of an array of ideological conceptions and structures that prevent us from seeing the numerous contradictions (and alternative developmental possibilities) contained in our present, "hypostatized" social reality.

For the Frankfurt School, then, the Kantian trope of "immaturity" was largely replaced by the more familiar Marxian trope of "false consciousness." Largely, but not entirely. From the beginning—indeed, starting with the work of Marx and Engels themselves—"critical" theory conceived itself explicitly as a form of political or "scientific" pedagogy in the service of the oppressed—those who, through their belief in certain religious, political, or cultural forms, were unknowingly complicit in their own domination.[4]

Contra the Leninist deformation of the "vanguard party," this pedagogy was never supposed to be a one-way hierarchical relationship between teachers and taught. Rather, the basic Marxian insight into the practical or *involved* nature of human understanding—its demystification of a disembodied Cartesian or "contemplative" view of reality[5]—entailed a complex and ongoing *pas de deux* between the oppressed working class and their erstwhile philosophical helpers. Theory "informed" the masses while being crucially informed by the masses "practical" struggles. Or such, at least, was the official line.[6]

This line—in which largely bourgeois thinkers act not as philosopher-kings, but rather as theoretical guides or tutors to their less well-educated working class comrades—broke down entirely with the popular endorsement of the Hitler regime. The tradition we know as the "Frankfurt School" is completely unthinkable outside the context provided by this fundamental trauma. The failure of the German proletariat not only to live up to their pre-assigned role in the class struggle, but to support the forces of civilization rather than barbarism, led Horkheimer, Adorno, and Marcuse to jettison the idea of an "immaturity" that could be overcome by political self-assertion or the therapeutic intervention of *Ideologiekritik*.[7] Even more consequentially, it led them to reject the idea that the political-public sphere could ever be the home of a dissolvent rationality, one which loosened the grip of ideology and which operated by means of critical rational debate.

Jürgen Habermas, the most illustrious of the "second generation" of Frankfurt School theorists, has attempted to make good this deficit. Starting from the early *Structural Transformation of the Public Sphere*, his theoretical work has attempted to rescue the idea of the public realm—and, more broadly, the notion of communicative action itself—from a too-inclusive Marxist "unmasking." While fully acknowledging the ways in which the public realm can become a mask for the interests of a particular class, Habermas has consistently focused his attention on the "rationalizing" or pedagogical potential contained in the discursive realm of public argument and deliberation. An historically developing capacity for "communicative rationality"—one based equally on social evolution and partially embodied in the concrete institutional reforms of so-called "bourgeois" democracy—promised to counter-balance the "encompassing ideology" thesis, as well as provide a vehicle for the self-education of citizens. Seen from this perspective, the failure of the proletariat's revolutionary project did not leave us stranded helplessly in an "administered world," the victims of an increasingly "reified" or ahistorical consciousness. Rather, this failure pointed to the absolute necessity of recovering the rational dialogical norms contained in language and the political-institutional landscape of modernity. Only in this way could an immanent critique of social reality proceed.

There is much to recommend this project. Habermas's recovery of the idea of the public sphere (in his early work) and the potentials of communicative action (in his "mature" theory) offer a much needed corrective to a tradition that seemed all too ready to write off both the genuine achievements of constitutional democracy and the "moral learning capacities" of ordinary citizens. That said, it must be acknowledged that Habermas's recovery is itself overly shaped by the same Weberian metanarrative of the "formalization of reason" that led Horkheimer, Adorno, and Marcuse into their respective cul-de-sacs. This leads him to place far too much weight on the idea that properly structured communication—freed from the distortions introduced by money, power, and ideology—can lead us to an "objectively guaranteed" concordance of interests, a rationally demonstrable universal interest.[8]

The "Culture Industry" and the Ideological Absorption of the Public Sphere in *Dialectic of Enlightenment*

It was the trauma of the working class abandonment of emancipatory struggle that accounts for the pathos—and the power—of Horkheimer and Adorno's *Dialectic of Enlightenment* (1947). This is a work of theoretical reorientation whose primary goal was to trace the roots of "false consciousness" back to the primordial origins of reason and Enlightenment itself. Growing out of the struggle for self-preservation in the face of overwhelming natural forces, Western rationality was, from its inception, bound up with domination—of nature, and of man who is also nature.[9] The ultimate expression of such "instrumental" reason was the all-inclusive "system" of late capitalist domination, a system that took Max Weber's idea of "administered society" to a level of unprecedented actualization, one that left few, if any, escape hatches or reasons for hope.

In this regard, Horkheimer and Adorno went so far as to ironically invoke Kant's maxim, seeing in it an unexpectedly sinister foreshadowing of the instrumentally rationalized (and substantively irrational) present.[10] Understanding without the direction of another, they wrote, is "understanding guided by reason." And reason, according to Kant and the Enlightenment, is nothing more than a mind "that combines its individual cognitions into a system in accordance with its own internal logic." As Horkheimer and Adorno put it: "For Kant, as for Leibniz and Descartes, rationality consists in 'processes of ascending to the higher genera and of descending to the lower species [by which] we obtain the idea of systematic connection in its completeness.'"[11] The bringing of all the manifold contents of nature (themselves pre-structured by the *a priori* categories of our cognitive understanding) into a systematic unity by means of the "regulative employment" of the "ideas of pure reason" is the task of science.[12] From Horkheimer and Adorno's perspective, the great sin of Kant and the Enlightenment is precisely this "critical" reduction of reason to scientific rationality.[13]

This "positivistic" reduction of reason to an essentially systematizing power, one built on the principle of noncontradiction, short-circuits any more "reflective" uses of reason, such as the dialectical conceptions of social reality proposed by Hegel, Marx, Lukács, and, of course, by the Frankfurt School itself. Ultimately, it yields the hegemony of "formal rationality," a development Weber saw as the inescapable destiny of the late capitalist West. This hegemony entails not just the identification of science/reason with "systematic" rationality, but the extension of this type of rationality to the most important subsystems (law, economics, government) of society itself.

Increasingly, Weber and the Frankfurt School argue, modern social reality has come to resemble the integrated, systematic branches of the "hypothetical" unity Kant outlined in the *Critique of Pure Reason*. Just as the "regulative use" of such systematic ideas of pure reason helped us gain control of nature through the creation of a universal natural science (one stripped of Aristotelian teleological anachronisms), so their implementation as the guiding principles for a restructured, "rationalized" social reality has yielded greater control, order, and capacity for domination. (Not for nothing is "systems theory" one of the great *bête noires* of the Frankfurt School.)

Now, one could argue—as Habermas does in his two-volume *Theory of Communicative Action*[14]—that the creeping infiltration or "colonization" of social reality by varieties of formal or "systematic" rationality is both very real and importantly incomplete. Our social reality is split between the rationalized-hierarchical subsystems of the economy and the state, on the one hand, and the more egalitarian domain of human interaction (the "lifeworld"), on the other. Money and power are the driving media of the first two, while argument and communicative interaction provide the medium for third. The latter consists of the broad public domain in which questions of political direction, the meaning of cultural values, and sociopolitical tensions have typically been addressed, at least in liberal democratic societies (the erosion of many of this domain's prerogatives notwithstanding). Such a view of social reality allows the critical theorist to insist that Weber's "iron cage" is only half-built. It is up to us to make sure that the creeping colonization of the political-cultural "lifeworld" by the "system" is *not* allowed to reach fulfillment.

Such a possibility is not even remotely suggested by the analyses offered by *Dialectic of Enlightenment*. The reason for this is not, or not simply, because Horkheimer and Adorno failed to make a crucial distinction between "instrumental" and "communicative" rationality (as Habermas has suggested). Rather, it is because they saw the "colonization" process as one that *had already reached completion* in the mass society spawned by late capitalism. Nowhere is this sense of completion—the "total system" character of the new society—more in evidence than in *Dialectic of Enlightenment's* famous chapter on the "culture industry," a chapter tellingly subtitled "Enlightenment as Mass Deception."

The burden of the "Culture Industry" chapter is to make the case that a new type of social formation has grown up on the ruins of both the *ancien régime* and classic, market and individual-centered, capitalism:

> The sociological view that the loss of support from objective religion and the disintegration of the last pre-capitalist residues, in conjunction with technical and social differentiation and specialization, have given rise to cultural chaos is refuted by daily experience. Culture today is infecting everything with sameness. Film, radio, and magazines *form a system*. Each branch of culture is unanimous within itself and all are unanimous together. Even the aesthetic manifestations of political opposites proclaim the same inflexible rhythm.[15]

In the place of atomization and anomie, we have a "total" society in which the work of social integration is achieved—uniformly and successfully—by the media and messages of mass culture. Who needs a common set of beliefs, old-fashioned community, or even what Charles Taylor has called a "post-industrial *Sittlichkeit*" when the culture industry provides a virtually total form of social integration?[16] The great aspiration of post-Kantian thinkers—the *unity* of universal and particular sought by Schiller, Hegel, and Marx—is achieved by contemporary culture, albeit in the "false" form of a consumer-worker who is at one with the system that created him. This is not to say that Horkheimer and Adorno think that mass culture utterly succeeds in producing "bundles of reflexes," agents who are little more than a set of preconditioned appetites and who (as a result) fit smoothly into the "machine." The argument of the "Culture Industry" chapter is more subtle than that, even though its conclusion—summed up by the subtitle—is just as hopeless.

The "mass deception" of the subtitle refers not just to the big lies of the advertising industry and the false promises of Hollywood films, both of which *are* designed to engineer our desires and guide us frictionlessly into the "system." It also refers to the "pseudo-individuality" that Horkheimer and Adorno see as a characteristic trait of the era of monopoly (cartelized) capitalism.[17] Mass culture provides us with innumerable ways of "distinguishing" ourselves—from the cars we drive, to the films we like, to the fashion labels we prefer, to our vacation destinations—all of which are no more than commodities aimed at specific markets or demographics. Even what counts as an "eccentric" characteristic—the funny hat, the bow tie, the unorthodox facial hair, the sultry walk or the "in your face" attitude—is no more than a codified signifier cribbed from television or film.

"Pseudo-individuality" designates a condition where virtually everything we do is, at some level, an imitation of the looks, attitudes, and behavioral types we have previously encountered in advertising and mass media. In such a world—a world of pervasive, unrestrained, and often unconscious mimesis—the peculiarity of the self (that is, what we take to a marker of "genuine" individuality) turns out to be, in fact, "a socially conditioned monopoly commodity misrepresented as natural."[18]

Pseudo-individuality reigns when the social preconditions of a more robust, genuine form of individuality—the free market conditions of "liberal" capitalism—no longer obtain. So-called "bourgeois" individuality may itself have been an ideological fiction. Nevertheless, it reflected a social reality in which a certain level of hard-won adult autonomy was necessary to realize the "two dimensional" profile of a self-interested bourgeois existence (leaving aside the Romantic-Idealist conception of genuine, "all-sided" individuality championed by Fichte, Schiller, and Marx).[19] Today, the aborted promise of bourgeois individuality issues in a regimentation and infantilization that—no matter how diverse its surface styles or colors—is more akin to a smoothly integrated input than to the quasi-Hobbesian subjects who strategically negotiated the treacherous shoals of market society in its nineteenth-century heyday.[20]

But how does this happen? How is a one-sided and distorted form of agency—bourgeois individuality—transformed into the mimetic *mass* form of "pseudo-individuality"?

True to their Marxist heritage, Horkheimer and Adorno provide something approximating a "base and superstructure" explanation. At the level of the base—that is, at the level of economic structures—the transition is one from unplanned, "anarchic" liberal capitalism to the quasi-planned, state-coordinated system characteristic of "advanced" or monopoly capitalism. In the latter, markets are regulated, protected, and regularized. Possibilities for crises of the sort that rocked nineteenth- and early-twentieth-century capitalism are vastly reduced—as is the need for a widely spread entrepreneurial form of self-reliance. At the level of super-structure, the transition is from *culture as commodified art* to *culture as all-inclusive cognitive schema*. It is this second thesis that drives the argument of the "Culture Industry" chapter, and which accounts for its tremendous power and continuing influence—the decisive categorial objection raised by Habermas and others notwithstanding.

What does it mean to characterize mass culture as a *schema*? The Kantian reference is explicit and pursued in depth by Horkheimer and Adorno.[21] For Kant, the "schematism of pure concepts" referred to the necessarily opaque process ("concealed in the depths of the human soul") by which the experience-shaping *a priori* categories of human understanding apply themselves to the seemingly heterogeneous order of sensuous intuition.[22] For Horkheimer and Adorno, this pre-structuring of experience is accomplished not by any mysterious cognitive faculty (one that somehow unites concepts and sensuous intuitions), but *by mass culture itself.* The (active) Kantian epistemological subject is thus reduced to a status even more passive than that portrayed by the classical empiricists (Locke, Berkeley, Hume).

> The active contribution which Kantian schematism still expected of subjects—that they should, from the first, relate sensuous multiplicity to fundamental concepts—is denied to the subject by industry. It purveys schematism as its first service to the customer. According to Kantian schematism, a secret mechanism within the psyche preformed immediate data to fit them into the system of pure reason. That secret has now been unraveled. Although the operations of the mechanism appear to be planned by those who supply the data, the culture industry, the planning is in fact imposed on the industry by the inertia of a society irrational despite all its rationalization. . . . For the consumer there is nothing left to classify, since the classification has already been preempted by the schematism of production.[23]

The fact that experience is now pre-structured in this fashion—that "the whole world is passed through the filter of the culture industry"[24]—has implications at the levels of both form and content. At the level of form, the culture industry—by which Horkheimer and Adorno mean the mass entertainment and advertising churned out by Hollywood, radio, journalism, and publishing[25]—proceeds mainly by formulas, styles, and familiar clichés. These are relentlessly imposed on every film, every script, and every popular piece of music, the better to obviate the need for any active engagement (in viewing, reading, or listening) by the audience.

What is at stake in the hegemony of the "formula" in all branches of the culture industry is not that it converts its audience into *consumers*, but that it converts them into intellectually *passive* consumers. No effort of assimilation, classification, or judgment is necessary, since it has all been done for you: "The spectator must need no thoughts of his own: the product prescribes each reaction, not through any actual coherence ... but through signals."[26] The result is a "crippling" of imagination and spontaneity.[27] The spewing out of ever new movies, music, and fashions is, in fact, predicated upon a rigorous avoidance of any genuine novelty, a novelty that still existed in the "liberal" bourgeois period. Thus Horkheimer and Adorno's claim that "what is new in the phase of mass culture compared to that of late liberalism is the exclusion of the new. *The machine is rotating on the spot*. While it already determines consumption, it rejects anything untried as a risk."[28]

The exclusion of novelty and the cultivation of passivity are basic preconditions for the proper functioning of mass culture within the "system" as a whole. And the essential "function" of mass culture, according to Horkheimer and Adorno, is to facilitate integration and conformity. It is to create a horizon of experience that relentlessly repeats the message that: (a) capital truly is omnipotent; and (b) that the greatest sin is failure to coordinate one's behavior with the demands of the system.[29] The former message is hammered home by the sheer scale and expense of the latest blockbuster, while the latter message takes more varied (but even more repetitive) forms.

For the most part, Horkheimer and Adorno stress the continuity of form and content in mass culture, the way they ironically approximate the classical ideal and the *Gesmantkunstwerk*. Thus, "The Culture Industry" places great stress upon tempo, editing, repetition, and genre as essential elements of the "formula." The message of these formal elements is that the present we encounter—a landscape of seemingly constant movement and endless novelty—is, in fact, an "eternal" one. "Nothing is allowed to stay as it was, everything must be endlessly in motion. For only the universal victory of the rhythm of mechanical production and reproduction promises that nothing will change, that nothing unsuitable will emerge."[30] Yet despite their fixation on the forms of mass culture as the primary mechanisms through which experience is both processed and truncated, Horkheimer and Adorno also provide a fair amount of what is now termed "content analysis." If the *forms* of mass culture deprive the cultural realm of any *antagonistic* relation to the larger social world (a message not lost on the audience), its *content* and everyday functioning propagate the "deception" Horkheimer and Adorno refer to in their subtitle.

In what ways, then, are we "deceived" by the culture industry? From Horkheimer and Adorno's perspective, the most fundamental would seem to be industry's effective effacement of the distinction between reality and its representation. The more sophisticated film and TV become, the more the "illusion" that "the world outside is a seamless extension of the one which has been revealed in the cinema" predominates.[31] The inability to distinguish between the movies and "real life" afflicts even our political leaders, a fact made much of in analyses of the Reagan and Bush presidencies, and (more abstractly) by post-modern theorists who have stressed the priority of the "virtual."[32] Yet however threatening such an "ontological" illusion may be (and it is threatening, since it deprives us of our first line of resistance to the reality "constructed" by advertising, mass media, and cinematic cliché), it does not reach to the actual ideological content of the world created by the culture industry.

What is the nature of *this* world? What lessons does it teach? The first lesson is found in the nature and temporality of cultural consumption in a "mass" age. Life is divided between work in the factory or office (on the one hand) and the pursuit and consumption of amusement or entertainment (on the other). "The only escape from the work process in factory and office is through adaptation to it in leisure time."[33] Ceaselessly alternating between the routines of work and mass culture consumption, the worker-consumer's life takes on specific and inescapable rhythm, one that imposes the "imprint of the work routine" on all our waking hours.[34] Clocking in, clocking out, a little commodified amusement (dinner out, a movie, TV or perhaps a club), sleep and clocking in again: this eternal return of the same is the underlying message of all mass culture consumption. As Horkheimer and Adorno put it in one of their more memorable aphorisms, "Entertainment is the prolongation of work under late capitalism."[35]

Second, the culture industry teaches the imperative of conformity, while simultaneously fostering a willingness to accept what is offered:

> Anyone who does not conform is condemned to an economic impotence which is prolonged in the intellectual powerlessness of the eccentric loner. Disconnected from the mainstream, he is easily convicted of inadequacy. Whereas the mechanism of supply and demand is today disintegrating in material production, in the superstructure it acts as a control on behalf of the rulers. The consumers are the workers and salaried employees, the farmers and petty bourgeois. Capitalist production hems them in so tightly, in body and soul, that they unresistingly succumb to whatever is proffered them. However, just as the ruled have always taken the morality dispensed to them by the rulers more seriously than the rulers themselves, the defrauded masses today cling to the myth of success still more ardently than the successful. They, too, have their aspirations. They insist unwaveringly on the ideology by which they are enslaved.[36]

This dual message is hammered home by the spunky positivism of a Mickey Rooney and the continually beaten and humiliated Donald Duck.[37] It is echoed and reechoed in the "churches, clubs, professional associations, and other relationships" that, according to Horkheimer and Adorno, "amount to the most sensitive instruments of social control."[38] The message of the movies is that society only rewards its loyal members—a message that is repeated and monitored at every level of civil society. Anyone who thinks Horkheimer and Adorno exaggerate here should reflect for a moment on the peculiarly unquestionable status, within our culture, of the thesis that "with hard work and persistence, you can accomplish anything you want." With one ideological catchphrase—endlessly recycled in TV and movie dramatizations of individuals who "overcome the odds"—the grounding myth of society is established. An entire landscape of structural inequality and injustice is banished from our horizon.

Third, the culture industry teaches a lesson which—at first glance—seems to contradict the ideological imperative of belief in success and a generalized "positivism" à la Mickey Rooney. The "contradictory" lesson is that individuals are fungible, a point driven home by the identification of the shop girl with the not necessarily more beautiful or talented screen goddess, and the generalized lust for celebrity. The people on the movie screen or TV aren't especially different from their audience, the "insuperable separation" between them notwithstanding. This is precisely the (misleading) point. There but for a lucky break (and the requisite publicity) go I. This lesson trickles down to everyday economic life, where the "religion of success" is both modified and supported by the idea that chance plays the leading role in opportunities offered or withheld. One can be what one is—utterly ordinary, not especially gifted, educated, or hard-working—and fortune may still smile. Such, at least, is the ideological message of the Hollywood "lucky break," a message supported by the reality of an increasingly planned economy and the apparent randomness with which training, educational opportunities, and careers are distributed.[39]

Of course, chance doesn't really rule here. It couldn't, given the demands for calculability, rational investment, and a profitable return on both capital and social resources. However, the pervasive idea that it does (purveyed by Hollywood) is crucial, Horkheimer and Adorno think, to providing "the masses" with the illusion that their lot in life is neither fixed nor structurally determined in any way.[40]

Fourth and finally, the culture industry teaches—through its character as ubiquitous and quasi-pornographic come-on—resignation to the present. It does this through its incitement of desire, which is both perpetually aroused and perpetually frustrated. Since growth is a functional imperative of the quasi-planned capitalist economy, "the masses" must be socialized to accept their new role as "eternal consumers." Advertising is the primary vehicle of this socialization, insuring that our needs endlessly proliferate even as (or precisely because) the products themselves fail to deliver any substantial fulfillment.[41]

In principle, this lack of fulfillment could lead to a rejection of consumerism. However, not only is the culture and advertising industry masterly at eroticizing everything (from beer and cars to cell phones and deodorants); it also inscribes and reinscribes the logic of the tease in virtually *all* its proffered entertainments. One goes to the movies or buys a video game on the hyped-up promise of a quasi-orgasmic experience—a *promesse de bonheur* that is never delivered on (nor could it be). This has important consequences for how one views life and responds to the dissatisfactions of an essentially unfulfilled existence. Thus, while the erotic "bait and switch" of 1940s movies may be long gone, the essential structure Horkheimer and Adorno describe is still immovably in place:

> The culture industry replaces pain, which is present in ecstasy no less than in asceticism, with jovial denial [amusement]. Its

supreme law is that its consumers shall at no price be given what they desire: and in that very deprivation they must take their laughing satisfaction. In each performance of the culture industry the permanent denial imposed by civilization is once more inflicted on and unmistakably demonstrated to its victims. To offer them something and to withhold it is one and the same. That is what the erotic commotion achieves. . . . What is decisive today is no longer Puritanism, though it still asserts itself in the form of women's organizations, but the necessity, inherent in the system, of never releasing its grip on the consumer, of not for a moment allowing him or her to suspect resistance is possible.[42]

Taken together, these four lessons—the encompassing temporality of work, the conformity essential to economic survival, the belief in the "religion of success" and its reigning god, Chance, and the quasi-ascetic acceptance of a life in which desire is permanently aroused but fulfillment is endlessly deferred—are driven home by the culture industry in a way which permanently infantilizes its audience, thereby "enslaving" them to the requirements of the "system."

If we connect these lessons back to the more encompassing thesis of a "schematism" performed by the culture industry, we can easily see why Horkheimer and Adorno consider Enlightenment's *telos* in late capitalist commodity culture a form of "mass deception." Our sense of reality, and our interpretation of our own existence, is so ideologically saturated that it can barely, if ever, emerge from the bubble. The Enlightenment's promise of autonomy has, without the least irony, been transformed into a virtually inescapable culture of heteronomy.

At this point, a skeptical reader—perhaps prompted by a faith in science, the market, God, or even "communicative rationality"—will want to shout, "Enough! Horkheimer and Adorno have gone too far." The apparently seamless web of domination they describe depends not only upon an unquestioned Marxian demonization of all things capitalist, but also upon an undifferentiated idea of instrumental or "systemic" rationality, one that absorbs the very possibility of a rational alternative or, indeed, of a rational critique.[43]

I have a certain amount of sympathy for the latter objection (see chapter 7 of this volume). However, before tarring, feathering, and disposing Horkheimer and Adorno as "totalizing critics" of late capitalism, we need to remember a couple of things.

First, the main lines of their critique are hardly original. In fact, they are prefigured by Tocqueville, who pointed not only to a potentially fatal "love of physical gratifications" in America, but also to an unprecedented degree of conformity in behavior and opinions—one he saw grounded in the emerging form of mass culture.[44] Tocqueville also pointed to the potential hegemony of an "aristocracy of manufacturers," something that even the most casual student of American history would have to admit has been partially realized in our day.[45] Finally, it was Tocqueville who warned of a new form of despotism—one that would keep us in "leading strings" and "perpetual childhood," one that would fasten less on our bodies than on our souls.[46] Not for nothing do Horkheimer and Adorno single out his critique of democratic culture as providing the *leitmotif* of their own.[47]

One may acknowledge this connection, and still object that it is a long way from Tocqueville's *fears* to Horkheimer and Adorno's *description* of a new form of "systemic" domination. Ideological structures may well reach into "the most hidden recesses" of our individual lives, but that is no reason to conclude—as Adorno evidently does in the "Dedication" to *Minima Moralia* (1951)—that "the subject is vanishing," or that most of us lead lives that resemble "component parts of machinery."[48]

In fact—and this is the second point we need to recall—neither Horkheimer nor Adorno is committed to a "strong" (Kantian) conception of individual autonomy, one whose contrasting pole is the complete determinism (or heteronomy) found in either the "mechanism of nature" (Kant) or the "mechanism" of late capitalism (Weber).[49] Despite a certain amount of rhetorical exaggeration, their theoretical goal is not to argue for a *Brave New World* level of "false consciousness." Rather, it is to trace the ideological and cultural roots of a new kind of conformism—one that is moralizing, frightened, obtuse, and "wised up" all at the same time. They want to show us the myriad ways we consciously and unconsciously coordinate ourselves to the requirements of the of a rationalized, post-laissez faire capitalism; a "system" run not by the *grand bourgeois* of yore, but by an interlocking directorate of corporate and state interests.[50]

Such coordination has important, and largely negative, consequences for the "learning potential" Kant and the Enlightenment associated with public debate. When our "reality principle" is colonized by the schema of mass culture and the "lessons" taught by the culture industry, the ground for a robust form of human plurality is largely effaced. As Hannah Arendt reminds us, such plurality is the *sine qua non* for any genuine public sphere. Where it doesn't exist, what we get instead is the "appearance of life" and the appearance of political debate. A "totality harmonious through all its antagonisms" results, one in which the sense of the public—of the "universal," general, or common (*allgemein*)—emerges not out of a variety of individual perspectives, but out of jargony fragments filtered from the top down.

Seen from this angle, Adorno's retreat to the "truth"of "damaged" individual experience makes perfect sense.[51] Similarly, his quixotic search for a non-totalizing, non-identity imposing form of aesthetic rationality makes sense in a world where a fictitious and omnipresent "universal" sets the rules of the game (whether in culture, politics, or society). *Pace* Habermas, the reason Adorno neglects intersubjectivity and communicative action as possible alternative sources of moral-political *Bildung* is not because he is entrapped in "the philosophy of the subject."[52] Rather, he spurns this path because he believes that "the public use of one's reason" leads nowhere when the debate is administered and the "audience" in question has been rendered passive and infantilized. To put the point in crude and only somewhat misleading terms, "rational adults" are lacking.

We are, of course, far from being ideological automatons or thought-controlled zombies. Adorno, however, would argue that most of us are all too immediately creatures of the false reality created by the culture industry to be able to take the step back necessary for critical reflection, discourse, and judgment. The usual response to such a stance is to denounce it as yet another instance of "old European" elitism, at odds with the fundamental presuppositions of a democratic culture.

Before we do this, however, we should take a good look at the state of our own public sphere, and the level of its discourse. The fact that politics today relies on advertising, focus groups, the marketing of personalities, and a relentless appeal to the lowest common denominator—to say nothing of outright lies and shameless fear-mongering—should be enough to convince even the most "patriotic" among us that the citizen was long ago absorbed by the "eternal" consumer. Spontaneous and inclusive rational critical debate is nowhere to be seen: what we have is the clash of jargons and advertising campaigns mounted by political parties, "action committees," and corporate interests. The merging of politics, entertainment, and mass culture—a merging Horkheimer and Adorno predicted—is now taken for granted by virtually everyone, even though it was unthinkable a mere thirty years ago.

Well, perhaps not entirely unthinkable. In the early 1960s, two works appeared by Frankfurt School theorists that addressed the current state and prospects of the "political public sphere." The first of these was *The Structural Transformation of the Public Sphere* (1963), the *Habilitation-schrift* of Adorno's former assistant, Jürgen Habermas. The second was Herbert Marcuse's *One-Dimensional Man* (1964). There are great differences in focus and method in these two works, to say nothing of the context and experience of their respective authors.[53] Nevertheless, both works can be fairly (if somewhat lopsidedly) described as attempts to apply the theoretical perspective developed in the "Culture Industry" essay to the reality of postwar society and politics. To what degree had Horkheimer and Adorno's suggestion that the public-political sphere was being absorbed by the culture industry been borne out? In what ways had they gone too far? In what ways had they not gone far enough?

I want to begin with *One-Dimensional Man* (I treat *Structural Transformation* in the next section). Despite its association with a long-dead student left, Marcuse's analysis merits a fairly detailed consideration. By foregrounding Horkheimer and Adorno's basic characterization of postwar society—the end of individuality, the rise of a "system" with which the workers identified—Marcuse was able to offer a striking picture of "advanced industrial society." This was a society in which capitalism, technology, and the national security state (born of the Cold War) were systemically integrated, producing a novel form of domination, one that legitimated itself in terms of productivity, efficiency, and the permanent presence of "the Enemy." These grounds of legitimation also served as the basic means by which this new social form contained any pressure for change from within.

Despite its somewhat dated quality, the Marcusean idea of a closed circle of scientific rationality, capitalist economics, and national security state paranoia still structures the views of many on the cultural or "theory" left.[54] This continuing influence is in part a function of Marcuse's striking assimilation of *Dialectic of Enlightenment's* most basic presuppositions and theoretical arguments. *One-Dimensional Man* is both a digest and extension of these arguments, conveyed in a style considerably less compressed than the original. Horkheimer and Adorno's kernels of truth are delivered in an updated package, one that was (and still is) relatively user-friendly.

Like *Dialectic of Enlightenment, One-Dimensional Man* assumes that certain things have irrevocably changed in the transition to late or "advanced" capitalism. Any theory that takes its inspiration from Marx's presentation of capitalism *as* a structure of domination must take note of the new constellation, or face the charge of historical irrelevance. Marcuse shares with Horkheimer and Adorno the presupposition of a far more organized form of capitalism, one that bears a greater resemblance to Weber's "iron cage" than it does to the contradiction-riven form analyzed in Marx's *Capital*. Hence Marcuse's—and Horkheimer and Adorno's— tense relation to *all* brands of orthodox Marxism. Before turning to Marcuse's updated formulation of the "administered society," I should note the key issues separating Critical Theory from Marxism proper.

First, as indicated at the beginning of this chapter, there is issue of the proletariat. This class had failed to live up to its revolutionary role. Not only that. World War I and the subsequent rise of fascism revealed the consciousness of the proletariat to be seriously if not fatally flawed. The Marxian social epistemology of praxis—in which the working class, by virtue of its place in the production process, is better placed to pierce the veil of commodity fetishism and the appearance of a "nature-like" social reality[55]—turned out to be mere wishful thinking. Critical Theory in its mature form thus departs from the assumption that the consciousness of the proletariat is every bit as reified as that of the bourgeoisie. There is no special epistemological kiss that can wake this particular sleeping beauty from a mystified sense of the world and its place in it. The advent of new bureaucratic structures of formal rationality serve only to solidify the sense of an impenetrable, pre-given, and fundamentally unchangeable reality, one that is hardly the "creation" of the worker.

Second, Marcuse—like Horkheimer and Adorno—assumes that many of capitalism's defining contradictions ("defining" at least from the quasi-Hegelian perspective of *Capital*)[56] have been either resolved or "put on ice." Most notably, planning and expansion of markets have eliminated the periodic crises of overproduction, and the central tension between forces of production and relations of production has been relaxed. In addition, the unequal distribution of socially generated wealth no longer bothers to legitimate itself in terms of the hoary ideology of the "exchange of equivalents." Rather, this unequal distribution (and the hierarchy it presumes) is justified in terms of the vastly increased productivity and efficiency of a technologically integrated, governmentally subsidized and regulated, economy.

Third, the "classical" Frankfurt School position drew on Freud to understand the libidinal investment that the dominated make in the very structures that oppress them. As both the "Elements of Anti-Semitism" chapter of *Dialectic of Enlightenment* and the chapter on "repressive desublimation" in *One-Dimensional Man* demonstrate, the "new forms of domination" (fascism, consumer society) are capable of channeling sexual or aggressive instinctual energy in direct and highly effective ways. The result is an immediate identification on the part of "the masses" with the society that oppresses them—an identification the disenfranchised and pauperized workers of the nineteenth century could never have experienced.

Fourth, the Frankfurt School presumes that images of what it likes to call an "emancipated future" have been increasingly absorbed by "the system," whether this takes the form of consumer society or a fascist *Volksgemeinschaft*. If, as Marx and Engels famously asserted, society sets itself only riddles it can solve, *socialism* can appear as a *concrete possibility* only on the basis of the fullest possible development of capitalist economic forces (and the creation of a "universal" working class that this development makes possible). It was up to the Frankfurt School to show how such transformative possibilities—including the idea of a society in which "the free development of each is the condition for the free development of all"[57]—were absorbed by a productive apparatus that was fully capable of assuring an existence (indeed, an often quite comfortable existence) "to its slave within his slavery."[58]

The commodification of emancipation—especially in the highly seductive form of the "American Dream"—demanded a certain skepticism toward Marx's faith in the "immanent" possibilities opened up by economic and technological development. It also demanded an imaginative-critical step back from the present in order to find non-reified images of happiness and freedom. From the perspective of Marcuse and Adorno, these could be brought to light only through the critical remembrance of a bourgeois and pre-bourgeois past.

Fifth and finally, Horkheimer, Adorno, and Marcuse see it as incumbent upon the Critical Theorist to explain the *end of the individual*. This theme received an influential and powerful formulation in Weber's "Parliament and Government in a Reconstructed Germany" (1917).[59] In that series of articles, Weber envisaged the possibility of private (corporate) and public bureaucracies fusing, creating a "shell of bondage" that "men will perhaps be forced to inhabit one day, as powerless as the fellahs of ancient Egypt." Such a return to the ant heap becomes probable if "a technically superior administration" is allowed to become the "ultimate and sole value" in the ordering of social and political affairs.[60] For Horkheimer and Adorno, there is little doubt that this development has come to pass. Moreover, the culture industry's colonization of our dreams and desires leaves little if any room for a distinctly private, nonconformist existence. The "mass" has absorbed the individual—a conclusion Marcuse accepts and retools for the analysis of consumer society built on a technological rationale.

These five points should be kept in mind as we trace Marcuse's development of the main theses from the "Culture Industry" essay. To anticipate just a bit: I argue that Marcuse's appropriation of the "Culture Industry" essay is more totalizing than anything Horkheimer and Adorno have to offer. On the basis of the assumptions listed above, it effectively denies (a) the continuing possibility of immanent critique; (b) the idea that privacy and autonomous individuality have any partial or concrete existence in the present; and (c) the "existentialist" notion that people retain the capacity to transcend—whether in language, thought, experience, or culture—the society that surrounds them. Marcuse's conception of a "total society"—a society dominated by means of social control as ubiquitous as they are insidious (advertising; the culture industry; the "phony" freedom manifest in consumer and political choices)—consummates and codifies the dystopian potentials set forth in *Dialectic of Enlightenment*. In the process, Marcuse manages to reiterate orthodox Marxism's peremptory dismissal of "bourgeois" (constitutional) democracy, delivering the verdict that our public sphere is the scene of manipulation and control, and nothing more.

Echoing a claim Horkheimer and Adorno make almost in passing in the "Culture Industry" essay, Marcuse notes that "as a technological universe, advanced industrial society is a *political* universe, the latest stage in the realization of a specific historical *project*—namely, the experience, transformation, and organization of nature as the mere stuff of domination." He goes on to state:

> As the project unfolds, it shapes the entire universe of discourse and action, intellectual and material culture. In the medium of technology, culture, politics, and the economy merge into an omnipresent system which swallows up or repulses all alternatives. The productivity and growth potential of this system stabilize the

society and contain technical progress within the framework of domination. *Technological rationality has become political rationality.*[61]

"Technological rationality" is, of course, a successor concept to Weber's notion of purposive or means/end rationality (*Zweckrationalität*). Born of the Enlightenment project of dominating nature, this form of rationality comes into its own when technology emerges not just as the leading edge of economic development and corporate profitability, but as the *primary* integrating agent of scientific research, capitalist expansion, and governmental planning. The establishment of a "universe of technics" is the establishment of a social reality in which the most important subsystems not only interlock, but legitimate themselves precisely in terms of the systemic efficiency their "technological" structuring affords. Politics is then absorbed by technics and by technocratic jargon. As a result, it loses much if not all of its appearance as domination. In an early essay, Habermas concisely summed up Marcuse's basic point concerning the "fusion of technology and domination":

> In industrially advanced capitalist societies, domination tends to lose its exploitative and oppressive character and become "rational," without political domination thereby disappearing. . . . Domination is rational in that a *system* can be maintained which can allow itself to make growth of the forces of production, coupled with scientific and technical progress, the basis of legitimation. . . . The existing relations of production present themselves as the technically necessary organization of a rationalized society. . . . [62]

Technology, in other words, is not simply an *ideology* masking domination, but a form of domination itself. The systemic character of technological civilization—the priority it gives to the values of expertise, efficiency, and operationalism in the context of the larger social "mechanism"—not only marginalizes democratic discourse and decision making. It also reduces the vast majority of citizens—those who are not part of the corporate-scientific-governmental "directorate"—to the status of "inputs" in the "system."[63] Marcuse insists on the *deformations* of a technological civilization, and not just the distortions of a technocratic ideology, because he is absolutely convinced that *the domination of nature through technology is inextricably linked to the domination of man.*

This, of course, is the fundamental thesis of *Dialectic of Enlightenment*, one that—despite Horkheimer and Adorno's rhetorical brilliance in advancing it—is obviously open to challenge. Marcuse's version of it, however, reveals an internal contradiction that Horkheimer and Adorno's formulation tended to conceal. On the one hand, there is Marcuse's quasi-Heideggerian insistence that technology is both a way of seeing and being in the world: in short, a "mode of revealing" (to use Heidegger's locution from his 1953 lecture *Die Frage nach der Technik*).[64] On the other, there is Marcuse's Marxian faith in technology's essential power (as *instrumentum*) to finally "pacify" the human struggle for existence.[65] Such pacification hardly guarantees the passage from the realm of necessity to the realm of freedom invoked by Marx in volume 3 of *Capital*.[66] It is, however, *the* essential precondition for anything like such a transition. Hence the semi-schizophrenic character of *One-Dimensional Man*, a book that holds onto technology as an essential means while decrying it as a "mode of revealing."

This combination of Heideggerian thought trains with Horkheimer and Adorno's basic argument yields Marcuse's description of advanced industrial society as "totalitarian" in nature. The nonmetaphorical intent of this description is confirmed by Marcuse's supposition of a pervasive "false consciousness," one grounded in the "false needs" we have absorbed (via advertising and media) and the numerous social controls we have "introjected."[67] Of course, Marcuse knows better than to argue that *our* lives are suffused with political terror. The "total society" bears not even a superficial resemblance to Nazi or Soviet totalitarianism. But that, in a sense, is precisely the point:

> By virtue of the way it has organized its technological base, contemporary industrial society tends to be totalitarian. For "totalitarian" is not only a terroristic political coordination of society, but also a non-terroristic economic-technical coordination which operates through the manipulation of needs by vested interests. It thus precludes the emergence of an effective opposition against the whole.[68]

Hyperbole aside, one might allow this as a broad characterization of our "liberal," monopoly-capitalist consumer society. Ours is a society, after all, in which governmental and corporate interests are often indistinguishable, thanks in part to the famous "revolving door" between Washington and the corporate sector. Moreover, it is a society economically driven by the feverish creation of ever new "factitious needs."

But such broad agreement can extend only to the most metaphorical use of the term "totalitarian." Marcuse's argument is not limited to the point that late capitalism is a "total" society insofar as state, civil society, and "cultural" life interpenetrate each other, leading to a limited "refeudalization" of social relations by the blurring of essential modern distinctions (like that between state and civil society). Rather, he is arguing that late capitalist-technological society is "totalitarian" because it is a total system, one defined not only by the coordination of science, government, and corporate interests, but also by the effective effacement of the gap between public and private life:

> In this society, the productive apparatus tends to become totalitarian to the extent to which it determines not only the socially needed occupations, skills, and attitudes, but also individual needs and aspirations. It thus obliterates the opposition between the private and public existence, between individual and social needs. Technology serves to institute new, more effective, and more pleasant forms of social control and social cohesion.[69]

Marcuse's entire argument in *One-Dimensional Man* thus hinges on his ability to convince his audience that, all things considered, we have become utterly "social"—and thus utterly heteronomous—beings. Individual consciousness does not stand apart from either "public opinion" or the media. Rather, today it is simply a function of these two forces working in tandem. We are, all of us, "preconditioned receptacles of long standing," the targets of highly sophisticated techniques of psychic manipulation. Indeed, Marcuse argues that, in our context, the Freudian idea of "introjection" is an anachronism, since it "implies the existence of an inner dimension distinguished from and even antagonistic to the external exigencies."[70]

Where desires have been aroused, shaped, and colonized by ubiquitous advertising, and where our behavior and identities are revealed as functions of a deeply mimetic (and non-antagonistic relation) to society as a whole—*there* it no longer makes sense to assume a private sphere in which the rudiments of a nascent individuality can be either preserved or cultivated. The "total society" announces not just the "end of the individual"—his absorption into the mass (as predicted by Tocqueville, Mill, and Weber). More frighteningly, it announces the extirpation of the human capacity for spontaneity as such. In Marcuse's eyes, we have virtually become those "bundle of reflexes" that Arendt—in her analysis of the concentration camps—argued was the ultimate goal of Nazi and Bolshevik totalitarianism.[71] Consumption, not terror, lies at the root of this "immediate identification of the individual with his society":

> The productive apparatus and the goods and services its produces "sells" or imposes the social system as a whole. The means of mass transportation and communication, the commodities of lodging, food, and clothing, the irresistible output of the entertainment and information industry carry with them prescribed attitudes and habits, certain intellectual and emotional reactions which bind the consumers more or less pleasantly to the producers and, through the latter, to the whole. The products indoctrinate and manipulate; *they promote a false consciousness which is immune against its falsehood.* And as these beneficial products become available to more individuals in more social classes, the indoctrination they carry ceases to be publicity; it becomes a way of life.[72]

There is much that one could say about passages such as this, and about Marcuse's related observation that Marxism's central critical category—alienation—ceases to obtain in a society able to foster "immediate" identification through its patent ability to "deliver the goods." Suffice it to note here that a mimetic relationship to social reality is hardly confined to the culture of late capitalism. Indeed, one can see the entire Western philosophical tradition of moral individualism—from Socratic moral individualism to Millian liberalism and Heideggerian existentialism—as insisting on the debilitating tyranny of custom, everydayness, and received opinion.[73] Marcuse is hardly unrelated to this tradition; nor is he unaware of its influence on his thought. He departs from it, however, insofar as he sees the "mimetic" individual less as a partial function of the pull of custom and convention, and more as the comprehensive creation of an increasingly "total" system.

Hence the arch-Marcusean ideas of the hegemony of "one-dimensional thought and behavior" and the "closing of the political universe." The former refers to the mimetic "individual" created by consumer capitalism, an "individual" whose thought and behavior stays entirely within the "established universe of discourse and action." Any contents that might transcend the status quo are reflexively repelled as irrational and dangerous. Reason is identified with the universe of established facts, and progress with the "dynamic capability of producing more and bigger facts of the same sort of life."[74] This positivism of everyday life extends to the dimension of behavior, insofar as each "individual" finds him- or herself cleaving ever more closely to the established codes of normalcy and good function both at home and in the workplace. To *not* do so is to risk being spat out by the "system" as a bad worker or neighbor. It also means sacrificing the contentment—the "happy consciousness," in Marcuse's ironic Hegelian construction—that comes from the relaxing consumption of an array of cultural goods, all of which have been stripped of their alienating (critical) power via the dual process of commodification and massification (otherwise known as "dumbing down").[75]

To these attitudinal-behavioral propensities correspond a set of changes in the sphere of material reproduction itself. These pave the way for the integration of the working class itself, and for the eventual suspension of any residual social tension between "bourgeois" and "proletarian." From Marcuse's perspective, the most important elements are: (a) the transformation of the labor process through technology and automation, a transformation that eliminates the more brutal dimensions of worker exploitation; (b) the integration of working class trades and occupations within an overall "technologized" system of production, one that creates a seemingly objective, functionally necessary hierarchy while simultaneously destroying the professional autonomy found in the old trades; (c) the cultural assimilation of blue- and white-collar workers (in terms of needs, aspirations, standard of living, leisure activities, and so on), a phenomenon that dissolves what remains of class consciousness while promoting the tendency of workers to identify with the corporation as such; and (d) the disappearance of what Marcuse calls "a tangible source of exploitation" behind the facade of objective rationality—that is, the transfiguration of domination into *administration*.[76]

The end result of these related transformations in the workplace is not simply the sealing of so-called "bourgeois" hegemony. More radically, they point to the suspension of the master/slave dialectic itself. The worker under late capitalism might well be reduced to the status of an "instrument" or "thing," utterly dependent upon the "machine" of the corporation and the integrated economy. But this is also the lot of his managing boss as well: "The organizers and administrators themselves become increasingly dependent on the machinery which they organize and administer."[77] Employees at *all* levels are "enslaved" to the economic mechanism, allowing Marcuse to pose the rhetorical question, "Do the technicians rule, or is their rule that of the others, who rely on the technicians as their planners and executors?"[78]

That question leads to another: "Is there any prospect that this growing chain of productivity and repression [of "rational," conformist behavior coordinated to an ever-more productive technological economy] may be broken?"[79] On the basis of everything Marcuse has said up to this point about the rationalization of domination and the spread of consumer "false consciousness," the answer is easy to guess. But it is not just a question of domination losing its oppressive profile, nor of extensive "preconditioning" of the exploited by advertising and media. It is also (and this marks *One-Dimensional Man* as a clear product of the Cold War era) a question of the seemingly permanent presence of "the Enemy." This is the "existential threat" that keeps the economy in a continuous state of mobilization, that accelerates technological development, and that spins out new products and consumer gadgets as quickly as it does ever more deadly weapons.

The welfare state—responsible for raising the standard of "administered" living—and the "warfare state" are thus internally linked. They are, in fact, interdependent halves of the "streamlined technical apparatus" whose survival depends upon ever-increasing productivity.[80] As long as the "administered society" delivers on its promise of an ever-rising standard of living, there is no reason to expect the slightest deviation from "one-dimensional" thought and behavior. As Marcuse writes:

> Rejection of the Welfare state [the administered society] on behalf of abstract ideas of Freedom is hardly convincing. The loss of the economic and political liberties which were the real achievement of the preceding two centuries may seem slight damage in a state capable of making the administered life secure and comfortable. If the individuals are satisfied to the point of happiness with the goods and services handed down to them by the administration, why should they insist on different institutions for a different production of goods and services? And if the individuals are preconditioned so that the satisfying goods also include thoughts, feelings, aspirations, why should they wish to think, feel and imagine for themselves?[81]

Provided with a rising standard of living, preconditioned to find satisfaction in what is offered, and supplied with an ever-widening array of consumer choices, the "one-dimensional" man or woman is, in Marcuse's view, utterly content in their one-dimensionality. The idea that there might be "higher" possibilities—for themselves or their society—simply does not signify. This is especially so in light of the "permanent presence" of "the Enemy." The ideological function of the latter phenomenon is to maintain a high degree of social unity, one that places America's celebrated pluralism within tightly circumscribed—and easily controllable—limits.[82] Thus, Marcuse can conclude his basic argument with the apparently outrageous statement that "democracy would appear to be the most efficient system of domination."[83]

This would indeed be true if social and political antagonisms had been "put on ice" (by economic growth, technological integration, and the Cold War presence of "the Enemy") to anywhere near the degree Marcuse stipulates. The seemingly invincible "system" turned out to be riven by a good deal more social and political tension than the émigré Marcuse—his eyes fastened firmly on the "setting" of the antagonism between bourgeois and proletarian in "late" capitalism—could possibly have imagined.[84] It is only if we accept the picture of an expanding technological society smoothly "delivering the goods" that we can understand the last and perhaps most characteristic twist in Marcuse's argument: his assertion of *closure* of our horizon of existential possibility, a closure intimately tied to the dissolution of high culture's critical message in a sea of commodification.

A good deal of the pathos of Horkheimer and Adorno's "Culture Industry" essay derived from the latter's never-repudiated faith in the critical capacity of high or "autonomous" art. In the post-bourgeois era, the fact that high art is not only commodified, but absorbed and functionally retooled as mass culture, means that this negative capacity is largely expunged. "Processed" by the culture industry, art loses even the semblance of autonomy. It becomes a storehouse of styles and motifs for popular culture, a mass-reproduced means of relaxation and leisure-time consumption.

Marcuse's reformulation of this argument in *One-Dimensional Man* provides a highly accessible guide to the Frankfurt School's expectations of high culture, and underlines the reasons for its postwar despair. It also dramatically illustrates just how marginal the institutionalized "public-political sphere" had become for the Frankfurt School. Viewed from the standpoint of "classic" Critical Theory, the public-political realm presented little more than administered debate, "mediatized" manipulation, and an essentially phony pluralism. The *Bildung* necessary for the emergence of a critical consciousness (and a widened sense of personal and social possibility) was hardly to be found here. In contrast, art—especially in its high bourgeois, early-nineteenth-century incarnation—represented an opposi-tional order, one "irreconcilably antagonistic to the order of business, indicting it and denying it."[85] It presumed a certain level of alienation or "unhappy consciousness," while simultaneously preserving subversive images of a genuinely "reconciled" existence (taken, in large part, from the pre-bourgeois past).[86] Broadly speaking, the high culture of the bourgeois epoch embodied what Marcuse calls the "rationality of negation," the "Great Refusal—the protest against that which is."[87]

And today? The novel feature of the present is

> the flattening out of the antagonism between culture and social reality through the obliteration of the oppositional, alien, and transcendental elements in the higher culture by virtue of which it constituted another dimension of reality. This liquidation of two-dimensional culture takes place not through the denial and rejection of "cultural values," but through their wholesale incor-poration into the established order, through their reproduction and display on a massive scale.[88]

By transforming the alien oeuvres of intellectual and artistic culture into "familiar goods and services," endlessly reproduced and consumed, mass culture invalidates the "subversive force," the "destructive content," the truth of the great anti-bourgeois works of art.[89] The result is that the "Great Refusal" is itself refused in technological society—not by any "abstract negation," but by a thorough incorporation and circulation in the channels of commerce and leisure-time consumption. Cherished images of transcendence of the kind we find in Bach or Beethoven, Shelley or Word-sworth, Baudelaire or the Surrealists, are invalidated by being incorporated into "omnipresent daily reality." The "essential gap" between the arts and the order of the day is "progressively closed by the advancing technologi-cal society."[90] Even language is reified to the point where the "communica-tion of transcending contents" becomes "technically impossible."[91] The only hope for an exit from this cultural/societal cul-de-sac would seem to lie with those "outcasts and outsiders, the exploited and persecuted of other races and other colors, the unemployed and the unemployable"—namely, those whom "the system" has either spat out or repelled from the beginning. As Marcuse puts it, "Their opposition is revolutionary even if their consciousness is not."[92]

This appeal to an Other who is "revolutionary" by the sheer fact of their otherness marks the end of immanent critique and the struggle for social justice as traditionally conceived. The logic and absorptive power of "the system" is such that only a "radical trembling from the outside" will do the trick.[93]

It is easy to caricature the "adolescent" quality of such a stance, and—mixing realism with a more status quo-friendly "idealism"—to point out the fundamental importance of "bourgeois" democracy's basic institutions as the *sine qua non* of any viable reform. It is easy, in other words, to play Hegel to Marcuse's (or Horkheimer and Adorno's) Marx. This is especially the case given Marxism's oft-noted lack of interest in the problem of institutionalizing freedom.[94] This lack of interest is manifest on virtually every page of *Dialectic of Enlightenment* and *One-Dimensional Man*. However, before we accuse Marcuse of throwing the liberal democratic baby out with the "technological" bath water (something he is, on the whole, guilty of), we should note a few things.

First, it is indeed dubious to view the political-public sphere as part of a closed circuit of technological rationality. Doing so reduces this sphere to the status of media-manipulated "appearances" and bogus electoral contests between Tweedle-Dee and Tweedle-Dum.[95] It is to posit—a priori, as it were—that this sphere can never be the home of a critical or dissolvent rationality, a rationality that helps cut through illusions rather than simply underwriting their proliferation. That said, it must be acknowledged that Marcuse—like Horkheimer and Adorno—gets certain aspects of our contemporary public sphere right. It is, essentially, a "mediatized" public sphere, one in which advertising and the manipulation of symbols and popular resentments plays a far greater role than anything approximating rational—or even rhetorical—debate. Our fundamental *political* reality is one of photo-ops, press releases reported as news, and the relentless testing of policy initiatives through focus group research.

Second, we are "pre-conditioned" to a surprising degree, even if we are not as herd-like in our conformity as Marcuse suggests. "Pre-conditioning" should be understood less as a form of brainwashing (an interpretation fostered by the bogus parallel between so-called "hard" and "soft" totalitarianism) than as what it unquestionably and irrefutably is: the shaping and manipulation of our desires by media. Our ideas of the lives we want to lead are often lifted wholesale from the "aspirational" advertising aimed at people of our "demographic." The array of consumer and lifestyle choices we confront may be far wider than anything Marcuse imagined, but the fact remains that we respond to cues we have been conditioned to accept since early childhood. Indeed, the fact that some of our most voracious and unreflective consumers have degrees from "elite" colleges and universities demonstrates that it is not merely the uneducated who respond more or less blindly to the false *promesse de bonheur* held out by the advertising and lifestyle industries.

Third, while it is all too easy to frame our pluralism as "false" or bogus, it is also easy to exaggerate its real presence in our political landscape and the workings of our political institutions. Reflexive invocations of Tocqueville and *Federalist* 10 should not blind us to the fact that neither a strong pluralism nor a truly viable system of "countervailing powers" exists in America today. Corporate power is too strong, and the press too fearful for its own survival, for anything like a robust pluralism (of either interests or views) to exist.

When we add to these factors the remarkable success the second Bush administration has had in cowing or co-opting the other branches of government, we are forced to acknowledge that our pluralism may be a mile wide, but it is often only an inch deep. Distracted by superficial differences of religious, ethnic, and racial identity, we let the government and the corporations have their way. "System" may be too strong and misleading a word for this non-edifying reality, but the domination of special interests, combined with the revolving door between government and the corporate sector, tells us much if not all of what we need to know about the contemporary health of our "pluralist" civil society.

Fourth and finally, the welfare/warfare state linkage has hardly survived in quite the form Marcuse envisaged. The discipline of the globalized market for labor, and not the comfort of an implicit or explicit social democracy, currently plays a far greater role in enforcing social "integration." This anxiety is everywhere on display, from newly arrived immigrants willing to do almost anything to get on the lowest rung of the economic ladder to the hysteria surrounding college and university admissions. The latter is as sure a sign as any that the American middle and upper middle classes are well aware of the increasingly caste-like character of our society, and are willing to pay almost any price to "guarantee" their children's permanent membership in the managerial class that serves the super-rich.

The "warfare state," on the other hand, is alive and well, achieving its integrating function through deployment of the simple Schmittian dichotomy of "friends" and "enemies." When a global threat to "our way of life" is relentlessly hyped, it is reasonable to expect the silencing of dissent and the emasculation of countervailing powers. Yet if democracy is about anything, it is about different political points of view and the arguments that arise between them. This is the content of any (even vaguely) democratic public sphere. The fact that our post–Cold War warfare state has repeatedly tried to portray disagreement as the moral equivalent of treason speaks volumes about the current condition of our political pluralism.

All of this is merely to state the obvious: namely, that our public sphere has been colonized and perverted, and not merely by a chance configuration of what Jeremy Bentham called "sinister interests." "False consciousness" may not be our problem, but consumer consciousness does threaten the minimal attentiveness to public-political matters that is essential for the survival of democratic forms. Pluralism exists, but it has been radically foreshortened by the increasingly unholy nexus of corporate and state power. Our public sphere has been whittled down to staged media events, shameless advertising, and orchestrated harangues à la Rush Limbaugh. The result is that the democratic promise of self-government has been replaced by impotent venting on call-in shows and in the blogosphere. Add to this the shameful state of literacy and public education in this country, and one might well conclude that the American *demos* is heading toward a permanent twilight of partly self-inflicted (and partly self-enforced) *Unmündigkeit*.

It was the latter possibility that Marcuse—and Horkheimer and Adorno—envisaged. This gives their work, for all its faults and rhetorical exaggerations, a continuing relevance. Indeed, confronted with the infantilization of our political debate, the absorption of the public realm by the media, and the cretinizing spread of a culture of "repressive desublimation," one might well argue that the only problem with "classic" Frankfurt School theory is that they didn't go far enough.

But that would be a mistake. However prescient the analyses of the "classic" Frankfurt School turned out to be with respect to the fate of the public in modern consumer societies, they are based on two flawed assumptions. The first is that there is a strong and distinct epistemic alternative to a public sphere soaked in ideology (call it *Ideologiekritik*, reflective consciousness, or "rational" discourse).[96] The second is that the "bourgeois public sphere" was, from the very beginning, fraudulent in character, the home of an illusory reconciliation of individual or sectional interests and the common good. From the perspective of the early Frankfurt School, recent historical tendencies only underlined the essentially ideological role played by the public realm and public opinion in effecting this bogus "reconciliation."[97]

Habermas and the "Bourgeois Public Sphere"

While retaining a certain amount of descriptive power, Marcuse's critique of "advanced industrial society" terminates in a critical dead-end. The same can be said of Horkheimer and Adorno's *Dialectic of Enlightenment*. As a number of writers have pointed out, the first generation Frankfurt School theorists were far too reliant upon Weber's formalization of reason metanarrative.[98] They fully and uncritically accepted the Weberian idea that rationalization meant the domination of an increasingly formal and purposive rationality—one that facilitated the workings of "self-regulating" economic and social systems, but which repulsed any effort by associated individuals to reassert even minimal control over their creations.[99]

In Weber's original formulation, the increasing predominance of *Zweckrationalität* in the modern age ultimately yielded a bureaucratic-economic "iron cage."[100] In Horkheimer and Adorno's reformulation, it was instrumental rationality which ran amok, creating the reified structures of an "administered society" bent on dominating both man and nature. Finally, in Marcuse's version, "technological rationality" establishes the closed universe of the "system," rebuffing not only alternative forms of consciousness and behavior, but the very possibility of immanent critique. No concrete set of standards or institutional practices existed through which the "false society" might be called to account or prodded to change in light of its own historic ideals.

Common to all three iterations of the "administered society" is the assumption that the values and institutions of the public-political sphere would be swallowed up by the relentless advance of bureaucratic-formal or "administrative" rationality. Hence Weber's appeal to charismatic leadership in "Politics as a Vocation." Hence Adorno and Marcuse's respective appeals to the aesthetic realm. Unless some alternative source of value—the "inwardly called leader," "aesthetic rationality," "autonomous" art—could be found, the "disenchantment of the world" apparently led to a new form of bondage. Public freedom, the autonomous individual, and the cherished Enlightenment linkage between reason and emancipation all seemed destined for extinction.

It fell to Habermas to find a way out of this impasse. As is well known, he did this by insisting on a two-track model of rationalization/modernization. On the one hand, there was formal or bureaucratic rationalization, a process that proceeded in pretty much the manner Weber and the early Frankfurt School described. But on the other hand there was communicative rationalization: the widespread tendency within the modernizing West for *argument and the giving of reasons all can accept* to take over the business of "redeeming" truth or rightness claims.[101] Alongside the phenomenon of formal or "system" rationalization, then, there emerges the characteristically modern practice of what Habermas calls the "discursive redemption of validity claims." This practice is deeply at odds with traditional (hierarchical) sources of meaning and authority, as well as the stripped down instrumental imperatives of the "system." In opposition to the latter, it privileges not authority or efficiency, but the *force of the better argument*. Historically speaking, this practice was concretely (if inadequately) instantiated in some of the central institutions of constitutional democracy—among them, the public sphere itself.

It would lead me too far astray to trace how Habermas uses the idea of communicative rationalization to (a) sketch an alternative path of modern social evolution; and (b) provide an "immanent" normative basis for a critical theory of society. This story has been well told by others, notably Benhabib, McCarthy, and Wellmer.[102] What I want to do is look at the historical-sociological investigations contained in Habermas's first book, *The Structural Transformation of the Public Sphere*, the better to grasp the concrete inspiration behind his later theory of communicative action. My (uncontroversial) preliminary thesis is that the idealized model of the "bourgeois public sphere" outlined in *Structural Transformation* provides Habermas with a normative ideal he never abandoned, throughout all the twists and turns of his subsequent development.[103] For complicated reasons—some good, some bad—this ideal gets repackaged as a quasi-transcendental set of arguments about the nature of communicative interaction as such.

My guiding questions in this section are thus as follows. First, what was Habermas trying to accomplish when he "recovered" the idea of the public sphere for a theoretical tradition that had largely dismissed it as ideology and anachronism? Second, why did he feel the need to "go transcendental" in his later theory? How had the sociological and historical approach of *Structural Transformation* "failed" him? Third, what is it about Habermas's construal of *opinion publique* in *Structural Transformation* that makes this later trascendentalizing move both possible and plausible to him?

With respect to the last question, my semi-controversial conclusion is that Habermas remains tied to the myth of an *ordre naturel*—that is, to the myth of a unitary and rationally discernable public good, a myth originally articulated by the physiocrats and *philosophes* in their efforts to instruct royal power about the "general interest" of society. This is not to say that there is anything strongly a priori about Habermas's conception of democratic deliberation and its outcomes (as there is, for example, in Rousseau). Nevertheless, he cleaves to the rationalist assumption that— freed from the coercion of the state, the interference of sectional interests, and the distortions of ideology—our arguments about the public good will tend toward consensus. Under such reformed conditions, the previously obscured general interest will (finally) be able to emerge.

◆

In a 1981 interview with Axel Honneth, Habermas remarked that "on the level of political theory, the old Frankfurt School never took bourgeois democracy very seriously."[104] This is an understatement. This lack of seriousness extends to the early bourgeois conception of the public sphere. For Horkheimer, Adorno, and Marcuse, this much-lauded arena of public argument and opinion formation appeared as little more than the site of a false reconciliation between the "universal" and the "particular"—a reconciliation effected through manipulative ideological means that clearly served the bourgeois class. Instead of providing a genuine *mediation* of particular and general interests, the bourgeois public sphere was—from the very beginning—a Trojan horse designed to create the *appearance* of universalism while maintaining the reality of class domination.

Habermas thought this cavalier dismissal was a grave mistake, which he sought to rectify with his *Habilitationschrift* on the public sphere.[105] The guiding intuition of *The Structural Transformation of the Public Sphere* was that the emergence of a "critical publicity" in England, France, and Germany in the eighteenth century marked an epoch in the (potential) rationalization of state power and public authority. The "proto-public spheres" created in London coffeehouses, Paris *salons*, and German *Tischgesellschaften* not only taught their habitués the all-important practices of public argument and "critical-rational" judgment. They also pointed toward the eventual integration of informed public opinion in the representative institutions of constitutional ("bourgeois") democracy. However, in the late nineteenth and early twentieth centuries, working class struggle and the expansion of the suffrage helped create a "mass" electoral politics, one characterized less by critical-rational debates than by bureaucratized political parties competing for plebiscitary acclamation.[106] The "critically reasoning" bourgeois gave way to Weber's "foot soldier on the battlefield of elections," who in turn gave way to the passive consumer of political advertising and staged candidate debates (of the sort we Americans are all too familiar with).

As we will see, this basic account of the "structural transformation" of the public sphere—from critically reasoning public to media-manipulated "public opinion"—owes much to the old Frankfurt School. What is crucial for Habermas, however, is the way in which the idea and practice of publicly *criticizing and rationalizing* laws and acts of state emerge during the early "bourgeois" period (roughly 1700–1830). This emergence marks an epoch in the politics of the West, signaling the beginning of the end of the monopoly on political power and judgment held by the sovereign European state. *Raison d'état* began to give way—gradually and fitfully, to be sure—to the principle of critical publicity and the idea that the state should pursue and protect society's interest, not merely its own.

The idea of an institutionalized space in which public opinion can organize itself, becoming a critical filter through which laws and enactments must pass if they are to have legitimacy, cannot be taken for granted. It is, rather, a contingent historical development, one we owe to a particular period. As Habermas puts it, "Public discussions about the exercise of political power which are both critical in intent and institutionally guaranteed have not always existed—they grew out of a specific phase of bourgeois society and could enter into the order of the bourgeois constitutional state only as a result of a particular constellation of interests."[107]

Before entering a discussion of the specifics of this historical constellation, a word must be said about the concept of the "public sphere" itself. Today, this concept is used fairly promiscuously, with little regard to societal "location" or historical context. Thus, the Greek ("agonistic") public sphere is sometimes juxtaposed to a more deliberative ("bourgeois") public sphere, with proponents of each trying to persuade us why one is better than the other. For Habermas, however, the concept of the public sphere is irreducibly *modern* in nature:

> By "the public sphere" we mean first of all a realm of our social life in which something approaching public opinion can be formed. Access is guaranteed to all citizens. A portion of the public sphere comes into being in every conversation in which private individuals assemble to form a public body. They then behave

neither like business or professional people transacting private affairs, nor like members of a constitutional order subject to the legal constraints of a state bureaucracy. Citizens behave as a public body when they confer in an unrestricted fashion—that is, with the guarantee of freedom of assembly and association and the freedom to express and publish their opinions—about matters of general interest.[108]

The key phrase in the above definition is: "in which *private individuals* assemble to form a public body." What this phrase points to is a distinctively modern configuration of public and private, state and civil society. We are private individuals and legal persons first, politically active citizens second. The Greek public realm, in contrast, gave the status of citizenship an unquestionable priority—a priority upheld by the restriction of economic activity to the *oikos* and the performance of the bulk of such activity by women and slaves. In contrast, the modern individual is (as Hegel, Constant, and Tocqueville all emphasized) a creature of civil society, one with interests of his own. He enters the public sphere *not* to perform glorious deeds on a public stage, for an audience of civic peers (the "agonistic" conception).[109] Rather, he enters it in order to assert the interests of society against the overweening prerogatives of the state, to make the interests of "the public" known.

In its basic character as the "place" where "private people come together as a public," the modern public sphere is a "sphere which mediates between state and society."[110] Initially a "part" of civil society (broadly construed), the modern public sphere gradually comes to include the basic deliberative and representative institutions of constitutional democracy.[111] It is through the latter, Habermas argues, that the "political public sphere" gains an "institutionalized influence" over the governmental and administrative functions of the state.[112]

So conceived, the modern public sphere has a vital political function, albeit one not nearly as glamorous as the ancient public realm. Through a variety of means—political associations, the press, media, representative institutions, and so on—it applies the principle of public information to governmental activity. This helps assure that state policies serve the interest of society, an interest that is articulated through the self-organization of public sphere itself. This broad conception has deep roots in the tradition of liberal constitutionalism going back to Locke. What is notable in Habermas's formulation, however, is how the public sphere has a function every bit as crucial as the press (the so-called "fourth estate") and political representatives themselves. Indeed, it is that larger "watch dog" and venue for "democratic will formation," one that includes the press and representative organs, rather than being merely ancillary to them.

It is the rise and decline of such a robustly active, critical public sphere that Habermas traces in *Structural Transformation*. In many respects, this rise and decline is a function of a certain kind of civic *Bildung*, one available in early decades of the public sphere's development but now increasingly rare. This education is not the "education to citizenship" familiar to us from the civic republican tradition (with its stress on patriotism, civic virtue, and military discipline). Rather, it is an education in the deliberative arts and "the public use of one's reason." Such an education, Habermas argues, could be had in the early stages of the formation of the "bourgeois public sphere." Unsurprisingly, he argues that the social and institutional preconditions for such an education are today simply lacking. As a result, the public sphere ceases to be a space in which rational deliberation plays a central role. Neither the negative function of critical interrogation of governmental policies nor the positive one of "democratic will formation" are carried out by "private people coming together as a public." Publicity, once an intrinsically critical principle, is now known to us only in its bastardized, Madison Avenue form, as public relations.[113]

One could argue, à la Hannah Arendt or Tocqueville, that the absence of such civic *Bildung* in our time is largely due to a lack of accessible public spaces. The people remain privatized and infantilized, locked within the horizon of their own self-interest, largely because they have been frozen out of meaningful public participation and debate. Give them something to do, and a place to do it, and the problem will begin to take care of itself.[114]

For Habermas, the contemporary decline of the public sphere is more complex, and the character of the *Bildung* he seeks is more involved. In order to understand the latter—namely, the skills and abilities cultivated in, and required for, a robust public sphere—we have to trace his story about the emergence of the "bourgeois public sphere" in eighteenth-century Europe. How was it that the bourgeoisie came to learn the art of critical-rational judgment, the art so crucial to a properly functioning public sphere?

The poignancy of this question is hard for us to appreciate, since—as Tocqueville reminds us—participation in public-political affairs had been a hallmark of American life even in colonial times. Yet the rise of absolutist monarchies in Europe destroyed what little remained of feudal representative structures (usually, assemblies of the "estates"). As a result, the "rising middle class" Guizot made so much of had no political experience, and no public consciousness, to fall back on. They were, in effect, *purely* private persons engaged in strictly economic activity—an activity overseen, sometimes directed, and frequently interfered with by an unresponsive public authority (the monarchical state). The liberty they had was "the liberty of a subject," a liberty Hobbes famously described as "the liberty to buy, and sell, and otherwise contract with one another; to chose their own aboad, the own diet, their own trade of life, and institute their children as they themselves think fit."[115]

Confined to the private sphere by the absolutist state's monopoly on political power and judgment, the emerging bourgeois class had to learn the art of the "public use of one's reason" elsewhere, in a *nonpolitical sphere*. The proto-public sphere that grew up in the coffee houses, salons, and *Tischgesellschaften* of the late seventeenth and early eighteenth centuries was, therefore, primarily a *literary public sphere*, one devoted to debating cultural productions and cultivating a new, bourgeois form of sociability. It was here that the educated (literate) members of the bourgeois class learned the arts of judgment and persuasion, and gradually came to form a "critical public" (albeit one often tutored, at least in its initial stages, by aristocratic elements).[116]

The various meeting grounds of the "literary public sphere" gave the bourgeoisie the opportunity not only to debate and exchange opinions about novels, poetry, painting, and plays (and thereby learn the art of *öffentliches Räsonnement*). According to Habermas, they also created the basic institutional structure necessary for ongoing debate amongst "private" persons. While obviously different in size and composition, the coffeehouses, salons, and *Tischgesellschaften* all had certain criteria in common—criteria that provided the institutional "blueprint," so to speak, for the soon-to-emerge political public sphere.

First, all these spaces were characterized by the bracketing of rank and unequal social status. In the diverse spaces of the literary public sphere, a fundamental trust and equality prevailed amongst discursive participants. The commoner could address the aristocrat as an equal partner in cultural debate, confident that only the "force of the better argument" would carry the day.[117] Second, the literary public sphere began the trend of *problematizing* topics and areas of culture (such as philosophy, literature, and art) that had previously been the sole preserve of church and court. The "commodification of culture" in the early bourgeois era was crucial to making an array of cultural contents available to a wider range of people than ever before. This was a basic precondition not only for the rise of public debate and criticism, but for the shattering of previously unquestioned interpretive monopolies. Third, the "culture-debating" literary public was, in principle, inclusive—open to anyone with access to books, plays, or journals (the literate and at least minimally propertied).[118]

According to Habermas's history, then, it was in the domains of art, theater, and literary criticism that two absolutely crucial ideas emerged: first, that *there was no higher authority than the force of the better argument*; second, that rational people were precisely those *who were willing to let themselves be persuaded by such arguments*.[119] These basic ideas underlie the developing notions of a "critical publicity," and of the public—and "public opinion"—as a critical authority.[120] Habermas suggests that it was only a matter of time before the bourgeois class, having tutored itself in the arts of critical judgment, would turn its attention to the state interventions, rules, and decrees that directly and negatively impacted the "social" sphere (the sphere of economic reproduction and commodity exchange). In other words, it was only a matter of time before the "public sphere in the world of letters" would be "functionally converted" for the task of criticizing public (state) authority.[121]

This reorientation of the nascent public sphere—the move from strictly cultural matters toward criticism of a hitherto sacrosanct public authority—was the result of an inevitable clash between bourgeois economic interests and the interventionist policies of the mercantilist state. The latter, it is true, had cultivated economic growth and the emergence of civil society. However, it was soon perceived as the source of impositions that distorted and damaged the *ordre naturel* of free commodity exchange. Thus, the "bourgeois" public-political sphere comes into existence at precisely at the moment when (as Hannah Arendt put it) "the fact of mutual dependence for the sake of life and nothing else assume public significance."[122] At this moment the long and increasingly tension-filled relationship between state and civil society was born. The "politicization" of the nascent public sphere—its turn to the critique of public authority and its support of the rule of law and more governmental transparency— was the result of a quarrel over how "civil society" (the "private" sphere of economic reproduction, trade, and the creation of value) should be regulated.[123]

Even at this early stage, two points must be emphasized regarding Habermas's genealogy of the bourgeois public sphere. First, Habermas makes no attempt to conceal the fact that the project of publicly institutionalized criticism of governmental authority has its origins in what, to our eyes, might well appear to be the strictly selfish interests of a specific, economically powerful, social class. The "bourgeois public sphere" was indeed bourgeois.[124] Its roots and impetus for expansion are to be found in the economic interest the bourgeois class had in making state power less arbitrary and more responsive. Of course, capitalism needed the state to "take off" in the seventeenth and eighteenth centuries, but it needed a less intrusive and more predictable state. The normative idea of the "public sphere" as we know it—as a space for the formation of public opinion and for the holding governmental authorities to account—has its origins precisely in the tense relations between early capitalism and the state.[125] This is something Habermas wants to highlight, the better to separate the rational kernel of the "bourgeois public sphere"—its focus on a public space of critical-rational debate—from the ideological chaff (the bourgeois pretense to represent society's interest as a whole).

Second, the state/society tension at the root of the bourgeois public sphere has important consequences for how we think of the *mission* of the public sphere—not only in its "bourgeois" incarnation, but in our own time as well. From the beginning, that mission was to articulate and defend *society's* interest against the (far less general) prerogatives of the state. The principles and practice of "critical publicity" and "critical-rational debate" may have grown up via the dubious equation of *society's* interest with those of the bourgeois class. Nevertheless, the key thing is less the tainted or ideological character of this equation than the idea that, first, *society has an interest contrary to the absolutist* state (a notion that forms the basis of Locke's *Two Treatises* and the subsequent development of all liberal constitutionalism); and second, that the only way to bring state and society into some kind of rough harmony is by restricting governmental power in accordance with the "general interest" discovered by and articulated in the public sphere itself.

With these two points in mind, we can turn to Habermas's exposition of the historical linkage between a universalizing (and "morally pretentious") rationality, and the emergent bourgeois public sphere:

Historically, the polemical claim of this kind of rationality was
developed, in conjunction with the critical public debate among

private people, against the reliance of princely authority on se-
crets of state. Just as secrecy was supposed to serve the maintenance of sovereignty based on *voluntas*, so publicity was supposed
to serve the promotion of legislation based on *ratio*. Locke already
tied the publicly promulgated law to a common consent; Montesquieu reduced it altogether to *raison humaine*. But it remained
for the physiocrats . . . to relate the law explicitly to *public opinion as the expression of reason*. A political consciousness developed in the public sphere of civil society which, in opposition to
absolute sovereignty, articulated the concept of and demand for
general and abstract laws and which ultimately came to assert itself
(i.e., public opinion) as the only legitimate source of this law.[126]

As Habermas notes, the physiocrats' thought played a key role in linking
the idea of universal legal norms to a rational (and rationalizing) public
opinion. Formed in a discursive realm in which claims of status, secrecy,
and authority were bracketed, *opinion publique* was—in the physiocrats'
view—well situated to discover the *ordre naturel* of both trade and civil
society.[127] The essential point was that *opinion publique* was not "just"
opinion, but rather "an opinion purified through critical discussion in
the public sphere."[128] As conceived by the physiocrats, *opinion publique*
was therefore the expression of a *publique éclairé*. Building on conceptual transformations performed by Hobbes, Bayle, Locke, and Burke,
they were able to abolish not only the distance between *opinion* and
critique, but also dismantle the more deeply set philosophical opposition between *opinion* and *truth*. *L'opinion publique* was "the enlightened
outcome of common and public reflection on the foundations of social
order," an outcome that "encapsulated [social order's] natural laws."[129]
The wise king would not rule by *voluntas* alone, but pass his ideas
through the critical filter provided by *opinion pubique* and its articulation of the *ordre naturel*.

For obvious reasons, the physiocratic doctrine of a "dual authority"
of royal *voluntas* and an enlightened, public *ratio* did not survive the
French Revolution. Yet however stop-gap this doctrine might appear in
retrospect, it is important to appreciate the extent of the physiocrats'
achievement. More than anyone else in Habermas's story, they can be
credited with performing the conceptual innovations necessary for the
idea and ideology of the "bourgeois public sphere" to take flight. It was
the physiocrats who established, at least in principle, the potential legis-

lative authority of a critical public opinion based on an *ordre naturel*.[130] Rousseau and the French Revolution attempted to cash out this legislative authority in terms of the *volonté générale*. In the process, however, they fatally undermined the importance of debate and deliberation to opinion formation. As a result, an acclamatory public took the place of a critical-rational public in the theoretical equation. Democracy was achieved, but at the cost of public debate and the process of mutual enlightenment.[131]

It remained for Kant to give full theoretical articulation to the idea of the public sphere as the mediating link between morality and politics, reason and policy. This he did, famously, in his "An Answer to the Question: What is Enlightenment?" (1784). There he argued not only for man's emergence from his "self-incurred tutelage," but for the freedom to make "public use of one's reason" in all matters. "The public use of man's reason must always be free," Kant categorically pronounced, "and it alone can bring about enlightenment among men."[132] Of course, Kant immediately circumscribed the "public use of one's reason" to the "man of learning" addressing "the entire reading public," the better to avoid the charge that his call for enlightenment encouraged disobedience.[133] From Habermas's perspective, the important point is that Kant makes a philosophical defense of the public sphere of critical argument, a defense which—at least in principle—encourages *everyone* to see themselves as potential contributors, as "learned individuals" no matter what their vocation.[134]

Kant, of course, was writing under the paternalistic surveillance of an "enlightened" despot, Frederick the Great. Hence the excessive prudence of his formulation, a prudence manifest in his complete rejection of the idea that a person in his private capacity (as soldier, as academic employee of the state, and so on) has any right to challenge authority, and in his denial that an oppressed people has any right to resistance or revolution.[135] This circumspection under absolutist conditions should not, however, blind us to Kant's great achievement as a theorist of the public sphere: his insistence that the principles of reason and publicity belong together, and together form a veritable moral test for *any* law or enactment of political authority. The famous universalizability criterion of the categorical imperative is given a concrete and (so to speak) three-dimensional existence in a public sphere constituted by critically reasoning citizens (a public sphere which, as Kant well knew, would come fully into being only with the advent of republican government).[136] This is the force behind Kant's well-known declaration that "*freedom of the pen* is the only safeguard of the rights of the people."[137] It is, moreover, the force behind his insistence on the importance of communicability as a standard for rational validity.[138]

For all his insistence on the importance of a critical publicity, and on man as a being possessed of intrinsic dignity, Kant could not bring himself to allow the propertyless into the discursive confines of the public realm.[139] From his perspective, the poor lacked the most basic conditions necessary for even the semblance of "disinterested," rational judgment. Insofar as Kant dealt with this aporia in his idea of the public realm, he did so by invoking "natural" forces at work in history, forces that would bring about—behind our backs, as it were—a more equitable juridical condition.[140]

It was up to Hegel and Marx to foreground the havoc that "civil society" and the interests of the propertied could play with the public sphere. The price of this foregrounding was a structural diminishment in the importance of *opinion publique* itself. For Hegel, "informed" public opinion was important, but hardly the sole or most important criterion of "the universal."[141] For Marx, public opinion was little more than a mask for class interests. The public would express the general interest only when class hierarchy itself was abolished. At that point in history, the interest of society would emerge more or less spontaneously, undistorted by faction, interest, or ideology. Debate and deliberation would become largely superfluous, since the interest of society would be as clear and distinct as Rousseau's "constant, unalterable, and pure" *volonté générale*.[142]

Like Rousseau, Marx's conception of the common good (or general interest) retains more than a few traces of the physiocrats' *ordre naturel*.[143] There *was* an objective, identifiable social interest out there, one that could be discovered by means of a *publique éclairé*, a civic "communion of hearts" (Rousseau), or a truly universal class (Marx). Habermas is acutely aware of the problems attending all three versions of this rationalist faith. Nevertheless, following Kant and the physiocrats' lead, he maintains his loyalty to the idea of a rationally discoverable "general interest," one that can be teased out and articulated through the basic structures of an egalitarian public sphere.[144]

From Habermas's point of view, then, the problems attending our contemporary public sphere have nothing to do with the grounding assumption on which the idea the "bourgeois public sphere" was based—namely, that there is indeed a "general interest" that reveals itself through undistorted communication or a "rationalized" public opinion. Rather, such problems arise from the "structural transformation" this sphere underwent in the period from 1850 to 1960, a period that witnessed the rise of party politics, plebiscitary democracy, and the corruption of public opinion through the art of public relations. It is this transformation—and not the elusive (or even fictional) quality of a rationally discoverable "general interest"—that has derailed the promise of the "bourgeois public sphere" in the present.

It is in his treatment of Tocqueville and Mill that the problematic nature of Habermas's formulation of the "kernel of truth" found at the heart of the bourgeois public sphere comes into sharpest focus.[145] As Habermas remarks:

> The model of a public sphere in the political realm that claimed the convergence of public opinion with reason supposed it to be objectively possible (through reliance on an order of nature or, what amounted to the same, an organization of society strictly oriented towards the general interest) to keep conflicts of interest and bureaucratic decisions to a minimum and, in so far as these could not be completely avoided, to subject them to reliable criteria of public evaluation.[146]

With electoral reform and the beginnings of a more genuinely inclusive political-public sphere, this supposition—and the ideological rationales of "virtual" representation on which it was based—could no longer be maintained. Moreover, the defeat of absolutism meant that one could no longer count on the seeming clarity of "society's" interest as it emerged in tension with the state: "The unity of public opinion and its unambiguousness were no longer guaranteed by the common foe."[147] The result was that the public sphere was "flooded" by a swarm of "unreconciled" interests and a divided public opinion. It was in response to this new constellation that Tocqueville and Mill developed their respective critiques of public opinion as a potentially and actually coercive force, as well as their distinctive formulations of what has since come to be called "liberal pluralism."

It was Tocqueville who most pointedly formulated the idea that public opinion had ceased to be a locus of critical reason and become, instead, "one power among other powers." The notion of the "tyranny of the majority" advanced in volume 1 of *Democracy in America* was intended to underline the conformist and uncritical character of majority opinion in a democratic *condition sociale*. The eclipse of traditional elites, the lack of confidence in an "atomized" individual judgment, the consequent readiness to "trust the mass"—these and other factors born of democratic equality conspired to make public opinion the "mistress of the world."[148] The crucial point for Tocqueville—and for Mill—was that the "compact mass" of such opinion proved to be distinctly resistant to both the claims of critical rationality and to any ideas that emerged from a minority perspective.

Faced with this ever-hardening monolith of public opinion, both Tocqueville and Mill sought to limit its effects through institutional restraints and the encouragement of social pluralism and nonconformity. Mill in particular sought to reformulate the idea of an agonistic public realm, one better suited to counter the tendencies toward congealment that haunted the emerging "mass" (democratic) public. Hence *On Liberty's* insistence on the need to give "heretical" ideas, no matter how seemingly offensive, a hearing, as well as its emphasis on the need to "keep the lists open" on all questions affecting morals and the good of society. Many voices and perspectives engaged in an ongoing, open-ended argument seemed to Mill to be the best defense against the new and growing dogmatism of the mass public. A public realm in which virtually absolute freedom of thought, discussion, and association reigned would institutionalize the all-important "gadfly" function first introduced to Western culture by Socrates' endlessly dissolvent dialectic.[149] One important epistemological consequence of this pluralism of perspectives was the discarding of the last residues of the *ordre naturel*, as well as the idea of a rational reconciliation of interests this *ordre* seemingly guaranteed.[150]

Habermas reads Mill's insistence on the need to give fair play to "all sides of the truth" less as a corollary of an "agonistic" conception of the public sphere than as a symptom of Mill's *resignation* in the face of increasingly sharp and varied conflicts of interest. As Habermas tellingly writes:

> For the opinions conflicting in the public sphere Mill developed a concept of toleration on the analogy of religious conflicts. The public engaged in critical debate was entirely prevented from attaining a rational opinion because "only through diversity of opinion is there, in the existing state of human intellect, a chance of fair play to all sides of the truth." This resignation before the inability to resolve rationally the competition of interests in the public sphere was disguised by a perspectivist epistemology: because the particular interests were no longer measured against the general, the opinions into which they were ideologically transposed possessed an irreducible kernel of faith. Mill demanded not

criticism but tolerance, because the dogmatic residues could indeed be suppressed but not reduced to the common denominator of reason. The unity of reason and of public opinion lacked the *objective guarantee of a concordance of interests existing in society: the rational demonstrability of a universal interest as such.*[151]

This is a remarkable passage, one that traces the gap not only between Habermas's version of Critical Theory and liberal "pluralism," but also between Habermas and more open conceptions of democratic discourse and the public sphere (such as Mill's or Hannah Arendt's). For the holder of the more open conception, a robust public sphere is one characterized by on-going debate and deliberation concerning not just means but the ends of political society itself. These ends—and the idea of the public good they point to—are constituted discursively, through public talk and argument, and as such are in a more or less constant state of modification and reinterpretation. The "essentially controversial" nature of the public good means that any attempt to find a common denominator for a variety of perspectives engaged in such debate is more or less doomed to failure.[152] Pluralism—or, to use Arendt's word, plurality—is the epistemological and ontological precondition of a robust public-political sphere.[153]

For Habermas, in contrast, the Millian emphasis on a "many-sided truth"—like Arendt's emphasis on a "plurality of perspectives"—signals a failure to find a way to "rationally resolve the competition of interests in the public sphere," a failure "disguised" by a "perspectivist epistemology." This critique makes sense only on the basis of two suppositions. First, that the essential function of the political-public sphere is to "rationalize" interests (rather than to provide an arena for the formation and clash of opinions). Second, that the "rational demonstrability" of a "universal interest" provides, at least in principle, an "objective guarantee of the concordance of interests existing in society."

As previous chapters in this volume indicate, I have more sympathy with the first supposition than the second. It makes (limited) sense to see one essential function of the public sphere as the "rationalization of interests," provided that we understand "rationalization" to mean something like the expansion of horizon that comes through associational life and participation in public-political discourse.[154] As Hegel and Tocqueville have taught us, spheres of interest and opinion intersect and overlap with one another in civil society, and can be conceived as forming a set of concentric circles, widening out to an ever-more general perspective (even or especially if there is no such thing as a final, fully or truly, general perspective).

It does not make sense, however, to insist that the "rational demonstrability" of a "universal interest" is the *sine qua non* of any political theory that desires to rise above (in however limited a sense) liberal interest-group pluralism. This assumption is a holdover from the rationalist tradition in modern political theory, a tradition that has deep roots in ancient and medieval political thought (with their joint emphases on concord [*homonoia*] and harmony).[155] To continue to cling to it makes no sense from either a descriptive or a normative perspective. Even where "sinister interests" have been bracketed (as they are in any "idealized" or normative conception of the public sphere), we should and indeed ought to expect "well-intentioned and competent participants" to "disagree about the common good."[156] This is a lesson we can learn from either Mill or Arendt, or from such sympathetic critics of Habermas as Craig Calhoun, Thomas McCarthy and Nancy Fraser.[157]

Why, then, does Habermas continue to cling to this assumption in *Structural Transformation*? The answer points us to a series of conceptual dichotomies Habermas inherited from what Isaiah Berlin has called the "monistic" (rationalist) tradition.[158] This tradition assumed that passions, interests, opinions, rhetoric, power, and force are on one side of the equation, and reason, truth, justice, the "general interest," and "undistorted communication" are on the other. The project of subjecting politics to morality thus appeared to demand not just the bracketing of the grosser forms of coercion and inequality, but also the elimination, reduction, or transcendence of moral-political pluralism as such. Just as there can be only one Truth (*unum verum*), so there can only be one correct iteration of the common good. It is the function of reason—whether "monological" (Plato, Hegel) or "dialogical" (Kant, Habermas)—to elucidate it. Hence Habermas's spurning of Mill's "perspectivism" as tantamount to a resigned (and, in a sense, defeated) relativism.

In Habermas's defense, it should be emphasized that he by no means insists—in *Structural Transformation* or anywhere else—on reducing the actual activity of politics to a search for "rational consensus." He does not seek the effacement of political differences of opinion. What he does seek, however, is the widest possible deployment of the ideal embedded in the "bourgeois public sphere," an ideal he reformulates as "the ideal speech situation" in his later work. This ideal—whether in its concrete historical or more formal-theoretical iteration—serves as a non-arbitrary normative standard against which the ideological manipulations and structural coercions of our present sociopolitical reality can be measured. We not only want our democratic institutions and procedures to be open to critical publicity—to be, as the current lingo has it, "transparent." We also want them to conform, as far as possible, to dialogical rather than strategic or merely instrumental norms.

The mistake Habermas makes—at least in *Structural Transformation*—is to assume that the institutionalization of such norms will lead us (asymptotically, as it were) toward increasing agreement about the nature of the "common good." The basic argument is quite simple. The more such norms find institutional embodiment—the more our public sphere resembles the "idealized" bourgeois version—the more "undistorted" our communication will be. This, in turn, will provide a relatively transparent linguistic-argumentative medium in which the "general interest" can appear with relative clarity and distinctness, through the "unforced force of the better argument."

◆

But such is not our fate. As the second half of *Structural Transformation* makes all too clear, the institutional and sociological preconditions for a "critical-rational" public sphere have not been preserved in contemporary society. In the phase of "organized" (Keynesian and post-Keynesian) capitalism, state and society increasingly penetrate one another, effacing the sharp distinction between public and private upon which the original "blueprint" of the bourgeois public sphere was based.[159] Corporations and private organizations wield an increasingly public power, while the state finds itself deeply implicated not only in the regulation and protection of markets, but in the provision of basic welfare, education, and research and development services.[160] The general strategy of crisis avoidance produces an increasingly coordinated relationship between the chief economic and political actors, one that resolves potential class conflicts through direct governmental negotiations with the major interests involved (unions; the corporate sector).[161] The result—at least in the constellation created by the postwar European welfare state—is the thorough marginalization of the public as a possible venue for the "generalization" of interests:

> The process of the politically relevant exercise and equilibrium of power now takes place directly between the private bureaucracies,

special-interest associations, parties, and public administration. The public as such is included only sporadically in this circuit of power, and even then it is brought in only to contribute its acclamation.[162]

The simultaneous "socialization" of the state and "stateification" of society thus produces a configuration in which the public sphere loses its original position ("between" state and civil society) and is functionally retooled.[163] Its primary purpose now is to provide plebiscitary legitimation for policies and compromises achieved "behind closed doors" by government ministers and technocrats. The original promise of its "critical publicity"—to reconcile conflicting interests in light of a rationally discoverable general interest—is thus rendered moot.

To this broad reconfiguration of the relation between state and society (which Habermas refers to as its "refeudalization"), a number of smaller but nevertheless critical sociological factors must be added. The "structural transformation" of the public sphere could never have been so thorough were it not for a set of subsidiary transformations that occur at the levels of work, private life, and culture itself.

The first of these transformations concerns what Habermas calls the "the polarization of the social sphere and the intimate sphere." By this Habermas means the tremendously altered configuration of family, work, and leisure in a world characterized by large-scale industrial enterprises and corporate actors. In such a world, the last remaining links between home and individual economic activity are severed. The *oikos* is transferred to the site of large-scale enterprises, many of which create their own communities, complete with residences, health and recreational facilities, and so on. In this way, the new "world of work" strips the family of many, if not all, of its traditional functions.[164]

One result of this transfigured social topography is that the "private realm" ceases to be a sphere in which a specific type of "audience-directed subjectivity" (and a joy in discursive sociability) is cultivated.[165] It becomes, instead, a site devoted primarily to leisure and the consumption of mass culture. The "quiet bliss" of "homeyness" replaces what was once (at least according to the "ideology" of the bourgeois family) a talkative sphere of "purely human" relations. Such a gradual and surreptitious "hollowing out" of the family's "intimate sphere" finds its architectural expression in suburbs and planned communities, where true privacy "dissolves before the gaze of the 'group.'"[166] In place of clearly defined public and private realms—with the latter providing a protected sphere necessary for the cultivation of adult autonomy and a discursive form of sociability—we have a diffuse "social" sphere, one that effaces boundaries and subjects all to the expectations of the group (such as one's neighbors or co-workers). Leisure behavior, Habermas writes, "supplies the key to the floodlit privacy of the new sphere, to the externalization of what is declared to be the inner life."[167]

Just as the private sphere is transformed through the "polarization" of the intimate and social spheres (with the former being absorbed by the latter), so the public sphere itself is transformed in terms of the activities for which it now provides a home. If, in former days, private individuals entered a "literary public sphere" constituted by coffeehouses, *salons*, and *Tischgesellschaften* in order to debate and judge a wide variety of cultural contents (books, plays, music, art), today they enter it as consumers of a mass culture resistant to any "discursive" appropriation whatsoever. One could easily argue—and Habermas comes close to doing so—that the defining characteristic of contemporary mass culture is that it renders all discursive appropriation and judgment superfluous.

Once culture (in whatever form) is identified with leisure, it becomes a matter of individual consumption rather than communicative appropriation.[168] In this way, "the public sphere in the world of letters was replaced by the pseudo-public or sham-private world of culture consumption."[169] The point about group leisure activities centered on the passive consumption of mass media is that they "do not require any further discussion." Even the most "stimulating" of such relaxations—the "enjoyable" book or the "really good" concert—is unlikely to demand or provoke a "public use of one's reason."[170] Indeed, the form of sociality produced by such activities is—like many a polite dinner party—characterized by an enforced "abstinence from literary and political debate."[171] The talkative world of the coffeehouses, *salons*, and *Tischgesellschaften* gives way to the crowd's consumption of the entertainment event or commodity, whatever it may be ("up-scale" or "down-market"). Indeed, insofar as public discussion and argument are still present in our society, they make their appearance as carefully produced and managed consumer items, such as candidate forums and so-called "town hall meetings." "Today," Habermas aptly observes, "the conversation itself is administered."[172]

A third transformation is intimately linked to the preceding two. The "socialization" of the private sphere, combined with the movement from a culture-debating to a culture-consuming society, gives rise to a "sham public sphere," one characterized above all by the mass media and their "culture of integration."[173] In this new constellation the public sphere—once an arena of critical communication amongst peers—increasingly "assumes advertising functions." Such a "mediatized public realm" is the logical extension of the closed circuit of interest bargaining and compromise sketched above. By-passed through the direct negotiations of governmental, corporate, and labor interests, the public is reduced to a status well below that of Weber's "foot soldiers." As "citizens," we are subjected to a barrage of publicity and public relations work "generated from above . . . in order to create an aura of good will for certain positions" or interests.[174] "Critical publicity is supplanted by manipulative publicity"—a truth currently born out by the ubiquitous corporate PR campaigns of British Petroleum, Archer Daniels Midland, and a host of other corporate lawbreakers too numerous to mention.[175]

These various evolutions have their bastard consummation in a fourth and final transformation: that of the political function of the public sphere itself. The "mediatized" public sphere aims not only at procuring an "aura of good will" for certain interests or positions. It also fundamentally transforms the role and character of public opinion—*opinion publique*—in contemporary "democratic" systems. In the (idealized) bourgeois public sphere, an "opinion" was not something one had prior to debate and deliberation with others. Rather, it was something formed in the process of argumentation and persuasion. Thus, "opinion" for the men of the eighteenth century had a connotation of both publicness and rationality: our faculty of opinion was a rational faculty.[176] Public opinion—*opinion publique*—was a collective judgment born of the process of deliberation, testing, and purification of judgments offered in the literary or political public spheres.

Thanks to the rise of a "sham public sphere" with advertising functions, these connotations have completely disappeared. In Habermas's view, public opinion is now little more than an input in an overall system of technocratic management and policy implementation. Systematically managed, massaged, and manipulated, it is targeted to assure higher poll numbers for particular candidates or policy proposals. The "opinions" measured in such polls are, of course, anything but the rational outcomes of extended processes of public argument. What is measured are the preferences and moods of the moment—preferences and moods that flow from the rawest mix of unfiltered interest, political predisposition or prejudice, and media-induced feelings of approval or disapproval. The "engineering of consent" is the essential task.[177]

None of this will be news to any inhabitant of a contemporary mass or "mediatized" democracy. What makes Habermas's version of what is now a widespread criticism interesting is its focus on how political advertising zeroes in on the "undecided" segment of the population—typically the most ill-informed and politically immature—the better to secure the necessary votes and requisite acclamation. The elision of any discursive intermediaries in this process (greatly facilitated by television) creates a false intimacy designed to let the privatized consumer-voter think they "know" the candidate.[178] The appeal is deliberately aimed at the un- or semi-conscious, at half-articulate likings and dislikings. And this, of course, is the essence of advertising itself. Hence Habermas can quite legitimately claim that "even the political realm is social-psychologically integrated into the realm of consumption."[179]

As an essentially raw, unfiltered, and pre-discursive formation, contemporary public opinion—the opinion of privatized consumers, themselves untutored and unpracticed in the arts of cultural and political judgment—is susceptible to a wide array of manipulative techniques, from the relatively sophisticated (for example, the campaign against so-called "Hillary Care" in the first years of the Clinton presidency) to the crude but effective ("Swift Boat Veterans for Truth"). The remarkable success of such techniques is a function of their ability to short-circuit even the most rudimentary forms of "critical publicity," appealing directly to half-conscious fears, hopes, and prejudices. That our "public sphere" will continue to be held captive to such techniques—and to the industries of advertising and public relations—for the foreseeable future is, unfortunately, a truism that even the most inveterate opponent of Critical Theory would likely acknowledge.

Such an opponent would, however, disagree with Habermas's Marcuse-like presentation of a conformist society based on a "false" consensus. If Habermas can be said to have exaggerated anything in his account of the "structural transformation of the public sphere," it is less the amount of manipulation that occurs than the coherence and predictability of the product it creates. "Public opinion" as we know it is massaged, managed, hyped-up, and tamped down. The last adjective anyone would use to describe it is "rational," even when it happens to agree with our particular point of view on a given issue. Yet however true this may be, it is hardly the case that the opinion managers of our day have succeeded in producing a "culture of consensus," one in which a bastardized general will repeatedly and predictably stands in for the real thing.

In this regard, a contrast Habermas draws toward the end of *Structural Transformation* is quite revealing. Writing about the way public relations secures the illusion that a "person, product, organization or idea" coincides with the "general interest," and thus deserves public acclamation, Habermas notes:

> The resulting consensus, of course, does not seriously have much in common with the final unanimity [!] wrought by a time-consuming process of mutual enlightenment, for the "general interest" on the basis of which alone a rational agreement between publicly competing opinions could be freely reached has disappeared precisely to the extent that the publicist self-presentations of privileged private interests have adopted it for themselves.[180]

The contrast drawn here is between the ad hoc feelings of good will generated by public relations (the "false" consensus that a particular interest or person is "good for society") and the genuine agreement produced by a "time-consuming process of mutual enlightenment." The *telos* of the latter process can be consensus—"final unanimity"—precisely because the "general interest" is its actual and not just pretended point of departure. We seem to be left with the either/or of an "integrated" society based on public relations and a "false" consensus (on the one hand) and a more deliberative society based on a revivified public sphere (on the other). The latter has its lode star in the idea and reality of a rationally demonstrable general interest that can be redeemed discursively, under conditions of relatively undistorted communication.

The final pages of chapter 6 of *Structural Transformation* somewhat undercut this black-and-white contrast between "true" and "false" consensus. There Habermas quite reasonably calls for the extension of the principle of transparency (or "publicity" in its original, "bourgeois" sense) from "the organs of the [constitutional] state to all organizations acting in a state-related fashion."[181] Not the foredoomed attempt to resuscitate the collapsed "bourgeois public sphere," but rather a "long march through institutions" seems to be the order of the day. The gradual spread of transparency in the bargaining and legislative processes of the modern state is apparently the best we can hope for. Indeed, Habermas goes so far as to acknowledge that the "unresolved plurality of competing interests" in contemporary society makes it "doubtful whether there can ever emerge a general interest of the kind to which a public opinion could refer as a criterion."[182]

This reformist bit of realism is, however, quickly circumscribed. For Habermas, Critical Theory loses its much of its *raison d'être* unless it can continue to speak in the name of a submerged or at least regulative idea of the "general interest." Writing in the early 1960s, he sees two slim historical reeds on which to fix his hopes. The first is economic growth and the advent of what J. K. Galbraith called "the affluent society." The second is the effect of the Cold War arms race and the continuing threat of nuclear destruction. Economic growth would, at least in principle, resolve many of society's more persistent "structural" conflicts of interest. That, in turn, would radically diminish the need for bureaucratic-ministerial high-handedness. The arms race, on the other hand, has the unexpected upside of bringing the minimal core of any society's *general interest*—the avoidance of mutually assured destruction and the creation of a more cosmopolitan international order—into the kind of sharp focus all can agree on.[183]

Given the possible "relativizing" of "structural conflicts of interest" and the general interest all presumably have in peace and prosperity, Habermas concludes that the struggle between a "critical publicity" oriented by a "standard of universal interest everyone can acknowledge" and a strictly manipulative publicity generated by special interests is by no means over. The problem is that everything he has said in his historical-sociological narrative suggests otherwise. The corruption of the public-political sphere by advertising and special interests; the transformation of governmental deliberative bodies into mere "public rostrums" in which previously achieved compromises are presented in a "voter-friendly" way; the loss of a distinctively discursive form of sociability; and the transformation of the civic public into so many consumer demographics: these and other factors all point to a sociopolitical reality in which the idea of the bourgeois public sphere can no longer put down roots.

Habermas's concluding rhetorical gesture thus cannot conceal what appears to be the *real* lesson of his historical genealogy. Instead of "saving" the concept of the public sphere—for Critical Theory, for political theory, and for us—he has managed, instead, to give us a highly persuasive catalog of all the reasons why it is and must be an anachronism. Once again, a Frankfurt School theorist sees the grounds of immanent critique dissolve under his feet.

Habermas knew this, and was unwilling to abide the apparent consequences. Rather than reformulate his conception of the public sphere in a more pluralistic direction *à la* Mill, he took the historical-sociological dissolution of the "general interest" embodied in *opinion publique* as a cue to "go transcendental." His subsequent theoretical work is thus an extended attempt to tease out a new (and only partly historical) ground for the dialogical norms which the "bourgeois public sphere" had so tantalizingly formulated yet so imperfectly realized. The quasi-transcendental strategy behind these various investigations—of societal rationalization processes, of communicative action, of "universal pragmatics," and "discourse ethics"—is intended not as a rejection of immanent critique, but as its necessary regrounding.

If, as the analysis of *Structural Transformation* suggests, contemporary political institutions and practices have been more or less drained of their normative content (the public sphere being a case in point), then the only alternative—besides Adorno-esque pessimism—is to look elsewhere for it. Perhaps, Habermas suggests, the normative ideal of the "unforced force of the better argument" is embedded in the structure of communicative action itself. And perhaps rationalization, when viewed from the standpoint of societal evolution, is a Janus-faced process, one involving not just "systemic" rationalization, but communicative rationalization as well.

Assuming either or both of these theses could be cashed out, then we need not be too depressed by the "structural transformation of the public sphere." For if Habermas's later "transcendental-evolutionary" research program were to bear fruit, the normative force of undistorted communication *and of reason itself* would be shown to be securely grounded in linguistic interaction—that is, in the assumptions every competent speaker must make in initiating a dialogue—and not in ephemeral sociohistorical institutions. Moreover, the principle that validity claims can be redeemed only discursively, through uncoerced public argumentation (and not through appeals to such pre-discursive authorities as religion, myth, or tradition) would be shown to be gaining ground throughout the modern period. True, such "communicative rationalization" often comes off as the weaker partner in the late modern struggle of the colonizing "system" with the "lifeworld." Nevertheless, the twofold nature of the rationalization process would provide reason for hope and (in theory, at least) an escape from the "iron cage" of bureaucratic rationalization. Finally, it would give us reason to believe that the search for generalizable interests through open and "symmetrical" dialogical processes is not a futile one.

Like many of Habermas's more sympathetic critics, I find his transposition of the normative bases of the bourgeois public sphere (including parity, openness, inclusiveness, and a shared commitment to "the force of the better argument") into functions of the human capacity for communication to be unconvincing.[184] Far too much weight is attached to the idea that the "undistorted speech situation"—an ideal whose historical and cultural roots Habermas investigated in *Structural Transformation*—is grounded in language and the pragmatics of speech itself. Similarly, the idea that the public sphere is, *qua* ideal, a "contingent product of the evolution of communicative action, rather than its basis," is open to skepticism.[185] There is nothing intrinsically democratic about the pragmatic structure of communication, nor are the dialogical dimensions of speech normatively determinative in quite the way Habermas imagines they are. We would do better to see such dialogical dimensions as something "read off" from the contingent and haphazard evolution of democratic institutions and practices, rather than embodying a "gentle, but obstinate . . . claim to reason" inscribed in the structure of communication and mutual understanding itself.[186]

Why then does Habermas reject historical-sociological concreteness and "go transcendental"? An answer has already been given. The sociological analysis seemed to bear out what Horkheimer, Adorno, and Marcuse had already argued, albeit at a much higher pitch of theoretical abstraction. Sociology and history apparently confirmed the more totalizing aspects of Frankfurt School criticism. Hence the need to look elsewhere if the grounds of immanent critique were to be recovered.

This is a highly counterintuitive progression. If anything has the power to undermine "totalizing critique," it would seem to be concrete historical and sociological investigations. And, indeed, starting with the 1992 collection *Habermas and the Public Sphere*, a veritable cottage industry has grown up consisting of such investigations, many devoted to questioning many of Habermas's earlier generalizations about the character of the "bourgeois public sphere" itself. Yet I would suggest that the reason Habermas comes so perilously close to totalizing critique in *Structural Transformation* is because of his excessive reliance upon Weber's "formalization of reason" metanarrative and the scarcely concealed philosophy of history that animates it. This theoretical debt accounts not only for the odd way the second half of the book shadows earlier Frankfurt School analyses. It also accounts for his transcendental turn in the face of the "re-feudalization" of state and society. Thus, Habermas's magisterial *Theory of Communicative Action* breaks out of the cul-de-sac represented by Weber's implicit philosophy of history, while remaining firmly grounded in the rationalization paradigm he established.[187]

This entrapment has important consequences not only for Habermas's vision of a democratic public sphere, but for his assessment of the prospects for civic education and the achievement of *Mündigkeit* as well. For Habermas, a democratic public sphere is not simply one characterized by equal access, inclusiveness, and a general absence of coercion. Its "job" (if one may put it that way) is not merely to provide a check on representatives and other governmental institutions. Nor is it simply to provide an arena for the discussion and "trickling up" of a variety of popular concerns. Rather, its essential task is to begin the work of "rationalizing" interests—that is, to separate out of those interests that are irreducibly particular from those that are authentically generalizable.

Viewing the public sphere in this way—seeing it as *primarily* a venue for the articulation of interests which are subsequently "tested" for their universalizability—is useful, up to a point. But it also dramatically limits the reach of public life and a more civic consciousness.

The problem with Habermas's conception is twofold. First, as noted above, the idea that a "discursive" public realm filters the irreducibly particular from the actually universalizable assumes the existence of a "genuinely universal" set of interests, one that all rational (communicatively competent) citizens could, in principle, agree on.[188] The result—at least from the perspective of a theory of the public sphere—is that a quasi-centralized "testing" process takes the place of a more decentralized mediation (and education) of particular and general interests. The latter conception—articulated, in different ways, by both Hegel and Tocqueville—suggests that the real "work" of the public sphere is not the isolation or identification of universal interests "all can agree on," but rather the gradual and decentered "education" to a wider horizon of interest—precisely through participation in public-political affairs and attention to public debates.[189]

Habermas spurns such a civil society-oriented approach because he thinks that something like a "testing board" conception of the public sphere is essential if there is to be anything like a valid process of democratic will formation. This conception—obviously indebted to both Rousseau and Kant—is notable for the way it equates an irreducible plurality of interests with what Habermas considers to be the relativistic assertion (by Weber and others) of an irreducible plurality of ultimate value commitments. As Habermas puts it in *Legitimation Crisis*, commenting on Hans Albert's "critical rationalism":

The discursively formed will may be called "rational" because the formal properties of discourse and of the deliberative situation sufficiently guarantee that a consensus can arise only through appropriately interpreted, *generalizable* interests, by which I mean needs *that can be communicatively shared.* The limits of a decisionistic treatment of practical questions are overcome as soon as argumentation is expected to test the generaliz*ability* of interests [*sic*], instead of being resigned to an impenetrable pluralism of apparently ultimate value orientations (or belief-acts or attitudes). It is not the fact of this pluralism that is here disputed, but the assertion that it is impossible to separate by argumentation generalizable interests from those that are and remain particular. Albert mentions, to be sure, various types of more or less contingent "bridge principles." But he does not mention the only principle in which practical reason expresses itself, namely, the principle of universalization.[190]

The insistence that practical reason expresses itself "only in the principle of universalization" and that this principle is the core of any and all communicative rationality in the public sphere culminates in Habermas's strong cognitivist assertion that "practical questions admit of truth."[191] The myriad perspectives and interests that make up the public realm most emphatically *can* be reduced to a common denominator. A "right answer" is, in principle, possible to even the most vexed of social-political questions.[192]

The reader will here recall Habermas's dismissal of J. S. Mill's "perspectivist epistemology." Mill, in Habermas's view, "gives up" on the idea of a rationally demonstrable general interest, and so resigns himself to the idea of a "gadfly" public realm. This is a public realm whose primary function is not simply to speak truth to power, but also to reveal the many dogmatic forms that society's "general will" can and does take. Seen from the perspective of a theory that views the value of the public sphere primarily in terms of its contribution to "democratic will formation," Mill's conception is clearly lacking. Yet Mill's emphasis on the negative or dissolvent function of the public sphere is essential to any conception that wants to do justice to both pluralism and the dangers born of mass public opinion. With apologies to Rousseau: the general will is not always right, even when it has been "enlightened" according to procedures akin to those Habermas suggests.

The second problem with the universalizing conception of the public sphere is that it radically constricts the interpretive indeterminacy of any given test or argument. As a number of commentators have noted, Habermas's later conception of practical discourse—while clearly inspired by elements of the "bourgeois public sphere"—takes as its implicit model the kind of free and unrestrained questioning, hypothesis formation, and testing we tend to associate with scientific discourses. Habermas suggests that, as practical agents, we are in a position roughly parallel to that of a community of inquirers: both are seekers after truth. And, as Richard J. Bernstein has noted, "when there are serious conflicts between competing scientific theories and hypotheses, research programs, or paradigms, we are committed to resolving such differences through non-manipulative and non-coercive argumentation."[193]

Habermas argues that this commitment needs to be extended to disagreements that crop up in the public-political world concerning both the validity of specific claims and norms and the "background consensus" of which they are a part. When such breakdowns in communication occur, it is important to jump from a "pre-theoretical" level of argument to a more "theoretical" one, the better to cash out the validity (or invalidity) of the specific claim or norm in question. In making the move to a more formal, theoretically inflected *Diskurs* the goal is hardly to reach unanimity over what to do or what policies to enact. However, this move does enable us to repair the argumentative context in which all such discussions occur, allowing the search for best or most universalizable policies to continue.[194]

Habermas's notion of *Diskurs* is thus intended to foreclose the possibility that moral pluralism or divergent conceptions of what is reasonable will derail the public in its search for universalizable interests and its attempts to "re-establish a lost consensus via argumentative processes in which reasons are advanced, debated, and evaluated."[195] Hence the questionable parallel with scientific discourses, which provide us with a model of what to do when confronted with a threatened breakdown in communication between two or more camps. The jump to a quasi-theoretical discourse is required if we want to preserve the conditions under which it even makes sense to speak of "the force of the better argument"—if we want, in other words, to avoid a slide into the discursive relativism that apparently arises whenever certain taken-for-granted norms (for example, the separation of church and state or equality under the law) are challenged. We may still disagree about which argument is the better one, but our disagreement will take place within a coherent and shared context. The tear in our discursive "lifeworld" will have been repaired.

The problem, of course, is that the "political public sphere" has little in common with a coherent (disciplinary) community of inquirers, even if argumentative practices are common features of both. As citizens, we are not essentially "seekers after truth." At best, we are seekers after justice, and justice—notoriously—is an "essentially controversial" notion. There are certainly better and worse arguments out there for social democratic, libertarian, liberal democratic, and multicultural conceptions of it. But the fact that we can broadly distinguish better and worse arguments in this regard (the job, typically, of political theorists, who rarely agree on any definitive ranking) does nothing to alter the more massive fact that our most basic intuitions about what justice entails will continue to radically diverge. Unlike a community of investigators that inhabits a relatively coherent and established paradigm of scientific inquiry—one with strictly codified canons of proof, argumentation, and verification—we inhabit a public-political world of conflicting ideas of justice, diverse conceptions of practical reasoning, and radically incommensurable notions of "the good life."

This fact, and not the presence of conflicting interests per se, guarantees that public-political discourse—even under the most "undistorted" conditions of communication—will often resemble the knocking of heads, with little, if any, chance for agreement on basic presuppositions or standards of what constitutes the "better argument." Under these conditions, the idea that political or practical discourse can, when properly construed and practiced, provide us with a "method" for generalizing interests (or at least identifying ungeneralizable ones) rings hollow.

The moral and, if I may put it this way, "methodological" pluralism of the political-public sphere—a pluralism that radically distinguishes it from any scientific or disciplinary discourse—is matched by its sociological and cultural pluralism. A "community of investigators" inhabits a shared, articulated, and very concrete "public" world: the world of their discipline, its practices, methods, institutions, honors, and so on. Citizens, in contrast, often seem to inhabit a wide variety of different "lifeworlds," with only the bogus *Lebenswelt* of mass media to unite them. Many have little access to education, deliberative skills, or the levers of power. And many continue to be structurally, if not legally-formally, excluded from "the political process."

In such a world, the "testing board" conception of a single, more deliberative public sphere falls short. The advantages of a more pluralistic, civil society-type conception of the public realm—one that thinks in terms of a plurality of competing publics, rather than a single, "comprehensive" public sphere—seem fairly obvious. Such a conception—laid out over fifteen years ago by the political theorist Nancy Fraser—pluralizes the public sphere by making room for a number of "subaltern counterpublics." Such "unofficial" discursive networks among women, gays, blacks, Hispanics, and other minorities can be seen to provide a form of civic self-education broadly parallel to that pursued by the European bourgeoisie in the coffeehouses, *salons*, and *Tischgesellschaften* of the eighteenth century.[196]

The upshot of these various considerations is that it no longer makes much sense to think of the public sphere as a kind of "rational tribunal," constituted by a relatively coherent group of educated private persons, who perform a clear "rationalizing" function with respect to state policies. Nor does it make much sense to think of the political-public sphere and democratic institutions as grounded on structures of communicative rationality, *if* by that we mean that public-political discourse, freed of the distortions introduced by money and power, approximates a form of dialogue or discourse in which the shared interests and underlying agreement of the participants can ultimately come to the fore. Habermas's linguistic-transcendental reformulation of the basic formal features of an "idealized" bourgeois public sphere is meant to save politics from drowning in a sea of manipulative publicity, ideology, and "colonization" by functionalist reason. But all it really does is preserve the ghost of the *ordre naturel*.[197]

Conclusion

In reflecting on the possibility of *Mündigkeit* in our time, it is important to remember that our lives and our discourses are saturated with ideology. It takes many forms and utilizes every conceivable vehicle—from "traditional" mass media (TV, radio), to fashion, to religion, to self-help books, to youth culture, to corporate PR, to the Internet and beyond. There is no such thing as an "ideology-free" zone in our or any other culture. One of the most important contributions of the Frankfurt School has been to sharpen our appreciation of this fact. Yet while enabling us to see more of the shape-shifting forms that ideology takes in our culture, Frankfurt School theorists have tended to perpetuate two conflicting myths. The first—represented by Horkheimer and Adorno's "Culture Industry" essay and Marcuse's *One-Dimensional Man*—is that ideological saturation indicates the presence of a "total society," one that uses mass culture in a planned and systematic way in order to achieve certain behavioral outcomes. The second—represented by Habermas's work on the public sphere—is that there exists a formal institutional or discursive structure which can plausibly be said to "bracket" or step beyond ideological claims.

The problem with the idea of a "total society" is that it systematizes what is, in fact, a far more decentered and insidious process. Ideology comes at us from every direction, often with conflicting contents and imperatives. Thus, while it makes sense to speak of certain large and overpowering forms in our culture (such as consumerism), it doesn't make sense to overly functionalize what is, in fact, a multilayered, messy, and often ineffectual process. We may be up to our proverbial eyebrows in the ideological content spewed out by mass culture, but that doesn't mean we necessarily reduce to the pseudo-subjects theorized by Horkheimer, Adorno, and Marcuse.

The seemingly "pure" instances of ideological pre-conditioning in our culture—the teen who is the sum of his or her consumption habits; the status-seeking denizens of the upper middle class; the "USA # 1" NASCAR crowd—are less quasi-Pavlovian entities than they are the partial victims of a deprivation in education and experience. The ideology purveyed by mass culture, religion, or "patriotism" is strongest when there are few alternative contents or perspectives inhabiting the minds of those it targets. And it is only acquaintance with scales of value outside the mainstream of one's own "demographic" that enables any of us to retain even the semblance of autonomy. Without such acquaintance—which can come via many avenues, not just educational ones—a kind of mental and moral vacuum is created, one that the ideological contents of mass culture rush to fill.

The choice, then, is not between a more or less "complete" autonomy and a similarly comprehensive heteronomy. What we face is a perpetual, Sisyphian task of partial critique and disillusionment: the never-completed overcoming of our own relative parochiality or "particularity." Only in this way is the necessary minimum amount of alienation, skepticism, and distrust maintained in the midst of our relentlessly "positive" culture, a culture that often seems to be little more than the sum of its myriad public relations campaigns.

Such an approach is hardly novel. As I have argued elsewhere, the need to perpetually resist the gravitational pull of custom and convention was first articulated by Socrates, and finds its "contemporary" echo in such early critics of mass culture as Tocqueville and Mill.[198] These thinkers were all well aware of how society may effect a "false" reconciliation of the universal and the particular, making it appear that something like a "general will" had emerged where what had really manifested itself was the tyranny of custom, a class, or a majority. To this perpetual threat they opposed not *Ideologiekritik*, but the twin ideas of a dissolvent rationality and an open or pluralistic public sphere, one that could be home to voices and arguments other than those that constitute hegemonic opinion.

Of course, in America "pluralism" is itself an ideology, a term we continue to invoke even as our public sphere and civil society function in less and less pluralistic fashion. It is quite wrong to assume that our sociological pluralism translates, in any meaningful way, into an open and multivoiced "discussion" in the public sphere. Sinister interests abound, and money and power continue to make a mockery of the claim that "here the people (or the law) rule." However, the answer to such grotesque asymmetries lies neither in a "great refusal" nor in appeals to "undistorted communication" and "the force of the better argument." The "great refusal" makes sense only in the framework provided by a totalizing critique, and totalizing critique (no matter how superficially warranted) is always an abandonment of political responsibility. Similarly, appeals to "undistorted communication" and "the force of the better argument" make sense only where other, more obviously "immanent," grounds of critique have failed. In the case of the "advanced" Western societies, these grounds are to be found in their respective democratic and constitutional traditions and in their continued allegiance to the ideals of the Enlightenment and the culture of human rights.

All the major Frankfurt School theorists aligned themselves with such ideals—even, or most especially, when they were questioning the "trajectory" of the Enlightenment in late modern times.[199] Habermas in particular had made substantial efforts to distance himself from the totalizing critiques of the first generation, and to recover the democratic potentials at the heart of the Enlightenment.[200] Yet the looming influence of Weber's "formalization of reason" metanarrative—together with its associated notions of "the system" and the hegemony of technocratic-bureaucratic rationality—skewed Habermas's recovery of the promise of the public sphere, directing it away from concrete cultures, traditions, and historical possibilities, and toward increasingly unlikely evolutionary and "transcendental" hypotheses.[201]

A further impetus in this direction comes from the critique of instrumental (or "functionalist") reason that has always been the Frankfurt School's *raison d'être*. However, once we see that critique as addressing merely one (albeit important) dimension of our current situation, we are less likely to be convinced of the need to "go transcendental," or to draw dubious analogies between the "moral maturation" process of the individual and that of societies. Indeed, we are less likely to think of "enlightenment" and *Mündigkeit* in terms of a discursive rationality that privileges universalizability, and more in terms of a culture of argument and debate—one that recognizes the value of political discussion as a means to a more "representative" form of thinking and (thus) to a more valid process of opinion formation.

This, of course, is what Hannah Arendt argued for in her appropriation of Kant, and in her insistence that the "rational" medium of political thinking, discussion, and judgment was opinion, not truth. In a famous passage from the "The Crisis in Culture," Arendt writes:

> Culture and politics . . . belong together because it is not knowledge or truth which is at stake, but rather judgment and decision, the judicious exchange of opinion about the sphere of public life and the common world, and the decision what manner of action is to be taken in it, as well as how it is to look henceforth, and what kinds of things are to appear in it.[202]

Opinion and judgment are faculties whose rationality does not depend upon on their ability to generate (or agree with) a generalizable interest so much as their ability to take the perspectives of others into account. The representative character of political thinking and opinion formation consists in the following:

> I form an opinion by considering a given issue from different viewpoints, by making present to my mind the standpoints of those who are absent; that is, I represent them. This process of representation does not blindly adopt the actual views of those who stand somewhere else, and hence look upon the world from

a different perspective; this is a question neither of empathy, as though I tried to be or to feel like somebody else, nor of counting noses and joining a majority but of being and thinking in my own identity where actually I am not. The more people's standpoints I have present in my mind while I am pondering a given issue, and the better I can imagine how I would feel and think if I were in their place, the stronger will be my capacity for representative thinking, and the more valid my final conclusions, my opinion.[203]

The interesting thing about Arendt's characterization of opinion formation and judgment is that it assumes communication with others while not assuming that such communication will yield an interest, argument, or opinion that all competent speakers must acknowledge as the most universal or valid. One forms one's opinion through anticipated communication with others, broadening one's opinion through representative thinking and the widening of one's perspective. The resulting judgment will be (relatively speaking) stripped of idiosyncrasy and selfish interests, and thus "impartial" in a broad sense. However, it will still be only my judgment. For others to share it, I must convince them through persuasion, and not by means of any formal test or jump to another level of discourse. The "public use of one's reason" takes us only so far.

Arendt's conception assumes, of course, that our capacity for representative thinking and persuasive "wooing" has not been utterly destroyed by privatization, the hegemony of interests, and the "colonization" of the public sphere by advertising and other nondiscursive forms of communication. Yet even if Arendt has failed to take sufficient account of such structural threats—the "transformation" Habermas so vividly describes—we can still appreciate the singular version of *Mündigkeit* she offers us. This is a version that depends on no special faculties beyond the ability to see a distinction between one's (pregiven) interest as a stockbroker, union member, public school teacher, or corporate executive and one's opinion about issues affecting the local or national (or indeed international) community. The latter is something that must be formed. It will have validity not because it conforms to an abstract standard of universalizability or has emerged in the course of a special argumentative protocol, but because it has passed through a (self-imposed) filtering process. In other words, *Mündigkeit* in the political world consists in the desire to inform oneself of basic facts, the capacity to think in something approximating "representative" fashion, and the willingness to use only honest (noncoercive) persuasive means.

There is both a convergence and a divergence here with Habermas.[204] Perhaps most strikingly, Arendt assumes these capacities lie, at least in principle, within the competence of every literate adult. We may all be vulnerable to ideological spinning and scare tactics, but we are all more or less capable of looking at things from a variety of angles, bracketing our more immediate material interests and (one hopes) our more inveterate prejudices. The problem with Arendt's conception lies not so much with her assumption that the political realm is populated by "adults," able to step back at least partially from their immediate interests. Rather, it lies with the fact that fewer and fewer of us ever feel called upon to "anticipate communication" with those who have actively disagreed with us, or who have genuinely different perspectives.[205]

Habermas is thus right to say that the "structural transformation" of the public sphere has reduced public opinion to reflexive responses offered to pollsters and others. Since we are not asked to think, deliberate, or actively argue, we have acquired the habit of offering up our most knee-jerk responses as "opinions." This fact, combined with the fragmentation of the public sphere according to interest, ideology, and demographic (a fragmentation only facilitated by new technologies) yields an increasingly shrill public discourse, one divided between substanceless bromides of our politicians and infotainment Punch-and-Judy shows that mime political debate.[206]

Here we have to face up to an uncomfortable truth. The culture industry does indeed provide a vehicle for all kinds of ideological contents, and the "structural transformation" of the public sphere has indeed been extreme. Nevertheless, there remains the issue of our active complicity in our collective infantilization. At the level of mass culture, it is less a question of the subliminal messages Horkheimer and Adorno identify than it is our massive desire to be distracted by the shiny surfaces of popular culture. I should stress that I am hardly arguing for the resurrection of long-dead, "antique" civic virtue. Rather, I am merely pointing to the fact that it is distraction—and the intellectual and civic laziness which it breeds—that is our biggest problem. We are treated like children by our leaders because they know in their bones that ours is an attention-deficit-disorder democracy, one born of the perpetual distractions of mass culture. It is a democracy in which sustained attention to public affairs has increasingly become the exclusive province of professional politicians, journalists, and academic specialists. The majority of us would prefer to be entertained, rather than face the grim realities of what is being done in our name, both at home and abroad. The greater part of our "tutelage" is and remains self-incurred.

Political maturity is something that can be gained, and it is something that can be lost. This is a truth that the civic republican tradition framed as the problem of "corruption"—that is, the gradual yet inevitable displacement of concern for "the public thing" by individual interests and the desire for material well-being. One can be rightly skeptical of any civic republican account of *virtu* yet still see the relevance of the thematic of corruption to our time. We are the most powerful and wealthy society the world has ever known, and yet in many ways the least public-spirited and least politically thoughtful. Needless to say, "patriotism" of a knee-jerk and militaristic sort is not the answer. Nor, for that matter, are new and increasingly sophisticated theories of ideology and/or communicative rationality. What is needed is the widespread acknowledgment that democracy does not exist for the sake of the "free enterprise system," and that the latter (at least in its contemporary, multinational corporate form) is a potent source of corruption of both government and people.

America, needless to say, will never be a social democracy of the Western European variety. But that fact, in and of itself, is no reason to stand by while the greatest experiment initiated by the European Enlightenment destroys itself in the name of power, money, and some of the most anti-intellectual forms of religious doctrine ever conceived by the mind of man. There are many ways in which the brakes might be applied to our accelerating "corruption." Paying attention and demanding accountability are but two obvious candidates. Recognizing our own complicity in the creation of the "society of the spectacle" is another. Blaming "the system" (or some of its correlates: ideology, the "culture industry," "instrumental" and "functionalist" reason) is no longer an option, precisely because it absolves us of what little remains of our collective sense of civic and social responsibility.

It is this sense—the sense of shared responsibility that comes, or should come, with being an adult citizen of a liberal democracy—that forms the core of any defensible idea of political *Mündigkeit* in our time.

Ours may not be a particularly "enlightened" society. It may even at times seem incapable of enlightenment. It remains, however, a very imperfect constitutional democracy. The institutional bases for reform and democratic change are there, despite what Horkheimer, Adorno, and Marcuse imply or (just as often) come right out and say. The only question is whether we have the will, the attention span, and the energy to use them.

7 | GENEALOGIES OF TOTAL DOMINATION: ARENDT, ADORNO, AND AUSCHWITZ

What was decisive was the day we learned about Auschwitz.
When was that?
That was in 1943. And at first we didn't believe it—although my
husband and I always said that we expected anything from that
bunch. But we didn't believe this because militarily it was unnecessary
and uncalled for. My husband is a former military historian, he
understands something about these matters. He said don't be
gullible, don't take these stories at face value. They can't go that far!
And then a half-year later we believed it after all, because we had the
proof. That was the real shock. Before we said: Well, one has enemies.
That is entirely natural. Why shouldn't a people have enemies? But this
was different. It was really as if an abyss had opened. Because we had
the idea that amends could somehow be made for everything else, as
amends can be made for just about everything at some point in
politics. But not for this. *This ought not to have happened.*
—Hannah Arendt to Günter Gaus[1]

All sorrows can be borne if you put them into a story or can tell
a story about them.
—Isak Dinesen, quoted by Hannah Arendt[2]

Comprehending the Incomprehensible

Sixty years on, it is difficult to recapture the shock that Auschwitz and other death camps had on the European intellect and imagination. Temporal distance (and the numerous intervening atrocities it entails) plays a role, as does the inevitable dying off not only of the survivors, but an entire generation whose formative years were unclouded by the thought of the industrial production of corpses. Though much recent writing on memory and trauma strains to preserve the shock of the unthinkable, Auschwitz has become all too familiar—and thus all too thinkable—for recent generations. The "culture of memory," with its attendant media apparatus, hasn't exactly helped, nor has the persistent injunction of "Never forget." Endlessly repeated, the cliché's hearers presume that the work of understanding has long since been accomplished. All that remains is to commemorate the victims, an exercise that quickly becomes as rote and ritualized as any Memorial Day at Arlington National Cemetery.

We may not, then, ever forget. But can we ever understand? This is the question that determined the nature and trajectory of Arendt and Adorno's work from the moment confirmation of the death camps reached the United States in 1944. If "shock and wonder at existence" lie, as Plato tells us, at the root of philosophy, then shock at the existence of Auschwitz lies at the root of Arendt's political thinking and Adorno's mature philosophy. Made concrete by the camps, the pure form of antipolitics determined not only the nature and scope of *The Origins of Totalitarianism* but also forced Arendt to rethink the nature of authentic political action and public freedom—tasks she took up in *The Human Condition* and *On Revolution*.[3] More directly, the camps led her to theorize the nature of the evil performed by totalitarian political movements and to ponder the apparent "superfluousness of motives" in many of the perpetrators (the theme of the Eichmann book).[4]

As *the* image of the totalitarian collective—its essence, so to speak— Auschwitz confirmed not only Adorno's fears about reason's increasing complicity with power (however irrational the end, the extermination process was carried out in a highly rationalized manner, with technically innovative means). It also confirmed his sense that the tendency to eradicate the particular was lodged in the very heart of conceptual rationality. To understand Adorno's polemic against the "universal" requires that we begin with his commitment to the creaturely particular—a commitment that becomes fully explicit only after 1944 (its foreshadowing in *Dialectic of Enlightenment* notwithstanding).[5]

But however much the shock of the camps may have influenced Arendt and Adorno, the routes they choose to follow in pursuing the "interminable dialogue with the essence of totalitarianism" could hardly be more different.[6] For Arendt, the road to the death camps and the realization of total domination was neither a straight nor a necessary one. Nor was it uniquely German. Explicitly eschewing teleologies of progress or doom, Arendt conceived *The Origins of Totalitarianism* as the elucidation of the specific constellation of elements that made totalitarianism possible, not inevitable.[7]

The main features of her story—the bourgeois fascination with the accumulation of power and limitless economic expansion; the decline of the nation-state under imperialism and the rise of the pan-ethnic movements; the growing influence of racial-nationalist conceptions of political identity across Europe; the dissolution of the class system because of war, revolution, and economic trauma; the creation of millions of stateless ("superfluous") people by governmental abuse of the principle of national sovereignty; the emergence of a fatal alliance between the "mob" and the elite—are well known. What is less well known is that Arendt did not conceive her work as a check list of necessary causes nor, indeed, a causal explanation of totalitarianism at all.

Her project was "merely" to begin the interminable process by which it might be *understood*. Whether viewed singly or in combination, the elements Arendt discusses do not—in and of themselves—"produce" totalitarianism. Most obviously (in the German case), they have to be amalgamated by what Arendt calls the "catalytic agent" of anti-Semitic ideology. But even then, the final outcome—total domination through the eradication of human individuality in the "laboratory" of the camps[8]— remained, like everything else in history and politics, contingent.[9] That the constellation crystallized in just this toxic manner, that certain pathologies of late European modernity (such as racism and imperialism) should give rise to the society of the camps—all this has nothing remotely "necessary" about it.

In stark contrast to Arendt, Adorno (and his partner Max Horkheimer) often seems as intent as Hegel in "eliminating the contingent."[10] This is not to say that Adorno crafts an encompassing narrative of "World History," the better to explain the camps.[11] He treats them and the phenomenon of total domination less as the culminating (and contingent) pathology in a history of pathologies (the history of late modern Europe) than as the quasi-necessary outcome of the evolution of culture and the rationalization of society. What appears at the end must somehow be contained in the beginning. Adorno takes this Hegelian principle to almost absurd lengths in *Dialectic of Enlightenment*, his primary effort to philosophically comprehend civilization's relapse into barbarism.

Of course, Adorno does not follow the quasi-Aristotelian lead of Hegel's self-embodying Spirit. The "dialectic of enlightenment" is more of a genealogy in the Nietzschean sense.[12] The "primal history of subjectivity" it presents (most fully adumbrated in the excursus on the *Odyssey*) reveals "how much blood and cruelty lies at the bottom of all good things." The formation of the rational subject—the liberation from myth through Odysseus's disenchanting form of cunning—sets the pattern for an endlessly repeated sequence of self-denial, self-violence, and self-sacrifice.

Hence *Dialectic of Enlightenment's* most famous thesis: scientific-Enlightenment rationality, as it dominates nature, inevitably dominates man, who is also nature.[13] Reason has its origin in the primordial struggle for self-preservation—in the painful process by which a unitary self gradually emerges and separates itself from the mythic powers of a primitive, animistic world. It is this identity-forming struggle against an overwhelming nature that creates, from the very beginning, an internal link between reason and domination, reason and power.

What, one might ask, does this have to do with the death camps? Originally, nothing at all, given the chronology of *Dialectic of Enlightenment's* composition and ultimate verification of the darkest and most unbelievable rumors from Europe.[14] But what the book's first four chapters clearly do accomplish is a deepening—via Nietzsche and Freud—of Max Weber's account of the centuries-long process of the formalization of reason. That is to say, these chapters illuminate the forces behind the modern divestment of the moral, political, and even religious content traditionally associated with the concept of reason in the West.

By showing how a thoroughly "disenchanted" rationality is bound up with man's primordial and ongoing self-cruelty, Horkheimer and Adorno revealed the "germ of regression" contained in the origins (and development) of civilization itself. Enlightened reason finds itself entangled in "blind domination" not by chance or an unfortunate concatenation of historical circumstances. Rather, this possibility is inscribed in its very origins. For Adorno and Horkheimer, recent history merely verified this fact in the most horrific manner imaginable.

From Adorno's perspective, the only way to prevent this particular fruit from appearing on reason's genealogical tree was to relentlessly apply reflective rationality to rationalization itself. Failing this, enlightenment winds up destroying itself through the creation of a closed system of formal rationality: the "administered society." Such a system makes regression at once more likely and more deadly. The unsustainable levels of self-denial and self-violence demanded by modern society create the need to let off steam by means of what Nietzsche called "orgies of feeling." This time, however, a new kind of "ascetic priest" (Hitler) would orchestrate such orgies, aimed at Enlightenment's original representatives (the Jews).[15]

Stepping back, we can see not only a vast difference in Arendt and Adorno's "methods," but also in their respective narrative frames. Arendt begins by constructing a history of the present, one in which the idea of historical causation ("if y—or even if a, b, c, and d—then x") has little, if any, place. Horkeimer and Adorno take up Weber's thesis about rationalization and extend it backward in time (by means of Nietzsche and Freud) to reveal the genetic link between reason, sacrifice, and total domination. This narrative on a grand scale—a metanarrative, to use Jean-François Lyotard's overused term—is comparable to Hegel's *Phenomenology of Spirit* in its sheer scope and ambition, if not exactly in its object or method. Indeed, so grand is Horkeimer and Adorno's speculative history of "impure" reason that one is tempted to say that Arendt, in comparison, has no metanarrative.

However, Arendt's encounter with totalitarianism—her dialogue with its "essence"—does begin from a very specific account of the nature of total domination. The story Arendt tells in *The Origins of Totalitarianism* is one predicated on her sense of the camps as the site of totalitarianism's most ambitious "experiments." These experiments, in her view, have one purpose: to eradicate the human capacity for spontaneity. They mean to change human nature, to turn humans into "bundles of reflexes" much like Pavlov's dogs. Thus it is not the sadism of the extermination per se but the rendering of human beings *superfluous as human beings* that is the "radical evil" represented by Auschwitz.

In this chapter I explore the nature and stakes of Arendt and Adorno's respective approaches to the problem Auschwitz posed, and continues to pose, for humanity in general and European humanity in particular. My desire is to illuminate how these two very different thinkers narrativized modernity's contribution to what looks (at first glance) like atavistic horror or sheer regression. For if Arendt and Adorno share one thing, it is the grounding conviction that total domination (*totale Herrschaft*) is a distinctively modern pathology.

Of course, neither Arendt nor Adorno blamed the Enlightenment or the modern age for Auschwitz. Fast and loose appropriations of both figures have made us familiar with such an argument, but it is not Adorno's and it is certainly not Arendt's. Both thinkers owe far too much to the spirit of the Enlightenment, and to its ideas of human dignity and the right to a domination-free existence, to be classed as out-and-out anti-modernists.[16] However, Adorno and Arendt do more to expose the extent of modernity's complicity with horror than any other thinkers. The issue that separates them is the source of this complicity: is it to be found in a secularization and formalization that empties reason of all ethical content? Or is it in a growing modernist-capitalist-imperialist impatience with all durable legal-political structures (an impatience born of the pro-totototalitarian thought that "everything is possible"[17] if only such limits are removed)? Around these themes Arendt and Adorno spin their respective narrative webs, the one concrete, historical, and bewilderingly multidimensional, the other fragmentary and forbiddingly abstract.

My aim is not to pass judgment on these two extraordinarily different accounts (although I will say at the outset that I find Arendt's more persuasive, Adorno's theoretical brilliance notwithstanding). Rather, it is to tease out certain "Hegelian" dimensions, the better to understand why Arendt and Adorno wind up constructing the kind of narratives they do and why they emphasize certain issues rather than others. In the case of Adorno, the recourse to Hegel is hardly surprising or unexpected. It is present not only in the contrast between "reflective" and "positivistic" reason but also in Adorno's recourse to grand narrative and in his conviction—fundamental to both German Romanticism and idealism—that only reconciliation with nature, rather than the "enlightened" attempt to dominate it, will heal the wounds of civilization.

Things are quite different with Arendt. Throughout her considerable oeuvre, she repeatedly castigates Hegel and Hegelian-type thinking. Most prominently (in *On Revolution*), she attacked his attempt to derive freedom from (rational) necessity, a deductive link she found operative in much totalitarian thinking. But she also attacked the related idea that realizing freedom somehow hinged on reconciliation with nature. Arendt's political thought is based on the idea that only a durable man-made world of laws, institutions, and culture prevents human beings from being assimilated to nature and natural necessity. Such assimilation would make them lose the very thing that makes them human: their capacity for freedom, for beginning. Yet despite this "contrastive" theory of freedom—despite Arendt's insistence on the importance of an artificial world that stands between man and nature—her argument in *The Origins of Totalitarianism* actually owes much to the very philosopher she loved to hate.

How Reason Reverts to Barbarism: Hegel, Weber, and Horkheimer

How does one begin to comprehend the incomprehensible? To fall back on faith is to abdicate the task of understanding at the outset. To cite the character of one person, one movement, or one nation merely localizes the problem of evil. The Holocaust was a pan-European phenomenon, one in which many nations took an active or supportive role. Hence the deeply unsatisfying quality of works like Daniel Goldhagen's *Hitler's Willing Executioners*. While many Germans lent themselves to Hitler's project of "eliminationist anti-Semitism," other nations were (clearly) more anti-Semitic. If anti-Semitism is the standard, the "national character" argument refutes itself. Similarly, while the idea of a German "special path"—a *Sonderweg*—to modernity has merit, the road to modernity has hardly been straight for any number of countries. Of course, good philosophical and historical reasons exist for maintaining the uniqueness of the Holocaust as an event in world history. But there are less good reasons for maintaining the uniqueness of the perpetrators or confining them to one national "species."

If we were still Hegelians, the project of understanding would pose difficulties, but they would hardly be insurmountable. As Hegel famously said, "God does not wish to have narrow-minded and empty-headed children."[18] The specific context of this remark, his lectures on the philosophy of world history, included a discussion of the knowability—or unknowability—of God's nature and His plans for humankind. Hegel emphatically asserts that Christianity has revealed what was formerly unknowable. God has, through Scripture, commanded us to know him.[19]

Given the pantheistic implications of God as a cosmic spirit (*Geist*) that must embody itself in nature and human history, the injunction to "know God" amounts to a command to understand the ways of Providence in world history. For Hegel, this entails grasping the final end or purpose of history and the means that Spirit deploys to realize it. This project can be accomplished only by a reason that neither stands trans-fixed at appearances nor contents itself with measuring natural regulari-ties (the kind of reason Hegel dismissed as the "mere understanding," *Verstand*). Reason must be able to penetrate to the dialectical core of things, to the necessary movement or development behind the flux of in-terests, appearances, and contingencies.[20]

That such a "super-science" actually exists Hegel takes to have been demonstrated by his *Phenomenology* and (later) by his *Logic*. The idea of it is implicit in philosophy's aspiration—first appearing in the pre-Socratics—to rise from existence to essence; to show, as Anaxagoras said, that reason (*nous*) rules the world.[21] Yet while this ambition spurred the growth of the natural sciences and comprehension of the "nonspiritual" realm, philoso-phy failed to deliver on its early promise to understand humanity's place in the world, let alone its peculiar destiny. Hegel's *Lectures on the Philoso-phy of World History*, like his philosophy generally, is a "scientific" (*wis-senschaftlich*) attempt to deliver on this unfulfilled promise.

The idea of such a super-science, one that reveals to us not only the end of history but its means of realization, now seems more than a little absurd. When it comes to events like the Holocaust, the explanatory pre-tensions of such a super-science—along with Hegel's conviction that reason governs the world[22]—border on the obscene. Confronted with the reality of the gas chambers, we have no need of yet another Pangloss, even if he is as intellectually high-powered as Hegel. Understandably, it has become a reflexive gesture among European and American theorists to say that Auschwitz definitively repudiates Hegel's philosophy of history, which sees civilization culminating in the objective institutionalization of the moral knowledge that "all are free." For close to fifty years, Auschwitz has been the rock on which all dialectical theodicies—with their promises of rationality, continuity, and meaning—are shattered.[23]

Yet however much Auschwitz may strike us as a radical break in the history of Western civilization (and it certainly struck Adorno and Arendt in this way), Hegel's philosophy of history is more than up to the task of accommodating it. It was, after all, Hegel himself who insisted that "his-tory is a slaughter-bench" on which the best of nations, peoples, and cul-tures have been sacrificed.[24] History's progressive movement—to realizing that all are free and to building a sociopolitical world on that principle—is not linear, but more like a spiral, complete with catastrophes and moments of (seemingly total) regression or loss. The fall of Rome and the subsequent Dark Ages provide only the most obvious examples. The idea that "freedom is on the march" along a straight road to democracy may be popular with American neo-conservatives, but it is certainly not Hegel's view.

Moreover—and even more Hegelian—Auschwitz has important "dialectical" effects for our world. As Michael Ignatieff reminds us, universal human rights culture really came into being only after World War II.[25] The United Nations Charter of Human Rights and the (painfully slow) acknowledgment of the need to limit the principle of national sovereignty are both direct effects of the extermination camps. The fragility of this accomplishment and the frequent failures to make good on the principles of the 1947 declaration are plain enough. My point here is not that we are being magically propelled into a better future by something called the "movement of history." It is, rather, that no list of civilization-shattering catastrophes is enough to disprove Hegel's basic contention: that we can understand who we are only in narrative retrospect and on the supposition that moral progress is being made (albeit in fits and starts). The very intensity with which Hegel is denounced in some quarters (for his supposed doctrine of historical inevitability, his flagrant Eurocentrism, his condescending attitudes toward women and non-white races) is as good a demonstration as any that the moral and political implications of the realization that "all are free"—a realization introduced, but hardly fulfilled, by Christianity—are still working themselves out in the roundabout way he described.

The weakness of Hegel's philosophy of history is not that he was blind to tragedy and catastrophe in the manner of Leibniz—nothing could be further from the truth.[26] Rather, the weakness is found in the narrative and epistemological assumptions he had to deploy to turn human history into a continuous (and, as such, meaningful) process of moral, cultural, and spiritual development. Most glaringly, a subject was needed to render the "bacchanalian whirl" of forms of consciousness into a plausible (not to say necessary) *Bildungsroman*. The idea of *Geist*, of a cosmic spirit forming and embodying itself through successive cultures and civilizations, provided a "hero" for the story, but only by imposing an unconvincing Aristotelian metaphysics onto history. Hence the narrative-metaphysical conceit of a "necessary" or "objective" unfolding, one in which the beginning always contains, somehow, the end.

But however incredible Hegel's idea of *Geist* is to us, it is ultimately surpassed by his supposition of a "reflective" rationality able to grasp reality in its innermost essence, in its full natural and historical development.[27] In Hegel, the limits to intelligibility imposed by Kant's critique and the *Ding an sich* are abolished by a speculative coup de grâce—the identification of thought and being in "the Idea"—and teleological judgment returns with a vengeance. This comes out most clearly in those pages of *Die Vernunft in der Geschichte* where Hegel blithely leaps from a law-regulated Nature to a History driven by Providence (that is, Reason). If, Hegel argues, we agree that reason governs the natural world in the form of laws, why do we find the idea of an objective rational schema structuring history implausible?

> It was indeed fashionable at one time to admire the wisdom of God as manifested in animals and plants. But to marvel at human destinies or products of nature is already an indication that we have some knowledge of God. If we admit that providence reveals itself in such objects and materials, why should we not do the same in world history? . . .
>
> To believe that God's wisdom is not active in everything is to show humility towards the material rather than towards the divine wisdom itself. Besides, nature is a theater of secondary importance compared with that of world history. Nature is a field in which the divine Idea operates in a non-conceptual medium; the spiritual sphere is its proper province, and it is here above all that it ought to be visible. Armed with the concept of reason [*Vernunft*], we need not fear coming to grips with any subject whatsoever.[28]

To move from Hegel's 1830 *Lectures on the Philosophy of World History* to Max Weber's 1917 lecture "Science as a Vocation" is to witness an epochal shift in the Western tradition's understanding of—and hopes for—reason itself. With Weber the Reason of the philosophers is replaced by the sociological concept of rationalization and by the cognate concept of the "disenchantment of the world" (*die Entzauberung der Welt*).

Rationalization and disenchantment are intimately tied, and not only because the growth of autonomous modern legal, bureaucratic, and economic structures demands calculation, regularity, and predictability of outcome. At a deeper level, the historical development of reason—from its Greek origins in the ideal of the *bios theoretikos*, to its medieval subordination to faith, to its sloughing off theological and metaphysical residue as it crosses the threshold of modernity—can be fairly characterized as a movement from a substantive or "emphatic" concept of reason (one that presumes an internal connection not only to truth but to justice, freedom, and the good life) to an increasingly scientific, formal, and instrumental conception of rationality (purposive rationality or *Zweckrationalität*).

Leo Strauss perhaps to the contrary, the movement from substantive to formal or means-end rationality was not the result of a plot by Machiavelli, Hobbes, or even Weber himself to undermine Aristotelianism and the possibility of an objective ranking of values. It was not, in other words, the product of a conspiracy of the "moderns" against the ancients.[29] Rather, this transition is inscribed *in the history of Western reason itself*, a subterranean history Nietzsche first brought to light in his *Twilight of the Idols*, and one that Weber brilliantly encapsulates in "Science as a Vocation."

Weber gave his lecture at the request of students at the University of Munich. After considering the demanding "external" and "internal" conditions for the pursuit of "science as a vocation" in the world of specialized scholarship, Weber turned to the broader Nietzschean question of what is the value or meaning of science within "the total life of humanity."[30] Here, he states, "the contrast between the past and the present is tremendous." Plato's *Republic* famously presented philosophy and science (*epistēmē*) as one and the same, an identity founded on the Greek discovery of the concept and its logic. The philosopher's emergence from the "cave" of everyday life through a strictly conceptual dialectic enabled "true being to be grasped." This, in turn, seemed to open the way "for knowing and for teaching how to act rightly in life, and, above all, how to act as a citizen of the state."[31] Well, Weber asks, "who today views science in such a manner?"—that is, as containing the key to how to live and how to act? For us, scientific rationality hardly facilitates the apprehension of "true being" in all its cosmic meaningfulness. Nor does it provide a guide to properly human conduct and the purpose of life.

Next, the discovery of the "second great tool of scientific work," the rational experiment, enabled men of the Renaissance like Leonardo to think of science as a path to true art and (thus) to "true nature." Art itself was raised to the rank of science. Yet (as Weber reminds his audience) the idea that scientific intellectualism opens the path to either "true art" or "true nature" sounds absurd to modern ears.

With Protestantism and the idea of a *deus absconditus*, the meaning of science takes yet another turn. Now, through scrutinizing the structure of the most humble of God's creatures, it seemed to show "the way to God."[32] As Weber puts it in one of his most pungent passages:

> God is hidden. His ways are not our ways. His thoughts are not our thoughts. In the exact sciences, however, where one could physically grasp His works, one hoped to come upon the traces of

what he planned for the world. And today? Who—aside from certain big children who are indeed found in the natural sciences—still believes that the findings of astronomy, biology, physics, or chemistry could teach us anything about the *meaning* of the world? If there is any such 'meaning,' along what road could one come upon its tracks? If these natural sciences lead to anything in this way, they are apt to make the belief that there is such a thing as the 'meaning' of the universe die out at its very roots.[33]

Puritanism and Hegel to the contrary, the natural and the historical sciences have nothing to tell us about the ultimate meaning of the world or the purposes of its Creator. The thrust of their development has been to make such questions appear as holdovers from an earlier (quasi-theological) stage of moral and intellectual culture.

Having dispatched the (once influential) ideas that science opened the way to true being, true nature, true art, or true God, Weber turns to the bourgeois notion that science, as a means to master life, is actually the "way to happiness." Such "naive optimism" gives way on the slightest interrogation of the bourgeois idea of happiness, or the consideration of the concrete possibilities of devastation opened up by a technologized world. Thus, only a "few big children in university chairs or editorial offices" could find convincing the idea that science and technology are the ways to happiness.[34] At the end of two thousand years of the self-undermining of science's original (Greek) pretensions, we must, Weber contends, own up to the truth of Tolstoy's observation: "Science is meaningless because it gives no answer to our question, the only question that is important for us: 'What shall we do and how shall we live?'"[35]

For Weber, it is self-evident historical fact that science (or "Reason") gives no answer to this question. The grandiose hopes of thinkers from Plato to Bacon, Leibniz to Hegel, have all come to naught. The disenchantment of the world does not stop when the world is rid of magic and animism. Rather, reason and science themselves undergo a relentless purging process. The end result is a world in which we moderns must face up to the reality that no "facts of value" exist—no cosmically inscribed laws or norms, no final purpose of the universe, history, or man—for our reason to discover.

Of course, the fact that this process produces increasingly astringent (and narrowly applied) notions of rationality has led many to bemoan the "relativism" that Weber's sternly upheld distinction between facts and values (apparently) implies. Stripped of the grandiose hopes of the Western philosophical tradition, reason/science seems—from a moral point of view—to have become utterly impotent. The very idea of an "end-constitutive" rationality—and, indeed, of objectively given rational ends—appears to have been abolished.[36] At the same time, instrumental or purposive rationality—inscribed in systematized law, bureaucratized administration, and ever-growing technological efficiency—is stronger than ever.

Weber was hardly unaware of this tendency. However, he staunchly refused to deal in rationalist nostalgia. The point of his insistence upon intellectual honesty was not to condemn us to a seemingly irrationalist "decisionism," but to force us to take up the burden of such choices, with a clear-eyed and sober view of the consequences (and shortcomings) of any particular value position.[37] Yet despite Weber's forceful articulation of this message in "Science as a Vocation" (and it is difficult to imagine a more forceful articulation), the myth of an irrationalist world of value choices closed off from any rational adjudication whatsoever still haunts his reputation. If Kant had limited reason "to make room for faith," Weber—it seemed—limited reason still further in order to make room for a politics of authentic (yet ultimately groundless) commitment.[38]

This charge was leveled at Weber by Strauss on the right and by Horkheimer on the left. One of the more surprising aspects of Horkheimer's *Eclipse of Reason* (the "popular" set of lectures he gave at Columbia in 1946, intended as a kind of layperson's guide to *Dialectic of Enlightenment*) is just how crudely, even dishonestly, it makes the case against Weber. Horkheimer, framing his lectures through a global contrast between a traditional "objective" conception of reason and a "subjectivist" view made predominant through the long historical process of the "formalization of reason," points out that the very distinction between a "functional" and "substantial" rationality derives from the "Max Weber school." Thus, "Weber . . . adhered so definitely to the subjectivistic trend that he did not conceive of any rationality—not even a 'substantial' one—by which man can discriminate one end from another."[39] Indeed, "Weber's pessimism with regard to the possibility of rational insight and action, as expressed in his philosophy [here Horkheimer cites "Science as a Vocation"], is itself a stepping-stone in the renunciation of philosophy and science as regards their aspiration of *defining man's goal.*"[40]

Even if one leaves aside the question of whether it is possible, in a modern pluralist context, to cleave to a traditional (Aristotelian) idea of a reason capable of defining humanity's *telos*, to state that Weber could not even *conceive* of a more substantial or end-discriminating rationality ignores the very premise of his account. As Albrecht Wellmer has pointed out, the "paradox" of rationalization—around which Weber constructs his social philosophy and which provides the core of all subsequent Frankfurt School theorizing—presumes that a more substantial, Enlightenment-generated idea of reason accompanies and is part of the formalization process itself.[41]

Thus, the disenchantment of the world does not imply that a narrowly scientific or instrumental rationality is the only permissible kind in the late modern world. Construed broadly, Weber's idea entails what Wellmer calls "the de-sacralization of society"—that is, the gradual destruction of bogusly "objective" systems of social meaning (such as those that reigned in the *ancien régime*). As a result, disenchantment must be seen not as a turn down a blind alley, but as a crucial component of humanity's emergence from its "self-incurred tutelage." It marks a critical step in human moral-political self-formation or *Bildung*.

Now, it is certainly true—as Weber repeatedly insisted—that we finds ourselves increasingly confined by a bureaucratic-economic "iron cage," whose main features are generated by purposive and formal rationality. But this broad tendency of rationalization hardly refutes the idea that emergence from falsely "objectivistic" accounts of society, morality, and politics is *the* precondition for anything like moral maturity (to say nothing of pluralist democracy). The promise of this moment—the modern moment, as captured by the separation of church and state in the French and American Revolutions—may well go unfulfilled. As Jürgen Habermas has argued, the imperatives of the "system" may well colonize the "life-world" that is the home of practical discursive contexts, or there may be a resurgence of objectivist (anti-modern and intrinsically intolerant) moral regimes. Both tendencies are amply in evidence today. The "paradox" of rationalization in the Weberian sense is that it clearly recognizes the cognitive achievement of the moderns while underscoring the ironies of a purposive rationality shorn of any traditionalist restraints.

Horkheimer's critique glosses over the fundamentally ambiguous nature of this modern moment and thus fails to do justice to the complexity of Weber's stance. Rhetorically, Horkheimer does this to create the misleading impression that unless we go back to the "right reason" of the philosophical tradition, we cannot distinguish the validity of one end or value claim against any other. This refrain is, of course, familiar from more conservative theorists, such as Leo Strauss, Eric Voegelin, and Alasdair MacIntyre. The only thing that really distinguishes Horkheimer's version from theirs is that his is neo-Hegelian rather than neo-Aristotelian or neo-Platonist.

Like his opposite numbers on the right, Horkheimer wants us to draw the following "inevitable" conclusion: a reason shorn of its end-adjudicating and end-defining power is a reason that will able to supply the most efficient means to any end whatsoever. To accept the lessons of the disenchantment of the world when it comes to reason or science is, then, not to take a crucial step forward in our moral-political *Bildung* (the realization that neither can absolve us of the task of thinking and judging for ourselves). It is, rather, to set ourselves up, one and all, as potential Adolf Eichmanns. In Horkheimer's view, unless reason is "objective"—unless it is capable of revealing the structure of the world and humanity's true end—then we are simply at sea, morally and politically speaking.[42] A disenchanted rationality leads to barbarism because it cannot provide the criteria necessary to distinguish civilized from barbaric ends.

This argument is the rationalist equivalent of Dostoevsky's "If God is dead, then all is permitted."[43] It holds that if reason cannot tell us how to live and how to act, then civilization devolves into barbarism. The catch, of course, is that neither Dostoyevsky's argument—nor Horkheimer's version of it—at all follows logically. Human values (and civilized behavior) are not logically dependent on faith in an omnipotent Lawgiver nor on the idea of an end-defining (substantive) Reason.

The idea of a substantial rationality capable of articulating the best way of life or the best political regime is, as Isaiah Berlin repeatedly pointed out, the inheritance of a "monistic" ethical-religious tradition.[44] This tradition gives birth to an idea of reason that presumes that there is one, and only one, correct answer to questions about humanity's end and proper sociopolitical arrangements. Such a conception has proved remarkably long-lived. Rhetorically, it is still quite powerful, the progress of disenchantment notwithstanding. Its appeal (which Horkheimer exploits to the fullest) hinges on the idea that modernity must be able to answer questions that theology, tradition, and metaphysics had previously raised and provided answers to. As Hans Blumenberg has suggested, we should view modern attempts to provide new "definitive" answers to ultimate questions as instances of a peculiar syndrome: the seeming "obligation of the heir" to "know what was known before."[45]

From Odysseus to Auschwitz: *Dialectic of Enlightenment* and the Holocaust

Like Strauss's *Natural Right and History* and Voegelin's *Order and History*, *The Eclipse of Reason* gives the impression that a return to a substantial (end-defining) rationality is a live option. Thanks to the formalization of reason, we have taken a wrong turn. All that is required to get back on track is to think once more in the substantial, comprehensive terms of a Plato, an Aristotle, or a Hegel—philosophers who believed in the rational structure not only of nature, but of society and human life as well. Teleology is not dead; it has simply been unjustly banished by an overly aggressive positivism. The idea that modernity has closed off certain paths (Weber's disenchantment thesis)—that intellectual honesty demands that we acknowledge the inability of either reason or science to provide answers to our most pressing social and existential questions—is anathema to Horkheimer.

All the more reason, then, to be surprised by the path he and Adorno take in *Dialectic of Enlightenment*. Unlike *The Eclipse of Reason*, *Dialectic* does not really trade in theoretical nostalgia, despite its constant invocation of the need for "reflective" rationality. Rather, it takes the critique of reason to previously unimagined depths. Conceptual rationality itself is in the dock, thanks to its impure origins in the struggle for self-preservation. This struggle fundamentally and irrevocably shapes conceptual rationality so that it might serve as an effective tool of domination (of nature, of other men, and of the self which is also nature). Civilization reverts to barbarism not because we are prey to an irreducible set of aggressive instincts (Freud's thesis in *Civilization and Its Discontents*) but because conceptual rationality—the subsumption of particulars by a universal—arises out of, and endlessly recapitulates, the master's distanced and abstract view of those he dominates.[46]

In *Dialectic of Enlightenment*, the "thoroughly enlightened" world— from which animism, myth, and metaphysics have been extirpated—is presented as an integrated, systematic apparatus for dominating nature, coordinating men, and eliminating otherness. Enlightenment, in Horkheimer and Adorno's memorable phrase, is "mythical fear radicalized."[47] That is the real content of the disenchantment of the world. In its inclusive, closed, and "totalitarian" character, the scientific-industrial civilization born of the Enlightenment inevitably reverts to myth. It becomes its own fetish as it relentlessly expunges everything (human, natural, or intellectual) that does not fit in with the systemic demands of the whole.[48]

For Horkheimer and Adorno, this remythologization is as manifest in the positivistic cult of fact and scientific rationality as it is in the culture industry's "idolization of the existing order."[49] The way out of the "administered society" is not through more conceptual rationality; nor is it through a more reflective version of discursive thinking. Rhetorical gesturing toward the "self-reflection of reason" aside, the analyses offered in *Dialectic of Enlightenment* support the thesis that discursive logic and conceptual thinking are themselves too geared toward domination and self-preservation to escape a built-in tendency toward reification and suppressing difference. According to Horkheimer and Adorno, the repressive logic of identity drives the development of Western *ratio* from the very beginning, culminating in the "total society's" elimination of everything that is irredeemably "other." Even Hegelian logic, with its assertion of the identity of identity and difference, does not escape this indictment.[50] What is needed is a new kind of rationality, one that offers a form of synthesis in which the mediation of the universal and the particular occurs without the latter's obliteration.[51]

This well-known and exceedingly bleak picture takes Weber's meta-narrative of the formalization of reason and gives it a distinctively Nietzschean twist. Enlightenment is now identified with the disenchantment of the world, and enlightened reason with a specifically corrosive form of rationality. The problem is not (simply) that enlightened rationality empties itself of content as it crosses the threshold of modernity (the formalization thesis); rather, it is that such rationality operates by actively destroying all concrete determinations of reason.[52] Wherever truth retains traces of an immanent connection to the just or the good, there disenchanted reason sees yet one more superstition to be destroyed.

In this "permanent twilight of the idols," every "definite theoretical view is subjected to the annihilating criticism that it is only a belief, until even the concepts of mind, truth, and indeed enlightenment itself have been reduced to animistic magic."[53] The "self-destruction of the enlightenment"—the regression of the civilization born of modern science, technology, and economics to a "new form of barbarism"—flows from the intrinsically dissolvent movement of an untethered, self-contained rationality. No values beyond power and systemic integration can survive the corrosive assault of enlightened reason's "will to truth."

As a program of radical disenchantment, enlightenment yields what Nietzsche described as an epistemology of nihilism: the truth that there is no truth beyond the reality of power and the fact of domination.[54] Horkheimer and Adorno conceive this movement not as a contingent fanaticism or intolerance (a kind of positivist Jacobinism, so to speak) but as contained in the logic of conceptual rationality itself. This Nietzschean point is driven home by the two excursuses to "The Concept of Enlightenment" essay. The first, by Adorno, examines the primal history of subjectivity via the figure of Odysseus. The second, "Enlightenment and Morality," by Horkheimer, investigates those "dark writers of the bourgeoisie" (Hobbes, Machiavelli, and Mandeville, but—more important—de Sade and Nietzsche) who first articulated "the merciless doctrine of the identity of domination and reason."

As Seyla Benhabib has pointed out, there is an implicit tension between the two excursuses, Horkheimer and Adorno's insistence on joint responsibility for virtually every line in *Dialectic of Enlightenment* notwithstanding.[55] It is Adorno who most rigorously theorizes that "the structure of Western reason as such is one of domination and sublimation," whereas Horkheimer makes the weaker claim that it is the bourgeois reduction of reason to an instrument of calculation—in service of selfish ends—that leads to nihilism and the betrayal of the Enlightenment's emancipatory potential.[56] Nevertheless, the two excursuses *do* complement each other, pointing (as Habermas has argued) to a clearly Nietzschean conclusion: reason—whether viewed in its origins or in its Enlightened maturity—equals domination.

Adorno's essay concentrates on the psychic archaeology of the self—that is, on tracing the effects of the early Western self's fear of being reabsorbed by the very natural powers it had so recently escaped. As Odysseus's travails demonstrate, emergent self-identity is perpetually under threat of dissolution by more powerful archaic, mythic forces. Confronting the Sirens, Circe, and Polyphemus (among others), Odysseus cunningly mimics the logic of acquiescent sacrifice. It is this very mimicry that allows him to create loopholes and (thus) evade entrapment. Indeed, exploiting these loopholes is enough to destroy these mythic powers of nature *as powers* and enable Odysseus to emerge intact from every threat to his selfhood's integrity. The price of Odysseus's success, however, is ceaseless instinctual renunciation and self-denial. He overcomes the logic of mythic sacrifice (which presupposes the superiority of natural powers) through the introversion of sacrifice.[57]

The psychic archaeology of the self—laid out as a kind of allegory in the Homeric text—reveals the need to perpetually reinscribe the principle of self-sacrifice if an enduring, self-identical subject is to be preserved. This is exactly the strategy Odysseus pursues, earning him Adorno's memorable, if unintentionally humorous, tribute as the "first bourgeois" (*erste Bürger*). Happiness and reconciliation—the twin goals of German Romanticism and Idealism, respectively—are infinitely deferred as "self-preservation destroys the very thing which is to be preserved": a self at once distinct from, yet also a part of, nature. Adorno concludes that Western subjectivity is founded on primordial and repeated self-violence, and that Western *ratio* emerged out of the need to dominate nature and suppress all otherness as existential threat.[58] Like Nietzsche and Freud, Adorno clearly implies that these genealogical origins cannot be transcended dialectically. On the contrary, their distorting and pathological power only becomes clearer with the triumph of scientific rationality and technological civilization.

If Adorno's excursus concentrates on reason's primordial origins (and determinative shaping) in the struggle for self-preservation, Horkheimer's focuses on the moral trajectory of Enlightenment rationality—a rationality that reduces the traditional bases of social morality to the status of mere superstition.

At the outset, Horkheimer cites Kant's definition of enlightenment. Man's "emergence from his self-incurred tutelage" consists in finding the "courage to use his own understanding" without authoritative guidance. Yet, as Horkheimer demonstrates by reference to Kant's appendix to his "Transcendental Dialectic," human reason, essentially "a faculty of deducing the particular from the universal," has as its goal the creation of a "unified scientific order," one that derives "factual knowledge from principles."[59] But—as we know from Bacon and, indeed, from Kant himself—science (even in its most elegant, sophisticated, and systematized form) is essentially a tool in the struggle for self-preservation. Controlling nature, bending it to our will, prevents scientific reason from reflecting on its own goals.[60] The conclusion seems to be that emergence from our self-incurred tutelage entails recognizing that *practical* reason will be just as geared toward domination—just as "instrumental"—as theoretical reason (that "lawgiver to Nature") is.[61]

Kant, of course, could not bring himself to this conclusion. Hence the second *Critique's* elaborate attempt to derive the duty of mutual respect from a "law of reason"—an endeavor that, Horkheimer notes, "has no support within the [epistemological doctrines of the first] *Critique*."[62] It fell to Hobbes, Machiavelli, and Mandeville to point out how social duties are ultimately rooted in prudence and self-interest, and how "public virtues" rise out of egoism and "private vices." And it fell to the self-consciously nihilistic Sade and Nietzsche to unmask not only Kantian moral "propaganda"—the fiction of the categorical imperative—but also the ideology that any social morality grounded on interests alone would tend toward harmony, equilibrium, and the greatest good for the greatest number. The "bourgeois" doctrine that both science and practical reason are mere tools for coordination and control—for getting what we want—leads inexorably to the recognition that the inescapable reality of social life is domination.

Much of Horkheimer's essay is devoted to drawing out Sade and Nietzsche's relentless demythologization of practical reason after Kant. Just as theoretical reason aims at a "systematic unity" of knowledge, one that enables us to control the natural world, so a disillusioned practical reason imagines a completely administered society, one whose relentless organization and brutal efficiency actualizes total domination. Prefigurations of this post-bourgeois, totalitarian society are found in Sade's orgies (sex as a joyless and hyper-organized team sport) and in Nietzsche's praise of those "strong natures" who realize that most people are suited to be means and nothing more.[63]

At its core, then, enlightenment is a disillusioning rationality, and disillusionment leads—with unvarying logic—not merely to a one-dimensionalization of reason (the formalization thesis) but to a global transvaluation of values. Pity, justice, and human solidarity are unmasked as the necessary superstitions of the "herd." Once these qualities are revealed as pieces of moralizing sentimentality, Sade and Nietzsche consign them to the ash heap of our unenlightened pre-history. Horkheimer does not condemn them for this. Rather, he sees their identification of reason with power as cutting through centuries of bourgeois cant. Their "pitiless doctrines are more compassionate than those of the moral lackeys of the bourgeoisie," since Sade and Nietzsche openly proclaim what "enlightened reason" demands. Horkheimer writes, "It is because they did not hush up the impossibility of deriving from reason a fundamental argument against murder, but proclaimed it from the rooftops, that Sade and Nietzsche are still vilified, above all by progressive thinkers." All they did was to take science at its word, and apply its findings in a way more consistent than any logical positivist.[64]

The introversion of sacrifice—the "original sin" of Odysseus's calculating reason—combined with the Enlightenment's fetish of systematic (scientific) rationality, yields the Frankfurt School nightmare of a "total society," one built on the twin pillars of self-denial and administrative despotism. The social machine works, but only by endlessly distorting human nature into an inhuman shape. To be sure, this is an intriguing and suggestive thesis. But what, if anything, does it contribute to understanding Nazi anti-Semitism? How does Horkheimer and Adorno's revision of Weber's formalization thesis illuminate—if that is what it does—the extermination of European Jewry?

In his excursus, Horkheimer develops Adorno's idea about the circular (and increasingly neurotic) relationship between self-preservation and self-denial. Civilization as we know it demands that this circle remain unbroken. Yet the demand that all fit smoothly into the apparatus exacts a horrible price, one that can lead (as Nietzsche noted in the *Genealogy*) to an almost suicidal nihilism.[65] Horkheimer asks: how does modern society avoid this terminus, the point where even the masses realize—albeit through a glass, darkly—that the technological "total" society built to ensure self-preservation actually "annihilates the subject," destroying "the very thing which is to be preserved"?[66]

Unsurprisingly, Horkheimer's answer echoes Nietzsche's. The "total society," most itself in the hyper-organized "fascist collectivity," promotes "orgies of feeling" in which the masses are allowed to participate in (or at least pantomime) the "right of the masters." Once pity has been eradicated by the triumph of "calculating reason" and a century of "bourgeois coldness," the way lies open to a temporarily revivifying revenge on those most removed from the stoic masculinity that characterizes the cogs in the social machine. As Horkheimer writes:

> Women and Jews show visible evidence of not having ruled for thousands of years. They live, although they could be eliminated, and their fear and weakness, the greater affinity to nature produced in them by perennial oppression, is the element in which they live. In the strong, who pay for their strength with their strained remoteness from nature and must forever forbid themselves fear, this incites blind fury. They identify themselves with nature by calling forth from their victims,

multiplied a thousandfold, the cry they may not utter themselves.[67]

An introverted sacrificial violence is—briefly and spasmodically, yet repeatedly—turned outward. Not, to be sure, on the masters or the social formation itself, but on those whose position at the bottom of the hierarchy enabled them to preserve the greatest amount of warmth and emotional solidarity.[68] The revenge wreaked on such "natural" victims is terrible and provides the tormentors with the simulacrum of a reconciliation with nature. This regression is undertaken to protect both a pathological civilization and a self perpetually uncertain of its own dearly purchased boundaries.

The kernel of truth contained in Horkheimer's analysis—that the dominated always reserve their most vicious kicks for those directly beneath them—also reveals its inadequacy. By explaining too much, it winds up explaining nothing at all. Weakness does call forth abusive and violent behavior—from the schoolyard to the matrimonial bed, from the lynch mob to the concentration camp. But sadism (in the clinical rather than philosophical sense) is, as Arendt noted, essentially sexual in nature. The same can be said of the "festive" cruelty that Nietzsche celebrated in the *Genealogy of Morals*.[69] Such spontaneous cruelty can, perhaps, account for pogroms, but it can hardly explain a massively planned and meticulously executed project of extermination. Further—and even more problematic for Horkheimer and Adorno's analysis—the link they strive to establish between systematic (or calculating) reason and human domination is here reduced to the status of an omnipresent background assumption. As a result, hardly a single modern instance of socially mediated violence exists that it is not capable of "explaining."

Only in "Elements of Anti-Semitism" do Horkheimer and Adorno narrow their focus, attempting to explain why the Jews had moved to "the storm center of history" (to use Arendt's phrase), becoming the martyrs of civilization. Six of the theses were written in summer 1943 (with the collaboration of Leo Leöwenthal), just as reports of the Holocaust were reaching America. Horkheimer added the seventh thesis in 1947.[70]

Readers expecting at least an intimation of the uniqueness of the extermination, or the novelty of totalitarian terror, will be sorely disappointed by "Elements of Anti-Semitism." Traces of Marxist economic determinism abound, framed by a sometimes heavy-handed use of speculative anthropology, psychology, and sociology. The result is a strangely functionalist account as to why Western civilization must have victims and why the Jews are its victims of choice. Horkheimer and Adorno are so determined to link anti-Semitism to their meta-narrative about the Enlightenment and the formalization of reason that they wind up effacing just about everything contingent, historical, or particular about the fate of European Jewry. This is a deeply ironic outcome, given *Dialectic of Enlightenment's* indictment of conceptual formalism and the ingrained habit of mechanically subsuming the particular under the universal.

The first thesis addresses the simultaneous truth and falseness of both the fascist and liberal idea of the Jews. "For the fascists," Horkheimer and Adorno write, "the Jews are not a minority, but the anti-race, the negative principle as such; on their extermination the world's happiness depends."[71] For the liberals, the Jews are a group formed by religious belief and cultural tradition, "free of national or racial features." The fascist thesis is true insofar as the Nazis have created a social reality grounded upon it; it is false in that all the predicates the fascist attaches to the Jews—the craving for exclusive ownership, endless appropriation, for unlimited power—form *his* essence, his will, not the Jew's.

The liberal thesis is true "as an idea," as the precipitate of a realized "unity of humanity." But it is patently untrue within the confines of "the existing order," in which a "hidebound particularism" constitutes "precisely the universal."[72] In other words, class society ensures that the "unity of humanity" remains a mere idea, while community—the "harmonious society" to which liberal Jews had pledged allegiance—takes the only form it can: that of a disfigured (and disfiguring) *Volksgemeinschaft*. Such a community enables the self-assertion of both worker and bourgeois in terms of race. Thus, the persecution of the Jews is built into the short-circuiting of the liberal order *qua* nation-state.[73]

The second thesis addresses the phenomenon of mass conformity within the confines of the "total society." "Anti-Semitism," Horkheimer and Adorno tell us, "as a popular movement has always been driven by the urge of which its instigators accuse social democrats: to make everyone the same."[74] This urge—in enraged, violent form—is cultivated and sanctioned by rulers, the better to deflect attention from the reality of domination and capitalist exploitation. Yet it is not simply a question of deflecting the understandable rage (and less understandable intolerance) of ordinary people at a substitute target, the "conspicuous and unprotected." Rather, "anti-Semitism is a well-rehearsed pattern, indeed a ritual of civilization, and the pogroms are the true ritual murders."[75]

They are the "true ritual murders" because the specific intention to persecute Jews is lacking. All that is needed is the feeling of power that comes from being a representative of the norm, and the presence of some "other"—Jews, vagrants, Catholics—who can serve as the "exceptions" to the inescapable rule. Thus it is that "the mindless pastime of beating people to death confirms the drab existence to which one merely conforms."[76] An inability to relax, to ever know reconciliation, drives the mass to project its own socially suppressed happiness onto some minority and to ruthlessly suppress that group in turn. As an omnipresent minority within Western civilization, the Jews serve this ritual function of projection and suppression all too well.

The third thesis departs from Horkheimer's earlier work on anti-Semitism. The most Marxist-economistic of the lot, it argues that the Jews—as merchants and bankers—provide a ready-made screen for the real capitalist swindle: the factory owner's extortion of "surplus-value." Historically relegated to the sphere of circulation, the Jews are a visible and easily exploited scapegoat for the entire capitalist class: "The merchant is the bailiff for the whole system, taking upon himself the odium due to others. That the circulation sphere is responsible for exploitation is a socially necessary illusion."[77]

The fourth thesis addresses the Christian roots of anti-Semitism, as well as the transformation (and preservation) of this structure under fascism. The fifth thesis—by far the most intellectually original and ambitious—deploys anthropology to argue that civilization's original proscription on the kind of uncontrolled mimesis characteristic of animism is both suspended and violently reinforced by anti-Semitism. The sixth focuses on the psychology of "false projection" characteristic of the paranoid imagination, while the seventh argues that late capitalism—in both its state and its monopoly form—has rendered the individual (whether as thinking subject or as ideologically motivated anti-Semite) an anachronism. Further, it has reduced thinking to a largely automatic process within the division of labor.

The result is a pervasive "thinking in stereotypes" and "ticket mentality" in which moral-political choices are presented as "inclusive" commodities to the (forever infantilized) consumer. The ticket mentality is "intrinsically anti-Semitic" because it reduces the most inhumane ideological ideas to the status of just one more plank in a party's platform. The voter then chooses among the commodified bundles. Any failure to participate, to accept the "petrified reality" of an electoral system in which the persecution of minorities can be framed in terms of a larger "program," leads to ostracism.[78]

This constellation of theses—the "reversibility" of the fascist and liberal ideas of the Jew; the rage of the conformist masses against anything "other"; the Jew as a handy scapegoat for capitalist exploitation; the Christian-fascist rage against the "older brother" (Judaism) who "knows better" and eschews "magical thinking"; the violent desublimation of proscribed mimetic impulse against those who originally banned it (the Jews as the people of the *Bilderverbot*); the reduction of the world to a closed circle of ideas via a paranoid structure of "false projection"; and the political domestication of anti-Semitism by means of the party system, which sells candidates and platforms (sometimes containing anti-Jewish "planks") like soap to voters—offers a strange combination of social-psychological insight, anthropological speculation, and Procrustean Marxist doctrine. Taken together, they render "the Jew" a highly charged symbol in the imaginary of Western civilization and in the fascist/capitalist present—so highly charged, in fact, that extermination becomes an all but predictable occurrence. The deceived and raging masses know not what they do. They are blindly and violently responding to the unhappiness wrought by "civilization" as a system of (now superfluous) self-denial. The Jews pay for this ignorance—this lack of thought, therapeutic insight, and self-clarity—with their lives.

What Horkeimer and Adorno offer in *Dialectic of Enlightenment*, then, is a theory in which liberal-market capitalism (and the "autonomous ego" its competition makes possible) is replaced by "total" societies in which planning, production, culture, and consumption are seamlessly integrated. If, as Lenin famously claimed, imperialism was the highest stage of liberal capitalism, for Horkheimer and Adorno the fascist collectivity is one side of the Janus-faced total society that emerges with monopoly capitalism. The other side is American consumer society and mass culture. Both versions—and this is the crucial proposition of both *Dialectic of Enlightenment* and Herbert Marcuse's *One-Dimensional Man*—are equally adept at churning out conformist *Ordnungsmenschen*.[79] Whether the regimentation of affect and desire is effected by Hollywood or Goebbels's ministry of propaganda ultimately makes little difference. In both cases, the need for "orgies of feeling"—for some form of repressive desublimation, whether violent or hedonistic—will be present. The libidinal economy of civilizationally repressed instinct simply demands it.

The price of this theoretical construct is the supremely dubious moral equation of fascism with consumer culture, Auschwitz with California. But there are other costs as well. Horkheimer and Adorno's "explanation" of Hitler's persecution and extermination of the Jews winds up being little more than a variation on the old theme of an eternal anti-Semitism. The sheer novelty of the Holocaust and the mass production of corpses is effaced under the rubric of recurrent pogroms as the outward projection of "introverted" sacrifice. To be sure, Horkheimer and Adorno's version of this thesis—in which the Jews are presented as the irredeemable "other" of Western civilization—has a certain cachet and might well be termed "postmodern" *avant la lettre*.

Horkheimer and Adorno are also overly reliant upon the idea of thoughtless, and easily manipulated, masses. Gathering themes from such diverse critics of bourgeois civilization as Tocqueville, Burckhardt, and Nietzsche, the authors of *Dialectic of Enlightenment* filter their critique of mass culture through the Marxist notion of false consciousness, the better to account for a pliant conformity easily mobilized in politically and culturally regressive ways.[80] Of course, to view the masses as masses—as emanations of an infernal "total society" that colonizes their dreams and desires, permanently infantilizing them in the process—is to eliminate any residual sense of moral agency or responsibility.

In *Dialectic of Enlightenment*, then, the "highly placed instigators" are held accountable, but the people are not.[81] Unable to judge and clearly unable to think, the masses in *Dialectic of Enlightenment* perpetually await their Svengali—the "ascetic priest" who will ease (or appear to ease) the accumulated pain of centuries of instinctual repression. We should hardly be surprised by what the "half-educated" masses do once they find their priest, nor should we should be surprised that it is the Jews who bear the burden of an "introverted sacrifice" sporadically and spectacularly turned outward.

◆

It may seem unfair to criticize Adorno's view of the Holocaust on the basis of *Dialectic of Enlightenment*, a work conceived and written (for the most part) before verifiable reports of the extermination of European Jewry reached America. There is, in fact, a change in tone and—to a lesser degree—a change in orientation in the later sections of *Minima Moralia*. Both changes are evident in the following passage, composed in 1947:

Criticism of tendencies in modern society is automatically countered, before it is fully uttered, by the argument that things have always been like this. . . . But even if things have always been so, although neither Timur nor Genghis Khan nor the English colonial administration in India systematically burst the lungs of millions of people with gas, the eternity of horror nevertheless manifests itself in the fact that each of its new forms outdoes the old. What is constant is not an invariable quantity of suffering, but its progress toward hell: that is the meaning of the thesis of the intensification of antagonisms. . . . He who registers the death camps as a technical mishap in civilization's triumphal procession, the martyrdom of the Jews as world-historically irrelevant not only falls short of the dialectical vision but reverses the meaning of his own politics: to hold calamity in check. . . . He who relinquishes awareness of the growth of horror not merely succumbs to cold-hearted contemplation but fails to perceive, together with the specific difference between the newest and that preceding it, the true identity of the whole, of terror without end.[82]

The bleakness of *Dialectic of Enlightenment* has here hardly dissipated. In fact, it has deepened. Adorno views the unprecedented tragedy of European Jewry no longer in terms of a meta-narrative about instrumental reason and its dialectical costs, but rather in terms of humanity's ever-expanding technical capacity to create hell on earth. "Horror," Adorno writes, consists in mass murder's "always remaining the same." However, it is "realized as constantly different, unforeseen, exceeding all expectation."[83] Here we move from the variation on Weber's "formalization of reason" meta-narrative to a position more in line with Freud's sober estimation of human nature and Benjamin's inversion of the notion of progress ("terror without end").

But despite the clear gain in moral depth and sobriety, Adorno still has difficulty with the relative uniqueness of the Holocaust (on the one hand) and the novelty of totalitarian terror (on the other). In the passage cited above, both are read back into the ever-widening gap between humanity's expanding technical capacity and its permanently stunted capacity for moral judgment and self-restraint. Thus, an aphorism that Adorno composed precisely to counter the argument that "things have always been like this"—that there is nothing new under the sun, least of all when it comes to man's inhumanity to man—winds up, curiously, supporting the claim he wanted to demolish.

Contra *Dialectic of Enlightenment*, Auschwitz can no longer be subsumed under the historical tendency of instrumental reason to issue in barbarism. It can be subsumed, however, under the "progress as recurrent disaster" schema installed by Benjamin in his *Theses on the Philosophy of History*. Adorno links technical progress to a Nietzschean-Freudian idea of a prehistory of cruelty that we never overcome. The result is that domination appears "the open secret of an enduring prehistory."[84] We are one step away here from the old saw *homo homini lupus*, which—however true as a proposition—does nothing to account for *why* the Holocaust happened, let alone when and where it did.[85]

In fact, the closest Adorno ever came to addressing the Holocaust in its specificity was in two radio lectures he gave after his return to Germany. In the 1960 lecture, "Working Through the Past," Adorno identifies a narcissistic, paranoid, and semi-obsolete nationalism as the precondition for all that followed: "Everything that took place between 1933 and 1945 goes together with pathological nationalism."[86] This thesis—together with Adorno's insistence that a disempowering, post-bourgeois economic order left many Germans anxious to "throw themselves into the melting pot of the collective ego," ridding themselves thereby of the painful obligation of autonomy—is no doubt true at a rudimentary psychological level. However, it adds little to standard liberal insights about the pathologies of strong group identity.[87]

The 1967 lecture, "Education After Auschwitz," describes the American "explanation" of National Socialism and Auschwitz by reference to a "characteristic German trust in authority" as "superficial." Adorno nevertheless insists that the end of the *Kaiserreich* found a people psychologically unprepared for self-determination: "They proved to be unequal to the freedom that fell into their laps."[88] Insisting on the importance of therapeutic self-clarification, Adorno suggests television programs and the mobilization of educational cadres aimed at the sons and daughters of the former peasant class. It was, after all, these groups that provided the most active and obedient enforcers of the Final Solution in the concentration camps. Finally, extending his critique of an inveterate German "immaturity" to bourgeois "coldness" and "reified consciousness," Adorno declares "the single genuine power standing against the principle of Auschwitz is autonomy, if I may use the Kantian expression: the power of reflection, of self-determination, of not cooperating."[89]

This praiseworthy call for dissent and non-cooperation with evil is, however, framed within a "top-down" schema of moral education, one that follows firmly in the steps of the Enlightenment/Idealist notion of the philosopher as "educator of the people" (*Volkserzieher*). In describing how education can be used to break up collective deformations of consciousness and structures of traditional "immaturity," Adorno seems unaware of the Tocquevillian-Millian lesson that the most vital part of political-moral education is learning by doing. Adorno's invocation of "autonomy" and "self-determination" as the only power standing against the "principle of Auschwitz" ultimately rings hollow because of his overall view of the German people—and, indeed, people everywhere—as children in need of guidance or patients in need of intervention (thanks to their "reified consciousness").

Such an attitude is, of course, hardly unique in the history of Western political thought. In Adorno's case, the crucial moment comes in identifying *autonomy* with *reflection* in the Hegelian sense—that is, with a form of thinking that is *not* available to everyone, and that can hardly be inculcated by general education or cultural practice.[90] Thus the public sphere remains a critically underutilized possibility for Adorno. It appears, when it appears at all, as the scene of relentless manipulation, mass *ressentiment*, and the conformist identification with the collective. The way out of the cave is not through anything like "the public use of one's reason," but through a guided program of sociological insight into the cultural and psychological roots of the "authoritarian personality" in Germany.[91]

Arendt: The Pathologies of Modernity, the Contingency of the Holocaust

In vivid contrast to Horkheimer and Adorno's speculative flights, *The Origins of Totalitarianism* is firmly rooted in modern European history and politics. There is no primordial history of the self, no speculative anthropology or meta-narrative of the formalization of reason, to contend with. Indeed, *Origins* is so rooted in European history that it has often been characterized as history, replete with causal pretensions.

This characterization is mistaken, and one that Arendt repeatedly tried to correct. In *Origins*, she is attempting to understand the constellation of factors that made a radically new political form—totalitarianism—possible in the heart of Europe. The emergence of this constellation was historically contingent, as were the disastrous political consequences that resulted from it.

This may give impression that *The Origins of Totalitarianism*—unburdened by Hegelian, Nietzschean, or Weberian pretensions—lacks any narrative frame, any "big story," whatsoever. Such an impression is strengthened by the disparate materials and topics addressed by the book, as well as by its less-than-transparent organization. This impression is also incorrect. Arendt does have a story to tell, and she deploys a narrative frame in order to make sense of what appears, at first glance, to be utterly incomprehensible. This resort to narrative should hardly surprise us, given Arendt's later observations on the importance of "story-telling" as a way of making sense of the world.[92] But what is Arendt's narrative? And how does it differ, if at all, from the more speculative constructions of *Dialectic of Enlightenment*?

To grasp Arendt's story, one has to begin at the end—in the section "Total Domination," which concludes the book's penultimate chapter.[93] The section tries to show why the concentration camps were the "central institutions" of totalitarian regimes. Everything Arendt says in *Origins* up to this point must be filtered through the lens provided by the camps, by their attempt to realize total domination concretely. Only with this point firmly in mind can we appreciate why she focuses on the phenomena and tendencies she does. And only then can we fully appreciate the abyss that separates her genealogy of total domination from Horkheimer and Adorno's.

What is total domination? What is its goal, and why do totalitarian regimes strive to achieve it?

For Arendt, total domination is certainly not something realized by the administered society. Indeed, in her view, Hitler and Stalin's regimes, even at their most murderous, did not achieve it. It remains an ideal type, one whose fearsome outline is glimpsed in the highly organized terror of the concentration camps. Total domination achieved a "local," limited reality in the *Lagers* and the Gulag. Thus, Arendt can claim that it was in the camps that the essence of totalitarianism revealed itself, even though this essence remained (as it were) unrealized in society at large.

Many of us, liberal in sensibility, would agree with the first half of this statement. The camps revealed the "essence" of totalitarianism because it was in the camps that the racism, brutality, and genocidal tendencies of these regimes were most clearly on display. Yet while she would hardly dispute the importance of these elements, Arendt did not see them as constituting the "essence" of totalitarianism in general (or the camps in particular). In her view, the focus on the camps' sheer brutality misleads us. It makes us think that the *raison d'être* of totalitarian regimes was hatred or sadism, when in fact these were distinctly secondary phenomena. What really went on in the camps—the reason why they were the "central institutions" of totalitarianism—was something much darker and more disturbing.[94]

According to Arendt,

> Total domination, which strives to organize the infinite plurality and differentiation of human beings as if all of humanity were just one individual, is possible only if each and every person can be reduced to a never-changing identity of reactions, so that each of these bundles of reactions can be exchanged at random for any other. The problem is to fabricate something that does not exist, namely, a kind of human species resembling other animal species whose only "freedom" would consist in "preserving the species." Totalitarian domination attempts to achieve this goal both through ideological indoctrination of the elite formations and through absolute terror in the camps. . . . The camps are meant not only to exterminate people and degrade human beings, but also [to] serve the ghastly experiment of eliminating, under scientifically controlled conditions, spontaneity itself as an expression of human behavior and of transforming the human personality into a mere thing, into something that even animals are not.[95]

Beyond humiliation, degradation, and extermination, the purpose of the camps was to conduct experiments that would ultimately transform human nature. Through systematic terror in a "controlled" environment, human beings were reduced to interchangeable "bundles of reactions." The transfer of this outcome to society at large would—if it could be effected—enable the totalitarians to remake the world according to their ideological "super-sense," the struggle of races or that of classes. The camps thus validated what Arendt calls "the fundamental belief of totalitarianism"—namely, that "everything is possible." They showed how far concrete dehumanization could be taken and just how plastic human nature actually is.[96]

The radical evil of totalitarianism's experiments in total domination cannot, then, be reduced to either selfishness or cruelty (the twin grounds of sin and evil in the Christian tradition). Totalitarian evil flows from an essentially ideological contempt for factuality and the "thrownness" of the human condition—its irreducible finitude or givenness. It is this very givenness—born of human plurality and mortality—that becomes the object of totalitarian "experimentation." Dehumanization is undertaken not to "puff oneself up" (as Augustine would say) but to transform human nature into a more pliant and efficient conductor of the "law of movement" laid down by either Nature (in the form of race struggle, as the Nazis believed) or History (in the form of class struggle, as the Bolsheviks believed).

The ultimate goal of totalitarian terror, then, was not the destruction of the Jews, the Kulaks, or any other group. The goal was to transform human beings into something subhuman, something incapable of resisting the "laws of movement" themselves. It is this replacement of a plural and active humanity with the interchangeable examples of the "animal species mankind"—examples prefigured by the "marionettes without the slightest trace of spontaneity" found in the camps—that constitutes the real goal of totalitarian domination.

This is a breathtaking (and counterintuitive) interpretation of the aim of totalitarian regimes and the role the camps played within them. Of course, outside the camps total domination was never achieved, nor was the desired eradication of spontaneity and the transformation of human nature accomplished. Yet despite their failure, the totalitarians revealed the path by which the human status could be destroyed. Their motivation was a distinctively modern (and distinctively pathological) desire to combine a feeling of infinite power ("everything is possible") with a total lack of responsibility. Such a feeling comes when we identify ourselves with, and abandon ourselves to, the superhuman forces of Nature or History.[97] Thus, while totalitarianism may, for the time being, "be history," the totalitarian temptation—the desire to throw off care for our common world and indulge in fantasies of a limitless power that comes from identifying with greater-than-human forces—remains with us.

Arendt's emphasis on the artificial character of our common world—the world of political and cultural institutions that stands between man and nature—distinguishes her later political thought, particularly her theory of political action. Thematically speaking, however, it is already present in *The Origins of Totalitarianism*. Indeed, this emphasis provides the key to understanding the by no means linear narrative Arendt provides concerning European modernity as a whole. It also provides the key to understanding why Arendt's genealogy of "total domination" diverges so sharply from the classical Frankfurt School analysis. The latter analysis sees totalitarianism emerging from a manipulative, "unreconciled" stance toward nature. In contrast, Arendt sees totalitarianism as nothing less than the attempt to "re-naturalize" humanity, to reduce it to the status of one animal species among others.

If we work backward from the section "Total Domination" and from "Ideology and Terror," Arendt's criteria of selection become immediately apparent. The developments and *mentalités* she emphasizes are all linked because they undermine both the idea and the reality of a spatially limited, durable, man-made public world. According to Arendt, it takes generations to build such a public-political world, which receives its primary articulation in law and a stable structure of rights. Political equality and identity are clearly functions of something that lies between us—laws, institutions, representative organs, and public spaces—not something inside us. The peculiar pathologies of European modernity—the pathologies that made totalitarianism possible—were all born (in Arendt's view) from a desire to transcend the spatial and institutional limits of the political association, as it has been understood in the West from the polis to the nation-state.

The growing impatience with a legally and institutionally bounded public realm is most apparent in the three developments that Arendt traces in part 2 of *The Origins of Totalitarianism*. These are: (1) the bourgeois fascination with the accumulation of power and limitless economic expansion; (2) the growing influence of racist and nationalist conceptions of identity in late-nineteenth- and early-twentieth-century Europe; and (3) the decline, not to say disintegration, of the nation-state.

I want to look briefly at each of these elements, with an eye toward how each one fits into Arendt's larger narrative about the factors and tendencies that give rise to the pure anti-politics of totalitarianism. To repeat, such an anti-politics is characterized—above all—by the effacement of limited, permanent institutional structures. But it is also characterized by the denial of human plurality and by the attempt to eradicate, via "experiments" in total terror, the human capacity for spontaneity.

One of the more startling aspects of the second part of *The Origins of Totalitarianism* is the degree of blame Arendt lays at the feet of the Continental bourgeoisie. Her indictment, however, has nothing to do with the standard Marxist complaint about bourgeois exploitation of the working class and connivance with right-wing extremists. The "political emancipation of the bourgeoisie" looms large in Arendt's story because it introduced categories from the sphere of business speculation into the political realm, with disastrous results. Imperialism may well be the "highest stage of capitalism," but it is so only because it signifies the moment when the arch-capitalist ideas of "expansion for expansion's sake" and a limitless accumulation of wealth became the guiding principles of the political realm.

That this was an event in itself, one relatively late in coming, is a thesis Arendt advances precisely against Marxist accounts. In her view, the European state was—for much of the nineteenth century—*not* "a committee for managing the common affairs of the whole bourgeoisie."[98] Rather, the essential story tells of the "latent fight between state and society" that becomes an open "struggle for power" only in the imperialist period (roughly, 1884–1914).[99] Throughout this period, "national institutions resisted . . . the brutality and megalomania of imperialist aspirations."[100] In the end, however, the bourgeoisie were triumphant. Imperialism and "expansion for expansion's sake" won out, but only at the cost of the virtual destruction of the nation-state (which, for Arendt as for Hegel, is essentially a spatially limited and legally articulated political entity).

The story of the imperialist age is, then, the story of the nation-state's struggle against society, with society—or at least its most powerful element, the bourgeois class—ultimately achieving victory. But this triumph did not simply deliver the powerful tool of the state into the hands of the bourgeoisie. On the contrary, Arendt traces what can only be described as a radical refoundation of the political association.

After the French Revolution, the European nation-state was characterized by territorial limitation, a stable institutional and legal structure, and representative institutions founded (broadly speaking) on the principles of consent and civic equality. In the imperialist period, it evolved into a constantly expanding entity, one that acquired new lands and new populations but did not extend the reach of political or even civil rights. The need to realize a return on "superfluous" capital led, in other words, to a root and branch transformation of the European political system. A plurality of nation-states, each recognizing the other's sovereignty and basic boundaries, gave way to what was (in effect) a constellation of competing "fully armed business concerns"—empires—each intent on outdoing the others in the grab for land, people, raw materials, and opportunities for investment. The "destruction of the political body of the nation-state" was inevitable once expansion became, with the victory of the bourgeoisie, the "permanent and supreme aim of politics."[101]

Arendt wants us to appreciate the devastating consequences of re-founding the political world on the essentially economic concepts of expansion and competition. When expansion and competition became the guiding realities of the political world—as they did between 1884 and 1914—all stable boundaries dissolved and the principle of consent became increasingly inapplicable. Annexation and domination now became the primary business of state apparatuses like the military and the civil service. These were constantly called upon to protect increasingly far-flung investment opportunities. Brutal exploitation of subject populations became the norm as the institutional means of political integration were stretched beyond the breaking point. It was only a matter of time before the "methods" of domination perfected abroad came home to roost in Europe itself.

What was the driving force behind this top-to-bottom transformation of the political realm? The principle of "expansion for the sake of expansion" would seem, *à la* Marx, to point to bourgeois greed as the chief culprit. But while greed was indeed operative—it lay at the root of what Arendt calls "the bourgeoisie's empty desire to have money beget money as men beget men"—it is hardly the whole story, or even the most interesting part. In the imperialist epoch, as business notions became the guiding principles of politics, these notions themselves underwent a transformation. They took on a life of their own, ultimately developing a relative autonomy vis-à-vis their economic determinants. Thus expansion, originally undertaken for economic reasons, became an "end in itself," as did the relentless accumulation of more and more power. The bourgeois or "instrumental" view of political power gave way to the much more threatening—and indeed crazy—idea that the "end" of the political association was the endless accumulation of power. As Arendt points out, "All political bodies appear to be temporary obstacles when they are seen as part of an eternal stream of growing power."[102]

Here we approach the inner pathological core of the bourgeois dream, which bears more than a passing resemblance to what the "dark writers of the bourgeoisie" had diagnosed. For the root of expansion for expansion's sake and the aimless accumulation of power was not mere greed, but a dream of domination, of ever-expanding or total mastery.

Power became the essence of political action and the center of political thought when it was separated from the political community which it should serve. This, it is true, was brought about by an economic factor. But the resulting introduction of power as *the only content of politics*, and of expansion as its only aim, would hardly have met with such universal applause, nor would the resulting dissolution of the nation's body politic have met with so little opposition, had it not so perfectly answered *the hidden desires and secret convictions* of the economically and socially dominant classes. The bourgeoisie, so long excluded from government by the nation-state and by their own lack of interest in public affairs, was politically emancipated by imperialism.[103]

The "secret conviction" Arendt speaks of here is the bourgeois belief that the endless accumulation of power is both the logical precondition and implicit goal of the endless accumulation of wealth. The prophet of this belief was Hobbes.

Arendt's reading of Hobbes in *Origins* is both one-sided and unapologetically anachronistic. Instead of a proto-liberal defender of the right to an unenslaved life, Arendt presents Hobbes as "the only great thinker who ever attempted to derive public good from private interest and who, for the sake of the private good, conceived and outlined a Commonwealth whose basis and ultimate end is the accumulation of power."[104] If man is driven by nothing but individual interest, then the desire for power "must be the fundamental passion of man."

Hobbesian man does not yield up his "natural right" to threat assessment, political judgment, and the use of force in order to partake in the stability of a lawful order guaranteed by sovereign power. Rather—according to Arendt—he supports tyranny because it frees him (the bourgeois) from any public duties or responsibilities whatsoever. Indeed, he supports the Sovereign's endless accumulation of power as the only real guarantee of the status quo.[105] The only public reality of the Hobbesian commonwealth is Sovereign power, which must either expand or die. This, according to Arendt, is the basis of Hobbes's uncanny prefiguration of later bourgeois attitudes toward the "state of nature" (read: state of war) that must always exist between nation-states. The dissolution of a stable public world—held together by law and shared civic responsibilities—in the cauldron of completely liberated self-interest leads, according to Arendt, to a societal celebration of power and to war without end. Hobbes was, at least, consistent enough to see this (unlike such liberal apologists as Benjamin Constant).[106] Hence Hobbes's symbolic importance for Arendt and his symptomatic anticipation of the bourgeois idolization of power as the only basis of political association.

If the bourgeoisie of the late nineteenth century were responsible for dispatching the idea of a limited (republican) political structure, the rise of racial ideology put an end to the republican idea of political membership (citizenship as an artificial legal status, predicated on the idea of equality of rights). "Race-thinking" dispatched not only the republic, but the nation itself. It deliberately cut across national boundaries, which it viewed as artificial in a strictly pejorative sense. From its theoretical roots in Boulainvilliers, the German Romantics, Burke, and Gobineau, race-thinking developed into its distinctively pathological (modern) form through the imperialist "scramble for Africa" and the rise of the "pan-movements" of Central and Eastern Europe.

If the conflict between society and state underlies Arendt's analysis of the bourgeoisie's projection of economic categories onto the political world, the conflict between state and nation is the ground of her examination of tribal nationalism in the late nineteenth and early twentieth centuries. The "tragedy" of the European nation-state is that rising national consciousness in this period overwhelmed the state's characteristic functions, which were to protect the lives and guarantee the rights of all inhabitants of a defined territory. The story of the late nineteenth century is, in fact, the story of the "conquest of the state by the nation": how an ethnic people makes itself the locus of sovereignty, thereby reducing legal and institutional structures to mere emanations of their (ever-fluctuating) will.[107] Nationalism, according to Arendt, is "essentially the expression of this perversion [sic] of the state into an instrument of the nation."[108] But nationalism is also a "precious cement" for holding together a society atomized by the market, class tensions, and liberal individualism. Facing atrophy by these forces, the centralized state found that it could survive only through the appeal to national spirit.

But what happens where there is no nation-state? Where there is no triad of people-territory-state?

The answer, according to Arendt, can be found in the history of the "belt of mixed populations" that stretched from the Baltic to the Adriatic. Here tribal nationalism came into its own in the form of the pan-movements—that is, in the form of a conception of political identity that was separate from, and intrinsically hostile to, any and all state structures.[109] For Slavs and Germans living as minorities within this zone—without either a territory of their own or a shared history of institution building—tribal nationalism provided a form of political identity utterly detached from national boundaries or national (state) institutions.

Appeals to German racial consciousness, or to the Slavic "soul," replaced identification with any worldly, tangible territory or man-made institutional structure. Such appeals "empowered" by making the national quality of the groups in question a "portable private matter, inherent in their very personality, [rather] than a matter of public concern and civilization."[110]

The appeal to the pseudo-mysticism of the Slavic "soul," or the pseudo-naturalism of the German "race," deterritorialized political identity and subjectified it. A resentful sense of tribal isolation effaces any sense of shared responsibilities and, indeed, any sense of humanity as a moral community politically divided into nation-states. On one level, this subjectification of political identity was unavoidable: the German and Slavic populations of the Dual Monarchy were "nations without a state and without visible institutions."[111] But, on another, it was a conscious choice—a turn away from worldly institutions toward an inward and pseudo-natural conception of political community.

In this sense, Arendt's analysis goes well beyond pointing out the baneful effects of political romanticism. It demonstrates how a contempt for law and legal institutions is always at the core of movements that have turned political identity inward. Government by decree, administrative despotism, and an overtly ideological politics of mass mobilization are the predictable political results of an "empowered" tribal nationalism. Impatience with institutional structures, a contempt for law, and the conviction that the party system is a sham are all characteristic features of ultra-nationalism. Together, they pave the way for a movement politics that cares not a whit about preserving rights or institutions in a shared public world. As the name implies, the main concern of movement politics is to keep moving: to create the illusion of a restlessly dynamic collective subject that is above and beyond all political parties, partial interests, and institutional structures.

Ultimately—which is to say, in its totalitarian form—the "movement" subsumes both people and state. Arendt quotes the Hobbesian Nazi Carl Schmitt: "The Movement . . . is State as well as People, and neither the present state . . . nor the present German people can even be conceived without the Movement."[112] The telos of political romanticism is not the deification of the *Volk*, but the sanctification of dynamism as such—movement for the sake of movement, endless "creative destruction" as the principle of the political world.[113] For Arendt, such a politics is, in fact, an anti-politics. It is predicated on the endless revolutionizing of that stable structure of institutions and laws that alone can make the world a fit "home" for mortal men and women.

This, however, is to jump ahead to part 3 of *Origins*. Moreover, it is to leave out of consideration one of the most original (and morally charged) chapters of Arendt's analysis, "The Decline of the Nation-State and the End of the Rights of Man."

If, in previous chapters of *Origins*, Arendt considered "external" threats to the stability of "Europe's nation-state system" (imperialism; the pan-movements), in this chapter she analyzes what she calls their "internal disintegration."[114] Both the codification of minority status for millions excluded from full participation in newly constituted nation-states of the former Dual Monarchy and the massive waves of refugees produced by civil wars, revolutions, and economic dislocation caught the European nation-state system off-guard. As the idea of second- and third-class citizenship spread throughout Europe, the legal and political equality previously guaranteed by the status of citizens disappeared in a maze of bureaucratic and police subcategories: "minority," *apatride*, and (finally) "stateless persons." Whether in the new nation-states (with their majority and minority populations) or the old (overwhelmed by fleeing Russians, Armenians, Spaniards, and Hungarians), the new reality was based upon the clear and irrevocable insistence that "only nationals could be citizens."[115] Everyone else was a sub-citizen, unequal and—as Arendt emphasizes—effectively without rights.

One way to explain the European nation-state's behavior during the interwar period is to say that the "system" was institutionally incapable of handling such an influx, one made even worse by the phenomenon of mass denationalization introduced by revolutionary or proto-totalitarian governments. The creation of internment camps in France, Holland, and elsewhere for "displaced persons" was (from this perspective at least) a sad but necessary measure in the face of an out of control situation.

Arendt was hardly unaware of such arguments. In *Origins* she agrees that the nation-state system was more or less "swamped" by the refugee problem. However, she argues that its response flowed from the original tension between state and nation, a tension finally (and firmly) resolved in favor of the latter. The idea and structure of the nation-state itself predicated enjoyment of full civil and political rights on membership (whether by birth, blood, or "naturalization") in the *ethnos*. Confronted by a large body of technically stateless people, the nation-state responded not by expanding legal protections to noncitizens but by placing the stateless in the legal and political limbo of a continent-wide system of the internment camps. And it was here that the rightlessness of the stateless—as well as the inherent inadequacy of the nation-state system—was revealed for all to see.

This inadequacy was moral as well as political. As Arendt points out in the most famous passages of *Origins*, the idea of intrinsic human dignity—the "right to have rights"—was, from the beginning of European modernity, bound up with (and finally subsumed by) the idea of a sovereign "people."[116] The inalienable Rights of Man, it quickly became clear, could be "guaranteed" only by a people that had emancipated itself and practiced self-government. Then and only then would what Burke called the "abstraction" of human rights find concrete reality in the civil and political rights articulated by a particular (sovereign) political community. Everywhere else, supposedly inalienable rights would prove utterly unenforceable. This point was driven home by the experience of the stateless—their absolute vulnerability—during the interwar period.

Not yet or no longer a member of a "sovereign people," the stateless were not simply deprived of a home and social context (a "place in the world"); they were deprived of any stable legal status whatsoever. They occupied a zone—the permanent "outside" of the nation-state—where the category of rights simply did not reach. Hence Arendt's conclusion that "the calamity of the right-less is not that they are deprived of life, liberty, and the pursuit of happiness, or of equality before the law and freedom of opinion—formulas designed to solve problems *within* given communities—but that they no longer belong to any community whatsoever."[117]

Arendt's analysis of how statelessness reveals the moral and institutional inadequacy of the nation-state might suggest that she favors strong international institutions as a way to bolster human rights. Yet her disillusion with the League of Nations and various "human rights philanthropists" of the interwar period was profound. What hopes she had for the rescue of human dignity from the abyss into which it fell during the 1930s lay not with supra-national organizations, but with the recognition by states the world over of the "right to have rights." And the ground of this right—what it fundamentally means—is that every person has the opportunity to belong "to some kind of [politically] organized community."[118] One can, Arendt observes, lose all the so-called Rights of Man and still retain one's human dignity. However, as the experience of the stateless testifies, it is the "loss of the polity" that can effectively expel one from humanity. The most important right—the *sine qua non* of all others—is, then, the right to membership in a political community. Without it, we all risk becoming a "superfluous human being," a candidate not only for exile or permanent homelessness, but for extermination.

◆

Stepping back, we can see how these three developments—the bourgeois endorsement of "expansion for expansion's sake," the deterritorialized and racialized conception of political identity flowing from the pan-movements, and the nation-state's "disintegration" into an administrative police-state in the face of refugee masses—paved the way for the practices and ideologies we call "totalitarian." Yet the most surprising aspect of Arendt's genealogy of totalitarianism does not concern bourgeois attitudes, political romanticism, nor even the failure of the European nation-state system in the interwar period. Rather, it concerns her (unexpected) commitment to the *idea of the state* as a legal-constitutional entity—a *Rechtsstaat*, as her erstwhile philosophical enemy Hegel would say.

This is surprising because Arendt is known (in the United States, at least) as the *doyenne* of participatory democracy. For the most part, political theorists have concentrated on her "Greek" theory of political action, ignoring or downplaying her intense concern with constitutions and the legal-institutional "housing" of freedom.[119] Yet it can be argued that such structures form the core of the "public world" that Arendt so vehemently urged us to actively care for. One can be "at home in the world" only if there is such a legal-institutional housing of freedom; a "human artifice" that not only guarantees rights, but preserves us from the shock of natural and "pseudo-natural" forces (such as race, ethnicity, or the "movement of history").

These characteristic themes of Arendt's mature political philosophy all have their roots in *The Origins of Totalitarianism*. Statelessness is the most radical form of homelessness one can imagine in the modern world. It is a condition of extraordinary vulnerability, the like of which had rarely been seen in previous European history, let alone become the norm for tens of millions. As a structure of law, the constitutional state is first and foremost the legal guarantor of rights for all; it is the artificial structure that makes civilization and a recognizably human life possible.[120] Strange as it might sound to our post-Foucauldian ears, for Arendt the "right to have rights" is guaranteed by the constitutional state. The *Rechtsstaat*

(Arendt would prefer "republic") eliminates the most extreme form of vulnerability.

Once we have this thought firmly in mind, the disparate strands of *The Origins of Totalitarianism* come together in a new and powerful way. Arendt's hostile treatment of the bourgeoisie and "expansion for the sake of expansion"; her investigation of the racialized conception of political identity emerging from the pan-movements; her analysis of the "disintegration" of the nation-state in the face of the interwar refugee crisis—each strand throws into sharp relief how the underpinnings of the European constitutional state were gradually swept away during five decades of imperialist expansion and political crisis.

Of course, it is only when totalitarian movements actually come to power that the stake is finally driven through the heart of the constitutional state. The story that Arendt tells in part 3 of *Origins* is the story of how endlessly dynamic, ideologically driven "movements" hollow out and make superfluous whatever "inert" institutional and legal structures they inherit from the "old-style" state. Totalitarianism in power is not what Ernst Cassirer thought it was—namely, a horrible instantiation of the "myth of the state." Rather, in Arendt's view, it was the dissolution of every stable, artificial political structure that had "humanized" life in the West for two centuries.

Totalitarianism levels whatever laws and institutions stand in the way of a ruthless and relentless "law of Nature" or "law of History." Such "laws"—the core of totalitarian ideology—are essentially laws of *movement.* Accelerating the "lawful" process of nature or history—the driving goal of totalitarian movements—demands the use of total terror. For only the systematic deployment of terror enables the forces of nature or history to "race freely through mankind, unhindered by any spontaneous human action."[121] Thus, the "experiments" of the camps were designed to produce *natural* men and women—human beings stripped not only of rights, of their legal and moral personalities, but of any protecting artifice of civilization whatsoever.[122] What is left over from these experiments in total domination are mere "specimens of the human animal" drained of all genuine humanity. As Arendt reminds us, "man's 'nature' is only 'human' insofar as it opens up to man the possibility of becoming something highly unnatural, that is, a man."[123]

Contra Giorgio Agamben and Michel Foucault, then, the camps do not reveal the hidden ground of the constitutional state.[124] Rather, they stand as testimony to European society's fatal attraction to a life untrammeled by legal and institutional structures, to a life unburdened by the restrictions of the constitutional state. This is a life ruled by suprahuman forces (Nature, History). It is a life "liberated" from the artifice of civilization, one that celebrates and endlessly embodies "creative destruction." It is, in a word, a "natural" life.

Conclusion

Trying to fit Adorno and Arendt's respective "genealogies" of totalitarianism into a common paradigm is an exercise fraught with difficulty. There is the obvious problem of reconciling a highly abstract and speculative anthropology with what has often been mistaken to be an idiosyncratic history of the imperialist and interwar periods. But once we get beyond the difference in genres—abstruse quasi-Hegelian *Geistesgeschichte* on the one hand, and what appears to be concrete historical "political science" on the other—an even more substantial difference emerges.

Throughout this chapter I have pointed to the Hegelian dimensions of Adorno's and Arendt's respective genealogies. In the case of *Dialectic of Enlightenment*, this pedigree is obvious, notwithstanding the healthy borrowings from Nietzsche and Freud. One simply cannot conceive of Horkheimer and Adorno's analysis independent of Hegel's critical chapters on the Enlightenment and "Absolute Freedom and Terror" in the *Phenomenology*. The entire Frankfurt School critique of instrumental reason derives directly from Hegel's critique of the standpoint of the "understanding" and "observing reason."

In the case of Arendt, the connection is a good deal more indirect. Yet her insistence on the "civilizing" role of the constitutional state, combined with her ferocious critique of political romanticism and the unfettered rule of civil society, points clearly—if surprisingly—to the *Philosophy of Right*. Arendt's concerns are Hegel's concerns: how to preserve the concrete freedom that the constitutional state makes possible, and how to contain the dissolvent forces of both the market and popular impatience with laws and institutions.

Yet even if we grant that the shadow of Hegel lies over both *Dialectic of Enlightenment* and *The Origins of Totalitarianism*, there is a clear sense in which the latter is a distinctly anti-Hegelian book. This has less to do with Arendt's relentless critique of the idea of historical necessity than it does with her total break with the Hegelian-German Romantic paradigm of reconciliation. Let me explain.

While Hegel was fiercely critical of Romanticism, he entirely endorsed the Romantic ideas that alienation must be overcome, and that reconciliation between humanity and an increasingly objectified nature must be possible. The point was not to read man back into nature, *à la* Rousseau. Rather, it was to create a narrative of human and cultural *Bildung* that would enable us to see the "necessity" of both opposition to, and reconciliation with, nature. In Hegel this reconciliation occurs through the figure of Spirit, an identity that unifies thought and Being in a *humanized* nature, one we can see ourselves in and be at home with at the end of history. Horkheimer and Adorno take up this same broad problematic, even though they reject Hegel's "spirit-centric" approach. The reconciliation with nature—the nature we ourselves already are—is essential if culture is not to ceaselessly return to barbarism. The lesson of *Dialectic of Enlightenment* is not that reason must become "reflective" but that it must become non-objectifying. Then and only then will the relentless subsumption of the particular under the universal cease; then and only then will human *Bildung* stop being coeval with domination and self-sacrifice.

Arendt will have none of this. For her, freedom—like rights and human dignity—is, and always will be, a function of the "artificial world" of laws and institutions that make up our public reality. It is the public realm that provides us, potentially, with a "home in the world." This home protects us from nature, and from the temptation to submit to pseudo-natural forces in the quest for some imagined state of originary integrity, immediacy, or authenticity. The enormous distance between Arendt's genealogy of totalitarianism and Horkheimer and Adorno's grows out of this absolutely fundamental issue. She sees barbarism not as the result of distance from nature (and denial of a self that is also nature), but rather as the result of an imagined (and all too seductive) *closeness* to nature. Such is the appeal of racial conceptions of political identity and of the *Volksgemeinschaft*.

Nothing marks the separation between Arendt and Adorno more than her appreciation of the role public institutions and legal structures play in creating a *human* life. It is here that Adorno's ethical sensitivity—his palpable shudder at every manifestation of "bourgeois coldness"—led him astray. Arendt's lesson is that solidarity must be mediated by an institutional, worldly reality. To think otherwise is to lapse into a fetish of the attitudes or mood with which we face the world and each other. The public world may (as Arendt never to ceased remind us) be fragile, but it is a stronger reed than the individual's aesthetic-ethical sensitivity, his or her "private life." This is a lesson Adorno forgot in his too-inclusive critique of Hegel, and it is a lesson that many of his followers—in the United States, at least—have never learned.

8 | FOUCAULT AND THE DYSTOPIAN PUBLIC

The "Formative Project" and the Liberal Critique of Docility

The forming of citizens through one mode or another of "civic education" has been a central theme of Western political thought since Plato and Aristotle. For the classical mind, such education was grounded on a presumed continuity between ethics and politics, between the life of the citizen and the "good life for man." The soul was its object, and virtue was its aim.

Nowhere is this more apparent than in the analogy between the structure of the individual soul and that of the polity in Plato's *Republic*. Of course, *genuine* virtue—the kind of virtue that characterizes the well-ordered soul of the philosopher—was out of reach for the auxiliary (military) and producer classes. But the tutorial state of the *Republic* provided an education in virtue suited to the limited intellectual capacities of these classes, and not just the philosophical ruling elite. A warrior-like civic virtue was to be inculcated into the "guardian" class, making them friendly to fellow citizens and fierce toward enemies. A sense of unity and temperance, combined with a deeply ingrained acceptance of the "naturalness" of the ruling hierarchy, provided the rudiments of a widely dispersed "civic virtue" for the mass, and, as such, was absolutely necessary (in Plato's view) for good political "health."[1]

The idea that a well-ordered soul is fundamental to politics, and can be produced by political means, is one that dies with the advent of Christianity. The early Christians famously withdrew from the political world, rendering unto Caesar that which was Caesar's, while making the state of their souls a function of their worshipful relationship to the divine. For a long time, the politics of virtue remained either dormant or subsumed by theological considerations.

It is only with the revival of public life in the Italian city-states of the fourteenth and fifteenth centuries that one begins to see a renewed emphasis on civic education and "virtue politics" of a non-Christian sort. Machiavelli's republicanism, with its neo-Roman emphasis on such "formative" institutions as the military and civil religion, is a case in point.[2] For Machiavelli, a small republican city-state such as Florence could survive only if its central social institutions were successful in stamping out fierce, patriotic, and freedom-loving citizen-soldiers. Surrounded by forces hostile to both its liberty and independence (including powerful emergent nation-states like Spain and France), a republic like Florence had no choice but to concern itself with the "virtue" of its citizens. Unless a morality of the common good was pervasive, and individual citizens were reflexively willing to sacrifice their particular interests for the good of the city, a small-scale republic had no chance of survival.

At first glance, this early modern concern with "educating" citizens to republican civic virtue looks like a return to the classical *topos* of moral-political education. Yet something happens to the politics of virtue with the emergence of the early modern republic. From Machiavelli's perspective, civic virtue must be deeply rooted and protected against the dissolvent forces of "corruption" (selfishness, wealth, and the ambitions of the powerful or well-born). Its "seat," however, is no longer the soul. The institutional-educational matrix set out by the *Discourses*—including military training and civil religion, as well as laws, customs, and an array of institutions designed to create and sustain high levels of energy and *ambizione* among the people—is one that aims at the bodies, beliefs, and energies of citizens, *not* their internal life. Whether the "good citizen" is also a "good man" in some absolute sense is no longer relevant. Machiavellian republicanism represents not the *demise* of virtue, as Leo Strauss and Catholic natural law theorists have argued, but its "externalization" (to use Sheldon Wolin's apt phrase).[3]

For obvious reasons, large monarchical nation-states could afford to be much less concerned with this "formative" project. A subject, after all, is not a citizen—something Machiavelli himself stresses in both *The Prince* and the *Discourses*. However, once the nation-state remakes itself *as a* republic—the moment of the French Revolution—the formative project returns with a vengeance. The public freedom created by a republican constitution was deemed to depend crucially upon the people's attainment of a high level of patriotic feeling, republican sentiment, and political unity. It was also deemed to depend on the ruthless eradication of all sources of "corruption," faction, and inequality. With the French Revolution, then, the Machiavellian image of republics as "small islands of freedom in a hostile world" was utterly transformed. The world remained hostile, however, and this meant that civic education had to take an increasingly simplified and massified form, one suitable to the "wholesale" level.

Once the wars of the Revolution and Napoleon were over—once *la patrie* was no longer *en danger*—it was possible for Benjamin Constant to look back at Rousseau's and Robespierre's obsession with civic virtue as a kind of category mistake, one that hinged upon the confusion of *morality* with *freedom*.[4] The liberal "freedom of the moderns" (including the negative freedoms of individual conscience, opinion, and profession) had little if anything to do with the kind of collective sovereignty civic republicans presented as *the* model of authentic freedom.[5] But even liberals like Constant acknowledged that some training in the art of *political* liberty was essential if "the moderns" were to avoid the trap of a new, deadening, form of paternalism. "The danger of modern liberty," Constant observed, "is that, absorbed in the enjoyment of our private independence, and in the pursuit of our particular interests, we should surrender our right to share in political power too easily."[6] It was against this peculiarly bourgeois temptation that Constant's fellow liberal, Tocqueville, wrote when he praised decentered, American-style democracy—a form of democracy dependent upon citizen engagement and the "schooling" provided by political and "civic" associations of all sorts.[7]

The liberal republicanism of Tocqueville and (to a lesser extent) Constant strives to guarantee individual rights and liberties while preserving a substantial place for public (political) freedom. If, at some level, these theorists agree with the basic republican point that "good" (that is, active and energetic) citizens are not found but "made," they both take great pains to distance themselves from the Platonic-Machiavellian idea that civic education is akin to the imposition of form on a blank canvas or an unblocked slab of marble.[8] Even in its "externalized" version, the cultivation of *virtu* by civic republicans has, historically, been guided by this highly dubious and morally repugnant metaphor—a metaphor whose persuasiveness depends on the availability of "political artists of character" (Plato) or "great legislators" (Machiavelli). For Constant and Tocqueville, human beings were definitely not raw material that had to be beaten into shape if a harmonious polity—one dedicated to virtue or political independence—was to emerge. Rather, they were adult individuals worthy of the rights and freedoms necessary to lead their own lives. They were also *citizens* entitled to sharing political power and (in the case of Tocqueville) to participating directly in the administration of local affairs.

That said, we can hardly deny the presence of a substantial "moralizing" dimension in Tocqueville, one that threatens to overshadow his commitment to individual rights and a pluralistic form of public freedom. As I noted in chapters 3 and 4, the distinctively political character of Tocqueville's conception of civil society is, to some extent, tamed and undercut by his emphasis on *moeurs* and the supposed necessity of shared belief. Yet even though Tocqueville thought that the possibility of building democracy on the basis of moral pluralism was a non-starter, the fact remains that he was more than happy to contemplate a fair amount of pluralism and indeed turbulence in public life, the better to avoid the looming prospect of administrative despotism.[9]

Tocqueville's essential point in this regard is that the new "species of oppression" will be nothing like the old absolutism. It will not actively repress those who seek to enter the public realm in order to participate in political judgment. Rather, it will attack the roots of civic life by offering us a benign paternalism, one that provides for our lives, necessities, and pleasures. In this way, it will facilitate the withdrawal from public life already built into democratic equality and the dissociative forces of "individualism." As Tocqueville writes toward the end of volume 2 of *Democracy in America*:

> The first thing that strikes the observation is an innumerable multitude of men, all equal and alike, incessantly endeavoring to procure the petty and paltry pleasures with which to glut their lives. Each of them, living apart, is as a stranger to the fate of all the rest; his children and his private friends constitute to him the whole of mankind. . . . Above this race of men stands an immense and tutelary power, which takes upon itself alone to secure their gratifications and to watch over their fate. That power is absolute, minute, regular, provident, and mild. It would be like the authority of a parent if, like that authority, its object was to prepare men for manhood; but it seeks, on the contrary to keep them in perpetual childhood: it is well content that the people should rejoice,

provided they think of nothing but rejoicing. For their happiness such a government willingly labors, but it chooses to be the sole agent and the only arbiter of that happiness; it provides for their security, foresees and supplies their necessities, facilitates their pleasures, manages their principle concerns, directs their industry, regulates their descent of property, and subdivides their inheritances: what remains, but to spare them all the care of thinking and all the trouble of living?[10]

The horror of such a benign despotism is that it unbends the springs of political action and public involvement, encouraging the human propensity toward docility and what Nietzsche would later describe as "herd behavior."[11] The democratic state has the potential to be the most despotic state of all, in that its solicitude for the lives and necessities of its citizens enables them to dispense with the responsibilities of citizenship—including action, judgment, decision, and opposition—once and for all. In its caring, but administratively despotic, form the democratic state undercuts free agency, replacing the joint action of democratic equals with an increasingly comprehensive network of rules and practices:

After having . . . taken each member of the community in its powerful grasp and fashioned him at will, the supreme power then extends its arm over the whole community. It covers the surface of society with a network of small complicated rules, minute and uniform, through which the most original minds and the most energetic characters cannot penetrate, to rise above the crowd. The will of man is not shattered, but softened, bent, and guided; men are seldom forced by it to act, but they are constantly restrained from acting. Such a power does not destroy, but it prevents existence; it does not tyrannize, but it compresses, enervates, extinguishes and stupefies a people, til each nation is reduced to nothing better than a flock of timid and industrious animals, of which the government is the shepherd.[12]

Tocqueville's vision of a democratic state in which the public realm—considered as a space for deliberation, debate, joint action, and dissent—withers away, leaving a "docile" citizenry cultivated and managed by state agencies, prefigures Foucault's analysis of the emergence of disciplinary society in eighteenth- and nineteenth-century Europe. As Tocqueville's text so clearly illustrates, the fear that democratic citizens might well allow themselves to be treated as subjects by governments that attend to their welfare and happiness is an old liberal concern. This concern is found not only in Tocqueville and Constant, but in Humboldt, Thoreau, and Mill as well. Indeed, one could easily trace its lineage back to the seventeenth-century proto-liberal John Locke, whose *Second Treatise of Government* presumed that the tendency of human beings to regard themselves as the subjects of paternalistic authority (albeit of a monarchical, not democratic, kind) is almost inveterate.[13] It will only be overcome when we see that we are not *born* subjects to any government, but rather put ourselves under what is clearly a conditional obligation through our "mature" agreements and consent.

From "Forming Citizens" to "Manufacturing Subjects"

It is at this juncture that the contemporary follower of Foucault might be tempted to pounce, pointing out that—surface similarities notwithstanding—there is an insuperable gulf between the liberal critique of docility and that offered by Foucault. The follower will also point to an apparent gulf between the "formative project" as conceived by civic republicanism (the formation of citizens) and the "constitution of subjects" as set out in Foucault's various genealogies. Indeed, from the Foucauldian point of view, the essential point is that the political formation of citizens actually presupposes the social construction of subjects, a construction performed by disciplinary institutions and practices dispersed throughout the social body.

From this perspective, the problem with the liberal critique of docility is that it is state-centric and hence superficial. It conceives power as a distinct and localizable commodity, one that can be limited by constitutional instruments (Locke) and/or a relatively autonomous civil society (Constant, Tocqueville).[14] Fixated on the Hobbesian model of sovereignty, liberal theory is apparently blind to the fact that the seventeenth and eighteenth centuries witness the emergence (indeed, a "veritable technological take-off") of a new type of power, one which Foucault calls non-sovereign or disciplinary power.[15] Such power strives not for a monopoly on the legitimate means of violence, nor for a monopoly on the definition and interpretation of public right (both central prerogatives of the Hobbesian sovereign). Rather, its goal is the more effective management and control of large populations.

This new type of power, Foucault tells us, presupposes a "tightly knit grid of material coercions."[16] By this he means an ensemble of knowledges, practices, and technologies of control, one that extends throughout the social body in a net-like organization.[17] This power is not exerted (at least not primarily) through the state, nor through the law, nor even through the economy (although it supports all three). Rather, it is exercised through a network of local institutions—prisons, schools, factories, hospitals, army barracks, asylums. In these diverse locations, "meticulous, often minute" techniques for the control, observation, and training of bodies are evolved, to be gradually linked up to one another by what Foucault calls "macrostrategies" of power.[18] Hence the well-known—and by now somewhat irritating—Foucauldian insistence that "power is everywhere," circulating in capillary form at the furthest extremities of the social body.[19] Hence the equally well-known Foucauldian thesis that the theory of sovereignty and everything related to it (including all theories of public right and political obligation) constitute "a great trap we are in danger of falling into when we try to analyze power."[20]

Disciplinary power—the kind of power that acts through constant surveillance; the kind of power first exercised on soldiers, prisoners, children, and factory workers and later extended to the population at large—is not essentially repressive in character. Rather, as Foucault insists in a number of places, it is productive.[21] One of its chief purposes is to train bodies for good functioning (as soldiers or workers) and thus increase their political and economic utility. The achievement of this purpose requires cultivating the powers and aptitudes of the individual body while simultaneously rendering it "docile," that is, disciplined, controllable, and predictable. As Foucault writes in *Discipline and Punish*:

> The historical moment of the disciplines [the emergence of the body as the "object and target of power" in the seventeenth and eighteenth centuries] was the moment when an art of the human body was born, which was directed not only at the growth of its skills, nor at the intensification of its subjection, but at the formation of a relation that in the mechanism itself makes it more obedient as it becomes more useful, and conversely. What was then being formed was a policy of coercions that act upon the body [in military training, in school, workshop and prison discipline], a calculated manipulation of its elements, its gestures, its behaviors. The human body was entering a machinery of power that explores

it, breaks it down, and rearranges it. A political anatomy, which was also a "mechanics of power," was being born; it defined how one may have a hold over others' bodies, not only so they may do what one wishes, but so that they may operate as one wishes, with the techniques, the speed, and the efficiency that one determines. Thus discipline produces subjected and practiced bodies, "docile" bodies. Discipline increases the forces of the body (in economic terms of utility) and diminishes these same forces (in political terms of obedience).[22]

Bodies are both empowered (through training) and captured (through surveillance and control) at the same time. As the passage above suggests, there is an internal link between increased aptitude and increased domination: "A body is docile that may be subjected, used, transformed and improved."[23]

In addition to producing docile bodies, disciplinary power aims at producing prison-like souls. This is one of Foucault's more controversial suggestions, and has been the source of a good deal of confusion. When Foucault states that "the soul is the effect and instrument of a political anatomy; the soul is the prison of the body," he is not completely reducing individuality or subjectivity to the status of a mere "effect" of disciplinary power (although he frequently talks that way).[24] Rather, like Nietzsche, he is tracing the origin of our sense of "responsible agency" to the concrete training and surveillance we receive as children, students, workers, or soldiers. And he is saying that what counts as an individual for us depends upon how various knowledges and practices in medicine, education, psychology, and criminology identify "certain bodies, certain gestures, certain discourses, certain desires" as individuals.[25]

What matters are the practices, training, and disciplinary techniques that work on the body, that "explore it, break it down, and rearrange it." In this sense, discipline can indeed be said to "make" or constitute individuals through training and the cultivation of specific aptitudes.[26] But Foucault goes further, arguing that the "soul" or our identity as responsible moral agents must be traced back to our internalization of the supervisory gaze of the parent, teacher, officer, or doctor. Insofar as the soul is a function of this internalization process (and Foucault argues this quite explicitly),[27] it can be seen as a mechanism of confinement for the body. Hence Foucault's famous declaration that "the soul is the effect and instrument of a political anatomy; the soul is the prison of the body."[28] Internalizing the supervisory gaze, we come to police ourselves.

Individuals, then, can be said to be "constituted" by power through the training of docile bodies and the creation of prison-like souls. "Subjectification"—the process by which we become (responsible) subjects— turns out to be inseparable from subjugation. In the end, we are what power makes us. It "manufactures" us through its techniques and strategies, its norms of good and poor function, and its definitions of normal and abnormal.[29]

If we put this quintessential Foucauldian thesis together with the more general one that power is everywhere, we can see why the liberal critique of docility might appear structurally deficient. Focused (not to say fixated) on the sovereign model of power, liberalism fails to see where modern power is and how it actually works. It looks at the state when it should be looking at everyday life—at how disciplinary power "individualizes" each of us through carefully maintained records of our performance as students, patients, employees, conscripts, welfare recipients, or prisoners. Contra Tocqueville, it is not the paternalism of a centralized state that we have to worry about. Rather, it is the ongoing constitution of docile bodies and prison-like souls through a wide array of "everyday" institutions and practices that renders us a "flock of timid and industrious animals."

From a Foucauldian perspective, then, liberal political theory has noted a pervasive and troubling phenomenon—the growth of docility— but doesn't have a clue as to how it is actually produced. Liberal theory focuses its attention entirely on the "daddy" (authoritarian-Hobbesian) or "mommy" (welfare democratic) state, when it should be looking instead at the "meticulous, often minute, techniques" that make up the "microphysics of power" in modern societies. Worse, liberal theory encourages our belief in a "power-free zone" (the private sphere), one marked out and protected by law and a set of supposedly inalienable individual rights. But—as the Foucauldian would again point out—even the strictest adherence to Mill's harm principle, with its expansive protection of negative liberty, allows the social production of docile subjects to continue unabated. Worries about state intrusiveness, "social" tyranny, and the hegemony of majority opinion and feeling always arrive on the scene too late.

One would think that this bill of particulars against liberalism was enough. But there is more. Not only does liberalism's focus on the state blind us to the workings of power. Foucault himself goes even further. The liberal codification and institutionalization of individual rights actually presupposes the disciplines. In one of the most striking and oft-cited passages of *Discipline and Punish*, he writes:

> Historically, the process by which the bourgeoisie became in the course of the 18th century the politically dominant class was masked by the establishment of an explicit, coded, and formally egalitarian juridical framework, made possible by the organization of a parliamentary, representative regime. But the development and generalization of disciplinary mechanisms constituted the other, dark side of these processes. The general juridical form that guaranteed a system of rights that were egalitarian in principle was supported by these tiny, everyday, physical mechanisms, by all those systems of micro-power that are essentially non-egalitarian and asymmetrical that we call the disciplines. And although, in a formal way, the representative regime makes it possible, directly or indirectly, with or without relays, for the will of all to form the fundamental authority of sovereignty, the disciplines provide, at the base, a guarantee of the submission of forces and bodies. The real, corporeal disciplines constituted the foundation of the formal, juridical liberties.[30]

Foucault here takes Marx's basic critique of liberal rights in "On the Jewish Question" and considerably ups the ante. It is not just that the "Rights of Man" and the "Rights of the Citizen" enable the structural inequalities and selfishness of civil society to continue unabated. Rather, Foucault's point is that the entire bourgeois-liberal order—an order freed from the corporate and caste character of feudal domination, an order predicated upon equality of rights—actually rests on the invention and pervasive implementation of the disciplines. The civil rights and individual liberties of which we are so proud are granted us only because our formation by disciplinary techniques "guarantees" (*a priori*, as it were) our ultimate submission. In case anyone misses the point, Foucault proceeds to drive it home: "The 'Enlightenment,' which discovered the liberties, also invented the disciplines."[31] The two go hand in hand; you can't have one without the other.

What are the implications of this? Foucault wants us to see that the entire tradition of liberal constitutionalism—a tradition that begins with the Levellers and Locke, that is built on by the American founders and the French Revolution of 1789, and that Constant, Tocqueville, and Mill tried to shore up and supplement with a focus on the importance of popular participation—is at once a blindfold (to how power actually works) *and* also a kind of Trojan horse. The liberties are granted us just at the historical moment that the disciplines effect their subjection of the entire social body to their "tightly knit grid of material coercions." The discourse of rights—and the distinctions between public and private, state and civil society—make possible a potentially infinite extension of apparatuses of surveillance and control into the social body.[32]

Seen from this perspective, liberalism and constitutionalism are hardly innocent. What began as an understandable response to theories of sovereignty *à la* Hobbes rapidly evolved into an "instrument of domination," one that crucially enabled the further extension and penetration of disciplinary power.[33] As such, liberal-constitutionalist discourse continues to mask the "multiple forms of subjugation" made possible by non-sovereign power.[34] Suffice it to note here that civic republicanism and the discourse of "strong" citizenship is equally suspect, and for many of the same reasons. Wherever we turn in the seventeenth and eighteenth centuries, we find new political vocabularies (royalist absolutism, liberal constitutionalism, civic republicanism) deployed in a way that camouflages the rise of disciplinary power and the achievement of a new—and hitherto undreamt of—level of social control.

While Foucault would modify aspects of this position in his later work, his broad critique of what he called the "juridical" paradigm of public right remained largely intact. As we shall see, it implied not just a distrust of the vocabulary of rights; it also entailed a severe skepticism toward the Arendtian-Habermasian idea of the public realm, conceived as a space of civic equality reserved for the debate, deliberation, and decision of citizens.[35] Just as the discourse of rights distracts us from what is really going on in the social body, so the ideas of the public realm and public freedom distract us from the grim reality of domination. They distract us, in other words, from the unpleasant but apparently indisputable fact that politics is war carried on by other means. With his famous inversion of Clausewitz, Foucault stands all "normative" understandings of the public realm and public freedom on their heads.

This chapter is devoted to examining these and other central claims from Foucault's work of the mid- to late 1970s. This is the period that extends from *Discipline and Punish*, through the 1975–76 lectures at the Collège de France, to (finally) Foucault's thematization of the problem of "governmentality" and the first volume of the *History of Sexuality*, with its concluding thesis about the emergence of "biopower." It is in these texts that Foucault makes some of his boldest and most characteristic arguments about how subjects are "manufactured" and how structures of domination actually operate in the contemporary world. And it is in these texts that we find Foucault's elaboration of the claim that politics is "the continuation of war by other means," as well as his analysis of how the vocabularies of public right and social contract act to conceal the workings of modern power.[36]

Such claims have, for better or worse, become identified with a "Foucauldian perspective" in the American academy. Taken together, they underline the apparent irrelevance of the public sphere (as a space of political or joint action) and public freedom (the freedom to share in political power [Constant] or be a "participator in government" [Arendt]). After all, if citizens have been constituted as "docile subjects" by the insidious workings of disciplinary power, what can we really expect from "joint action" in the public realm? Genuine resistance must occur elsewhere—not at the level of citizenship, but at the level of bodies resisting their "subjectification" in schools, barracks, factories, and so on.[37] It must occur, in other words, at the various local sites where the "material operators of domination" are actually being applied to bodies and their forces.[38]

Even more disturbing than Foucault's implicit "refutation" of a civic republicanism modified *à la* Tocqueville or Arendt is his apparent rejection of the entire inherited vocabulary of liberal constitutionalism—a vocabulary that, he reminds us, emerged entirely as a response to the idea of sovereign right.[39] As I noted above, individual rights and "negative freedom" always come on the scene too late, after the processes of subjectification/subjugation have done their work. Hence Foucault's well-known conclusion that "the man described for us, who we are invited to free, is already in himself the effect of a subjection much more profound than himself. A 'soul' inhabits him and brings him to existence, which is a factor in the mastery that power exercises over the body."[40]

As "constituted" subjects, positive political freedom is beyond our grasp: the *citoyen* is always already a subject—in the political sense—thanks to implementation of power effects at the local or "micro" level. But negative freedom—the freedom from interference, the freedom for self-development so central to Constant, Humboldt, and Mill—turns out to be a myth as well. Since power's actual workings do not respect the boundary between public and private, the liberal ideal is revealed as bogus, dependent on the fiction of the individual "as a sort of elementary nucleus, a primitive atom or some multiple, inert matter to which power is applied."[41] The individual, as we now know thanks to Foucault, is not the "*vis à vis* of power." Rather, he is a "power-effect."[42]

The "Foucauldian revolution" in the discussion of power thus seemed to render many of the central concepts underlying republican and liberal political thought irrelevant. Citizenship, public freedom, and limited government all look increasingly dubious to Foucault's more intent readers, those who have been rigorously tutored in "how actual relations of subjugation manufacture subjects."[43] In similar fashion, Foucault's step beyond the "trap" of the sovereign model of power apparently reduced the distinctions between state, civil society, and the public sphere to the status of quaint (and largely obfuscating) anachronisms.

Foucault's critical recasting of the "formative project" in terms of the "manufacture of subjects" by various local "operators of domination" thus seemed to warrant a grand, demystifying de-differentiation. The more structuring distinctions of the old political theory we got rid of, the more clearly we could see the actual workings of power in everyday life. This was a lesson many of Foucault's followers in Europe and the United States were happy to draw, gratified by the discovery of a theory that provided a quick end-run around the last three hundred years of Western political thought.

Here several important questions present themselves. Does the Foucauldian focus on disciplinary power (and its cognate, the notion of "biopower") really suspend or undercut the claims of active (dissident) citizenship, public freedom, and limited government? Can we, *should* we bid farewell to the public/private distinction and the discourse of rights once we see how modern forms of disciplinary power actually operate? Is the Italian philosopher Giorgio Agamben right when he claims that Foucault's notion of "biopower" reveals an underlying structural continuity between liberal constitutionalist and totalitarian regimes? Does the appearance of concentration camps in our time (as "zones of exception" that manifest the modern state's power over "bare life") tell us something crucial about the "political space of modernity" as such, and not just about the "essence" of totalitarian regimes?[44]

In response to these questions, I will argue that Foucault's middle-period thought traces an intriguing arc from a hyperbolic de-differentiation (the strategy of *Discipline and Punish*); to the reintroduction of a number of substantive (and more or less traditional) "political theory"-type distinctions (in his lectures at the Collège de France in 1975–76); to, finally, a new "meta-level" de-differentiation (in the last chapters of volume 1 of *The History of Sexuality*, which introduce the notion of biopower).

This dialectic of de-differentiation and re-differentiation makes Foucault's thought from this period both more complex and more interesting than it has sometimes been portrayed on this side of the Atlantic. At the same time, however, it also makes possible the kind of appropriation performed by Agamben, an appropriation in which the complicated legal and institutional apparatus deployed by totalitarian regimes to strip their intended victims of their legal persona, moral personality, and sheer individuality is either not addressed or prematurely conflated with supposedly parallel liberal institutions. The juxtaposition of "the carceral archipelago" with "biopower" and "bare life" encourages us to think of ourselves as occupying—in principle and in *potentia*—the same conceptual and political space as actual concentration camp inmates.[45]

Foucault—like Adorno and like Agamben, but unlike Arendt—is dangerously attracted to the identification of late modernity with a condition of "total domination." This comes out most clearly in his stipulation of a "carceral network" underlying "panoptic society" (in *Discipline and Punish*), and in his suggestion that any political power that cares for the life of its population invariably dreams of exposing this population to destruction.[46] It is also apparent in his broader conception of disciplinary power pervading the entire social body, as well as his inversion of Clausewitz. When Foucault writes that "politics is the continuation of war by other means," he is inviting us to view the political world along an appealingly simple (not to say simplistic) axis: that of domination and resistance to domination.[47]

Needless to say, only the most dogmatic of normative political philosophers—someone who really believed in the legitimating powers of consent, no matter how dubious the form in which it is supposedly expressed—would deny that social struggle and various forms of domination (governmental, economic, sexual) are permanent features of life in contemporary liberal democracies. Similarly, only the most shameless apologist for corporate power or the prerogatives of the super-rich would pretend that all is for the best in the "opportunity society" created by globalization and the "free enterprise system."

But even the candid acknowledgment that domination and exploitation remain with us hardly refutes the thesis that there is more to politics than practices of governance (in the specific Foucauldian sense of "maintaining domination") and resistance to such practices. Rhetoric aside, this is something Foucault himself knew quite well. It emerges not only in the remarkably self-conscious genealogy of the of the "politics is war" metaphor he provides in *"Society Must Be Defended,"* but also in his all too brief engagement with liberal political theory. And, of course, this knowledge is clearly on display in his remarkably full life as a public actor and political activist.[48]

From a Public "Space of Appearances" to a Space of Surveillance

The concept of the public sphere can hardly be said to loom large in Foucault's thought. All the more reason, then, to be surprised by the fact that the historical narrative of *Discipline and Punish* hinges on the idea of a simultaneous *transformation* and *subsidence* of the public realm in the seventeenth and eighteenth centuries.

In some respects, this idea is parallel to Hannah Arendt's thesis concerning "the rise of the social" in the modern age.[49] Like Arendt, Foucault argues that the pre-modern public sphere was characterized by a certain theatrical or performative quality. Above all, the public realm was a "space of appearances." However, the transition to modernity witnesses a distinct rise in governmental attention to what were, previously, "household" matters. Life and productivity—in both the economic and biological senses—move to the forefront of political and administrative concern.

"Discipline" was one of the primary means deployed by governmental rationality for the cultivation and care of the "forces" of its population, the training and expansion of which were essential to success in economic and military competition. The "theatrical" public realm—whether conceived as a stage for the debate and deliberation of equal citizens (the *polis*), or as a platform for the ceremonies of kingly power (the *ancien régime*)—gives way to a *social* regime of normalizing visibility. This regime combines the bureaucratic administration of a mass society (Arendt) with the architecture and practices of a continuous, individualizing surveillance (Foucault).[50]

One's response to this modern eclipse of the public realm will determine, to a large extent, the kind of theory and politics one will espouse. For Arendt, as for Tocqueville and even Constant, the horror of a hyperbureaucratized welfare state is not that it undercuts "free enterprise" (the lament of contemporary libertarians) but that it leaves so little space for self-government and active citizenship. For Foucault, on the other hand, the nostalgia for a genuinely political space of appearance is itself a form of bad faith. We are no longer dealing with "realms of freedom" vs. "realms of necessity" (if, indeed, we ever were). Rather, from Foucault's perspective, we are dealing with an ever-shifting spectrum of social forces—forces which invest, utilize, and resist an array of disciplinary techniques. To repeat, these techniques are deployed throughout the social body, in sites (such as the office, school, hospital, or barrack) that are neither purely "public" nor "private."

Viewed from this angle, the public realm long ago ceased being the essential *topos* of political life. The inversion of Clausewitz's dictum merely drives this fact home. It points us toward a "politics of everyday life"—that is, toward a dimension of social conflict that is *prior to* and *constitutive of* any institutionally defined public realm. If politics is about domination and if power "is everywhere," then it follows that the obsessive concern with the relative "health" of public sphere (as a space of debate, contestation, and popular will formation) is grossly misplaced.

One can see this concern—along with the liberal entanglement with questions of public right—as deriving more or less directly from the sovereign model of power. As Foucault observes, in the *ancien régime* the public realm was reserved for the ceremonials of sovereign power (most spectacularly manifest in public executions).[51] After the revolution, the public realm is supposedly reserved for the self-manifestation of the sovereign people in all its virtuous unity.[52] In reality, however, the idea of a "public" realm in which single or plural actors appeared on stage was subsumed by what Foucault calls "the Rousseauist dream" of a "transparent society, visible and legible in each of its parts."[53] In such a society, the ratio of civic virtue to corruption would be immediately apparent, as would the sources of the latter.

This is the background for what is unquestionably the most widely discussed chapter of *Discipline and Punish*. In "Panopticism," Foucault suggests how Bentham's idea for prison reform spawned a veritable revolution in the modalities of social control. If the early modern era responded to threats (plague, say, or local uprisings) in the mode of "quarantine," blocking off the infected area and applying a kind of "discipline blockade," the Enlightenment, via Bentham, came up with a much lighter and more efficient way of achieving "perfect government" and control. In an interview, Foucault described Bentham's basic architectural innovation:

A perimeter building in the form of a ring. At the center of this, a tower, pierced by large windows opening into the inner face of the ring. The outer building is divided into cells each of which traverses the whole thickness of the building. These cells have two windows, one opening onto the inside, facing the windows of the central tower, the other, outer one allowing daylight to pass through the whole cell. All that is then needed is to put an overseer in the tower and place in each of the cells a lunatic, a patient, a convict, a worker, or a schoolboy. The back lighting enables one to pick out from the central tower the little captive silhouettes in the ring of cells. In short, the principle of the dungeon is reversed; daylight and the overseer's gaze capture the inmate more effectively than darkness, which afforded after all a kind of protection.[54]

This "panoptic" mechanism makes it possible to "see constantly and recognize immediately." It does so in a manner that makes it impossible for an inmate, worker, or student to know *if and when* he is actually being watched. The panoptic idea, initially embodied in the new architecture of prisons, created a "system of isolating visibility" in which visibility itself "is a trap."[55]

Thanks to its efficiency and economy (the architecture did most of the work, hence less supervisory personnel were needed) the panoptic scheme was "destined to spread throughout the social body; its vocation was to become a generalized function."[56] And this, indeed, was how Bentham himself "sold" the idea: "Morals reformed—health preserved—industry invigorated—instruction diffused—public burthens lightened . . . all by a simple idea in architecture!" The inmate's "isolating visibility," combined with the apparent constancy of the overseer's surveillance, created a "power situation of which they themselves [the inmates] are the bearers."[57] "He who is subjected to a field of visibility, and who knows it, assumes responsibility for the constraints of power; he makes them play spontaneously upon himself; he inscribes in himself the power relation in which he simultaneously plays both roles."[58] In this way the gaze is effectively internalized by its "objects."[59]

Anyone who has ever worked in a factory, an "open plan" office, a hospital, or (indeed) a prison will know precisely what Foucault is talking about. Instant legibility and maximum control were the goals of Bentham's invention, and any impartial observer will have to admit that these have been achieved to a remarkable extent.[60] The extraordinarily rapid migra-tion of the Panoptic technique to a vast array of social sites—the fact that it was (and is) "an indefinitely generalizable mechanism"—allows Foucault to speak of "the formation of a disciplinary society," one characterized by a generalized surveillance.[61]

Such a society is, indeed, a "transparent" society.[62] As in Rousseau's vision of a virtuous community, there are fewer and fewer places to hide. True, our mores and practices are not monitored by our fellow citizens, as in the ideal "republican" community dreamt of by Rousseau. Rather, they are the object of a more anonymous and professionalized apparatus. The norm of good function or behavior is installed by the hierarchical obser-vation of the overseer, doctor, teacher, or officer. It replaces both the law and one's fellow citizens as the chief instrumentality of social control.[63] The liberal idea of a sacrosanct private realm, one marked out by legal rights, is thus given the lie by the supervisory and therapeutic practices of everyday life.

In Foucault's view, it was hardly a coincidence that the Enlighten-ment initiated many such disciplinary practices (including projects like Bentham's) all in the name of "reform." In response to a question from Michelle Perrot, Foucault goes so far as to claim that "a fear haunted the latter half of the eighteenth century: the fear of darkened spaces, of the pall of gloom which prevents the full visibility of things, men and truths."[64] The Enlightenment sought to "break up the patches of dark-ness that blocked the light, eliminate the shadowy areas of society, demolish the unlit chambers where arbitrary political acts, monarchical caprice, religious superstitions, tyrannical and priestly plots . . . were fomented."[65]

Seen from this angle, Bentham's Panopticon was not a betrayal of the Enlightenment project, but one of its most straightforward and literal expressions. The idea of a "public sphere" in which *bürgers* or *citoyens* came together to expose the secret policies of *raison d'état* to the light of day and critical argument (Habermas) is here given a new twist. Adjacent to or underpinning this sphere is a new "public" realm of disciplinary visibility, one constituted by the relentless gaze of rational experts and humanitarian overseers, who are specialists in the dynamics of "normal human function." The "light" of the Enlightenment thus simultaneously liberates and captures, empowers and disempowers.

This line of argument led Habermas to charge Foucault with promot-ing a "totalizing" critique of modernity, and to brand him a "Young Conservative" in the mode of a Carl Schmitt, Martin Heidegger, Ernst Jünger, or Hans Freyer.[66] There is some bite to this criticism, since Foucault, like Horkheimer and Adorno in *Dialectic of Enlightenment*, often seems to be conflating instrumental or "objectivizing" reason (the kind of reason characteristic of psychology, criminology, and the more intrusive "human sciences") with communicative or deliberative rationality (the kind of reason we deploy as civic equals in the public sphere). He appears not to notice that there is a wide and important gap between the fixing, dominating gaze of the positivistic Enlightenment (the "light" of the human sciences and various disciplinary knowledges) and the freedom of *speech* and *communication* given partial, imperfect expression in the new "bourgeois public sphere."[67] It obviously makes a huge difference whether we conceive the "Enlightenment project" in the objectifying terms suggested by Foucault's ocular metaphors (the disciplinary "gaze") and examples (the Panopticon), or in terms of speech and argument (which are intersubjective phenomena par excellence).

In Foucault's defense, it must be said that he isn't really interested in denying the potential of critical argument in the public sphere.[68] He is far more interested in drawing our attention to a crucial historical transformation in the *general character* of the public realm. Drawing on the 1831 *Leçons sur les prisons*, Foucault cites the French jurist F. H. Julius in order to draw a fundamental contrast between the principle animating the ancient public realm and that animating the modern public sphere:

> Antiquity had been a civilization of spectacle. 'To render accessible to a multitude of men the inspection of a small number of objects': this was the problem to which the architecture of temples, theaters, and circuses responded. With spectacle, there was a predominance of public life, the intensity of festivals, sensual proximity. In these rituals in which blood flowed, society found new vigor and formed for a moment a single great body. The modern age poses the opposite problem: 'To procure for a small number, or even a single individual, the instantaneous view of a great multitude.' In a society in which the principal elements are no longer the community and public life, but, on the one hand, private individuals and, on the other, the state, relations can be regulated only in a form that is the exact reverse of a spectacle: 'It was to the modern age, to the ever-growing influence of the state, to its ever more profound intervention in all the details and all the

relations of social life, that was reserved the task of increasing and perfecting its guarantees, by using and directing towards that great aim the building and distribution of buildings intended to observe a great multitude of men at the same time."[69]

In other words, the essential *modern* transformation of the public sphere concerns a reversal of the "optics" of public life. The ancient, stage-like "space of appearances"—so well suited to public argument and decision, as well as to kingly ceremony—gives way to a Panoptic-type "space of surveillance," one in which various disciplinary techniques (like the hierarchical observation and normalizing judgment Foucault describes at length in *Discipline and Punish*) enable a compulsory yet individualizing visibility.[70] Architecture, institutions, and the configuration of public space itself all have critical roles to play in this transformation: the creation of a new, essentially asymmetrical, public space. Indeed, the perfected *Polizeistaat* would be the Panopticon writ large, a "network of gazes" from which there was no escape.[71] As Foucault points out, this would be the realization of Napoleon's dream of a "world of details" organized, observed, and controlled from a single (but forever opaque) point.[72]

This is a breathtaking thesis, one that apparently captures an essential and epochal difference. We seem, however, to have wandered fairly far from both liberalism and the Enlightenment.[73] However much the concepts and distinctions central to these traditions may obscure the everyday workings of power, it seems implausible to accuse either of secretly desiring or covertly working for a police-state of the Napoleonic sort.[74] We may well live in a world in which the optics of public life have been reversed, exposing us as never before to a "network of gazes" and a "general visibility." But, it would appear, we can hardly blame *liberalism* or the Enlightenment for this reversal. Or can we? More to the point, can Foucault?

On the Prehistory of "Politics is the Continuation of War by Other Means"

Here we have to acknowledge that Foucault's various genealogies—of the clinic, of the prison, of the asylum, of psychiatry—are driven by a fundamental desire. He wants to demonstrate "how every victory of enlightenment was also a triumph of a new and insidious form of domination."[75]

This desire underlies Foucault's narrative conflation of reason, rights, military discipline and juridical punishment in *Discipline and Punish*. It also accounts for his seamless presentation of Frederick and Napoleon, Bentham and Beccaria, Rousseau and Tocqueville as collectively (and more or less equally) implicated in the "Enlightenment project" of achieving a society of total or "generalized" visibility.

One might well see this as yet another instance of a "postmodernist" throwing the Enlightenment baby out with the bath water, were it not for one simple fact. Every advance in legal, medical, military, or psychological rationalization *is also* (as Foucault argued) an advance in the knowledge and techniques of control. It is the assertion of this underlying continuity—similar, in certain respects, to *Dialectic of Enlightenment's* positing of an internal link between enlightened reason and increased domination—that accounts for much of the power of Foucault's analysis in *Discipline and Punish*. Yet, as I have already suggested, the very power of this analysis is inextricably tied to a radical and a strategic de-differentiation of social spheres. Let me explain.

Foucault's relentless focus on the "micro-techniques of discipline" revealed a dimension of social reality that had rarely, if ever, became an object of theoretical attention, let alone the center of a theory of "modernization." Rusche and Kirchheimer's precedent notwithstanding, Foucault could rightly claim to be the first social theorist to map the "carceral network"—made up of prisons, schools, orphanages, factory convents, reformatories, alms houses, workers' estates, and courts—that constituted the disciplinary underside of modern society. The need for such a network is obvious. From the early nineteenth century on, the major European nations required not only an endless supply of disciplined conscripts for their mass armies, but also an endless supply of disciplined workers for their increasingly gigantic industrial concerns.[76]

However, bringing this carceral underside into focus meant *dropping* the basic distinctions between state, civil society, and the public sphere, distinctions upon which a good deal of post-Rousseauian political and social theory has been built. These distinctions had to be dropped if the network of disciplinary institutions that cuts across all three spheres was to emerge as a totality.[77] They had to be dropped if we were to see clearly that the discipline of an army or a prison represented "a continuation and intensification of what goes on in more ordinary places."[78] Finally, they had to be dropped if the distinctive profile of modern (disciplinary) domination were to come into view. To hold onto these distinctions—worse, to structure one's analysis of domination around them—would put us back in the orbit of the "sovereign model of power," with all its misleading metaphors and concealing categories. "De-differentiation" is therefore not simply an effective rhetorical trope deployed by Foucault (and by countless epigoni). It constitutes, rather, a theoretical imperative of the first order. We simply cannot see what he wants us to see without it.

It is to Foucault's credit that, having accomplished his primary task of thematizing the disciplinary dimensions of modern society, he later qualified and, to a degree, reined in this theoretical strategy. This shift away from a radically de-differentiating analysis is evident in the series of lectures Foucault gave at the Collège de France in 1975–76. It becomes even more explicit in lectures he gave in 1977–79 on the topics of "governmentality" and "political reason."[79] I turn now to consider how these lectures constitute a significant moment of "re-differentiation" in Foucault's thought.

◆

Foucault's inversion of Clausewitz's dictum is well known, and underlies what some have called his "ontology of power." What is less well known is that Foucault saw Clausewitz himself as being an "inverter." The Clausewitzian formula ("War is the continuation of politics by other means") is not the original. Rather, what Clausewitz had done was to take a far older, more widely circulating thesis and stood *that* on its head.[80] The greater part of Foucault's 1975–76 lectures at the Collège de France are thus given over to a genealogy of the maxim that "*politics* is the continuation of war by other means"—a maxim based on the old and now seemingly discredited idea that *war is the basis of social relations.*[81]

Foucault knows that, by inverting Clausewitz's dictum, he too is hardly being original. In certain key respects he is merely recovering a once widespread but now nearly forgotten "historico-political discourse." This discourse challenged—from both the "left" and the "right"—the dominant vocabulary of sovereign power, contractual obligation, and public right (the latter being a juridical discourse based—in the European context—on Roman law). In taking up this discourse, Foucault realizes that he is following in the footsteps of some rather odd, and occasionally quite reactionary, characters. Thus, even though he situates himself at the same *point de départ* as people like Edward Coke and John Lilburne, the Comte de Boulainvilliers and the Comte d'Estaing, the Abbé Sieyès and Buonarroti, his archaeology of the thesis that "war is the basis of social relations" effectively relativizes (and problematizes) his own "Nietzschean" standpoint.[82] Once we, like Foucault, attempt to answer the question "Who came up with the idea that the civil order is an order of battle?" we realize that we can no longer deploy this trope naively or non-metaphorically (or, as some might say, "radically").[83]

Where does the "historico-political discourse" grounded on the idea that "war is the basis of social relations" come from? What is this discourse saying, and what are its implications, both historically and in the present? These are the questions Foucault confronts in his Collège lectures of 1975–76.

According to Foucault, this rhetoric dates from the end of the civil and religious wars of the sixteenth century in Europe.[84] It figures prominently in the revolutionary and pre-revolutionary arguments of the Puritans and the Levellers in England (from about 1630 on), and reemerges "on the other side" (that of the aristocracy in France) as a protest against the "great absolute-administrative monarchy" put in place by Louis XIV.[85] In all cases, whether "progressive" or "reactionary," this rhetoric relied upon history and the traditional rights claims of specific social groups, the better to attack the injustices of the new juridical-sovereign discourse of public right.

The absolutist state's victory in successive "local" struggles—against the nobility, against the peasants, against the Church, municipalities, *parlements*, "heretics," and previously independent cities or regions—led it to clothe its might in right. This was the "public right" of the crown jurists, who presented the sovereign state as entitled to a monopoly on political power as a means to guaranteeing social peace. In opposition to the legalistic discourse of the crown jurists (and political theorists like Hobbes and Pufendorf), a historical counter-discourse emerged, one that—in its various iterations—made the following general claims:

No matter what philosophico-juridical theory may say, political power does not begin when war ends. The organization and juridical structure of power, of States, monarchies, and societies, does not emerge when the clash of arms ceases. War has not been averted. War obviously presided over the birth of States: right, peace, and laws were born in the blood and mud of battles. This should not be taken to mean the ideal battles dreamed up by philosophers or jurists: we are not talking about some theoretical savagery. The law is not born of nature, and it was not born near the fountains that the first shepherds frequented: the law is born of real battles, victories, massacres, and conquests which can be dated and which have their horrific heroes; the law was born in burning towns and ravaged fields.[86]

One may grant this broad historical point—what nation-state ever came into existence except on the basis of blood and conquest?—and still draw a generally Hobbesian conclusion: the State born of violence puts an end to ubiquitous (and otherwise ceaseless) violence. The practitioners of the "historico-political discourse" that holds that war is the basis of social relations could hardly disagree more. The emergence of the centralized, sovereign state is not the end of war, but its continuation:

> This does not, however, mean that society, the law, and the State are like armistices that put an end to wars, or that they are the products of definitive victories. Law is not pacification, for beneath the law, war continues to rage in all the mechanisms of power, even in the most regular. War is the motor behind institutions and order. In the smallest of its cogs, peace is waging a secret war. To put it another way, we have to interpret the war that is going on beneath peace; peace itself is a coded war. We are therefore at war with one another; a battlefront runs through the whole of society, continuously and permanently, and it is this battlefront that puts us all on one side or the other. We are all inevitably someone's enemy.[87]

Such a discourse of "perpetual war" may well appeal to angry partisans of the radical left or right: people who think that the worst—and most characteristic—things about liberal democracy are its love of procedural mechanisms and juridical mind-set.[88] The forgotten voices of the seventeenth and eighteenth centuries remind us that, behind the legalistic facade, there lies the reality (and blood) of irreducible historical conflict and injustice. This injustice hardly disappears with one side's "victory" and the creation of new institutions. What began as war continues as war: a war of perpetually evolving tactics and configurations of forces; a war that involves the assertion of "singular" rights against a bogus (state-serving) juridical universality.[89] It was the proto-Nietzschean quality of this perspective that Foucault evidently embraced when he famously declared that he was interested in using the "model of war" for his analysis of the "how" of power.[90]

However, things become more complicated the moment Foucault presents us with the analytical architecture deployed by his seventeenth- and eighteenth-century predecessors in "the discourse of history that made war the primary, and almost exclusive, analyzer of political relations."[91] For men as different as the radical John Lilburne and the aristocratic Comte de Boulainvilliers, the analysis of society as perpetual war actually (and, one might say, necessarily) took the form of an ongoing struggle between *races*: Saxons vs. Normans, Gallo-Romans vs. Franks.[92] It was in terms of historical "peoples," their various conquests and subjugations, that the "discourse of permanent war" proceeded, articulating its specific rights claims in terms of the wrongs done by one "race" to another (for example: the "Norman yoke," or the usurpation of the French nobility's traditional rights by the collusion of the monarch with the Church).

Much of the 1975–76 Collège lectures are devoted to teasing out the discursive possibilities opened up by the coding of social struggle not simply as war, but as "race war" or (indeed) "race struggle." Foucault does not shy away from the questionable character of these origins, even though he is quick to point out how—in the seventeenth and eighteenth centuries—the term "struggle of the races" did not have the unsavory associations it has today. One crucial point of the lectures is to show how this discourse—initially a particularist, "plural," and revolutionary counter-discourse deployed by a specific estate or "nation" against the pseudo-universality of the State—opened up a rhetorical field subsequently inhabited by nationalist, class-based, and (finally) race-based politics of the sort we are familiar with from the nineteenth and twentieth centuries.

In this regard, Foucault cites the "tactical generalization of historical knowledge" that emerged in the fight against the Sovereign's deployment of public right.[93] A rhetorical and analytical approach that arose fully formed in the "nobiliary reaction" of the early eighteenth century soon revealed its effectiveness (as well as its "tactical polyvalence") in a broad array of struggles—from those between the estates of the *ancien régime*, to the French Revolution, to 1848 and beyond. Indeed, one of Foucault's primary points is that this entire discursive field—an obvious precursor of his own approach—evolves in such a way that it is finally taken up by the state itself and deployed to induce a paranoiac concern with biological racial purity among the nation's populace.[94]

These various evolutions and appropriations are, of course, contingent. There is nothing "necessary" about them—no deep, underlying tie between the origins of a discursive field in the nobiliary reaction and the later uses to which it will be put. In other words, there is no straight line from the discourse of "race struggle" in Boulainvilliers to what Foucault calls the "Nazi transformation" of this discourse.[95]

This insistence on contingency is a basic "genealogical" point, one that Foucault owes explicitly to Nietzsche.[96] From the genealogical point of view, discourses—like practices, signs, and institutions—are invested and mastered by a variety of forces over time, each of which supplies a new purpose to the vocabulary (or entity) in question. As a result, the meaning of any given discourse, practice, or institution is fluid, never fixed or singular.[97]

That said, the discursive transformations Foucault traces in "Society Must Be Defended" are more than a little curious. We are unlikely to conclude that, if only the "Nazi transformation" had not occurred, we could still be deploying the "historico-political" discourse of "race struggle" for a variety of progressive political causes. The problem is that the discursive field of politics as war rests on a fundamental and irreducible asymmetry. The rights and freedoms of the aggrieved "race," nation, estate, or class can only be purchased at the expense of those of their dominators and enemies. The relationship of force is never overcome; it can only be reversed.

This problem is brought to the fore in Foucault's treatment of Henri, Comte de Boulainvilliers, one of the master practitioners of the "historico-political" discourse of war and "race struggle" as the great analyzer of political relations. While Boulainvilliers can hardly be said to have invented this discourse, Foucault clearly thinks that he was responsible for casting it into a theoretically sophisticated form, one that ultimately made it possible for this discourse to become a "general instrument" in the political and social struggles of the eighteenth, nineteenth, and even twentieth centuries. Without Boulainvilliers's systemic elaboration of a new mode of historical analysis in his *L'état de la France*, the discourse of "permanent war" would never have become the counter-discourse par excellence for both left and right, both before and after the French Revolution. Or so Foucault argues in "Society Must Be Defended."

Foucault's treatment of Boulainvilliers as a uniquely important predecessor in the "war as social analyzer" paradigm is detailed and highly instructive. It fully reveals the extent of Foucault's methodological debt. It also makes clear that "discourse of permanent war" rests on some fairly dubious historical and theoretical presuppositions and can, as a result, give birth to some profoundly unpleasant offspring.

The Comte de Boulainvilliers was the most gifted of the historians and propagandists allied to the "nobiliary reaction" in France during the late seventeenth and early eighteenth centuries. Assigned the task of providing the Duc de Bourgogne a digest of the massive *intendants'* reports to Louis XV, Boulainvilliers produced his *L'état de la France* in two volumes in 1727, which were followed by a third in 1728.[98] These volumes were, in effect, a "filleting and abridging" of the reports of the intendants. Boulainvilliers's work thus quite self-consciously colonized the "hateful knowledge" of court clerks and state bureaucrats, the better to turn the "State's knowledge of itself" against the forces of monarchical centralization and bureaucratization.[99]

But it is not simply a matter of contesting the "State's knowledge of the State" through the "subversive" appropriation of the knowledge of the intendants. Rather, Boulainvilliers's originality—his epoch-making importance, in Foucault's estimate—is to be found in the way he opens up a new field of history. Against juridical knowledge—the knowledge of right deployed by the clerk of the court, the *greffier*—Boulainvilliers introduces "another form of knowledge," a historical knowledge "whose nature will allow it to get outside right, to get behind right and to slip into its interstices." This history will be unlike any previous history. It will not provide a "pictorial or dramatized account of the development of public right," such as we find in history textbooks. Rather, it will be (quite explicitly) a counter-history. It will demonstrate "that the very edifice of right— even in its most valid institutions, its most explicit and widely recognized ordinances—is the product of a whole series of iniquities, injustices, abuses, dispossessions, betrayals, and infidelities committed by royal power, which reneged on its commitment to the nobility."[100]

History so conceived reveals not just a totally new field of objects—the "dark history" of alliances, rivalries, usurpations, betrayals, debts, trickery, and stupidity that lies beneath the official, State-sponsored "glorious history of power"[101]—but a *new subject* as well:

> With Boulainvilliers and the reactionary nobility of the late eighteenth century, a new subject of history appears. This means two things. On the one hand, there is a new speaking subject: someone else begins to speak in history, to recount history; someone else begins to say "I" and "we" as he recounts history; someone else begins

to tell the story of his own history; someone else begins to reorganize the past, events, rights, injustices, defeats and victories around himself and his own destiny.[102]

In recent decades, we have become so familiar with the idea of history written "from below"—from the point of view of workers, women, blacks, or the "subaltern"—that it comes as a bit of a shock when Foucault credits a reactionary French aristocrat with the creation of this entire genre, this new "discursive possibility." The feminist and multiculturalist concern with "voice" here receives an unexpected and no doubt unwanted forebear. From Boulainvilliers's perspective, it is the weakened French aristocracy that must learn how to speak and recover its lost capacity for agency. In order to do that, it must first remember who it is, and what it was. Hence the importance of a history that unmasks the "glorious history" of the State and of public right, that "talks about events that occur beneath the State, that ignore right, and that are older and more profound than institutions."[103]

But who—or, more precisely, what—is this new "subject of history," this new speaking subject that appears in Boulainvilliers's *L'état de la France*?

The obvious answer would be "the French nobility." However, for this question to be theoretically interesting, we must tease out a higher level of generality in Boulainvilliers's text. That is why Foucault reminds us that the nobility, considered collectively, were members of what eighteenth-century French historians would have called a "society"—that is, an association or grouping of individuals "governed by a statute," with "its own manners, customs, and even its own laws." Thus, "the something that begins to speak in history, that speaks of history, and of which history will speak, is what the vocabulary of the day called a 'nation.' "[104] But this new "speaking subject" of history—a subject that revolts against the "glorious" and misleading history of State power and public right, a subject that uses history as a weapon to reveal and redress a catalog of past injustices—is not a nation in anything like the contemporary sense of the word:

At this time, the nation is by no means something that is defined by its territorial unity, a definite political morphology, or its systematic subordination to some imperium. The nation has no frontiers, no definite system of power, and no State. The nation circulates behind frontiers and institutions. The nation, or rather "nations," or in other words the collections, societies, groupings of individuals who share a status, mores, customs, and a certain particular law—in the sense of regulatory statutes rather than Statist laws. History will be about this, about these elements. And it is those elements that will begin to speak: it is the nation that begins to speak. The nobility is one nation, as distinct from the many other nations that circulate within the State and come into conflict with one another. It is this notion, this concept of the nation, that will give rise to the famous revolutionary problem of the nation; it will, of course, give rise to the basic concepts of nineteenth-century nationalism. It will also give rise to the notion of race. And, finally, it will give rise to the notion of class.[105]

Foucault here occupies a terrain very similar to that explored by Arendt in part 2 of *The Origins of Totalitarianism*.[106] He is exploring the origins of the now widespread idea that the political identity of a people or group has nothing to do with the set of laws or institutions it inhabits (the "State"), but is rather a function of some pre-legal, pre-institutional historical origin, status, or quasi-natural characteristic (such as aristocratic blood, race, or the "Slavic soul").

Foucault, however, isn't interested in making an Arendtian case for the nation-state and the artificial (public and legal) character of political membership. Quite the contrary: he wants to explore the potential for resistance to the universalistic discourse of "the State" that is contained in Boulainvilliers's "historico-politico discourse." A good deal of this potential lies precisely in the "vague, fluid, shifting notion of the nation" that Boulainvilliers's analysis puts into play. This "shifting notion" of a people or group—a "mass of individuals" who "move from one frontier to another," perpetually deterritorialized and deterritorializing—becomes, according to Foucault, the "subject-object of a new history," a "disruptive principle" diametrically opposed to the "Statist organization of discourse."[107] From now on, history need not concern kings, their power and institutions. It can be a "history of subjects or peoples," that is, a look at power from the other side of the relationship.[108]

It's easy to see why Foucault is so attracted to this move, to Boulainvilliers's *coupure epistémologique* in the writing of history. Never mind that the "multiplicity" this discourse introduced was not the pluralism of civil society, but that of races or "nations" (the nobles vs. everyone else). Never mind that, as a strictly historical discourse, Boulainvilliers's analysis might be shown to be "wrong as a whole and wrong about the details" concerning the historical roots of aristocratic rights and freedoms. For however absurd the story Boulainvilliers tells—a story in which a Frankish "warrior aristocracy" without a king liberates their "brother Gauls" from "Roman absolutism," setting up a benign feudal system with a contented military caste and peasant body, only to be subsequently cheated out of their lands and privileges by an ambitious monarch in cahoots with the old Gaulish aristocracy—his analysis succeeds in one very important but ultimately ambiguous respect.[109]

The historical analyses offered in *L'état de la France* establish the primacy of the "relationship of war" as "a general social analyzer." That is, they take what had previously figured in the linear narrative of the evolution of public right as a "disruption, an enigma, a sort of dark mass or raw event" and transform it into a powerful "grid of intelligibility."[110] This grid makes sense of an otherwise incomprehensible past, reminding the nobility of who they are (the descendants of a proud Germanic warrior caste) and how they—the most powerful, privileged, and free, the liberators of Gaul—came to lose their power (thanks to the nefarious deployment of law and right by the State). It also enables them to calculate the current configuration of forces so that they might regain at least some of their power. This intelligibility, and the strategic knowledge it makes possible, are the results of what Foucault calls Boulainvilliers's "threefold generalization of war."[111]

First, Boulainvilliers's analysis generalizes war with respect to right and the foundations of right. Instead of portraying war as either a disruption or a "ferryman" between systems of right, Boulainvilliers's historical approach shows how "war in fact completely conceals right, and even natural right, to such an extent that right becomes unreal, abstract, and, in a sense, fictive."[112] "Conceals" is a very unfortunate translation in this context.[113] What Foucault is trying to say is that Boulainvilliers's approach reveals how war is not a simple *interruption* or break between discrete systems of right and law; rather, it is their *underlying common denominator*. War is the historical "base" of every legal "superstructure" that presents itself as grounded on natural right—that is, on something nonsocial and nonhistorical.

Boulainvilliers establishes this generalization by three arguments. First, he argues that, from a historical point of view, natural right simply does not exist. In effect, Boulainvilliers says "you can study history as long as you like, and in any way you like, but you will never discover any natural rights. . . . No matter where we look, we find only either war itself . . . or the inequalities that result from wars and violence. . . . Inequality is everywhere, violence creates inequality everywhere, and wars are everywhere."[114] History itself debunks the idea of natural right, and with it the effort to see systems of right as rooted in something other than the brute fact of social conflict.

Second, the generalization of war with respect to right is carried forward by a more theoretical argument to the effect that freedom and equality are diametrically opposed. Thus, while Boulainvilliers thinks it is conceivable that a "primitive freedom" existed prior to any and all domination, such freedom (in which "every individual is the equal of every other individual") would have been without force and without content. "What would be the point of being free and what, in concrete terms, would it mean if one could not trample on the freedom of others? That is the primary expression of freedom"—at least according to Boulainvilliers.[115]

Third, Boulainvilliers establishes the generalization of war with respect to right and law by the following argument. Even if egalitarian freedom did or could exist—even if natural right were not a self-serving fiction—it would invariably be defeated by "the historical force of a freedom that functions as non-equality." Freedom as equality—the dubious presupposition of natural law and of the State's ideological undermining of aristocratic privilege—is, in fact, "powerless to resist the law of history, which states that freedom is strong, vigorous, and meaningful only when it is the freedom of the few and when it exists at the expense of others."[116] According to Boulainvilliers, the egalitarian "law of nature" will always lose to the anti-egalitarian "law of history."[117]

Boulainvilliers's historical generalizations thus reveal that there is no other foundation for right than inequality, equality itself being little more than an ideological fiction. Hence, right—even egalitarian right—is always and everywhere the product of a relationship of inequality and domination. Thrasymachus and Callicles were correct: justice is the interest of the stronger, a proposition Boulainvilliers believes is historically undeniable. Indeed, he would say—and Foucault would apparently agree—that the truth of this proposition has been demonstrated by *L'état de la France*.

The second dimension of the "war as social analyzer" paradigm established by Boulainvilliers centers on what Foucault calls the "generalization of the battle form." Boulainvilliers persistently draws our attention to the fact that, while every battle or conquest results in a relation of force (dominator and dominated), a relationship of force also clearly preceded the contest of arms.

What, then, established the prior relationship of force, the relationship that "guarantees that one nation will win the battle and the other will lose it"? Boulainvilliers's answer—based on his reading of French history—is quite simple. It is the "nature and organization" of military institutions that establishes the prior relationship, and that clearly indicates who will be the winner and who the loser. The Franks won because they possessed a warrior aristocracy and an armed people; the Romans lost because they had been reduced to using mercenaries after they had disarmed the Gauls.[118] So, in order to make sense of any particular configuration of social forces, one must ask a basic question: who has the weapons? What is the precise economy of armed and unarmed? Boulainvilliers as presented by Foucault would affirm Mao's dictum that all power grows out of the barrel of a gun.

The third and final generalization concerns what Foucault dubs the "invasion-rebellion system."[119] Boulainvilliers gives systematic expression to the idea that, when one looks at any given political entity, one should look at it through the dual lenses of invasion and rebellion. These categories enable the interested historian—the historian who has taken sides—to "rediscover the war that goes on within societies."[120] Of course, the point is not simply to recall ancient battles between Normans and Saxons, Franks and Romans, or Franks and Gauls. Rather, it is to render transparent how it happened that a certain relationship of force—say, that of the Frankish warrior aristocracy toward the king and the people—came to be inverted. How did the strong become weak and the weak become strong? The "invasion-rebellion system" foregrounds this reversibility of power relationships, and thus aids the partisan historian in answering this most important of political questions. History, as Foucault writes, "now looks essentially like a calculation of forces."[121]

Boulainvilliers's revolution in historical-political analysis is now clear. Taken together, his three analytical "generalizations of war" yield an entirely new optic on social groups and the tensions between them. The result is a history not of power, but of "peoples" caught up in power relationships within the social body. As Foucault sums up Boulainvilliers's achievement:

> Until the seventeenth century, a war was essentially a war between one mass and another mass. For his part, Boulainvilliers makes the relationship of war part of every social relationship, subdivides it into thousands of different channels, and reveals war to be a sort of permanent state that exists between groups, fronts, and tactical units as they in some sense civilize one another, come into conflict with one another, or on the contrary, form alliances. There are no more multiple and stable great

masses, but there is a multiple war. . . . With Boulainvilliers . . . we have a generalized war that permeates the entire social body and the entire history of the social body; it is obviously not the sort of war in which individuals fight individuals, but one in which groups fight groups. And it is, I think, this generalization of war [in three broad and overlapping senses] that is characteristic of Boulainvilliers's thought.[122]

The reader will probably feel that one could substitute "Foucault" for "Boulainvilliers" in this passage and have a tolerably accurate description of the approach in works like *Discipline and Punish*. After all, the goal of Boulainvilliers's "threefold generalization of war" is to demonstrate how politics—and law and right—are, in fact, the "continuation of war by other means."[123] As we have seen, this a thesis with which Foucault largely concurs. It is a thesis, however, that rests completely on Boulainvilliers's distinction between state and *societies*. On the one hand, there is "the State": the monarch, his intendants and administrators, his military and legal apparatus. On the other, there are the "nations" that make up the political entity that is France: the "estates" or "races" of the nobility, clergy, peasants, and bourgeoisie. In the course of the eighteenth century, this reactionary distinction between the centralized state and its subsidiary "nations" becomes the more familiar (and less freighted) distinction between state and society (the latter considered not as a set of warring "races," but as an "association of associations" or estates).[124]

Thus, it becomes possible to say that Boulainvilliers's historical discourse, with its "disruptive principle" of a plural "nation" or "societies," points toward two quite distinct moments or political-theoretical possibilities. First, it points toward what we might call a liberal or "bourgeois" critique of the absolutist state—that is, toward a critique of sovereign power and *raison d'état* delivered from the standpoint of the "nations," estates, or associations that make up the social body. Second, it points toward the eventual absorption of the vocabulary of political struggle by a rhetoric of race or class struggle—that is, by a rhetoric that presupposes a radical separation of political identity from law and institutional frameworks (a rhetoric analyzed by Arendt in *The Origins of Totalitarianism*).[125]

These two possibilities come to the fore the moment Foucault historicizes Boulainvilliers's discourse of "permanent war." While the type of history practiced by Boulainvilliers (and his inheritor, the Comte de Buat-Nançay) succeeded in making war the "primary, and almost exclusive, analyzer of social relations in the [French] eighteenth century," it also posed what Foucault calls a "great threat," a "great danger." However useful and "tactically polyvalent" this discourse was, it implied that "we would be caught up in a war without end" and that "all our relations, whatever they might be, would always be of the order of domination"—the domination of one "race" or group over another.[126] As France navigated the path to republican nationhood, there was a pressing need to reduce, restrict, and ("up to a point") pacify the historical discourse of "permanent war," bringing the warring "peoples" back into the ambit of law and shared institutions. In other words, there was a need not so much to eliminate or repress struggle in the political realm, but to think it in what Foucault describes as "purely civilian terms." This meant its relocation within the public-institutional structures of the newly republican state.[127]

This work of relocation—what Foucault describes as the "embourgeoisement" of the discourse of historico-political struggle[128]—was begun by Sieyès in *Qu'est-ce que le Tiers état?* According to Foucault, Sieyès accomplished this specific task by pursuing a dual strategy. The first was to ask a broadly transcendental question: What are the conditions of possibility for a nation (in the modern sense of the word) to exist? Sieyès's answer is that neither a king nor, indeed, a government is necessary for the emergence of a nation (they can come later).

What is needed is a common law (an inclusive law for all estates) and a legislative body—or, as Foucault puts it, "explicit laws and agencies to formulate them."[129] But the "law-legislature couple" is only the "formal" precondition of the nation. It must be supplemented by a fairly extensive set of "substantive" preconditions. These include the "works" of agriculture, industry, trade, and the liberal arts, plus the "functions" of the army, justice, the church, and administration. Who performs these works and fulfills these functions? In the case of France, the answer (with some minor exceptions for the clergy and aristocracy) is the Third Estate. "The Third Estate is in itself the historical precondition for the existence of a nation."[130]

Thus, whereas the "historico-political discourse" of Boulainvilliers and the nobiliary reaction "extracted" from the monarchical unity of the state the "singular right of the nobles" to make good its claims, Sieyès and the Third Estate (according to Foucault) practice a strategy of immanence:

> We are no more than one nation among other individuals. But the
> nation that we constitute is the only one that can effectively con-

stitute the nation. Perhaps we are not, in ourselves, the totality of the social body, but we are capable of guaranteeing the totalizing function of the State. We are capable of Statist universality.[131]

For a nation (as opposed to "nations"—that is, nobles, peasants, clergy) to exist, its essential social class must embody universality as well as particularity. By blood and privilege, the nobility exempts itself from this role. By virtue of its substantive, functional contributions to society, the Third Estate is, in Sieyès's estimation, uniquely qualified to be the "active, constituent core of the State."[132]

Sieyès's text thus constructs a new relationship between universality and particularity. This specific "nation"—the Third Estate—is, in a concrete sense, just as universal as the state itself. In Foucault's view, *Qu'est-ce que le Tiers état?* completes the transformation of the "historico-political discourse" it cribs from Boulainvilliers by reorienting the temporal axes of its "history with practical intent." The present, not the past, is privileged as the "fullest moment," the moment in which "the universal makes its entry into the real."[133] With the prospect of a common law replacing feudal privilege and political rights for the Third Estate, France is about to be reborn as a "concrete universal"—that is, as a nation-state rather than a State composed of endlessly warring nations.

Qu'est-ce le Tiers état? is thus a continuation, inversion, and—in certain respects—a transcendence of the mode of analysis created by *L'état de la France.* Summing up the contrast between Boulainvilliers and Sieyès, Foucault writes:

> In Boulainvilliers' analysis, the clash between different nations that exist within a single social body is of course mediated by institutions. . . . But the use of civil institutions was . . . purely instrumental, and the war was still basically a war. Institutions were merely the instruments of a domination which was still a domination of the warlike kind, like an invasion. We now have, in contrast, a history in which war—the war for domination—will be replaced by a struggle that is, so to speak, of a different substance: not an armed clash, but an effort, a rivalry, a striving toward the universality of the State. The State, and the universality of the State, become both what is at stake in the struggle, and the battlefield. This will therefore be *an essentially civil struggle* to the extent that domination is neither its goal nor its expression, and to the extent that the State is both its object and its space. It will

take place essentially in and around the economy, institutions, production, and the administration. We will have a civil struggle and the military struggle or bloody struggle will become no more than an exceptional moment, a crisis or episode within it.[134]

Now, even though Foucault is delineating the "problematic" installed by Sieyès and the Third Estate here, this passage is remarkable for its clear and unapologetic grasp of the distinction between politics as the continuation of a literal war between social groups (a war begun long ago and continued "by other means," a permanent war), and politics as the (generally) peaceful or "civil" struggle for control of leading public institutions and the policymaking apparatus. This distinction is all the more remarkable given Foucault's official position in *Discipline and Punish*, namely, that politics is war continued by other means, and that the only thing that really matters is the strategic configuration of forces—and possibilities for "local resistance"—at any given moment.

In recognizing this distinction, Foucault has hardly become a civic republican or liberal democrat. He has, however, indicated his awareness of the need to revise his paradigm of social conflict. The "politics is war" formula must be transposed into a more metaphorical key.

It would be silly to say Foucault finally recognizes the difference between bullets and ballots (although, given the tumultuous political history of France, such recognition is hardly to be taken for granted). Rather, the passage cited above indicates his growing awareness that social conflict must be institutionally mediated if it is to be politically meaningful, and not just fall back into the catch-all category of a "politics of everyday life." It indicates, in other words, Foucault's clear grasp of the fact that politics does not begin and end with "disciplinary mechanisms" and the "contestation of identities." Politics, rather, is institutionally mediated conflict— conflict that arises in the "social" domain of civil society, and plays out in the "public" domain of the republican state and its institutions. This is what separates it from war (a point the Machiavelli of the *Discourses* would have fully agreed with). The races/history/war series installed by Boulainvilliers thus gives way to a new series: associations/common law/institutionalized political struggle.

The "domestication" of the "politics as war" schema should not, however, make us complacent. The specter of "permanent war" may have been too much to bear, politically speaking. But this fact hardly prohibits the possibility that "politics as war" will reemerge within the confines of the republican nation-state or the *Rechtsstaat*. Even where social conflict is mediated by constitutional instruments, it is possible that the state will colonize life and civil society, arrogating to itself the role of cultivator and protector of both. This is the possibility Tocqueville articulated in the last part of *Democracy in America,* with its invocation of "administrative despotism." It is, moreover, a possibility Foucault gives an ingenious twist to in the last lecture (March 17, 1976) of the 1975–76 series at the Collège de France.

Foucault begins by noting how the "politics as war" schema emerged in the eighteenth century as a "struggle between the races," only to submerge in the early nineteenth century thanks to the rise of a discourse of "national universality" (the discourse of Sieyès, the Revolution, and the Declaration of the Rights of Man and the Citizen). "Sovereign" power—the King's "right of life and death," his power to "let" his subjects live and his power to kill them, when need be[135]—gives way to the rule of law, the recognition of individual rights (including the "right to life"), and a circumscribed state power (although hardly as circumscribed as the "liberal" revolution of 1789 would have liked). How, then, Foucault asks, does it come to pass that the modern, lawful state—the state that claims to work for the interests of all—wields a power over life that far exceeds that of the sovereign power of the *ancien régime*? Is this merely a fluke of the history of technology, the inevitable result of the development of atomic bombs and thermonuclear weapons?

Foucault's response to this question is a categorical "no." In fact, he argues, the modern democratic state wields the power of mass death largely, if not solely, because it wields the power of life. Technically speaking, death is not an "object" of modern political power at all: life is. Over the course of the nineteenth century, the modern state increasingly concerns itself with the health, hygiene, birth rate, and mortality of its population. The state attacks illness and epidemics (which sap the strength of the social body) by centralizing medical knowledge, coordinating care, making public health interventions, and generally "medicalizing" the population at large.[136] "Biopolitics" is the name Foucault gives to this new set of techniques and statistical knowledge, and to the interventions that the emerging welfare state carries out on the body of the population as a whole. Biopolitics focuses on the "the population as a political problem," that is, as *the* essential resource of the state. In so doing, it introduces a new form of political power: biopower.

At first glance, "biopower" appears to simply displace Foucault's earlier conception of "disciplinary" power. In fact, he insists, the two complement each other. Disciplinary power deals with individual bodies and their forces in the "sub-state" arena of schools, hospitals, barracks, and workshops. Biopower, in contrast, is what Foucault calls a "massifying" power. It works by utilizing techniques such as forecasts and statistical surveys, mechanisms that enable it to intervene in the care of a mass population, which it views as a "body with many heads." The object here is not to discipline, but to regularize the essential biological processes of man-as-species.[137] Biopower is thus the state taking control of life itself through its growing interventions in matters of public health. It replaces the sovereign power of "taking life and letting live" with a "power of regularization" that consists in "making live and letting die."[138] Biopower's "regulatory technology of life" aims at the body of the population as a whole, whereas the "microtechniques" of disciplinary power aimed at the training and normalization of individual bodies.

The dark side of this new form of power should be evident. Not only does biopower enable the state to subject its population to a whole range of "objectifying" statistical-medical surveillance techniques; it also raises the possibility that the state will detect a threat to the health of the nation from within. While "care for life" is the essential aim of biopower and the medicalized welfare state, state racism can now intervene in the name of the biological health of the mass. It can demand the liquidation of threats to the racial health and purity of the nation.[139] The concern with health thus paves the way for the reemergence of the discourse of race struggle, now properly "medicalized" and given a scientific veneer. The old sovereign right to kill is reintroduced, but this time in the name of life itself. The most obvious and dramatic example of this transformation is the Nazi state, which used "biopower" not only in order to attack other (inferior) races, but to "expose its own race to the absolute and universal threat of death."[140]

At this point in Foucault's analysis, two distinct paths present themselves. His introduction of biopower as the "massifying," state-centered complement to localized and capillary disciplinary power could provide a novel point of entry into the concrete investigation of the historical emergence of *raison d'état* and specific modes of governmental rationality. In other words, it could lead to an enlightening investigation of how modes of seeing and acting like a state dramatically change in the eighteenth and nineteenth century, at once enabling the relative autonomy of civil society while maintaining an overarching control. This would provide a more supple grid for understanding transformations in the state/civil society relationship than is typically provided by liberal theory. At the same time, however, this investigation would be entirely consonant with classically liberal concerns—namely, the tracing of the subtle yet pervasive extension of state power into ever new domains of everyday life.

This is indeed the path Foucault takes in the 1979 Tanner lectures at Stanford and in his earlier lecture on "governmentality." The latter provides a searching historical analysis of the shift (during the seventeenth and eighteenth centuries) from a Machiavellian or princely form of *raison d'état* to an "art of government" that aims at managing increasingly autonomous social and economic spheres.[141] The state's "management" of the population as a resource is only one dimension of this new form of political rationality, an administrative rationality whose emergence provides the focal point for the cognate analyses offered by Max Weber, Hannah Arendt, and Sheldon Wolin.[142] This, it must be said, is a rich field for research. It traces the creation of new, "lighter," and more socially oriented modes of political rationality, modes that both presume and transgress the emergent distinction between state and society.

However, Foucault's programmatic introduction of biopower also points in another direction, toward what can only be described as a new and radicalized strategy of de-differentiation. This strategy comes into sharpest focus in remarks Foucault makes at the conclusion of volume 1 of *The History of Sexuality*. More recently, it has become prominent through the appropriation of Foucault performed by Agamben in his enormously influential book *Homo Sacer*. I want to conclude this section by saying a word about each.

In the last section of *The History of Sexuality*, volume 1, Foucault returns to the problematic of "the right of death and the power over life" he opened in the 1975–76 lectures. His explicit intention is to synthesize this problematic with his previous analysis of disciplinary power, the better to provide a "global" model of power in the modern age. In this new model, individual bodies are not only trained and subjugated. In addition to the "anatomo-politics of the human body," there emerges a form of power—biopower—focused on the body of the species. This power sets up an "entire series of interventions and regulatory controls," the better to "invest life through and through."[143] Our individual bodies and our species-life are colonized and controlled by what Foucault calls "this great bipolar technology—anatomic and biological." Is it any wonder that the politics of the twentieth century—the century of the welfare state and totalitarianism— revolve around power's ability to both manage life and destroy it *en masse*, all in the name of a healthier, more functional, more flourishing life? Foucault draws a startlingly dystopian conclusion:

> Wars are no longer waged in the name of a sovereign, who must be defended; they are waged on behalf of the existence of everyone; entire populations are mobilized for the purpose of wholesale slaughter in the name of life necessity [sic]: massacres have become vital. It is as managers of life and survival, of bodies and the race, that so many regimes have been able to wage so many wars, causing so many men to be killed. . . . The atomic situation is now at the end point of this process: *the power to expose a whole population to death is the underside of the power to guarantee an individual's continued existence.* . . . If genocide is indeed the dream of modern powers, this is not because of a recent return of the ancient right to kill; it is because power is situated and exercised at the level of life, the species, the race, and the large-scale phenomena of the population.[144]

A state that cultivates and manages life, that is indeed the "shepherd" of its population, not only produces docile subjects whose forces can be exploited (the Tocquevillian nightmare). It also produces a mass body fit for possible sacrifice or extermination.[145]

It is this "biopolitical" figure—in which any modern state is, by virtue of its welfare and public health interventions, a potential Moloch—that Agamben seizes upon in *Homo Sacer*. Indeed, his starting point is a passage from volume 1 of *The History of Sexuality* in which Foucault sums up what we might call the "world historical" significance of the emergence of biopolitics. "For millennia," Foucault writes, "man remained what he was for Aristotle: a living animal with an additional capacity for political existence; modern man is an animal whose politics places his existence as a living being in question."[146] For Agamben, the modern entry of what the Greeks called *zoē* into the space of politics effectively undercuts the all-important distinction between public and private. What had previously been excluded from the public realm—"bare" life—now becomes, in some sense, the principle and justification of the modern state. Indeed, by "placing biological life at the center of its calculations," the modern state "does nothing other than to bring to light the secret tie uniting power and bare life."[147]

The result of this biopolitical transformation is that our "species existence" takes the place of civic identity as *the* subject of politics. "Bare life" replaces both the citizen and the juridical subject of rights. And this, according to Agamben, sets up an "inner solidarity between democracy and totalitarianism," a "contiguity between mass democracy and totalitarian states."[148] For "only because biological life and its needs had become the *politically* decisive fact is it possible to understand the otherwise incomprehensible rapidity with which twentieth-century parliamentary democracies were able to turn into totalitarian states and with which this century's totalitarian states were able to be converted, almost without interruption, into parliamentary democracies."[149]

For the average reader, Agamben's conclusion will appear to trace the outer limits of the de-differentiating potential built into Foucault's "biopolitical" thesis. After all, what grander and more "daring" theoretical de-differentiation could there be than the reduction of parliamentary or liberal democracy to the same fundamental basis as Nazi or Soviet totalitarianism? The latter becomes the flip side of the former. Entire libraries of European history and Western political theory since the English Civil War are thereby rendered moot. But Agamben—relying on Foucault, yet also making perverse use of Arendt's work on totalitarianism—goes further still.

Since the modern state wields a power over "bare life," it is in the position of being able to decide (on a case by case basis, so to speak) who is part of the nation's "healthy" biological life and who is a threat to the body of "the people." According to Agamben, this power of inclusion/exclusion makes the concentration camp the "very paradigm of political space at the point at which politics becomes biopolitics."[150] Every modern polity structurally demands a camp-like "zone of indistinction," one in which the boundaries between outside and inside, exception and rule, licit and illicit are utterly unclear, one in which the "very concepts of subjective right and juridical protection" no longer make any sense.[151] Such "zones of indistinction" are a crucial part of the modern state's biopolitical armory. They invariably crop up during time of emergency or "crisis," initially as holding centers for groups of individuals whom the state neither wants to recognize (as subjects with rights) nor immediately expel (as aliens or illegal immigrants).

Thus, "bare life" and "juridical rule" themselves enter a "zone of indistinction" in the concentration camp, and it is this fact—rather than the specific activities that went on in the Nazi or Soviet facilities—that makes the concentration camp the emblematic "political space of our time."[152] Such camps—whether they hold Albanian refugees (as in Bari in 1991), or "enemy aliens" (as in Gurs, France, in 1939–40), or Jews, Communists, and

homosexuals (as in the Nazi *Konzentrationslagers*)—have their justification and purpose in the protection of the nation's biological life from a
variety of internal and external "threats." These threats are defined by the
"biopolitical" state, a state that also wields the monopoly on threat assessment that defined the Hobbesian sovereign. The "biopolitical transformation" of the modern state thus brings together sovereign power and "bare
life," in such a way that we are all, potentially, concentration camp inmates
and victims. Or so, at least, Agamben would have us believe.

In the light of Guantánamo and other such "holding" facilities (many
of them secret), it would be premature to dismiss Agamben completely out
of hand. Nevertheless, his appropriation of Foucault's biopolitical thesis
reveals the enormous deficits that result when we base political theory on
a *reductio*—to life, to power, or to anything else. Of course, the cynicism
of the modern state—whether constitutional monarchy, sovereign republic, or "liberal" democracy—can rarely if ever be overestimated. Again
and again in European and American history, we encounter the shame-
inducing spectacle of an "official" attachment to individual rights and
limited state power grotesquely undercut by *Realpolitik* or "geopolitical"
considerations. Yet there is an enormous gap between this cynicism—the
willingness to cut moral corners and to profligately spend the lives of
other people's children in unnecessary wars—and the all-out assault on
entire races or classes that characterize the totalitarian movements of the
last century.

Our civil and political rights may not be as secure as a few of us, in
whatever remains of our liberal complacency, sometimes assume. Nevertheless, we need to remember a few things that Agamben and Foucault (at
least in his more "radical" moments) encourage us to forget. First, there is
the historical fact that liberalism, as a tradition of political thought and
practice, emerged out of the struggle to contain *raison d'état* and the cynicism of the state. If liberal democracy means nothing else, it means a commitment to individual rights and the replacement of "sovereign" power
with the rule of law and *some* set of constitutional checks and balances.
The fact that there are no guarantees that the resulting machine will in any
sense "run by itself" is something liberal theorists have been alerting us to
at least since Mill. As recent American experience has demonstrated, the
legal "machine" can be hijacked to serve what are essentially illiberal ends
and practices (like torture).

Second, the kind of political regime a particular nation has matters,
even though "regime form" is hardly a guarantee of humane treatment or,

indeed, of humanity. The *reductio* to biopolitics, or to "bare life," works only insofar as it persuades us that this is not the case. From the biopolitical perspective, a state is a state is a state. It wields what is in truth a form of absolute power over our lives, rights, and identities. If nothing else, Agamben is to be commended for teasing out this (highly arguable) implication of Foucault's biopolitical paradigm.

Third, we are not all equally vulnerable. We are not equally vulnerable because citizens of liberal or parliamentary democracies have, relatively speaking, enormous legal and political resources available to challenge mistreatment by either their government or governing majorities. The vocabulary of individual rights, and the entire legal-constitutional system built upon it, hardly guarantees fair or just treatment in every case. But it does offer a variety of procedural avenues (and judicial precedents) for redress. This is something the victims of the last century—who, for the most part, lived and died in the shadow of group rights, the supposed rights of "peoples"—did not have, as Arendt's analysis in *The Origins of Totalitarianism* makes abundantly clear. If, as citizens of liberal or parliamentary democracies, we allow our governments to pursue policies that undermine civil and political liberties (whether of some ethnic or racial minority, or of us all), we have only ourselves—and our insufficient moral and political vigilance—to blame.

Finally, there are worse things than the "pastoral power" of the welfare state. Life has indeed become an "object" of government in a new and unprecedented way in the course of the last hundred and fifty years. However, the real danger of the "pastoral power" wielded by government comes not from its interventions in public health, nor from its collection of statistics on birth and death rates, epidemics, and so on. Rather, it comes from governmental *abuse* of that knowledge and of the instrumentalities that such an expanded role makes possible.

Once again, we find ourselves on venerable liberal terrain. The answer to such abuse is not the denial of the effectivity of legal rights, constitutional restraints, or "traditional" political theory distinctions such as those between state, civil society, and the public sphere. Such a denial is, I am afraid, built into Agamben's Foucault-inspired reduction of the complex story of nineteenth- and twentieth-century politics to "the rise of biopower." A more appropriate response—one that sees biopower less as the essence of modern political power and more as a supplementary field of governmental activity—would be to remind our governors that their power is strictly bounded; that it is not, in any sense, their property, nor is it to be used for personal ends; that it is, in effect, a conditional grant, one that ought to be revoked should they violate the terms of their "trust." This is the language of Locke and liberal constitutionalism, and it is a language we abandon at our peril.

Conclusion

In an interview, Foucault once said that the point of his work was not to say that everything is bad, but rather that everything is dangerous. Taken at face value, this sentiment is generally harmonious with liberalism's traditional distrust of state power and state instrumentalities. To this distrust Foucault can be said to add a salutary skepticism about many of the practices and institutions that go to make up what liberals and political theorists like to call "civil society." Contra Tocqueville, it turns out that docility—a perpetual danger, from any consistently liberal standpoint—is promoted by a large number of nonstate agencies. This is the essential contribution of Foucault's retheorization of power in *Discipline and Punish*.

Perhaps surprisingly, there is indeed a "Foucault for liberals." However, Foucault also turned his skeptical eye toward the vocabulary of rights, suggesting that discipline or dressage underlay the various Enlightenment principles of which we are so proud. The proper response to this suggestion is not a reflexive repudiation. But neither is it the certainty that Foucault has provided the definitive unmasking of liberal constitutionalism and vocabularies of public right. Like Marx in "On the Jewish Question," all Foucault has really done is to highlight a dimension of this vocabulary that has hitherto received little attention.

Of course, the radical Foucault—like the radical Marx—wanted to claim much more than this. In each case, the stronger claim is that this liberal vocabulary—and the set of practices and institutions that go along with it—is actually a Trojan horse for power. For Foucault, this power is originally disciplinary in nature, an analysis later supplemented by his discovery of the "biopolitics" of the modern state. For Marx, this power is wielded by the economically most powerful class: the bourgeoisie. As "On the Jewish Question" argues, the bourgeois commitment to civil rights and the "Rights of Man" is no more than a self-serving scrim for the most rapacious forms of self-interest. Given this fundamental similarity (differences regarding the "relational" vs. the "commodity" character of power notwithstanding), it comes as no surprise that both Foucault and Marx deploy the analytics of war "discovered" by Boulainvilliers. This enables them to give a sharper profile to the modes of domination they have uncovered, and to make sense of the configuration of forces in any given political-historical conjuncture.[153]

When social struggle is coded as war, the primary concerns of what is usually called "normative political theory" go out the window. "Legitimacy" and its preconditions cease to be the necessary (one might even say privileged) objects of theory. Contrary to what many have maintained, there is nothing the slightest bit incoherent about such a "bracketing" of the "legitimacy problematic." Focusing on the "how" of power has a long and illustrious history in both political and social theory. This is obviously what Foucault is up to, and it is what Marx and Max Weber were up to before him. In none of these cases does one have to go ransacking their work in order to discover their animating moral passion. The concern with freedom is there in plain sight.[154] Neither Marx, nor Weber, nor Foucault have to appeal to Kantian principles of autonomy or Lockean ideas of consent in order to persuade us that, at the end of the day, "struggle is preferable to submission."[155]

Where domination constitutes the takeoff point for analysis, the only real "normative" question is "Which side are you on?" Have you allied yourself with "class rule," "bureaucratic domination," or the "disciplinary apparatus"? If not, how might one best go about resisting such phenomena? The reason why critics like Nancy Fraser have accused Foucault (but not Marx or Weber) of being "normatively confused" is that Foucault insists that there is no "outside" of power. To philosophers and political theorists who have been brought up on clear-cut distinctions between legitimate and illegitimate power, this assertion seems one step away from nihilism. If there is no "outside" of power, then it must be domination all the way down—a relativism of various "power-knowledge regimes."

In hindsight, Marx offered what looked like a "scientific" analysis of socioeconomic domination, yoked to an eschatological promise of a future without domination. Weber and Foucault, on the other hand, were honest enough to reject this possibility. We can be honest enough to acknowledge that—even where fundamental political institutions conform to the most basic standards of legitimacy—social domination can and does continue. The central question is not whether our basic political institutions are "legitimate" according to an abstract theoretical standard, but whether they provide a public space for the exercise of political freedom and (thus) the institutional mediation of social conflict. We return here to the basic insights of Constant, Tocqueville, Hegel, Mill, and Arendt—that is, to the recognition that the only way to prevent "legitimate" structures of political power from devolving into structures of domination is to make sure we provide for both individual rights and the institutionalization of public freedom.

It is Foucault's lack of concern with the last issue that makes his "philosophy of power" ultimately problematic. His analytical strategy of de-differentiation has the advantage of bringing previously unnoticed power operations and strategies into sharp focus. But it has the disadvantage of suggesting that there is a kind of "base" out there that no institutional "superstructure" can begin to alter or contain. Insofar as the world of law, right, and institutions are more than a scrim for domination, Foucault suggests that they are nevertheless being endlessly colonized by disciplinary power and "biopolitical" strategies. The fight for what Arendt called the "objective, public world" seems to be over before it is even begun. We are thus thrown back upon ourselves and the politics of everyday life, a politics that—as Foucault never ceased to remind us—is a politics of dispersed, never-ending, "local" resistance.

"*Résistez, résistez toujours*" is a slogan easy to endorse in times such as our own. The dangers we face, however, are far greater than the "microphysics of power" and the disciplinary institutions that deploy them. They are greater than the "massifying" power deployed by the biopolitical/welfare state. These dangers include the decline of the rule of law and effective constitutional checks and balances; the accelerating erosion of civil rights; the enormous and growing legislative influence of corporate special interests; and the absorption of our public sphere by what Guy Debord famously called the "society of the spectacle."

In combating these dangers, it pays to remember that the "politics of everyday life" and "contesting identities" take us only so far. Their capacity to effect meaningful change in the way our deficient public institutions operate is either minimal or nonexistent. It also pays to remember that docility has sources that are far deeper, and far more intransigent, than the type of disciplinary institutions Foucault analyzes. The deepest reserves of civic docility are found in the human, all-too-human tendency to submit to the gravitational pull of custom and convention—to what is, in effect, a decidedly social and "participatory" form of authority.

It is misleading, then, to say that docile subjects are "manufactured" or produced. More often than not, they are self-willed and, to a degree, self-created. We are docile because we want, if not to be like everyone else, then to be admired for the things everyone else wants and admires. We desire the socialization of our desires, even or especially when those desires invest themselves in the project of self-development. In this way, "self-fashioning" has become one of the most superficial of all herd animal behaviors. The ancient "arts of the self"—so full of promise to a Foucault who, in his later years, increasingly turned his back on the public realm— return to be marketed as so many techniques for individual fulfillment. This is the predictable result of a modern form of life that is less "disciplined" than it is, put simply, shallow. It is shallow not because it lacks self-concern or self-care, but because it lacks the depth that only a viable public realm can give it.

9 | ARENDT AND HEIDEGGER, AGAIN

In 1996 I published a book titled *Arendt and Heidegger: The Fate of the Political*.[1] I had spent a lot of time as a graduate student and junior faculty member reading and thinking about Arendt, and I was consistently surprised by how little had been written in English (or any other language, for that matter) about her debt to existentialism, and to Heidegger's philosophy in particular. Where the debt was noted, it was usually done so in passing, or in order to indicate elitist or even "reactionary" political tendencies.[2]

This situation surprised me, particularly given *The Human Condition*'s clear appropriation and reworking of many Heideggerian themes. First, there was Arendt's rethinking of freedom, a rethinking which stressed the radical, nonsovereign, and "worldly" character of political freedom. While deeply opposed to some of the more individualistic themes of *Being and Time*, Arendt's rethinking clearly presupposed that work's displacement of the cognitive and practical subject in favor or a more "involved" conception of "being in the world." Second, the later Heidegger's unmasking of the Western tradition's view of freedom as one or another form of sovereignty, with action as essentially telic or goal-driven, clearly provided the rudiments of Arendt's own critique of the teleological concept of action. It also provided the basis for her charge that the tradition has persistently effaced the contingency and plurality that are essential components of (public) freedom. Third, Heidegger's critique of technological modernity, while clearly mired in images of pastoral wholeness, provided something of a template for

Arendt's own critical view of the pathologies of the modern age. For her as for Heidegger, ours is an age in which the "will to mastery" and the "resentment of the human condition of finitude and plurality" loom especially large.[3]

With these thoughts in mind, I set out to situate Arendt's thought in relation to the German philosophical tradition as a whole, and to Heidegger in particular. At the time, I thought I was filling an enormous gap in the literature—a literature that (at least in the Anglo-American world) generally shied away from making any such connections. This "modesty," if I can call it that, was largely a function of a widespread ignorance of the "tradition of German philosophy" that Arendt herself had identified as her intellectual point of origin.[4] Little did I know that I was wading into the middle of what we can call, in retrospect, the "Hannah Arendt wars" of 1995–97. This conflict was ignited by the publication, in America, of Elsbieta Ettinger's *Hannah Arendt/Martin Heidegger*, a slim volume devoted not to the intellectual relationship between Arendt's political theory and Heidegger's philosophy (the subject of my own work), but to their romantic and sexual relationship during 1924–26, a period when Arendt was a student of Heidegger's at Marburg and (subsequently) of Jaspers at Heidelberg.[5]

Ettinger's psychologizing work had no particular political agenda, other than to wonder why such a "smart woman" as Arendt had made such a "foolish choice" as Heidegger, allegedly remaining under his spell for the rest of her life. Nevertheless, it provided Arendt's detractors—and they are still legion in the United States—with a new and powerful round of critical ammunition. Here we have to remind ourselves of the fact that, insofar as Arendt is known to a non-academic audience in the United States, it is as the author of *Eichmann in Jerusalem*. Around this book, a quite unsavory legend has grown, a legend that shows few signs of dying.

The legend is quite simple. In *Eichmann in Jerusalem*, her detractors say, Arendt did her best to minimize Adolf Eichmann's role in the Holocaust, all the while blaming the victims—the Jews themselves—for a good part of the disaster. This is, of course, nothing short of slander, based on a willful misreading—or, more accurately, nonreading—of eight pages in the middle of a three-hundred-page book. In those eight pages, Arendt paused in her account of the Eichmann trial in order to ruminate on how the disaster of European Jewry might have been much less had not certain leaders of the Jewish communities in Poland and elsewhere (whom the

Nazis had organized into *Judenräte*) been so willing to do what Eichmann, the SS, and the German army asked them to do. Their job was to administer the ghettos in accordance with Nazi demands, a task that included drawing up lists of less-well-connected members of the community for the transport trains to the East, where they would receive "special treatment" in the death camps.[6]

Arendt no doubt exaggerated the ultimate effect that simple non-cooperation with the Nazis would have had.[7] Even so, her pages on the *Judenräte* are a digression from the main theme of the book. What attracted Arendt's attention was Eichmann's inability to think and to judge, to realize that he was doing anything wrong in his capacity as "transport czar" for the Holocaust. Yet however peripheral to Arendt's main theme, it was around the pages on the *Judenräte* that the legend about the Eichmann book grew. An organized wave of criticism, the initial goal of which was to prevent the book from even being published, succeeded in making Arendt *persona non grata* amongst a substantial section of the American Jewish community.[8] This remains her status for many today. The situation is even worse in Israel, where, until recently, her work has been studiously ignored and left untranslated.[9]

The "Eichmann controversy" earned Arendt her most vehement and relentless critics, critics who—to this day—would like to see her reputation tarnished beyond redemption. Forget the fact that Arendt had worked in Paris with Youth Aliyah during the 1930s, training young Jewish émigrés to Palestine.[10] Forget that, after the war, she headed up Jewish Cultural Reconstruction and—in that capacity—helped to recover over 1.5 million articles of Judaica and Hebraica from a war-ravaged Europe.[11] Forget, finally, that her *Origins of Totalitarianism* (published in 1951) did more to jumpstart a public conversation about the concentration and death camps (which Arendt called the "central institutions of totalitarian rule") than the work of almost any other author, with the possible exception of Primo Levi. The verdict was already in: Hannah Arendt was bad for the Jews. As I have already indicated, it is a verdict to which many still cleave.

It is in this broader context that the so-called "Hannah Arendt scandal," occasioned by Ettinger's volume, erupted. Hannah Arendt, the headlines screamed, was in love with a Nazi! Not only that, she remained loyal to him after the war! After six million dead! How could she?!

This, one might say, was the lowbrow version of the "scandal." But we have to remember that this version came to the public's attention through such supposedly highbrow publications as the *New York Times, The Nation*, and even the *Chronicle of Higher Education*. A somewhat more specialized version of the "scandal" came in the form of reviews of Ettinger's work and other volumes on Arendt by people like Richard Wolin and Peter Berkowitz in the *New Republic*.[12]

What these reviews argued was that Hannah Arendt was not only Heidegger's lover and loyal lieutenant (helping to get him translated and rehabilitated after the war). *Even worse*, she was a "Heideggerian"—and thus radically suspect—in her most characteristic theories and ideas. Thus, according to Wolin, Arendt was the "ultimate political existentialist," contemptuous of the constitutional and institutional strictures of liberal ("bourgeois") democracy.[13] Like Nietzsche, like Schmitt, and like Heidegger, she supposedly wanted something more "noble," more dramatic, more radically spontaneous than constitutional democracy could offer. And, according to Berkowitz, she was even willing to risk "permanent revolution" to get it.[14] She was, in Wolin's highly revealing phrase, a "non-Jewish Jew" whose political thought offered little more than "a parallel, if slightly left-leaning, version of Heideggerian revolutionary vitalism."[15] She was even portrayed as an enemy of political egalitarianism and universal suffrage—the *sine qua non* of democracy and a democratic culture.[16]

However shocking these charge may appear, they are remarkably flimsy and easy to refute. As anyone who has read either *The Origins of Totalitarianism* or *On Revolution* knows, the last thing Hannah Arendt desired was "permanent revolution." That idea—the logical outgrowth of totalitarian ideology—was predicated on contempt for the stable, man-made world of public-political laws and institutions, a durable world that stood between man and nature and made a civilized life possible. The *leitmotif* of Arendt's thought, "care for the public world," is directed specifically against both the totalitarian and capitalist celebrations of endless (political or economic) "creative destruction." In this conservative concern with the durability, stability, and law-governed character of the public world, Arendt remained true to her civic republican roots—a fact well documented by Margaret Canovan's work.[17]

Similarly, the idea that Arendt was a worshiper, *à la* Nietzsche or Heidegger, of unrestrained "great" action performed by exceptional individuals who are "a law unto themselves" is given the lie by her definition of action as "acting together," and by her numerous strictures against violence and coercion as (supposed) forms of political action. As *The Human*

Condition makes amply clear, action for Arendt essentially means speech, and it occurs in the modes of debate, deliberation, and persuasion amongst civic equals. Violence is the enemy of what Jürgen Habermas has rightly called Arendt's "communications concept of power"—the idea that political power is generated by diverse equals talking about, and caring for, the public world or "public thing" (*res publica*).[18] Violence destroys power, just as tyranny—the logical outcome of those who act as "laws unto themselves"—destroys the public realm by making political action and judgment the prerogative of a single actor.[19]

True, Arendt writes of the "boundlessness" and "unpredictability of outcome" of genuine or *initiatory* action. But that is why she insists so strenuously that only a framework of laws and the "space" provided by durable institutions can be a proper place for "great" action.[20] It is why, in *On Revolution*, she takes such pains to distinguish the violent struggle for liberation from the (properly revolutionary) creation of a "new space for freedom" through constitutional means. Freedom—which Arendt, following Tocqueville, calls "the *raison d'être* of politics"—appears only with the founding and preserving of such a legally and institutionally articulated space for the interaction of diverse equals.[21]

The charges, then, are more notable for their willful distortion of Arendt's thought than anything else. They are also surprisingly derivative. The "elitist" charge—the idea that Hannah Arendt was *au fond* no friend of democracy—was made by the political theorist Sheldon Wolin back in 1983, while the "political existentialist" charge was lodged by the intellectual historian Martin Jay as early as 1978. The former charge questions Arendt's basic commitment to an open public realm (one accessible to ordinary people), while the latter suggests that she was an unwitting fellow traveler of such radical and anti-Semitic European thinkers from the 1920s as Carl Schmitt (who also asserted a version of the "autonomy of the political"). The "scandal" triggered by Ettinger's volume provided Arendt's more ideologically inspired detractors to reiterate these criticisms, albeit in vulgarized form.

The fact that such eminently responsible scholars as Sheldon Wolin and Martin Jay detect an anti-democratic dimension in Arendt's work should, however, give us pause. Have Wolin and Jay simply misread Arendt, or have they detected a real moral weakness in her thought? Does Arendt's philosophical background—her anti-foundationalist *Bildung*, at the hands of Heidegger and Jaspers—militate against her more explicitly egalitarian pronouncements, rendering them either half-hearted or empty?

Partly in response to such questions, Seyla Benhabib has suggested a redistribution of interpretative emphasis, one that plays down what Arendt owed to Heidegger while underlining her debt to the ethical rationalist Kant.[22] But even if we take this tack, aren't we forced to admit that Arendt's relationship to her Jewishness is weirdly distant, submerged by her education in the German philosophical tradition? At its "universalist" best—in Kant—this tradition cleansed moral and political questions of any taint of "particularity" (what we would today call "difference"). At its *völkisch* worst—in Division II of *Being and Time* and much of Heidegger's work of the 1930s—it indulged in celebrations of mysterious communal "destinies," with little or no regard for the rights of individuals and minorities.

Forced to make a choice, most readers would opt for a "Kantianized" Arendt. True, Kant was not an especially political thinker, whereas Arendt devoted her entire career to thinking about politics and "the political."[23] This major difference aside, the thesis that Arendt was really a Kantian at heart holds an obvious attraction. It allows us to place the more questionable ("elitist" or existentialist) aspects of her intellectual background within the reassuring folds of a human rights universalism. This, after all, is the broad ethical-political orientation that appears to emerge naturally from *The Origins of Totalitarianism*—specifically from Arendt's biting critique of "tribal nationalism" and her unwavering focus on the plight of the stateless in the interwar period.

Intellectual honesty, however, demands that we acknowledge that the influence of two other traditions—existential philosophy and civic republicanism—far outweighs the Kantian heritage in Arendt's thought. While it is dubious to label Arendt as a "Heideggerian," the fact remains that his influence on her was profound, regardless of whether she was thinking "with" him or against him (as she often was).[24] This can be seen by the briefest survey of her intellectual trajectory.

When, after the publication of *The Origins of Totalitarianism*, Arendt turned to the project of identifying the "proto-totalitarian elements" in the thought of Karl Marx, she discovered that the Marxian bias against human plurality and the public realm had deep roots within the Western tradition of philosophy and political thought. It is no exaggeration to state that Heidegger's "deconstruction" of Western metaphysics provided her with a kind of map—and, indeed, a kind of "method"—with which to reveal the tradition's hostility to plurality, contingency, and the very phenomenon of political action amongst diverse equals. In Arendt's view, the

Western canon of political philosophy devalued the faculties of opinion and judgment (preferring a monological Reason instead); repeatedly sought to find ways around the "obstacle" presented by the fact of human plurality; and desired, above all, to reduce political action to the status of instrumental appendage to a philosophically derived discourse of "Truth."

It should not surprise us, then, that Arendt found the staunch anti-Platonism of Heidegger helpful in overcoming the authoritarian and hierarchical tendencies of the Western tradition, a tradition rooted in Plato's and Aristotle's revolt against the civic life of Athenian democracy.[25] Nor should her radical appropriation of the Heideggerian idea of "authentic *Existenz*" be seen as a source of potential embarrassment. This appropriation was performed expressly against what she viewed as the solipsistic spirit of *Being and Time*, and precisely in order to reassert the dignity of the public realm and a life devoted to "acting with others."[26] And it was precisely the dignity of the public realm—and the robust human plurality on which it depended—that Arendt saw as repeatedly attacked by a philosophical (and theological) tradition hostile to all things "worldly."

Of course, "human plurality" is not a phenomenon that looms large in Heidegger's thought, his rather undernourished concept of *Mitdasein* notwithstanding. The reason Hannah Arendt, rather than Heidegger or any other figure in the tradition, became *the* thinker of human plurality is quite simple. She saw in the destruction of European Jewry not just an irrationalist assault upon an allegedly "alien" minority or barely tolerated "other." As the penultimate chapter of *The Origins of Totalitarianism* makes clear, even darker forces were at work.

The totalitarians (both Nazis and Communists) systematically deployed terror as a way of eliminating the institutionally and legally defined space between individuals, the better to create a more easily dominated "One Man of gigantic dimensions."[27] The ultimate goal was to reduce discrete individual humans to the status of interchangeable "bundles of reflexes," incapable of spontaneous action or initiation themselves.[28] It was in the "laboratories" of the camps that the most gruesome and advanced "experiments" in such total domination occurred. These experiments aimed at eliminating not just plurality and the space between individuals (one source of unpredictability) but the distinctively human capacity for spontaneity as well. For only when human beings were no longer capable of initiating action could the supposed "laws" of Nature or History (the struggle of the races for the Nazis; of classes for the Bolsheviks) achieve their predestined ends (Aryan domination; a classless society) without further interference.[29]

It was, then, the totalitarian attempt to destroy human plurality and spontaneity in the camps—the *fact* of Auschwitz—that propelled Arendt to undertake her investigations in political theory. Again and again, these investigations circle back to the idea of the public realm as an institutionally articulated space between individuals; to political action conceived as spontaneous and joint action undertaken to either found or preserve such a constitutional space; and to the phenomenon of human plurality as the most basic constitutive element of the political world as such. Arendt draws deeply from civic republican tradition in order to understand the nature and prerequisites of such a "space of freedom," and from Heidegger and existentialism in order to understand both the "initiatory" dimension of action and the tradition's hostility to plurality, contingency, and the idea of a "radical beginning."

Say all this is true: that Arendt's theoretical ambitions were formed in large part as a response to the totalitarian attempt to uproot plurality and spontaneity, thereby forever altering the human status; that these concerns led her, ultimately, to engage the anti-political strands of the Western tradition itself; and that the radically critical nature of her reading of the tradition would be unthinkable without the appropriation and transformation of certain key Heidggerian categories.[30] However laudable these motivating factors may be, might not some highly undesirable bath water come with the adoption of this particular baby? Even if her critical appropriation of Heidegger is undertaken in order to overcome certain hierarchical and authoritarian dimensions of the Western tradition, might not specific categorial structures—such as the notion of "purified praxis" as a form of authentic *Existenz*—carry with them an array of anti-democratic, and even anti-Jewish, implications? It is this possibility, I think, that both Sheldon Wolin and Martin Jay set out to explore in their critiques.

I want to look a bit more closely at Wolin's and Jay's readings, the better to show how both critics tie a perceived elitism back to "existential" categories they see Arendt adopting from either Heidegger or Nietzsche. With this genealogy in mind, I demonstrate how the elitist reading of the "existential" Arendt hinges on a strategic fudging of some of her most central categories and distinctions. Once these are restored to their proper place in her thought, we see how misguided it is to frame Arendt as the passive receptacle, rather than a transformative appropriator, of either Nietzschean and Heideggerian ideas. We also see just how wrong it is to suggest—as both Richard Wolin and Peter Berkowitz have in the pages of the *New Republic*—that Arendt was, at heart, a kind of Nazi or Marxist fellow traveler, deluded by love of German *Kultur* and a bad case of Jewish self-hatred.

In addition to answering her critics, I want to suggest that there is a moral context—or, better, a moral-existential context—that frames Arendt's recovery of the public realm and her theorizing of political action as a kind of end-in-itself. The "autonomy of the political" she so famously champions is neither faux-aristocratic nor existentially amoral in character. There is nothing remotely "fascistic" about it. Rather, it flows directly from her deep desire to preserve the sense and context of a tangible freedom that can be known by diverse equals acting in a shared public world. It is this freedom that totalitarianism effectively destroyed, and that much of our philosophical tradition has helped "cover-over" through a series of anti-political (that is, hierarchical and authoritarian) concepts. Arendt's response to the destruction of the Jews was not to abandon the standpoint of politics to the enemy (the totalitarians) and cleave to the Kantian/moral high ground. Rather, it was to rethink the nature and conditions of political relations as such. The resulting legacy is a morally egalitarian one—the normative ideal of a "polis without slaves"—even if it is not, as some of her contemporary defenders might claim, a morally universalist one.

Elitism and Existentialism: Wolin and Jay

In "Hannah Arendt: Democracy and the Political," Sheldon Wolin states flatly that "many of the major categories that compose and distinguish [Arendt's] political outlook were either critical of or incompatible with democratic ideals."[31] The primary problem is the Arendtian distinction between the political and the social, a distinction that embodies what Wolin calls Arendt's "critical attitude toward democracy." This attitude is based on the "correct intuition" that the "impulse toward democracy overrides that distinction." In Wolin's words, "Historically, democracy has been the means by which the many have sought access to political power in the hope that it could be used to redress their economic and social lot."[32] Not only does Arendt's distinction run against what Wolin views as the primary "impulse" toward democracy; it also delegitimates the political goals of "the many" and works to deny them access to the public realm. She is an enemy of the fundamental democratic tendency that would "extend the broad egalitarianism of ordinary lives into public life."[33]

What does Arendt want instead? What is her "anti-democratic" alternative? According to Wolin, it is a heroic conception of a "pure" politics, one untainted by such "vulgar" concerns as socioeconomic betterment; one that concerns itself solely with "lofty ambition, glory, and honor."[34]

Such charges will be familiar to any to student of Arendt's work. They have their basis in the agonistic or "Greek" conception of political action we find in *The Human Condition* (1958). In that work, Arendt does not merely go out of her way to distinguish action from work and labor (the other, "lesser" components of the *vita activa*). She also lays out what some have called a "dramaturgical" conception of political action, a conception that focuses on the identity- and world-disclosing capacity of "great" words and deeds in the public realm. Arendt argues that the disclosure of the individual's unique identity occurs through performances that take place upon a public stage. She even invokes Achilles, whose great words and deeds give the poets—and the public realm—something to remember long after he's gone.[35] If we combine this theatrical conception of political action—political action as the performance of great deeds on a public stage—with Arendt's strictures against social matters becoming the primary "content" of the public realm, we seem to have all the evidence we need to verify Wolin's charge of an anti-democratic elitism.[36]

But Wolin goes further. Not only does Arendt apparently ban the "ordinary" concerns of life and economic reproduction from the public sphere; she also treats power superficially (as something that "grows up" between acting men, rather than as the institutional instantiation of political-economic might) and justice not at all.[37] However, according to Wolin, it is justice that is "the main objective of political action" in its democratic mode.[38]

Why would Arendt spend so much time describing the "words and deeds" of a privileged few, rather than engaging more fundamental questions of power, justice, and democratization? The answer, Wolin states, is that her "archaic" vision of a "new polity" in *The Human Condition* was actually "inspired by the version of pre-Socratic [Homeric] Hellenism associated with Nietzsche and Heidegger."[39] That this is no aberration—a kind of Graecophilic detour from the more participatory and inclusive thrust of her thought—is made clear, Wolin claims, if we look at both *The Origins of Totalitarianism* (1951) and *On Revolution* (1963).

In the former work, we find Arendt combining Nietzschean, Heideggerian, and Tocquevillian themes. She blames an atomized, privatized, and security-craving "mass man" for the triumph of totalitarian movements.[40] In the latter work, we find Arendt praising the American founders not just for creating a new "space of freedom," but also for keeping "the rabble and their social concerns" out of this newly constituted public sphere.[41] This is the true meaning of her famous contrast between the "social" French Revolution, which futilely tried to use violence to solve the question of poverty, and the properly "political" American Revolution, which stuck to the *constitutio libertatis* and bracketed the "social question."

In all three of Arendt's major works of political theory, then, we find what Wolin calls an "antipathy towards material questions." Moreover, we find an unconcern with justice and a tendency to blame "the masses" for bringing ruin to the otherwise durable structures of the public-political world.[42] Once again, Wolin leaves little question as to what he sees as the source of these deplorably anti-democratic tendencies in Arendt's thought. Her "elitist" and "exclusionary" reflexes are grounded in the existentialism of Heidegger and Nietzsche, an existentialism built on the contrast between the authentic *Existenz* of a courageous few and the herd-like behavior of the conformist many.

Thus, Wolin charges, even when Arendt praised "the people" for spontaneous political action and organization of new political structures (as she did in the final chapter of *On Revolution*), she did so in a way that conformed to the strictures of a "heroic" or existentialist account of political action. The striking contrast she draws between political parties and "professional revolutionaries" (on the one hand) and revolutionary soldiers' and workers' councils (on the other) in *On Revolution* is a contrast grounded solely in the existentialist preference for a politics of spontaneous, initiatory appearances; for grand gestures (however futile) instead of the long, slow march toward greater justice.[43]

Against an image of the political derived from such extraordinary moments in which ordinary people act heroically against overwhelming odds, Wolin offers one that refers us to the strictly human roots of democratic solidarity. "The nature of the political," he writes, "is that it requires renewal. It is renewed not by unique deeds whose excellence sets some beings apart from others, but by rediscovering the common being of human beings. The political is based on this possibility of commonality: our common capacity to share, to share memories and a common fate. *Our common being is the natural foundation of democracy*."[44] Wolin thus concludes his critique of the "elitist" Arendt on what is, in fact, a strangely Heideggerian note.

In "The Political Existentialism of Hannah Arendt," Martin Jay takes what Wolin presents as the background of Arendt's "elitism" and places it front and center. Originally published in *Partisan Review* in 1978, less than three years after Arendt's untimely death, this essay stands out as one of the most informed early assessments of Arendt's *oeuvre*. Noting the confusion plaguing those who tried to "pigeonhole" her thought in ideological terms, and taking issue with Margaret Canovan's early identification of Arendt as a republican "in the eighteenth century sense," Jay turned to the tradition of *Existenzphilosophie* (and especially Heidegger and Jaspers) in order to illuminate the often perplexing contours of Arendt's political thought. Focusing on the explicit politicization this tradition undergoes during the 1920s in the work of Carl Schmitt, Ernst Jünger, and Alfred Bäumler, Jay suggests that Arendt is best read, like them, as a "political existentialist" (albeit of a "tender" rather than a "tough" variety).[45]

While it's hard not to agree with Jay's main thesis (namely, that the influence of *Existenzphilosophie* on Arendt's thought has been underappreciated), one can legitimately be taken aback by a "contextualization" that puts her in the company of fascists and fascist fellow-travelers such as Schmitt and Bäumler. It is this move that, more than any other, made the far less reliable Arendt critique offered by Richard Wolin possible. What enables Jay to argue that Arendt not only has a background in *Existenzphilosophie* (an indisputable and, I think, noncontroversial claim), but also that her thought bears more than a "family resemblance" to the reactionary *political* existentialists" of the 1920s?

Jay cites four main features of Arendt's political thinking in this regard. First, there is Arendt's assertion of the primacy of the political over the social. For Jay, this assertion resonates with the "reaction" of Pareto and Mosca, the Action Française clique, and the German "political existentialists" against the "typical nineteenth-century tendency to downgrade politics to a function of socioeconomic trends."[46] Like all of these groups—and, indeed, like Lenin and the Italian Fascists—Arendt wanted to "rescue politics" and assert its "relative autonomy." Hence her claim that action is the highest of human capacities, and that the essence of freedom is to be found only in a public sphere where men share words and deeds.

Second—and following from the first tendency—there is Arendt's "yearning to free politics from all extraneous considerations." This is a yearning she evidently shares with the political existentialists, who were also anxious to assert the "utmost possible autonomy" of action and politics.[47] Jay knows that he is on fairly firm ground here, as any reading of Schmitt's *Concept of the Political* (with its strong assertion of the autonomy of the political) and Arendt's essay "What Is Freedom?" will bear out. Arendt does delineate a "theatrical" concept of political action, one that focuses on the performance of the deed itself, and that makes the strongest possible distinction between this performance and its informing motives or ultimate goal.[48] It is precisely this "theatrical" or performative conception of action that I focused on in *Arendt and Heidegger*. Jay has at least a *prima facie* case that this conception links Arendt to people like Schmitt— even though Arendt's version of the "autonomy of the political" explicitly distinguishes between *violence* and political action, and hardly relies upon the Schmittian distinction between "friends" and "enemies."

Third, there is the distaste for rationalism shared by Arendt and the political existentialists. Indeed, Arendt—like the Sophists, John Adams, Edmund Burke, Lessing, Oakeshott, Gadamer, and a raft of others— thought that a "strong" rationalism in politics could only lead to tyranny. Plato's "tyranny of Truth" and Marx's "theorization" of French Revolutionary violence loom in her imagination as warning signs to those who would prefer firm rationalist foundations to the "relativity" of the plural realm of opinion. But—needless to say—it is a long way from Lessing's rejection of a singular Moral Truth (and the coercive logic that flows from it) to what Jay calls "Heidegger's resurrection of the pre-Socratic Greeks" and his "concomitant denigration of *Logos*."[49]

As any reader of *The Origins of Totalitarianism* or the essay "Truth in Politics" knows, Arendt strongly emphasizes the essential role of factual truth in the dual processes of political argument and opinion-formation. Likewise, there is a tremendous emphasis on the rationality of speech, argument, and opinion throughout her work—the denigration of which she calls one of the primary sins of our "Platonic" tradition of political theory.[50] Jay's suggestion that Arendt will have nothing to do with the "introduction of rational considerations" into the political sphere is thus surprisingly easy to refute—unless, of course, we define "rational considerations" Platonically; that is, in opposition to opinion and judgment.[51] While Heidegger was no champion of either opinion or judgment as rational faculties, Arendt's recovery of these capacities was (as she herself recognized) in no small part enabled by Heidegger's assertion that—at the end of the metaphysical (Platonic) tradition—"We have left the arrogance of all Absolutes behind us."[52]

Fourth and finally, there is Arendt's "existentialist" struggle against historicism. As Jay notes, political existentialism was "to a significant extent . . . directed against the prevailing historicist orthodoxy, bourgeois or Marxist, which dominated German thought from the time of Herder to the 1920s."[53] Broadly speaking, Arendt is certainly part of this anti-historicist movement, as her essay "The Concept of History" and chapter 2 of On Revolution attest. She struggled mightily against the dominant intellectual tendency (instituted by Hegelianism) to "dissolve" all human actions, institutions, and cultural achievements in the flux of the historical process.[54] Similarly, she viewed any attempt to reduce the "realm of human affairs" to the working out of all-determining historical "laws" as implicitly totalitarian.

Jay approves of this aspect of the "political existentialist" heritage, but expresses perplexity as to why Arendt did not opt for the "alternative view," namely, that men—not laws—make history.[55] The simple answer is that Arendt saw the Vico/Marx view of mankind as a demiurgic subject, giving birth to himself and shaping the world, as promoting a "productionist"— and ultimately violent—conception of political action. If "man makes history" in the way a craftsman makes a table, then violence winds up being the fundamental mode of all "initiatory" or creative action. This is a view—and a metaphor—Arendt spent a lifetime repudiating, ultimately tracing its routes back to the beginning of the tradition in Plato.[56] As Aristotle insisted in the Nicomachaean Ethics, praxis is not poiēsis. To think that it is, as Plato and Marx both do, is to reduce fellow human beings to the status of raw material awaiting the shaping hand of the philosopher-king or the revolutionary party.[57]

Thus, while Jay's four main criticisms are designed to create a common context for Arendt and the "political existentialists," it turns out that only two of them—the assertion of the "relative autonomy" of the political, followed by the stronger assertion of the virtually complete autonomy of "genuine" or "great" political action—hold any water. Arendt did indeed devote enormous theoretical energy to distinguishing political action (praxis) from other modes of human activity. And she insisted time and again that the "public-political world" should be distinguished from the social or economic realms.

Her strenuousness in this regard gives the impression that (as Jay puts it) she was a champion of *politique pour la politique*—that is, of an essentially aesthetic conception of the political, one that does not draw any content from outside herself. And—if that *is* the case—then it appears hard to avoid Sheldon Wolin's conclusion: namely, that Arendt was an "elitist" thinker, one more concerned with the "great deeds" of a gifted and virtuosic few than with political inclusion of the many and the broad democratization of everyday life.

It is precisely this nexus of existentialism with what seemed a form of aestheticism that I highlighted in *Arendt and Heidegger*. What earlier commentators had identified as among the more dubious tendencies of Arendt's thought, I identified as its theoretical core, its *raison d'être*. Arendt, I argued, tries to provide us with a notion of "self-contained" action, of political action viewed as "an end in itself."[58] And this leads to her focus on what she sometimes calls "great" action; that is, to the performative dimension of political action, a dimension where meaningfulness does not depend on the means/end schema or upon the achievement of an external goal. Writing of the ancient Greek experience, she states: "The point of the matter is that only human deeds were supposed to possess and make apparent a specific greatness of their own, so that no 'end,' no ultimate telos, was needed or could even be used for their justification."[59]

Even Aristotle, then—with his all-important distinction between *praxis* and *poiēsis*—gets it partly wrong. The Aristotelian definition of *praxis*—"authoritative throughout the tradition"—is telic in nature. His emphasis on the performance as the work notwithstanding, Aristotle winds up reducing action and its specific meaningfulness to the category of an instrument (albeit a relatively noble one) which the virtuous man deploys in pursuit of the good life and happiness.[60] So long as action *qua* activity is viewed in such teleological terms, its character as an "end it itself" can never be fully recognized or appreciated.

But why is this important? Unless we want to turn politics and political action into a "leisure time sport for aristocrats," as Berkeley political theorist Hanna Pitkin once put it, what can possibly be gained by asserting the intrinsic value of politics and political action? With this question we approach the heart of Hannah Arendt's political thinking, her self-positioning vis-à-vis the "great tradition" of Western political thought, and the controversial character of her intellectual debt to Heidegger.

The Autonomy of the Political, the Tradition, and Heidegger

In what follows, I want to suggest that the antagonism many critics feel toward Arendt's attempt to conceptualize action as an end in itself rests on a fairly basic misunderstanding.

What is this misunderstanding? It is the idea that Arendt's theory of political action is primarily a normative theory directed against either (a) the advent of mass democracy and its attendant pathologies or (b) the rise of the social and the reduction of politics to economics that accompanies it. To be sure, both these events—the former emphasized by Wolin, the latter by Jay—play a central role in Arendt's thought. But her theory of political action is misunderstood if it is seen as essentially a reaction to one or both of these "late modern" tendencies. Framed in this way, there seems little doubt that Arendt is pursuing a rearguard "elitist" (that is, exclusionary) strategy against the increasingly inclusive—and increasingly social—character of politics in the modern age.

This framing of Arendt's political theory is, however, wrong. While useful to her critics, it fails to take sufficient account of her intellectual trajectory. As I noted above, this was a trajectory from the attempt to understand how the supremely destructive political phenomenon of totalitarianism became possible in the heart of civilized Europe; to a deeper engagement with the proto-totalitarian tendencies underlying the thought of Karl Marx; to—finally—a full-fledged and remarkably deep engagement with the Western tradition of political thought from Plato to Marx. This is a tradition that Arendt increasingly came to view as anti-pluralistic and (indeed) anti-political in many of its most characteristic tropes, concerns, and conclusions.

We can characterize the main phases in this intellectual trajectory in "methodological" as well as substantive terms.[61] Arendt, we might say, moves from the hermeneutic-analytic attempt to understand the constellation of events, practices, and *mentalités* that made totalitarianism possible; to the genealogical attempt to locate proto-totalitarian tendencies in the thought of Karl Marx (the inheritor of many of the Enlightenment's most cherished political and social hopes); to, finally, a "deconstructive" encounter with the Western tradition of political thought itself. This encounter is driven by the desire to recover the experiential basis of a "genuine" or authentic politics centered on human plurality, speech, and the exchange of opinion in the public sphere. This layer of experience—"the political" in its original (Greek) incarnation—had been "covered over" by a fabrication model of action, a model installed by a philosophic tradition deeply hostile to human plurality and the "irresponsibility and uncertainty of outcome" it apparently created in the public-political realm.

It is at this level—and not at the level of any supposed existentialist contempt for the "inauthentic" they-self (*das Man*)—that we encounter Arendt's real debt to Heidegger. This debt has, *pace* Wolin and Jay, nothing to do with the politics of either Heidegger or the "political existentialists." Indeed, as I tried to demonstrate in the third part of *Arendt and Heidegger*, it is difficult to think of a deeper critic of Heidegger's philosophical politics—not to mention other fascist-leaning intellectuals—than Hannah Arendt.[62] Rather, the debt is more methodological in character. It concerns not the substance of the political (about which Heidegger and Arendt were in total disagreement), but the manner in which one might go about recovering experiences and meanings that a layer of obfuscating tradition had plunged into obscurity, if not complete oblivion. To quote Arendt's well-known characterization of her friend Walter Benjamin's "method," a method that had remarkable affinities to both Heidegger and her own:

> This thinking, fed by the present, works with the "thought fragments" it can wrest from the past and gather about itself. Like a pearl diver who descends to the bottom of the sea, not to excavate the bottom and bring it to light but to pry loose the rich and the strange, the pearls and the coral in the depths and to carry them to the surface, this thinking delves into the depths of the past— but not in order to resuscitate it the way it was and to contribute to the renewal of extinct ages. What guides this thinking is the conviction that although the living is subject to the ruin of time, the process of decay is at the same time a process of crystallization, that in the depth of the sea, into which sinks and is dissolved what once was alive, some things "suffer a sea-change" and survive in new crystallized forms and shapes that remain immune to the elements, as though they waited only for the pearl diver who one day will come down to them and bring them up into the world of the living—as "thought fragments," as something "rich and strange," and perhaps even as everlasting *Urphämomene*.[63]

This passage gives a more or less precise description of what Arendt herself was up to when she attempted—against the entire weight of the tradition from Plato to Marx—to "recover" *praxis* in its "pure," prephilosophic form. This recovery finds its fullest articulation in the chapter on action in *The Human Condition*. The point of that chapter is not—as many of her critics have charged—to resurrect a long-gone *polis* politics. Rather, it is to delve behind or beneath the intervening layer of our philosophic tradition—a tradition in many respects hostile to politics—in order to bring forth, in "crystallized" form, the phenomenological bases of politics as practiced by diverse equals in a public space. As Arendt says in her Benjamin essay, "The Greek *polis* will continue to exist at the bottom of our political existence—that is, at the bottom of the sea—for as long as we use the word 'politics'."[64]

Like Heidegger, whose own thinking was characterized by a "digging quality peculiar to itself," Arendt's thought was driven by a desire to "get to the bottom," to bring up something "rich and strange" that would serve not as a model, but as a means to put our most ossified prejudices about the nature of politics into question. The value of a book like *The Human Condition* is not to be found in any set of prescriptions it supposedly offers about the public realm (what to let in, what to keep out—or, more pointedly, who to let in and who to keep out). Rather, it is to be found in the glimpse it offers us of a "pure" *praxis*, a *praxis* prior to its philosophical conceptualization and subsequent "dis-essencing."[65] This project—which proceeds, to quote Arendt, through an enormous "distillation" of Greek and Roman "non-philosophical literature . . . poetic, dramatic, historical, and political writings, whose articulation lifts experience into a realm of splendor which is not the realm of conceptual thought"[66]—has a quite specific, "non-normative" goal. In the words of George Kateb, it aims to "do what has never been done." It aims to "supply a philosophical account of the *meaning* of political action" considered as an "end in itself"—that is, as the center of a certain lost or forgotten way of life.[67]

But why the need to "go to the bottom," to seek out the "rich and strange"? Why is providing us with a glimpse of "pure" *praxis* so important? In order to understand Arendt's "deconstructive" strategy (and I use the word "deconstructive" in its original Heideggerian, not Derridean, sense),[68] I have to say a word or two about Arendt's reading of the "great tradition" of political thought from Plato to Marx. For it is only with this reading in mind—a reading found in *The Human Condition*, but also in *On Revolution* as well as the essays in *Between Past and Future*—that we can make sense of her theory of political action, her conception of the public realm, and her debt to Heidegger.

In *The Human Condition*, Arendt notes that political action, as performed by a plurality of actors in a defined public space, such as the

Athenian assembly or agora, has several irreducible features. First, it presupposes a condition of civic equality or "no-rule"—*isonomia*, as the Greeks would call it.[69] This means that an authentically political public space is one characterized not only by the absence of coercion or violence (such as master inflicts on a slave, or a ruler imposes on his subjects), but by the absence of the sort of authoritarian hierarchy Plato and (to a lesser degree) Aristotle wished to introduce into the Greek political world through their political philosophies.[70]

Second, it presumes a genuine plurality of actors—that is, a wide range of individual citizens who see "the public thing" from different perspectives. As Arendt puts it, "The reality of the public realm relies on the simultaneous presence of innumerable perspective and aspects."[71] Such perspectives are not a given, nor are they a function (as we like to think today) of one's "identity" or affinity group. Rather, such perspectives are the articulation of an individual point of view, an articulation that occurs only through the active formation and exchange of opinions with others. "Opinions," Arendt writes, ". . . never belong to groups but exclusively to individuals. . . . [They] will rise whenever men communicate freely with one another and have a right to make their views public."[72] *Doxa* is not a deficient mode of appearance, somewhere between genuine knowledge of reality and complete ignorance or nonbeing.[73] It is, rather, the essential medium of a political way of being-together.[74]

Third, and following from the previous two, the essential *mode* of political action is persuasive speech. It is through argument, deliberation, and rhetoric that political equals not only communicate and decide what to do, but also reveal themselves—their unique identities—and their understanding of the world they share. This is the arch-Arendtian theme of action as both world- and self-disclosive, a theme that Arendt obviously borrows from Heidegger's conception of human being as essentially disclosive or revelatory in nature (the *Da* of *Dasein*).[75] We should not, however, allow Arendt's strong emphasis on the "revelatory" character of speech and action to obscure her essential point. This is that persuasive speech—the kind of speech found in assembly debates, political argument in the marketplace, and constitutional deliberations of all sorts—is the only mode of political action befitting a world of civic equals.[76] As is well known, her entire conception of political action—elicited in large part from the talkative political world of Periclean Athens—is one that places all forms of violence, coercion, and hierarchy outside the sphere of distinctly political relations.

Fourth, political speech—understood as the open-ended debate and deliberation of diverse equals—is, "properly speaking," about politics. That is, political speech is, at least implicitly, about the structure of laws and institutions—the constitution, if you will—of a particular public-political world.

The thesis that "the content of politics is politics" strikes us as paradoxical. It is seen by many of Arendt's critics as the *reductio ad absurdum* of her misguided insistence on a "pure" or self-contained conception of action and the public realm. The thesis becomes less paradoxical when we realize that Arendt is talking about the legal and institutional structure that makes the public and private freedom of citizens—not to mention their equality—possible in the first place.[77] Political speech is speech about the creation, preservation, and health of this institutionally articulated public world. Of course, "social" concerns are important in their own right. However, at a moment in America when the constitutional structure of our public world is under attack by a "unitary Executive branch," such a "narrow" focus on the public-political world is perhaps not entirely misplaced.[78]

Fifth and finally, political action thus understood—as the speech and action of diverse equals, taking place in a constitutionally articulated public realm, and concerning the health and care of this very "space of freedom"—is subject to what Arendt (in *The Human Condition*) calls a pervasive *frailty*.[79] The basic fact of human plurality suffuses the political world entirely. As political actors, we "always move among and in relation to other acting beings." Hence the political actor is, as Arendt reminds us, "never merely a 'doer' but always and at the same time a sufferer."[80] Indeed, "to do and to suffer are like opposite sides of the same coin."[81]

This dual quality of political action flows from what Arendt calls its "boundlessness." Any given action in the public sphere generates unlimited consequences, if only because it acts into a medium "where every reaction becomes a chain reaction and where every process is the cause of new processes."[82] Hence, in the public realm, "one deed, and sometimes one word, suffices to change every constellation." This boundlessness of political action is one reason why action rarely, if ever, achieves its goal. Arendt refers to this dimension of action as its apparent futility. Finally, the "boundlessness" of action—itself a function of action's occurrence in a context of a plurality—yields an inherent unpredictability of outcome. We can never know in advance what action—with its ability to "change every constellation" and create potentially "boundless" consequences—is going to result in.

Taken together, the futility, boundlessness, and uncertainty of outcome that characterize action make it appear one of the most vulnerable, if not ephemeral, of all human activities. Indeed, it was precisely because of this vulnerability and ephemerality—and the apparent lack of moral responsibility they generated—that philosophers from the time of Plato and Aristotle on down have "recoded" political action, substituting making or fabrication for a form of activity originally grounded in the human condition of plurality.[83] By treating *praxis* as a form of *poiēsis*, and the political actor as more like a solitary craftsman than an agent interacting with other agents, the Western philosophical tradition has succeeded in eliminating many of the various "calamities" of action. As Arendt puts it in a supremely important passage from *The Human Condition*:

> It has always been a great temptation, for men of action no less than for men of thought, to find a substitute for action in the hope that the realm of human affairs may escape the haphazardness and moral irresponsibility inherent in a plurality of agents. The remarkable monotony of the proposed solutions throughout our recorded history testify to the elemental simplicity of the matter. Generally speaking, they always amount to seeking shelter from action's calamities in an activity where one man, isolated from all others, remains master of his doings from beginning to end. This attempt to replace action with making is manifest in the whole body of argument against "democracy," which, the more consistently and better reasoned it is, will turn into an argument against the essentials of politics.[84]

In *The Human Condition*, Arendt is quite emphatic about the importance of what she calls "the traditional substitution of making for acting," even titling a central section (number 31) after it. And, as the last line of the passage cited above demonstrates, she is equally emphatic about the profound and anti-democratic consequences that such a rebellion against the "human condition of plurality" entails. For the "calamities of action"—"the unpredictability of its outcome, the irreversibility of its process, and the anonymity of its authors"—all arise from "the human condition of plurality, which is the *sine qua non* for the space of appearance which is the public realm." Hence, Arendt concludes, "the attempt to do away with this plurality is *always tantamount to the abolition of the public realm itself.*"[85]

In Arendt's telling, it is Plato who initiates the traditional and long-lived "substitution of making for acting." Seeing in fabrication an activity in which the beginner remains the master of the process he has initiated, Plato, according to Arendt, was the first to draw a systematic analogy between the specialized knowledge of the craftsman and the political wisdom of the statesman or ruler. Like the craftsman, the wise or moral ruler "knows" what he wants to accomplish—what ideals he wants to give concrete reality to—before any action takes place. Plato's entire theory of transcendent ideas, as well as his allegory of the cave, is nothing less than the attempt to draw out this analogy between the political actor and the fabricator who first "sees" his product as an ideal or blueprint, and then sets about to actualize it concretely.[86]

As Plato realized, within the schema of fabrication, knowledge is quite distinct from the activity of execution. Whereas democratic citizens in Periclean Athens exemplified a unity of thought and action in their amateur, nonspecialist way, the Platonic-philosophical conceptualization presupposed a radical separation—and hierarchical ranking—of these two faculties.[87] The Platonic ruler monopolized political and moral knowledge (in the form of science or *epistēmē*). *Knowing* and *doing* became two separate things, the latter reduced to the merely "instrumental" effectuation of what the former spelled out.[88] Every subsequent attempt to postulate a relation of deduction or derivation of "practice" or action from a theoretically determined ("scientific") discourse of Truth or Justice reiterates, in effect, the basic Platonic schema—and with it, the "traditional substitution of making for acting."

It is for this reason that Arendt can claim that the "substitution of making for acting" characterized not just ancient philosophy, but modern as well. And this leads her to make an even more general claim: namely, that the desire to overcome the "frailty" of human affairs and avoid the "calamities of action" is philosophically so strong that "the greater part of political philosophy since Plato could easily be interpreted as various attempts *to find theoretical foundations and practical ways for an escape from politics altogether.*"[89]

It is in this claim—with its more or less explicit indictment of the "inauthenticity" of political philosophy since Plato—that we encounter Arendt's most radical and suggestive appropriation of Heidegger's "deconstructive" approach to the tradition.

Like Heidegger, Arendt thought that traditional philosophy had projected an alien metaphorics onto a sphere of life that is, in some sense, the unique locus of an "authentic" *Existenz*; of a distinctly human life. For Heidegger, this sphere was the individual's care for his own being, a dimension of existence that needed to be radically distinguished from the preoccupation and "concernful absorption" of everyday life.[90] For Arendt, this sphere was the public realm, a realm of freedom in which the automatism of everyday life (biological and economic reproduction) was overcome and "transcendence"—in the worldly form of a spontaneous action with others—achieved. In this regard, one can see Arendt as, in effect, "spatializing" the central distinction of *Being and Time*, locating man's distinctively human freedom in the public realm, that is, over against both the social sphere of everyday activity and the private realm of "care for the self."[91]

Traditional philosophy, on the other hand, refused to acknowledge the "groundless" freedom of either individual *Existenz* or acting with others. It preferred, instead, to install a set of evidently secure metaphysical standards ("first principles") in order to guide both individual conduct and political life. It saw political action not as something with inherent value but, at best, as a mere means by which to realize "an allegedly higher good."[92] In this sense, philosophy turns its back on the non-sovereign character of human freedom, preferring instead to chase after images—not to say fantasies—of mastery and control.[93] Arendt, in other words, takes Heidegger's basic theme—the tradition's substitution of a "grounded" mastery of being for a groundless existential freedom—and applies it to the Western canon of political philosophy. In so doing, she reveals a persistent effacement of action, plurality, and the non-sovereign freedom of the public-political realm. As she puts it in a central passage from her essay "What Is Freedom?":

> Within the conceptual framework of traditional philosophy, it is indeed very difficult to understand how freedom and non-sovereignty can exist together, or, to put it another way, how freedom could have been given to men under the condition of non-sovereignty. Actually it is as unrealistic to deny freedom because of the fact of human non-sovereignty as it is dangerous to believe that one can be free—as an individual or as a group—only if he is sovereign. . . . Under human conditions, which are determined by the fact that not man but men live on the earth, freedom and sovereignty are so little identical that they cannot even exist simultaneously. . . . If men wish to be free, it is precisely sovereignty they must renounce.[94]

Now, one may allow that Arendt is onto something here, but still object that she has grossly overstated her case. To be sure, Plato and a certain "anti-political" strand of the Western philosophical tradition wanted to escape from the vagaries of the public realm and the uncertainties born of human plurality. They clearly prefer the image of the craftsman/sovereign, in complete control of the political world and the shaping of his subjects' character. But the tradition as a whole, from "Plato to Marx"? How can she possibly make such a claim?

Here we have to acknowledge that Arendt, under the sway of Nietzsche and Heidegger's metanarratives of Western philosophy, succumbed to the idea that philosophy is Platonism.[95] Whitehead's famous one-liner— "All philosophy is a footnote to Plato"—aside, it is hardly clear that Western tradition of political philosophy can be so reduced. Plato was extraordinarily influential in shaping that tradition, but there are clearly resources within it—beginning with Aristotle, as Arendt knew—for thinking politics and plurality at least partially together.[96]

Yet despite a certain exaggeration, Arendt's Heidegger-inspired reading of the tradition is, I think, for the most part on target. Even professors of political theory who love the canon (as I do) have to admit that the bulk of the tradition—like the bulk of European culture prior to the French Revolution—is explicitly anti-democratic and anti-egalitarian. Over and over again, it has embraced not only hierarchy, but the rationalist chimera of one set of correct answers to man's most enduring moral and political problems—a habit of mind that makes it inherently monist rather than pluralist.[97] As a result, it has habitually devalued the public realm and the exchange of opinion, equating this sphere and this activity with ignorance, relativism, and moral irresponsibility.

This is obviously the case with Plato. The basic tendency, however, is also manifest in Augustine, Hobbes, Hegel, and Marx. They all have little use for human plurality or a "doxastic" (opinion-based) rationality. The thinkers who opt out of this "scientific" (or faith-based) devaluation of plurality and the public sphere—one thinks of Montesquieu, Tocqueville, and Mill—are generally either not philosophers, or are more concerned with private rather than public liberty.[98] Nor should we be surprised that even such "nonphilosophical" thinkers as Max Weber see political action as essentially strategic in character, just as they see political power entirely in light of the "sovereign" model, namely, as the ability to "enforce one's will" upon another.[99] The debate, deliberation, and judgment of equal citizens in the public realm has little if any place in their thought. This is also the case with respect to the civic republican tradition, a tradition well known for its assertion of the importance of public liberty, but equally well known for its insistence that a freedom-loving citizen body must be united, militarily and morally.[100]

In the Western tradition, then, political liberty and the public realm suffer a peculiar fate. They are either bracketed in favor of a ruler who monopolizes action and judgment (the case of Plato and Hobbes); or they are repudiated as "pagan" values (as in Augustine and Christianity's polemic against Roman "worldliness").[101] Alternatively, political freedom and the public realm are demoted to a second-rank status (as in Constant, Mill, and liberalism generally); or they are asserted as positive values, but made contingent upon the curbing of human plurality in favor of a united, strong, and morally homogeneous citizen body (Machiavelli and Rousseau).[102]

Marxism hardly escapes this traditional and deeply set tendency to devalue plurality and the public realm. Not only did Marx absorb the category of *praxis* or human interaction in his concept of labor. He also thought that the transcendence of class divisions (brought about by the overthrow of capitalism and the rule of the bourgeoisie) would issue in the spontaneous emergence of a clear and palpable "general interest" of society as a whole. The entire domain of the political could then be reduced to the "administration of things" performable "by any cook."[103] As Albrecht Wellmer has rightly observed, in Marx and the Marxian tradition generally, there is little if any concern with the problem of the institutionalization of freedom.[104]

◆

Plurality, then, does not do well by the tradition, no matter which segment of it we care to examine. The image of a sovereign will, of a singular moral truth, or of a morally homogenous "people" loom far too large in our tradition for this all-important dimension of political life to be given its due. Margaret Canovan is thus absolutely correct to single out the "emphasis on the plurality of human beings and the political space between them" as "the most distinctive feature of Arendt's political thought."[105]

This emphasis is not only distinctive; it is revolutionary and far-reaching in its implications. As Arendt reminds us, the public realm, phenomenologically construed, does not know the distinction between rulers and ruled. Nor does it know any "collective subjects" such as a "sovereign" people, the *Volk* or the proletariat. As plural (individual) citizens, we are brought together by what lies between us—an institutionally articulated public realm. This realm "relates and separates" us, as a table does those who sit around it.[106] This relation and separation makes the formation of opinions possible, and opinions—the stuff of the talkative politics Arendt celebrates—are held by individuals, not groups or collective subjects.[107]

The extraordinary salience of plurality in Arendt's thought raises an immediate question. If this notion distinguishes her from an overly "Platonic" tradition of political philosophy in general, does it not also distinguish her from her teacher, Heidegger, in particular?

The answer to this question is assuredly "yes." While Heidegger was quite aware of the importance of the distinction between *praxis* and *poiēsis*, drawing attention to the "productionist" character of ancient Greek ontology as far back as his Marburg lectures of 1927, his notion of authentic *Existenz* was surprisingly devoid of a robust interactive dimension (his identification of *Mitsein* as a structural characteristic of human existence notwithstanding).[108] If, as Jacques Taminiaux has suggested, Heidegger's notion of authentic vs. inauthentic *Existenz* was based on the reappropriation of Aristotle's distinction, it is a reappropriation that washes out the importance of human plurality and interaction—what Arendt calls "the sharing of words and deeds." The largely individualist character of authentic *Dasein* we find in Div. II of *Being and Time* (at odds, in certain respects, with the relational and anti-Cartesian ontology of Div. I) is reproduced in the "authentic" community that emerges in Ch. V ("Temporality and Historicality"). The image of a unitary people taking on the role of an authentic self reappears in the notorious *Rektoratsrede* (1933) and in the *Introduction to Metaphysics* (1935).[109]

In these texts, Heidegger emerges as an increasingly *völkisch* thinker, one who attributes to the state an essentially speculative function, namely, "clearing" a space within which the unique destiny of a particular historical people can come to light. The "world" of an historical people is manifest in its political organization. Its laws, customs, and institutions do not simply articulate a public realm. They trace an ontological horizon for the culture as a whole. Thus, the political association is a "space of disclosure" for Heidegger (as it is for Arendt), but a "space of disclosure" in the most fundamental ("primordial") sense possible. A formulation taken from

Heidegger's 1942 seminar on Parmenides brings this speculative-ontological function of the political association into sharp focus:

> What is the *polis*? . . . *Polis* is the *polos*, the pivot, the place around which gravitates, in its specific manner, everything that for the Greeks is disclosed amidst beings. . . . As this location, the pivot lets beings appear in their Being subject to the totality of their involvement. The pivot neither makes nor creates beings in their Being, but as the pivot, it is the site of the unconcealedness of beings as a whole. . . . Between *polis* and Being, a relation of the same origin rules.[110]

This conception relates back to the idea of the *polis* as an example of what Heidegger (in "The Origin of the Work of Art" [1936]) calls the "setting-into-work-of-truth." A genuine work of art neither represents nor expresses; rather, it "opens" the "world of an historical people." As Heidegger puts it: "To be a work means to set up a world."[111]

The *polis*, then, is a unique, indeed privileged, instance of such a "world-disclosing" artwork. As such, it is made possible not by the interaction—the *praxis*—of citizens within an institutional-legal context of civic equality. Rather, it is the most fundamental and uncanny instance of *poiēsis* imaginable. The *polis* is the work of a "creator" who engages in a *polemos* or conflict with the dark background of nature and myth, struggling to create a human world—a space of disclosure—amidst the surrounding darkness, which Heidegger calls "earth." The original agon is not between equal but competitive citizens (Arendt's "aristocratic" or Greek conception in *The Human Condition*). Rather, it is between "world" and "earth" as such, between "concealedness" and "unconealedness." "It is this conflict," Heidegger writes in 1935, that

> first projects and develops what had hitherto been unheard of, unsaid, and unthought. The battle is then sustained by the creators, poets, thinkers, statesmen. Against the overwhelming chaos they set the barrier of their work, and in their work they capture the world thus opened up. It is with these works that the elemental power, *physis*, first comes to stand. Only now does the essent become essent as such. This world-building is history in the authentic sense.[112]

Such "world-revealing" or "world-building" *poiēsis* can take many forms. It can occur in the words of a thinker, a poet, a priest, or a playwright. But, as already indicated, it is the city's founder—the "lonely" figure who brings forth a political world in the form of a new *polis*—who is most important. For the *polis* is "the historical place, the there *in* which, *out* of which, and *for* which history happens."[113] Such a radical or foundational beginning can occur, Heidegger states, only if there are "violent men" willing to "use power, to become pre-eminent in historical being as creators, as men of action."[114] Such men—founders such as Sophocles' Theseus—are, strictly speaking, *apolis*, "without city and place, lonely, strange, and alien."[115]

I cite these passages because they reveal how Heidegger, his thematization of the "productionist" prejudices of Greek ontology notwithstanding, himself succumbed to the lure of *poiēsis*, albeit in a "radicalized" form.[116] Plurality and equality are effaced, as the "poetic" founder-legislator performs his lonely, quasi-divine work. Using Sophocles as his departure point (specifically, an interpretation of the first choral ode from *Antigone*), Heidegger comes to a "conclusion" surprisingly reminiscent of Machiavelli and Rousseau. Everything, it turns out, depends on the availability of a singular founder-legislator. Without him, no *polis* or republic can come into being and grow into a "world" of its own.

Nothing could be further from the Arendtian conception of a constitutional founding than this emphasis of the "lonely, strange, and alien" man of creative, radically poetic, violence. In *On Revolution* Arendt takes enormous pains to separate the violence that accompanies liberation from oppression from the debate, deliberation, and argument that precedes the constitutional creation of a new (legally and institutionally articulated) "space of freedom." Hence the paradigmatic stature of the American founders for her; hence her approving citation of their debates at the constitutional convention in Philadelphia as exemplary instances of political speech. Plurality and equality, in other words, attend even the *ur*-political moment of foundation. This is a remarkable deviation, not only from Heidegger, but also from the French and Marxian revolutionary traditions (with their emphasis on the violence of the beginning), and from the Western tradition of political thought as a whole (where the myth of the "founding legislator" looms very large indeed).

Since plurality marks not just the preservation of a new "space of freedom" but its very founding as well, are we not safe to claim it as Arendt's "master idea"?

In part, yes. Seen in the context of the tradition, to say nothing of existential philosophy, Arendt is indeed the champion of human plurality, just as she is a champion of the dignity of the political life as such. That said, however, we have to note that there are important limits to Arendt's concept of plurality, limits that tie her back to the tradition she struggled so hard both to appropriate and overcome.

Here it is helpful to be reminded of the "perspectival" effects of human plurality in a public sphere that has *not* been reduced to the spectacle of an authoritarian regime, nor to the privatism of a consumerist one. In *The Human Condition* Arendt writes:

> The reality of the public realm relies on the simultaneous presence of innumerable perspectives and aspects in which the common world presents itself and for which no common measurement or denominator can ever be devised. For though the common world is the common meeting ground of all, those who are present have different locations in it and the location of one can no more coincide with the location of another than the location of two objects. Being seen and being heard by others derive their significance from the fact that everybody sees and hears from a different position. This is the meaning of public life, compared to which even the richest and most satisfying family life can offer only the prolongation or multiplication of one's own position with its attending aspects and perspectives. . . . Only where things can be seen by many in a variety of aspects without changing their identity, so that those who are gathered around them know they see sameness in utter diversity, can worldly reality truly and reliably appear.[117]

This passage evidently provides us with a way of conceiving that "community without unity" which has been the elusive lodestar of so many contemporary champions of "difference." However, Arendt's perspectival, quasi-Nietzschean formulation depends on two things. First, as already indicated, it presupposes a shared world—a "human artifice," a public-political world that is legally and institutionally articulated.[118] Second—and more problematically—it presumes the presence of a substantial degree of public-spiritedness. Only the latter guarantees that our different perspectives on the common world will be worthy of the title "opinion" in Arendt's sense. Without it, the potential actualization of a rich politics of debate, deliberation, and opinion aborts, issuing in the vastly more familiar politics of divergent interests and identities.

It is possible to chastise Arendt for wanting a plurality-based politics while eschewing what liberals commonly refer to as pluralism: the pluralism of interests and group identities. This is a "realist" objection that any robustly republican idea of politics (and Arendt's is certainly that) must contend with. But I want to take the plurality/pluralism distinction one step farther and suggest that the real problem with Arendt is not that she asks us to partially bracket our economic and group interests when we attend to the public-political world. This, I think, is something every reasonably good citizen tries to do, partly in horrified response to the exploitative/strategic approach to the public realm that currently reigns supreme in our cynically "pluralist" democracy.

No, the deeper problem has to do with a political formulation of plurality that leaves little to no room for the recognition of genuine, and deep-seated, moral pluralism. Arendt hardly yearns for a world in which our self-conception as political beings overcomes the distinction between *homme* and *citoyen* (the Marxian fantasy of a "human emancipation" from all the differences that divide us). But she does want a world in which strong citizenship, and the "free *moeurs*" that sustain it (Tocqueville), have a clear and distinct moral priority. "Care for the world," not for our souls, should be the dominant passion.

As Isaiah Berlin has pointed out in his essay "The Originality of Machiavelli," this is a perfectly plausible moral stance to take. However, it is not only at odds with the rampant materialism of our world. It is also at odds with what many take to be their ultimate and most sustaining moral commitments. To put the point in Aristotelian terms: "Care for the public world," as Arendt intends the phrase, presupposes a vision of the good life, and an attachment to public freedom, that few in our increasingly religious, and increasingly privatized, culture can be said to share. Citizenship has lost its luster, and it seems there is little we can do to restore it. So long as Arendt's vision of a diverse public world restricts the expression of "plurality" to those sharing a strong civic and constitutional commitment to "the public thing"—so long as it fails to address the fragmentary and divided character of our public world, the depth of moral disagreement and the divergence of its various "tables of value" within it—there will be clear limits to its applicability.[119]

I do not want to be understood as offering a variation on Sheldon Wolin's critique, namely, that Arendt is fundamentally motivated by a desire to exclude certain concerns, values, or agents from her excessively "purified" public realm. Rather, I am trying to point out the degree to which her conception of a vibrant public sphere, and a richly articulated plurality, depends upon the presence of a shared civic ethos—a "horizon-sustaining" set of *moeurs* or myths—and not just upon a set of common institutions or basic laws.

This idea—the "foundational" quality of public spirit, as manifest in the "worship" of the founding moment and attempts to "preserve and augment" it—is a mainstay of the civic republican tradition. Whatever Arendt's departures from that tradition—and they are substantial—they do not extend to this supremely important dimension.[120] A culture or group that lacks public spirit or "worldliness" in this specific sense will find themselves not expelled from the Arendtian public sphere (a charge trumped up by Arendt's critics), but they will find themselves with little, if anything, to contribute. Until and unless they "recalibrate" their values, giving "care for the public thing" a place of priority on their list, their voice will be curiously absent from the talkative politics Arendt hopes to recover—pearl-diver-like—from the depths of our heritage.

Conclusion: A "Heideggerian" Republican?

In pointing out the limits of Arendt's concept of plurality, I do not mean to endorse a "politics of difference" that questions the very idea of a "universal" or inclusive category of citizenship. Nor do I intend to substitute a multicultural perspective for either the "radical" or social democratic agendas that have hitherto motivated many of Arendt's academic critics. Rather, I am merely trying to draw attention to the built-in limits of the civic republican tradition, a tradition grounded upon a heavily freighted "positive" or civic conception of freedom. Thanks in no small part to her transformative appropriation of existentialism, Arendt was able to unburden herself of the more dubious aspects of the republican legacy, such as those targeted by Constant in his famous lecture "The Liberty of the Ancients Compared to that of the Moderns" (1819). But the insistence upon a certain form of worldliness—an essentially *public* form of being—remains. It is at once the most characteristic feature of her thought—the thing that distinguishes her from both Heidegger and liberalism—and the most problematic. "Worldliness" as Arendt uses the term has a certain philosophical affiliation with Heidegger's notion of *being-in-the-world*, an existential category of *Dasein* that took direct aim at the disembodied and atomistic Cartesian subject. But "worldliness" for Arendt has a broader cultural context. It is intended to fight not just the distortions of the modern epistemological tradition, from Descartes to Kant (one of Heidegger's primary projects in *Being and Time*). Rather, it is intended to reveal the anti-worldly, anti-political bias of Western culture from the fall of Rome to the present. It targets Socratic conscience, Stoicism, Christian otherworldliness, the modern focus on will and labor, all forms of romanticism, privatism, and narcissistic self-absorption. Arendt wants us to stop caring so much about ourselves or our souls, and start caring a lot more about our world. Overcoming the "world-alienation" of the modern age—an alienation with deep cultural roots in Christianity—was her largest and most ambitious goal.

I would like to suggest that in this project, Arendt had an important—and generally overlooked—predecessor. Hegel's *Phenomenology of Mind* was nothing if not a blistering attack on the notion of freedom as independence or (self) sovereignty.[121] Obsessed with demolishing the Western attraction to ideas of autonomy or self-sufficiency, Hegel set out to reveal the social and public roots of reason, morality, and (of course) freedom itself. He even set out to show how our persistent tendency to misunderstand ourselves in "sovereign" or self-sufficient terms was itself a function of historical-cultural context. Last but not least, he wanted to show how the spirit of the "Unhappy Consciousness" of Christianity continued to hang over our world, producing romantic self-absorption (the "beautiful soul"), a (Protestant) cult of inwardness, and world-alienation on a gigantic scale.

Arendt generally had little use for Hegel, seeing him as a fount of the kind of rationalism and historicism that helped pave the way for doctrines of totalitarian "historical necessity." But, like him, she drew on the Greeks and the Romans in order to combat all forms of Western world-alienation, beginning with Christianity and ending with the ravages of a privatized consumer culture.[122] Like Hegel, she reserved a special scorn for, and wariness of, any and all forms of romantic individualism.[123] And—once again like Hegel—she warned against conceptions of political identity that base themselves not on something objective and shared, such as laws and institutions, but rather "personal" or "portable" (one's race or ethnicity, one's Slavic "soul" or German "blood").[124]

This wariness of romantic individualism—a reaction to a former self, perhaps—is especially evident in *Rahel Varnhagen: The Life of a Jewess*, a book Arendt wrote largely in the 1930s.[125] It recurs in her early critique of

Heidegger in the 1946 *Partisan Review* essay "What Is *Existenz* Philosophy?"[126] The latter essay is noteworthy for the way Arendt traces Heidegger's involvement with the Nazis—which she is tempted to dismiss as an instance of sheer stupidity based on "lack of character"—back to German Romanticism, with its "lack of responsibility" and "spiritual playfulness."[127] The pattern was already set in the "solipsistic" version of existential philosophy put forth in *Being and Time*, a version which— unlike that of Arendt's other teacher, Karl Jaspers—substitutes the idea of "being a Self" for the idea of being part of the community of mankind.[128] Heidegger, as Arendt writes in the essay, is "the last (let us hope) Romantic"—a purveyor of a potentially quite dangerous form of "world alienation."[129]

This critique of romantic world-alienation has some unlikely targets as well. In her essay on "On Humanity in Dark Times," Arendt addresses the temptation faced by those who have the misfortune to live in "dark times"—that is, in times when public life is a locus of shame rather than pride; when Heidegger's "perverse sounding statement" that "the light of the public obscures everything" actually goes "to the very heart of the matter."[130] In such times, Arendt warns, we are all too likely to look for sources of human solidarity not in the worldly structures that actually define a shared public world, but in "human nature," human feeling, or human reason. *Fraternité* based on such supposed "universals" is, in fact, an illusion, and a dangerous one at that. Unlike commitment to a constitutionally defined public sphere, such "feelings of brotherhood" can promote a range of what Arendt calls "enthusiastic excess." This excess is documented extensively in *On Revolution's* critique of revolutionary compassion.[131]

A less dangerous, but equally seductive, form of world-alienation is found in the warmth of "pariah peoples"—such as the Jews—who find themselves forcibly excluded from the "bright light of the public." This warmth—an intensity of feeling and concern for others in what is a strictly "private" existence—is likely to be envied as a superior reality by those who can actually enter the public sphere they are ashamed of. As Arendt writes:

> It is true that in "dark times" the warmth which is the pariahs' substitute for light exerts a great fascination upon all those who are so ashamed of the world as it is that they would like to take refuge in invisibility. And in invisibility, in that obscurity in

which a man who is himself hidden need no longer see the visible world either, only the warmth and fraternity of closely packed human beings can compensate for the weird irreality that human relationships assume wherever they develop in absolute worldlessness, unrelated to a world common to all people.[132]

It is this loss of a common—politically and legally articulated—world that Arendt dreads most. She sees it, however, as the spirit of our age and, indeed, of much of Western history. There are exceptions, of course; moments when civic equals devoted their best energies to creating and preserving their "space of freedom" out of love for the world. But such moments are rare. "World-alienation" and "resentment of the human condition" are the norm, both now and in the past. The former affect characterizes Christianity and Romanticism; the latter what I have called "productionist metaphysics" as well as the relentlessly revolutionizing forces of modern technology and capitalist economics. The one point on which Arendt would agree with Marx is that capitalism is, above all else, a dissolvent force, undermining the stability and durability of the public world that stands between man and nature. "All that is solid melts into air . . ."

Worldlessness and resentment of the human condition fuel political pathology. Romantic nationalism leads to tribal nationalism; revolutionary compassion and "brotherhood" lead to terror and a proto-totalitarian contempt for constitutional instruments. We seem to be condemned to swinging between the active worldlessness of revolutionary terrorism and tribal nationalism and the passive worldlessness of Christian withdrawal and "pariah" solidarity. Hence Arendt's rueful observation that "nothing, it seems to me, is more questionable than our attitude toward the world."

Unless Arendt's critics engage the importance of the themes of world-alienation and resentment of the human condition in her thought, their critiques will largely miss the mark. And this, in turn, means grappling with the depth and breadth of her engagement with the Western tradition of political and philosophical thought. I am afraid that the latter task is one fewer and fewer American academics are either competent or willing to take up.

Sheldon Wolin and Martin Jay are important exceptions to this rule. However, neither places Arendt in the contexts her thought so obviously demands: the broad historical-cultural shift away from publicness per se, and the "deconstructive" engagement with the roots of our tradition of political thought. Focusing on more immediate, ready-to-hand contexts (the prospects for radical democracy in the late twentieth century; the "political existentialists" of the twenties), they produce an elitist Arendt who fetishized spontaneity and *politique pour la politique*; an Arendt who gave little thought to justice for either ordinary people or, indeed, her own people.

As I have argued, this picture has little to do with the reality of Arendt's thought, a reality that comes to the fore only when we pay attention to her appropriation of the distinction between *praxis* and *poiēsis,* and her concern with preserving the *ur*-political phenomenon of human plurality. That so many of Arendt's critics barely mention the role plurality plays in her thought is in itself quite revealing. In my view, to write about Arendt's concept of the political without discussing human plurality or the problem of "world-alienation" is like writing about Hobbes without discussing sovereignty or the state of nature. Whatever else results, we can be sure it is not Arendt or Hobbes.

Of course, the temptation to approach any political theorist through the lens of our current concerns is a strong one. A case can be made, via Gadamer, that understanding depends upon the projection of "prejudices" in the Burkean sense. But the process of understanding is short-circuited if we allow this initial projection permanently to define the context—the hermeneutical backdrop—without subsequent revision and correction. In understanding the political thought of Hannah Arendt, "participatory democracy" and "political existentialism" only get us so far. At a minimum, they have to be supplemented by a consideration of Arendt's notion of plurality, and by a serious examination of her critique and appropriation of Heidegger's thought.

While I can claim to have at least initiated the latter project, I cannot pretend to have sufficiently examined the implications of plurality in *Arendt and Heidegger.*[133] Margaret Canovan's *Hannah Arendt: A Reinterpretation* has, however, provided readers with a full-scale, "plurality-centric" reading of Arendt's political theory. In the course of rereading Canovan's work and my own, I have often been struck by the fundamental problem confronting any interpreter who desires to "get Hannah Arendt right": how to give due weight to the influence of civic republicanism and existentialism on her thought, while recognizing the originality of her appropriation of both traditions.

We are now at a place, in the academic world, at least, where the influence of these two traditions on Arendt's thought is widely recognized.

Indeed, the most interesting recent scholarly work on Arendt centers on sorting out the implications of her stunningly original synthesis of these two (quite opposed) schools of thought. As a result, we have reason to hope that we have heard the last of complaints about her "elitism" and the "dangerous" or "anti-democratic" character of her debt to existentialism and Heidegger. I would not, however, bet on it.

10 | THE "AUTONOMY OF THE POLITICAL"

RECONSIDERED

As the political theorist George Kateb has written, Hannah Arendt's work is "shocking and foreign to the prepossessions of most of us."[1] Kateb is not referring to those moments of enraged misunderstanding that have marred Arendt's reception in this country (the controversy over the Eichmann book being the most obvious example). Rather, he is referring to Arendt's approach and primary concerns as a political theorist. Both in terms of content and "method," Arendt's work retains a strangeness, an unfamiliarity, that almost encourages misunderstanding. Nowhere is this more evident than in her effort to think "the political" as a separate and distinct domain of human life, one possessed of an intrinsic value and dignity.

For many Americans—and certainly for many American academics—this would seem an incomprehensible project. In what sense can politics or political action be an "end in itself"? Doesn't Arendt know the basic modern lesson, taught by both Adam Smith and Karl Marx, that "the political" is really an epiphenomenon of the social or the economic? And even supposing it makes sense to demarcate "politics" from economics, what happens to the claims of *justice* when politics is seen as an end in itself?

More to the point, isn't political action—always and everywhere—fundamentally instrumental in character? Whether we approach the problem of politics in either strategic or moral terms—that is, whether we approach it as Machiavellians or Kantians—we seem unable to escape the conclusion that political action is essentially a means to an end. To view it, as Arendt would have us do, as an end in itself runs the risk of aestheticism (on the one hand) or immoralism (on the other). Arendt doesn't help matters when she writes about the "shining glory of great deeds," or when she characterizes the freedom of political action in strictly performative terms. As she writes in her essay "What is Freedom?" "Men are free as long as they act, neither before nor after; for to be free and to act are the same."[2]

To anyone brought up in the liberal tradition (with its emphasis on individual rights, limited government, and freedom from interference)—or the social democratic tradition (with its focus on social justice), Arendt's insistence on the inherent value of political action will look both strange and beside the point. Yes, such readers might acknowledge, Arendt has something to teach us about the importance of positive political freedom, and also about the need to properly institutionalize this freedom—to create and sustain a durable public realm in which equal yet diverse political actors can engage in the collective (deliberative) determination of their fate. But, they insist, Arendt's focus on the neglected meaning of political action leads her to neglect the most important source of political energy and progressive democratic political change. That source is the desire of "the many" to gain political power and redress their economic and social lot.[3]

Such doubts about her project turn into outright disbelief when Arendt's readers encounter her categorical distinction between the social and the political. This distinction is theoretically articulated in *The Human Condition* (1958), which is also the text where Arendt lays out her conceptions of action and the public realm. It is then given uncomfortable historical flesh in *On Revolution* (1963), which is Arendt's extended rumination on the fate of the modern revolutionary tradition.

In *The Human Condition*, Arendt presents what we might call a contrastive theory of freedom. According to Arendt, freedom—considered as a tangible, worldly reality—was experienced by the ancients whenever they entered the assembly or conversed in the agora. These were public spaces predicated upon the equality of citizens. Such civic equality was an equality of peers, and—as such—stood in the sharpest possible contrast to the (seemingly natural) hierarchy that pervaded the private or household realm. Devoted to debate, deliberation, and decision of common affairs by citizens, the public realm was a man-made space of positive freedom. The private or household realm, on the other hand, was devoted entirely to the tasks of biological reproduction and material subsistence. Natural necessity determined all its activities. Thus, unlike ourselves, the ancient Greeks and Romans had the almost daily experience of leaving one realm—the private, the sphere of necessity—and crossing over into another—the public, the realm of freedom. They had the daily experience, in other words, of moving from a "natural" realm of hierarchy and coercion to an artificial realm of equality, speech, and persuasion.

Of course, Arendt was well aware that the equality and freedom found in the classical world was purchased at the price of excluding slaves, women, and children from the "realm of freedom." She sometimes gives the impression that she—like Rousseau—is almost willing to pay this price.[4] If civic equality and political freedom unavoidably rest upon relations of domination and coercion in the household realm, so be it. Yet—and this is an important point overlooked by critics who see Arendt as suffering from an acute case of "polis-envy"—she welcomed the emancipation of women and workers in nineteenth- and early-twentieth-century Europe.

This would seem to align Arendt normatively with figures like Hegel, Marx, and the Frankfurt School—that is, with thinkers from the German tradition whose normative ideal remained a "polis without slaves." And it would seem to align her with those welfare state liberals (such as Rawls or Amy Gutmann) who value deliberative democracy and the public provision of services necessary to enable full political participation (services such as public education, health care, and adequate housing).

Yet while Arendt thought—like Marx and Hegel—that modern economic growth was clearly a precondition for a "polis without slaves," she also thought that this growth fundamentally—and irrevocably—perverted the public realm. The modern age witnesses, in Arendt's view, the increasingly unfiltered admission of "household" issues, problems, and activities to the public realm. Starting in the eighteenth century, the "life process" of subsistence and material reproduction is no longer relegated to the private realm; rather, it becomes a central—indeed, the central—concern of the state or commonwealth.

Here one can speak, as Arendt does, of the emergence of a kind of "national household"—of an economic polity devoted to the expansion of markets, productivity, and (in the European case, at least) material welfare. From Arendt's perspective, the problem—as previously "private" concerns flow endlessly into the public arena—is that the all-important distinction between public and private is increasingly blurred and (ultimately) effaced. The rhythms and imperatives of the "life process" steadily displace our concern for public freedom and collective decision making, our "care for the public world." Instead of inhabiting a world with clearly demarcated realms of freedom and necessity—a world with distinct public and private spheres—we find ourselves in one whose main phenomenological domain is "the social."

The social, according to Arendt, is a kind of bastard hybrid of public and private. It is a realm that reduces the public sphere to bureaucratic administration of the "national household," and which replaces the private sphere with the experience of intimacy. One can speak, in this regard, of the "eclipse" of an authentically public sphere as well as an authentically private one in the modern age. One could even go so far as Richard Sennett did in his very Arendtian book, *The Fall of Public Man*. There Sennett writes of the "*end* of public life."

Arendt's central point in this regard—that our public realm is dominated by social concerns, and hence is no longer authentically public or political—has elicited the charge of essentialism from such sympathetic critics as Seyla Benhabib and Richard Bernstein. Benhabib and Bernstein are moved to make this charge because they both want to assimilate Arendt's political theory to more traditional (social democratic) concerns.[5] More amusingly, perhaps, Arendt's concept of the social has led the political theorist Hanna Pitkin to burlesque her idea as the "attack of the blob."[6]

While it is doubtful that 1950s science fiction exerted the shaping influence on Arendt's thought that Pitkin suggests, her tongue-in-cheek characterization does get certain things right. For Arendt, the "social realm" does indeed devour more and more areas of life as modernity proceeds. It puts the bureaucratic welfare state in the place previously reserved for citizens and the activity of self-government. Worse, it imposes heavy demands for conformity on the part of citizens, who now figure largely as "jobholders" or as mere specimens of the "laboring animal." As Arendt puts it in *The Human Condition*, "Society has conquered the public realm." And society (to again quote Arendt) "excludes the possibility of action. . . . [It] expects of each of its member a certain kind of behavior, imposing innumerable and various rules, all of which tend to 'normalize' behavior and exclude spontaneous action."[7] The echoes of Tocqueville, Nietzsche, and Heidegger here are plain. The prefiguration of Foucault is even plainer.

If Arendt had left it at this, it would be fairly easy to bracket what Pitkin and others view as her implausible metanarrative about the "rise of the social." This would leave us free to concentrate on the suggestiveness of her account of political action: political action as initiatory action, as a form of acting together that takes place on (or actually creates) a public stage, a "public space of freedom." Such a stage is accessible, in principle, to all. The problem, of course, is that Arendt doesn't leave it at this. In *On Revolution* her idea of "the social" returns with a vengeance, this time in the guise of what she terms the "Social Question."

What is the "Social Question"? Essentially, it is the existence of poverty on a massive scale, as well as various attempts to eliminate such poverty by political means. Arendt deploys the "Social Question" in order to draw a fundamental (and much debated) contrast between the French and American Revolutions. According to Arendt, the French Revolution began as all true modern revolutions do: as the attempt to constitute a "new space of freedom," a new public-political world predicated upon civic equality. In this sense, it was indeed a "radical beginning," initiatory political action in the best (and most authentic) sense. But the French Revolution soon went off the rails, veering toward terror and class warfare—all as a result of the increasing weight of the "Social Question" in the minds of men like Robespierre.

Arendt makes the not very congenial argument that it was the very compassion that French Revolutionary leaders felt for the poor which led them to abandon the project of constructing a new and durable public realm. The civic republican project of the "constitution of freedom"—the *constitutio libertatis*—came to seem secondary, if not self-indulgent, in the face of such dire need. Moreover, compassion for the legions of poor seemed to dictate submission to overwhelming historical and (as it were) natural forces, forces that had never before entered the world of politics. This was the experience of the *tempête révolutionnaire*: the masses of the hunger-driven poor who—entering the public realm for the first time—swept all before them.

In Arendt's view, the experience of this seemingly elemental force gave rise to the illusion that freedom can result from the unleashed forces of necessity. This illusion is one that Arendt sees as afflicting not only the leaders of the French revolution, but also those theorists who took this revolution as the paradigm for political struggle and social change (Hegel, but also Karl Marx himself, whom Arendt views as the theorist of the French Revolution *après la lettre*). The fact that compassion for the poor trumped the *constitutio libertatis* and care for the public world is what ultimately sent the French Revolution (and all its progeny) to their doom. The hard truth, Arendt writes, is that poverty can never be eliminated by "political" means—that is, by violence or revolutionary struggle.

In stark contrast to the French Revolution and the Marxist tradition, Arendt poses the example of the American Revolution. This revolution remained, from start to finish, a political, and not a social, revolution. Freed from the crushing burden of Old World poverty, the American revolutionaries focused—after the initial violent work of liberation—on the constitution of a new public realm, on building a "new house for freedom." Seen from this angle, the primary achievement of the American Revolution was the Constitution, which Arendt understands less as a formula for limited government than as an ingenious "system of power." Our Constitution uses checks and balances between institutions to generate more power and (thus) to create and sustain a new public-political realm, one in which the activity of self-government takes place.

Reading Arendt's praise of the American Revolution, one is tempted to cast her as an all-too-grateful émigré to this country, one whose very gratitude blinded her to the Republic's structural injustices, past and present. We should note, however, that Arendt was well aware that the absence of poverty that made the American "constitution of liberty" possible was, to no small extent, a function of the existence of slavery. More to the point, we should note that in *On Revolution* the American Revolution appears less as a giant step forward in the "march of freedom" than as a kind of avoidable tragedy.

The original project of the French Revolution—the creation of a new public space of freedom—was quickly aborted, thanks to the hegemony of the Social Question in the minds of its moving political actors. The American Revolution, in contrast, was successful in both its goals of liberation (from the British Empire) and constitution (of a new public world). Yet the second half of the project—the genuinely revolutionary half—remained, in Arendt's view, importantly unfulfilled. After the revolutionary generation, the focus of American life quickly shifted from a concern with public freedom and public happiness to a focus on individual rights and what Tocqueville would call "the taste for physical gratification." In other words, we move from an emphasis on political rights and "positive" freedom—the freedom to be a "participator in government"—to an emphasis on civil rights and "negative" freedom, the freedom from politics. We move, in short, from a civic republican self-understanding to a liberal (and increasingly economic) one.

The final irony in Arendt's story comes in the shape of the masses of poor immigrants—the "huddled masses yearning to breathe free"—who arrive from Europe in the late nineteenth and early twentieth century. According to Arendt, these immigrants forever altered the meaning and promise of the "American Dream." This dream no longer signified the "foundation of freedom" and the pursuit of public happiness. It did not even signify the blessings of limited government. Rather, for the masses of Old World poor, America was a material "promised land," one where milk and honey flowed. It was, first and foremost, a land where wrenching poverty did not exist; a land where anyone could become rich.[8]

Even if one is convinced, as I am, that Arendt points out a fatal lacuna in the European revolutionary tradition—namely, a lack of concern with the institutionalization of public freedom—it is hard not to feel somewhat appalled by her general stance. In *On Revolution* she seems to be blaming the failure of the modern revolutionary tradition—its largely abortive result in both France and, ultimately, America—on the poor. Made abject by poverty, driven by "constant want" and "the absolute dictate of their bodies," the multitude, in Arendt's words, "rushed to the assistance of the French Revolution, inspired it, drove it onward, and eventually sent it to its doom."[9] The tragedy is repeated on an even grander scale with the Russian Revolution.[10] And it is repeated yet again in the case of the American Revolution—although this time *sotto voce*, in the form of a persistent confusion of consumerism and free enterprise with freedom itself.

What are we to make of this apparent tendency to "blame the victim" in Arendt's thought? Some theorists (like Pitkin or Sheldon Wolin) would argue that she was an inveterate elitist, one who thought of political action—the "sharing of great words and deeds"—as a kind of "leisure time sport for aristocrats."[11] Struggles for social justice seem not to concern her. Indeed, in her thought they generally appear as the channels by which natural or quasi-natural forces colonize, and then overwhelm, the carefully built up artificial reality that is the public world. Rather than seeking ways to realize a "polis without slaves," Arendt spends a suspiciously large amount of time and theoretical energy warning us about the dangers that the liberation of the "slaves" pose to her cherished "public realm."

To leave it at this, however, would do Arendt a grave injustice. Her perplexing strictures against "the social" and her disturbing critique of revolutionary compassion for the poor are not the expression of any faux-aristocratic contempt for the struggles of ordinary people. On the contrary, they are motivated by her intense (one might even say exclusive) "care for the public world." As her exuberant praise of the "council system" that emerged in the February Revolution of 1848, the 1871 Paris Commune, the 1905 strikes in Russia, the February Revolution of 1917, and the short-lived "council republic" of Bavarian Revolution in 1918–19 demonstrates, her faith in the political instincts of ordinary people is almost unlimited.

In situations where the authority of the old state collapses, Arendt argues, ordinary people have again and again organized themselves—spontaneously and successfully—for the business of self-government. Sadly, this success is evanescent. The forces of reaction or the party system (whether in its parliamentary or Leninist form) quickly overwhelm such "amateur apparatuses" (to use Max Weber's condescending phrase). The point we should note, however, is that Arendt had far greater faith in the political instincts of ordinary people than, say, the founders of the American Republic did. As Arendt points out, it was the founders who neglected to include the townships in their otherwise extraordinary system of power.[12] In so doing, they deprived ordinary people of a public space in which they could be "seen and heard," in which they could concretely realize their political freedom by becoming "participators in government."

But if Arendt is untainted by the elitist preference for rule of the "gentlemen," why does she insist on such a hard and fast distinction between the social and the political? And why does she seem to place struggles for social justice at the extreme margin of "authentic" politics? To answer the second question first, Arendt is more than willing to concede that every social problem has, so to speak, a political "face."[13] She also recognizes that social struggles can help cultivate an increased concern on the part of ordinary people for the health of their public realm and its institutions. But—and the qualification is crucial—such struggles can just as well result in the creation and perpetuation of interest group politics. Worse, they can foster a radical impatience with the "wearisome" processes of debate, deliberation, and compromise that constitute the core of political speech and political action.[14] Such impatience is, of course, to be expected where what is at stake is not the creation and preservation of durable institutions for public freedom, but bread and the most elemental needs of the human body.

In other words, wherever the "social question" exists in its most pressing form—in the wrenching poverty of hundreds of thousands if not millions—there the political processes of debate and exchange of opinion will seem an insult, little more than an excuse for not taking immediate, direct, and—if need be—violent action. But it is precisely this fact which leads Arendt to insist that human beings must be relatively free from basic issues of subsistence and survival if they are to make the freedom of the public world, rather than the necessity of the human body, the focus of even their episodic attention. As jarring and as retro as it might sound to our ears, liberation "from" the body must—in this basic sense—come first. Only then can we be "free for the world"; only then can we make "care for the world" the focus of our attention.

If the struggle for social justice is not elemental in this sense—if it concerns not the struggle for bread but for the enfranchisement of women, workers, and minorities as citizens with political rights—then Arendt has no problem whatsoever with it. Quite the contrary. As the passionate pages in *The Origins of Totalitarianism* on the plight of "stateless" peoples between the wars testifies, she views full membership in a political community as the essential precondition of all other civil, political, and indeed "human" rights. Full membership in such a community provides what Arendt called "right to have rights." Without this right—born of membership and the recognition it bestows—the various philanthropic and international proclamations made concerning the natural "dignity of man" aren't worth the paper they're written on.[15]

Arendt's insistence on political membership as the *sine qua non* of so-called human rights was born of her own experience as a stateless person for eighteen years, an experience she shared with millions of others in the interwar period. Rendered politically "homeless" by economic and political dislocation—by war, revolution, and economic crisis—these millions were stripped of civil and political rights by proto-totalitarian governments, governments that had no use for them and denaturalized them *en masse*. Denied membership in the established nation-states of Western Europe, they found themselves embodying a pure, almost limitless, vulnerability—a vulnerability that resulted from having no guaranteed place in the world, no political "home."

But if the struggle for enfranchisement—for full citizenship and the array of civil and political rights that come with it—is properly "political" in Arendt's sense, we should still not confuse it (as we are currently wont to do) with the fight for various benefits and entitlements. However essential programs like Medicaid, Medicare, and Social Security are, and however essential it is to protect and preserve them against assaults by unscrupulous administrations, we should remember that the object of their care is life itself. Such programs are, so to speak, pre-political: they concern the frailty and vulnerability of the human body and not the constitution or institutionalization of public freedom. From an Arendtian point of view, a politics whose central concern is to either build up or knock down the welfare state fails to engage the most important political consideration of all: the institutional housing of political freedom. Such housing makes the participation of ordinary citizens possible by providing accessible public spaces for debate and deliberation. It was the availability of such spaces that—as *On Revolution* testifies in a hundred places—was Arendt's chief obsession as a political theorist.

The fact that so much of contemporary American and European politics is taken up with welfare state–related issues may make us question the sheer tenability of Arendt's social/political distinction. Thus far, I have limited myself to responding to those who see this distinction as irreducibly elitist in character. As I have tried to show, it isn't. Rather, it testifies to Arendt's deeply held conviction that unless we care for the public world—unless we create and preserve a set of laws, institutions, and public spaces that make active citizenship possible for anyone who wants to pursue the *bios politikos*—we are likely to find ourselves relegated to the status of clients or consumers of various social services offered by the state. We are likely, in other words, to find ourselves dependent on what Foucault called the "pastoral power of the state," on that "immense and tutelary power" which—as Tocqueville warned—is "absolute, minute, regular, provident, and mild."[16]

The political life, in contrast, has to do with active participation in debates and decisions concerning our collective fate and—more to the point—the fate of our public institutions. The central paradox of Arendt's thought—her insistence that the content of politics is politics—dissolves when we realize that the objects of her concern are the institutions, laws, and spaces that make public freedom and a "shared public world" a tangible reality for all. Political action concerns the care and augmentation of this world, this reality, this set of institutions. That is what distinguishes it from social activism of various kinds. At a time when the supposed imperatives of national security and CEO-style management have restricted access and the transparency of public institutions as never before, Arendt's notion of "care for the public world" can hardly be dismissed as idiosyncratic or irrelevant. The struggle for social justice is one thing; the struggle to preserve and protect a structure of democratic governance—a structure that is quickly slipping from our grasp—is another.

Our public sphere has not only been "mediatized," to use Habermas's phrase. It has also been neutralized to a surprising degree. The press and a wide range of civic and political associations—the twin pillars of the Toc-quevillian idea of "civil society"—have not exactly been shut down. But they have been sidelined, domesticated, and "tamed" to a degree rare in American history. What we are left with is less constitutional government (in either the Arendtian or liberal sense of the term) than a new corporat-ist version of plebiscitary democracy (albeit this time minus the charis-matic leadership that made it Weber's preferred mode).

In the understanding of our leaders—and, indeed, of many of our fel-low citizens—the "public realm" has been squeezed down to little more than an "accountability moment" that occurs once every four years. The rest of the time, they say, the "unitary executive branch" (Hobbes would have liked the phrase) should be free to do its thing—to judge and respond to threats—more or less unimpeded by constitutional restraints. The gov-ernmental right to a monopoly on threat assessment and response has, of course, been a hallmark of authoritarian thinking from Hobbes to Schmitt. In our case, it is as if the current "state of emergency" had brought about what Hobbes always insisted was the defining characteristic of sovereign power and the state, namely, a monopoly on political judgment, decision, and action by one (clearly supreme) branch of government.

The response of some on the left to this situation has been to bemoan the lack of sixties-style activism. Indeed, the old SDS chestnut that "de-mocracy is in the streets" was partly inspired by Arendt's theory of politi-cal action. But to frame the problem at the level of activism and passion is, I think, to remain at the surface of things. For all her praise of the active life (and the life of political action in particular), Arendt never succumbed to the vulgar existentialist idea that the deed is everything. Even at her most "dramaturgical"—that is to say, even in the extraordinarily theatri-cal account of political action she gives in *The Human Condition*—Arendt never lost sight of the fact that authentic political action demanded a du-rable institutional home. Only then would the debate and deliberation of diverse equals have a tangible reality and a lasting effect. This intense con-cern with the durability of institutions of public freedom is, I think, the most poignant and bracing aspect of Arendt's political thought in the present moment. It reminds us of just what we are losing, and just how large our responsibility is for the care and preservation of the public world.

When Arendt uses the phrase "care for the world," it is this responsi-bility she is referring to. This care can be—and, historically, has been—ab-dicated in a variety of ways. One can, as did the early Christians, see "worldliness" as a sin and the political life as a distraction from the only thing that mattered: the care and salvation of one's soul. Or one can see the civic life as a distraction from the more pressing business of making money and securing physical gratifications—the response of the continental bourgeoisie that Tocqueville so reviled. Finally, one can see the public world instantiated in constitutional law and durable institutions as little more than an obstacle to such galvanizing forces as economic growth; racial, ethnic, or religious self-assertion; or globalization. In the nineteenth and twentieth centuries, the worldlessness of Christianity gave way to a new form of *ressentiment*. This is the resentment of stability and limitation as such—two factors that have always been crucial humanizing aspects of organized political life in the West.

The idea that unchained technological and economic forces will bring about a better, "post-political" form of life has been the stock-in-trade of a remarkable variety of thinkers and commentators. In its more extreme forms, it is a dream in which mankind wins through to God-like power by submitting to historically (or naturally) determinist forces. If only we allow economic, technological, or other such quasi-natural forces to grow without impediment, these thinkers promise, life on earth will be revolutionized. Poverty will be eliminated, the nation-state will be rendered obsolete, and the warring identities of the past will dissipate in the endlessly accelerating (and increasingly universal) process of production and consumption. This is the shared faith of the *Communist Manifesto* and Thomas Friedman.

It was this dream of a "post-political world"—perhaps first articulated by Benjamin Constant in his 1819 lecture "The Liberty of the Ancients Compared with that of the Moderns"—that Carl Schmitt memorably savaged in his *Concept of the Political* (1932). Schmitt asserted that the heart of liberalism was a set of thoroughgoing "depoliticalizations," the ultimate goal of which was to create a world in which the political association would be merely one association among many. Technology, economic integration, and global markets would reduce the political community to the status of a tenement building in which "citizens" come and go, tending to their disparate affairs minus any essential connection whatsoever.[17] Against this archetypally "liberal" dream, Schmitt vehemently asserted the autonomy and irreducibility of the political.

However desirable the liberal vision of a "depoliticized" world might seem to some, Schmitt argued that it rested on a crucial blindness and on what was, at bottom, a logical impossibility. The political association could never really subside to the status of "one association amongst many," since the political association was predicated upon—indeed, defined by—the *jus belli*: the right to make the decision as to who is a friend and who is an enemy. With this right—traditionally, the right of the sovereign European nation-state—comes the power "over the physical life of men," a power that effectively makes the political association existentially supreme over all others. As long as the possibility of conflict remains, the political association retains this priority, however much it may have retreated in everyday life. Only on a "completely pacified globe"—one from which the distinction between friend and enemy had been truly eradicated—would it be possible to claim that the political association was merely one association among many, the humble servant of an array of economic and social interests.

From Schmitt's point of view, such a world (if ever it could be achieved) would be lacking in existential depth and meaning. It would be a world from which both authentic identity and community had been expunged. After all—and this is Schmitt's essential argument—the identity of every "we" depends crucially upon the presence (or possibility) of enemies; upon the existence of some "other" that either is, or can be judged to be, a threat to "our" way of life. The elimination of the possibility of enemies logically demands the creation of global government—a dictatorship of global technological integration, if you will.[18] However, as long as there are distinct communities or particular identities—as long as the political world remains a "pluriverse" and not a universe[19]—the possibility of the "intensification" of the friend/enemy distinction (the defining distinction of "the political") remains. In Schmitt's view, this ever-present possibility simultaneously haunts and mocks the liberal dream of a "totally depoliticalized" world.

Schmitt's argument for the priority and autonomy of the political—a sphere of life that cannot be reduced to the social, the economic, or the moral—bears more than a passing resemblance to Arendt's. Both Arendt and Schmitt wage war on the ascendent tendency of liberal modernity: the tendency to make the political realm an appendage of society and economics. In order to fight this tendency, they each try to demonstrate that the life of political action, or that of the political association, is existentially supreme. A life devoid of a robust political dimension is, to use Arendt's phrase, "dead to the world." It cannot claim to be a fully *human* life. According to both Arendt and Schmitt, the "sublimation of the political" performed by liberal modernity is tantamount to the sublimation of our true humanity.

This broad agreement raises a very uncomfortable question. Is Hannah Arendt, with her exaggerated fear of the social and her disdain for economism, merely (as one prominent scholar once put it to me) "Carl Schmitt in drag"? Insofar as Arendt and Schmitt both assert the autonomy of the political they are, indeed, engaged in parallel projects. The similarity, however, ends there. The core of Schmitt's idea of the political is, of course, the concept of sovereignty, a concept Arendt definitively (and repeatedly) repudiates. It is not simply that she—like the American founders and Tocqueville—worried about the centralization of power and the tension between the idea of the sovereign state and constitutional government. Her objection goes much deeper, and penetrates to the roots of the Western tradition of political thought itself. As Arendt reminds us, what that tradition denied—in its concepts of sovereignty and rulership, patriotism and authority—was the politically all-important fact of human plurality.

We can see—with Arendt's help—the Western tradition as struggling, from Plato and Aristotle down, to find ways to efface the dimension of human plurality—of diverse and talkative equals—from our conception of political community. Such a plurality of individuals necessarily entails an array of conflicting opinions on what constitutes the public good. This, in turn, gives public life the cast of a perpetual argument about ends as well as means. Repelled by such a prospect, many (if not all) of the canonical theorists present the political association as something more like a family, a school, an army, or a corporation. From Arendt's perspective, all these metaphors have an explicitly anti-political intent. They are deployed to make us think that the heart of political association is found in the concept of rule, or in some putatively "natural" relation of authority and obedience. Thus, the paradigmatically political relationship of speech and persuasion between diverse equals is replaced by the hierarchical relationship between rulers and ruled, teachers and taught, managers and employees, commanders and patriotic citizen-soldiers.

With the idea of rulership comes the idea of a commanding will: the so-called "sovereign will" of the monarch, the aristoi, or even the people themselves. The point about the "sovereign will"—as Hobbes emphasized and as Arendt entirely agrees—is that it is always unitary, no matter how many (or how few) people are actually vested with "sovereign power" in a given form of government. Thus, Arendt is as repelled by Rousseau's General Will—an active version of a popular sovereignty that sees dissent as a "mistake"—as she is by Plato's philosopher-kings or Hobbes's Leviathan.

Always and everywhere, the tendency to erect "One man of gigantic dimensions"—a unanimous or harmonious "we" from which disagreement, debate, and dissent have been largely expunged—is operative.

The idea of community that haunts the Western tradition, then, is one that repeatedly sacrifices the fact of human plurality on the altar of unity, wholeness, or oneness. It is an idea of political community that is not, in Arendt's view, political at all. A political community is precisely a "community without unity." It is an association of diverse equals whose shared care for the public world takes the form of intense and open-ended debate, deliberation, and decision. What is at stake in these political discussions and decisions is the best way to "preserve and augment" the space of public freedom these citizens have either constructed or inherited.

The image of the political life we find in Arendt, then, is the furthest thing imaginable from what we find in Schmitt. It is decidedly not the collective banging of spears on shields that happens when we confront an "other" who seems to threaten us and "our way of life." Rather, the political life is a life of talk and argument, a life that takes place in a public space that is—at least in principle—open to all. It is this space—and the institutions and laws that articulate it—that we have in common. Not our identity, not our "values," not our religion, and not our material interests. The object of our political speech is the set of policies, institutions, and laws that mark out and structure this sphere, this durable "space of freedom." As citizens, we actively and discursively care for this world, this space, this realm: the public.

Plurality, not sovereignty, is the precondition of the political world. To uproot it or make it superfluous—as all manner of authoritarian, totalitarian, and class-dominated politics have tried to do—is to create a world without the possibility of authentic politics. For authentic politics—and however unfashionable, the phrase is unavoidable with Arendt—is possible only where diverse perspectives on a common world have a durable and institutionalized space for their free play. We know that our public sphere is healthy when, first, everyone who wants to be a "participator in government" can in fact have access to it; and second, when the talk that takes place there is viewed not as mere *bavardage* or spin, but as the one of the chief and most valuable expressions of public liberty.

We are, of course, far from Arendt's utopia of ongoing, care-full, political talk. Our political talk is cheap, ideology-laden, and (more often than not) aimed at the lowest common denominator. The response of any cynical freshman is to say that political speech was always thus, and that to hope for the concrete realization of public freedom *in speech and action* is to court disappointment and disillusionment. Political speech rarely reaches to heroic or truly edifying heights. Even Thucydides knew that Pericles—with his unique combination of idealism, practical wisdom, and rhetorical virtuosity—was one in a million.

To look at the matter this way—to see Hannah Arendt as celebrating "great words and deeds on a public stage"—is to confuse her with the plague of "edifying" historians and political biographers we have had to endure for the last twenty years. Arendt is no Garry Wills, nor is she David McCullough or (heaven forbid) Doris Kearns Goodwin. While she admires the speeches in Thucydides and the debates of the founders, she admires them for their spirit and devotion to "the public thing"—not for the character, idiosyncrasies, or style of the men who spoke them. What those speeches were about was the creation, preservation, or augmentation of spaces of positive, public liberty.

Authentic political speech—especially the kind that alerts us to threats to the freedom and durability of our public world—is the enactment of public freedom, its "preservation and augmentation." At a time when our public world is under attack by an array of economic, technological, and ideological forces (to say nothing of the cabal of unwitting Schmittians currently occupying the executive branch), it is important to realize that "care for the public world" is the furthest thing from a "leisure-time sport for aristocrats." It is, it turns out, a responsibility we all share; a responsibility that grows heavier each day as the boundaries of our public world—and the attention span of many of our fellow citizens—perpetually contracts.

NOTES

1 | Introduction: Public Freedom Today

1. See Isaiah Berlin's classic essay "Two Concepts of Liberty" in Berlin, *Liberty*, ed. Henry Hardy (Oxford: Oxford University Press, 2002). While the early sections of Berlin's essay clearly present the contrast between "negative" and "positive" liberty (liberty as freedom from interference vs. the liberty to be autonomous or genuinely self-directed), and the middle sections trace how a Kantian or individualist idea of autonomy can easily morph into something collective and proto-totalitarian, the fact that Berlin hardly intended his contrast to be exhaustive is often overlooked. In referring to public liberty as a "positive" form of freedom, I am not appealing so much to Berlin's discussion as to Hannah Arendt's in *On Revolution* (New York: Penguin, 1990), pp. 31–33. Cf. also Hannah Arendt, "What is Freedom?" in Arendt, *Between Past and Future: Eight Exercises in Political Thought* (New York: Penguin, 1968), especially pp. 145–146.

2. See Machiavelli, *Discourses on the First Ten Books of Titus Livius,* in *The Portable Machiavelli,* ed. Peter Bondanella and Mark Musa (New York: Penguin, 1979), especially book 1, chap. 11 (on the civil religion of the Romans), and book 2, chaps. 15–18, 49 and 54 (on the republic as a "structure of virtue" and the role the military plays in staving off corruption). See also J. G. A. Pocock's illuminating discussion of Machiavelli's understanding of the "sociology of liberty"— the social preconditions for civic virtue and patriotic citizens—in his *The Machiavellian Moment: Florentine Political Thought and the Atlantic Republican Tradition* (Princeton: Princeton University Press, 1975), chap. 7, especially pp. 196–204. For Rousseau's image of the peasants, see *The Social Contract* in *Jean-Jacques Rousseau: Political Writings*, ed. and trans. Frederick Watkins (Madison: University of Wisconsin Press, 1986), book 4, chap.1.

3. See Pocock, *The Machiavellian Moment*, which (in many respects) corrected the overly sanguine picture presented by Louis Hartz in his *The Liberal Tradition in America* (New York: Harcourt, Brace and World, 1955).

4. Benjamin Constant, "The Liberty of the Ancients Compared with That of the Moderns," in Constant, *Political Writings*, ed. Biancamaria Fontana (Cambridge: Cambridge University Press, 1988), pp. 308–328.

5. Ibid., pp. 310–311.

6. Ibid., p. 311.

7. Ibid., p. 316.

8. Of course, as the recent "war on terror" has amply demonstrated, *with* the excuse of war all bets are off. Even *habeas corpus*, the foundation of every civilized government from the thirteenth century onward, has become fodder for the anti-liberal fearmongers of today.

9. Constant, *Political Writings*, p. 326.

10. Ibid., p. 323.

11. See Jürgen Habermas, *The Structural Transformation of the Public Sphere*, trans. Thomas Burger (Cambridge, Mass.: MIT Press, 1989), and my discussion in chap. 6 of this volume.

12. Constant, *Political Writings*, p. 313.

13. See chap. 3 of this volume.

14. Alexis de Tocqueville, *Democracy in America*, vol. 2, ed. Phillips Bradley, trans. Henry Reeve (New York: Vintage, 1990), pp. 298, 304, 318 (hereafter cited as *DAII*).

15. Ibid., p. 141.

16. See Louis Uchitelle's *The Disposable American* (New York: Knopf, 2006).

17. Uchitelle cites the figure of 30 million layoffs since the 1980s.

18. See *DAII*, book 2, chaps. 2–7. See also chap. 2 in this volume.

19. *DAII*, p. 159.

20. Ibid., p. 319.

21. See Charles-Louis Secondat Baron de Montesquieu, *The Spirit of the Laws*, trans. Anne Cohler, Basia Miller, and Harold Stone (Cambridge: Cambridge University Press, 1989), book 3.

22. Immanuel Kant, "What is Enlightenment?," in *Kant's Political Writings*, ed. Hans Reiss (Cambridge: Cambridge University Press, 1970), pp. 54–60.

23. *DAII*, p. 318.

24. See Robert Dahl's classic study, *Who Governs?* (New Haven: Yale University Press, 1963).

25. As I have remarked elsewhere, the extent of Arendt's Graecophilia have been grossly exaggerated by her critics, the better to dismiss her groundbreaking political theory as an exercise in nostalgia and nothing more.

26. By the phrase "higher levels of generality" I mean not a testing for "universalizability" of the sort Kant, Rousseau, and Habermas all advocate (in separate but related ways). I mean, instead, the gradual education of interests to a less parochial, and less grotesquely self-interested, perspective on public affairs. Such education—which occurs through a variety of avenues, including civil

society, political participation, the attentive reading of newspapers, and so on—does not lead to anything like a unitary interpretation of the "common good." Rather, it creates a plane of genuinely political discourse, one in which there is a clash of interpretations about the public good, and not just a struggle of naked interests. See my discussion in chapter 6 in this volume.

27. Karl Marx, "On the Jewish Question," in *The Marx-Engels Reader,* ed. Robert Tucker (New York: Norton, 1978), p. 34.

28. *DAII*, p. 142. See chap. 3 below.

29. See Marx, "On the Jewish Question," pp. 41–43.

30. These criticisms of the "Rights of Man" were anticipated by F. H. Jacobi's *Zugabe an Erhard O———*. See Frederick Beiser's analysis in his *Enlightenment, Revolution, and Romanticism: The Genesis of Modern German Political Thought, 1790–1800* (Cambridge, Mass.: Harvard University Press, 1992), p. 151.

31. See Shlomo Avineri's discussion in his *The Social and Political Thought of Karl Marx* (Cambridge: Cambridge University Press, 1968), chap. 3.

32. Marx, "On the Jewish Question," p. 43.

33. See, in this regard, Marx's extraordinarily detailed and lengthy attack on Hegel's idea of mediation through public institutions in Karl Marx, *Critique of Hegel's Philosophy of Right*, ed. and trans. Joseph O'Malley (Cambridge: Cambridge University Press, 1970).

34. Marx, "On the Jewish Question," p. 45.

35. See Sheldon Wolin, "Democracy and the Welfare State: Theoretical Connections between *Staatsrason* and *Wohlfahrtsstaatsrason*," in *The Presence of the Past* (Baltimore: Johns Hopkins University Press, 1990), pp. 151–179.

36. For Hannah Arendt's strong assertion of the autonomy of the political—and its disturbing resonance with Carl Schmitt's parallel project—see chap. 10 of this volume.

37. Constant, *Political Writings*, p. 328.

38. See Machiavelli, *Discourses*, book 1; Rousseau, *Social Contract*, book 4.

39. Machiavelli, *Discourses*, book 1, chaps. 17–18.

40. See Rousseau, *Social Contract*, book 3, chap. 15.

41. Constant, *Political Writings*, p. 326.

42. Ibid.

43. *DAII*, p. 141.

44. G. W. F. Hegel, *Elements of the Philosophy of Right*, ed. Allen Wood, trans. H. B. Nisbet (Cambridge: Cambridge University Press), sec. 311.

45. See chaps. 2 and 5 below.

46. J. S. Mill, *Considerations on Representative Government*, in Mill, *On Liberty and Other Essays*, ed. John Gray (Oxford: Oxford University Press, 1998), pp. 254–255.

47. See chap. 5, below, and chap. 2 of my *Socratic Citizenship* (Princeton: Princeton University Press, 2001).

48. See my discussion of Tocqueville's political conception of civil society in chap. 2.

49. Michael Hardt and Antonio Negri, *Multitude: War and Democracy in the Age of Empire* (New York: Penguin, 2006).

50. See chap. 8 below.

51. See Foucault's comparison of Bentham and Rousseau in "The Eye of Power," in Michel Foucault, *Power/Knowledge*, ed. Colin Gordon (New York: Pantheon, 1980), pp. 146–165.

52. Ibid., p. 156. Cf. Michel Foucault, *Discipline and Punish*, trans. Alan Sheridan (New York: Pantheon, 1979), p. 222.

53. The founders, after all, were intent on finding a way out of—or around—the logic of the "sovereign state" as it had developed in early modern Europe, a logic theoretically articulated by Hobbes and Bodin.

54. This passage was written prior to the congressional elections of November 2006.

55. Mill, "Considerations on Representative Government," in *On Liberty and Other Essays*, p. 207.

56. This is how it sometimes appears in the work of Hannah Arendt. See, for example, her *On Revolution*, pp. 234–238.

57. Locke's status as a "proto-liberal" is due, in part, to his lack of a theory of citizenship and his acceptance of a largely virtual form of representation. Thus, while chap. 19 of his *Second Treatise on Government* famously invests the people with the right to judge when a government has "betrayed the trust" and exercised political power in way destructive to lives, rights, and properties, it has next to nothing to say about how such a judgment is arrived at, or how a people wielding such a power actually acts collectively to contain the "rebellion" of its magistrates. See John Locke, *Two Treatises of Government*, ed. Peter Laslett (Cambridge: Cambridge University Press, 1988), pp. 426–429. The implied "self-evidence" of when a government employs "force without authority" is carried over into the rhetoric of the American Declaration of Independence, even though that document is careful to contain a long list of the various "abuses and prevarications" committed by the government of George III.

2 | Tocqueville and Civil Society

1. See Peter L. Berger and Richard John Neuhaus, "To Empower People: From State to Civil Society" in *The Essential Civil Society Reader,* ed. Don Eberly (Lanham, Md.: Rowman and Littlefield, 2000), pp. 143–181.

2. See Michael Walzer, "The Civil Society Argument," in *Theorizing Citizenship,* ed. Ronald Beiner (Albany: State University of New York Press, 1995), p. 163.

3. See Jean Cohen and Andrew Arato, *Civil Society and Political Theory* (Cambridge, Mass.: MIT Press, 1992), chap. 1.

4. For a concise critique of the American debate, see John Ehrenberg, *Civil Society: The Critical History of an Idea* (New York: New York University Press, 1999), chaps. 8 and 9.

5. On the topic of the role and value of voluntary association in American life, see Amy Gutmann, ed., *Freedom of Association* (Princeton: Princeton University

Press, 1998), and Nancy Rosenblum, *Membership and Morals* (Princeton: Princeton University Press, 1997).

6. See the discussion in Larry Siedentop's *Tocqueville* (Oxford: Oxford University Press, 1994), chap. 2.

7. See Ehrenberg, *Civil Society*, p. 169.

8. G. W. F. Hegel, *Elements of the Philosophy of Right*, trans. H. B. Nisbet (Cambridge: Cambridge University Press, 1991), addition to sec. 182.

9. John Locke, *Two Treatises of Government*, ed. Peter Laslett (Cambridge: Cambridge University Press, 1988), sec. 87.

10. Ibid., sec. 89.

11. See Peter Laslett's introduction to *Two Treatises*, pp. 113–115.

12. Locke, *Two Treatises*, sec. 222.

13. See Ehrenberg, *Civil Society*, chap. 4.

14. See Jean-Jacques Rousseau, *The Social Contract* in *Political Writings*, trans. and ed. Frederick Watkins (Madison: University of Wisconsin Press, 1986), book 2, chaps. 3–4. Cf. Lucio Colletti, "Rousseau as a Critic of Civil Society," in *From Rousseau to Lenin* (New York: Monthly Review Press, 1971).

15. Jürgen Habermas, *The Structural Transformation of the Public Sphere*, trans. Thomas Burger (Cambridge, Mass.: MIT Press, 1989).

16. Immanuel Kant, "An Answer to the Question, 'What is Enlightenment,'" in Kant, *Political Writings*, ed. Hans Riess (Cambridge: Cambridge University Press, 1970).

17. Hegel, *Elements of the Philosophy of Right*, sec. 183.

18. Ibid., secs. 184, 238–246, 289.

19. Ibid., secs. 195, 241; addition to 244.

20. Ibid., secs. 187, 289. See Cohen and Arato, *Civil Society and Political Theory*, chap. 2.

21. Hegel, *Elements of the Philosophy of Right*, secs. 207, 253–256.

22. See Z. A. Pelczynski, "The Hegelian Conception of the State," in *Hegel's Political Philosophy: Problems and Perspectives* (Cambridge: Cambridge University Press, 1971), p. 23.

23. Hegel, *Elements of the Philosophy of Right*, secs. 290 and 302.

24. See Jean-Jacques Rousseau, "Discourse on the Origin of Inequality" in Rousseau, *Discourses*, ed. and trans. Roger Masters (New York: St. Martin's Press, 1964). As for Hegel, he retained the distinction between *bourgeois* and *citoyen*, albeit in much softened form. This was made possible, in part, by the dual sense of the adjective *bürgerliche* in German, which has the connotations of both civil or civic (on the one hand) and middle-class or bourgeois (on the other). Hence, for Hegel, the term "civil society"—*bürgerliche Gesellschaft*—already contained individualist and "civic" elements.

25. See, however, Siedentop, *Tocqueville*, p. 58.

26. G. W. F. Hegel, *Vernunft in der Geschichte*, ed. J. Hoffmeister (Hamburg, 1952), p. 207. See G. A. Kelly's essay "Hegel's America" in Kelly, *Hegel's Retreat from Eleusis* (Princeton: Princeton University Press, 1978), pp. 184– 223.

27. Tocqueville, *Democracy in America*, vol. 1, ed. Phillips Bradley, trans. Henry Reeve (New York: Vintage, 1990), author's introduction (hereafter cited as *DAI*).

28. A quote from *DAI* nicely captures this shift of terrain: "The political activity that pervades the United States must be seen in order to be understood. No sooner do you set foot upon American ground than you are stunned by a kind of tumult; a confused clamor is heard on every side, and a thousand simultaneous voices demand the satisfaction of their social wants. Everything is in motion around you; here the people of one quarter of a town are met to decide upon the building of a church; there the election of a representative is going on; a little farther, the delegates of a district are hastening to the town in order to consult upon some local improvements; in another place, the laborers of a village quit their plows to deliberate upon the project of a road or a public school." *DAI*, p. 249; Alexis de Tocqueville, *De la Démocratie en Amérique*, in *Oeuvres II, Bibliothèque de la Pléiade* (Paris: Éditions Gallimard, 1992) (one-volume edition, hereafter cited as *Pléiade*), p. 278.

29. *DAII*, p. 110; *Pléiade*, p. 625.

30. *DAII*, p. 106; *Pléiade*, p. 621.

31. See Siedentop's discussion in *Tocqueville*, pp. 76–77.

32. *DAI*, p. 191; *Pléiade*, p. 212.

33. *DAI*, p. 192; *Pléiade*, p. 213.

34. *DAII*, p. 106; *Pléiade*, p. 621.

35. See Roger Boesche's discussion in his *The Strange Liberalism of Alexis de Tocqueville* (Ithaca: Cornell University Press, 1987), p. 127.

36. *DAII*, p. 304; *Pléiade*, pp. 822–823. Cf. Alexis de Tocqueville, *ORR* (trans. Kahan), pp. 118–119.

37. *DAI*, p. 70; *Pléiade*, p. 77.

38. *DAI*, p. 61; *Pléiade*, p. 65. In *ORR*, Tocqueville traces the genealogy of the New England township back to the medieval parish. See Tocqueville, *ORR*, 1 (trans. Kahan), p. 129.

39. *DAI*, p. 40; *Pléiade*, p. 44.

40. *DAI*, pp. 55–58, 62; *Pléiade*, pp. 60–63, 67.

41. *DAI*, p.65; *Pléiade*, p. 71.

42. *DAI*, pp. 66, 72; *Pléiade*, pp. 72, 80.

43. *DAI*, p. 68; *Pléiade*, p. 75.

44. *DAI*, p. 299; *Pléiade*, p. 330.

45. *DAI*, p. 299. Cf. also p. 319; *Pléiade*, p. 354.

46. *DAI*, pp. 191–192; *Pléiade*, pp. 212–213.

47. *DAI*, p. 192; *Pléiade*, p. 214.

48. *DAI*, p. 194: *Pléiade*, p. 216. Of course, Tocqueville was hardly an enemy of political association in France or Europe generally. What he feared was the way governmental restrictions served to encourage the growth of demagogic "factions." Political association became "dangerous" when limits on press freedom and the franchise deprived it of its public or deliberative character and the experienced citizen body it demanded. Thus, the July monarchy only made matters worse by imposing such restrictions.

49. *DAII*, p. 106; *Pléiade*, p. 621.

50. *DAII*, p. 99; *Pléiade*, pp. 613–614.

51. *DAII*, pp. 98–99; *Pléiade*, p. 612.

52. See Siedentop, *Tocqueville*, p. 89.

53. See Pierre Manent, *Tocqueville and the Nature of Democracy* (Lanham, Md.: Rowman and Littlefield, 1996), p. 25.

54. *DAII*, p. 118; *Pléiade*, p. 633.

55. *DAII*, p. 104; *Pléiade*, p. 618.

56. *DAII*, p. 102; *Pléiade*, p. 616. I should note that, for Tocqueville, the line between "civil" and political associations is sometimes clear, sometimes not, given the "public" character of the ends often pursued by the former type of association. For a different reading of Tocqueville on associations, one that stresses the *continuity* between political and civil associations, see Boesche, *Strange Liberalism*, pp. 128–129.

57. *DAII*, p. 103; *Pléiade*, pp. 617–618.

58. The burden of Hobbes's *Leviathan* was, of course, to argue precisely for such a monopoly of judgment.

59. *DAII*, p. 319; *Pléiade*, p. 837. Cf. Boesche, *Strange Liberalism*, pp. 221–225.

60. See Siedentop's discussion, *Tocqueville,* pp. 22–23.

61. *DAII*, p. 116; *Pléiade*, p. 631.

62. *DAII*, p. 119; *Pléiade*, pp. 633–634. Cf. Tocqueville's verdict on the French in 1840, delivered in a letter to his mentor Royer-Collard: "I have never seen a country in which the first manifestation of public life, *which is the frequent contact of men among themselves*, is less to be found." *Oeuvres Complètes* (Paris: Gallimard, 1951-), vol. 11, p. 89.

63. See Alan Kahan, *Aristocratic Liberalism: The Social and Political Thought of Jacob Burckhardt, John Stuart Mill, and Alexis de Tocqueville* (New Brunswick, N.J.: Transaction Publishers, 2001), pp. 41–46.

64. *DAII*, p. 141; *Pléiade*, p. 653.

65. Ibid.

66. See *Recollections: The French Revolution of 1848*, ed. J.-P. Mayer and H. P. Kerr, trans. George Lawrence and Roger Boesche (New York: Anchor Books, 1971), pp. 5–6; *Alexis de Tocqueville: Selected Letters on Politics and Society,* ed. Roger Boesche, trans. Roger Boesche and James Taupin (Berkeley: University of California Press, 1985), p. 129. For Tocqueville's general attitude toward the antagonistic relationship between bourgeois "virtues" and political freedom, see the preface to *ORR* (trans. Kahan), pp. 3–4:

> People today are no longer attached to one another by any ties of caste, class, guild, or family, and are all too inclined to be preoccupied with their own private interests, too given to looking out for themselves alone and withdrawing into a narrow individualism where all public virtues are smothered. . . . In these kinds of societies, where nothing is fixed, everyone is constantly tormented by the fear of falling and by the ambition to rise. . . . Liberty alone can effectively combat the natural vices of

these kinds of societies and prevent them from sliding down the slippery slope where they find themselves. Only freedom can bring citizens out of the isolation in which the very independence of their circumstances has led them to live, can daily force them to mingle, to join together through the need to communicate with one another, persuade each other, and satisfy each other in the conduct of their common affairs. Only freedom can tear people from the worship of Mammon and the petty daily concerns of their personal affairs and teach them to always see and feel the nation above and beside them; only freedom can substitute higher and stronger passions for the love of material well-being, give rise to greater ambitions than the acquisition of a fortune, and create the atmosphere which allows one to see and judge human vices and virtues.

67. For an account of Tocqueville's distrust of the bourgeoisie, and his reservations about *laissez-faire* economics, see Boesche, *Strange Liberalism*, especially pp. 134–135.

68. *DAII*, p. 142; *Pléiade*, p. 655.

69. See especially *DAI*, pp. 242–243, 250; *Pléiade*, pp. 270–271, 279.

70. See the famous discussion in *DAII*, book 2, chap. 7. I should note that, in general, Tocqueville was much less sanguine about the possibility of private and public interest dovetailing (see the passage from *ORR* cited in note 66). The general tenor of his discussion of "self-interest, rightly understood" in *DA* is gently ironic: he thinks the Americans invoke self-interest even in the most unlikely times and places, as if a disinterested concern for the public good would somehow tell against them or invite the charge of hypocrisy.

71. See *DAII*, pp. 22–23; *Pléiade*, pp. 532–533.

72. See *DAI*, pp. 305–306; *Pléiade*, pp. 335–337. See also *DAII*, p. 22; *Pléiade*, p. 532.

73. Indeed, Tocqueville was well aware that respect for religion and devotion to family could, in the context of bourgeois life, be compatible with the complete abdication of public responsibilities and public life generally. See Boesche, *Strange Liberalism*, p. 87.

74. See Siedentop's discussion in *Tocqueville*, pp. 63–64. Docility and worldlessness have been the civic republican tradition's standard objections to Christianity. Variations on the theme are to be found in the work of Machiavelli, Rousseau, Hegel, and Arendt.

75. It is in the moralizing potential of political action and citizenship that Rousseau's influence is most strongly felt.

76. See *DAII*, p. 324; *Pléiade*, p. 843.

77. *DAII*, p. 112; *Pléiade*, p. 627.

78. Boesche is, however, right to question the assimilation of Tocqueville to the kind of liberal pluralism popular among social scientists in the 1950s and early 1960s. See *Strange Liberalism*, p. 128.

79. See Siedentop's illuminating discussion in *Tocqueville*, p. 83. For Hegel's pluralism, see Shlomo Avineri's *Hegel's Theory of the Modern State* (Cambridge: Cambridge University Press, 1972), pp. 161–175.

80. Despite the influence of Plato, it is important *not* to read this as a subsumption of society *by* the state; as the return to a pre-modern idea of "civil society" in which the social achieves integration and order only through a more comprehensive and inclusive *political* order.

81. This point engages Sheldon Wolin's charge that Tocqueville—in his conception of civil society and "intermediary organizations"—is guilty of *ancienneté*: a nostalgic anti-modernism that yearns for the lost world of aristocratic-feudal powers and "freedom." See Sheldon Wolin, *Tocqueville Between Two Worlds: The Making of a Political and Theoretical Life* (Princeton: Princeton University Press, 2001), pp. 450–453. It is important, however, to see that the "young" Tocqueville was capable of looking to the future as well as the past, and of transporting Montesquieu's basic conception into an altogether different terrain—that of modernity.

82. Hannah Arendt, *The Human Condition* (Chicago: University of Chicago Press, 1958); Richard Sennett, *The Fall of Public Man* (New York: Vintage, 1977).

83. See Habermas, *Structural Transformation of the Public Sphere*, chaps. 5 and 6.

84. *DAII*, p. 6.; *Pléiade*, pp. 516–517.

85. See, however, *DAII*, p. 22, where Tocqueville locates the "great utility" of religion in its ability to "inspire diametrically contrary principles" to the atomization, individualism, and love of material gratification promoted by a "democratic social condition."

86. *DAII*, p. 290; *Pléiade*, pp. 809–810.

87. G. W. F. Hegel, *The Phenomenology of Mind*, trans. J. B. Baillie (New York: Harper and Row, 1967), pp. 391–400. See Judith Shklar, *Freedom and Independence* (Cambridge: Cambridge University Press, 1976), chap. 3.

88. See *DAII*, chap. 15. As Cheryl Welch points out, there are some indications in *DAII* that Tocqueville would not be wholly surprised by the trajectory of modern American Protestantism. See her discussion in *De Tocqueville* (New York: Oxford University Press, 2001), pp. 95–101.

89. This alien quality is perhaps most compactly evident in Tocqueville's declaration (in *ORR*) that "whoever seeks for anything from freedom but itself is made for slavery" (p. 217). The notion of public freedom as an end in itself has an important twentieth-century echo in the work of Hannah Arendt. See chap. 10 of this volume.

90. See Benjamin Constant, "The Liberty of the Ancients Compared with That of the Moderns," in Constant, *Political Writings*, ed. Biancamaria Fontana (Cambridge: Cambridge University Press, 1988), pp. 309–328.

3 | Hegel, Tocqueville, and "Individualism"

1. G. W. F. Hegel, *Über die wissenschaftlichen Behandlungsarten des Naturrechts,* in Hegel, *Werke 2: Jenaer Schriften, 1801–1807* (Frankfurt: Suhrkamp Verlag, 1970); English translation in *Hegel: Political Writings*, ed. Laurance Dickey and H. B. Nisbet (Cambridge: Cambridge University Press, 1999), pp. 102–180.

2. See Steven Lukes, *Individualism* (Oxford: Basil Blackwell, 1973), for a concise analytical and historical survey of the various (moral, methodological, epistemological, and political) strands of "individualism."

3. G. W. F. Hegel, *Grundlinien der Philosophie des Rechts*, ed. Johannes Hoffmeister (Hamburg: Felix Meiner Verlag, 1995), addition to sec. 273; *Elements of the Philosophy of Right*, ed. Allen W. Wood and trans. H. B. Nisbet (Cambridge: Cambridge University Press, 1998), p. 312 (hereafter cited as *PR*).

4. It would, however, be hard to think of an eighteenth- or nineteenth-century philosopher more methodologically self-aware than Hegel.

5. See Judith Shklar, *Freedom and Independence: A Study of the Political Ideas of Hegel's 'Phenomenology of Mind'* (Cambridge: Cambridge University Press, 1976).

6. See Robert Fine, *Political Investigations: Hegel, Marx, Arendt* (New York: Routledge, 2001), p. 34.

7. Cf. Benjamin Constant, "On the Liberty of the Ancients Compared with That of the Moderns," in Constant, *Political Writings*, ed. Biancamaria Fontana (Cambridge: Cambridge University Press, 1988), pp. 309–328.

8. For the "civic humanist" reading of Hegel, see Dickey's introduction to *Hegel: Political Writings,* and Alan Patten, *Hegel's Idea of Freedom* (New York: Oxford University Press, 2001). While an important corrective to other, more metaphysical, readings of Hegel, the civic humanist interpretation has its limits, as Hegel's diverse criticisms of Rousseau and civic republicanism in *PR* make clear. See Georg Lukács, *The Young Hegel*, trans. Rodney Livingstone (Cambridge, Mass.: MIT Press, 1976), pp. 31–56.

9. At the end of the day, neither did Constant. See Constant, *Political Writings*, pp. 326–329.

10. Alexis de Tocqueville, *The Old Regime and the Revolution*, trans. Alan S. Kahan (Chicago: University of Chicago Press, 1998), p. 87 (hereafter cited as *ORR*).

11. Roger Boesche, *The Strange Liberalism of Alexis de Tocqueville* (Ithaca: Cornell University Press, 1987), p. 53.

12. Alexis de Tocqueville, *De la Démocratie en Amérique,* in *Oeuvres II, Bibliothèque de la Pléiade* (Paris: Éditions Gallimard, 1992) (one-volume edition, hereafter cited as *Pléiade*); *Democracy in America*, ed. Phillips Bradley, trans. Henry Reeve (New York: Vintage, 1990) (two-volume edition, hereafter cited as *DA*); see especially vol. 2, book 4, chap. 3 (p. 293).

13. *DA II*, p. 3; *Pléiade*, p. 513.

14. *DA II*, p. 99; *Pléiade*, p. 613.

15. *DA II*, pp. 129, 122; *Pléiade*, pp. 643, 635.

16. *DA II*, p. 99; *Pléiade*, p. 613.

17. Of course, Tocqueville admired the habit of self-reliance he found in the Americans, but largely because it inured them to the siren song of a tutelary state, one that ministered to all their needs, whether public or private.

18. *DA II*, p. 98 (my emphasis); *Pléiade*, p. 612.

19. *DA II*, p. 103; *Pléiade*, p. 617.

20. *DAII*, p. 104; *Pléiade*, p. 618.
21. See *DAII*, book 2, chap. 5 ("Of the Use Which the Americans Make of Public Associations in Civil Life").
22. See *DAI*, pp. 241–244, 250; *Pléiade* edition, pp. 269–272, 279.
23. *DAII*, p. 122; *Pléiade*, p. 635.
24. *DAII*, p. 122; *Pléiade*, p. 636.
25. *DAII*, p. 123; *Pléiade*, p. 637.
26. *DAII*, p. 122; *Pléiade*, p. 636.
27. *DAII*, p. 102. Tocqueville provides an explanation for this reductionism by noting the affection Americans have for simple, all-explaining general ideas.
28. *DAII*, p. 142; *Pléiade*, p. 655.
29. Ibid.
30. *DAI*, p. 250; *Pléiade*, p. 279.
31. *DAI*, p. 68; *DAII*, pp. 108–109.
32. *DAII*, p. 3; *Pléiade*, p. 513.
33. *DAII*, p. 4; *Pléiade*, p. 514.
34. *DAII*, pp. 10–11; *Pléiade*, pp. 520–521.
35. Ibid.
36. *DAI*, p. 263; *Pléiade*, pp. 292–293.
37. Tocqueville's chapter on the necessity of "dogmatic" beliefs (*DAII*, book 1, chap. 2) ends, however, by reiterating his concerns about the potentially "despotic" rule of "authoritative" public opinion.
38. *DAII*, pp. 5–6; *Pléiade*, pp. 515–516.
39. See *ORR*, pp. 196–208.
40. *DAII*, p. 11; *Pléiade*, p. 522. Tocqueville writes: "Thus, intellectual authority will be different, but it will not be diminished; and far from thinking it will disappear, I augur that it may readily acquire too much preponderance and confine the action of private judgment within narrow limits than are suited to either the greatness or the happiness of the human race."
41. See *DAI*, p. 300; also *DAII*, p. 21.
42. *DAII*, p. 22; *Pléiade*, pp. 532–533.
43. See Cheryl Welch, *De Tocqueville* (New York: Oxford University Press, 2001), p. 243. Cf. Larry Siedentop, *Tocqueville* (Oxford: Oxford University Press, 1994), p. 64.
44. *DAII*, p. 22; *Pléiade*, p. 532.
45. *DAI*, chap. 1, pp. 34–44: "Liberty regards religion as its companion in all its battles and its triumphs, as the cradle of its infancy and the divine source of its claims. It considers religion as the safeguard of morality, and morality as the best security of law and the surest pledge of the duration of freedom." (*Pléiade*, p. 48.) Cf. *ORR*, p. 206.
46. *DAI*, pp. 299–305. I should note that Tocqueville saw the potential tyranny of majority opinion as being contained, chiefly, by the spirit of American Christianity. See *DAI*, p. 305; *Pléiade*, p. 337.
47. *DAII*, p. 99; *Pléiade*, p. 613.
48. *DAII*, book 2, chaps. 5–7.

49. *DAII*, pp. 138, 263; *Pléiade*, pp. 650, 780–781. The (perhaps counterintuitive) case that Tocqueville presents a democratic form of *Sittlichkeit* is made by Albrecht Wellmer in his essay "Models of Freedom in the Modern World" in Wellmer, *Endgames*, trans. David Midgley (Cambridge, Mass.: MIT Press, 1998).

50. Georg Wilhelm Friedrich Hegel, *Die Vernunft in der Geschichte*, ed. Johannes Hoffmeister (Hamburg: Felix Meiner, 1955), p. 209; Hegel, *Lectures on the Philosophy of World History: Introduction*, trans. H. B. Nisbet (Cambridge: Cambridge University Press, 1975), p. 170. Tocqueville's initial impressions of America oddly coalesce with Hegel's. See his letter of June 9, 1831, to Ernest de Chabrol in *Alexis de Tocqueville: Selected Letters on Politics and Society* (Berkeley: University of California Press, 1985).

51. These functions compose, in part, the activity of the *polizei* in Hegel's conception of civil society.

52. *PR*, sec. 260. It is important to note at the outset Hegel's distinction between the *political* state (*der politische Staat* mentioned in sec. 267) and the state as ethical totality. The former comprised the legal apparatus, governmental powers, and coercive authority we normally identify with "the state," while the latter pointed to the collective ethical life of a specific, differentiated form of political community. See Pelczynski's essay "The Hegelian Conception of the State," in *Hegel's Political Philosophy: Problems and Perspectives*, ed. Z. A. Pelczynski (New York: Cambridge University Press, 1971), pp. 1–29.

53. *PR*, sec. 260 (my emphasis).

54. *DAII*, p. 319; *Pléiade*, p. 837.

55. This assessment has been made from the most diverse ideological standpoints. See, for example, Don Eberly, ed., *The Essential Civil Society Reader* (Lanham, Md.: Rowman and Littlefield, 2000), and Jean Cohen and Andrew Arato, *Civil Society and Political Theory* (Cambridge, Mass.: MIT Press, 1994).

56. In his Introduction to Hegel's *Political Writings*, Laurence Dickey presents Hegel as intensely committed to the principle of popular participation, if not self-government. This is a useful correct to the usual "statist" interpretations, but I think Allen Wood is more on target when he observes (in his editor's introduction to *PR*) that "Hegel plainly intends real political power to be in the hands neither of the prince nor of the people, but of an educated class of professional civil servants" (p. xxiv).

57. G. W. F. Hegel, *Political Writings*, ed. Zbigniew Pelczynski (Oxford: Oxford University Press, 1964), pp. 163–164.

58. Ibid. See p. 161, where Hegel writes of the ideal state in "recent theories": "A state is a machine with a single spring which imparts movement to all the rest of the infinite wheelwork." Cf. *PR*, sec. 303.

59. For the Tocqueville/Weber connection, see J. P. Mayer, *Alexis de Tocqueville* (New York: Harper and Brothers, 1960). For the Hegel/Weber connection, see Fred Dallmayr's essay "Max Weber and the Modern State," in *The Barbarism of Reason: Max Weber and the Twilight of Enlightenment*, ed. Asher Horowitz and Terry Maley (Toronto: University of Toronto Press, 1994), pp. 49–67.

60. *PR*, addition to sec. 290.

61. This characteristically "liberal" critique of Hegel is echoed by—of all people— Theodor Adorno in his *Negative Dialectics*, trans. E. B. Ashton (New York: Seabury Press, 1973), pp. 349–350.

62. See Hegel, *PR*, sec. 260. Here Hegel notes that the "concrete freedom" of the modern state requires that "personal individuality and its particular interests should reach their full development and gain recognition of their right." See also the additions to secs. 184, 185, 206, 261, 262, and 273 ("the principle of the modern world at large is freedom of subjectivity").

63. See Hegel's letter from November 1807 where he complains to his friend Niethammer that "so far we have seen that in all the imitations of the French only half the example is ever taken up. The other half, the noblest part, is left aside: liberty of the people; popular participation in elections; governmental decisions taken in full view of the people; or at least public exposition, for the insight of the people, of all the reasons behind such measures." In *Hegel: The Letters*, trans. Clark Butler and Christine Seiler (Bloomington: Indiana University Press, 1984), p. 151.

64. *PR*, addition to sec. 302.

65. Ibid., sec. 303.

66. Ibid., sec. 302. Cf. addition to sec. 290.

67. By "corporation" Hegel primarily meant trade or professional groups. However, he also included churches and municipal governments in this classification. See *PR*, secs. 250–256; 270 and 288.

68. *DAI*, pp. 64–71; *Pléiade*, pp. 70–75; see also *DAII*, pp. 103–104; *Pléiade*, pp. 617–618.

69. *DAII*, p. 104; *Pléiade*, p. 618.

70. See Siedentop's discussion in *Tocqueville*, pp. 66–67.

71. *PR*, sec. 261. For the speculative principle underlying this formulation, see *PR*, addition to sec. 270: "The state is actual, and actuality consists in the fact that the interest of the whole realizes itself through the particular ends. Actuality is always the unity of universality and particularity, the resolution of universality into particularity."

72. As Hegel writes in *PR*, sec. 187, the essence of "education" (*Bildung*) consists in the "elimination" of the "immediacy and individuality in which spirit is immersed, so that this externality may take on the rationality of which it is capable."

73. In the addition to sec. 255, Hegel says: "In our modern states, the citizens have only a limited share in the universal business of the state; but it is necessary to provide ethical man with a universal activity in addition to his private end. This universal [activity], which the modern state does not always offer him, can be found in the corporation." Cf. *PR*, addition to sec. 301, where Hegel expresses his dubiousness about the idea that the "people themselves" necessarily "know best what is in their own interest"; also sec. 309.

74. *PR*, secs. 309, 315, and 319.

75. Ibid., addition to sec. 279.

76. Hence the claims in the famous preface to *PR* about *comprehension* as the proper task of a *philosophical* approach to the state. Cf. additions to secs. 258, 268, and 270.

77. Shlomo Avineri, *Hegel's Theory of the Modern State* (Cambridge: Cambridge University Press, 1972), p. 102.

78. *PR*, sec. 279; see also secs. 308, 318.

79. Ibid., sec. 269.

80. Ibid., secs. 317 and 318.

81. Georg Wilhelm Friedrich Hegel, *Vorlesungen über die Geschichte der Philosophie I* (Frankfurt: Suhrkamp Verlag, 1971), pp. 442–443; *Lectures on the History of Philosophy*, vol. 1, trans. E. S. Haldane (Lincoln: University of Nebraska Press, 1995), p. 386.

82. Hegel, *Early Theological Writings*, pp. 157; 162–165 Cf. Hegel, *The Philosophy of History*, trans. J. Sibree (New York: Dover Books, 1956), p. 317.

83. Ibid., p. 157.

84. See Lukács, *Young Hegel*, pp. 9, 21–23.

85. See Charles Taylor, *Hegel and Modern Society* (Cambridge: Cambridge University Press, 1979), p. 90.

86. In sec. 273 of *PR*, Hegel makes both these points with respect to the constitution of the state. First, it is wrong to view a state's constitution as a product of a mere "aggregate" of individuals (the atomistic/social contract fallacy); second, that "the principle of the modern world" is "freedom of subjectivity," and that (therefore) any constitution that does not "sustain within itself" the principle of "free subjectivity" is "one-sided," defective.

87. For the first item on this list, see *PR*, addition to sec. 182; for the second, see *PR*, addition to sec. 270; for the third, see *PR*, preface.

88. See Shklar, *Freedom and Independence*, chap. 1.

89. See Jean-Claude Lamberti's discussion in his *Tocqueville and the Two Democracies*, trans. Arthur Goldhammer (Cambridge: Harvard University Press, 1985), pp. 57–58. That Hegel was not unaware of this "German" contribution—he loathed it—is made clear by his remarks about the German character and its "stubborn insistence on independence." See Hegel, "The German Constitution," in *Political Writings*, p. 57. Cf. Hegel, *Philosophy of History*, pp. 350–351 (on German "subjective freedom" as "self-will" or willfullness [*Eigensinn*]).

90. See *PR*, addition to sec. 150.

91. Hegel, *Die Vernunft in der Geschichte*, pp. 63–64; *Lectures on the Philosophy of World History*, p. 55.

92. Shklar's book emphasizes—rightly, I think—this dimension of the *Phenomenology*.

93. Hegel, *Die Vernunft in der Geschichte*, p. 76; *Lectures on the Philosophy of World History*, pp. 65–66. See also the well-known abuse Hegel directed at Fries in the preface to *PR* and the less well-known abuse he directs at Haller's *Restauration der Staatswissenschaften* in the note to *PR* sec. 258.

94. See Allen Wood, "Editor's Introduction," in *PR*, p. xvii.

95. Hegel, *Die Vernunft in der Geschichte*, p. 55: "Frei bin ich, wenn ich bei mir selbst bin"; *Lectures on the Philosophy of World History*, p. 48. See Allen Wood's discussion in his *Hegel's Ethical Thought* (Cambridge: Cambridge University Press, 1995), pp. 45–46.

96. G. W. F. Hegel, *Phänomenologie des Geistes*, ed. Johannes Hoffmeister (Hamburg: Felix Meiner Verlag, 1988), pp. 136–140 (Stoicism); 144–156 ("unhappy consciousness"); 157–163 (Cartesian rationality and egoism); 277–287 (Kantian morality); 379–384 (Enlightenment utilitarianism); 385–393 (Jacobin radicalism as "absolute freedom and terror"); *The Phenomenology of Mind*, trans. J. B. Baillie (New York: Harper and Row, 1967), pp. 242–246; 252–267; 273–280; 440–453; 594–600; 601–610.

97. Hegel, *Die Vernunft in der Geschichte*, p. 111; *Lectures on the Philosophy of World History*, p. 94.

98. See Wood's discussion in *Hegel's Ethical Thought*, p. 207.

99. See Taylor, *Hegel and Modern Society*, pp. 89–94.

100. Hegel, *Die Vernunft in der Geschichte*, pp. 48, 55–61, 66–67; *Lectures on the Philosophy of World History*, pp. 42, 48–53, 57–58.

101. See Taylor, *Hegel and Modern Society*, pp. 83, 91.

102. *PR*, addition to sec. 136.

103. Ibid., addition to sec. 138.

104. Ibid., preface, secs. 136–137.

105. See Wood, "Editor's Introduction," *PR*, p. xvi.

106. See Hegel, *Early Theological Writings*, pp. 69–75, 91–108, for his critique of "positivity."

107. *PR*, addition to sec. 261. Cf. note 112. Also Hegel, *Die Vernunft in der Geschichte*, p. 64; *Lectures on the Philosophy of World History*, p. 55.

108. As Hegel observes in *Die Vernunft in der Geschichte*, p. 64: "The substance of spirit is freedom. From this, we can infer that its end in the historical process is the freedom of the subject to follow its own conscience and morality, and to pursue and implement its own universal ends; it also implies that the subject has infinite value and that it must become conscious of its supremacy. The end of the world spirit is realized in substance through the freedom of each individual" (*Lectures on the Philosophy of World History*, p. 55).

109. See Wood, "Editor's Introduction," Hegel, *PR*, p. xiii.

110. Cf. Hegel's description of "liberalism" in *Philosophy of World History*, p. 452.

111. *PR*, preface, p. 17. See also Hegel, *Die Vernunft in der Geschichte*, p. 111; *Lectures on the Philosophy of World History: Introduction*, p. 93.

112. See Hegel's *Philosophy of Mind*, trans. William Wallace (Oxford: Oxford University Press, 1971), sec. 514: "But the person, *as an intelligent being*, feels the underlying essence [of the "spirit of the nation"] to be his own very being . . . looks upon it as his absolute final aim. In its actuality he sees not less an achieved present, but something he brings about by his own action."

113. See George Grote, *Plato and other Companions of Sokrates*, vol. 1 (London: Thoemmes Press, 1998), p. 303; Michael Walzer, *The Company of Critics* (New York: Basic, 1988), pp. 14–15.

114. See my discussion in Villa, *Socratic Citizenship* (Princeton: Princeton University Press, 2001), chap. 1.

115. The canard that Hegel was an apologist for the reactionary Prussian state of Frederick William IV goes back to Rudolf Haym's 1857 work, *Hegel und seine Zeit*. As Avineri points out, even Haym had to admit that "though Prussia was not yet a constitutional state" (Hegel's goal), it was "surely one of the relatively enlightened ones" amongst the European states after the final defeat of Napoleon. See Avineri, *Hegel's Theory of the Modern State*, pp. 115–116.

116. See Hegel's letter to K. F. Göschel, Dec. 13, 1830, in *Hegel: The Letters*, p. 544. Cf. Tocqueville's letter to Mme. de Circourt, cited by Mélonio and Furet in their introduction to *ORR*, p. 5.

117. See Boesche, *Strange Liberalism*, p. 139. As Boesche emphasizes, Tocqueville is quite critical of independence in this "English" sense—at least insofar as it lends itself to an ideology of privatism and self-interest. Cf. Tocqueville's statement, "There is nothing less independent than a free citizen" (cited by Furet and Mélonio in their introduction to *ORR*, p. 7). "Independent" here refers to the illusion of self-sufficiency or autonomy—the illusion fostered by *individualisme*.

118. *DAI*, chap. 12; *Pléiade*, vol. 1, part 2, chap.4.

119. *DAI*, pp. 194–195; *Pléiade*, p. 216.

120. *DAII*, p. 319; *Pléiade*, pp. 837–838.

121. See *DAII*, p. 318 (*Pléiade*, p. 837), where Tocqueville famously writes of the advent of "an immense and tutelary power, which takes upon itself alone to secure [men's] gratifications and to watch over their fate. That power is absolute, minute, regular, provident, and mild." This is Tocqueville at his most proto-Weberian and, indeed, proto-Foucaultian—a link I discuss at the beginning of chap. 9 of this volume.

122. See Alan Kahan, *Aristocratic Liberalism: The Social and Political Thought of Jacob Burckhardt, John Stuart Mill, and Alexis de Tocqueville* (New Brunswick, N.J.: Transaction, 2001).

123. Unlike some of his inheritors, Tocqueville's hopes for the future hinge on the Janus-faced nature of democratic equality itself. In chap. 1, book 4 of vol. 2 of *DA*, he tells us that "the principle of equality, which makes men independent of each other, gives them a taste for following in their private actions no other guide than their own will. This complete independence . . . tends to make them look upon all authority with a jealous eye and speedily suggests to them the notion and love of political freedom." Tocqueville concludes by stating, "Far from finding fault with equality because it inspires a spirit of independence, I praise it primarily for that very reason."

124. Hence Napoleon was always, for Hegel, a symbol of the progressive forces in history, whereas for Tocqueville the Empire supplied the basic model of "administrative despotism." Some of Foucault's most Tocquevillian pages are to be found in his characterization of Napoleon's significance for the emergence of a "disciplinary society." See Michel Foucault, *Discipline and Punish*, trans. Alan Sheridan (New York: Vintage, 1979), and chap. 8 of this volume.

125. See Otto Pöggeler, *Hegels Kritik der Romantik* (Munich: Wilhelm Fink Verlag, 1998), pp. 45–69. Of course, Hegel did appropriate the fundamental Romantic idea of self-actualization (the "expressive" subject), making it the cornerstone of both his metaphysics of *Geist* and his social and political philosophy. The importance of this appropriation provides the takeoff point for Charles Taylor's *Hegel* (Cambridge: Cambridge University Press, 1975), chap. 1, "Aims of a New Epoch."

126. *DAII*, p. 293; *Pléiade*, p. 812.

127. See Boesche, *Strange Liberalism*, chap. 11.

128. But not, of course, to Hegel the youth. See Lukacs, *The Young Hegel*, pp. 43–72.

129. *PR*, sec. 279.

130. See Tocqueville's letter to Eugène Stoffels (February 21, 1835), in Tocqueville, *Selected Letters*, pp. 98–99.

131. *DAI*, pp. 254, 260; *Pléiade*, pp. 282, 289.

132. *DAI*, pp. 195, 305; *Pléiade*, pp. 216, 338.

133. *DAI*, pp. 263–264; *Pléiade*, p. 293.

134. *DAI*, pp. 266–267; *Pléiade*, p. 296.

135. See Harvey Mansfield and Delba Winthrop's analysis in the introduction to their translation of *DA* (Chicago: University of Chicago Press, 2000), p. lxxi.

136. *DAII*, p. 11; *Pléiade*, p. 522.

137. *DAI*, pp. 242–243; *Pléiade*, p. 270.

138. *DAI*, p. 243; *Pléiade*, p.270. Cf. *PR*, addition to sec. 260: "Everything depends on the unity of the universal and the particular within the state." The rest of the addition, like *PR* generally, makes it clear that this is a *mediated* unity, quite unlike Rousseau's General Will.

139. See Tocqueville's explanation of what he means by *moeurs* in *DAI*, p. 299; *Pléiade*, p. 331. The priority of *moeurs* as a "cause" that helps maintain a "democratic republic" in the United States is never in doubt for Tocqueville—a fact well documented by Siedentop.

140. Tocqueville, quoted in Siedentop, *Tocqueville*, p. 49.

141. *DAII*, pp. 143–147, 149–150; *Pléiade*, pp. 657–658, 662–663.

142. *DAI*, p. 306; *Pléiade*, pp. 338–339. Cf. J. S. Mill, *On Liberty and Other Essays*, ed. John Gray (Oxford: Oxford University Press, 1998), pp. 34–35, where he condemns in no uncertain terms the court's "refusal of redress" to an unbeliever who had been robbed.

143. Mill, *On Liberty*, pp. 68–82.

144. See the passage from Pierre Paul Royer-Collard's article "On the Liberty of the Press," *Discours*, January 2, 1882 [cited in Siedentop, *Tocqueville*, p. 26].

145. Hannah Arendt, "Civil Disobedience," in *Crises of the Republic* (New York: Harcourt, Brace, Jovanovich, 1972), p. 92.

146. Taylor, *Hegel and Modern Society*, pp. 111, 125.

147. I borrow from Isaiah Berlin here. See his essay "The Originality of Machiavelli" in Berlin, *Against the Current: Essays in the History of Ideas*, ed. Henry Hardy (New York: Penguin 1979).

148. See Taylor, *Hegel and Modern Society*, pp. 112, 115, 118.

149. See Hegel, *Die Vernunft in der Geschichte*, p. 75; *Lectures on the Philosophy of World History*, p. 65.

150. The more exotic strands—Black Africans and native Americans—were ruthlessly enslaved or exterminated, as Tocqueville knew all too well. See *DAI*, chap. 18.

151. See Taylor, *Hegel and Modern Society*, p. 90.

152. Hegel, *Die Vernunft in der Geschichte*, p. 67; *Lectures on the Philosophy of World History*, p. 58. The whole idea of a *Volksgeist* that underlies and animates the "religion, ritual, ethics, customs, art, constitution and political laws—indeed the whole range of its [a nation's] institutions, events, and deeds" is there to convey a sense of the aesthetic/moral coherence of a "people's" spiritual creations.

153. See Max Weber, "Science as a Vocation," in *From Max Weber: Essays in Sociology*, ed. H. Gerth and C. Wright Mills (New York: Oxford University Press, 1958), p. 149.

154. This (highly Tocquevillian) account received its classic formulation in Hannah Arendt, *The Origins of Totalitarianism* (New York: Harcourt Brace, 1951), pp. 305–326.

155. See Taylor, *Hegel and Modern Society*, pp. 116–17; Michael Sandel, "The Procedural Republic and the Unencumbered Self," *Political Theory* 12, no. 1 (February 1984), pp. 81–97.

156. See Max Horkheimer and Theodor W. Adorno, *Dialectic of Enlightenment*, trans. Edmund Jephcott (Stanford: Stanford University Press, 2002), p. 97.

157. See Herbert Marcuse, *One-Dimensional Man* (Boston: Beacon Press, 1965).

158. Horkheimer and Adorno, *Dialectic of Enlightenment*, p. 94.

159. See Immanuel Kant, "An Answer to the Question: 'What is Enlightenment?'" in *Kant: Political Writings*, ed. Hans Reiss (New York: Cambridge University Press, 1970), pp. 54–60.

160. See Martin Heidegger, *Sein und Zeit* (Tübingen: Max Niemayer Verlag, 2001), sec. 38, "*Das Verfallen und die Geworfenheit.*" Cf. sec. 44.

4 | Tocqueville and Arendt: Public Freedom, Plurality, and the Preconditions of Liberty

1. See Jürgen Habermas, *The Structural Transformation of the Public Sphere*, trans. Thomas Burger (Cambridge, Mass.: MIT Press, 1989), pp. 27–43.

2. Ibid., pp. 89–108.

3. Ibid., pp. 102–107. See Immanuel Kant, "An Answer to the Question: What is Enlightenment?," in Kant, *Political Writings*, ed. H. S. Reiss (Cambridge: Cambridge University Press, 1970), pp. 54–60. See my discussion of Habermas in chap. 6 of this volume.

4. Hannah Arendt, *On Revolution* (New York: Penguin, 1990), p. 225 (hereafter cited as *OR*); Alexis de Tocqueville, *Democracy in America*, ed. Phillips Bradley, trans. Henry Reeve (New York: Vintage, 1990), vol. 1, pp. 258–261 (hereafter cited as *DA*).

5. *OR*, pp. 74–79; *DAI*, pp. 106–110; 322–330.

6. *DAII*, p. 147.

7. Ibid., pp. 121–124. Of course, Rousseau framed this distinction largely as a criticism of modern societies, arguing that we can be happy only as either fully *men* or *citizens*. As Rousseau puts it in "Le bonheur public": "What makes human miserable is the contradiction that exists between our situation and our desires, between our duties and our inclinations, between nature and social institutions, between man and citizen"

8. The phrase "private individuals appearing in public" comes from Habermas. In chaps. 5–8 of vol. 2 of *DA*, Tocqueville emphasizes the continuity between the energies that power political associations and those that give rise to business and social associations. Contrary to contemporary American civil society writers (e.g., Robert Putnam), he stresses how political associations serve as schools in which the art of association is learned, and from which a vibrant civil society is generated. See my discussion in chap. 2 of this volume.

9. Seyla Benhabib, *The Reluctant Modernism of Hannah Arendt* (Thousand Oaks, Calif.: Sage Publications, 1996), pp. 123–130.

10. *DAII*, book 2, chap. 7. See also note 8.

11. This is also the case with some of Tocqueville's British admirers. See, for example, Jack Lively's otherwise excellent *The Social and Political Thought of Alexis de Tocqueville* (Oxford: Oxford University Press, 1962), pp. 1–22.

12. For the contrast between "instrumental" accounts of political action and those (such as Arendt's) that treat action as intrinsically valuable, see my *Arendt and Heidegger: The Fate of the Political* (Princeton: Princeton University Press, 1996), chap. 1.

13. See, for example, Hannah Arendt, *The Human Condition* (Chicago: University of Chicago Press, 1958), pp. 38–46, on "the rise of the social" and the creation of a society of laborers and "jobholders," all subject to rule by bureaucracy.

14. *DAII*, book 2, chap. 1.

15. See *DAII*, book 2, chap. 3; and Hannah Arendt, *The Origins of Totalitarianism* (New York: Harcourt Brace, 1979), pp. 305–318.

16. As Larry Siedentop notes in his excellent short study, "By writing *Democracy in America*, Tocqueville attempted something extraordinary—the overturn of the established European idea of the state." See Siedentop, *Tocqueville* (New York: Oxford University Press, 1994), p. 41. See also Lively, *Social and Political Thought of Tocqueville*, pp. 143–182.

17. The most obvious convergence (already mentioned) is their joint emphasis on the importance of the townships. The widest divergence has to do with Arendt's overly pessimistic assessment of representative democracy, an assessment that leads her to resurrect Jefferson's ward proposal in the form of council government. See *OR*, pp. 235–239.

18. See Robert D. Putnam, *Bowling Alone* (New York: Simon and Schuster, 2000), and Peter L. Berger and Richard John Neuhaus, *To Empower People: From State to Civil Society* (Washington, D.C.: AEI Press, 1996), pp. 157–208. See also the writings collected in Don E. Eberly, ed., *The Essential Civil Society Reader* (Lanham, Md.: Rowman and Littlefield, 2000).

19. *DAII*, p. 115.
20. Ibid., p. 116.
21. See, for example, Arendt, *Human Condition*, pp. 188–192 (hereafter cited as *HC*); Arendt, *OR*, pp. 173–175; and Hannah Arendt, *Crises of the Republic* (New York: Harcourt Brace, 1972), pp. 94–97.
22. *DAII*, pp. 318–319.
23. Sheldon S. Wolin, *Tocqueville Between Two Worlds: The Making of a Political and Theoretical Life* (Princeton: Princeton University Press, 2001), p. 415.
24. See, in this regard, the author's preface to vol. 2 of *DA*.
25. *DAI*, p. 263.
26. *DAII*, p. 10.
27. *DAI*, p. 263.
28. Ibid., pp. 264–265.
29. Ibid., p. 263.
30. Habermas, *Structural Transformation*, sec. 15.
31. Thus Tocqueville could cite the court of Louis XIV as a veritable utopia of free speech compared to America, since the aristocrats were more than willing to have their vices aired in plays and books. See Tocqueville, *DAI*, p. 265.
32. The rapturous response to Robert Putnam's work on the decline of membership in contemporary America signals just how far the idea of individualism—construed as a kind of social disease—has wormed its way into the American imagination and public discourse. For some characteristic diagnoses of the "pathology" of individualism, see the essays collected in Eberly, *The Essential Civil Society Reader*, especially those by Nisbet, Bellah, and Elshtain.
33. *DAII*, p. 98.
34. Ibid.
35. Ibid. As Tocqueville notes, "Aristocracy had made a chain of all the members of the community, from the peasant to the king; democracy breaks that chain and severs every link of it" (*DAII*, p. 99).
36. Tocqueville's point here, both epistemologically and in terms of social ontology, is similar to Hegel's critique of "atomism" or "atomicity" in *The Philosophy of Right*. They both want to point out the fallacy of reducing moral and social life to the interactions of discrete, "unencumbered" selves. See my discussion in chap. 3 of this volume.
37. *DAII*, p. 98.
38. See Wolin, *Tocqueville Between Two Worlds*, p. 351. Tocqueville qualified his analysis of individualism in two significant ways. First, he noted the tendency of egalitarian isolation to be greatest in the transitional phases from an aristocratic to a democratic society—a transition the Americans had been spared. Second, because individualism is more of an epistemological than a moral shortcoming, it can be corrected by participation in public affairs: "As soon as a man begins to treat of public affairs in public, he begins to perceive that he is not so independent of his fellow men as he had at first imagined, and that in order to obtain their support he must often lend them his cooperation" (*DAII*, p. 102).

39. Tocqueville, *DAII*, p. 141. For a lucid analysis of Tocqueville's thoughts on how the "bourgeois" taste for material comfort undermines liberty, see Roger Boesche, "Tocqueville on the Tension Between Commerce and Citizenship," in *Tocqueville's Road Map: Methodology, Liberalism, Revolution and Despotism* (Lanham, Md.: Lexington Books, 2006), pp. 59–84.

40. Ibid., p. 142.

41. Ibid., book 1, chap. 5, which contains Tocqueville's most startling endorsement of "dogmatic belief"; see also book 2, chaps. 11, 15. See also *DAI*, p. 303.

42. See Cheryl Welch, *De Tocqueville* (New York: Oxford University Press, 2001), p. 243. Cf. Siedentop, *Tocqueville*, p. 64.

43. *DAI*, p. 305.

44. *DAII*, p. 147. I borrow the phrase "most basic political institution" from Siedentop, *Tocqueville*, p. 64.

45. *DAII*, book 2, chaps. 15 and 17.

46. Jean-Jacques Rousseau, *The Social Contract*, in Rousseau, *Political Writings*, trans. and ed. Frederick Watkins (Madison: University of Wisconsin Press, 1986), book 2, chap. 12. See Roger Boesche's discussion of the priority of mores in *Tocqueville's Road Map*, pp. 7–8, 97–101, 117–119. Cf. the important discussion of the same topic in George Armstrong Kelly's *The Humane Comedy: Constant, Tocqueville, and French Liberalism* (New York: Cambridge University Press, 1992), pp. 46–55.

47. See Tocqueville, *DAI*, pp. 304–305: "Christianity, therefore, reigns without obstacle, by universal consent; the consequence is . . . that every principle of the moral world is fixed and determinate."

48. *OR*, pp. 166–172.

49. For a consideration of Arendt's critique of Christianity and an account of how her thought can "enrich" Christianity, see James W. Bernauer, S.J., "The Faith of Hannah Arendt: *Amor Mundi* and its Critique-Assimilation of Religious Experience," in *Amor Mundi: Explorations in the Faith and Thought of Hannah Arendt* ed. James Bernauer (Boston: Martinus Nijhoff, 1987).

50. The locus classicus of this argument is Arendt's essay "What Is Authority?" in Hannah Arendt, *Between Past and Future* (New York: Penguin, 1968). See my discussion in *Arendt and Heidegger: The Fate of the Political* (Princeton: Princeton University Press, 1996), pp. 157–165.

51. See especially Arendt's essay "Understanding and Politics" in Hannah Arendt, *Essays in Understanding, 1930–1954*, ed. Jerome Kohn (New York: Harcourt Brace, 1994) (hereafter cited as *EU*).

52. *EU*, pp. 315–316.

53. *OR*, pp. 117–119.

54. Ibid, p. 116, speaking of Montesquieu: "in short, *mores* and morality, which are so important for the life of society and so irrelevant for the body politic. . . ."

55. See Jeremy Waldron, "Arendt's Constitutional Politics," and Albrecht Wellmer, "Hannah Arendt on Revolution," both in *The Cambridge Companion to Hannah Arendt*, ed. Dana Villa (Cambridge: Cambridge University Press, 2000).

56. It also led some liberal theorists to dismiss the book. See, for example, Judith Shklar's characterization of *OR* as "this embarrassing book" in her essay "Hannah Arendt as Pariah" in Shklar, *Political Thought and Political Thinkers*, ed. Stanley Hoffman (Chicago: University of Chicago Press, 1998), p. 371.

57. *OR*, p. 218. For a consideration of the baneful effects of Arendt's overly "concretized" opposition of participatory and representative democracy, see Albrecht Wellmer, "Hannah Arendt on Revolution," in *Cambridge Companion to Hannah Arendt*.

58. *OR*, p. 224.

59. Ibid., p. 225 (my italics).

60. Ibid., pp. 225–226.

61. Ibid., p. 227.

62. Ibid., p. 228. For the centrality of the idea of human plurality in Arendt's thought, see *HC*, pp. 175–192. In many respects, Arendt's political thought is motivated by the desire to reinscribe the phenomenon of human plurality—a phenomenon she thinks Western political thought has assiduously covered over, from Plato to Marx—at the root of political thinking. See chap. 9 in this volume.

63. *OR*, p. 227.

64. Ibid., pp. 27–229. See also *HC*, pp. 57–58.

65. Arendt sees this instrumental attitude as bourgeois in origin, and highly destructive to the (relative) autonomy of the public-political realm in a republic. See especially Hannah Arendt, *The Origins of Totalitarianism*, pp. 135–147.

66. *OR*, pp. 74–78. See also Arendt, *Between Past and Future*, pp. 163–164.

67. Michael Sandel, *Democracy's Discontent* (Cambridge, Mass.: Harvard University. Press, 1996), p. 6.

68. See, for example, Arendt's critique of Aristotle in the essay "What Is Authority?" in Arendt, *Between Past and Future*, pp. 115–119.

69. *OR*, p. 93.

70. *HC*, pp. 57–58.

71. Pericles' Funeral Oration is testimony to one side of this individualism, as is Plato's *The Apology of Socrates*. For an analysis, see my *Socratic Citizenship* (Princeton: Princeton University Press, 2001), chap. 1.

72. See J. S. Mill, Review of Grote's *History of Greece*, in Mill, *Collected Works*, ed. J. M. Robson (Toronto: University of Toronto Press, 1978), vol. 11, pp. 324–325.

73. Margaret Canovan, "Politics as Culture," in Lewis Hinchman and Sandra Hinchman, eds., *Hannah Arendt: Critical Essays* (Albany: State University of New York Press, 1994), pp. 179–205.

74. Hannah Arendt, "The Crisis in Culture," in Arendt, *Between Past and Future*, p. 223.

75. It is this Arendtian thought that leads Richard Sennett to speak, despairingly, of the end of public life in his groundbreaking *The Fall of Public Man* (New York: W. W. Norton, 1992).

76. I have chap. 3 of *OR* in mind, which attempts to account for the mysterious shift from public to private happiness on the American scene. The shift must

seem mysterious for anyone who claims, as Arendt does, that the primary motivation of the Revolution was the desire for a new form of government and a new space of freedom. This pretty much brackets both economic interests and the "liberal" desire for limited government. Arendt accounts for the switch by noting the ambiguity—not to say confusion—in the minds of the founders themselves. Hence what she calls Jefferson's "slip of the pen" in the Declaration of Independence, in which the pursuit of public happiness—made possible by a new set of free institutions—is elided to "the pursuit of happiness." More controversially, she blames the waves of immigration from Europe during the nineteenth and early twentieth centuries for substituting the materialist ideals of the poor for the more noble political ideals of earlier (Anglo-) Americans.

77. *OR*, pp. 138–139.

78. Ibid., p. 158.

79. Ibid., p. 175.

80. Ibid., pp. 149–150. See also Arendt, "On Violence," in Hannah Arendt, *Crises of the Republic* (New York: Harcourt Brace, 1972), p. 143.

81. Arendt, "What Is Authority?," in *Between Past and Future*, p. 93.

82. Ibid., p. 97: "The source of authority in authoritarian government is always a force external and superior to its own power; it is always this source, the external force which transcends the political realm, from which the authorities derive their 'authority,' that is, their legitimacy, and against which their power can be checked."

83. *OR*, p. 206.

84. John Adams, quoted in *OR*, p. 146.

85. Ibid., p. 201.

86. Ibid.

87. Ibid., p. 199.

88. Arendt, "What Is Authority?," in *Between Past and Future*, p. 121. Cf. Friedrich Nietzsche, *On the Genealogy of Morals*, trans. Walter Kaufmann (New York: Vintage, 1989), essay 2, secs. 19–20.

89. Arendt, "What Is Authority?," p. 95.

90. Hence, Arendt begins her essay "What Is Authority?" by noting that "it might have been wiser to ask in the title: What was—and not what is—authority? For it is my contention that . . . authority has vanished from the modern world" (*Between Past and Future*, p. 91).

91. *OR*, p. 204. Arendt is weirdly close to both the Nietzsche of the *Untimely Meditations* and Sorel here (her categorial repudiation of Sorelian politics as violence notwithstanding).

92. Ibid.

93. Ibid., p. 213.

94. Ibid. Cf. Arendt, "Tradition and the Modern Age," *Between Past and Future*, p. 18.

95. Arendt's overall argument here is etymological and vaguely Heideggerian. She is playing on the double sense of the Greek word *archē*, which can mean both beginning *and* foundation.

96. See my discussion in chap. 6 of this volume.

97. See, for example, Amy Gutmann and Dennis Thompson, *Democracy and Disagreement* (Cambridge, Mass.: Harvard University Press, 1996).

5 | Maturity, Paternalism, and Democratic Education in J. S. Mill

1. Michel Foucault, "Two Lectures," in *Power/Knowledge* (New York: Pantheon, 1980), p. 98.

2. For a rehearsal of the relevant issues, see Charles Larmore's *The Morals of Modernity* (Cambridge: Cambridge University Press, 1996), chaps. 6 and 7.

3. J. S. Mill, "Utilitarianism," in *On Liberty and Other Essays*, ed. John Gray (Oxford: Oxford University Press, 1998), p. 140.

4. J. S. Mill, "On Liberty," in *On Liberty and Other Essays*, pp. 14–15 (my emphasis).

5. John Locke, *Two Treatises of Government*, ed. Peter Laslett (Cambridge: Cambridge University Press, 1988), secs. 54–61.

6. Ibid., sec. 60.

7. Mill, *On Liberty*, p. 15.

8. Indeed, even Mill's champions have seen this as proof of his eminent good sense. See, for example, Michael St. John Packe's *The Life of John Stuart Mill* (New York: Macmillan, 1954), p. 388. Writing of James and J. S. Mill's attitude toward India, and the role of the East India Company, St. Packe states that "they were convinced that in India, as in primitive communities of the ancient world, despotism was the only possible system for the time, and in this sense they believed the Company to be unrivaled. . . . They had faith in its record of systematic expansion, of slow and steady enlightenment, and in its long tradition of loyal service."

9. J. S. Mill, *Considerations on Representative Government*, in *On Liberty and Other Essays*, p. 233 (henceforth cited as *CRG*).

10. Ibid.

11. Ibid.

12. Immanuel Kant, "What is Enlightenment?," in Kant, *Political Writings*, ed. Hans Reiss (New York: Cambridge University Press, 1970), p. 54.

13. Ibid., pp. 56–57.

14. Ibid., p. 59.

15. J. S. Mill, "The Spirit of the Age," in Mill, *Essays on Politics and Culture*, ed. Gertrude Himmelfarb (Gloucester: Peter Smith, 1973), p. 23.

16. There is an obvious connection here to the hopes Mill had for a "science of ethology," one that discovered supposedly universal laws for the formation of character.

17. Mill, *CRG*, p. 202.

18. Ibid.

19. Mill, *On Liberty and Other Essays*, p. 71.

20. Ibid., p. 80.

21. Ibid.

22. Ibid., p. 78: "The greater part of the world has, properly speaking, no history, because the despotism of Custom is complete. This is the case over the whole East." This remark seemingly reinscribes the basic schema found in Hegel's *Lectures on the Philosophy of World History*, but—as I argue in the text—there is an all-important difference. For Hegel, Mill's point—that the West is gradually sliding toward a "despotism of Custom" much like the East—would have seemed a non sequitur, a judgment that failed to take account history as indeed the evolution of consciousness. Mill and Hegel's joint emphasis on the importance of *development/Bildung* (a concept Mill imbibed from Humboldt) tends to mask this crucial difference.

23. See Martin Heidegger, *Being and Time*, trans. John Macquarrie and Edward Robinson (New York: Harper and Row, 1962), secs. 35–37. Of course, Mill is careful to qualify the exact nature of the "fate" awaiting us: "If a similar change should befall the nations of Europe, it will not be in exactly the same shape: the despotism of custom with which these nations are threatened is not precisely stationariness" (*On Liberty and Other Essays*, p. 79). However that may be, the overall fear is surprisingly reminiscent of Heidegger.

24. See Alan S. Kahan, *Aristocratic Liberalism: The Social and Political Thought of Jacob Burckhardt, John Stuart Mill, and Alexis de Tocqueville* (New Brunswick, N.J.: Transaction Books, 2001), pp. 119–125.

25. Mill, *On Liberty and Other Essays*, p. 80.

26. Ibid., p. 72.

27. Ibid., p. 71. Since the 1960s, it has been *de rigueur* for leftist intellectuals to call for such "shock therapy" for the West. See, for example, Jacques Derrida's Vietnam War inspired call for a "radical trembling from the outside" is his famous May 1968 essay, "The Ends of Man," in Derrida, *Margins of Philosophy*, trans. Alan Bass (Chicago: University of Chicago Press, 1982), p. 134.

28. See G. W. F. Hegel, *Lectures on the Philosophy of World History: Introduction*, trans. H. B. Nisbet (Cambridge: Cambridge University Press, 1975), pp 58–61.

29. Ibid., p. 59.

30. Indeed, if Mill is close to anyone here, it is Max Weber and his gloomy assessment that "freedom of the individual" is radically and inevitably diminished by the dominant tendencies of (rationalized) modernity. See Max Weber, *Economy and Society*, ed. Guenther Roth and Claus Wittich (Berkeley: University of California Press, 1978), p. 1402.

31. For the recognition that every post-Enlightenment theory of politics rests on a "philosophy of history," see J. S. Mill, *Autobiography*, ed. John M. Robson (New York: Penguin, 1989), p. 130.

32. *CRG*, p. 207.

33. Ibid., pp. 207–208.

34. Ibid., p. 208.

35. Ibid.

36. Ibid.

37. Ibid., p. 210.

38. For a contrasting view, see E. P. Thompson's epic *The Making of the English Working Class* (New York: Vintage, 1966).

39. *CRG*, pp. 228–229.

40. Ibid., p. 232. Of course, the opposite of such "savage independence" is a people that has been enslaved for decades if not centuries. In this case, Mill notes, "a despotism, which may tame the savage, will, in so far as it is a despotism, only confirm the slaves in their incapacities. Yet a government under their own control would be entirely unmanageable by them. Their improvement cannot come from themselves, but must be superinduced from without. They have to be taught self-government, and this, in its initial stage, means the capacity to act on general instructions. What they require is not a government of force, but one of guidance." See *CRG*, p. 233.

41. Thus, chap. 1 of *On Liberty* is devoted to setting out the broad context of European-American political development, from tribal to feudal to early modern times. The point here is that the problem of the "tyranny of the majority"—whether political or social in character—is one that emerges relatively late on the scene, and at a relatively late stage of political development. Hence, the "principle of liberty" has relevance and application only when a number of preliminary stages have been passed through, and the abuse of popular will and majority opinion becomes a clear possibility of *modern* politics. In other words, Mill takes care to *historicize* the principle of liberty in *On Liberty*'s introductory chapter. For the stereotyping characterizations, see *CRG*, pp. 250–251.

42. Ibid., pp. 226–227.

43. Ibid., p. 229.

44. This should not be surprising, given how large the ideas of autonomy and self-development loom in Mill's political thought. Cf. Wilhelm von Humboldt, *The Limits of State Action*, ed. J. W. Burrows (Indianapolis: Liberty Fund, 1993), and Benjamin Constant, "The Liberty of the Ancients Compared with That of the Moderns," in Benjamin Constant, *Political Writings,* ed. Biancamaria Fontana (Cambridge: Cambridge University Press, 1988), p. 327.

45. *CRG*, p. 243.

46. See Judith Shklar's discussion of this problem in *Men and Citizens: A Study of Rousseau's Social Theory* (New York: Cambridge University Press, 1985).

47. Alexis de Tocqueville, *Democracy in America*, vol. 2, ed. Phillips Bradley, trans. Henry Reeve (New York: Vintage, 1990), pp. 102–105.

48. For Mill's evolving attitude toward the question of universal suffrage (which he once called "trash"), see J. H. Burns, "J. S. Mill and Democracy," in *Mill: A Collection of Critical Essays*, ed. J. B. Schneewind (Garden City, N.Y.: Doubleday, 1968).

49. A student of John Rawls once told me that Rawls himself found Mill's manner of writing insufferably elitist.

50. See Alan S. Kahan's fine work, *Aristocratic Liberalism*, chap. 5.

51. Although, to be sure, he was extraordinarily sensitive to the need for inclusion and *self*-representation of previously marginalized groups. See, for example, *CRG*, pp. 245–246.

52. Ibid., p. 111.

53. See Maurice Mandelbaum, *History, Man, and Reason: A Study in Nineteenth Century Thought* (Baltimore: Johns Hopkins University Press, 1974), and John M. Robson, *The Improvement of Mankind* (Toronto: University of Toronto Press, 1968).

54. *CRG*, p. 224.

55. Ibid., p. 208.

56. John Stuart Mill, *Autobiography*, ed. John M. Robson (New York: Penguin, 1989), pp. 111–118.

57. Ibid., pp. 130–131. Cf. J. S. Mill, "Coleridge," in Mill, *Essays on Politics and Culture*, ed. Gertrude Himmelfarb (Gloucester, Mass.: Peter Smith, 1973), especially pp. 141–147. See also Nicholas Capaldi, *John Stuart Mill: A Biography* (Cambridge: Cambridge University Press, 2004), p. 252. I should note that the mature Mill's psychology remained, on the whole, associationist and even "determinist" in a broad sense. See Mill, *System of Logic*, book 6, chap. 2. What we might call the "pendulum swing" in the other direction—against psychological determinism and passivity—is found in his *Examination of Sir William Hamilton's Philosophy*. Here the idea of autonomy or self-determination again comes to the fore. What Mill obviously never did was to argue, *à la* Kant, that autonomy or self-determination hinged on a human ability to overcome *all* inclination (or associations of pleasure, happiness, and so on) via the faculty of a "pure" practical reason and the motivation of duty alone. Both utilitarianism and romanticism, as well as Mill's unique synthesis of these two schools, rejected Kant's vision of a "radical" human freedom divorced from all determining ("heteronomous") considerations of happiness or fulfillment.

58. See Capaldi, *John Stuart Mill*, pp. 267–271.

59. See Frederick C. Beiser, *Enlightenment, Revolution, and Romanticism* (Cambridge, Mass.: Harvard University Press, 1992), pp. 128–134.

60. Mill, *On Liberty and Other Essays*, p. 14.

61. *CRG*, pp. 251–252.

62. Mill contrasts the envy of "Orientals" and "Southern Europeans" to the "self-helping and struggling" character of the "Anglo-Saxons." See *CRG*, pp. 250–251. For the paean to "energy," see Mill, *On Liberty and Other Essays*, pp. 66–67.

63. *CRG*, p. 238.

64. Ibid., pp. 240–241.

65. As Hannah Arendt reminds us, *idiotes* originally referred to a strictly private life, one with no public dimension. See Hannah Arendt, *The Human Condition* (Chicago: University of Chicago Press, 1958), sec. 7.

66. *CRG*, p. 244 (my emphasis).

67. Ibid.

68. See Isaiah Berlin's essay, "John Stuart Mill and the Ends of Man," in *Liberty*, ed. Henry Hardy (New York: Oxford University Press, 2002).

69. See Himmelfarb's "Introduction" to *Essay on Politics and Culture*. Cf. Burns, "J. S. Mill and Democracy," pp. 305–306.

70. J. S. Mill, "Tocqueville on Democracy in America (vol. 2)," in Mill, *Essays on Politics and Culture*, p. 230.

71. Ibid. (my emphasis).

72. *CRG*, p. 254.

73. Ibid., p. 255 (my emphasis).

74. They are, however, closer to the former than to the latter's military-pagan civic ideal. See, for example, Mill's praise of the Athenian *demos* in his review of George Grotes's *History of Greece* in *The Collected Works of John Stuart Mill*, vol. 11, ed. John M. Robson (Toronto: University of Toronto Press, 1978), pp. 316–317.

75. Alexis de Tocqueville, *Democracy in America*, vol. 1, ed. Phillips Bradley, trans. Henry Reeve (New York: Vintage, 1990), pp 30–31; 35; 39–40; 43–44 (hereafter cited as *DAI*).

76. See Sheldon Wolin, *Tocqueville Between Two Worlds* (Princeton: Princeton University Press, 2001), p. 227.

77. *CRG*, p. 327.

78. Ibid., p. 313.

79. Ibid., p. 328.

80. *DAI*, pp. 200–201.

81. *CRG*, p. 312.

82. Mill to Hare, quoted by R. J. Halliday in his *John Stuart Mill* (London: George Allen and Unwin, 1976), p. 135. See Mill's article "Recent Writers on Reform," in *Essays on Politics and Culture*, especially pp. 353–367.

83. Halliday, *John Stuart Mill*, p. 135.

84. *CRG*, p. 215.

85. See, for example, Mill's statement in the "The Spirit of the Age" (1831), in *Essays on Culture and Politics*, pp. 8–9: "The multitude are without a guide; and society is exposed to all the errors and dangers which are to be expected when persons who have never studied any branch of knowledge comprehensively and as a whole attempt to judge for themselves upon particular parts of it." And, as he says in the same essay: "Society may be said to be in its natural state, when worldly power, and moral influence, are habitually and undisputably exercised by the fittest persons whom the existing state of Society affords."

86. See Leo Strauss, "Liberal Education and Responsibility," in Strauss, *Liberalism Ancient and Modern* (Chicago: University of Chicago Press, 1995), p. 17. Strauss would not have been too far off if he had been addressing the younger, "conservative" Mill—the Mill of the essay on Coleridge and the 1840 review of Tocqueville, where the "tyranny of public opinion" and the resulting danger of "Chinese stationariness" loom quite large.

87. See Wolin, *Tocqueville Between Two Worlds*, pp. 375–377.

88. The phrase in quotation marks is from Mill, *On Liberty*, p. 75.

89. *CRG*, pp. 271–284. Mill devotes a good deal of space to arguing that not only is the work of public administration too specialized for elected representatives to do well, but so is the activity of legislation. The writing of laws, in his view, should be undertaken by cabinet members who make up a legislative commis-

sion. These draw up the laws, which would then be approved and enacted by Parliament and (more ceremonially) the constitutional monarch. The "proper function" of a representative assembly, consisting neither in administration nor legislation, would be criticism and control of the government. See *CRG*, pp. 282–283.

90. Mill, *On Liberty and Other Essays*, p. 74. It is interesting to compare this passage to Tocqueville's observations on who can be counted on to initiate new projects in aristocratic and democratic societies, respectively. See Tocqueville, *DAII*, p. 109. The absence of much substantive discussion of civil society in Mill—except, of course, when he is reviewing Tocqueville—is striking in this regard.

91. J. S. Mill, in the *Examiner*, July 4, 1832. Quoted in J. H. Burns, "J. S. Mill and Democracy, 1829–1861," p. 284. In a second article (July 15, 1832), the young Mill writes: "We know that the will of the people, even of the numerical majority, must be supreme . . . but in spite of that the test of what is right in politics is not the *will* of the people, but the *good* of the people, and our object is, not to compel but to persuade the people to impose, for the sake of their own good, some restraint on tn the immediate and unlimited exercise of their own will." Without such restraints on popular will, Mill thinks, "human weaknesses and passion" would turn representative democracy into a "mere mob government." The appeal to the "good of the people themselves" as justification for limitation of the democratic principle has a long history in paternalist, anti-democratic thought.

92. Mill, *Essays on Politics and Culture*, p. 195.

93. See J. S. Mill, *Dissertations and Discussions* (London: John W. Parker and Son, 1859), vol. 1, p. 470: "It is not necessary that the many should themselves be perfectly wise. . . . It is sufficient that they be aware, that the majority of political questions turn upon considerations of which they, and all persons not trained for the purpose, must necessarily be very imperfect judges; and that their judgment must in general be exercised rather upon the characters and talents of the persons whom they decide to appoint to decide these questions, than upon the questions themselves."

94. See *CRG*, pp. 315–316: "The great difficulty of democratic government has hitherto seemed to be, how to provide, in a democratic society, what circumstances have provided hitherto in all societies which have maintained themselves ahead of others—a social support, a *point d'appui*, for individual resistance to the tendencies of the ruling power; a protection, a rallying point, for opinions and interests which the ascendent public opinion views with disfavor." Hare's plural voting scheme, by ensuring the "instructed classes" *some* place in Parliament, would (in Mill's opinion) remedy this defect, and provide the following advantages: "A separate organization of the instructed classes, even if practicable, would be invidious, and could only escape from being offensive by being totally without influence. But if the *élite* of these classes formed part of the Parliament, by the same title as any other of its members . . . their presence could give umbrage to nobody, while they would be in the position of the

highest vantage, both for making their opinions and counsels heard on all important subjects, and for taking an active part in public business." In this way, "modern democracy would have its occasional Pericles, and its habitual group of superior and guiding minds."

95. Mill, *Essays on Politics and Culture*, p. 197 (note).

96. *CRG*, p. 284.

97. Ibid.

98. See Alan Ryan, *J. S. Mill* (London: Routledge, 1974), pp. 193–196. Cf. Mill's invocation of "the government of Prussia—a most powerfully and skillfully organized aristocracy of all the most highly educated men in the kingdom," in his 1835 *London Review* article (quoted in Burns, "J. S. Mill and Democracy," p. 292). As Burns points out, Mill imbibed the distinction between a *public* and an *administration* from the French author Charles Duveyrier, whose work he reviewed in 1846. The former is characterized by the interests of, and competition between, individuals and classes, while the latter has "the general interest" as its "supreme law." And this, as Burns rightly points out, mirrors what Hegel has to say about the professional bureaucracy of his "rational state" in the *Philosophy of Right*.

99. Mill, *On Liberty and Other Essays*, pp. 68–69.

100. See my discussion in Villa, *Socratic Citizenship* (Princeton: Princeton University Press, 2001), chap. 2.

101. Mill, *On Liberty and Other Essays*, p. 72.

102. Ibid., p. 74.

103. Ibid., p. 37.

104. Ibid., p. 39.

105. See Villa, *Socratic Citizenship*, chap. 2.

106. Mill, *Inaugural Address at St. Andrews*, quoted in Robson, *The Improvement of Mankind*, p. 197.

107. It is important to remember that universal manhood suffrage did not become a reality in England until after the First World War. See Michael Bentley, *Politics Without Democracy, 1815–1914* (Oxford: Blackwell, 1996).

108. Mill, "Recent Writers on Reform," quoted in Robson, *The Improvement of Mankind*, pp. 197–198.

109. *CRG*, p. 254. Cf. Cleon's speech castigating the Athenians for their reversal of policy in the Mytilenian debate in Thucydides, *History of the Peloponnesian War*, trans. Rex Warner (New York: Penguin, 1972), p. 220.

110. See, in this regard, M. I. Finley, "Leaders and Followers" in Finley, *Democracy Ancient and Modern* (New Brunswick, N.J.: Rutgers University Press, 1984), pp. 3–37.

111. Mill, *Logic*, in *Collected Works*, vol. 13, p. 864.

112. See Cass Sunstein's analysis in *Republic.com* (Princeton: Princeton University Press, 2002).

113. See Mill's comparison of the national political sphere, with its newspapers and railways, to the agora of the Greeks in *CRG*, p. 210.

114. For a comprehensive articulation, see George Kateb, "The Moral Distinctiveness of Representative Democracy" in Kateb, *The Inner Ocean* (Ithaca: Cornell University Press, 1994).

115. *CRG*, p. 207.
116. See Nadia Urbinati, *Mill on Democracy* (Chicago: University of Chicago Press, 2002), p. 10. Cf. Phillip Pettit, *Republicanism: A Theory of Freedom and Government* (New York: Oxford University Press, 1999, chaps. 1 and 2.
117. *CRG*, p. 228.
118. Ibid., p. 257.
119. The shocking results of a study of adult literacy in America (reported in a December 16, 2005, article by Sam Dillon in the *New York Times*) probably only reveal the tip of the iceberg concerning the decline of this absolutely essential capacity. Not only are roughly a third of Americans only minimally literate; the relative literacy of college graduates has also dropped precipitously.

6 | The Frankfurt School and the Public Sphere

1. Immanuel Kant, "An Answer to the Question: 'What is Enlightenment,'" in *Kant's Political Writings*, ed. Hans Reiss (New York: Cambridge University Press, 1970), p. 54.
2. Max Horkheimer, "Traditional and Critical Theory," in Horkheimer, *Critical Theory: Selected Essays*, trans. Matthew J. O'Connell et al. (New York: Continuum, 1986), pp. 225–229, 237. See Rolf Wiggerhaus, *The Frankfurt School: Its History, Theories, and Political Significance*, trans. Michael Robertson (Cambridge, Mass.: MIT Press, 1998).
3. See Karl Marx and Friedrich Engels, "The German Ideology," in *The Marx-Engels Reader*, ed. Robert Tucker (New York: Norton, 1978), pp. 172–174.
4. See Marx and Engels, "Manifesto of the Communist Party," in ibid., pp. 481–482; Horkheimer, "Traditional and Critical Theory," pp. 221–222.
5. Karl Marx, "Theses on Feuerbach," in *The Marx-Engels Reader*, pp. 143–145. See Richard Bernstein's classic work *Praxis and Action* (Philadelphia: University of Pennsylvania Press, 1973), for a lucid analysis of the implications of Marx's "practical" epistemology.
6. This is the line already laid out in the *Manifesto*, and stands behind all iterations of the "dialectic of theory and practice." Biographically speaking, Marx often expressed his contempt for working-class leaders such as the tailor Wilhelm Weitling. See David McLellan, *Karl Marx: A Biography* (New York: Palgrave Macmillan, 2006), pp. 142–146.
7. In *Knowledge and Human Interests*, Habermas resurrected the "therapeutic" model of Critical Theory, explicitly invoking the parallel between Freudian psychotherapy and the attempt of *Ideologiekritik* to overcome "systematically distorted communication." See Habermas, *Knowledge and Human Interests*, trans. Jeremy Shapiro (Boston: Beacon Press, 1971), chap. 10.
8. Jürgen Habermas, *The Structural Transformation of the Public Sphere*, trans. Thomas Burger (Cambridge, Mass.: MIT Press, 1989), p. 135 (hereafter cited as *ST*).
9. This is the "lesson" of Adorno's brilliant allegorization of *The Odyssey* in the first "excursus" on the "Concept of Enlightenment" essay in *Dialectic of Enlightenment*. See chap. 7 of this volume.

10. Max Horkheimer and Theodor W. Adorno, *Dialectic of Enlightenment: Philosophical Fragments*, ed. Gunzelin Schmid Noerr (Stanford: Stanford University Press, 2002), p. 63 (hereafter cited as *DE*).

11. Ibid. The quotation in this passage is from Kant, *Critique of Pure Reason*, trans. Norman Kemp Smith (New York: St. Martin's Press, 1965), p. 542 [B686]. The full passage runs as follows: "Reason thus prepares the field for the understanding: (1) through a principle of the *homogeneity* of the manifold under higher genera; (2) through a principle of the *variety* of the homogenous under lower species; and (3) in order to complete the systematic unity, a further law, that of the *affinity* of concepts—a law which prescribes that we proceed from each species to every other by gradual increase of the diversity. These we may entitle the principles of *homogeneity, specification,* and *continuity* of forms. The last names arise from the union of the other two, inasmuch as only through the processes of ascending to the higher genera and of descending to the lower species do we obtain the idea of systematic connection in its completeness. For all the manifold differences are then related to one another, inasmuch as they one and all spring from one highest genus, through all degrees of a more an more widely extended determination."

12. Kant, *Critique of Pure Reason*, pp. 532 [B 670] ff.

13. This critique of Kant's "critical" philosophy was originally made by Hegel in *The Phenomenology of Mind*. See G. W. F. Hegel, *The Phenomenology of Mind*, trans. J. B. Baillie (New York: Harper and Row, 1967), pp. 281–336 (on "observing reason"). For the immediate predecessor of Horkheimer and Adorno's Hegelian-Marxist critique of the "antinomies" of the Kantian position, see Georg Lukács, *History and Class Consciousness*, trans. Rodney Livingstone (Cambridge, Mass.: MIT Press, 1971), pp. 121–131.

14. Jürgen Habermas, *The Theory of Communicative Action*, 2 vols., trans. Thomas McCarthy (Boston: Beacon Press, 1984 and 1987).

15. *DE*, p. 94.

16. Charles Taylor, *Hegel and Modern Society* (New York: Cambridge University Press, 1980).

17. *DE*, p. 125.

18. Ibid.

19. See Friedrich Schiller, *On the Aesthetic Education of Man*, ed. and trans. Elizabeth M. Wilkinson and L. A. Willoughby (Oxford: Oxford University Press, 1967), letters 6, 12, and 15. Cf. Marx and Engels, "The German Ideology," in *Marx-Engels Reader*, p. 160.

20. *DE*, p. 125.

21. Ibid., p. 98.

22. Kant, *Critique of Pure Reason*, pp. 182–183 [B 179-B 181]. As Kemp Smith notes, there is something artificial about Kant's set up of this particular problem: "if category and sensuous intuition are really heterogeneous, no subsumption is possible; and if they are not really heterogeneous, no such problem as Kant here refers to will exist." See Norman Kemp Smith, *A Commentary to Kant's "Critique of Pure Reason"* (Atlantic Highlands, N.J.: Humanities Press, 1962), p. 334.

23. *DE*, p. 98.

24. Ibid., p. 99.

25. Television had been invented, but had yet to take on its contemporary (and absolutely central) cultural role. Nevertheless, Horkheimer and Adorno were acute enough observers to see the writing on the wall. See *DE*, p. 97.

26. Ibid., p. 109.

27. Ibid., p. 100.

28. Ibid., p. 106 (my emphasis).

29. Ibid., pp. 98, 121.

30. Ibid., p. 107. Horkheimer and Adorno continue in a telling passage: "It is as if some omnipresent agency had reviewed the material and issued an authoritative catalog tersely listing the products available."

31. Ibid., p. 99.

32. See, for example, Michael Rogin's *Ronald Reagan, the Movie: And other Episodes in Political Demonology* (Berkeley: University of California Press, 1997), in which the "determinism of the signifier"—if I may coin a phrase—is taken all too literally.

33. *DE*, p. 109.

34. Ibid., p. 104.

35. Ibid., p. 109.

36. Ibid., p. 106.

37. Ibid., p. 110.

38. Ibid., p. 120.

39. Ibid., p. 117.

40. Horkheimer and Adorno's argument about the diffusion of "chance" as an ideological notion of the first order in contemporary society depends on a more general argument about the interpenetration of state and society in the Keynesian and social welfare–oriented economies of the immediate postwar era. Chance is the "other side" of planning in the sense that it provides a necessary illusion of spontaneity for those whose economic prospects are largely determined "from above," by either capitalists or technocrats. In our more market, stockholder value-oriented economy, the ideology of chance—of the individual's "good" or "bad" luck—still rules. This is most apparent in the way downsized workers tend to individualize their fate in terms of "luck," a phenomenon documented years ago in Richard Sennett's and Jonathan Cobb's *The Hidden Injuries of Class* (New York: Vintage, 1973) and more recently in Louis Uchitelle's *The Disposable American: Layoffs and Their Consequences* (New York: Vintage, 2007).

41. *DE*, p. 113.

42. Ibid.

43. The "performative contradiction" charge is one often leveled against *Dialectic of Enlightenment*'s "too inclusive" critique of instrumental and conceptual rationality (which Horkheimer and Adorno tend to conflate). See, for example, Jürgen Habermas, *The Philosophical Discourse of Modernity*, trans. Frederick Lawrence (Cambridge, Mass.: MIT Press, 1987), pp. 127–130. Cf. Seyla Benhabib,

Critique, Norm and Utopia (New York: Columbia University Press, 1986), pp. 169–171.

44. Alexis de Tocqueville, *Democracy in America*, vol. 1, ed. Phillips Bradley, trans. Henry Reeve (New York: Vintage Press, 1990), p. 264.

45. Ibid., vol. 2, pp. 158–161.

46. Ibid., pp. 318–319.

47. *DE*, p. 105.

48. Theodor Adorno, *Minima Moralia: Reflections from Damaged Life*, trans. E. F. N. Jephcott (London: Verso Editions, 1978), pp. 15–18.

49. See Immanuel Kant, *Foundations of the Metaphysics of Morals*, trans. Lewis White Beck (New York: Macmillian, 1985), pp. 64–72.

50. See Friedrich Pollock, "State Capitalism: Its Possibilities and Limitations," in *Zeitschrift für Sozialforschung*, 1941, Institute for Social Research, ed. A. Schmidt (Munich: Deutscher Taschenbuch-verlag, 1980).

51. See Adorno, *Minima Moralia*, p. 17. See also J. M. Bernstein, *Adorno: Disenchantment and Ethics* (New York: Cambridge University Press), pp. 41–42.

52. See Habermas, *Philosophical Discourse of Modernity*, chap. 11 (pp. 294–326).

53. Marcuse addressed "advanced industrial society," whereas Habermas looked at the history and fate of "the bourgeois public sphere." At the time of composition, Habermas was a "junior member" of the Frankfurt School, just starting his career. *ST* addresses a strictly West European historical experience and contemporary situation. *One-Dimensional Man*, on the other hand, was written by an established name in the Frankfurt School constellation, one who chose to stay in America after the period of exile in the 1930s and 1940s. Unsurprisingly, it focuses more on the American experience (references to Europe and the Soviet Union notwithstanding). Marcuse's work was a bestseller, tremendously influential on the student left that would shortly emerge in the 1960s. In contrast, Habermas's work had to wait thirty years for an English translation, the subsequent fame of its author notwithstanding.

54. For an analysis of this phenomenon, albeit one that does not invoke Marcuse at any great length, see Richard Rorty, *Achieving Our Country: Leftist Thought in Twentieth Century America* (Cambridge, Mass.: Harvard University Press, 1999).

55. See Georg Lukács, "Reification and the Consciousness of the Proletariat," in Lukács, *History and Class Consciousness*, pp. 97–103, 145–150.

56. See Marcuse's discussion of Hegel's dialectical notion of the concept in Herbert Marcuse, *Reason and Revolution* (Boston: Beacon Press, 1960), pp. 158–159: "There is no more adequate example of the formation of the dialectical notion than Marx's concept of capitalism. . . . The notion of capitalism is no less than the three volumes of *Capital*, just as Hegel's notion of the notion comprises all three books of his *Science of Logic*."

57. Marx and Engels, "Manifesto of the Communist Party," in *Marx-Engels Reader*, p. 491. For the "development" argument and the preconditions for overcoming a fundamental estrangement, see Marx and Engels, "The German Ideology," *Marx-Engels Reader*, pp. 161–162.

58. Ibid., p. 483.

59. Max Weber, "Parliament and Government in a Reconstructed Germany," in Weber, *Economy and Society*, ed. Guenther Roth and Claus Wittich (Berkeley: University of California Press, 1978), vol. 2, p. 1402.

60. Ibid.

61. Herbert Marcuse, *One-Dimensional Man* (Boston: Beacon Press, 1964), p. xlviii (my emphasis) (hereafter cited as *ODM*). The concluding sentence echoes Horkheimer and Adorno's observation (*DE*, p. 95) that "technical rationality today is the rationality of domination."

62. Jürgen Habermas, "Technology and Science as 'Ideology,'" in Habermas, *Toward a Rational Society*, trans. Jeremy J. Shaprio (Boston: Beacon Press, 1970), pp. 82–83. Cf. *ODM*, p. 32. The absorption of politics by technics is, of course, a primary theme of much of Habermas's early work. See, in this regard, Thomas McCarthy, *The Critical Theory of Jürgen Habermas* (Cambridge, Mass.: MIT Press, 1978), chap. 1, pp. 1–16.

63. *ODM*, p. 33.

64. Marcuse was a student of Heidegger's prior to his affiliation with the Frankfurt School. He cites Heidegger on pp. 153–154 of *ODM*. See Martin Heidegger, *Die Frage nach der Technik* in Heidegger, *Vorträge und Aufsätz* [*Gesamtausgabe*, Band 7] (Frankfurt am Main: Vittorio Klostermann, 2000), pp. 7–36.

65. *ODM*, pp. 2, 4, and 6.

66. See Karl Marx, "On the Realm of Necessity and the Realm of Freedom," in *The Marx-Engels Reader*, pp. 439–441.

67. *ODM*, pp. 5, 9.

68. Ibid., p. 3.

69. Ibid., p. xlvii.

70. Ibid., p. 10.

71. See Hannah Arendt, *The Origins of Totalitarianism* (New York: Harcourt Brace, 1973), p. 438.

72. *ODM*, p. 12.

73. See Dana Villa, *Socratic Citizenship* (Princeton: Princeton University Press, 2001), for an analysis along these lines.

74. *ODM*, p. 11.

75. Ibid., pp. 64–65.

76. Ibid., pp. 25–26, 32.

77. Ibid., p. 33.

78. Ibid.

79. Ibid., p. 34.

80. Ibid., p. 48.

81. Ibid., p. 50.

82. Ibid., p. 51.

83. Ibid, p. 52.

84. This is not to deny the attempt of the administration of George W. Bush to, in effect, create a new version of the Cold War—namely, a great, long-term ideological and physical struggle against a "totalitarian" enemy. It is sobering

to realize how successful this ploy was in its initial stages, and just how ready the "loyal opposition" was willing to lay down its opposition for the sake of a "necessary" unity in the face of a willfully inflated threat.

85. *ODM*, p. 58.
86. Ibid., p. 61.
87. Ibid., p. 63.
88. Ibid., p. 57.
89. Ibid., p. 61.
90. Ibid., p. 64.
91. Ibid., p. 68.
92. Ibid., p. 256.
93. See Jacques Derrida, "The Ends of Man," in Derrida, *Margins of Philosophy*, trans. Alan Bass (Chicago: University of Chicago Press, 1982), p. 134.
94. See Albrecht Wellmer, "Reason, Utopia, and the *Dialectic of Enlightenment*," in *Habermas and Modernity*, ed. Richard J. Bernstein (Cambridge, Mass.: MIT Press, 1985), especially pp. 35–40.
95. This was a view of things taken by many of my academic colleagues on the left in the presidential election of 2000—much to their later regret.
96. Such a distinction has deep roots, going back to the Greeks. Cf. Plato's distinction between rhetoric and dialectic in the *Gorgias*.
97. See Wellmer, "Reason, Utopia, and the *Dialectic of Enlightenment*," pp. 37, 46.
98. See, amongst others, Benhabib, *Critique, Norm, and Utopia*, pp. 163ff.; Jürgen Habermas, *The Theory of Communicative Action*, vol. 1, *Reason and the Rationalization of Society*, trans. Thomas McCarthy (Boston: Beacon Press, 1984); Martin Jay, *Marxism and Totality: The Adventures of a Concept from Lukács to Habermas* (Berkeley: University of California Press, 1984); Thomas McCarthy, *The Critical Theory of Jürgen Habermas*; Albrecht Wellmer, "Reason, Utopia, and the *Dialectic of Enlightenment*."
99. See Karl Löwith, *Max Weber and Karl Marx* (New York: Routledge, 1993).
100. Max Weber, *The Protestant Ethic and the Spirit of Capitalism*, trans. Talcott Parsons (New York: Charles Scribner's Sons, 1958), p. 181.
101. For the distinction between communicative and instrumental or "system" rationalization, see Jürgen Habermas, *Communication and the Evolution of Society* (Boston: Beacon Press, 1979), pp. 117–120. The distinction between two types of rationalization presupposes the distinction between work or purposive-rational action and communicative action (or symbolic interaction), a distinction Habermas made in his 1968 critique and appreciation of Marcuse. See Habermas, "Technology and Science as 'Ideology,'" pp. 91–92. It is also intimately related to the distinction Habermas draws between *system* and *social* integration. See Jürgen Habermas, *Legitimation Crisis*, trans. Thomas McCarthy (Boston: Beacon Press, 1975), p. 4.
102. See Benhabib, *Critique, Norm, and Utopia*, pp. 228–343; Wellmer, "Reason, Utopia, and the *Dialectic of Enlightenment*," pp. 51–57.
103. I say "uncontroversial" because *Structural Transformation's* prefiguration of themes in Habermas's later thought has been widely recognized. See, for

example, C. Calhoun's "Introduction" to *Habermas and the Public Sphere*, ed. Craig Calhoun (Cambridge, Mass.: MIT Press, 1992), pp. 1–3.

104. Jürgen Habermas, "The Dialectics of Rationalization," interview with Axel Honneth, Eberhard Knödler-Bunte, and Arno Widmann in *Autonomy and Solidarity: Interviews with Jürgen Habermas*, ed. Peter Dews (London: Verso, 1986), p. 98.

105. *Strukturwandel der Öffentlichkeit* appeared as a book in 1963, published by Hermann Luchterhand Verlag. Pointedly, the *Habilitationschrift* intended for Horkheimer and Adrono at Frankfurt had to be undertaken with the political scientist Wolfgang Abendroth at Marburg. See Wiggerhaus, *The Frankfurt School*, pp. 555–556.

106. This development is traced by Habermas in chap. 5 of *ST*, an analysis that owes much to the detailed genealogy Max Weber provides in his lecture "Politics as a Vocation." See Max Weber, "Politics as a Vocation," in *From Max Weber: Essays in Sociology*, ed. H. H. Gerth and C. Wright Mills (New York: Oxford University Press, 1958), especially pp. 96–112.

107. Jürgen Habermas, "The Public Sphere: An Encyclopedia Article," in *Critical Theory and Society: A Reader*, ed. Stephen Eric Bronner and Douglas MacKay Kellner (New York: Routledge, 1989), p. 137. Cf. Habermas, *ST*, p. xvii: "We conceive bourgeois public sphere as a category that is typical of an epoch. It cannot be abstracted from the unique developmental history of that 'civil society' (*bürgerliche Gesellschaft*) originating in the European High Middle Ages."

108. Habermas, "The Public Sphere," p. 136.

109. See *ST*, pp. 3–4, and—more generally—Hannah Arendt, *The Human Condition* (Chicago: University of Chicago Press, 1958), pp. 38–49.

110. *ST*, p. 27; Habermas, "The Public Sphere," p. 137.

111. *ST*, p. 30.

112. Habermas, "The Public Sphere," p. 136.

113. *ST*, p. 195.

114. This tack is suggested not only by Arendt's argument about the American Constitution in *On Revolution*, but also by Tocqueville's argument about associational life and civil society more generally in *Democracy in America*. See chaps. 2 and 4 of this volume.

115. Thomas Hobbes, *Leviathan*, ed. Richard Tuck (Cambridge: Cambridge University Press, 1996), chap. 21, p. 148.

116. *ST*, p. 29.

117. Ibid., p. 36.

118. Ibid., p. 37.

119. Ibid., pp. 40–43.

120. Ibid., p. 40.

121. Ibid., p. 51.

122. Arendt, quoted in *ST*, p. 19. There is, of course, a tremendous irony in Habermas's invocation of Arendt's thesis about the "rise of the social" in this context. Habermas uses it to pinpoint the moment when the ancient dichotomy between public and private ceases to obtain; the moment when "civil society" as we know it begins its long dialectical relationship with the modern state. The

"bourgeois public realm" emerges in response to the problem of *regulating* civil society. For Arendt, in contrast, an authentically public sphere must largely eschew social/economic concerns.

123. *ST*, p. 52.
124. Ibid., p. 56.
125. Ibid., p. 52.
126. Ibid., p. 54.
127. Ibid., p. 55.
128. Ibid., p. 95.
129. Ibid., p. 96.
130. See, in this regard, J. L. Talmon, *The Rise of Totalitarian Democracy* (Boston: Beacon Press, 1952), chap. 1.
131. *ST*, pp. 98–99. Cf. Hannah Arendt's reading of Rousseau in Arendt, *On Revolution* (New York: Penguin, 1990), pp. 74–81, and my discussion in Dana Villa, *Arendt and Heidegger: The Fate of the Political* (Princeton: Princeton University Press, 1996), pp. 73–77.
132. Kant, "An Answer to the Question: 'What is Enlightenment?,'" in *Political Writings*, pp. 55.
133. Ibid., p. 56.
134. *ST*, pp. 105–106: "Each person was called to be a 'publicist,' a scholar 'whose writings speak to his public, the world.'"
135. Immanuel Kant, "On the Common Saying: This May be True in Theory, but it Does not Apply in Practice," in *Political Writings*, pp. 80–81.
136. *ST*, p. 108; Kant, "Idea for a Universal History with a Cosmopolitan Purpose," in *Political Writings*, pp. 44–51. Cf. Immanuel Kant, "Perpetual Peace, A Philosophical Sketch," in *Political Writings*, pp. 112–113, 126–127.
137. Kant, *Political Writings*, p. 85.
138. Kant, *Critique of Pure Reason*, B850. Cf. Immanuel Kant, *Critique of Judgment*, trans. J. H. Bernard (New York: Hafner Press, 1951), sec. 40, pp. 135–138. On the importance of "communicability" in Kant, see Hannah Arendt, *Lectures on Kant's Political Philosophy*, ed. Ronald Biener (Chicago: University of Chicago Press, 1982), pp. 63–64, 67–70, 73–75.
139. *ST*, pp. 110–111; Kant, *Political Writings*, p. 78.
140. *ST*, p. 115.
141. See G. W. F. Hegel, *Elements of the Philosophy of Right*, ed. Allen W. Wood and trans. H. B. Nisbet (Cambridge: Cambridge University Press, 1998), sec. 318.
142. See Rousseau, *The Social Contract*, book 4, chap. 1.
143. *ST*, p. 140. See also Craig Calhoun, "Introduction," in *Habermas and the Public Sphere*, p. 19.
144. As Calhoun points out, "The very idea of the public was based on the notion of a general interest sufficiently basic that discourse about it need not be distorted by particular interests (at least in principle), and could be a matter of rational approach to an objective order, that is to say, of truth." See Calhoun, "Introduction," *Habermas and the Public Sphere*, p. 9.
145. *ST*, sec. 15.

146. Ibid., p. 130.

147. Ibid., p. 133.

148. Tocqueville, *Democracy in America*, vol. 1 (quoted in *ST*, p. 134).

149. For a fuller development of these themes—and, in particular, the "Socratic" dimensions of Mill's liberal public sphere—see Villa, *Socratic Citizenship*, chaps. 1 and 2.

150. See Calhoun, "Introduction," p. 20. Of course, Mill himself took pains to constrict the "perspectivist" implications of the agonistic public sphere outlined in *On Liberty*, suggesting an additive conception of truth and moral progress. At the same time, however, he insisted on the need for an open and "rough process of struggle" to ensure that fair play be given to "all sides of the truth." See my discussion in *Socratic Citizenship*, pp. 94–99.

151. *ST*, p. 135 (my emphasis).

152. See, in this regard, the important passage in Hannah Arendt, *The Human Condition*, pp. 57–58. The phrase "essentially controversial nature of the public good" is borrowed from Leo Strauss. See Strauss, "What is Political Philosophy?," in *What Is Political Philosophy and Other Studies* (Chicago: University of Chicago Press, 1988), p. 17.

153. There is, of course, a further distinction to be made between Arendtian "plurality" and more radical forms of liberal pluralism, such as the moral pluralism described by Isaiah Berlin. For a discussion of the distinction, see chap. 4 of this volume.

154. See chap. 2 of this volume.

155. See *From Alexander to Constantine: Passages and Documents Illustrating the History of Social and Political Ideas 336 B.C.-A.D. 337*, translated with introductions, notes, and essays by Ernest Barker (Oxford: Oxford University Press, 1956). For the "classic" formulation, see Plato, *Republic*, 441C-445B.

156. See Thomas McCarthy, "Practical Discourse: On the Relation of Morality to Politics," in Calhoun, *Habermas and the Public Sphere*, p. 66.

157. In *Habermas and the Public Sphere*, the essays by Craig Calhoun, Thomas McCarthy, and Nancy Fraser are all critical of this central Habermasian assumption. Calhoun's "Introduction" comes closest to the perspective I offer here.

158. See Isaiah Berlin, "The Pursuit of the Ideal," in Berlin, *The Crooked Timber of Humanity* (Princeton: Princeton University Press, 1998), pp. 1–19.

159. This theme goes back to Friedrich Pollock's 1941 article, "State Capitalism: Its Possibilities and Limitations." See Benhabib's discussion in *Critique, Norm, and Utopia*, pp. 158–159.

160. *ST*, pp. 145–146.

161. Ibid., p. 147.

162. Ibid., p. 176. It would be premature to exempt America—and its more "entrepreneurial" form of capitalism—from the broad dynamic Habermas describes.

163. Ibid., p. 142.

164. Ibid., p. 155.

165. Ibid., pp. 43–51.

166. Ibid., p. 157.

167. Ibid., p. 159.

168. Ibid., p. 161.

169. Ibid., p. 160.

170. Ibid., p. 170.

171. Ibid., p. 163.

172. Ibid., p. 164. Anyone who has sat through the mind-numbing contentlessness of a recent American presidential debate would be hard put to disagree with Habermas on this point.

173. Ibid., p. 175.

174. Ibid., p. 179.

175. Ibid., p. 178.

176. This is something Arendt stresses in her discussion of opinion vs. interest in *On Revolution*, pp. 228–229.

177. *ST*, pp. 192–194.

178. Ibid., pp. 216–218.

179. Ibid., p. 216. The oldest saw in modern campaign wisdom is that candidates are "sold like soap." The only thing that has changed in recent memory is the sophistication of the selling techniques—for both soap and politicians.

180. Ibid., p. 195.

181. Ibid., p. 232.

182. Ibid., p. 234.

183. Ibid., pp. 234–235.

184. See, for example, Calhoun, "Introduction," *Habermas and the Public Sphere*, p. 31; Jay, *Marxism and Totality*, p. 508.

185. Calhoun, *Habermas and the Public Sphere*, p. 32.

186. Jürgen Habermas, "Historical Materialism and the Development of Normative Structures," in Habermas, *Communication and the Evolution of Society*, p. 97.

187. What I am suggesting here is that, important as Habermas's radical revision of the "critique of instrumental rationality" paradigm is, the distinction between *communicative* and *instrumental* rationalization fails to break as decisively as it should with an underlying conception of society as a subject capable (at least ideally) of self-transparency. As a result, the corrective focus on intersubjectivity Habermas introduces to Critical Theory remains, in crucial respects, undernourished, less robust than that offered (for example) by Hannah Arendt.

188. This may be a little hard on Habermas. Seyla Benhabib suggests that Habermas's "discourse ethics" approach to practical reasoning is designed not so much to discover generalizable interests as to provide a test for uncovering non-generalizable interests. She admits, however, that the distinction between "the Rousseauian and the critical models" is "extremely blurred" in the formulation found in *Legitimation Crisis*. See Benhabib, *Critique, Norm and Utopia*, pp. 312–313.

189. See chaps. 2 and 3 of this volume.

190. Habermas, *Legitimation Crisis*, p. 108.

191. Ibid., p. 111.

192. Cf. Hannah Arendt's contrary claim in *The Human Condition*, p. 58.

193. Richard J. Bernstein, "Introduction," in *Habermas and Modernity*, p. 19.

194. See Benhabib's discussion, *Critique, Norm and Utopia*, pp. 239–241. For Habermas's definition of what he means by a "discourse" in this context, see *Legitimation Crisis*, p. 107.

195. Ibid., p. 241.

196. Nancy Fraser, "Rethinking the Public Sphere," in *Habermas and the Public Sphere*, pp. 109–142. See especially pp. 125–126.

197. See, in this regard, Benhabib's general characterization of Habermas's theoretical project: "Since *The Structural Transformation of the Public Sphere* . . . Habermas has focused on the inconsistency between the utopian kernel of the early bourgeois political tradition—the consensus of all as the basis of a just order—and the institutional contradictions of capitalism which constantly violate this utopian promise through relations of exploitation" (Benhabib, *Critique, Norm and Utopia*, p. 228).

198. See Villa, *Socratic Citizenship*, especially chaps. 1 and 2.

199. See Horkheimer and Adorno, *DE*, preface.

200. See Habermas, "The Dialectics of Rationalization," pp. 98–101, on the "deficiencies" of first generation Critical Theory. Cf. also Habermas, "The Entwinement of Myth and Enlightenment," in *Philosophical Discourse of Modernity*, pp. 106–130.

201. It must be acknowledged that Habermas's most recent major work goes some distance in answering these criticisms. See Jürgen Habermas, *Between Facts and Norms: Contributions to a Discourse Theory of Law and Democracy*, trans. William Rehg (Cambridge, Mass.: MIT Press, 1998).

202. Hannah Arendt, *Between Past and Future* (New York: Penguin, 1968), p. 223.

203. Ibid., p. 241.

204. An anecdote told by Jerome Kohn illustrates this divergence. Stopping by her apartment in the early 1970s to take Arendt out to dinner, Kohn (then her teaching assistant) spied a huge manuscript sitting on a side table. "What's that?" he asked. "Jürgen Habermas's latest book," Arendt replied, adding: "He thinks we're doing the same thing, *but we're not.*"

205. In *ST*, Habermas claims that it is precisely the fact that "the political task of the bourgeois public sphere was the regulation of civil society (in contradistinction to the *res publica*)" (p. 57). Yet the contrast of ancient and modern public spheres, while essential, is overdrawn. For any citizen of a modern democracy, concern with "the public thing"—the health and functioning of their political institutions and civic culture—is, or ought to be, every bit as important as the rules regulating civil society.

206. See Cass Sunstein, *Republic.com* (Princeton: Princeton University Press, 2002).

7 | Genealogies of Total Domination: Arendt, Adorno, and Auschwitz

I would like to thank Martin Jay, Peter Gordon, Josh Dienstag, and Andy Rabinbach for critical comments on an earlier draft of this chapter.

1. Hannah Arendt, "What Remains? The Language Remains," in *Essays in Understanding, 1930–1954*, ed. Jerome Kohn (New York: Harcourt Brace, 1994), pp. 13–14.
2. Hannah Arendt, *The Human Condition* (Chicago: University of Chicago Press, 1958), p. 175.
3. See Mary Dietz's essay, "Arendt and the Holocaust," in *The Cambridge Companion to Hannah Arendt*, ed. Dana Villa (Cambridge: Cambridge University Press, 2001).
4. Despite the impression given by the published exchange between Arendt and Gershom Scholem in *Encounter*, the Arendtian ideas of totalitarian "radical evil" and the "banality of evil" (the case of Eichmann and certain other perpetrators) are not in any direct contradiction. See Richard Bernstein's lucid presentation in his *Hannah Arendt and the Jewish Question* (Cambridge, Mass.: MIT Press, 1996). See also my essay "Conscience, the Banality of Evil, and the Idea of a Representative Perpetrator" in *Politics, Philosophy, Terror* (Princeton: Princeton University Press, 2000).
5. Most of *Dialectic of Enlightenment* was drafted in exile in Santa Monica during the years 1942–43. The concluding section—on "Anti-Semitism and the Limits of Enlightenment"—was a later addition, and not (evidently) part of the original conception of the book. See Rolf Wiggershaus, *The Frankfurt School: History, Theory, Politics* (Cambridge, Mass.: MIT Press, 1994), and Anson Rabinbach, "Why Were the Jews Sacrificed?: The Place of Anti-Semitism in *Dialectic of Enlightenment*," *New German Critique* 81 (Fall 2000), pp. 49–64.
6. Hannah Arendt, "Understanding and Politics," in *Essays in Understanding, 1930–1954*, p. 323.
7. Hannah Arendt, *The Origins of Totalitarianism* (New York: Harcourt Brace, 1973), p. vii (hereafter cited as *OT*).
8. Ibid., pp. 437–438, 441. Arendt famously describes the concentration and death camps as the "central institution" of totalitarianism, as the laboratory in which "the fundamental belief of totalitarianism that everything is possible is being verified."
9. From Machiavelli onward, the contingency of politics and political action has been one of the primary themes of political (as opposed to philosophical) thought. See J. G. A. Pocock, *The Machiavellian Moment: Florentine Political Thought and the Atlantic Republican Tradition* (Princeton: Princeton University Press, 1975). Arendt's own hostility to Hegelian narratives of "necessary" outcomes is well known, and vividly on display in both *OT* and her essay "The Concept of History," in *Between Past and Future* (New York: Penguin, 1968). For a discussion of the centrality of contingency to Arendt's thought, see Villa, *Arendt and Heidegger: The Fate of the Political* (Princeton: Princeton University Press, 1996), chaps. 2 and 3.
10. See Georg Wilhelm Friedrich Hegel, *Lectures on the Philosophy of World History: Introduction*, trans. H. B. Nisbet (Cambridge: Cambridge University Press, 1975), p. 28 (hereafter cited as *WH*).

11. Adorno's later philosophy is devoted, in no small part, to the radical critique of these central Hegelian notions. See Theodor W. Adorno, *Negative Dialectics*, trans. E. B. Ashton (New York: Seabury Press, 1973), part 3, chap. 2, "World Spirit and Natural History."

12. Jürgen Habermas, *The Philosophical Discourse of Modernity*, trans. Frederick Lawrence (Cambridge, Mass.: MIT Press, 1992), chap. 5, "The Entwinement of Myth and Enlightenment."

13. Max Horkheimer and Theodor W. Adorno, *Dialectic of Enlightenment: Philosophical Fragments*, trans. Edmund Jephcott (Stanford: Stanford University Press, 2002), p. 43 (hereafter cited as *DE*).

14. See note 2 and Rabinbach, "Why Were the Jews Sacrificed?"

15. Friedrich Nietzsche, *On the Genealogy of Morals*, trans. Walter Kaufmann (New York: Random House, 1989), essay 3, secs. 18 and 19. Cf. Rabinbach, "Why Were the Jews Sacrificed?"

16. In my book *Arendt and Heidegger* I argued that Arendt, following some of Heidegger's thought trains, was an "anti-modernist" of sorts. I think this largely holds true of *The Human Condition*, the primary articulation of her ideas on political action and the public realm. It is obviously less true of *The Origins of Totalitarianism*, which is a book that elucidates both the hopes and the horrors of European modernity. In this regard, Seyla Benhabib's characterization of Arendt as a "reluctant modernist" strikes me as felicitous.

17. *OT*, pp. 440–441.

18. *WH*, p. 42.

19. Ibid., p. 36. The scriptural reference is to I Corinthians 2, 10.

20. Ibid., pp. 30–31, 139.

21. Ibid., p. 34.

22. Ibid., pp. 28, 33.

23. See, for example, Philippe Lacoue-Labarthe, *Heidegger, Art, and Politics* (London: Blackwell, 1990).

24. *WH*, p. 69.

25. See Michael Ignatieff, *The Warrior's Honor: Ethnic War and the Modern Conscience* (New York: Metropolitan, 1998).

26. See, in this regard, Susan Neiman's recent *Evil in Modern Thought: An Alternative History of Philosophy* (Princeton: Princeton University Press, 2004).

27. For a sympathetic yet nevertheless incredulous account of Hegel's *Geist qua* "cosmic subject," see Charles Taylor, *Hegel and Modern Society* (New York: Cambridge University Press, 1979), part 1.

28. *WH*, pp. 37–38.

29. See Leo Strauss, *Natural Right and History* (Chicago: Chicago University Press, 1959).

30. See Max Weber, "Wissenschaft als Beruf," in *Gesammelte Aufsätze zur Wissenschaftslehre*, ed. Johannes Winckelmann (Tubingen: J. C. B. Mohr Verlag, 1988), p. 595: "*Welches ist der Beruf der Wissenschaft innerhalb des Gesamtlebens der Menschheit? und welches ihr Wert?*"; "Science as a Vocation," in *From Max*

Weber: Essays in Sociology, ed. H. H. Gerth and C. Wright Mills (New York: Oxford University Press, 1958), p. 140.

31. Weber, "Science as a Vocation," pp. 140–141.

32. Ibid., p. 142. Weber cites Swammerdam's famous statement, "Here I bring you the proof of God's providence in the anatomy of a louse."

33. Ibid.

34. Ibid., 143.

35. Ibid.

36. This is, at least, one lesson to be learned from Nietzsche's famous "How the Real World becomes a Fable" in *Twilight of the Idols*—a metaphorical and telegraphic account of the same self-undermining process Weber recounts in "Science as a Vocation."

37. I deal with this point at greater length in chap. 4 of *Socratic Citizenship*.

38. See, in this regard, Harvey Goldman's *Politics, Death, and the Devil: Self and Power in Max Weber and Thomas Mann* (Berkeley: University of California Press, 1992).

39. Max Horkheimer, *The Eclipse of Reason* (New York: Continuum, 1974), p. 6.

40. Ibid. (my emphasis).

41. See Albrecht Wellmer, "Reason, Utopia, and the *Dialectic of Enlightenment*," in *Habermas and Modernity*, ed. Richard J. Bernstein (Cambridge, Mass.: MIT Press, 1985), p. 42.

42. Cf. Herbert Marcuse's parallel reconstruction of Hegel in *Reason and Revolution* (Atlantic Highlands, N.J.: Humanities Press, 1983), pp. 16, 147–151.

43. See Horkheimer's discussion of Sade's *Juliette* in *DE*, pp. 81–82.

44. See Isaiah Berlin, "The Pursuit of the Ideal," in *The Crooked Timber of Humanity*, ed. Henry Hardy (Princeton: Princeton University Press, 1998), pp. 1–19.

45. Hans Blumenberg, *The Legitimacy of the Modern Age* (Cambridge, Mass.: MIT Press, 1982), p. 48.

46. *DE*, p. 10: "The generality of the ideas developed by discursive logic, power in the sphere of the concept, is built on the foundation of power in reality." Cf. p. 16.

47. Ibid., p. 11.

48. Ibid., pp. xviii, 9, 11.

49. Ibid., p. xix.

50. See G. W. F. Hegel, *Differenz des Fichte'shen un Schelling'shen Systems des Philosophie*, ed. G. Lasson (Leipzig, 1923), p. 75: "Das Absolute selbst aber ist darum die Identität der Indentität und der Nichtindentität; Entgegensetzen un Einssein ist zugleich in ihm."

51. See Wellmer, "Reason, Utopia, and the *Dialectic of Enlightenment*," p. 48.

52. This is, of course, an idea borrowed from Hegel. See G. W. F. Hegel, *Phenomenology of Mind*, trans. J. B. Baillie (New York: Harper and Row, 1967), "Absolute Freedom and Terror."

53. *DE*, p. 7.

54. See Tracy Strong's discussion in chap. 3 of his *Friedrich Nietzsche and the Politics of Transfiguration* (Berkeley: University of California Press, 1975).

55. *DE*, p. xi. Cf. Seyla Benhabib, *Critique, Norm, and Utopia: A Study of the Foundations of Critical Theory* (New York: Columbia University Press, 1986), pp. 163–164.
56. Benhabib, *Critique, Norm, and Utopia*, p. 164.
57. *DE*, p. 43.
58. Nietzsche, *Genealogy of Morals* 2, 16. Cf. Sigmund Freud, *Civilization and its Discontents*, trans. James Strachey (New York: W. W. Norton, 1989), pp. 84, 97.
59. *DE*, pp. 63–64.
60. Ibid., pp. 66, 68.
61. Immanuel Kant, *Critique of Pure Reason*, trans. Norman Kemp Smith (New York: St. Martin's Press, 1965), Bxiii.
62. *DE*, p. 67.
63. Ibid., pp. 69, 79–80. Cf. Friedrich Nietzsche, *Beyond Good and Evil*, trans. Walter Kaufmann (New York: Harper and Row, 1968), sec. 212.
64. *DE*, p. 93.
65. See Nietzsche, *Genealogy of Morals*, 3, secs. 18–22. Nietzsche's analysis of the "ascetic priest" and his various palliatives addresses precisely this problem.
66. *DE*, p. 43.
67. Ibid., p. 88.
68. See Arendt's discussion of Jewish warmth and "unworldlness" in her essay on Lessing, "On Humanity in Dark Times," in *Men in Dark Times* (New York: Harcourt, Brace, and World, 1968).
69. See Hannah Arendt, *Eichmann in Jerusalem: A Report on the Banality of Evil* (1963; New York: Penguin, 1994), p. 26.
70. See Rabinbach, "Why Were the Jews Sacrificed?," p. 49.
71. *DE*, p. 137.
72. Ibid., p. 138.
73. Ibid., p. 139.
74. Ibid.
75. Ibid., p. 140.
76. Ibid.
77. Ibid., p. 143.
78. Ibid., p. 170.
79. See my discussion in chap. 6 of this volume.
80. For an investigation of the roots and philosophical coherence of the idea that "the masses" are complicit in their own domination, see Michael Rosen, *On Voluntary Servitude: False Consciousness and the Theory of Ideology* (Cambridge: Harvard University Press, 1996).
81. *DE*, p. 140.
82. Theodor Adorno, *Minima Moralia: Reflexionen aus dem beschädigten Leben*, in Adorno, *Gesammelte Schriften* 4, ed. Rolf Tiedemann (Frankfurt: Suhrkamp, 1997), pp. 226–68; *Minima Moralia*, trans. E. F. N. Jephcott (London: Verso), pp. 233–235.
83. Ibid., p. 90.
84. Rolf Tiedemann, "Introduction," in Theodor Adorno, *Can One Live After Auschwitz?: A Philosophical Reader* (Stanford: Stanford University Press, 2003), p. xxii.

85. See Freud, *Civilization and its Discontents*, p. 69.

86. Adorno, "Working Through the Past," in *Can One Live After Auschwitz?*, p. 13.

87. For a development of liberal insights concerning the pathologies arising from strongly held group identities, see George Kateb, *The Inner Ocean* (Ithaca: Cornell University Press, 1994).

88. Adorno, "Education After Auschwitz," in *Can One Live After Auschwitz?*, p. 22.

89. Ibid., p. 23.

90. Hence *Dialectic of Enlightenment*'s repeated appeal to reason or a form of reflection that is *higher than* mere scientific rationality—an appeal that largely reiterates Hegel's speculative twist on the Kantian distinction between *Vernunft* and *Verstand*.

91. It is to Habermas's credit that he took the Frankfurt School's basic story about the manipulation of public opinion in the "administered society" and complicated it. He did this through the historical study of the "bourgeois public sphere" and its animating notion of the critical (public) use of one's reason. See Jürgen Habermas, *The Structural Transformation of the Public Sphere*, trans. Thomas Burger (Cambridge, Mass.: MIT Press, 1989) and chap. 6 of the present volume.

92. See Arendt, *The Human Condition*, pp. 181–192. See also David Luban's essay "Explaining Dark Times," in *Hannah Arendt: Critical Essays*, ed. Lewis P. Hinchman and Sandra K. Hinchman (Albany: State University of New York Press, 1994), and Stan Spyros Draenos's essay in *Hannah Arendt: The Recovery of the Public World*, ed. Melvyn Hill (New York: St. Martin's Press, 1975).

93. Arendt's replacement of the abbreviated "Conclusion" of the original edition by the lecture/essay "Ideology and Terror" should not distract us from the fact that the original conception of the book ended with chap. 12's consideration of the place of the concentration and extermination camps in totalitarian regimes.

94. As Judith Shklar observed in her book *Ordinary Vices* (Cambridge, Mass.: Harvard University Press, 1984), liberals think that "cruelty is the worst thing we do to each other." For Arendt, the *summum malum* represented by totalitarianism is much worse, and far less generic. See my essay "Totalitarianism, Modernity, and the Tradition" in *Politics, Philosophy, Terror*, pp. 198–203 (hereafter cited as *PPT*).

95. *OT*, p. 438.

96. See Primo Levi's memoir *Survival in Auschwitz* for "eyewitness" confirmation of Arendt's basic take on the camps; also my essay "Terror and Radical Evil," *PPT*.

97. I borrow here from Margaret Canovan. See her insightful analysis in Canovan, *Hannah Arendt: A Reinterpretation of Her Political Thought* (Cambridge: Cambridge University Press, 1992), p. 62.

98. Karl Marx and Friedrich Engels, "Manifesto of the Communist Party," in *The Marx-Engels Reader*, ed. Robert Tucker (New York: Norton, 1978), p. 475.

99. *OT*, p. 123.

100. Ibid., p. 124.

101. Ibid., p. 125.

102. Ibid., p. 138.

103. Ibid. (my emphasis).

104. Ibid., p. 139.

105. Ibid., p. 142.

106. Ibid., p. 146.

107. Ibid., p. 230. Arendt expands on this analysis in chap. 4 of *On Revolution*.

108. Ibid., p. 231.

109. Ibid., p. 237.

110. Ibid., p. 231.

111. Ibid., p. 240.

112. Ibid., p. 266.

113. See Arendt's analysis in "Ideology and Terror" in *OT* and my own reading of that analysis in *Arendt and Heidegger*, pp. 253–260.

114. Ibid., p. 270.

115. Ibid., p. 275.

116. Ibid., p. 291.

117. Ibid., p. 295.

118. Ibid., p. 297.

119. See Jeremy Waldron's essay "Arendt's Constitutional Politics" in *The Cambridge Companion to Hannah Arendt*, pp. 201–219.

120. See Canovan, *Hannah Arendt*, p. 32.

121. *OT*, p. 465.

122. Ibid., pp. 446–454.

123. Ibid., p. 455.

124. Giorgio Agamben, *Homo Sacer: Sovereign Power and Bare Life*, trans. Daniel Heller-Roazen (Stanford: Stanford University Press, 1998), p. 123.

8 | Foucault and the Dystopian Public

1. Plato, *The Republic of Plato*, trans. F. M. Cornford (New York: Oxford University Press, 1945), 441C-445B (pp. 139–143).

2. See Niccolo Machiavelli, *The Discourses*, in *The Portable Machiavelli*, ed. Peter Bondanella and Mark Musa (New York: Penguin, 1979), pp. 207–213.

3. See Sheldon Wolin, *Politics and Vision*, expanded ed. (Princeton: Princeton University Press, 2004), pp. 212–213.

4. Benjamin Constant, *Political Writings*, ed. Biancamaria Fontana (Cambridge: Cambridge University Press, 1988), pp. 317–319.

5. Ibid., p. 311.

6. Ibid., p. 326.

7. See chap. 2 of this volume.

8. See Plato, *Republic*, 501a (p. 209), and Machaivelli, *Discourses*, pp. 223–228.

9. See Roger Boesche, *Tocqueville's Road Map: Methodology, Liberalism, Revolution and Despotism* (Lanham, Md.: Lexington Books, 2006), pp. 48–49.

10. Alexis de Tocqueville, *Democracy in America*, vol. 2, ed. Phillips Bradley, trans. Henry Reeve (New York: Vintage, 1990), p. 318 (hereafter cited as *DAII*).

11. See Roger Boesche, "Hedonism and Nihilism: The Predictions of Tocqueville and Nietzsche," in *Tocqueville's Road Map*, pp. 127–144.

12. *DAII*, p. 319.

13. John Locke, *Two Treatises of Government*, ed. Peter Laslett (New York: Cambridge University Press, 1988), p. 346.

14. For Foucault's critique of power conceived as a kind of (transferable) commodity, see Michel Foucault, *"Society Must be Defended": Lectures at the Collège de France, 1975–1976*, trans. David Macey (New York: Picador, 2003), p. 14 (hereafter cited as *SMd*). For just how wrong the point about the "liberal" conception is vis-à-vis Tocqueville, see Jack Lively, *The Social and Political Thought of Alexis de Tocqueville* (Oxford: Oxford University Press, 1962), pp. 15–16.

15. Michel Foucault, *Power/Knowledge*, ed. Colin Gordon (New York: Pantheon, 1980), p. 104 (hereafter cited as *PK*). See *SMd.*, pp. 35–36, for a contrast of "sovereign power" with the "new mechanism of power" that arose in the seventeenth and eighteenth centuries, a power "exercised through constant surveillance and not through chronologically defined systems of taxation and obligation."

16. *PK*, p. 104.

17. Ibid., pp. 104–105.

18. Michel Foucault, *Discipline and Punish*, trans. Alan Sheridan (New York: Vintage, 1979), p. 139 (hereafter cited as *DP*).

19. *PK*, p. 96. I say "irritating" not because of the claim itself, which points to a dimension of power's functioning that many of us would rather forget. Rather, it has become irritating in the mouths of Foucauldians who presume that the rest of us are trapped in liberal or Marxist conceptions of power as commodity, centered in the state or "held" by a particular social class. Needless to say, one can grant Foucault his primary point—that power does indeed circulate throughout the social body, through many of the mechanisms he describes—without having to deny that state or economic power exists, and that these forms of power have to be limited (by constitutional instruments, or by legislation that moves us—ever so slightly—toward capitalism with a human face). It is, obviously, a question of levels and types of power, not of who gets something called "power" right and who gets it wrong.

20. *SMd.*, p. 34.

21. *PK*, pp. 59, 119, 125.

22. *DP*, pp. 137–138.

23. Ibid., p. 136.

24. Ibid., p. 30. For a good example of Foucault in hyperbolic mode, see *PK*, p. 98: "The individual is not to be conceived as a sort of elementary nucleus, a primitive atom, a multiple and inert material on which power comes to fasten or against which it happens to strike, and in so doing subdues or crushes individuals. In fact, it is already one of the prime effects of power that certain bodies, certain gestures, certain discourses certain desires, come to be identified

and constituted as individuals. The individual, that is, is not the *vis à vis* of power; it is, I believe, one of its prime effects. The individual is an effect of power." Cf. *SMd.*, pp. 28–30, for the unexpurgated passage.

25. *PK*, p. 98.
26. *DP*, p. 170: "Discipline 'makes' individuals; it is the specific technique of a power that regards individuals both as objects and as instruments of its exercise." Note the scare quotes around the word "makes." Cf. Foucault, *SMd.*, pp. 45–46: "The manufacture of subjects rather than the genesis of the sovereign: that is our general theme."
27. Ibid., p. 29: "It would be wrong to say that the soul is an illusion, or an ideological effect. On the contrary, it exists, it has a reality, it is produced permanently around, on, with the body by the functioning of a power that is exercised on those punished—and, in a more general way, on those one supervises, trains, and corrects, over madmen, children at home and at school, the colonized, over those who are stuck at a machine and supervised for the rest of their lives. This is the historical reality of the soul, which, unlike the soul represented by Christian theology, is not born of sin and subject to punishment, but is born rather out of methods of punishment, supervision, and constraint."
28. Ibid., p. 30.
29. *SMd.*, p. 45.
30. *DP*, p. 222.
31. Ibid.
32. *SMd.*, pp. 27, 37: "This theory [of sovereignty], and the organization of the juridical code centered upon it, made it possible to superimpose on the mechanism of discipline a system of right that *concealed its mechanisms* and erased the element of domination and the techniques of domination involved in discipline, and which, finally, guaranteed that everyone could exercise his or her own sovereign rights thanks to the sovereignty of the State" (my emphasis).
33. *PK*, p. 95.
34. Ibid., p. 105. Cf. *SMd.*, pp. 26–27.
35. See Hannah Arendt, *On Revolution* (New York: Penguin, 1990), pp. 30–33.
36. See, especially, *SMd.*, pp. 26–29, for a brief and straightforward précis of Foucault on the problem of sovereignty, how law and right both mask and are vehicles for domination, and how it is necessary to look at the "capillary" level of power techniques if one is to "grasp the material agency of subjugation insofar as it constitutes subjects."
37. See Foucault, "The Subject and Power," in *Essential Works of Foucault, 1954–1984*, vol. 3: *Power*, ed. James D. Faubion (New York: New Press, 2000), pp. 326–348.
38. Hence the well-known Foucauldian dictum about "local" resistance and the "local" knowledges that make such resistance possible.
39. *SMd.*, p. 59.
40. *DP*, p. 30.
41. Ibid., p. 29.

42. This, of course, is merely a reiteration of the basic Hegelian critique of "atomism," albeit this time substituting "practices of power" for "social relations" or "forms of consciousness." The much commented upon "overcoming" of the "three Hs—Hegel, Husserl, and Heidegger" in recent French thought notwithstanding, Foucault never disavowed the centrality of Hegel and Hegelian thought to his own *Bildung*. See, for example, Michel Foucault, *The Hermeneutics of the Subject: Lectures at the Collège de France*, trans. Graham Burcell (New York: Picador, 2005), p. 524. For general background, see Vincent Descombes, *Philosophy in France* (Cambridge: Cambridge University Press, 1981).

43. *SMd.*, p. 45.

44. Giorgio Agamben, *Homo Sacer: Sovereign Power and Bare Life*, trans. Daniel Heller-Roazen (Stanford: Stanford University Press, 1998), pp. 174–175.

45. See, in this regard, Hannah Arendt's famous analysis of the legal and institutional means by which totalitarian and proto-totalitarian regimes strip various "enemy" populations of their legal rights, moral personality, and (finally) capacity for individuality in Arendt, *The Origins of Totalitarianism* (New York: Harcourt Brace, 1976), pp. 447–455.

46. See *DP*, p. 301; Agamben, *Homo Sacer*, vol. 1, p. 137: "If genocide is indeed the dream of modern powers, this is not because of a recent return to the ancient right to kill; it is because power is situated and exercised at the level of life, the species, the race, and the large-scale phenomena of population."

47. *SMd.*, pp. 15–16.

48. See David Macey's excellent biography, *The Lives of Michel Foucault* (New York: Vintage, 1995). It is tempting, then, to say that in theory Foucault unmasked the public realm and liberal rights as so many fictions, while in practice he continued to act and organize with various reformist groups in the name of prisoners' rights, immigrant rights, student rights, and so on. Tempting, but not really true. For his "theory of domination" actually registers the importance of both the public realm and the vocabulary (or "discourse") of rights, even though its preponderant sense is to make us skeptical of both.

49. See Hannah Arendt, *The Human Condition* (Chicago: University of Chicago Press, 1958), and her *On Revolution* (hereafter cited as *HC* and *OR*, respectively).

50. See, in this regard, *HC*, p. 40.

51. *DP*, pp. 7–10.

52. See Jean-Jacques Rousseau, *On the Social Contract*, book 4, chap. 1.

53. *PK*, p. 152. Foucault is drawing on the interpretation of Rousseau found in Jean Starobinski, *Transparency and Obstruction* (Chicago: University of Chicago Press, 1988). For a somewhat different but related criticism of Rousseau and the Rousseauian-democratic public sphere, see Reinhardt Koselleck, *Critique and Crisis: Enlightenment and the Pathogenesis of Modern Society* (Cambridge, Mass.: MIT Press, 1988), pp. 162–164.

54. *PK*, p. 147.

55. *DP*, p. 200.

56. Ibid., p. 207.

57. Ibid., p. 201.

58. Ibid., p. 202.

59. *PK*, p. 154.

60. This is true even though the most powerful surveillance mechanisms of our time are on a different technological plane, viz., computerization and omnipresent video cameras.

61. *DP*, p. 216.

62. *PK*, pp. 152–154.

63. *DP*, p. 171 (where Foucault describes the creation of institutions that are, in effect, *observatories*); p. 178 (where he describes how all "deviation from the norm" in schools, workshops, and the army was subjected "to a whole micro-penalty of time [lateness, absences, interruption of tasks], of activity [inattention, negligence, lack of zeal], of behavior [impoliteness, disobedience], of speech [idle chatter, insolence], or the body ["incorrect" attitudes, irregular gestures, lack of cleanliness], of sexuality [impurity, indecency])."

64. Ibid., p. 153.

65. Ibid.

66. Jürgen Habermas, "Modernity vs. Postmodernity," *New German Critique* 22 (Winter 1981): 3–14. See Nancy Fraser's insightful analysis in her *Unruly Practices* (Minneapolis: University of Minnesota Press, 1989), pp. 35–54.

67. See the editor's "Introduction" to *What is Enlightenment? Eighteenth Century Answers and Twentieth Century Questions*, ed. James Schmidt (Berkeley: University of California Press, 1996), p. 29.

68. See, in this regard, Michel Foucault, "What is Enlightenment?," in Schmidt *What is Enlightenment?*

69. *DP*, pp. 216–217.

70. Ibid. pp. 187–192.

71. Ibid., p. 171.

72. Ibid., p. 141.

73. I have here followed the contemporary habit of associating liberalism/rights-based individualism with the Enlightenment. It is important to remember that, historically speaking, these two movements were often separate (and occasionally contradictory) in the minds of their respective proponents. See Schmidt's "Introduction" to *What Is Enlightenment?* (Berkeley: University of California Press, 1996), p. 12. Cf. Frederick C. Beiser, *Enlightenment, Revolution, & Romanticism: The Genesis of Modern German Political Thought 1790–1800* (Cambridge, Mass.: Harvard University Press, 1992), part 1 ("Liberalism").

74. For the French, the connection appears somewhat more natural given the rationalization of French law by Napoleon in the Civil Code of 1804, the *Code d'instruction criminelle* of 1808, and the *Code pénal* of 1810.

75. Schmidt, "Introduction" to *What is Enlightenment?*, pp. 26–27. As Schmidt explains (summarizing the primary points of Foucault's genealogies): "Tuke and Pinel arrived in eighteenth-century prisons to separate criminals from the

insane—and forced the insane 'to enter a kind of endless trial for which the asylum furnished simultaneously police, magistrates, and torturers.' Freud shattered the silence surrounding sexuality—and inaugurated the 'nearly infinite task of telling—telling oneself and an other, as often as possible,' anything that might be linked in the remotest way to the body and its pleasures. In *Birth of the Clinic*, the light that penetrates the dark interior of the body in search of life finds only death, just as in *Discipline and Punish* the prisoners who have been freed from the darkness of the dungeon are captured all the more securely in the light that floods through the Panopticon. Like the 'dark writers of the bourgeoisie,' everywhere Foucault looked he found a complicity between enlightenment and domination."

76. *DP*, pp. 24; 298–299.

77. See Michael Walzer's essay "The Politics of Michel Foucault" in *Foucault: A Critical Reader*, ed. David Couzens Hoy (Oxford: Blackwell Publishers, 1986), p. 59.

78. Ibid., p. 58.

79. See Michel Foucault, *Power: Essential Writings of Foucault, 1954–1984, Vol. 3*, ed. James B. Faubion (New York: New Press, 2000), pp. 201–222 and 298–325.

80. *SMd.*, p. 48.

81. Ibid., p. 49.

82. The Comte de Boulainvilliers was an aristocratic French reactionary who wrote at the beginning of the eighteenth century, and whose writing appeared only after his death. He is best remembered for his argument that France was not one nation, but two, the outcome of a racial struggle between native Gauls and invading (Germanic) Franks. He sought to reestablish the eroding rights and power of the French aristocracy under Louis XIV and his successors by appealing to the original "right of conquest" and racial superiority of the Franks (the ancestors of the French nobility). See Arendt, *The Origins of Totalitarianism*, pp. 162–164.

83. *SMd.*, p. 47.

84. Ibid., p. 49. Cf. pp. 126–127, where Foucault importantly qualifies this assertion.

85. Ibid., pp. 49, 59.

86. Ibid., p. 50.

87. Ibid., pp. 50–51.

88. Ibid., p. 57.

89. Ibid., p. 52.

90. Ibid., pp. 23–24.

91. Ibid., p. 215.

92. Ibid., pp. 59, 61, 81. For Foucault's discussion of the English (pre-Civil War) discourse, see *SMd*, pp. 99–111. Here he presents the set of "domination" issues arising from the Norman Conquest; how these issues (and "Conquest" trope) were used by opponents of Charles I; and the significance of Hobbes's denial that there is any normative distinction between "sovereignty by institution" (i.e., contract) and "sovereignty by conquest" (a denial made possible by his inflation of the idea

of consent to include the case of life-threatening duress, and specifically designed to undercut those who deployed the "Conquest" discourse).

93. Ibid., p. 190.
94. Ibid., p. 81: "I think that racism is born at the point when the theme of racial purity replaces that of race struggle, and when counterhistory begins to be converted into a biological racism. . . . Whereas the discourse of races, of the struggle between races, was a weapon to be used against the historico-political discourse of Roman sovereignty, the discourse of race (in the singular) was a way of turning that weapon against those who had forged it, of using it to preserve the sovereignty of the State, a sovereignty whose luster and vigor were no longer guaranteed by magico-juridical rituals, but by medico-normalizing techniques. Thanks to the shift from law to norm, from races in the plural to race in the singular, from the emancipatory project to a concern with purity, sovereignty was able to invest or take over the discourse of race struggle and reutilize it for its own strategy." Hence what Foucault calls "State racism" as a general phenomenon, and the "Nazi transformation" of State racism in the twentieth century (*SMd.*, p. 82).
95. Ibid., p. 82. Cf. Arendt, *The Origins of Totalitarianism*, chap. 6, "Race-Thinking Before Racism."
96. See Michel Foucault, "Nietzsche, Genealogy, History," in Foucault, *Language, Counter-Memory, Practice*, ed. Donald F. Bouchard (Ithaca: Cornell University Press, 1977) (hereafter cited as *LCP*). Cf. Gilles Deleuze, *Nietzsche and Philosophy*, trans. Hugh Tomlinson (New York: Columbia University Press, 1983), pp. 156–164.
97. The *locus classicus* here is, of course, Friedrich Nietzsche, *On the Genealogy of Morals*, trans. Walter Kaufmann (New York: Vintage, 1989), 2, secs. 12 and 13 (pp. 77–79).
98. For a historical account of the Comte de Boulainvilliers and his relationship to the "Burgundy Circle," see Harold A. Ellis's *Boulainvilliers and the French Monarchy: Aristocratic Politics in Early Eighteenth-Century France* (Ithaca: Cornell University Press, 1988).
99. *SMd.*, p. 128.
100. Ibid., p. 131.
101. Ibid., p. 135.
102. Ibid., p. 133.
103. Ibid., p. 134.
104. Ibid.
105. Ibid.
106. See my discussion in chap. 7 of this volume.
107. *SMd.*, p. 142.
108. Ibid., p. 168.
109. For Foucault's summary of Boulainvilliers's history of the Franks in France, see *SMd.*, pp. 146–154.
110. Ibid., p. 163.
111. Ibid., p. 155.

112. Ibid., p. 156.

113. In the original French text, the sentence in question runs: "La guerre, en fait, recouvre entièrement le droit, recouvre même entièrement le droit naturel, au point de le rendre irréal, abstrait, et en quelque sorte fictif" (Michel Foucault, *"Il faut défendre la société": Cours au Collège de France, 1976* [Paris: Gallimard Seuil, 1997], p. 138). "Recouvre" has the connotation of subsuming or absorbing, rather than simply "concealing." The problem with "concealing" is that it makes it sound as if Foucault is saying that war is the appearance and right is the reality, when in fact he is saying the opposite: war is the fundamental reality in Boulainvilliers's analysis, one that underlies all law and right.

114. *SMd.*, p. 156.

115. Ibid., p. 157.

116. Ibid.

117. These terms (law of nature; law of history) are, of course, reversible when it comes to the issue of moral equality. Thus, for Plato, Aristotle, and (in a different way) Nietzsche, nature was essentially hierarchical, a measure of the high and the low, the noble and the base. For Hegel, Tocqueville, and Marx, history is essentially a movement toward greater and greater moral equality (the historical realization that "all are free" pointing to the fact that all are equal as well).

118. *SMd.*, pp. 158–159.

119. Ibid., p. 160.

120. Ibid.

121. Ibid., p. 161.

122. Ibid., pp. 162–163.

123. Ibid., p. 165.

124. See John Ehrenberg, *Civil Society: The Critical History of an Idea* (New York: New York University Press, 1999), chap. 6.

125. *SMd.*, pp. 142–143.

126. Ibid., p. 215.

127. Ibid., p. 225.

128. Ibid., p. 216.

129. Ibid., p. 218.

130. Ibid., p. 221. For a thorough consideration of Sieyès's project in its own right, see Murray Forsyth's *Reason and Revolution in the Political Thought of the Abbé Sieyès* (New York: Holmes and Meier, 1987).

131. *SMd.*, p. 222.

132. Idid., p. 223.

133. Ibid., p. 227.

134. Ibid., p. 225.

135. Ibid., p. 240.

136. Ibid., p. 244.

137. Ibid., p. 247.

138. Ibid.

139. Ibid., p. 255.

140. Ibid., p. 259.

141. See Michel Foucault, "Governmentality," in Foucault, *Power: Essential Writings*, pp. 201–222.

142. See Max Weber, *Economy and Society*, ed. Guenther Roth and Claus Wittitch (Berkeley: University of California Press, 1978); *HC*; Sheldon Wolin, *The Presence of the Past* (Baltimore: Johns Hopkins University Press, 1988), chap. 5.

143. Michel Foucault, *The History of Sexuality: An Introduction*, trans. Richard Howard (New York: Vintage, 1990), p. 139.

144. Ibid., p. 137.

145. For the importance of the figure of the shepherd to the kind of "pastoral" power exercised by the modern state, see Michel Foucault, "*Omnes et Singulatum*: Toward a Critique of Political Reason," in Foucault, *Power: Essential Writings*, pp. 298–325.

146. Foucault, *History of Sexuality*, p. 143; Agamben, *Homo Sacer*, p. 3.

147. Agamben, *Homo Sacer*, p. 9.

148. Ibid., pp. 10, 121.

149. Ibid., p. 122.

150. Ibid., p. 171.

151. Ibid., p. 170.

152. Ibid., p. 174.

153. Isaiah Berlin drew attention to Marx's basic "strategy and tactics" approach well over sixty year ago in his *Karl Marx: His Life and Environment* (London: Home University Library, 1939).

154. This is perhaps clearer in Foucault and Marx than Weber, whose advocacy of supposedly "wertfrei" social science continues to haunt his reputation. For a discussion of Weber's central moral concerns, see chap. 4 of Dana Villa, *Socratic Citizenship*.

155. See Nancy Fraser, "Foucault on Power: Empirical Insights and Normative Confusions," in *Unruly Practices*, p. 29.

9 | Arendt and Heidegger, Again

1. Dana R. Villa, *Arendt and Heidegger: The Fate of the Political* (Princeton: Princeton University Press, 1996).

2. See Sheldon Wolin, "Hannah Arendt: Democracy and the Political," in *Hannah Arendt: Critical Essays*, ed. Lewis P. Hinchman and Sandra K. Hinchman (Albany: State University of New York Press, 1994); also Martin Jay, "The Political Existentialism of Hannah Arendt," in *Permanent Exiles: Essays on the Intellectual Migration from Germany to America* (New York: Columbia University Press, 1986). Wolin's essay—in which the "elitist" charge is made—originally appeared in 1983 in *Salmagundi*. Jay's essay originally appeared in 1978 in *Partisan Review*. These are two of the sharpest—in the critical sense—appreciations of Arendt's debt to existentialism. Other early appreciations include the Hinchmans' "Existentialism Politicized: Arendt's Debt to Jaspers," *Review of Politics* 53, no. 3 (1991), which focused on Arendt's other existentialist teacher, and Bhiku Parekh's *Hannah Arendt and the Search for a New Political*

Philosophy (Atlantic Highlands, N.J.: Humanities Press, 1981), which focused, in a general way, on Arendt's phenomenological approach to political theory.

3. See my essay "The Anxiety of Influence: On Arendt's Relationship to Heidegger" in *Politics, Philosophy, Terror: Essays on the Thought of Hannah Arendt* (Princeton: Princeton University Press, 1999), pp. 61–86.

4. See Arendt's response to Gershom Scholem's misguided charge that she emerged from the milieu of the radical German (Weimar) Left in "An Exchange of Letters," in Hannah Arendt, *The Jew as Pariah*, ed. Ron H. Feldman (New York: Grove Press, 1978), pp. 250–251.

5. Elsbieta Ettinger, *Hannah Arendt/Martin Heidegger* (New Haven: Yale University Press, 1995).

6. See Hannah Arendt, *Eichmann in Jerusalem: A Report on the Banality of Evil* (New York: Penguin, 1983), pp. 117–125.

7. In *Eichmann in Jerusalem*, she estimates that fewer than half of the six million ultimately murdered would have died if there had been simple non-cooperation with the Nazis by Jewish "elites."

8. For the basics of this highly unedifying story, see chap. 8 of Elisabeth Young-Bruehl's *Hannah Arendt: For Love of the World* (New Haven: Yale University Press, 1982), especially pp. 347–377.

9. Thanks to the efforts of scholars such as Steven Aschheim, this situation is beginning to be remedied. See *Hannah Arendt in Jerusalem*, ed. Steven Aschheim (Berkeley: University of California Press, 2000).

10. See Young-Bruehl, *Hannah Arendt*, pp. 137–139.

11. Ibid., pp. 187–188: "Hannah Arendt became executive director of the Jewish Cultural Reconstruction organization after its establishment in 1948 and retained the position until 1952. She traveled to Europe for six months in 1949 and 1950 to direct the operation that eventually recovered 1.5 million volumes of Hebraica and Judaica, thousands of ceremonial and artistic objects, and over a thousand scrolls of law."

12. See Richard Wolin, "Hannah and the Magician," *New Republic*, October 15, 1995 (review of Ettinger); and Peter Berkowitz, "The Pearl Diver," *New Republic*, June 14, 1999 (review of Hanna Pitkin's *The Attack of the Blob: Hannah Arendt's Concept of the Social*).

13. Richard Wolin, *Heidegger's Children: Hannah Arendt, Karl Löwith, Hans Jonas, and Herbert Marcuse* (Princeton: Princeton University Press, 2001), p. 67.

14. This is a charge made by Berkowitz in his review of Pitkin—a charge that is not only baseless, but that signals an ignorance of Arendt's fundamental critique of totalitarian anti-politics; to wit, that totalitarianism destroys all durable, man-made political institutions in the misbegotten attempt to directly channel the race-selecting "law of nature" or the class-selecting "law of history" directly into the realm of human affairs. See Hannah Arendt, *The Origins of Totalitarianism* (New York: Harcourt Brace, 1973), pp. 460–467 (hereafter cited as *OT*). Cf. Margaret Canovan's excellent piece, "Hannah Arendt's Theory of Totalitarianism: A Reassessment," in *The Cambridge Companion to Hannah Arendt*, ed. Dana Villa (Cambridge: Cambridge University Press, 2000), pp. 25–43.

15. Wolin, *Heidegger's Children*, pp. 5, 68.

16. Ibid., pp. 68–69. After reminding us of Heidegger's invocation of "the great creators"—the poetic, philosophical and political "disclosers of Being" who are "the violent ones . . . who use force to become pre-eminent in historical Being"—in his *Introduction to Metaphysics*, Wolin states that Arendt "fully preserves" what he calls "the Master's emphasis on authentic leader-types" who are "laws unto themselves." He then goes on to cite the concluding pages to Arendt's *On Revolution*, where Arendt writes of a "self-selecting" political elite. The implication is twofold. First, that Arendt engaged in romantic hero-worship *à la* Heidegger, and was willing to let the heroes use violence against ordinary people to achieve their ends; second, that the notion of a "self-selecting" political elite is intended to overturn universal suffrage as such.

    Both charges are irresponsible and ungrounded. As I argue at length in *Arendt and Heidegger*, Arendt's theory of political action as a kind of "end in itself" was directed precisely against the instrumental or means/end conception that justifies violence as a primary vehicle for the achievement of goals (think of Plato's reliance on "noble lies" and coercion to achieve the rightly ordered—"just"—polity in the *Republic*, or Machiaveilli's endorsement of a strategic—and notably violent—conception of action in *The Prince* and the *Discourses*). A brief glance at Arendt's essay "On Violence" makes absolutely clear how opposed she was to the idea of "creative" violence, and even to the idea that violence *in any form* is a legitimate part of political action.

    As to the second charge (the idea that a "self-selecting" political elite spells the end of democracy as we know it): Arendt's point here is that the public realm must be open and available to all, but that no one should be forced to be an "active" citizen. Thus, "leading" political actors will be "self-selecting" in the sense that they will be people animated by public spirit and an interest in politics. Those who are not interested, or more concerned with business and material affairs, will have less influence in Arendt's "ideal" republic, simply because they choose not to become "active." While Arendt highly values the "positive" freedom manifest in becoming a "participator in government," she also recognizes the importance of the "negative" freedom to choose *not* to engage in politics. See Arendt, *On Revolution* (New York: Penguin, 1990), pp. 277–280 (hereafter cited as *OR*), where she makes it clear that the "excluded" are "self-excluded"—i.e., excluded by their own choice.

17. See Margaret Canovan, *Hannah Arendt: A Reinterpretation of Her Political Thought* (Cambridge: Cambridge University Press, 1992), chap. 6.

18. See Jürgen Habermas, "Hannah Arendt's Communications Concept of Power," in *Philosophical-Political Profiles*, trans. Frederick Lawrence (Cambridge, Mass.: MIT Press, 1987).

19. See Hannah Arendt, *The Human Condition* (Chicago: University of Chicago Press, 1958), pp. 202–203 (hereafter cited as *HC*).

20. Ibid., pp. 192–199. Cf. Arendt, "Ideology and Terror," in *OT*, pp. 461–464, where she contrasts the endlessly destructive dynamic of totalitarian "lawfulness"— the attempt to direct the "law of nature" or the "law of history" *directly* into

human affairs, and so to "speed up" the process of natural or historical evolution—with the durability and stability created by structures of positive law.

21. See Hannah Arendt, "What Is Freedom?," in *Between Past and Future: Eight Exercises in Political Thought* (New York: Penguin, 1977), p. 146 (hereafter cited as *BPF*).

22. See Seyla Benhabib, *The Reluctant Modernism of Hannah Arendt* (Thousand Oaks, Calif.: Sage Publications, 1996).

23. The unfinished *Life of the Mind* is, of course, the exception to this rule.

24. See part 3 of Villa, *Arendt and Heidegger* ("Arendt's Critique of Heidegger's Philosophical Politics").

25. See Hannah Arendt, "What Is Authority?," in *BPF*, especially pp. 104–120. Arendt sees Plato and Aristotle as both attempting to introduce something like the concept of authority into Greek political life—that is, to replace the idea of the "no rule" of civic equals with a supposedly "natural" distinction between rulers and ruled, adopted from either the household (*oikos*) or from the "educational" relation between generations.

26. See Villa, *Arendt and Heidegger*, pp. 130–143.

27. *OT*, p. 465.

28. Ibid., pp. 465–466.

29. Ibid., p. 465.

30. Even Benhabib would not disagree with this. See her *The Reluctant Modernism of Hannah Arendt*.

31. Sheldon Wolin, "Democracy and the Political," p. 289.

32. Ibid.

33. Ibid., p. 290.

34. Ibid., pp. 292–293.

35. See *HC*, pp. 189–194.

36. For the "theatrical" component of Arendt's theory of political action, see *BPF*, pp. 150–153.

37. Wolin, "Democracy and the Political," p. 295.

38. Ibid. A similar point is made by Hanna Pitkin in her article "Justice: On Relating Public and Private," also in Hinchman and Hinchman, *Hannah Arendt: Critical Essays*, pp. 261–288.

39. Wolin, "Democracy and the Political," p. 292.

40. Ibid., pp. 291–292. See *OT*, pp. 311–318: "The chief characteristic of the mass man is not brutality and backwardness, but his isolation and lack of normal social relationships." To this depiction of isolated and privatized "mass man," Arendt will add a yearning for certainty and security born of economic and political trauma during the interwar years (*OT*, pp. 351–352), along with a desire to "escape from reality," a desire born of their "situation of spiritual and social homelessness" (*OT*, p. 352). The operative referent here is, of course, Heidegger's analysis of *das Man* in *Being and Time*. See Martin Heidegger, *Being and Time*, trans. John Macquarrie and Edward Robinson (New York: Harper and Row, 1962), sec. 27.

41. Wolin, "Democracy and the Political," p. 298.
42. See especially Arendt, *On Revolution*, pp. 59–73; 111–114.
43. Wolin, "Democracy and the Political," p. 299.
44. Ibid., pp. 303–304.
45. Jay, "Political Existentialism," p. 240.
46. Ibid., p. 241.
47. Ibid., p. 242.
48. See Arendt, "What Is Freedom?," in *BPF*, pp. 151–156. See especially Arendt's claim on p. 153: "Men *are* free—as distinguished from their possessing the gift for freedom—as long as they act, neither before nor after; for to *be* free and to act are the same."
49. Jay, "Political Existentialism," p. 243. There is a tremendous irony in Jay leveling the "relativism" charge against Arendt. Arendt does reserve a central place for factual truth in politics (in large part as a response to the totalitarian preference for fictions). She disputes only the idea that if we could somehow discover the authentic Moral Truth (or order of History or the Cosmos), politics could somehow be deduced from that. In this, she is entirely in agreement with Isaiah Berlin. Indeed, Arendt's assertion of plurality and a politics of opinion looks pale indeed when contrasted to Berlin's robust assertion of moral pluralism. The idea that not all human goods are commensurable, and that the conflict of values cannot be rationally adjudicated, is an arch-Berlinian idea, one that bears a far more striking resemblance to what the proverbial "man in the street" would call relativism than anything Hannah Arendt ever wrote.
50. See Arendt, *On Revolution*, pp. 227–229. As Arendt writes on p. 229: "Opinion and judgment obviously belong among the faculties of reason, but the point of the matter is that these two, politically most important, rational faculties had been almost entirely neglected by the tradition of political as well as philosophical thought." Arendt sees herself as quite self-consciously attempting to "reassert the rank and dignity of opinion in the hierarchy of human rational abilities." And, by "opinion," she does not mean our unthought reflexive responses to current events (what pollsters measure when they measure "public opinion"). Rather, she means something that belongs to *individuals* who "'exert their reason coolly and freely'.... Opinions will rise wherever men communicate freely with one another and have the right to make their view public" (p. 227). This insistence on "communicative rationality" makes Arendt an important precursor of Jürgen Habermas. The latter, however, insisted on calling the outcome of "unconstrained dialogue" *truth*, thereby reasserting the rationalist prerogative of measuring the "realm of opinion" against something that stood (in some ultimate sense) outside of it. See my discussion in chap. 6 of this volume.
51. See Hannah Arendt, "Socrates," in Arendt, *The Promise of Politics*, ed. Jerome Kohn (New York: Schocken, 2005), pp. 4–15 (hereafter cited as *PP*).
52. Heidegger, from *Das Ding*, cited in Arendt, "Concern With Politics in Recent European Philosophical Thought," in Arendt, *Essays in Understanding, 1930–1954*, ed. Jerome Kohn (New York: Harcourt Brace, 1994), p. 432.

53. Jay, "Political Existentialism," p. 244.

54. See *OR*, pp. 51–52.

55. Jay, "Political Existentialism," p. 244.

56. See Villa, *Arendt and Heidegger*, chap. 2 and sec. 4 of chap. 5.

57. This is one reason why Jay's additional charge that Arendt's anti-historicism leads her to believe in infinite "human malleability" is so off-base. Indeed, I can think of few ideas more anathema to Arendt than this one. While eschewing metaphysical definitions of human nature, she nevertheless insisted—time and again—on man's "conditioned" nature, and upon his essential finitude. Such an emphasis on our finite, conditioned nature is to be expected from someone who identified the notion that "everything is possible" as the totalitarian idea par excellence.

   To insist, against various doctrines of natural or historical determinism, that man has the capacity to initiate or begin is far from insisting that he is free to transform himself any way he wants. Such a doctrine has much deeper roots in the Hegelian-Marxist idea of man's "anthropogenetic" nature—that is, in man's capacity to create himself through labor and his "metabolism with nature." See Alexandre Kojève, "In Place of an Introduction," in his *Introduction to the Reading of Hegel*, ed. Allan Bloom and trans. James H. Nichols (Ithaca: Cornell University Press, 1980), pp. 23–28.

58. Ibid., chap. 1, especially pp. 36–41.

59. Arendt, "The Tradition of Political Thought," in *PP*, p. 45.

60. Ibid. Cf. *HC*, pp. 195–196, 206. Cf. my discussion in *Arendt and Heidegger*, pp. 17–25.

61. Arendt's trajectory is well documented by Margaret Canovan Magaret Canavan in *Hannah Arendt: A Reinterpretation of Her Political Thought*.

62. See Villa, *Arendt and Heidegger*, part 3, "The Critique of Heidegger's Philosophical Politics," pp. 212–270.

63. Arendt, "Walter Benjamin, 1892–1940," in Hannah Arendt, *Men in Dark Times* (New York: Harcourt Brace, 1968), pp. 205–206.

64. Ibid., p. 204.

65. In this respect, Seyla Benhabib is partly correct when she charges Arendt with practicing a kind of "phenomenological essentialism." See Benhabib, *The Reluctant Modernism of Hannah Arendt*.

66. *BPF*, p. 165.

67. See George Kateb, *Hannah Arendt: Politics, Conscience, Evil* (Totowa, N.J.: Rowman and Allenheld, 1984), p. 7. As Kateb rightly adds: "Her ambition is enormous."

68. See Martin Heidegger, *The Basic Problems of Phenomenology*, trans. Albert Hofstadter (Bloomington: Indiana University Press, 1982), pp. 21, 29.

69. *OR*, pp. 30–31.

70. Arendt, "What Is Authority?," in *BPF*, pp. 104–120. I deal with Arendt's treatment of Plato and Aristotle in this regard in *Arendt and Heidegger*, pp. 157–165.

71. *HC*, p. 57.

72. *OR*, pp. 226–227. Cf. Arendt, *HC*, p. 57.

73. Cf. Plato, *Republic*, trans. F. M. Cornford (New York: Oxford University Press, 1945), 509b-511e.

74. See Arendt's treatment of a "maieutic" Socrates—a Socrates who tried to help others "give birth" to their own opinions, their own perspective on the world— in her essay "Socrates," in PP, pp. 20–24. Arendt's anti-Platonic revaluation of *doxa* and a doxastic rationality is one of the most striking, anti-traditional features of her thought.

75. See Heidegger, *Being and Time*, sec. 43. As Heidegger famously declares, "*Dasein* [human existence] is its disclosedness." See, in this regard, Jacques Taminiaux's important essay, "The Reappropriation of the Nicomachean Ethics: *Poiesis* and *Praxis* in the Articulation of Fundamental Ontology," in Taminiaux, *Heidegger and the Project of Fundamental Ontology*, trans. and ed. Michael Gendre (Albany: State University of New York Press, 1991), pp. 110–137. Also see my discussion in *Arendt and Heidegger*, pp. 117–143.

76. For the "revelatory" character of political speech, see *HC*, p. 180; also my discussion in *Arendt and Heidegger*, pp. 89–98.

77. Such a position obviously entails the rejection of so-called "natural rights," a rejection we find in various forms in such other canonical thinkers as Hobbes, Rousseau, Hegel, and J. S. Mill. See *OR*, pp. 30–32.

78. See Joan Didion's very informative piece, "Cheney: The Fatal Touch," *New York Review of Books* (Oct. 5, 2006).

79. *HC*, sec. 26.

80. Ibid., p. 190.

81. Ibid.

82. Ibid.

83. See *HC*, p. 195: "Though it is true that Plato and Aristotle elevated lawmaking and city-building to the highest rank in political life, this does not indicate that they enlarged the fundamental Greek experiences of action and politics to comprehend what later turned out to be the political genius of Rome: legislation and foundation. The Socratic school, on the contrary, turned to these activities because they wished to *turn against politics and against action* [my emphasis]. To them, legislating and execution of decisions by vote are the most legitimate political activities because in them men 'act like craftsmen': the result of their action is a tangible product, and its process has a clearly recognizable end. This is no longer or, rather, not yet action (*praxis*), properly speaking, but making (*poiēsis*), which they prefer because of its greater reliability."

84. Ibid.

85. Ibid.

86. Ibid., pp. 225–226. Cf. Arendt, "What Is Authority?," in *BPF*, pp. 104–114.

87. See J. Peter Euben, "Creatures of a Day: Thought and Action in Thucydides," in *Political Theory and Practice: New Perspectives*, ed. Terrence Ball (Minneapolis: University of Minnesota Press, 1977). Cf. Cornford's "Introduction" to his translation of Plato's *Republic*.

88. *HC*, p. 225.

89. Ibid., p. 222 (my emphasis).

90. See Taminiaux, "The Reappropriation of the Nicomachean Ethics," p. 124.

91. See Villa, *Arendt and Heidegger*, pp. 130–149.

92. *HC*, p. 229: "The substitution of making for acting and the concomitant degradation of politics into a mere means to obtain an allegedly 'higher' end—in antiquity the protection of the good men from the rule of the bad in general, and the safety of the philosopher in particular, in the Middle Ages the salvation of souls, in the modern age the productivity and progress of society—is as old as the tradition of political philosophy."

93. For Heidegger's conception of metaphysics as a "science of grounds," see Otto Pöggeler, "Being as Appropriation," in *Heidegger and Modern Philosophy*, ed. Michael Murray (New Haven: Yale University Press, 1978); for an explanation of the basic *Eigentlichkeit/Uneigentlichkeit* distinction, see Karsten Harries, "Fundamental Ontology and the Search for Man's Place" and "Heidegger as a Political Thinker,"also in Murray's volume.

94. Arendt, "What Is Freedom?," in *BPF*, pp. 164–165.

95. See, in this regard, Friedrich Nietzsche, "How the 'True World' Finally Becomes a Fable," in *Twilight of the Idols*, in *The Anti-Christ, Ecce Homo, Twilight of the Idols and other Writings*, ed. Aaron Ridley and Judith Norman (Cambridge: Cambridge University Press, 2005), p. 171, and Martin Heidegger, *The End of Philosophy*, trans. Joan Stambaugh (New York: Harper and Row, 1973). Heidegger's idea of the "onto-theological tradition" is, in many respects, a riff on Nietzsche's idea that Christianity is "Platonism for the masses."

96. See, for example, Aristotle's critique of Plato in book 2 of the *Politics*.

97. See Isaiah Berlin, "The Pursuit of an Ideal," in Berlin, *The Crooked Timber of Humanity* (Princeton: Princeton University Press, 1998), pp. 1–19.

98. Hence the Arendtian charge—echoed by Sheldon Wolin in his magisterial study of the Western tradition of political thought, *Politics and Vision*—that the liberal tradition is "non" political.

99. See Weber's definition of power in *Economy and Society*, ed. Guenther Roth and Claus Wittich (Berkeley: University of California Press, 1978), p. 53. Cf. Habermas's discussion in "Hannah Arendt's Communications Concept of Power."

100. See especially J. G. A. Pocock's chapter on Machiavelli's *Discourses* in *The Machiavellian Moment* (Princeton: Princeton University Press, 1975).

101. Augustine, *City of God*, trans. Gerald G. Walsh et al. (New York: Image Books, 1958), pp. 110–114; 308–311; 321–322; 437–471.

102. For Arendt's critique of Rousseau, and the fetish he makes of a morally homogenous "popular" sovereign will, see *OR*, pp. 73–81 and 182–184. Cf. *BPF*, pp. 163–165. The case of Machiavelli—a key voice in the civic republican tradition, within which Arendt locates herself—is more complicated. On the one hand, Machiavelli's *Discourses* is responsible for introducing the radical idea into Western political thought that conflict and dissensus between social groups might be a good thing, rather than a self-evidently bad one. See, in this regard,

Quentin Skinner, *Machiavelli* (New York: Oxford University Press), 2000. On the other hand, the nexus of military discipline, civil religion, and enforced patriotism that Machiavelli so admires in the Romans is hardly a recipe for a "robust" appreciation of human plurality.

103. A parallel conception is found in the utilitarianism of Bentham and James Mill, who were convinced that the elimination of "sinister interests" and the implementation of the "method" of democracy would yield a clear and unproblematic indication of where the "greatest good of the greatest number" resided.

104. See Albrecht Wellmer, "Reason, Utopia, and the *Dialectic of Enlightenment*," in *Habermas and Modernity*, ed. Richard Bernstein (Cambridge, Mass.: MIT Press, 1985).

105. Canovan, *Hannah Arendt*, p. 205.

106. *HC*, p. 52.

107. See again *OR*, p. 227.

108. For *Mitsein*, see Heidegger, *Being and Time*, sec. 26. For Heidegger's identification of the "naive" quality of Greek ontology—its projection of modes of being derived from the fabrication experience onto the cosmos at large—see Heidegger, *The Basic Problems of Phenomenology*, pp. 109–116 and 153–160. Finally, see Taminiaux's discussion of the naive quality of Greek ontology in his *Heidegger and the Project of Fundamental Ontology*, pp. 121–128.

109. See Taminiaux, *Heidegger and the Project of Fundamental Ontology*, pp. 133–136; and Harries, "Heidegger as Political Thinker." Cf. my discussion in *Arendt and Heidegger*, pp. 212–230.

110. Heidegger, *Gesamtausgabe*, 54: 132–133 (quoted in Taminiaux, *Heidegger and the Project of Fundamental Ontology*, p. 134).

111. Heidegger, "The Origin of the Work of Art," in *Poetry, Language, Thought*, trans. Albert Hofstader (New York: Harper and Row, 1971), p. 44.

112. Heidegger, *Introduction to Metaphysics*, trans. Ralph Manheim (New Haven: Yale University Press, 1959), p. 62.

113. Ibid., p. 152.

114. Ibid.

115. Ibid. I should note that this passage, quoted by many of Heidegger's more vehement critics, occurs in a passage unpacking the first choral ode from Sophocles' *Antigone*. The most we can say is that it gives us clues to Heidegger's thinking about politics and founding—not that it embodies this thinking.

116. For Heidegger and "radical" *poiēsis*, see Werner Marx's *Heidegger and the Tradition*, trans. Theodore Kiesel and Murray Greene (Evanston: Northwestern University Press, 1971).

117. *HC*, p. 57.

118. See Jeremy Waldron's essay in *The Cambridge Companion to Hannah Arendt*, ed. Dana Villa (Cambridge: Cambridge University Press, 2001).

119. See chap. 4 of this volume.

120. Hence the analysis she gives in chap. 5 of *On Revolution*, an analysis couched entirely in the terms of the "preservation and augmentation" of the "sacred" moment of the founding.

121. See Judith Shklar, *Freedom and Independence: A Study of the Political Ideas of Hegel's 'Phenomenology'* (Cambridge: Cambridge University Press, 1976).

122. See Arendt's essay "The Crisis in Culture," in *BPF*.

123. For example, her critique of Rousseau's *âme déchirée* in *On Revolution* is exceedingly Hegelian. See *OR*, p. 80.

124. See *OT*, pp. 231–237.

125. Hannah Arendt, *Rahel Varnhagen: The Life of a Jewess*, ed. and trans. Lilianne Weisberg (Baltimore: Johns Hopkins University Press, 1997).

126. Arendt, "What Is *Existenz* Philosophy?," in *Essays in Understanding*, pp 163–187.

127. Ibid., p. 187.

128. Ibid., p. 181.

129. Ibid. See my essay "The Anxiety of Influence: On Arendt's Relationship to Heidegger."

130. Arendt, preface to *Men in Dark Times*, p. ix (*Das Licht der Öffentlichkeit verdunkelt alles*).

131. *OR*, pp. 79–90.

132. Arendt, *Men in Dark Times*, p. 16.

133. Although I do, of course, make note of it. See Villa, *Arendt and Heidegger*, pp. 20, 33, 70, 78, 82, 84, 86–87, 141, 211, 249, and 259–260. Also pp. 122–123 and 89–90.

10 | The "Autonomy of the Political" Reconsidered

1. George Kateb, *Hannah Arendt: Politics, Conscience, Evil* (Totowa, N.J.: Rowman and Allanheld, 1984), p. 1.

2. Hannah Arendt, "What is Freedom?," in *Between Past and Future* (New York: Penguin Press, 1968), p. 153.

3. Sheldon Wolin, "Hannah Arendt: Democracy and the Political," in *Hannah Arendt: Critical Essays,* ed. Lewis P. and Sandra K. Hinchman (Albany: State University of New York Press, 1994), p. 289.

4. See Jean-Jacques Rousseau, *The Social Contract,* in Rousseau, *Political Writings*, trans. and ed. Frederick Watkins (Madison: University of Wisconsin Press), p. 105 (book 3, chap. 15).

5. See Seyla Benhabib, *The Reluctant Modernism of Hannah Arendt* (Thousand Oaks, Calif.: Sage Publications, 1996), and Richard Bernstein, "Rethinking the Social and the Political," in *Philosophical Profiles* (Philadelphia: University of Pennsylvania Press, 1986).

6. See Hanna Pitkin, *The Attack of the Blob: Hannah Arendt's Concept of the Social* (Chicago: University of Chicago Press, 1998).

7. Arendt, *The Human Condition* (Chicago: University of Chicago Press, 1957), p. 40.

8. Arendt, *On Revolution* (New York: Penguin, 1990), p. 139.

9. Ibid., p. 60.

10. Ibid., pp. 57–58.

11. See Hanna Pitkin, "Justice: On Relating the Private and the Public," in *Arendt: Critical Essays*, p. 270.

12. Arendt, *On Revolution*, pp. 251–253.
13. See Arendt's remarks included in *Hannah Arendt: The Recovery of the Public Realm*, ed. Melvyn Hill (New York: St. Martins Press, 1979), pp. 316–318.
14. Arendt, *OR*, pp. 90–91.
15. See Hannah Arendt, *The Origins of Totalitarianism* (New York: Harcourt, Brace, Jovanovich, 1973), pp. 274–299. See especially pp. 297–298.
16. Alexis de Tocqueville, *Democracy in America*, vol. 2, ed. Phillips Bradley, trans. Henry Reeve (New York: Vintage, 1990), p. 318.
17. Carl Schmitt, *The Concept of the Political*, trans. George Schwab (Chicago: University of Chicago Press, 1996), p. 57.
18. Ibid., pp. 53–54; 57–58.
19. Ibid., p. 53.

INDEX

Adams, John, 314

Adorno, Theodor, 11–12, 143; on the administered society, 173, 214; on advertising/public relations, 149, 151, 154; on the archaeology of self, 227–28; and Arendt, 156, 211, 214–15, 238, 239, 252, 253; on art, 168, 173; on authoritarianism, 238; on autonomy, 155, 156, 168, 173, 234, 237, 238; on barbarism, 226; on bourgeois coldness, 237, 253; on the bourgeoisie, 149; and Burckhardt, 235; on capitalism, 146, 148–50, 152–54, 156, 159, 160, 232, 234; on chance, 154; on Christianity, 234; on civilization, 225, 226, 228, 233; on communication, 157; on conceptual rationality, 211; on conformity, 151, 153, 155, 156, 232–35, 238; on consumers/consumer culture, 153–55, 157, 160; on corporations, 156; on culture, 148–58, 161, 168, 213, 226; on the death camps, 211–14; on debate, 156; on desire, 154, 155; on domination, 22–23, 25, 146, 147, 155, 156, 159, 160, 163, 173, 212–13, 215, 225–28, 231, 232, 237, 253, 275; on the economic sphere, 149–50, 153, 154; on empiricism, 150; on the Enlightenment, 155, 156, 213–15, 225–27, 232, 238; on the eradication of the particular, 211–12; on false consciousness, 146, 235; on false projection, 233, 234; on the formation of the rational subject, 213; and Foucault, 268, 275; on freedom, 173, 237; and Freud, 213, 214, 228, 237; on Germany, 237, 238; and Habermas, 196, 197; and Hegel, 212, 213, 215, 226, 252; on heteronomy, 155; on the Holocaust, 235; on Idealism, 228; on identity, 157; on ideology, 155, 156; on the individual, 160–61, 173; on individualism, 149; on institutions, 25; on integration, 148; on intersubjectivity, 157; and Kant, 146, 147, 150, 156, 237; and Marcuse, 158–61, 170; on the market, 148–50; and Marx, 149, 155; and Marxism, 231, 233–35; on mass culture, 148–52; on the masses, 154, 232–35; on maturity, 145, 237, 238; and Nietzsche, 213, 214, 226–28, 235, 237; on the media, 148, 149, 152, 153, 170; on mimesis, 233, 234; on morality/ethics, 215, 238; on myth, 213, 225–26; on nationalism, 237; on nature, 146, 147, 215, 225, 227, 228; on particulars vs. universals, 225, 226, 253; on power, 213, 227; on progress, 237; on public freedom, 173; on the public realm, 170, 175, 238; on rationality, 148, 155, 211, 214, 226–28, 230; on the rationalization of society, 213; on reason, 146, 147, 157, 173, 213–15, 225–27, 231, 232, 275; on religion, 154; on Romanticism, 228; on science, 146–47, 225, 226, 228; on self-preservation, 226, 228, 230; on self-reliance, 150; on sexuality, 154; on society, 226; on the state, 156; on subjectivity, 213, 228; on sublimation, 227; on technology, 226, 228; and Tocqueville, 156, 235; on totalitarianism, 211, 212, 225, 236; on truth, 227; on the universal, 211; and Weber, 147, 156, 160, 213, 214; on workers, 148, 152, 153, 155

Adorno, Theodor, works by: *Dialectic of Enlightenment,* 146–61, 170, 173, 203, 212, 222, 225–36, 239, 252, 253, 275; "Education After Auschwitz," 237–38; "Elements of Anti-Semitism," 231–35; *Minima Moralia,* 156, 235–36; "Working Through the Past," 237

advertising/public relations, 5; and Arendt, 206; and contemporary America, 172; and Habermas, 176, 178, 185, 192–95; and Horkheimer and Adorno, 149, 151, 154; and Marcuse, 161, 163, 164, 167, 171

Agamben, Giorgio, 251, 267, 268, 297; *Homo Sacer,* 293, 294–96

Albert, Hans, 198–99

alienation, 72–74, 82, 83, 165, 169, 253

America: and Arendt, 85, 87, 344; Christian, 81; consumer culture in, 234, 235; contemporary, 11, 16, 25–26, 139–42, 170–72, 193, 204, 207–9, 347; and the Enlightenment, 33; governmental checks and balances in, 9–10; and Hegel, 33, 65; and Marcuse, 168; and Marx, 13, 15; and Mill, 121; political associations in, 38; public-political life in, 33; and Tocqueville, 13, 33, 45, 52–58, 65, 76–78, 80, 85, 87, 89–91, 93–94

American founders: and Arendt, 98, 101, 103, 104, 312, 329, 345; and checks and balances, 10; and Habermas, 86; and Tocqueville, 77, 78, 91

American Revolution, the, 14, 88, 97, 99, 102, 105, 223, 342, 343

Amis, Martin, 139

Anaxagoras, 217

anti-Semitism, 212, 216, 230–35, 306

Arendt, Hannah, 99, 210, 300; on action, 96, 100, 302, 305–6, 308–11, 314, 316–24; and Adorno, 156, 211, 214–15, 238, 239, 252, 253; on advertising/public relations, 206; on alienation, 334, 335; on America, 85, 87, 344; on the American founders, 98, 101, 103, 104, 312, 329, 345; on the American Revolution, 88, 97, 99, 102, 105, 342, 343; on ancient Greece, 100, 250, 316, 319, 320, 339–40; on ancient Rome, 104; on anti-Semitism, 212, 306; on argument, 206, 314, 320, 329; and Aristotle, 99, 308, 316, 320, 322, 331, 351; on association/ associations, 20, 88, 106, 242, 243; on Athens, 100; on atomism, 101; and Augustine, 325, 326; on Auschwitz, 210; on authoritarianism, 310, 320; on authority, 97, 101–5; on barbarism, 253; and Bäumler, 313; and Benjamin, 318; and Berlin, 413n51; on the bourgeoisie, 212, 242–46, 250, 251; on bureaucracy, 248; and Burke, 249; on capitalism, 243, 305, 335; on care for the

public world, 18, 19, 99, 331, 333, 341, 345, 347–49; and Cassirer, 251; on the centralized state, 246; and Christianity, 95–97, 240, 326, 333, 335, 348–49; on citizens, 24, 88, 248; on civic republicanism, 11–12, 97–100, 103, 305, 307, 309, 326, 332, 342; on civilization, 250; on civil society, 88; on class, 212, 309; on coercion, 305–6, 320, 340; on the common world, 241; on communication, 206, 320; on community, 247, 352; on consensus, 100; on consent, 243, 244; and Constant, 245, 326; on the council system, 345; on culture, 100, 215–16; on dark times, 334–35; on the death camps, 211, 212, 214, 239–40, 251, 309; on debate, 96, 98, 100, 306, 321, 329, 330, 339, 345; on decentralization, 89; on deliberation, 96, 98–100, 306, 320, 321, 329, 330, 339, 345; on democracy, 87, 97, 98, 106, 250, 305, 306, 309–13, 317, 322, 323; and Descartes, 333; on despotism, 107, 247; on domination, 212, 214, 215, 239–42, 244, 251, 308–9, 340; on the economic sphere, 242, 244, 246; on elites, 107, 306, 307, 309, 316, 317, 336, 344, 345; on the Enlightenment, 97; on equality, 95, 97, 102, 242, 243, 246, 248, 249, 310, 311, 320, 321, 339, 340; on Europe, 101, 104, 238, 241, 242, 246–48; on evil, 240–41, 396n4; on existentialism, 97, 305–7, 309, 313–16, 318, 332, 348; on expansionism, 243–45, 250, 251; on factionalism, 100; and Foucault, 265, 266, 269, 283, 287, 293, 341, 347; on the foundational act, 102–5; and the Frankfurt School, 242, 340; on freedom, 5, 87, 89, 95, 97, 101–5, 215–16, 252, 253, 302, 306, 310, 314, 321, 324, 326, 329, 339, 340, 342, 343, 346; on the French Revolution, 243, 312, 329, 342–44; and Habermas, 85, 86, 178, 180, 187, 188, 205, 207, 306, 413n52; and Hegel, 88, 215–16, 243, 250, 252–53, 315, 325, 340, 342; and Heidegger, 302–12, 314–16, 318–20, 323–25, 327–29, 332, 334, 336, 341; on history, 214, 241, 251, 252; and Hobbes, 245, 325, 326, 336, 351–52; and Horkheimer, 156, 238, 239; on human dignity, 249, 253; on human nature, 240–42; on human plurality, 12; on human spontaneity, 214, 240–42, 251, 308–9, 312; on identity, 23, 242, 247, 251, 311; on imperialism, 212, 243–45, 248, 251; on independence, 87, 100; on the individual, 98; on individualism, 100, 104, 212, 245; on institutions, 95, 97, 101, 102, 215–16, 242, 247, 248, 252, 253, 306, 311, 321, 347; on interests, 331; and Jaspers, 303, 306, 313, 334; on the Jews, 303–5, 308–10, 334; on joint action, 90; on judgment, 87, 100, 205,

206, 308, 315; on the judiciary, 103; and
Jünger, 313; on justice, 311, 312, 338, 345,
346; and Kant, 205, 307, 310, 333, 338; on
labor, 311; on law, 97, 106, 215–16, 243,
247, 248, 252, 253, 305, 306, 321, 347; on
legislation, 103; on legitimacy, 101; on
liberalism, 86, 97, 99, 104, 339; on limited
government, 105; on local administration,
101; and Locke, 97; and Machiavelli, 96, 99,
326, 338; on making, 322, 323; and
Marcuse, 164–65; and Marx, 96, 97, 242,
243, 307, 314, 318, 319, 325, 326, 335, 338,
340, 342; and Marxism, 310, 329, 331; on
the masses, 312; on material interests, 101;
and Mill, 99, 100, 325, 326; on *moeurs,* 107;
and Montesquieu, 96, 325; on morality/
ethics, 215, 241, 310; on mores, 96, 97; on
movement politics, 247–48; on a narrative
frame, 239; on nationalism, 212, 242,
246–47, 307; on the nation-state, 242, 243,
245, 247–51; on nature, 215–16, 241, 242,
251–53; and Nietzsche, 105, 305, 309–12,
325, 330, 341; on opinion, 205–6, 308, 314,
315, 317, 320, 330; on pan-movements, 23,
212; on patriotism, 100; on perspective,
diversity of, 99, 100, 205–7, 320, 330; on
persuasion, 306; on philosophy, 307, 308,
310, 318–20, 322–25; and Plato, 96, 105,
308, 314, 315, 317–20, 322, 323, 325–27, 351;
on plurality, 87, 95, 99, 100, 106, 156–57,
187, 241, 242, 302, 307–9, 317, 320–22,
324–26, 329–32, 336, 351, 352; on political
action, 15, 88, 307–21, 324, 338–39, 342,
344; on political participation, 87, 89, 95,
97–99, 106; on political parties, 247; on
political romantics, 23; on the political vs.
the social, 310, 313, 317, 338, 339, 341–42,
344, 345, 347, 350, 351; on poverty, 342–43;
on power, 101, 102, 212, 241, 242, 244–45,
306, 311; on the priority of the political, 96;
on private interests, 245; on the private
sphere, 95, 101, 107, 206, 254; on the private
vs. the public, 16, 99, 340–41; on public
freedom, 97, 101, 344, 347; on the public
good, 245; on public opinion, 87, 98–100;
on the public realm, 86, 88, 96, 97, 101, 102,
106, 156–57, 242, 247, 250, 253–54, 269,
305–11, 314, 317, 319–25, 330–32, 339, 340,
342, 343, 346, 347; on public spirit, 99–101,
104, 330, 332; on race, 23, 212, 242, 246–47,
250, 251, 309; on racism, 212; on rationalism, 314–15; on rationality, 205; on reason,
206, 215; on refugees, 250, 251; on religion,
95–97, 104, 106; on representation/
representative government, 105, 242; on
representative thinking, 205–7; on
republicanism, 96, 97, 246; on revolution,
97, 101, 102, 305, 329, 342–43; on rights, 97,
106, 242, 243, 246, 248, 250, 251, 253, 297,
343; on the right to have rights, 249, 346;
on romantic individualism, 333–34; on
Romanticism, 334, 335; and Rousseau, 86,
88, 96, 99, 104, 326, 340; on the Russian
Revolution, 344; on sadism, 231; and
Schmitt, 305, 306, 313, 350–52; on self-
government, 88, 89, 249; on self-interest,
245; on the Slavic soul, 247; on the social
contract, 102; on social interests, 15; on the
social vs. the political, 88; on society, 239,
243, 246; and Socrates, 100, 333; on
sovereignty, 212, 246, 249, 351, 352; on the
state, 242, 243, 245, 246, 248–52, 269–70;
on statelessness, 212, 248–50, 307, 346; on
the state of nature, 245; and Tocqueville,
85–90, 95–99, 101, 105–7, 306, 312, 325, 331,
341; on totalitarianism, 25, 89, 211, 212,
214, 238–53, 295, 305, 308–9, 312, 317, 333;
on townships, 101; on tribalism, 23, 246–47,
307; on truth, 98, 205–6, 314; on the U.S.
Constitution, 104, 343; on violence, 305–6,
312, 314, 315, 320; and Weber, 102; on the
welfare state, 347; on women, 340, 346; on
work, 311; on workers, 340, 346; on
worldliness, 332–33; on the world of
appearance, 100

Arendt, Hannah, works by: *Between Past
and Future,* 319; "The Concept of
History," 315; "The Crisis in Culture,"
100, 205–7; *Eichmann in Jerusalem,* 211,
303–4; *The Human Condition,* 46, 88, 96,
100, 211, 302, 305–6, 311, 319–22, 328,
330, 339, 341, 348; "On Humanity in Dark
Times," 334; *On Revolution,* 87, 95, 97,
101, 105, 211, 215, 305, 312, 315, 319, 329,
334, 339, 342–44, 347; *The Origins of
Totalitarianism,* 23, 211, 212, 214, 238–39,
241, 283, 287, 297, 304, 305, 307, 312, 314,
346; "Philosophy and Politics," 100;
Philosophy of Right, 252; *Rahel Varnhagen,* 333; "Truth in Politics," 314; "Walter
Benjamin," 319; "What Is *Existenz*
Philosophy?," 334; "What Is Freedom?,"
314, 324, 339
argument: and Arendt, 206, 314, 320, 329;
and civic republicanism, 3; and Foucault,
273; and Habermas, 106, 145, 147, 174, 175,
179, 180, 187, 189, 192, 196, 200, 201, 204,
205; and Mill, 186. *See also* debate
aristocracy, 34–36, 39, 59, 66, 91, 128, 130,
132, 134
Aristotelianism, 220
Aristotle, 147, 222, 225, 255, 294; and Arendt,
99, 308, 316, 320, 322, 331, 351; and Hegel,
62; and Heidegger, 327; and Mill, 123;
Nicomachaean Ethics, 315; *Politics,* 30
art, 168–69, 173, 180

civic religion, 2, 17
civic republicanism: and active citizenship, 2–3; and Arendt, 11–12, 97–100, 103, 305, 307, 309, 326, 332, 342; argument in, 3; and citizen formation, 17; common good in, 17; electoral participation in, 18; and Foucault, 266; and Habermas, 178; and Hegel, 11–12, 51; and interests, 6; and liberalism, 2; and Machiavelli, 51; and Mill, 118, 120; pluralism in, 3; and private sphere, 24; and public good, 3; and Rousseau, 51; and Tocqueville, 11–12, 51, 257
civic virtue, 28, 67, 122, 255
civilization: and Adorno, 225, 226, 228, 233; and Arendt, 250; and Hegel, 218; and Horkheimer, 224–26, 230, 231, 233; and Mill, 110, 112, 114. *See also* culture
civil society: and Arendt, 88; and associational life, 27–29; defined, 27, 28; and economy, 31, 45; in the Enlightenment, 31; and Foucault, 275, 290, 292–93; and government, 33; and Habermas, 180; and Hegel, 30, 32, 34, 59, 60, 359n24; and the individual, 177; and Kant, 31; and Locke, 31; and Marx, 12–15; and Montesquieu, 35; and morality/ethics, 32, 45; as political society, 31; political vs. nonpolitical, 28–30; priority of the political in, 30; and public opinion, 31–32; and public-political life, 33; and the public realm, 28–29, 177; and the state, 12–15, 27–29, 34; and Tocqueville, 12, 27–48, 52, 63–64, 86, 88, 258, 348
class: and Arendt, 212, 309; and Foucault, 279; and the Frankfurt School, 175; and Habermas, 189; and Marcuse, 166; and Mill, 112, 131, 132; and Tocqueville, 38, 94
Clausewitz, Karl von, 265, 268, 270, 276
Coke, Edward, 276
Cold War, 158, 167, 168, 195
Coleridge, Samuel T., 113, 125, 132
common good, the: in civic republicanism, 17; and Habermas, 86, 188, 189; and Hegel, 51; and Machiavelli, 256; and Marx, 184; and Rousseau, 31, 184; and Tocqueville, 40, 44, 51, 52, 55, 93
communication: and Arendt, 206, 320; and Foucault, 273; and Habermas, 145–47, 196, 197, 199, 200, 202, 204; and Horkheimer and Adorno, 157
communicative rationalization, 174
communitarianism, 91, 92, 95
conformity: and Adorno, 151, 153, 155, 156, 232–35, 238; in contemporary America, 170; and Habermas, 193; and Horkheimer, 151, 153, 155, 156, 232–35; and Marcuse, 170, 234; and Mill, 114; and Tocqueville, 57, 91, 95, 156, 185

conscience, 66, 70, 71, 72, 74
consensus, 86, 100, 193, 194
Constant, Benjamin, 26, 51, 260, 300; on active surveillance of representatives, 26; and Arendt, 245, 326; on citizens, 24; on civic education, 257–58; despotism in, 10; on the education of citizens, 17–18; and Foucault, 266; on freedom, 3–5, 257, 258; "The Liberty of the Ancients Compared with that of the Moderns," 3–5, 332, 349; and Marx, 14; and Mill, 127, 138; on morality/ethics, 257; on paternalism, 257; on private independence, 18; on the private sphere, 24; on public freedom, 11, 17–18, 20; on rights, 258; and Rousseau, 3; on the state, 269; and Tocqueville, 47
consumers/consumer culture, 7, 92, 107, 140; and Adorno, 153–55, 157, 160; American, 172, 234, 235; and the Frankfurt School, 172, 203; and Habermas, 191, 193; and Horkheimer, 153–55, 157, 160; and Marcuse, 160, 161, 165–67, 170–71
corporations, 6, 21, 24, 29, 46, 268; and contemporary America, 141, 171, 172; and Habermas, 189; and Horkheimer and Adorno, 156; and Marcuse, 162–64, 166
critical theory, 168, 195
culture: and Adorno, 148–58, 161, 168, 213, 226; and Arendt, 100, 215–16; in contemporary America, 207; and Habermas, 86, 147, 179–80, 191; and Hegel, 50, 218, 253; and Horkheimer, 148–58, 161, 168, 226; and Kant, 113; and Marcuse, 161, 168–69; and Mill, 112, 116–18. *See also* civilization; mass culture

death/concentration camps, 211–14, 239–40, 251, 267, 295–96, 309. *See also* Jews
debate: and Arendt, 96, 98, 100, 306, 321, 329, 330, 339, 345; and contemporary America, 139; and Foucault, 265, 270; and Habermas, 86, 106, 180, 181, 183, 187, 198, 205; and Hegel, 64; and Horkheimer and Adorno, 156; and Marx, 184; and Mill, 137–38; and Tocqueville, 46, 259. *See also* argument
Debord, Guy, 300
decentralization: and Arendt, 89; and Tocqueville, 35, 36, 45, 78, 86, 87, 89, 90, 95, 130. *See also* centralization
deliberation: and Arendt, 96, 98–100, 306, 320, 321, 329, 330, 339, 345; and Foucault, 265; and Habermas, 145, 178, 187; and Marx, 184
democracy: and Arendt, 87, 97, 98, 106, 250, 305, 306, 309–13, 317, 322, 323; and contemporary America, 141, 142; and

democracy (continued)

decentralization, 29–30; and despotism, 10, 35; and Foucault, 291; and Habermas, 145, 147, 174, 178, 183, 185, 192, 197–99, 202; and Hegel, 51, 63, 66, 73, 74, 76; legal protections in, 297; and Marcuse, 161, 162, 168, 170; and Marx, 23; and Mill, 121, 124, 132, 138–40, 186; and pluralism, 85; and the public realm, 177; and Rousseau, 45; and Tocqueville, 6, 13, 29–30, 33, 34, 36–40, 42, 43, 51–55, 57–60, 63, 66, 78, 80, 87, 89–95, 106, 185–86, 258, 259; and the warfare state, 171–72

demographics, 82, 149, 170, 195, 203

Descartes, René, 56, 57, 146, 333

desire, 154, 155, 164, 170

despotism: administrative, 6, 40, 52, 90, 230, 258, 291; and Arendt, 107, 247; bureau-cratic, 20; in Constant, 10; democratic, 10, 35; and the Frankfurt School, 230; and Hegel, 63; and Mill, 111, 112, 119, 125–27, 136; and Napoleon I, 42; and Tocqueville, 6, 10, 39, 40, 51–52, 58, 60, 75, 77, 89, 90, 93, 107, 156, 258, 259, 291

Dickey, Laurence, 366n56

Diderot, Denis, 31

Dinesen, Isak, 210

disenchantment, of the world, 173, 219, 221, 223–27

dissent, 68, 72, 80, 95, 259. See also argument

domination: and Adorno, 22–23, 25, 146, 147, 155, 156, 159, 160, 163, 173, 212–13, 215, 225–28, 231, 232, 237, 253, 275; and Arendt, 212, 214, 215, 239–42, 244, 251, 308–9, 340; and Foucault, 22, 25, 262, 266, 268, 270, 274, 276, 288, 299, 300; and the Frankfurt School, 22–23, 175; and Horkheimer, 22–23, 146, 147, 155, 156, 159, 160, 163, 173, 225–27, 229, 231, 232, 253, 275; and institutions, 24, 25; and Marcuse, 22, 158–63, 166–68; and Marx, 299; and reason, 228, 231; and Weber, 25, 173, 299

Dostoevsky, Fyodor, 224

duty, 58, 73, 229

economic sphere, the: and Adorno, 149–50, 153, 154; and Arendt, 242, 244, 246; and civil society, 29, 31, 45; and Habermas, 179–81, 195; and Hegel, 80; and Horkheimer and Adorno, 149–50, 153, 154; and Marcuse, 158, 162, 166–68; and Marx, 21; and Mill, 115; and the Scottish Enlightenment, 32, 33; and Tocqueville, 42, 80

egoism, 16, 21, 32, 92, 229. See also selfishness

Eichmann, Adolf, 72, 224

elites: and Arendt, 107, 306, 307, 309, 316, 317, 336, 344, 345; and Mill, 110, 121, 122, 127, 128, 132, 137; and Tocqueville, 56, 107, 185

Engels, Friedrich, 144, 160

Enlightenment, the: and Adorno, 155, 156, 213–15, 225–27, 232, 238; and America, 33; and Arendt, 97; civil society in, 31; and Foucault, 270, 272–75, 298; and the Frankfurt School, 204; and Habermas, 86, 204; and Horkheimer, 155, 156, 225–27, 229, 232; independent thought in, 57; and Marx, 317; and reason, 223; utilitarian philoso-phies of, 50

equality: and Arendt, 95, 97, 102, 242, 243, 246, 248, 249, 310, 311, 320, 321, 339, 340; and Foucault, 264, 285; and Habermas, 184; and Hegel, 80; and Locke, 112; and Mill, 112, 115, 121; and Tocqueville, 34, 39, 40, 42, 43, 52–54, 56, 58, 75, 78, 80, 87, 91, 95, 185–86, 259

Estaing, Comte d', 276

Ettinger, Elsbieta, Hannah Arendt/Martin Heidegger, 303–6

Europe: and Arendt, 101, 104, 238, 241, 242, 246–48; aristocracy in, 34–35; the bourgeoisie in, 34; the estates of, 34–35; and Mill, 110, 114–15, 117, 118; permanent associations in, 34–35; political associa-tions in, 38; and Tocqueville, 59, 89

existentialism. See under Arendt, Hannah

false consciousness, 144, 146, 156, 163, 165, 167, 172, 235

false projection, 233, 234

fascism, 22, 141, 159, 160, 233, 235, 313

fear, 9–10

Ferguson, Adam, 31

feudalism/feudal society, 7, 16, 30, 52, 60, 125, 164, 179, 190, 197, 264, 284, 289

Fichte, Johann Gottlieb, 149

Florence, 256

Foucault, Michel, 11–12, 61, 251; and Adorno, 268, 275; and Arendt, 265, 266, 269, 283, 287, 293, 341, 347; and Bentham, 270–72; on biopolitics, 291, 294–97, 300; on biopower, 267, 268, 291–93, 297–98; on the bourgeoisie, 264; on a carceral network, 268, 275; on citizens, 265; on civic docility, 261–63, 266, 300–301; on civic republican-ism, 266; on civil society, 275, 290, 292–93; and Clausewitz, 265, 268, 270, 276; on class, 279; on common law, 288–90; and Constant, 266; on control, 275; on debate, 265, 270; on de-differentiation, 267–68, 275, 276, 295, 300; on deliberation, 265; on democracy, 291; on the disciplinary gaze, 273; on the disciplinary society, 23–25, 259–62, 265–70, 272, 275, 276, 290–93, 298, 300; on domination, 22, 25, 262, 266, 268, 270, 274, 276, 288, 299, 300; on the Enlightenment, 270, 272–75, 298; on equality, 264, 285; on freedom, 264–67, 270,

273, 285, 299; on the French nobility, 279, 280, 282, 284, 288; and the French Revolution, 270, 279, 291; and Habermas, 265, 272–73; on history, 281–82; and Hobbes, 265, 277, 278; and Horkheimer, 275; and Humboldt, 266; on the individual, 262, 263, 266–67, 291; on individualism, 110; on juridical knowledge, 281; on juridical punishment, 275; on the law, 261; on liberalism, 260, 263–67, 269, 274, 293, 298; on local institutions, 261; and Machiavelli, 290, 293; and Marx, 298–99; on massifying power, 292, 300; and Mill, 266; on military discipline, 275; and Napoleon I, 274; on the nation, 283, 288–89; on nationalism, 279; on national universality, 291; on the nation-state, 291; and Nietzsche, 25, 262, 276, 280; on panopticism, 268, 273, 274; on particulars vs. universals, 289; on "politics is war," 268–70, 276, 290; on power, 267, 268, 270, 271, 276, 286, 291–94, 297–300; on the power over death and life, 291, 293, 294; on the private vs. the public, 266, 267, 270; on public freedom, 266; on public health, 292, 297; on the public realm, 265–67, 269, 270, 273–75, 290; on the public right, 260, 261, 265, 266, 270, 276, 277, 279, 281, 282, 284, 298; and Pufendorf, 277; on race, 279, 280, 283, 290, 292; on *raison d'état*, 272, 287, 292, 293, 296; on reason, 273, 275; on re-differentiation, 268; on republicanism, 267; on rights, 264–67, 275, 291, 298; and Rousseau, 270, 275; on the rule of law, 291; on the social contract, 266; on social control, 270–72; on society, 270, 271, 287; on sovereignty, 261, 263, 265–67, 291; on the state, 261, 267, 275, 277–79, 282–85, 287, 288, 291–94, 297; on subjectification, 263; on subjectivity, 262; on subjects, constitution of, 260; on subjects, manufacture of, 266, 267; on subjugation, 263, 265, 267, 293; on the supervisory gaze, 262, 263; on surveillance, 261, 262, 265, 269, 271, 274, 292; on the Third Estate, 288–90; and Tocqueville, 75, 90, 266, 275, 294, 298; on totalitarianism, 293, 296; on training, 262, 293; on transparency, 24, 270, 272; and Weber, 293; on the welfare state, 291, 292, 300

Foucault, Michel, works by: *Discipline and Punish*, 22, 261–62, 265, 267–70, 274, 275, 287, 290, 298; *History of Sexuality*, 265, 268, 293–94; lectures (1977–79), 276; "Panopticism," 270–72; *"Society Must be Defended": Lectures at the Collège de France, 1975–1976,* 269, 276, 277, 279, 280, 291; Tanner lectures (1979), 293

France, 76; and Hegel, 61, 65; and Marx, 13, 15; and Mill, 119, 121, 138; and Tocqueville, 29, 42, 52–54, 59, 65, 76, 90, 122, 130

Frankfurt School, the, 46, 143–45; and Arendt, 242, 340; on autonomy, 203; on the bourgeois public sphere, 172; on class domination, 175; on consumers/consumer culture, 172, 203; on contemporary America, 172; on culture, 168; on despotism, 230; on dialectics, 147; on domination, 22–23; on the Enlightenment, 204; and Freud, 160; and Habermas, 176, 197; and Hegel, 252; on ideology, 172, 202–3; on instrumental reason, 252; and Marx, 144; and Marxism, 144; on mass culture, 203; on maturity, 144, 145; on the media, 202; on public opinion, 172; on the public realm, 172; on the total society, 148, 161, 163, 164, 203, 226, 230, 232, 234, 235; and Weber, 173

Fraser, Nancy, 188, 202, 299

Frederick the Great, 183, 275

freedom: and Adorno, 173, 237; and Arendt, 5, 87, 89, 95, 97, 101–5, 215–16, 252, 253, 302, 306, 310, 314, 321, 324, 326, 329, 339, 340, 342, 343, 346; of choice, 2; and Constant, 3–5, 257, 258; and contemporary America, 141; and Foucault, 264–67, 270, 273, 285, 299; and Hegel, 49, 50, 62, 66–70, 72, 74, 80, 217–18, 333; individual, 4; from interference, 2; local, 7, 40, 41, 43, 45, 54, 58, 60; and Locke, 112; and Machiavelli, 257; and Marcuse, 167; and Marx, 14, 299; and Mill, 2, 110, 112, 116–17, 123, 125, 141, 186; negative, 2, 51; positive, 2; public, 4; and Rousseau, 4; subjective, 51; and Tocqueville, 5, 40, 41, 43–47, 54, 57, 58, 60, 68, 69, 75, 78, 80, 87, 89, 91, 94, 95, 257, 258. *See also* independence; public freedom

French Revolution, the, 25, 33, 223; and Arendt, 243, 312, 329, 342–44; and civic education, 256, 257; and Foucault, 270, 279, 291; and freedom, 4; and Hegel, 61; independent thought in, 57; and Marx, 14; and physiocrats, 182, 183; and Tocqueville, 48, 60

Freud, Sigmund, 160, 164, 213, 214, 228, 236, 237, 252; *Civilization and Its Discontents,* 225

Freyer, Hans, 273

Friedman, Thomas, 349

Gadamer, Hans-Georg, 314, 336

Galbraith, John Kenneth, 195

Gaus, Günter, 210

general will (*volonté générale*), 64, 86, 99, 183, 184, 193, 199, 204, 351

Germany, 65, 145, 216, 237, 238, 247

Horkheimer, Max (*continued*)
consciousness, 146, 235; on false projection, 233, 234; on feeling, 230; and Foucault, 275; and Freud, 214; and Habermas, 197; and Hegel, 224, 226; on heteronomy, 155; and Hobbes, 227, 229; on the Holocaust, 235; on ideology, 155, 156; on the individual, 160–61; on individualism, 149; on integration, 148; on interests, 229; on intersubjectivity, 157; and Kant, 146, 150, 156, 228; and Machiavelli, 227, 229; and Mandeville, 227, 229; and Marcuse, 158–61, 170; on the market, 148–50; and Marx, 149, 155; and Marxism, 231, 233–35; on mass culture, 148–52; on the masses, 154, 230, 232–35; on maturity, 145; on the media, 148, 149, 152, 153, 170; on the middle class, 149; on mimesis, 233, 234; on myth, 225–26; on nature, 146, 147, 225, 228, 230–31; and Nietzsche, 214, 226, 227, 229–30, 235; on particulars vs. universals, 225, 226, 253; on power, 227, 229; on the public realm, 170, 175; on rationality, 148, 155, 222, 225–27, 230; on reason, 146, 147, 157, 173, 213, 214, 222–27, 229–32, 275; on religion, 154; and Sade, 229; on science, 146–47, 225, 226, 228, 229; on self-preservation, 226, 230; on self-reliance, 150; on sexuality, 154; on society, 226, 229; on the state, 156; on technology, 226, 230; and Tocqueville, 156; on totalitarianism, 225, 229; on truth, 227; on values, 229; on violence, 231; and Weber, 147, 156, 160, 214, 222–23; on workers, 148, 152, 153, 155
Horkheimer, Max, works by: *Dialectic of Enlightenment*, 146, 148–61, 170, 173, 203, 212, 222, 225–36, 239, 252, 253, 275; *Eclipse of Reason*, 222, 225; "Elements of Anti-Semitism," 231–35; "Traditional and Critical Theory," 144
Humboldt, Wilhelm von, 125, 260, 266
Hume, David, 31

idealism, 215, 228
identification, 72, 73, 74, 81, 82, 83
identity, 39, 242, 246, 247, 251
ideology, 145, 155, 156, 172, 202–4
Ignatieff, Michael, 218
imperialism, 23, 110–12, 115–17, 212, 243, 244, 245, 248, 251
independence, 69, 70, 74–79, 83, 87, 100. *See also* autonomy; freedom
India, 112, 114, 118, 138
individual, the: and Adorno, 160–61, 173; and Arendt, 98–100; and civil society, 177; and Foucault, 262, 263, 266–67, 291; freedom of, 4; and Habermas, 177; and Hegel, 33, 61,

66, 71; and Horkheimer, 160–61; and Marcuse, 160–61, 164; modern, 177; and Tocqueville, 33, 34, 39, 44, 47, 66, 185
individualism: and Arendt, 100, 104, 212, 245; and Foucault, 110; and Hegel, 49–51, 60, 65–66, 69, 70, 72, 75, 80, 83; and Horkheimer and Adorno, 149; and Marcuse, 158, 165; methodological, 49, 51; and Mill, 109–12, 114, 117, 121, 136; moral, 49; and Rawls, 111; and subjectivism, 66, 68, 69, 72, 83; and Tocqueville, 39–40, 50–60, 65–67, 75, 78, 80, 83, 87, 90–93, 100, 258
institutions: and Adorno, 25; and Arendt, 95, 97, 101, 102, 215–16, 242, 247, 248, 252, 253, 306, 311, 321, 347; and domination, 24, 25; and Habermas, 189; and Hegel, 73; and sovereignty, 91; and Tocqueville, 78, 95
interest(s): and Arendt, 331; and civic republicanism, 6; competing, 194, 195; in contemporary America, 5; general, 184, 185, 194–96, 199; generalizable, 198; general vs. particular, 12; and Habermas, 186, 188, 189, 194–96, 198, 199; and Horkheimer, 229; individual vs. general, 63, 79; and Mill, 124, 130, 131; particular vs. general, 64, 186; private, 19–20, 59, 245; private vs. general, 54, 55, 63; and the public realm, 6; pursuit of, 16–17; rationalization of, 187, 198; of society, 177, 181; and Tocqueville, 44, 54, 59, 79; universal, 195, 198
Italian city-states, 256

Jacobins, 45, 70
Jaspers, Karl, 303, 306, 313, 334
Jay, Martin, 306, 309, 315, 317, 318, 335–36; "The Political Existentialism of Hannah Arendt," 313–16
Jews, 230–36, 303–5, 308–10, 334. *See also* death/concentration camps
judgment: and Arendt, 87, 100, 205, 206, 308, 315; and Habermas, 175, 178; and Hegel, 68, 72; and Mill, 124; private, 53, 56–58; and Tocqueville, 54, 56, 57, 67, 78, 87, 92, 185
Julius, F. H., 273
Jünger, Ernst, 273, 313
justice, 43, 58, 93, 122, 170, 201, 311, 312, 338, 345, 346

Kahan, Alan, 115
Kant, Immanuel: and Adorno, 146, 150, 156, 237; and Arendt, 205, 307, 310, 333, 338; on authority, 113; on the categorical imperative, 183, 229; on civil society, 31; on the common good, 188; on culture, 113; and Frederick the Great, 183; and Habermas, 86, 184, 198; and Hegel, 69, 70,

218; and Horkheimer, 146, 150, 156, 228; on maturity, 10, 113, 143, 144; on paternalism, 10, 113; on the public realm, 183–84; on reason, 31, 113, 150, 183, 184, 228–29; and Weber, 222

Kant, Immanuel, works by: "An Answer to the Question: What is Enlightenment?," 10, 183; *Critique of Practical Reason,* 228–29; *Critique of Pure Reason,* 147, 229

Kateb, George, 319, 338

Kirchheimer, Otto, 275

law, the: and Arendt, 97, 106, 215–16, 243, 247, 248, 252, 253, 305, 306, 321, 347; and Foucault, 261, 288, 289, 291; and Habermas, 86, 182; and Hegel, 59, 60, 64, 67, 72, 73; and Mill, 118, 119; and public right, 260, 261, 265, 266, 270, 276, 277, 279, 281, 282, 284, 298; and Tocqueville, 37, 77, 106

League of Nations, 249

Leibniz, Gottfried Wilhelm, 146, 218, 221

Lenin, Vladimir Ilyich, 144, 234, 313

Leonardo da Vinci, 220

Levi, Primo, 304

liberalism, 107; and Agamben, 268; and Arendt, 86, 97, 99, 104, 339; and civic docility, 260; and civic republicanism, 2; and disciplinary society, 24–25; and Foucault, 260, 263–67, 269, 274, 293, 298; and Habermas, 86; and Hegel, 80; and Hobbes, 260; and individual rights, 263–64; and juridical mind-set, 278; and Marx, 23; and mass culture, 91; and Mill, 110, 122, 138; and pluralism, 85; power, 24; and private sphere, 272; and procedural-ism, 278; and *raison d'état,* 296; and Rawls, 110, 111; and Schmitt, 349–50; and Tocqueville, 80, 86

Lilburne, John, 276, 279

Limbaugh, Rush, 172

local administration: and Arendt, 101; and Tocqueville, 36, 37, 52, 55, 63–64, 76, 95, 101, 258

local autonomy: and Tocqueville, 88–89

local freedom: and Tocqueville, 54

local institutions: and Foucault, 261; and Tocqueville, 122

localism: and Tocqueville, 75, 78

local organizations: and Tocqueville, 30, 35

local self-government, 82

Locke, John, 15, 79, 177; and active surveil-lance of representatives, 26; and Arendt, 97; on citizens, 24; on civil society, 31; on equality, 112; on freedom, 112; and Hegel, 73; and Horkheimer and Adorno, 150; and Mill, 112; on paternalism, 112, 260; and physiocrats, 182; on reason, 112; on rights, 112; *Second Treatise of Government,* 112,

260; on society and government, 47; on state of nature, 31 *Two Treatises,* 181

Louis XIV, 33, 77, 277

Löwenthal, Leo, 231

Lukács, Georg, 147

Luther, Martin, 57

Lyotard, Jean-François, 214

Machiavelli, Nicolò: and Arendt, 96, 99, 326, 338; and associational life, 19; and citizen formation, 17; and civic education, 256; civic religion in, 2; and civic republican-ism, 51; and the common good, 256; *Discourses,* 2, 129, 256, 290; and Foucault, 290, 293; on freedom, 257; and Hegel, 66; and Heidegger, 329; and Horkheimer, 227, 229; military in, 2; and Mill, 129; *The Prince,* 256; on rationality, 220; on republicanism, 256, 257; and Tocqueville, 43, 257

MacIntyre, Alasdair, 224

Madison, James, 99; *Federalist* no. 10, 12, 44, 98, 171; *Federalist* no. 50, 98

majority tyranny, 36, 38, 57, 76–78, 83, 86, 91, 93, 95, 99, 132, 185

Mandeville, Bernard, 227, 229

Marcuse, Herbert, 11–12, 83, 143, 172; on the administered society, 173; on administra-tion, 166; and Adorno, 158–61, 170; on advertising/public relations, 161, 163, 164, 167, 171; on alienation, 165, 169; on America, 168; and Arendt, 164–65; on art, 168–69; on autonomy, 161; on the bourgeoisie, 166, 168–70; on capitalism, 158–60, 162, 164, 165, 168; on citizens, 162; on classes, 166; on conformity, 170, 234; on consumers/consumer culture, 160, 161, 165–67, 170–71; on corporations, 162–64, 166; on culture, 161, 168–69; on democ-racy, 161, 162, 168, 170; on desire, 164, 170; on domination, 22, 25, 158–63, 166–68; on the economic sphere, 158, 162, 166–68; on false consciousness, 163, 165, 167; on freedom, 167; on government, 164; and Habermas, 193, 197; and Hegel, 166, 170; and Heidegger, 163, 165; on heteronomy, 164; and Horkheimer, 158–61, 170; on the individual, 160–61, 164; on individualism, 165; on justice, 170; and Marx, 170; and Marxism, 161, 165; on mass culture, 166, 169; on maturity, 145; on the media, 163, 164, 167, 170; and Mill, 164, 165; on mimesis, 164, 165; on nature, 161; *One Dimensional Man,* 25, 158–73, 203, 234; on one-dimensionality, 165, 167; on pluralism, 168, 171; on the private sphere, 161, 164; on the private vs. the public, 164; on the proletariat, 166, 168; on public opinion, 164;

Marcuse, Herbert *(continued)*
on the public realm, 161, 170, 175; on
rationality, 158, 162, 170; on reason, 146,
165; on science, 158, 162, 164; on society,
163, 165, 168; and Socrates, 165; on the
state, 167; on technology, 158, 161–64,
166–70, 173; and Tocqueville, 164; on
totalitarianism, 25, 163–65, 170; on the
warfare state, 167; and Weber, 160, 162,
164; on the working class, 166
market, the: and Hegel, 32; and Horkheimer
and Adorno, 148–50; and Marx, 13, 15, 159;
and Mill, 21; pressures of, 6, 8; and
Tocqueville, 41–42
Marx, Karl, 8, 58, 147, 148, 160; and Adorno,
149, 155; on America, 13, 15; on the
American Revolution, 14; and Arendt, 96,
97, 242, 243, 307, 314, 318, 319, 325, 326,
335, 338, 340, 342; on civil society, 12–15;
on the common good, 184; and Constant,
14; on debate, 184; on deliberation, 184; on
democracy, 23; on domination, 299; on the
economic sphere, 21; on egoism, 16; on the
Enlightenment, 317; and Foucault, 298–99;
on France, 13, 15; and the Frankfurt
School, 144; on freedom, 14, 299; on the
French Revolution, 14; and Habermas, 145,
184; and Horkheimer, 149, 155; on
liberalism, 23; and Marcuse, 170; on the
market, 13, 15; on power, 299; on the
private realm, 15; on public opinion, 184;
on the public realm, 184; on republics, 13;
on rights, 14, 15; on species-being, 14, 16
Marx, Karl, works by: *Capital,* 159, 163;
Communist Manifesto, 349; "On the Jewish
Question," 12, 264, 298
Marxism, 144; and Adorno, 231, 233–35; and
Arendt, 310, 329, 331; and Horkheimer,
231, 233–35; and Marcuse, 161, 165
mass culture: and the Frankfurt School, 203;
and Habermas, 190, 191; and Horkheimer
and Adorno, 148–52; and liberalism, 91; and
Marcuse, 166, 169; and Mill, 83, 136, 204;
and Tocqueville, 156, 204. *See also* culture
masses, the: and Adorno, 154, 160, 232–35;
and Arendt, 312; and Horkheimer, 154,
160, 230, 232–35; and Marcuse, 160; and
Tocqueville, 89
material interests: and Arendt, 101; and
Tocqueville, 7, 18, 42, 55, 87, 90, 92, 94, 101
maturity: and Adorno, 237, 238; and
contemporary America, 139, 142; and
falsely objectivist accounts, 223; and the
Frankfurt School, 144, 145; and Habermas,
193, 205; and Kant, 10, 113, 143, 144; and
Mill, 110, 113–14, 117, 119, 124, 130, 133,
138, 139, 142. See also *Bildung;* civic
education

McCarthy, Thomas, 174, 188
McCullough, David, 353
media: and Adorno, 148, 149, 152–54; 170;
and contemporary America, 172; and
feeling, 234; and the Frankfurt School, 202;
and Habermas, 176, 178, 191–93, 201; and
Horkheimer, 148, 149, 152–54, 170; and
Marcuse, 163, 164, 167, 170; modern, 46;
and political freedom, 5
middle class, the, 117, 122, 123, 130
Mill, James, 122, 124–25, 130–31
Mill, John Stuart, 107, 260, 263, 300; on
action by citizens, 26; on agon, 136; on
America, 121; on ancient Greece, 129, 138;
on Anglo-Americans, 117, 119; and Arendt,
99, 100, 325, 326; on argument, 186; on
the aristocracy, 128, 130, 132, 134; on
aristocratic liberalism, 122; and Aristotle,
123; on association/associations, 18–20,
186; on Athens, 129, 135, 138; on authority,
118, 134, 137; on autonomy, 109, 110, 121,
123, 125; on barbarism, 111, 112, 118, 119,
126, 129; and Bentham, 120, 124–25,
130–31; on *Bildung,* 125; and Carlyle, 125;
on China, 114, 115, 119, 138; on civic
education, 22, 113, 119–27, 129, 131–33,
135–38, 140, 238; on civic republicanism,
118, 120; on civic virtue, 122; on civilization, 110, 112, 114; on classes, 112, 131, 132;
and Coleridge, 113, 125, 132; on the
common good, 188; on conformity, 114;
and Constant, 127, 138; on a constitution,
117, 120; on cultural-historical development, 113–14; on cultural stagnation, 114,
115; on culture, 112, 116–18; on custom,
114, 115, 136; on debate, 137–38; on
democracy, 121, 124, 132, 138–40, 186; on
despotism, 111, 112, 119, 125–27, 136; on
diversity, 110; on the economic sphere, 115;
on elites, 110, 121, 122, 127, 128, 132, 137;
on equality, 112, 115, 121; on Europe, 110,
114–15; and Foucault, 266; on France, 119,
121, 138; on freedom, 2, 110, 112, 116–17,
123, 125, 141, 186; on the free market, 21;
on genius, 114–17; and Goethe, 125; on
government, 113, 120–21; and Habermas,
185–88, 195, 199; and Hare, 131–32; and
Hegel, 113, 115, 117, 123–24, 126; on
history, 117; on humanism, 110, 117; on
imperialism, 110, 115–17; on India, 112,
114, 118, 138; on individualism, 109–12,
114, 117, 121, 136; on interests, 124, 130,
131; and James Mill, 124–25, 130–31; on
judgment, 124; on justice, 122; on law, 118,
119; on liberalism, 110, 122, 138; on a
liberal public, 12; and Locke, 112; and
Machiavelli, 129; on majority tyranny, 132;
and Marcuse, 164, 165; on mass culture, 83,

136, 204; on maturity, 110, 113–14, 117, 119, 124, 130, 133, 138, 139, 142; on the middle class, 117, 122, 123, 130; on morality/ethics, 114; on native Americans, 118; on obedience, 134, 136; on originality, 114; on parties, 132, 134; on paternalism, 110, 115–16, 119, 121, 123, 125, 126, 133–34; on patriotism, 129; on perspectivism, 188, 199; and Plato, 123, 137; on pluralism, 130, 185, 186; on political participation, 117, 123, 124, 127–29, 131, 132, 135, 138, 140; on popular government, 127; on popular sovereignty, 131; on the private sphere, 121; on the private vs. the public, 16; on privatism, 126–27, 140; on progress, 110, 117; on psychology, 125; on public opinion, 114, 115, 127, 130, 134–36, 185, 186; on the public realm, 123, 124, 135, 136, 186–87; on public spirit, 118, 121, 122, 124, 129, 132; and Rawls, 110–11; on reason, 112; on representation/representative government, 118–19, 121–23, 128, 131–34, 139, 142; on rights, 122; and Romanticism, 113, 139; and Rousseau, 121, 123; on self-government, 112–13, 121, 124, 130, 133, 138; on selfishness, 130; on self-reliance, 126; on the social contract, 110; on society, 111; and Socrates, 136, 137; on southern Europe, 117, 118; on Spain, 138; and Tocqueville, 57, 74, 75, 79, 91, 121–24, 126–28, 130, 133–35, 138; on the tutorial state, 112; on utilitarianism, 125, 139; on the vote, 131; and Weber, 379n30; on the working class, 118, 122, 123

Mill, John Stuart, works by: *Autobiography,* 125; "Civilization," 108, 121; *Considerations on Representative Government,* 109, 114, 117, 120, 122, 123, 125–26, 128, 129, 131–35, 141, 142; "Inaugural Address," 137; *On Liberty,* 108–9, 114–17, 122, 123, 125, 126, 129, 133, 135–37, 186; *Principles of Political Economy,* 21; "Recent Writers on Reform," 137; *Representative Government,* 112–13, 120; review of Tocqueville's *Democracy in America I,* 134–35; "The Spirit of the Age," 113; *Utilitarianism,* 111

mimesis, 164, 165, 233, 234

Montesquieu, Charles-Louis de Secondat, baron de, 10, 30, 33, 35, 36, 45, 96, 325

morality/ethics: and Adorno, 215, 238; and Arendt, 215, 241, 310; and civil society, 32, 45; and Constant, 257; and Hegel, 59, 70, 71, 79, 80, 82, 218; and Mill, 114; objectivist accounts of, 223; and Tocqueville, 58, 79, 80, 82, 93, 94, 258

Mündigkeit, 198, 202, 205–8

Napoleon I, 18, 33, 42, 60, 61, 74, 257, 274, 275, 370n124

nation: and Foucault, 283, 288–89; and state, 248

nationalism: and Adorno, 237; and Arendt, 212, 242, 246–47, 307; and Foucault, 279; and Hegel, 69

nation-state: and Arendt, 242, 243, 245, 247–51; and civic education, 256–57; and Foucault, 291

natural law, 50, 256

natural order, 180, 182, 183

nature: and Adorno, 146, 147, 215, 225, 227, 228; and Arendt, 215–16, 241, 242, 251–53; and Hegel, 219; and Horkheimer, 146, 147, 225, 228, 230–31; and Marcuse, 161; and Weber, 220

Nazism, 165, 230, 234, 280, 292, 295, 304, 308–10, 334

Negri, Antonio, 23, 24

neo-absolutism, 25

Nietzsche, Friedrich, 83, 230, 252, 259; and Adorno, 213, 214, 226–28, 235, 237; and Arendt, 105, 305, 309–12, 325, 330, 341; and Foucault, 25, 262, 276, 280; *Genealogy of Morals,* 230, 231; and Horkheimer, 214, 226, 227, 229–30, 235; and Tocqueville, 75; *Twilight of the Idols,* 220; and Weber, 220

Nozick, Robert, 49

opinion: and Arendt, 205–6, 308, 314, 315, 317, 320, 330. *See also* public opinion

Paine, Thomas, 15, 73

pan-movements, 23, 212, 246–47

particulars vs. universals, 225, 226, 228, 232, 253, 289

paternalism: and Constant, 257; and Kant, 10, 113; and Locke, 112, 260; and Mill, 110, 115–16, 119, 121, 123, 125, 126, 133–34; and Tocqueville, 258, 263

patriotism, 78, 79, 100, 129

Perrot, Michelle, 272

philosophes, the, 33, 79, 175

physiocrats, the, 175, 182–84

Pitkin, Hanna, 341–42, 344

Plato, 188, 211, 221, 225; *Apology,* 74, and Arendt, 96, 105, 308, 314, 315, 317–20, 322, 323, 325–27, 351; *Laws,* 105; and Mill, 123, 137; *Republic,* 30, 65, 220, 225; and Tocqueville, 257

pluralism: and civic republicanism, 3; and contemporary America, 172; and democracy, 85; and Habermas, 187, 188, 194, 200–202; and Hegel, 44, 74, 80–81; as ideology, 204; and liberalism, 85; and Marcuse, 168, 171; and Mill, 130, 185, 186; and Rawls, 110, 111; and Tocqueville, 75, 77, 78, 80–81, 87, 94, 95, 106, 107, 130, 185, 186, 258 plurality: and Arendt, 87, 95, 99, 100, 106, 156–57, 187, 241, 242, 302, 307, 308, 309, 317, 320–22, 324–26, 329–32, 336, 351, 352; and Habermas, 198

Pocock, J. G. A., *The Machiavellian Moment*, 355n2, 356n3

political participation: and Arendt, 87, 89, 95, 97–99, 106; and Hegel, 62, 64, 65, 67; and Mill, 117, 123, 124, 127–29, 131, 132, 135, 138, 140; and Tocqueville, 55, 65, 67, 80, 87–89, 95, 106, 122, 135, 178–79

political parties: and Arendt, 247; and Habermas, 176, 185; and Mill, 132, 134; and Tocqueville, 35

popular sovereignty, 37, 65, 66, 76, 90, 131. *See also* sovereignty

positivism, 147, 165–66, 225

postmodernism, 22, 152, 275

power: and Adorno, 213, 227; and Arendt, 101, 102, 212, 241, 242, 244–45, 306, 311; and Foucault, 267, 268, 270, 271, 276, 286, 291–94, 297–300; and Horkheimer, 227, 229; legitimate vs. illegitimate, 299; and liberalism, 24; and Marx, 299; and reason, 229; and republicanism, 24; and Weber, 299

pre-Socratics, the, 217, 311

press/newspapers, the, 35, 44, 64, 75, 178

private sphere, the: and Arendt, 95, 101, 107, 206, 254; and civic republicanism, 24; and Constant, 24; and Habermas, 86, 178, 179, 193; and liberalism, 272; and Marcuse, 161, 164; and Marx, 15; and Mill, 121, 127–28; and Tocqueville, 43, 47, 52, 56, 92, 93, 95, 101, 107

private, the, vs. the public: and Agamben, 294; and Arendt, 16, 99, 340–41; and Foucault, 266, 267, 270; and Habermas, 189–91; and Marcuse, 164; and Tocqueville, 54, 55, 79

privatism, 20; and Hegel, 71; and Mill, 126–27, 140; and Tocqueville, 8, 34, 39, 53, 66

progress, 110, 117, 237

proletariat, 159, 166, 168

Prussia, 65, 74

public freedom: and active surveillance of representatives, 26; and Adorno, 173; and Arendt, 97, 101, 344, 347; and Constant, 4, 5, 11, 17–18, 20; contemporary neglect of, 7; and Foucault, 266; and Hegel, 66, 80; post-Rousseauian, 12; provision for, 300; and rights, 12; and Tocqueville, 42, 47, 66, 67, 80, 90. *See also* freedom

public good, 3, 15, 33, 56, 59, 174–75, 187, 245

publicity, critical: and Habermas, 175, 176, 178, 180, 181, 189, 190, 192–95

public opinion, 20, 21, 30; and Arendt, 87, 98–100; and civil society, 31–32; and the

Frankfurt School, 172; and Habermas, 86, 174–76, 180, 182, 184, 185, 187, 192–94, 196, 207; and Hegel, 32, 65, 184, 187; and Marcuse, 164; and Marx, 184; and Mill, 114, 115, 127, 130, 134–36, 185, 186; modern manipulation of, 46; and Tocqueville, 56–58, 78, 79, 86, 87, 90–95, 185–87. *See also* opinion

public realm, the: and Adorno, 170, 175, 238; and Agamben, 294; and ancient Greece, 176, 177; ancient vs. modern, 273–74; and Arendt, 86, 88, 96, 97, 101, 102, 106, 156–57, 242, 247, 250, 253–54, 269, 305–11, 314, 317, 319–27, 330–32, 339, 340, 342, 343, 346, 347; autonomy of, 16–17; care for, 19; and civil society, 28–29, 177; and contemporary America, 139, 172; and democracy, 177; and Foucault, 265–67, 269, 270, 273–75, 290; and the Frankfurt School, 172; and Habermas, 46, 85–86, 105–6, 147, 174–77, 179–81, 196, 198, 200, 205, 207, 272; and Hegel, 51, 66–67, 69, 80, 184; and Horkheimer, 170, 175; interests in, 5, 6; and Kant, 183–84; and Marcuse, 161, 170, 175; and Marx, 184; mediatized, 46; and Mill, 123, 124, 135, 136, 186–87; modern, 46; and social interests, 15; and the state, 177; and the state/civil society distinction, 20; as theatrical, 269; and Tocqueville, 39, 40, 51, 52, 75, 80, 87–89, 92, 93, 106, 186, 257–59; withdrawal from, 39, 40, 87, 89, 92, 258. *See also* bourgeois public sphere, the

public spirit: and Arendt, 99–101, 104, 330, 332; and Mill, 118, 121, 122, 124, 129, 132; and Tocqueville, 43, 55, 89

Pufendorf, Samuel, 277

Puritans, 58

Putnam, Robert, 89

race: and Arendt, 23, 212, 242, 246–47, 250, 251, 309; and Foucault, 279, 280, 283, 290, 292

rationality: administrative, 21, 173, 293; and Adorno, 148, 155, 211, 214, 226–28, 230; and Arendt, 205; communicative/deliberative, 273; conceptual, 225–27; end-constitutive, 222; end-discriminating, 223; and Habermas, 181–82, 192, 199, 202; and Horkheimer, 148, 155, 222, 225–27, 230; instrumental, 219, 222; and Marcuse, 158, 162, 170; means-end, 220; purposive and formal, 223; and Weber, 220, 223

rationalization, 390n101; bureaucratic, 173; communicative, 174; and disenchantment, 219; and Habermas, 173, 196; and Weber, 219, 223

rational subject, formation of, 213

Rawls, John, 49, 95, 110–11; *Political Liberalism,* 110; *A Theory of Justice,* 110
reason: and Adorno, 146, 147, 157, 173, 213–15, 225–27, 231, 232, 275; and Arendt, 206, 215; and domination, 228, 231; empathic concept of, 219; end-defining, 224; and the Enlightenment, 223; formalization of, 146, 173, 197, 204, 213, 215, 222, 223, 225, 226, 229, 230, 232, 236, 238; and Foucault, 273, 275; and the Frankfurt School, 252; and Habermas, 86, 105–6, 146, 174, 178, 179–82, 184, 185, 187, 194, 196, 197, 199, 200, 205; and Hegel, 66, 73, 74, 217, 219; the historical development of, 219–20; and Horkheimer, 146, 147, 157, 173, 213, 214, 222–27, 229–32, 275; instrumental, 236, 237, 252, 273; and Kant, 31, 113, 150, 183, 184, 228–29; and Locke, 112; and Marcuse, 146, 165; and Mill, 112; and objectivity, 224; and particulars vs. universals, 228; and power, 229; practical, 228; private, 57; theoretical, 228; and Tocqueville, 57, 185, 186; and Weber, 146, 173, 197, 204–5, 213, 215, 219, 221–23, 225, 226, 229, 230, 232, 236, 238
religion: as an antidote to modern pathologies, 46; and Arendt, 95–97, 104, 106; contemporary, 47; and Horkheimer and Adorno, 154; and Tocqueville, 42, 43, 46–47, 56–58, 76, 77, 87, 90, 93–96, 105, 106
representation/representative government: accountability in, 140, 141; and Arendt, 105, 242; and contemporary America, 140, 142; and Habermas, 185; and Hegel, 64, 65; and Mill, 118–19, 121–23, 128, 131–34, 139, 142; and Tocqueville, 37, 80
republic, 13, 24, 53
republicanism: and Arendt, 96, 97, 246; and Foucault, 267; liberal, 25; and Machiavelli, 256, 257; and power, 24; and Tocqueville, 46
revolution, 57, 76, 94, 97, 101, 102, 305, 329, 342–43
Riesman, David, 91
rights: and Agamben, 295; and Arendt, 97, 106, 242, 243, 246, 248, 250, 251, 253, 297, 343; and Boulainvilliers, 284–85; and Constant, 258; in contemporary America, 5, 141; and Foucault, 264–67, 275, 291, 298; and Hegel, 51, 60; and liberalism, 263–64; and Locke, 112; and Marx, 14, 15; and Mill, 122; provision for, 300; and public freedom, 12; and Tocqueville, 51, 106, 257, 258
Robespierre, Maximilien, 257, 342
Romanticism, 76, 113, 139, 149, 215, 228, 246, 253
Rome, ancient, 3, 11, 17, 20, 66, 67, 69, 70, 104, 340

Rousseau, Jean-Jacques, 183; and Arendt, 86, 88, 96, 99, 104, 326, 340; on associations, 19, 44; on the bourgeois and the citizen, 33; on censorship, 17; on citizen formation, 17; on civic religion, 17; on civic republicanism, 51; on civic virtue, 257; on the common good, 31, 184; and Constant, 3; on corruption, 17; on democracy, 45; *Emile,* 123; and Foucault, 270, 275; on freedom, 2, 4; and Habermas, 184, 198, 199; and Hegel, 66, 67, 253; and Heidegger, 329; and Mill, 121, 123; on the military, 17; *Social Contract,* 2; on self-interest, 31, 33, 64; on a Sovereign People, 86; and Tocqueville, 43, 44, 63–64, 79, 86, 88, 94; on transparency, 270, 272; on *volonté générale* (general will), 64, 86, 99, 183, 184, 351
Rusche, Georg, 275
Russian Revolution, the, 344

sacrifice, introversion of, 227, 230, 231, 235
Sade, Marquis de, 227, 229
Saint-Simonians, 132
Sandel, Michael, 99, 111
Scarry, Elaine, 25
Schiller, Friedrich, 67, 148
Schmitt, Carl, 25, 26, 247, 273, 305, 306, 313, 348, 350–52; *The Concept of the Political,* 1, 314, 349–50; *Political Theology,* 1
science: and Adorno, 146–47, 225, 226, 228; and Hegel, 217, 221; and Horkheimer, 146–47, 225, 226, 228, 229; and Marcuse, 158, 162, 164; and meaning, 221; and self-preservation, 228; and Weber, 220–22
Scottish Enlightenment, the, 31, 32, 33, 42
self-government: and Arendt, 88, 89, 249; and Hegel, 67; and Mill, 112–13, 121, 124, 130, 133, 138; and Tocqueville, 37, 56, 67, 75, 78, 87–89, 130
self-interest, 31–33, 40, 42, 52–56, 64, 69, 79, 88, 93, 99, 229, 245
selfishness, 53, 92, 130. *See also* egoism
self-preservation, 225, 226, 228, 230
self-reliance, 126, 150
Sennett, Richard, *The Fall of Public Man,* 46, 341
September 11, 2001 attacks, 9
sexuality, 154, 160
Sieyès, Abbé, 276, 290, 291; *Qu'est-ce que le Tiers état?,* 288–89
Sittlichkeit, 55, 59, 71, 73, 81
Smith, Adam, 31, 338
social contract, 67, 73, 79, 102, 110, 266
social vs. political, 310, 313, 317, 338, 339, 341–42, 344, 345, 347, 350

society: the administered, 46, 173, 214, 226,
229, 239; and Adorno, 226; the affluent,
195; and Arendt, 239, 243, 246; and the
bourgeoisie, 176; the de-sacralization of, 223;
and Foucault, 270, 271, 287; the government
as serving, 47; and Habermas, 189–90; and
Hegel, 72–73; and Horkheimer, 226, 229; the
interests of, 177, 181; and Marcuse, 158, 163,
165, 168; and Mill, 111; objectivist accounts
of, 223; the rationalization of, 213; as separate
from the state, 30; and the state, 246; the
total, 148, 161, 163, 164, 203, 226, 230, 232,
234, 235; and war, 276–80
Socrates, 66, 70–74, 100, 136, 137, 165, 186,
204, 333
Sophocles, *Antigone,* 329
sovereignty, 23, 95, 212, 218, 246, 249, 261,
263, 265–67, 291, 351, 352. *See also* popular
sovereignty
Soviets, the, 295
Spain, 138
Stalin, Joseph, 239
state: administrative, 60, 78; and Adorno, 156;
and Arendt, 242, 243, 245, 246, 248–52,
269–70; biopolitical, 296; bureaucratic, 6, 33,
46, 89, 90, 90; bureaucratic/authoritarian,
28; bureaucratized welfare, 269–70;
centralized, 33, 52, 263; centralizing, 60; and
civil society, 12–15, 27, 28–29, 34; and
Constant, 269; and contemporary America,
172; decentered, 20; and Foucault, 261, 267,
275, 277–79, 282–85, 287, 288, 291–94, 297;
and Habermas, 86, 179–82, 185, 189–90; and
Hegel, 20–21, 32, 34, 45, 59–63, 65–68, 70,
71, 80; and Horkheimer, 156; and the
interests of society, 177, 181; and Marcuse,
158, 167; and Mill, 112; and nation, 248;
national security, 9, 158; neo-Hobbesian, 10;
and the public realm, 177; as separate from
society, 30; and social interests, 15; and
society, 246; and Tocqueville, 6, 33, 38, 39,
42, 46, 60, 61, 78, 89, 90, 263, 269; tutelary,
45, 78, 90, 258, 347, 364n17; tutorial, 112;
warfare, 167, 171–72; welfare, 167
statelessness, 212, 248–50, 307, 346
Steuart, James, 31
Stoicism, 70
Strauss, Leo, 220, 224, 256; "Liberal
Education and Responsibility," 132;
Natural Right and History, 225
subjectivism: and Hegel, 66, 68, 69, 72, 83;
and individualism, 66, 68, 69, 72, 83; and
Tocqueville, 83
subjectivity: and Adorno, 228; and Foucault,
262; and Hegel, 49, 60, 62, 63, 67–72, 76

Taminiaux, Jacques, 327
Taylor, Charles, 111, 148

technology, 222; and Adorno, 226, 228; and
Horkheimer, 226, 230; and Marcuse, 158,
161–64, 166–70, 173; and Weber, 221
Thoreau, Henry David, 260
Tocqueville, Alexis de, 85, 171, 300; on
administrative despotism, 6, 40, 52, 90; on
the administrative state, 60, 78; and Adorno,
156, 235; on America, 13, 33, 45, 52–58, 65,
76–78, 80, 85, 87, 89–91, 93–94; and Arendt,
85–90, 95–99, 101, 105–7, 306, 312, 325, 331,
341; on the aristocracy, 36, 39, 59, 66, 91; on
association/associations, 8, 18–20, 33–46,
52, 55, 56, 58, 59, 62, 63, 65–67, 75, 86–88,
89–90, 95, 106, 130, 257; on atomism, 8, 52,
53, 75, 79–80, 101; on the bourgeoisie, 52–53,
55–56, 63, 76; on the bureaucratic state, 6,
33, 89, 90; and Burke, 79; on capitalism, 8–9;
on centralization, 29–30, 36, 38, 40, 45, 60,
61, 75, 76, 87, 95, 263; on centralized
organizations, 30; on the centralized state,
52; on central power, 7; on Christianity, 43,
58, 79, 87, 93–95; on citizens, 22, 41, 55, 63,
88, 259; on civic docility, 6–8, 75, 259–60; on
civic education, 18, 22, 37, 45, 56, 65, 75, 88,
90, 113, 131, 238, 257–58; on civic republicanism, 11–12, 51, 257; on civic spirit, 43; on
civil associations, 38, 40, 41, 43–44; on civil
society, 12, 27–48, 52, 63–64, 86, 88, 258,
348; on class struggle, 38, 94; on commerce,
41–42, 55; on the common good, 40, 44, 51,
52, 55, 93; on conformity, 57, 91, 95, 156, 185;
and Constant, 47; on corporate identity, 39;
on the courtier spirit, 57, 77, 91; on debate,
46, 259; on decentralization, 35, 36, 45, 78,
86, 87, 89, 90, 95, 130; on democracy, 6, 13,
29–30, 33, 34, 36–40, 42, 43, 51–55, 57–60,
63, 66, 78, 80, 87, 89–95, 106, 185–86, 258,
259; on democratic despotism, 35; on
despotism, 10, 39, 40, 51–52, 58, 60, 75, 77,
89, 90, 93, 107, 156, 258, 259, 291; on dissent,
95, 259; on duty, 58; on the economic sphere,
42, 80; on egoism, 92; on elites, 56, 107, 185;
on equality, 34, 39, 40, 42, 43, 52–54, 56, 58,
75, 78, 80, 87, 91, 95, 185–86, 259; on Europe,
59, 89; on family/friends, 7, 39, 40, 53, 58, 89,
92, 258; on federalism, 52; and Foucault, 75,
90, 266, 275, 294, 298; and France, 29, 42,
52–54, 59, 65, 76, 90, 122, 130; on freedom, 5,
41, 43, 44, 46, 47, 57, 58, 68, 69, 75, 78, 80, 87,
89, 91, 94, 95, 257, 258; on free enterprise,
42–43; on the French Revolution, 48, 60; on
government, 28, 36; and Guizot, 41; and
Habermas, 85, 86, 91, 178, 185, 198; and
Hegel, 43, 44, 50, 59, 60, 62–69, 75–76,
79–84; and Hobbes, 74; and Horkheimer,
156, 235; on identification, 74, 83; on
independence, 74–79, 83, 87; on the
individual, 33, 34, 39, 44, 47, 66, 185; on

individualism, 39–40, 50–60, 65–67, 75, 78, 80, 83, 87, 90–93, 100, 258; on the individual vs. the general interest, 79; on institutions, 78, 95; on integration, 82; on interests, 44, 54; on intermediate institutions, 29–30; on judgment, 54, 67, 78, 87, 92, 185; on justice, 43, 58, 93; on the law, 37, 77, 106; on liberalism, 80, 86; on local administrations, 36, 37, 52, 55, 63–64, 76, 95, 101, 258; on local autonomy, 88–89; on local freedom, 7, 40, 41, 43, 45, 54, 58, 60; on local independence, 68; on local institutions, 122; on localism, 75, 78; on local organizations, 30, 35; and Machiavelli, 43, 257; on majority tyranny, 36, 38, 57, 76–78, 83, 86, 91, 93, 95, 185; on manufactures, 21; and Marcuse, 164; on the market, 41–42; on mass culture, 156, 204; on the masses, 89; on material interests, 7, 18, 42, 55, 87, 90, 92, 94, 101; on mediating institutions, 28, 89–90; and Mill, 57, 74, 75, 79, 91, 121–24, 126–28, 130, 133–35, 138; on *moeurs*, 21, 28, 34, 45–48, 52, 55, 59, 74, 75, 79–84, 88, 89, 93, 94, 96, 106, 107, 122, 130, 133, 140, 258, 331, 332; and Montesquieu, 30, 33, 35, 36, 45; on morality/ethics, 58, 79, 80, 82, 93, 94, 258; on municipalities, 37; and Nietzsche, 75; on paternalism, 258, 263; on patriotism, 78, 79; on permanent associations, 54; and the *philosophes,* 79; on physical gratification, 7, 18, 42, 53, 90, 92–93, 156, 343; and Plato, 257; on pluralism, 75, 77, 78, 80–81, 87, 94, 95, 106, 107, 130, 185, 186, 258; on the political, the priority of, 88–90; on political associations, 38, 40–41, 43–44; on political participation, 55, 65, 67, 80, 87–89, 95, 106, 122, 135, 178–79; on political parties, 35; on popular sovereignty, 37, 66, 90; on the press/ newspapers, 35, 44, 75; on private interests, 59; on private judgment, 53, 56–58; on the private sphere, 43, 47, 52, 56, 92, 93, 95, 101, 107; on private vs. general interest, 55; on the private vs. the public, 13, 16, 54, 55, 79; on privatism, 8, 34, 66; on privatization, 39, 53; on public freedom, 42, 47, 66, 67, 80, 90; on the public good, 33, 56, 59; on public opinion, 56–58, 78, 79, 86, 87, 90–95, 185–87; on the public realm, 51, 52, 75, 80, 88, 93, 106, 186, 257–59; on public spirit, 55, 89; on public virtue, 34; on reason, 57, 185, 186; on religion, 42, 43, 46–47, 56–58, 76, 77, 87, 90, 93–96, 105, 106; on representation, 37, 80; on the republic, 53; on republicanism, 46; on revolution, 94; on rights, 51, 106, 257, 258; and Rousseau, 43, 44, 63–64, 79, 86, 88, 94; on self-government, 37, 56, 67, 75, 78, 87–89, 130; on self-interest, 40, 42, 52–56, 64, 79, 88, 93, 99; on selfishness, 53, 92; on

shared belief, 57, 79, 258; on society and government, 47; on sovereignty, 95; on the state, 38, 39, 42, 46, 60, 61, 78, 89, 263, 269; on subjectivism, 83; on townships, 55, 63, 66, 87, 101; on the tutelary state, 45, 78, 90, 258, 347, 364n17; on understanding vs. experience, 58; on utility, 54; on values, 44; on voluntary associations, 45; on the vote, 122; and Weber, 75; on withdrawal from society, 39, 40, 87, 89, 92, 258; on workers, 8–9

Tocqueville, Alexis de, works by: *Democracy in America,* 6–10, 18, 33, 52, 56, 87, 91–92, 127, 291; *Democracy in America I,* 28, 35, 76–78, 134–35, 185; *Democracy in America II,* 28, 41, 44, 45, 68, 79, 88, 92–93; *The Old Regime and the Revolution,* 51–52, 79

Tolstoy, Leo, 221

totalitarianism: and Adorno, 211, 212, 225, 236; and Agamben, 267, 268, 295; and Arendt, 25, 89, 211, 212, 214, 238–53, 295, 305, 308–9, 312, 317, 333; and Foucault, 293, 296; and Horkheimer, 225, 229; and Marcuse, 25, 163–65, 170; the rise of, 82; soft, 25

townships, 36–37, 55, 63, 66, 82, 87, 101

tribalism, 23, 246–47, 307

truth, 98, 182, 199–201, 205–6, 227, 314

U.S. Constitution, 26, 101, 102, 104, 343

utilitarianism, 67, 70, 110, 125, 139

Villa, Dana, *Arendt and Heidegger,* 302, 314, 316, 318, 336, 397n16

Voegelin, Eric, 224; *Order and History,* 225

Voltaire, 31, 57

vom Stein, Heinrich Friedrich Karl, 74

vote, 65, 122, 131, 175, 193

Waldron, Jeremy, 97

Walzer, Michael, 28, 73

Weber, Max, 325, 345; on the administered society, 173; on administrative rationality, 21, 173, 293; and Adorno, 147, 156, 160, 213, 214, 226; on ancient Greece, 220; and Arendt, 102; on the bourgeoisie, 221; on the disenchantment of the world, 173, 219, 221, 223, 225, 226; on domination, 25, 173, 299; on facts of value, 221–22; and Foucault, 293; on fragmentation, 81; and the Frankfurt School, 173; and Habermas, 146, 192, 198, 204–5; on happiness, 221; and Horkheimer, 147, 156, 160, 214, 222–23, 226; on the iron cage metaphor, 21, 22, 147, 159, 173, 196, 223; and Kant, 222; and Marcuse, 160, 162, 164; and Mill, 379n30; on nature, 220; and Nietzsche, 220; "Parliament and Government in a Reconstructed Germany," 160–61; and

Weber, Max *(continued)*
Plato, 220; on power, 299; on rationality, 220, 223; on rationalization, 219, 223; on reason, 173, 197, 204–5, 219, 221–23, 226, 236; on science, 220–22; "Science as a Vocation," 219–22
on technology, 221; and Tocqueville, 75
Welch, Cheryl, 363n88
Wellmer, Albrecht, 97, 174, 223, 326
Whitehead, Alfred North, 325
Wiggerhaus, Rolf, 144

Wills, Garry, 353
Wolin, Richard, 305, 310, 313
Wolin, Sheldon, 16, 256, 293, 306, 309, 316–18, 331, 335–36, 344, 363n81; "Hannah Arendt: Democracy and the Political," 310–13
women, 230–31, 340, 346
workers, 8–9, 148, 152, 153, 155, 158, 340, 346
working class, the, 118, 122, 123, 146, 159, 166, 175
World War I, 159